Approaches to Human Communication

Approaches
to
Human Communication

Edited by
RICHARD W. BUDD
and
BRENT D. RUBEN

 Spartan Books

---

HAYDEN BOOK COMPANY, INC.
Rochelle Park, New Jersey

TP
90
,B8

ISBN 0-8104-5796-2 (soft-bound edition)
0-8104-5797-0 (hard-bound edition)
Library of Congress Catalog Card Number 70-176222
Copyright © 1972

Printed in the United States of America

Spartan Books are distributed throughout the world by Hayden Book Company, Inc., 50 Essex Street, Rochelle Park, N.J. 07662, and its agents.

2   3   4   5   6   7   8   9   PRINTING

74 75 76 77 78   YEAR

To Bev and Jann

Contents

PREFACE

It is clear the way one thinks about communication can make a difference to the course of human affairs. With a similar conviction, scholars have pursued the construction of models of the process of communication from a wide variety of disciplinary bases, ranging from biology to electronics, seeking to develop frameworks for explaining and better understanding human communication.

For the most part, the more widely used literature on communication does not draw upon this diversity. All too often, the literature suggests that the process of communication must be understood from a particular disciplinary vantage point. As it is clear that the way we think about communication is important, it is equally clear that there is no single correct approach.

Indeed, it is because of the existence of this variety that *Approaches to Human Communication* was conceived. The volume is at once a response to the vast range of literature available within each of the several disciplines, and an effort to take advantage of the cross-disciplinary approach to the study of communication. The broader the perspective one brings to bear in his thinking about the process of communication, the more adequate his conception is likely to be. Emerging from this basic fact, the book reflects and draws upon the supradisciplinary heritage that distinguishes communication at both a theoretical and operational level. Between its covers, *Approaches to Human Communication* makes a succinct statement regarding the scope of communication, and points to an ever-increasing trend in cross-disciplinary scholarship. Additionally, it provides the student the opportunity to develop an integrated and highly useful understanding of human communication in all of its diversity.

In its twenty-four chapters, *Approaches to Human Communication* spans the broad range of concern for and application of communication theory from anthropology through zoology. In each of the original pieces prepared for this book we asked each author to review the mainstream thinking of his discipline's approach to communication, to sketch the dimensions of that concern, and the problems and the potential for the future of communication study in his field. We did not expect, nor do any of the authors intend, that each piece speak for an entire discipline. What we did intend is that the book be organized around its contributors, each of whom has established himself as a serious scholar in his own field and each of whom has applied his disciplinary knowledge toward advancing an understanding of human communication.

As the reader works his way through this volume, whether alphabetically or by sequencing chapters into a particular pattern he finds otherwise useful, he will come across diverging, and in several instances, opposing, understandings of human communication. The chapter on General Systems, for example, argues for variety and multiple understanding of reality, and suggests communication is something that occurs within people. The chapter on Journalism suggests communication is a phenomenon that occurs between people, and urges a quest for singular truth. That such opposing viewpoints exist within the same volume in not accidental. The book was designed to present a forum from which the widest range of understandings of communication might be pursued. Having completed this volume, the reader will have the basics and the background necessary to begin a meaningful study of human communication and the requisite variety to build his own integrated understanding of "how communication works."

To facilitate the student's development, we asked each author to prepare a list of suggested readings of basic primary sources necessary to provide a meaningful entrée into the study of human communication from the viewpoint of each of the fields. By so doing we hoped, in effect, to give the book a "second life," to make it useful not only for the student at the introductory level, but for the graduate student by providing more generic guidelines in the advanced stages of his work in communication. In three previously published chapters (those by Herbert Blumer, Robert Mueller, and J. Z. Young) the bibliographies were supplemented by the editors.

In a great number of ways, the editing of this book was both a joy and a learning experience. The cooperation of our contributors in meeting the most stringent deadlines and their concern for ensuring an integrated conceptual framework for the book must stand as some sort of a monument to multiauthored volumes. Our only loss comes in being unable to present the reader with the benefits of the intellectual ferment that accrued to us while working with the contributors to this book.

We are deeply saddened by the untimely death of our colleague and friend Dr. James W. Markham during the preparation of this book. Jim Markham was internationally recognized as a leading scholar in his field. It is with both a great deal of pride and sorrow that his chapter "International Behavior: An Approach to Human Communication" is offered in this volume as his final contribution to a field that was his life's work.

In addition to our contributors, we wish to extend our thanks to our many colleagues and friends who offered us their suggestions, criticisms, and support throughout the development of this project. While they are too numerous to list by name here, we want each of them to know we are grateful for their participation.

We would like to recognize in particular Henry LaBrie, Jae Won Lee, Dan Spillane, and Terrell Taylor, Ph. D. students at the University of Iowa, and Vera C. Stek of Rutgers for providing important material contributions to the book.

Because the preparation of a manuscript of the size required for this volume is such a thankless task, we wish to acknowledge and thank Carol Schrage of the University of Iowa and Barbara Duska of Rutgers University for the many hours they invested, often in sheer frustration, working on our behalf.

Any acknowledgements we might make would be woefully incomplete if we failed to recognize the invaluable contributions made by Dianne Littwin, Editor-in-chief of Spartan Books. Her patience as a person and her unquestionable skills as an editor have both left their mark on this volume. The shortcomings must be attributed to our own naiveté concerning the translation of an idea into a tangible form that would prove useful to others.

RICHARD W. BUDD
BRENT D. RUBEN

Rutgers University

ACKNOWLEDGMENTS

Grateful acknowledgment is made for permission to use the following material:

Chapter 2: Copyright © 1967 by Robert E. Mueller. Reprinted from *The Science of Art* by Robert E. Mueller, by permission of the John Day Company, Inc., publisher. Originally titled "The Communication of Art."

Chapter 3: First presented as one of six lectures in the Reith Lecture Series, BBC. Later published in J. Z. Young, *Doubt and Certainty in Science: A Biologist's Reflection on the Brain,* "A Biologist's Approach to Man," by permission of the Clarendon Press, Oxford.

Chapter 14: Copyright © 1969 by José M. R. Delgado. Reprinted from *Physical Control of the Mind: Toward a Psychocivilized Society* by José M. R. Delgado by permission of Harper & Row, Publishers, Inc., publisher. Originally published as Chapter 5, "Extracerebral Elements of the Mind: When and How the Mind Is Formed"; and Chapter 7, "Sensory Dependence of the Adult Mind."

Chapter 20: Adapted by the authors from "Mass Communication and the Social System," in *Sociology Today* edited by Robert K. Merton, Leonard Broom, and Leonard Cottrell, Jr., © 1959 by Basic Books, Inc. Publishers, New York, by permission.

Chapter 22: Copyright © 1969 by Prentice-Hall. Reprinted from *Symbolic Interactionism: Perspective and Method* by Herbert Blumer by permission of Prentice-Hall, Inc. Originally titled "The Methodological Position of Symbolic Interactionism."

Chapter 24: Especially revised and updated for inclusion in this volume, an earlier version appeared in *Communication: Concepts and Perspectives,* edited by Lee Thayer, © 1967 by Spartan Books.

Dr. Alfred G. Smith is Professor of Anthropology at the University of Oregon. He served the U.S. government as a specialist in Far Eastern and Pacific area affairs. He is the author of numerous publications in anthropology and has been a university teacher for twenty years. His most recent book is *Communication and Culture*.

1

ANTHROPOLOGY: AN APPROACH TO HUMAN COMMUNICATION

ALFRED G. SMITH

To all approaches there are approaches in turn. Even the anthropological approach to communication is not a first step. Rather, let us step into the stream with a conception of anthropology itself, a conception specific to the needs of studying human communication.

A STUDY OF HUMAN RESPONSES

When author James A. Michener was trying to understand the people of Spain, he had to learn the significance of the phrase *"Viva yo."* He recalled that "some time ago there was a competition for the cartoon which best expressed the Spanish character, and the winner, without a close second, was one showing an arrogant little boy urinating in the middle of the street and spelling out the words *'Viva yo,'* which could be translated as 'Hurray for me,' except that the guts of the phrase is implied in the second half, 'and to hell with everyone else.' A comprehension of the Spaniard's addiction to *viva yo* will help anyone trying to make his way in Spain. When the little car barrels right down the middle of the highway, forcing everyone else into the ditch, you don't swear at the driver. You say *'Viva yo'* and you understand what happened and why." [28, pp. 56-57]

But suppose one tries to make his way not in Spain but in Japan? The self-assertive *"Viva yo"* is quite different from the Japanese concept of *enryo*. This concept, according to anthropologists Bennett, Passin, and McKnight, is "loosely translatable as 'hesitance' or 'reserve.' " [6, p. 230] It is part of the traditional Japanese way of showing respect to superiors, submitting to social proprieties, controlling oneself, and maintaining a behavioral reserve. The traditional Japanese used the concept of *enryo* particularly when duties and relationships were unclear.

1

Thus the 'shyness' [of the Japanese student] or reserved behavior often found on the American campus can be due either in the fact that the Japanese views Americans, or certain Americans, as superior people; or to the fact that he is simply not sure how to behave in American social situations, regardless of status." (6, p. 231)

Viva yo and *enryo* represent two different ways of making one's way, and not necessarily differences between Spaniards and Japanese. Many Japanese urinate in the street, and many Spaniards are reserved. These are not necessarily national or group differences, nor are they differences between people who are self-assertive and those who are submissive. All people are a mixture of both. Different ways of making one's way are simply different responses.

There are a thousand and one responses to human circumstances. Neanderthal man made physical responses; sometimes his molars were ground down by his rough diet, and from that it can be inferred that his bowels must also have responded to that diet. Many North American Indians responded to a grievance by committing suicide as a form of revenge. In every period of human history and in every region of the earth, man has responded biologically and socially to the environment he lived in. Some men have toughened their intestines, some have bowed humbly, and others have marched in protest.

The male responds if a blond he admires bats her eyelashes at him. An American responds when he sees Neil Armstrong stepping onto the moon. The addict responds to heroin, and both student and faculty to a confrontation on campus. Some responses, for example, that to the blond, could be immediate while others might be delayed. Some are inherited and others are learned. Some are parts of characteristic sets of responses, parts of fixed-action patterns. Like a bicycle rider on a corduroy road, man responds to stimuli from his environment in order to maintain his balance and momentum.

Anthropology is the study of these responses. To some extent this conception of anthropology is novel. It is also fruitful, and it relates anthropology more closely to the study of human communication. Anthropologists often claim that anthropology is the study of man.[17; 24] If it were the study of total man it could claim the lion's share of attention. But that claim is either an affectation or a delusion. The claim is too brash and vain, too broad and vague.

Some social scientists claim that anthropology is the study of *primitive* man.[8, p. 9] That could include monkeys and apes, Americans, Russians, and other semiprimitives. Where does one draw the line between the primitive and the advanced?

Other anthropologists claim that anthropology is the study of culture or of race. But race and culture, like man and primitive man, tend to be regarded as entities—as fixed things. The sciences, however, recognize that the specialist in each field can best study processes rather than entities. The most fruitful subject of inquiry is not things, but actions; not man nor culture, but human interaction.

Because human responses are processes, let us begin by examining anthropology as the *study* of human responses. That conception leads to the anthropological approach to communication, the subject of this chapter.

ANTHROPOLOGY AS NATURAL HISTORY

The study of human responses is valuable to man in order for him to get along with his fellowman and to understand himself. There are those who specialize in specific kinds of responses: economists who study how people respond to a rise in prices or to automation in industry; psychologists who study responses to approval, to ambiguity, or to isolation. The anthropological approach is a part of this common enterprise. What these studies hold in common far outweighs their differences, the differences being less in what is studied than in how it is studied. To illustrate: The physicist and the physiologist study the color red in quite different ways. The physicist begins by measuring wavelengths, while the physiologist dissects the rods and cones of the retina. The difference is in method and orientation. Some specialists also study human responses by measuring them. A sociologist, for example, might administer a questionnaire about drugs to a hundred sophomores and then scale their responses. Poll-taking and attitude measurement, however, are not basic methods of study by the anthropologist. Other specialists conduct experiments. A psychologist might remove part of a rat's brain to study the effect on its responses. But the conducting of experiments is not a prevalent basic method of study for the anthropologist either. He has taken an apple off another tree.

The anthropologist studies human responses by using the methods and orientations of natural history. Some anthropologists might shake their heads at this, yet the natural-history approach has been the most common among anthropologists for the last 100 years.[39, chap. 1; 10, pp. 281–289, pp. 243–259; 22, pp. 172–178] Natural history is an anciént science that studies and compares plants, rocks, and animals. It used to mean collecting and identifying caterpillars and pine cones, and it generally entailed excursions into the country. Anthropology, like natural history of old, is one of the more humane branches of science.

In various museums of natural history—such as in New York, Chicago, and San Diego—stuffed birds, preserved insects, animals, plants, and rocks are displayed either in an evolutionary order, or by means of variations and comparisons. The anthropologist observes and describes human responses in a similar way.

Contemporary natural history is more concerned with living birds and insects than with dead ones, and it is primarily concerned with their behavior. A naturalist and ethologist like Konrad Lorenz [25] observes aggressive responses among birds and other animals, and Niko Tinbergen [38] observes the male stickleback fish staking out a nesting territory and changing its colors from dull gray to red, white, and blue in order to attract the female sticklebacks in the spring. There is a gradual and natural progression from the study of responses in birds and fish to the study of human responses. For example, Stuart A. Altmann [1] spent two years on an island off the coast of Puerto Rico studying a colony of rhesus monkeys, recording their behavior. George B. Schaller [32] did the same with the mountain gorilla of Africa. In a similar way, the anthropologist is a naturalist and ethologist of human communication.

THE NATURAL CONTINUUM OF RESPONSES

Like the fish, the bird, and the monkey, man responds to his environment—physically, socially, biologically, and symbolically. One kind of response can hardly be distinguished from another. Responses do not come in different colored packages: blue for biological and brown for symbolic; green for primitive and yellow for advanced. When the little boy spells out *viva yo* in the street, that is both a physical and a social response. There is a natural continuum.

When the anthropologist studies human communication, he assumes there is unity in responses. The responses of a mountain gorilla and of a Neanderthal man, of a Spaniard and of a Japanese are first cousins to each other. It is difficult to tell, and it seldom matters, whether a response is a product of nature or of nurture, whether it is genetically inherited or learned in a library, whether it is conscious or unconscious. A man communicates as well with an involuntary blush as with a calculated speech. Thus, a natural continuum is assumed. The same methods and orientations of natural history are used to describe and compare verbal responses, body movements, spatial relations, and many other forms of communication that are even less obvious. The same methods are used in the study of monkeys and people.

The idea of a natural continuum broadens vision and, incidentally, increases tolerance. It prevents us from making sharp distinctions between the normal and the deviant, the primitive and the civilized, the emotional and the rational. The principles of behavior of a schizophrenic patient in a mental hospital are the same principles that govern the behavior of the average saleslady in a dress shop. At least there is a natural continuum of responses.

In the study of human communication, the idea of a continuum indicates that communication processes cannot be separated from other processes; it indicates that agriculture, commerce, and warfare are also forms of communication.

Consider, for example, the introduction of a money economy into a community in East Africa. It changes all the processes of communication. Such communities used to practice *lobola,* the giving of cattle by a boy's family to a girl's family as a kind of bride price. *Lobola* compensated the girl's family for the loss of her services, as she would no longer cook for them, draw water, or make pots. It also compensated them for the investment they had made in her, the equivalent of the American investment in ballet lessons, braces on the teeth, and a hope chest. *Lobola* always took the form of cattle, because these were the prized possession among East Africans.

With the introduction of a money economy, everything is changed. First, money becomes the most important medium of contact with the outside world and increases that contact. With money, anyone in the community can write to Sears Roebuck in Chicago and order anything from a refrigerator to a corset. People can buy magazines, radios, and other sources of information, thus enlarging the world to which they respond.

Second, money changes responses in the local world of the community. Suppose a father refuses to give cattle for his son's bride. Perhaps he does not approve of the girl, or wants his boy to marry into another family, or wants the boy to keep working only for him. With the introduction of a money economy, the boy can go off and get a job, perhaps in the mines or on a plantation, and earn the money for the *lobola* cattle. Thus in a money economy, parental authority is reduced and a boy's response to his father is changed.

Responses become more impersonal. Traditionally, the boy works beside his father, erecting a new corncrib or tending a sick calf. If he goes off and gets a job, he might send a little money home each month, but that is much more impersonal than father and son building a wall together. And working for wages on a plantation also makes responses much more impersonal there. Father and son relations are replaced by employer and employee relations. There are employers and employees rather than fathers and sons.

Third, money becomes the covert common denominator for all things. Goods and services that used to be unmeasurable and incommensurable, such as a cow, a family heirloom, and a day's work, can all be evaluated in shillings. And in a money economy, a man can hide all his wealth in a sock under his mattress, while formerly his wealth—his house, his cattle, and his other goods—was on public display. This changes the whole process of bargaining and trading. Before, one could estimate how much the bride price should be, but now it is not so easy to tell how wealthy each family is and where the bargaining should begin.

Human responses are not isolated and detached—unrelated to family or friends. When a boy sees a picture of a bicycle in a mail-order catalog, his response is related to tending his father's sick calf, to the possibility of wages for labor, and to courting a girl. Communication processes are inextricably connected to all the other processes of living—to urinating in the street or to building a wall. Anthropological approaches to communication are the natural history of the continuum of human responses.

Nevertheless, some anthropologists look only for a special kind of response. Some emphasize biological responses, while others emphasize social ones. Cutting across this dichotomy is a second one: Some anthropologists emphasize the history of responses, while others emphasize comparisons among responses. These divisions yield four different kinds of anthropologists. Many biologically oriented anthropologists are concerned with man's adaptations in the course of biological evolution from a fish to a primate. Other biologically oriented anthropologists emphasize the similarities and differences among men today—differences in skin color, in hat size, and in blood type. In the same way, many socially oriented anthropologists follow a historical course of study, while others follow a comparative one. The history of social adaptations and responses is largely a matter for archaeologists. Since many ancient societies have left no written records, the anthropologist literally has to dig for his data, scavenging for potsherds in an Indian mound, his hands blistering and his back aching. And from that mound and its relics, he has to deduce how human beings responded to their environment in the past.

Cultural and social anthropologists may compare the habits of a band of Australian aborigines with those of an African tribe. The concerns of such cultural anthropologists include what different peoples know and feel and what they are anxious about. This can sometimes be deduced from language, art, folklore, and religion. Despite differences between the biological approach and the cultural approach, between historical and comparative approaches, the aim of anthropology as a whole is to understand the continuum of human responses.

WHAT ANTHROPOLOGISTS LOOK FOR

It is all very well to say that anthropologists study human responses as a part of natural history, but what do these anthrolopogists actually look for? Individual anthropologists study human communication through specific forms of responses. For example, Ray L. Birdwhistell [9] studies the use of body motion, or kinesics, in communication; Edward T. Hall [18; 19] studies spatial relations, or proxemics; Eliot D. Chapple [12; 13] has emphasized the rhythms of interaction; Ward H. Goodenough's [15] componential analysis dissects the structure of verbal categories; and Dell H. Hymes [20; 21] has related linguistics to ethnography by describing a speech community and its verbal repertories. But what kinds of observations do these anthropologists make in general? What do they look for?

Looking for Nothing

Anthropologists look for four things. First, they look for nothing. When an anthropologist begins to dig, he does not know what he is going to find or what may be relevant or crucial in a particular case. He may find something quite different from anything yet known to man. Therefore, he expects anything—and nothing in particular.

Consider an anthropologist who specializes in the study of verbal responses and who comes across the Bimbams, a group of people who have never before been studied. Does he look for nouns and verbs, infinitives and participles in the Bimbam language? No, perhaps the Bimbams do not distinguish these parts of speech, but make other distinctions instead.

Anthropologists do not begin their observations with prepared questions or with hypotheses to be tested in the classic tradition. Such questions and hypotheses can distort the information that, say, the Bimbam may give. A preformulated hypothesis is what courtroom lawyers speak of as "leading the witness." It prejudices the testimony. And it is not in the tradition of natural history.

Ordinarily, anthropologists do not set out to prove that *lobola,* for example, is an African form of capitalism or of male chauvinism. Yet it is, of course, dangerous to look for nothing. When questions and hypotheses are not explicitly stated, they may still be there, hidden beneath the surface like the agenda of a "free and unstructured" committtee meeting or a line of questioning that unobtrusively leads the witness. The unstated hypothesis or question is the most insidious and prejudicial of all.

Therefore, paradoxically, it takes much knowledge and experience to look for nothing. Ignorance and inexperience lead us to look at other people's responses as projections of our own. If we know only Freudian psychology, everything becomes Freudian to the point of distortion. If we know only English, and only one way of analyzing the structure of English, when we encounter the Bimbam language we will be prejudiced by our ignorance. We will be unable to look for nothing.

Looking for Differences and Distinctions

The second thing anthropologists look for is differences and distinctions. The Eskimo and the Zulu build houses that are round, while the English and the Iroquois build houses that are rectangular. Human responses differ. There are differences and distinctions not only between groups, but also within groups. There are distinctions made between what is summer work and what is winter work, what is sacred and what is profane, between plebeians and patricians, and between generations. In fact, the more advanced a group is, the more differences there are within it. English-speaking groups include bus drivers, priests, captains of finance, and spot welders. In comparison, the Eskimo are undiversified as a group. An anthropologist does not want to impose a preconceived set of distinctions on his findings. He does not know what differences and distinctions he will come across, but he generally assumes that he will find some.

Basically, he believes in the self-structured field. The bases of that structure are differences and distinctions. Variations and dissimilarities lay before our eyes the structure of language, of courtship, and of all other patterns of response. In English, for example, a difference between nouns and verbs is revealed by the fact that adding an *s* to one creates a plural (hat, hats), but to the other creates a singular (sit, sits). In East Africa, there is a difference between the *lobola* for the oldest daughter and for the younger ones, which is generally revealed by the number of cattle given. The anthropologist looks for no particular structure, but he expects differences and distinctions to reveal one.

Anthropologists have generally found antitheses and binary oppositions in their studies of groups. This is particularly true today, although there is a long historical tradition behind it. Bachofen [2] noted the distinction between matrilineal and patrilineal; McLennan [26] between exogamous and endogamous; Morgan [29] consanguineal and affinal and also classificatory and descriptive; Baudouin de Courtenay [4] and Pike [30] etic and emic; van Gennep [41] rites of passage and of intensification; Bateson [3] schismogenesis or polarization of ethos; Linton [24] ascribed and achieved status; Benedict [5] continuities and discontinuities in child-training; Redfield [31] folk and urban societies; and Levi-Strauss, [23] the raw and the cooked categories in myths. These are only ten examples of the hundreds of differences and distinctions that anthropologists find in social relations, language, mythology, and other habitual responses. When they find these distinctions, they often formulate theoretical points of departure after the fact. In other words, they discover their approach after they have arrived.

Looking for Contexts

In studying the natural history of the continuum of responses, anthropologists not only look for nothing and for differences and distinctions, they also look for contexts. Benjamin Lee Whorf, a student of anthropology who also worked for a fire insurance company, found that factory workers were careful of fire hazards around gasoline drums, but around empty gasoline drums they smoked and tossed about cigarette stubs. Wrote Whorf:

> Yet the empty drums are perhaps the more dangerous, since they contain explosive 'vapor.' Physically the situation is hazardous, but the linguistic analysis according to regular analogy must employ the word 'empty,' which inevitably suggests lack of hazard. (42, p. 75)

Whorf found differences and distinctions in the workers' responses and then looked for the context of each response. He found that part of the context was simply linguistic. Looking for contexts is based on the assumption that responses are not isolated and detached, without family or friends.

Looking for contexts is a matter of seeing relationships and searching out meanings. When an anthropologist digs for arrowheads in an Indian mound, he is not interested in the arrowheads for their own sake, not according to the canons of scholarship. When an anthropologist studies the body movements of two Japanese greeting one another, he is not concerned with a singular incident. Any event, of itself, is meaningless for the anthropologist. Things have meaning only when they are related to other things. How is the arrowhead related to the technology and the economy of the Indians? How are the two Japanese related to one another, and what is the occasion of their meeting? Contexts give meanings.

An anthropologist does not look for just any context. He looks at responses in their own contexts. He does not want to *give* things a meaning, he wants to *find* a meaning within the contexts of responses. He hears a Zulu click, for example, and he relates that sound to its own context, to the other sounds of Zulu language. He does not relate it to the sound of English because that is not the click's own context. Relating Zulu to English sounds means seeing another language in terms of the linguistic differences and distinctions of English. That projects the structure of English on Zulu, and for an English-speaking anthropologist, that is a form of self-centeredness. Ethnocentrism and linguacentrism are cardinal sins for the anthropologist.

Nor does he study those responses in the context of anthropological theories and hypotheses. That, too, would distort the response; it would lead the witness. Anthropologists look for things in their own contexts, believing in the self-structured field and the self-meaning field.

In anthropology, seeing things in their own contexts is part of seeing cultures as wholes, seeing the contribution of each individual response to an entire repertory of responses. Anthropologists look for contrasts and distinctions in a repertory of responses in order to see the pattern of those responses, and that pattern becomes the context in which each of the individual responses has meaning. Some anthropologists assume that each culture has a unique system of perceiving and organizing the world, that it has a special cognitive code.[40] Some anthropologists are also concerned with emotional or affective codes and with codes of human interaction.[33] These codes are the responses' own contexts.

All scholars study things in their own contexts. In physics, that is in a sense what is called "field theory"; students of business administration call it "systems theory." Anthropologists relate each response to its own environment.

Looking for Freedom and Order

The fourth thing anthropologists look for when they study responses is freedom and order. In some situations, there are responses that *must* be made; in other situations, there are responses that *may* be made. This is a matter of redundancy and entropy, and in human communication, the two are always intertwined.

Without freedom, we would be bound to routines and traditions. We would have no choices and options. We would respond to new things in old ways, and we would not learn anything. Without order, we could not know anything. We could not know that summer follows spring. We could not know what response would be effective or appropriate in a given situation. For us, the world would be chaos.

What are the freedoms and the constraints that frame any response? To understand the Spanish boy writing out *viva yo,* the anthropologist looks for the latitude the boy has and also for his restrictions. The fashion designers of New York and Paris are in part creative and deviant and in part traditional. The anthropologist asks, "Which part is which?" When all the children in one family learn the same responses, each child's response in a given situation is still different. The anthropologist asks, "How?" This present sentence is constrained by the structure of English, yet it is a sentence that has never been made before. Every response is both redundant and entropic.

There are traditions and norms in responses, and there are also variations and changes. Anthropologists generally find order and custom where people need security and predictability in their relations. And they find that changes and variations follow relatively unchanging and invariant traditions. [27; 36]

APPLYING ANTHROPOLOGICAL APPROACHES TO COMMUNICATION

Now how useful are anthropological approaches to communication? We may just as well ask, "How useful are mathematical approaches to algebra?" An utter tautology. How appropriate is a legal approach to jurisprudence? A sheer redundancy. Like teaching fish to swim!

Anthropology and communication are not solitary islands separated by deep waters. We need no bridge to span a chasm between them, nor even stepping-stones from one to the other. To negotiate an approach there would be like breaking down doors that were already open.

Nevertheless, let us break them down by taking a second look at the main points made earlier. The first point was that anthropology is a study of human responses. Now we can also regard the study of communication as a study of human responses.

A more widespread view is that communication is the eliciting of a response.[7, p. 16; 14, p. 289] A television commercial communicates when it induces people to buy Dimple's Dumplings. But the idea of eliciting responses can present awkward problems involving the nature of purposes and intentions.

We can avoid some problems by viewing the study of communication as a study of human responses. That view is akin to Goyer's [16] operational approach and to Thayer's conception of communication as taking something into account.[37, pp. 26ff] And as we have seen, this can also be a view in anthropology. In fact, when an anthropologist is on a South Sea island, it is easier for him to see people responding to each other, to see them communicating, than it is to see their culture, their heredity, or some other hypostatized quiddity.

The second point made earlier was that anthropology studies human responses with the same methods and orientations used in studying communication. Although most communication studies also use other methods, such as experiments, some have used the relatively unstructured approach of natural history. It has been used particularly in studying monkeys and apes, but in studying human interaction as well.[34] It should be further used to compare and classify communication patterns around the world. We have anthropological classifications by kinship system, by level of energy utilization, and by language group for the Navaho, for the Nuer, and for other peoples; but we have no comparable classifications by communication type. The natural history of communication and the science of comparative communication both need to be fostered.

Third, as anthropology studies the continuum of human responses, so does communication. Instead of fragmenting the world and balkanizing our concerns by making sharp distinctions between biological, social, and humanistic responses, we can better understand them as a continuum. There are also natural continuums between graffiti and poetry, between the physical expression of human aspiration in a ballet and the mating dance of the stickleback fish. They are all well-founded and legitimate forms of communication, each significant in its own context and all part of the human spectacle.

The fourth point described what anthropologists look for. The simple empiricism of natural history and its relatively open and unstructured approach lead anthropologists to look for nothing, for differences and distinctions, for contexts, and for freedom and order. Or, in more ontological terms, they look for the self-structured and self-meaning field. Communication studies can be equally free of prestructuring and closure. When we look without anticipating what we will see, the world opens up and expands. We could see whales in the desert, languages that have no verbs, emotions that have never been known before. And when we think we see new responses, we also have to consider how we see them. When we conceive of a field as open, we emphasize the process of looking at it as much as the content at which we look. Thus Richard W. Budd has shown that the most productive study of communication is "an open learning experience." [11, p. 32]

But how relevant is any of this in a world beset by wars and galled by inequality in cities that have become uninhabitable? Anthropological approaches to communication can do more than study facts for their own sake. In at least two ways, they are relevant to the problems we face as citizens.

The questions we pose and the problems we face are largely determined by the way we look at the world. A paranoid person, for example, asks, "Why is everyone looking at me?" The person in love hopes he can give enough. Generally we try to answer questions using the same viewpoints from which these questions arose in the first place. We leave where we came in, unable to get outside of ourselves, on a treadmill leading nowhere. Anthropology, however, teaches us Hausa, Hottentot, and Hopi points of view, giving us broader perspectives in which to reorient ourselves. It gives us alternatives to our own habitual ways of looking at things, and when we are faced with problems we need to perceive alternatives. By providing a catharsis through perspective, anthropology helps resolve our daily perplexities.

Even when anthropological approaches do not solve our problems directly, they can help more generally in the long run. Botanists help us to increase the quantity of corn we can grow per acre, not by studying corn directly, but by studying photosynthesis and genetics, by uncovering basic principles that can later be applied for the betterment of corn. In the same way, anthropologists can uncover basic principles about communication that may be used for the betterment of man.

REFERENCES AND SUGGESTED READINGS

1. Altmann, Stuart A., "Sociobiology of Rhesus Monkeys," *Journal of Theoretical Biology,* Vol. 8, 1965.

2. Bachofen, Johan Jacob, *Das Mutterrecht*. Basel: Benno, Schwabe, 1861.
3. Bateson, Gregory, "Culture Contact and Schismogenesis," *Man,* Vol. 199, 1935.
4. Baudouin de Courtenay, J., *Versuch einer Theorie der phonetischen Alternationen*. Strassburg, 1895.
5. Benedict, Ruth, "Continuities and Discontinuities in Cultural Conditioning," *Psychiatry,* Vol. 1, 1938.
6. Bennett, John W., Herbert Passin, and Robert K. McKnight, *In Search of Identity: The Japanese Overseas Scholar in America and Japan*. Minneapolis: University of Minnesota Press, 1958.
7. Berlo, David K., *The Process of Communication*. New York: Holt, Rinehart and Winston, 1960.
8. Bierstedt, Robert, *The Social Order*. New York: McGraw-Hill, 1957.
9. Birdwhistell, Ray L., *Kinesics and Context*. Philadelphia: University of Pennsylvania Press, 1970.
10. Boas, Franz, *Race, Language and Culture*. New York: Macmillan, 1940.
11. Budd, Richard W., *Communication, Education and Simulation,* Institute for Communication Studies, University of Iowa, 1970, prepublication copy.
12. Chapple, Eliot D., *The Interaction Chronograph: Its Evolution and Present Application*. New York: American Management Association, 1949.
13. Chapple, Eliot D., *Culture and Biological Man*. New York: Holt, Rinehart and Winston, 1970.
14. Dance, Frank E. X., *Human Communication Theory*. New York: Holt, Rinehart and Winston, 1967.
15. Goodenough, Ward H., "Componential Analysis," *Science,* Vol. 156, 1967.
16. Goyer, Robert S., *Communication, Communicative Process, Meaning: Toward a Unified Theory,* Special Report No. 20, Center for Communication Studies, Ohio University, 1969.
17. Haddon, Alfred C., *The Study of Man*. London: Murray, 1908.
18. Hall, Edward T., "A System for the Notation of Proxemic Behavior," *American Anthropologist,* Vol. 65, 1963.
19. Hall, Edward T., *The Hidden Dimension*. Garden City, N.Y.: Doubleday, 1966.
20. Hymes, Dell H., "Introduction: Toward Ethnographies of Communication," in *The Ethnography of Communication,* ed. by John Gumperz and Dell H. Hymes; *American Anthropologist,* Vol. 66, Pt. 2, 1964, special publication of the American Anthropological Association.
21. Hymes, Dell H., "On Anthropological Linguistics and Congeners," *American Anthropologist,* Vol. 68, 1966.
22. Kroeber, Alfred L., *An Anthropologist Looks at History*. Berkeley and Los Angeles: University of California Press, 1963.
23. Levi-Strauss, Claude, *The Raw and the Cooked*. New York: Harper & Row, 1969.
24. Linton, Ralph, *The Study of Man*. New York: Appleton-Century, 1936.
25. Lorenz, Konrad, *On Aggression*. New York: Harcourt, Brace, 1966.
26. McLennan, John Ferguson, *Primitive Marriage*. Edinburgh: Adam and Charles Black, 1865.
27. Mead, Margaret, *Continuities in Cultural Evolution*. New Haven: Yale University Press, 1964.
28. Michener, James A., *Iberia*. New York: Random House, 1968.
29. Morgan, Lewis H., *Systems of Consanguinity and Affinity of the Human Family*. Washington, D.C.: Smithsonian Institution, 1870.

30. Pike, Kenneth L., *Language in Relation to a Unified Theory of the Structure of Human Behavior*. The Hague: Mouton, 1967.
31. Redfield, Robert, "The Folk Society," *American Journal of Sociology*, Vol. 52, 1947.
32. Schaller, George B., *The Mountain Gorilla: Ecology and Behavior*. Chicago: University of Chicago Press, 1963.
33. Smith, Alfred G., ed., *Communication and Culture*. New York: Holt, Rinehart and Winston, 1966.
34. Smith, Alfred G., *Communication and Status*. Eugene, Oreg.: University of Oregon, 1966.
35. Tax, Sol, Loren C. Eiseley, Irving Rouse, and Carl F. Voegelin, eds., *An Appraisal of Anthropology Today*. Chicago: University of Chicago Press, 1953.
36. Textor, Robert B., *A Cross-Culture Summary*, New Haven: Human Relations Area Files, 1966.
37. Thayer, Lee, *Communication and Communication Systems*. Homewood, Ill.: Irwin, 1968.
38. Tinbergen, Niko, "The Curious Behavior of the Stickleback," *Scientific American*, Vol. 187, 1952.
39. Tylor, Edward Burnett, *Primitive Culture*. London: Murray, 1871.
40. Tylor, Stephen A., ed., *Cognitive Anthropology*. New York: Holt, Rinehart and Winston, 1969.
41. van Gennep, Arnold, *The Rites of Passage*. Chicago: University of Chicago Press (1908), 1960.
42. Whorf, Benjamin Lee, "The Relation of Habitual Thought and Behavior to Language," in *Language, Culture, and Personality: Essays in Memory of Edward Sapir*, ed. by Leslie Spier *et al*. Menasha, Wis.: Sapir Memorial Fund, 1941.

Robert E. Mueller is both a scientist and an artist, and contributes significantly in both realms. He is the author of *Eyes in Space, Inventor's Notebook,* and *Inventivity.* His most recent book is *The Science of Art.* Another volume, *Mind Over Media,* is now in preparation. Mr. Mueller is an active artist as well. Some of his work has been shown in the New York Museum of Modern Art.

2

ART: AN APPROACH TO HUMAN COMMUNICATION

ROBERT E. MUELLER

FLETCHER PRATT [37] tells a fascinating story in his classic book on cryptology, *Secret and Urgent,* about an indecipherable manuscript written by Roger Bacon. Discovered by an Italian rare-book dealer in 1912, the manuscript eventually reached the United States, where many scholars attempted to decipher its meticulous and mysterious scrawl. In the manuscript were contained a series of unusual pictures which did not contribute much to its meaning. Finally, a medieval scholar at the University of Pennsylvania, Dr. William Newbold, acquired the manuscript and turned his hand to the problem. He worked long and hard, absorbing the difficult text and trying to determine its connection with the illustrations. At last he began to have success, but what he discovered was too amazing to be true! Roger Bacon had evidently invented a microscope in the thirteenth century, well before the "official" invention in 1677, and the telescope long before Galileo! Dr. Newbold felt that the accompanying drawings could be nothing other than spiral nebulae or one-celled animals. After carefully rechecking his method, Dr. Newbold published his finds, much to the amazement and skepticism of the academic community. Cryptologists who checked out his method could find no error until finally a brilliant English astronomer named Proctor took up the problem. He showed that using Dr. Newbold's method it was possible to "decipher" Shakespeare and make it mean practically anything one desired. In all innocence, Dr. Newbold had actually manipulated the manuscript by Roger Bacon to satisfy his own unconscious wish for particular facts!

Art is sometimes such indecipherable material; it is possible to read

15

anything into it you desire. Is such art uncommunicative? Art sometimes seems to be private or to be a hoax. You have to have superhuman abilities, wide knowledge, and some talent as a cryptologist to understand the "message" of works belonging to certain schools of art. Is this a failure on the part of the artist or on the part of the viewer? Was Roger Bacon really trying to fool us and create a massive hoax by dreaming up utter nonsense, complete with fantastically imaginative pictures? Did he realize that for centuries scholars would attempt to unravel the mystery? (To my knowledge, Bacon's manuscript is still not deciphered.)

If you have a fertile imagination, or if you are sufficiently motivated, as was Dr. Newbold, you can see things in cloud shapes or in random art, much the way you can see faces or animals in rolling clouds in a Rorschach inkblot. Leonardo da Vinci knew the value of the random. He suggested that to throw a sponge charged with paint at canvas would give many interesting shapes to an area. *Sfumato,* his method of creating an ambiguity by blurring, is like the Japanese method of *shibuyi,* which allows for a resolution of an order beyond a rough confusing exterior. *Sfumato* is a useful method for an artist in search of original form. It was pursued methodically by the English painter Alexander Cozzens, who actually set it up as a "principle" of creativity. [13]

But after the fact—when you look at a finished work of art—you expect it to have more value and more independence than that which requires the complete application of your imagination. There must be in randomness some suggestion of form which the artist somehow calls to our attention in order to transcend the purely accidental. If we have to read all the meaning into a work of art ourselves, why do we need the work in the first place? Anything ought to do as well. What communication is possible with random art, if not this limited, reflected opportunity for our own imagination to work? What if an artist probes his own inner randomness—his own psychophysiological entropy—and tries to manifest it directly in an art form? Are there not degrees of randomness? The communication theorist who applies Wiener's cybernetic methods, called autocorrelation techniques, is able to discover order beneath impossible confusion, like radar signals beneath radio noise or cryptologists' secrets beneath difficult ciphers.* Dr. Newbold would have envied modern cryptologists and their deciphering techniques, which make it possible to rank even noise.

Pure randomness is called *gaussian,* and it is achievable only by mechanical means, like the throw of a die, the toss of a penny, or the motion of electrons in a vacuum tube which amplifies electronic shot-effect randomness. Humans, on the other hand, always create something this side of

---

* See *The Science of Art* for an evaluation of the applicability of information theory to aesthetics. See also Chapter 10 in this volume.

perfect randomness when left to their own devices. Theoretically at least, we see that something of ourselves is always communicated, even in our most haphazard production. Even our most chaotic moments exhibit our particular entropy figure. Try as we may, we cannot transcend a certain minuscule order which is somehow characteristic of each of us, even if we do the random walk.

Now if an artist probes his own inner randomness and tries to put himself into a shot-effect mode in which he is externalizing his psychophysical randomness in some artistic form, he still usually creates some kind of order in his act. The so-called Action painters who go at their canvases with pure motor movements, or the Surrealists who try to capture dreams, are not as arbitrary as they may think: the lines of an Action painting often suggest the pivot points of an arm, and from Surrealism comes forth a dreamlike logic with symbolic content. Aleatory music that leaves freedom of choice to the performing artist, for instance, adds not accident but the statistic of the performer to the statistic of the composer. The same is true of Baroque music, which leaves ornamentation up to the performer. It is not as easy as many people think to transcend the intrinsic organizing abilities of the mind, especially if an artist has been trained for years or has inherited a strong artistic tradition.

Modern schools that try to put randomness into their art do so only with limited results—they are less chaotic than they think. This time of confusion in which we live forces some artists who think that art should reflect its age to turn to the random in art instead of creating still another new degree of confusion that could have its own meaning. They imply, as Ben Shahn [39] suggests in *The Shape of Content,* that they have an affinity for the unknown, that they are "revealing the mystical paroxysms of nature," and are in touch with the great sea of unconscious unknowns which engulfs us all. But, as Shahn also suggests, they are only communicating their own romantic desires to be associated with the unknown—and also building certain orders of randomness. Their art becomes but an imitative thing, albeit imitating something chaotic. Modern science seems to corroborate or enhance artistic effort toward randomness by suggesting the essential randomness of nature and its limitations as far as causal certainty is concerned. One is reminded, however, of Einstein's famous remark that he believed that God does not play dice with us. In this case, our unconscious probably does not play dice with our imagination; and if we allow it to do so, we are missing the point of artistic meaning.

There is, however, a certain respect we always pay to chaos as the source of all order. Too much emphasis on order and perfection can lead to sterility; the impulse to destroy an old art form can be a healthy impulse if it leads toward a new creative vision. Ben Shahn once gave a talk to a group of architects in Aspen, Colorado, who were planning a new art center dedicated to perfection. In his talk Shahn emphasized the importance of a little chaos. That this applies to our scientific theorizing also becomes patently obvious when we begin to accumulate new facts which cannot be ordered by old theories. Art is not so lucky as science in this respect. Science looks to explain the order of nature, but when chaos rears its ugly head, science must begin to take it into account. Art can deny chaos by keeping attention focused on the ordered creations of the past, but chaos makes its secret entry through the imagination of man, and it appears in new artistic productions. This chaos is but a disguised brother to previous ordered creations, unrecognizable because of man's unfamiliarity with its strange costume. That is, if it has any final creative meaning for man.

EXTRA-ART MEANING

Extra-art information, arising when the title, name, or caption of a work of art carries important communicative suggestions about the work itself, can be more meaningful than we suspect. Given a near-random work of art—even one as inchoate as the mad Professor Frenhoefer could create—the title can actually define it. Countless meanings can therefore be communicated by virtue of a simple title, and the meanings actually arise due to the work of art's being given a "name." Consider, for instance, an entirely black canvas called "Death Riding a Black Horse on a Moonless Night." Most people who read the title and then looked at the picture would think they actually saw a creature lurking there in the blackness. It is possible to conjure up in our minds an entire image—to see the "figure in the carpet," as Henry James called it—and to think that the artist actually put it there. This is one degree less than a hallucination, however, because it is a controllable mode of the brain, like a hypnotic suggestion. We are not carried away into an unreality of image despite our better judgment, as in hallucination; but even though we are firmly anchored in our own reality, we find that the caption pulls us into a newly imagined reality. Max Ernst took this idea to its logical yet ridiculous extreme when he gave poetic and lengthy titles to some of his pictures. One amusing title is "The Transfiguration of the Chameleon on Mount Tabor Takes Place in an Elegant Limousine While the Angels and Halcyon Fly from the Houses of Men and While the Very Holy Costume of Our Lord Exclaims *de Profundis* Three Times Before Whipping The Exhibitionist's Flesh."

The power of the extra-art clue is very strong because it actually *assigns* communicative meaning to a work of art. This applies both to nonobjective art and to realistic art, although we most easily accept the suggestion when the picture is vague or random or surrealistic. This is perhaps the best sense in which the word *symbol* can be applied to art, because the caption defines the symbolic intent of art—which is the meaning we generally attach to the idea of symbolization today. I have purposely avoided using the word *symbol* because I feel that art is more complex than the symbolic assignment of meaning or the symbolization of emotions through an analogous morphological correspondence. Symbolism in poetry or symbolization of form is but a part of the story. The actual creative act is more properly called "encoding" because it partakes of that for which it stands. If we are familiar with an artist's body of work and know his past symbolic assignments through his captions or through a familiarity with his subject matter, we can guess about any new work of his we see. We continue to appreciate this symbolic meaning without really experiencing the work of art at any deeper level—which seems to me to demand a separation from the more apparent meanings that are contained in successful new works.

Extra-art meaning can be quite relevant if, for instance, it concerns some cause or idea which is important to us. Such causes obviously affect us as human beings, but they do so as simple messages which describe themselves, not as perceptual communications whose insights are built out of the actual communicative elements—as is art. Such causes and ideas are important, but art is not the only way to communicate ideas which are important, nor is it the only way in which we build our humanity; science, both as description of conjectured facts and as the revelation of natural forces, also influences us profoundly.

Captions or titles may or may not always coincide with the image which the artist has tried to capture in his art, but they most certainly change our response to the art. We react differently toward a titled canvas than toward one which is not, and captions deserve more care in their assignment than most gallery directors or artists give them. Banal novels with biblical titles often seem more profound than they are. In a sense, the caption or title of a work tells you something about the artist, if you care to study it as a symptom or hint of his philosophical orientation.

In the last analysis—and this should be our concern when we approach art—we must accept the title *de facto* as part of the active communication situation of all art. When an artist gives a title to a picture, a name to a book, and so on, we must assume that he does so for a very specific purpose, although he himself may not understand what he is doing or how it affects the communication situation. He must realize, however, that someone will read the caption or the title and be influenced by it during the time that he is considering the work of art. If a purist paints two chartreuse squares of different shades on canvas and calls his picture "Glory Arising," he must realize that two out of three museum-goers will actually see images of women on high, or God apotheosized, or other lofty images.

If the picture is close to the title in some literal way—for instance, a random picture that conjures up images of cloud shapes and is called "Chaos Apotheosized"—then there is a good chance that people will actually see what the artist thought *he* saw, however indefinite his title, much as we recognize the profile of Lincoln in a cloud shape if someone points it out. The artist may have chosen his title because he himself thought he saw something in his canvas after its production which we, too, can see because of common experience. We must recognize that this is part of the communication situation in art, although it is not necessarily part of *creativity* in art.

This may seem trivial, but it is actually at the heart of the question of whether everyone should react to a work of art in the same way, and whether art should be universal and should always be reacted to by man in constant fashion. When there is a discrepancy between the extra-art meaning of the title or caption and the work of art itself, the viewers or audiences are confused. They suspect the artist of false motives when it was only sloppy titling. When different levels of meaning are going on in the art situation—one called forth by the title and one suggested by the work of art itself—the conflict is sometimes to the detriment of the art.

Obviously there are many possible levels of meaning in a work of art, and all these can confuse (or enhance) the general communicative situation of art. A story can be understood at one level by, say, a child and at another by an adult, as is *Gulliver's Travels*. Some people react to art at one level and others at another level; each depends on his information about the artist and his intent and on the various suggestions and success of the artist. People feel cheated when they learn that they have missed some part of the communication in a multimeaning work of art; or they feel snobbishly self-satisfied if they can detect some new level which has escaped everyone else's attention. A recent analysis by Paul Tannenbaum of Edward Albee's *Who's Afraid of Virginia Woolf* shows how far it is sometimes possible to hide meanings in art, or to what extent meanings can be read into art.* Whether or not Albee consciously thought these meanings through to the extent that Tannenbaum suggests is unimportant, but their embodiment in the characters is one of the sources of the play's creative success. The main characters are George and Martha (parents of our nation); the play is set in New Carthage (built on the ruins of the Old World) University; and the couple's imaginary child plays an important role (as the "American Dream"). Martha (crass materialistic society) is wedded to George (intellectual, democratic liberalism). Their friends, a young scientist, who is seduced by Martha, and his mousy wife (inheritor of the church and its money), who is full of a fear that gives her a false

---

* Paul Tannenbaum, "Letter to the Editor," *The New York Times* (July 24, 1966).

pregnancy, are educated by Martha and George. The use of the name of Virginia Woolf, herself a novelist who wrote about the English upper classes, is another symbol of the American Dream.

Various art forms have developed different ways for generating levels of meaning and for encoding them in individual communication situations. Meanings are more than just by-products of art; more than just accidental facts which can be used or not, depending on the whim of the artist and his desire to hide ideas in his art. As suggested earlier, a true creative meaning in art arises when various encoded levels relate in a new way to reveal a new perception, and this is due to the particular media and its possibilities for multilevel encoding. But before actually considering how the arts achieve encoding, we must go back to the problem of how, in skirting on the edge of randomness or the unfamiliar in art, the artist can successfully forge art which does, in fact, communicate beyond randomness—although not necessarily creatively.

ENCODING IN ART

The desire to define a new work of art or a new artistic vision that at first glance appears random, or so unfamiliar that we are lost, is the reason why some artists (for instance, Picasso) always include something known, something recognizable, in their art. Unconsciously, artists often feel adrift if their current work does not have continuity with previous work, with reality, or with some predetermined logic (including socially accepted logic). They feel that when they make a new departure, they must define what they are now doing right in the work itself by including some of the old ideas, the easily communicated and well-understood elements. Picasso [20] suggested that this vague contact leads the viewer more easily into the realm of the unknown. It informs the viewer that a departure is occurring, but that it is a connected departure in the way shown— like including a cipher in art by which to decode the entire work. The recognizable form defines the artist's style and provides a gateway into his new imaginings, and at the same time, it allows the artist to deviate even more extremely. Even the vaguest suggestion of a past idea is sufficient to tie a work of art down to something familiar; this is liberating in some instances, permitting an artist to be even more radical, abstract, or bizarre if he desires. His stylistic deviations must be consistent in some way, but it is an easy matter for an artist to hide inconsistencies with stylistic devices. In the epochal "Les Demoiselles d'Avignon," Picasso does this by painting heads derived from exotic African sculpture on his recognizable Cubistically influenced nudes. We accept the canvas because we recognize the Cubist nude bodies, but the heads jar us. In addition, Picasso calls our attention to what he is doing by painting the heads thick impasto rather than thinly painted like the bodies, technically justifying their joint representation on the same canvas.

Calling a work by a number gets around the difficulties of extra-art meaning in the caption or title, and it makes it more important that the work of art itself have its own significance. Opus numbers for string quartets or numbers for paintings shift communication back to the art. Now pure randomness palls, and something more than nothing must get across.

An art form such as classical music presents its encodings in easily understood modes because society has encouraged music as an art form for centuries. Surprises or radical new departures in our own art forms are not welcome because they are not understood. (Neither can we appreciate the subtleties of a primitive culture unless we have exposed ourselves to its art for considerable time.) When a painter uses lines and dots, endlessly varying images in a completely nonobjective though inventive way, as I have done with the illustrations in this chapter, it takes slow exposure to his images—a gradual appreciation of their formal qualities—before it is possible to sense their perceptual meanings and creative communication. It is all a matter of form. Lines and dots communicate, among other things, the endless possibilities to create the new and beautiful in a simple way. For instance, the brilliance of a Bach sonata may be appreciated most by string players, not as much for its emotional range or even its articulation as for the endless imaginative complexities in so simple a form.

Recently, Milton Babbit announced that public enthusiasm for electronic music is nil, and he suggests that various composers working with electronic sounds should content themselves with composing for each other. This "ivory-tower" attitude has the merit of lifting the artist from the competitive realm of mass-communication media (which is apt to distort their motives or destroy their values anyway), but it has the disadvantage of forcing art into more and more esoteric and sterile areas. It also deprives the general public of the necessity to learn how to perceive new music. The deeper currents in creative communications are such that they can be appreciated on a larger scale than many practitioners suppose. Babbit underestimates the general audience for electronic music, perhaps drawing his conclusions from audience reaction to poor electronic music. We hear electronic music on television commercials and do not know it; our children hear it as sound effects on their programs. We probably cannot react to electronic music because it is essentially a young art form which even the artists do not yet fully know. Nevertheless, I can imagine more interesting compositions being created now by some gadget-musician, perhaps still in his teens, fiddling away in his basement; and when such a composer begins to have an opportunity to present his music to a more responsive audience, then the world will see a new art form come to fruition.

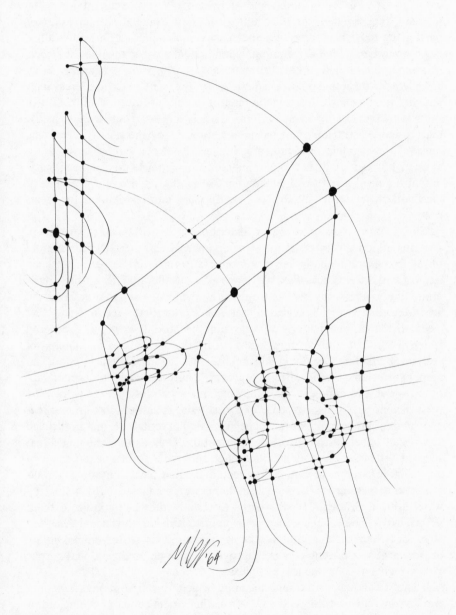

Figure 2.1   (c) Robert E. Mueller

The fundamental element in a work of art is the medium—the medium is the message, as McLuhan suggests. The most elementary reaction to a work of art is to its medium, and at least the *first* message of art is the medium. The sonority of sound, the texture of oils, the syntax of sentences, the movement in dance, the structure of materials in a building— these are what is initially communicated when a work of art is first perceived. The reason we like to see and hear a symphony orchestra is that considerable meaning is attached to seeing the conductor, the musicians, and the total visual display in the concert hall, and most of all to seeing the live performers in action—all of which is lost on records. Perhaps the reason many performing musicians are horrified by the idea of electronic music is not so much that they are worried about being replaced by automation, but that such music eliminates what Clarence Moore suggests is one of the most meaningful communicative facts of music: the presence of the human performer with all his imperfections and possibilities for greatness.

The problem becomes one of determining to what extent one sense communication can be substituted for another when we try to translate old terms like *music* to new ones like *electronic music*. If we see a musician playing, we are not actually experiencing the tactile qualities in his touching of the instrument, but we are directly aware of the kinesthesia of the act. McLuhan [29, p. 282] suggests that the modern tape-recording system meets the tactile challenge of television because it restores the depth which the old, scratchy record lost. He mistakes, I think, a broadening of the aural channel for the inclusion of the tactile communication; no amount of stereophonic effects, however "sculpturesque" the sound appears to our two ears, can make up for not seeing musicians at work. The eye's vision, which gives a sense of kinesthesia, is entirely lost on any record, and a broadening or a deepening of the sound of music through stereo can never restore this lost information. It is almost axiomatic that the symbol for a sense datum does not substitute for the experience of sensation in art. A second axiom could be that new sensations always give rise to new arts. The so-called hotness or coolness of the media, by which McLuhan means media with wide bandwidths as opposed to those with narrow bandwidths (telephone: cool; television: hot), only has the effect of tightening human involvement, because it decreases the possibility of extraneous disturbing effects, improving the communication, making the requirements of encoding less complex.

There is another important meaning which our first impression of a work of art communicates to us, even if that art is either unintelligible or extremely poor. The work of art is recognized as being a link between us and another personality. We are more impressed by the art if that personality has something special to offer us—even though it may not be carried in this particular work. The productions of people who have been deemed great by society have a magical communicative quality. It is most powerfully carried by the name or, when there is a signature, by the actual form of signed letters on the canvas or paper. Plagiarism, although it is, as Northrop Fry [19] suggests, one of the fundamental elements in all literary creations, is frowned upon because the communication of one person's essence is thereby confused with another's. Man Ray carried the idea of the importance of the signature in a painting to its final point when he made a picture that was actually composed of the letters and numbers, MAN RAY 1914. [24] Anonymous art, such as the sculpture that adorns medieval cathedrals in Europe, puts us in contact with an entire era.

The essence of greatness is somehow embodied in art done by great people, and we react to it initially for this reason. Before we get a glimpse of the actual work, before we hear the poem or read the story or see the play, we are disposed to accept it favorably in a certain way. We treasure every scrap of art from the recognized great, almost as if they were fetishes. Picasso can get away with murder in his art—and he sometimes does—and the world buys it and even reveres it; his buffoonery is a healthy reaction to the world's blind acceptance of his art. The greater the artist—at least, the greater the *myth* of the artist—the greater we value his productions, whatever they may be, and the more excited we become at the prospect of any art communication from him.

This is why success breeds success in art; why, as Picasso realized quite early in his career, the myth of the artist is actually quite important for the communication of art; why some artists concentrate more on creating a personality than they do on creating meaningful works of art. Death, too, is often the necessary condition for placing the artist into this extra-human mode we call the "mythical genius."

The physical and social problems which notoriety entails have compelled some artists to seek anonymity. For instance, B. Traven, the novelist who wrote *The Treasure of Sierra Madre,* has managed to preserve his anonymity all these years, and J. D. Salinger, author of *Catcher in the Rye,* avoids interviews and publicity. An artist's reasons for avoiding the public eye may be idiosyncratic, but the fact remains that such an attitude extols the art and diminishes the personality of the artist.

The world accepts an artist for many reasons, but paradoxically, acceptance gives him license to communicate in new and more powerful ways. Works of art which might normally be overlooked are given greater attention in the world art market. Success gives the artist license to communicate in high gear, with full confidence that he will be accepted. Some artists are overwhelmed by success and rendered impotent as creators, but this may be because their creative abilities were quite poor in the first place. Or perhaps they have, like certain *nouveau riches,* lost their ability

Figure 2.2   (c) Robert E. Mueller

to cash in on vital art. An artist may also have a sufficient body of work left over from his more creative youth to keep his art going, even after fame reaches him. Or he could be that rare artist who manages to maintain and deepen his artistic vision in the face of fame and fortune; then, our hopes for the all-powerful artistic genius are truly justified, and mankind is rewarded with great art.

This side of the extracommunicative suggestions mentioned thus far, and short of chaos, how are the bulk of important meanings built in art for the edification of mankind? The various media have manipulative possibilities which provide for artistic encoding to carry the human meaning of art. To assume that the encoding of art is just the literal use of artistic elements to express corresponding ideas—as rough-textured reds might convey aggression—is to miss the point of art communication and to vastly underestimate the communicative possibilities of art, not to mention its creative potential.

The encoding of meaning in art is always formal, that is, established through conventions. The conventions of a particular encoding are usually so familiar that we have forgotten we learned them, but in all cases they have been building up in our minds during our normal perceptual development or have built up during a new and intimate association with a given work of art. Although the conventions are formal, they are not arbitrary. We learn the conventions of art by an exposure to art—although help can be given to facilitate this learning process. The sensuousness of the conventions in art encoding usually allows us to detect them at the same time we are sensing the art itself.

The various possibilities for encoding different levels of meaning in a given medium compound the problem and also test the abilities of the artist to invent meanings within meanings that will be significantly and creatively related. Nature is the "experience" with which all artists are most familiar, and there is a long history of artists who have used nature directly in their work. The gamut of art begins with nature itself and extends through all human experience, including the psychic worlds of man; it also embraces the communicative art medium itself, with all the theoretical possibilities for encoding the relations of form which it presents. Problems of society, human redemption, the evolution of psyches, and the entire range of intellectual ideas also become an integral part of the encoding of art. This is important because communication allows the encoding not only of natural phenomena, but also of phenomena from other art.

That which art encodes is not static because man, as he lives and grows, as he experiences more and more art, as he learns to respond to art more meaningfully, influences art. We all contribute to the establishment of new meanings in current works of art, partially by our acceptance or rejection of these works, but mainly by our absorption of their essence to pass on to the next generation. Sometimes an art experience is overlooked or denied, and a succeeding generation takes it up and attaches new meaning to it. An artist can sometimes anticipate our changing sensitivities to a medium and take advantage of them by creating a new art which will only have meaning when it is understood—perhaps by the next generation. The artist is predicting how future generations will react to an art-encoding method. It is necessary, in fact, that every artist have complete faith that his encoding methods will be perfectly grasped by someone, although perhaps such an understanding can only be reached in the future. That art derives its basic form from a convention forces some artists to try to deny communication in their art; but they do not realize that even this denial will someday be understood and that their art, too, will be comprehended, if only for its perversity.

Since the encoding of art meaning is a question of formal conventions and not an inherent, immutable quality of the media, it is reasonable to assume that the meaning of art will change. Not only do the conventions of art change, but the interpretation which successive generations put on them change. This is counter to the idea that art is ageless, but not to the idea that art is forever human. Those who have not as yet grasped the meaning of a given art form—the uninitiated and also the very young—still have an opportunity to grow through a contact with old art. Music illustrates this difficulty of comprehending the unfamiliar: Eastern tonalities are generally not appreciated by the Western ear, and vice versa.

One of the functions of the critic is to sharpen the awareness of a culture to the encoding schemes of its artists. Through an educational process which leads to a better knowledge of the aims and operations of the artist, and to an understanding of the formal communicative means he uses, the critic helps us to respond to the creative communication in art. He cannot, of course, do other than indicate; the rest is up to us. Since this is a problem of actual perceptual reaction, we must have the necessary psychophysical tools at our mental disposal before we can react to art—and this sometimes requires a lot of experiential conditioning: looking at art, listening to music, attending plays and movies, reading books and poetry, and so on. The theoretician can help, too, by pointing out what the artist is up to from a technical standpoint, how he actually brings meaning to full bloom in his art.

The actual evaluation of a work of art cannot be made immediately upon perceiving it, since it is the function of great art to affect us in a creative way. Only after art has had its cumulative effect on us, sometimes only after generations have had an opportunity to drink from the creative springs and assimilate the effects, only then can it be grasped in all of its significance. In our age, the entire act can perhaps be speeded up through the prudent use of the mass media.

The advice of the critic is not like the extra-art meanings communicated by the title or signature on a work of art or the personality associated with the artist. The critic can only indicate what may have escaped attention; he cannot have the art experience by proxy for us and pass on his veneration with no justification. Once we begin to explore the jungle of a work of art, we are entirely on our own, although an understanding derived from the critic can serve us like a map. Experience obviously aids the art explorer as it does the African explorer, but maps save considerable time —although they do not indicate the location of ferocious animals or exotic flowers.

This concept of the function of the critic and teacher is considerably less broad than that of some art historians who, like Panofsky, feel that a total historical-human-social knowledge is necessary to understand art. I do not think that it is possible to say, categorically, that all art must be approached only in the terms of the art itself, excluding all historical or psychological insights which might be gotten from a study of the culture of its time or a knowledge of the personality of the artist. D. H. Lawrence is, for instance, ubiquitous in most of his novels, and his life can enlighten us about his characters, give us many important clues about his encoding motifs, and also enlighten us about why he wrote. On the other hand, James Joyce is the opposite. We can easily apply to his work this statement:

> The personality of the artist, at first a cry or a cadence or a mood and then a fluid and lambent narrative, finally refines itself out of existence, impersonalizes itself, so to speak. . . . The artist, like the God of the creation, remains within or behind or beyond or above his handiwork, invisible, refined out of existence, indifferent, paring his fingernails. (25, p. 168)

The improved reaction of succeeding generations is due to conditioning to art, which becomes more and more spontaneous as it becomes more an integral part of our perceptual apparatus. Since man desires to bind himself to previous generations, he will usually regard art approved by previous generations more favorably than he will new and unfamiliar art. As the freshman physics student today easily understands the theory of relativity, once only grasped by a few men in the world, so very sophisticated art of the past is comprehended because of a generally higher level of art awareness. The broader environment provided for children today by communication media and modern education actually speeds up awareness of art, allowing us a greater potential for future fulfillment. Sense-stretching profits from time-binding.

LEVELS OF ENCODING

Various artistic means for encoding demand most of our attention when we try to understand the actual ways in which creative communications are fabricated. It must be emphasized that this knowledge does not provide an artist or an audience with all that is required to make or detect great art. That is a question of talent and of experience—as are all acts of true creation. The Sunday painters, the Thursday-night string quartet, the amateur poet, the dilettante, however serious are their motives, however high their aspirations, often get trapped by a static view of their art which prevents growth. The Sunday painter may paint only what his eye sees, never giving his imagination or soul or even his heart a chance; the amateur string quartet may play only Mozart or the simplest, standard works because the moderns are too difficult; the poetaster may compose maudlin sonnets that imitate some admired master. The usual in art is what becomes accepted by the most "serious" culture lovers, and they often disdain a more creative fad or fashion which the uninformed will accept. The informed view of the serious culture lover, however, has allowed him to go only so far—forcing him to err on the side of conservatism and poor taste rather than overenthusiasm.

The reason it is not possible to set up standards for art production or to derive practical methods from present theories is that the situation always changes; the practical situation of art is always different from the theoretical basis which might explain it. We do not always necessarily respond to certain artistic elements in one way and to others in a different way. For example, blue can be thought of as cool and red as warm, musical rumbles as fears, bearded men as prophets; but established conventions can be accepted as important elements for future artistic encoding only to a limited extent. Artists have a way of taking up the wrong notions and using them in incorrect but powerful new ways; this is the very nature of artistic creativity. Familiar elements, the well-known elements of past art, are given new twists and taken to surprising extremes in all new, creative art which deserves our respect. The painter loves to push reds back and bring blues forward; a musician can use a rumble as he might use the sound of a flute; a writer might make a wise-looking man into a fool. The creative jumps made by an artist destroy previous conceptions and build new attitudes in his art, always out of the unexpected.

In considering the various encoding possibilities of art, it is useful to divide them into two main classes: those existing at the primary level of physical sensation and those once removed to a secondary level where a physical sensation is suggested and rebuilt in our minds. This is not always a simple division to apply to the arts, since the one can sometimes be reduced to the other. If the sensual arts like music and painting are thought of as primary-level arts, and those arts which use words, secondary level, some valuable theoretical distinctions can be made when discussing the encoding of art forms. The overlap between primary and secondary levels in some art forms—such as opera, which uses words and music, or even movies and theater, which have their visual elements—gives us another level of encoding, but one which can be more clearly outlined when its components are clearly recognized.

To distinguish painting and music as primary phenomenal arts is not to revert to the "innocent-eye" (or ear) theory of Ruskin and Berkeley. Conceptually, all art forms must be sensual-mental organizations. Nevertheless, most encoding in painting and music is achieved directly at the level of the physical sensation, whereas in the language arts, encoding is more conventionally achieved at the sensation level, and only sensually suggested at the mental level. Similar sensations at the word level in language can be produced in various ways. A novel can be put into braille or into Morse code; it can be written in green ink or on an electric typewriter; it can be translated into another language. If sense is preserved and form is accurate in the literary and verbal arts, the arts still remain valid, whatever their physical medium. (An exception would be poetry that uses its sounds as a kind of music.) No such translation is possible in the arts that depend directly on physical qualities for their meaning: To translate or even to reproduce is to destroy in music or painting or any other art qua physical in this sense.

Although painting suggests depth, it does so by means of illusion residing point by point across the two-dimensional canvas. A painting may be realistic and literal or it may suggest worlds that are dreamlike or mythical, but it is always primarily physical. The eye-brain rationalizes painting, and it functions as the data-processing system. On the other hand, when we read a story, we forget the visual scratches on paper—the dots of braille, if we are blind. Higher mental processes, relieved of a dependence on physical sensations, are brought into play. The difficulties in these arts lie in trying to discover just how their perceptual communications are meaningful to us in a direct way as they are in other arts, and to discover how these arts can be autonomous (whereas mathematics is not). What is the difference between art and science, if we have to learn symbols to read literature just as we have to learn rules to understand mathematics? The answer is that the illusion of writing causes a secondary sensation which is manipulated by the brain in the same way that the physical arts are manipulated in a physical form, and that the physical arts can attach themselves to other literal encodings in a more direct way within the brain than can the other arts, whose suggestive qualities are more clearly established by their actual physical reality.

BOUNDARIES OF ART

The boundaries of art—in the sense of beginnings and ends manifest in frames, introductions, codas, prologues, and epilogues—are the means by which art is built into closed systems. The establishment of a strict frame of reference reinforces the formality of art and sometimes also establishes some of the actual encoding qualities. For instance, the rectangularity of the canvas in its frame gives greater meaning to rectangles and also to vertical or horizontal lines within the picture by virtue of this emphasis or repetition of them at the outer edge.

A clear and decisive boundary is as necessary to art as it is to life; without it a sense of urgency would be missing. A life without death would radically transform the role of man and give new meaning to everything. It would be absolutely meaningless to do many things which we now consider vital, if there were an eternity in which to do absolutely everything.

All attempts to destroy the boundaries of art, to break down the "apartness illusion" of art, leave us with a sense of failure. Reality is never as strange and wonderful as Cinerama, replete with stereophonic sound. We are loath to return to the real world after such an experience. The drug experience is similar: Given an infinitely enhanced unreality that seems interminable in a drugged state, we may want to try to keep it indefinitely. There is danger of psychological addiction to drugs probably because our very humanness is built on such perceptual expansions, and people may be willing to pay any price to be "human," even the ultimate one which means loss of all contact and resignation from the human race.

Art, instead, must heighten the real experiences of our conscious, normal selves—normal because experience is always with us, disappearing only in sleep (where it echoes in our dreams). An art which consistently draws us out of ourselves serves not to build up our perceptual apparatus so that we can cope better with experience, but rather to satisfy the most immediate need for sensation—a strong need, it is true, but one which cannot dominate life to the exclusion of all else.

Expressing the infinite in art is another matter. The artist strives to encode more and more in smaller and smaller packages, and the infinite is sometimes his goal. But when a work of art leads you right off into infinity and leaves you there, it has lost all communicative value. If the art form strives to lull you into the redundancy of the constant and never-ending—like popular music that simply fades away or a pattern that seems to start at infinity left and extend to infinity right—it does so at the sacrifice of information content. The infinite or repetitive, like the zero, is boring and empty. There may be an unusual initial impression on seeing such art, an initial pulse of meaning due to the unexpectedness of its occurrence, but that quickly fades once the pattern has established itself. The repetitive quality of Op art causes an initial wave of curiosity, then a sudden zoom to zero curiosity, as does a fun-house novelty or a very poor pun.

The secret of meaningful art communication is unlocked when one knows the cipher, which is hidden in the artlike figures in a children's game but easily available if given sufficient attention. It is necessary to build these ciphers and learn to recognize them in art in order to establish a human continuity and an extended awareness of the possibilities for the enlargement of the human psyche. The revolt against man's fate, which Malraux [28] says is art's purpose, is more naturally a consequence of our desire for order than our desire to conquer death.

REFERENCES AND SUGGESTED READINGS

1. Allport, Floyd H., *Theories of Perception and the Concept of Structure*. New York: Wiley, 1955.
2. Apel, Willi, *Harvard Dictionary of Music*, 2nd ed. Cambridge, Mass.: Harvard University Press, 1969.
3. Arnheim, Rudolf, *Art & Visual Perception: A Psychology of the Creative Eye*. Los Angeles: University of California Press, 1954.
4. Arnheim, Rudolf, *Film as Art*. Berkeley: University of California Press, 1957.
5. Aschenbrenner, K., and A. Isenberg, eds., *Aesthetic Theories: Studies in the Philosophy of Art*. Englewood Cliffs, N.J.: Prentice-Hall, 1965.
6. Beardsley, Monroe C., *Aesthetics from Classical Greece to the Present: A Short History*. New York: Macmillan, 1966.
7. Beardsley, Monroe C., and Herbert M. Schueller, *Aesthetic Inquiry: Essays on Art Criticism and the Philosophy of Art*. Belmont, Calif.: Dickenson, 1967.
8. Bronowski, Jacob, "The Discovery of Form," in *Science and Literature: New Lenses for Criticism*, ed. by Edward M. Jennings. Garden City, N.Y.: Doubleday, Anchor Books, 1970.
9. Burnham, J. W., "The Aesthetics of Intelligent Systems," in *On the Future of Art*, ed. by Guggenheim Museum. New York: Viking, 1970.
10. Cage, John, *Silence*. Cambridge, Mass.: M.I.T. Press, 1967.
11. Collingwood, R. G., *The Principles of Art*. New York: Oxford University Press, 1958.
12. Copland, Aaron, *What to Listen for in Music*, rev. ed. New York: New American Library, Mentor Books, 1957.
13. Cozzens, Alexander, "A New Method of Assisting the Invention in Drawing Original Compositions of Landscape" (1785), in *Alexander and John Robert Cozzens*, ed. by Paul Oppé. London, 1952.
14. Croce, Benedetto, *Guide to Aesthetics*, trans. by Patrick Romanell. Indianapolis: Bobbs-Merrill, 1965.
15. Daiches, David, "The New Criticism," in *A Time of Harvest: American Literature, 1910-1960*, ed. by Robert E. Spiller. New York: Hill and Wang, 1962.
16. da Vinci, Leonardo, *Treatise on Painting*, ed. by A. Philip McMahon. Princeton: Princeton University Press, 1956.
17. Eisenstein, Sergei, *Film Form and the Film Sense*, ed. and trans. by Jay Leyda. Cleveland: World Publishing, Meridian Books, 1957.
18. Eliot, T. S., *The Sacred Wood: Essays on Poetry and Criticism*. London: University Paperbacks, 1960.
19. Frye, Northrop, "Language of Poetry," in *Explorations in Communication*, ed. by Edmund Carpenter and Marshall McLuhan. Boston: Beacon Press, 1960.
20. Gilot, Francoise, and Carolton Lake, *Life with Picasso*. New York: McGraw-Hill, 1964.

21. Goodman, Nelson, *Language of Art: An Approach to a Theory of Symbols.* Indianapolis: Bobbs-Merrill, 1968.
22. Grierson, John, *Grierson on Documentary,* rev. ed., ed. by Forsyth Hardy. Berkeley: University of California Press, 1966.
23. Hyman, Stanley E., *The Armed Vision: A Study in the Methods of Modern Literary Criticism.* New York: Knopf, 1948.
24. Jean, Marcel, *The History of Surrealist Paintings.* Paris: Grove Press, Editions du Seuil, 1950.
25. Joyce, James, *A Portrait of the Artist as a Young Man.* New York: Penguin, Signet Books, 1948.
26. Kepes, Gyorgy, ed., *Sign, Image, Symbol.* New York: Braziller, 1966.
27. Langer, Susanne K., *Philosophy In a New Key: A Study in the Symbolism of Reason, Rite, and Art.* New York: New American Library, Mentor Books, 1951.
28. Malraux, André, *Voices of Silence.* Garden City, N.Y.: Doubleday, 1953.
29. McLuhan, Marshall, *Understanding Media: The Extensions of Man.* New York: McGraw-Hill, 1964.
30. Mehlis, George, "The Aesthetic Problem of Distance," in *Reflections on Art: A Source Book,* ed. by Susanne K. Langer. London: Oxford University Press, 1958.
31. Meyer, Leonard B., *Emotion and Meaning in Music.* Chicago: The University of Chicago Press, Phoenix Books, 1961.
32. Meyer, Leonard B., *Music, the Arts, and Ideas.* Chicago: The University of Chicago Press, 1967.
33. Moles, Abraham, *Information Theory and Esthetic Perception,* trans. by Joel E. Cohen. Urbana: University of Illinois Press, 1966.
34. Moore, Henry, "Notes on Sculpture," in *The Creative Process,* ed. by Brewster Ghiselin. New York: New American Library, Mentor Books, 1952.
35. Osborne, Harold, *Aesthetics and Art Theory.* New York: Dutton, 1970.
36. Peckham, Morse, *Man's Rage for Chaos.* Philadelphia: Chilton Books, 1965.
37. Pratt, Fletcher, *Secret and Urgent.* Indianapolis: Bobbs-Merrill, 1939.
38. Seawright, James, "Phenomenal Art: Form, Idea, and Technique," in *On the Future of Art,* ed. by Guggenheim Museum. New York: Viking, 1970.
39. Shahn, Ben, *The Shape of Content.* New York: Random House, Vintage Books, 1957.
40. Sontag, Susan, *Against Interpretation.* New York: Dell, 1966.
41. Stravinsky, Igor, *Poetics of Music.* New York: Random House, Vintage Books, 1947.
42. Valentine, Charles W., *The Experimental Psychology of Beauty.* London: Methuen, 1962.
43. Valery, Paul, *The Art of Poetry,* trans. by Denise Folliot. New York: Random House, Vintage Books, 1958.
44. Whitehead, Alfred N., *Modes of Thought.* New York: Free Press, 1966.
45. Winters, Yvor, *The Function of Criticism,* 2nd ed. Denver: Alan Swallow, 1957.
46. Wright, Edward, *Understanding Today's Theatre.* Englewood Cliffs, N.J.: Prentice-Hall, 1959.
47. Wright, Frank Lloyd, *The Future of Architecture.* New York: New American Library, Mentor Books, 1953.
48. Zervos, Christian, "Conversation with Picasso," in *The Creative Process,* ed. by B. Ghiselin. New York: New American Library, Mentor Books, 1952.

Dr. J. Z. Young is Professor of Anatomy at University College, London. He is author of *The Life of Mammals, The Life of Vertebrates, Doubt and Certainty in Science,* and numerous other books, articles, and papers in biology and human communication. His most recent books include *Memory System of the Brain* and *From Molecule to Man.*

3

BIOLOGY: AN APPROACH TO HUMAN COMMUNICATION

J. Z. YOUNG

WHEN I was asked whether I would consider undertaking the series of Reith lectures, I said that it might be possible to give some idea of the methods of science by describing the various sorts of work being done on the brain. Frankly I did not consider that this would be a matter of research. The scientist does not usually think of the writing of books or preparing of lectures as research. Writing seems to him to be a rather tiresome labor that he must do after the fun of laboratory research and discovery is over. I therefore sat down to write more in the hope of making a summary than a discovery. But once I began, I came to realize the extent to which having to describe the results of one's thoughts to others is a part of the process of discovery itself. We are social creatures, depending far more than we realize on communication with each other. If we realize how deeply our whole life is influenced by this necessity of communication, we can understand better both the workings of the brain and the nature of scientific inquiry itself. Paying attention to this fact has made me think in a way that is new and helpful to me, and I hope it may be for others, also.

One of the characteristics of scientists and their work, curiously enough, is a certain confusion—almost a muddle. This may seem strange if you have come to think of science with a capital *S* as being all clearness and light. However, in a most important sense science does stand for law and certainty. Scientific laws are the basis for the staggering achievements of technology that have changed the Western world, making it, in spite of its dangers, a more comfortable and happier place. But when you talk to a scientist you may soon find that his ideas are not all so well ordered. He

35

loves discussion, but he does not always think with complete, consistent schemes, as do philosophers, lawyers, or clergymen. Moreover, in his laboratory, the scientist is not likely to spend much of his time thinking about scientific laws at all. He is busy trying to get some piece of apparatus to work, finding a way of measuring something more exactly, or making dissections that will show the parts of an animal or plant more clearly. He himself may hardly know what law he is trying to prove. He is continually observing, but his work is a feeling out into the dark, as it were. If pressed to say what he is doing, he may present a picture of uncertainty or doubt, even of confusion.

DOUBT AND CERTAINTY

This mixture of doubting with the certainty of scientific laws is not a new phenomenon for the scientist. On the occasion of the celebration of the third centenary of Sir Isaac Newton's birth in 1642, The Royal Society asked a number of learned men to write about Newton. Some placed great emphasis on the fact that Newton would not speculate "beyond the limits where quantitative confirmation could be sought from nature." They quoted Newton's now famous remark, *"hypotheses non fingo"* ("I do not make hypotheses"). By this he meant that he derived laws only from observations of nature, a process that he considered to be distinct from framing a hypothesis about the causes of a phenomenon. Those attracted by this side of Newton's character emphasized his constant work in the laboratory, how he made his own mirrors, his experiments with light, and endless other matters. He was one of the most exact, practical, and knowledgeable persons who ever lived. "I do not deal in conjectures," he said. Evidently for some people this is the typical picture of a scientist. But wait a minute. At the time Newton said that he did not deal in conjectures, he was *eighty-one years old*. Other learned men investigating his writings have attested that what he said about himself was not true. He *did* make hypotheses and conjectures; from his young and most fruitful period onward, he made them endlessly. Some of them were very good hypotheses. Newton, for instance, developed a general theory that matter is made of atoms—we can hardly make a better one today. But because he could not prove his atomic theory (he could neither see the atoms nor detect the forces that bind them together, as we can now), his theory was therefore a sort of guess, a conjecture. He made another guess about an ether that pervades all space, and he puzzled over much more curious matters than these. He spent a great deal of time studying the writings of mystics, theologians, and alchemists. For weeks on end he worked in his laboratory making experiments to find the philosophers' stone that would turn lead into gold. He left a mass of writings on these magical and alchemical subjects, writings so diffuse that they have never been published. The late Lord Keynes has commented that Newton was not so much one of the first men of the Age of Reason, as he was the last of the magicians. He seems to have thought of the universe as a riddle posed by God which could be solved if one looked hard enough for the clues. Some of the clues he sought in nature; others, he thought, had been revealed in sacred and occult writings. The search for answers was a continual struggle and an anxiety, which drove Newton to the edge of madness.

The point for us is that Newton did not spend his time merely observing nature. Besides doing so, his brain also tried to put all the observations together, to fit them into general schemes. This search is the process that I call "doubting." It is a process of exploration, and when only significant resemblances are found, it can be said that a new law has been promulgated, that some degree of certainty has been achieved.

What I hope to be able to demonstrate here is that this mixture of doubt and certainty is not an accident; it is the very nature and essence of the scientific method. Moreover, it is not by any means a characteristic peculiar to science. Science is only the latest product of the human brain, which has been working in essentially the same way for the last ten thousand years: that is, for as long as man has been a social animal. Still the matter does not end there. This method of proceeding is a development of the way in which all brains work. I shall try to show that there is something corresponding to the discovery of certainty through doubt in all the operations of living things.

This is a formidable task, and as I proceeded, I became aware of how much more the biologist needs to know of history, psychology, anthropology, mathematics, and related subjects. However, the ability to see in perspective the range of phenomena from the nature of human thinking and scientific inquiry to the facts of evolution (and perhaps even of cosmology), I thought, would be of such value that the task would be worth the attempt. I believe I have made some progress in this direction and cannot do less than to ask the reader to share the results with me, and to accept whatever may be wrong along with anything that appears to be right.

A BIOLOGIST'S APPROACH TO MAN

The method I have followed is to look at man as a modern biologist looks at a plant or an animal. How do biologists work and what language do they use to describe their view of the world? We might say that they examine how each sort of animal and plant manages to keep its kind alive. Every creature maintains its organization distinct from the surroundings: It prevents itself from returning to dust. Biologists study how even the humblest plant is a wonderfully organized system of roots, stems, leaves, and flowers arranged to do this. These parts act together to extract from the materials of soil and air the means to build the plant and to help it propagate its kind. In animals, similarly, the various parts act together to nourish and protect the organization and enable it to continue.

In examining man, the biologist's question is, How does man get *his* living on the earth? What are the means by which the continuity of human life is assured? In answering, some biologists might say: "Man is an omnivorous, terrestrial, and bipedal mammal." I believe that such phrases show where some biologists have been wrong. They have been concentrating on those features of man that are merely like those of the animal: his digestion, his locomotion, and so on. They have been loath to realize that they can apply the same methods of examination to man's higher functions. Eating and walking are not the really important features in man. It is far more significant that he is a thinking creature or a worshipping one. What biologists have not sufficiently considered is that it is just these traits, comprising what we commonly call man's "mind," that are also his peculiar and important *biological* characteristics. These are the features by which he gets his living: these are the ones that should attract more attention from the biologist.

Each animal has some special way of conducting its life. The cow and the sheep have special stomachs that store grass for later digestion; the tiger has its teeth, the elephant its trunk and its tusks. What then are the distinguishing characteristics of modern man? Surely, the chief one is his ability to cooperate with his fellows. Man's large brain is used to develop an intricate social system, based mainly on communication by words. Man has other special features, such as eyes good for acquiring information, and hands good for doing intricate things. But it is chiefly through cooperation that two billion human beings scattered over nearly all regions of the earth obtain a living. Sophocles expressed it long ago in these few words: "Of all the wonders none is more wonderful than man—who has learned the arts of speech, of windswift thought, and of living in neighborliness." These are indeed the matters that should engage the biologist in his serious study of man. On the subject of human cooperation, a vast mass of knowledge has been collected by generations of anthropologists, psychologists, sociologists, and others. But there is as yet no coherent body of knowledge about the biology of man that sets him in his proper place in the living world. Biologists are only now beginning to study what may be called the higher attributes of man: language, social behavior, religion, and science. We may find valuable new ideas by applying the biological method to the highest of man's activities and correlating these with the study of the organ that mediates them—the brain.

THE IMPORTANCE OF COMMUNICATION

What has been ignored is that these special features of man are due to the fact that he has developed the power of communication far beyond other animals. Biologists have so far neglected to give full attention to the significance of communication in our species. The subject has been forced on their attention in recent years by developments in mechanical aids to communication. There has already been useful cooperation between biologists studying the brain and engineers and mathematicians who developed radio, television, and similar devices. One analogy has been the comparing of the brain to a calculating machine, but this is only a minor detail. What is more important is that the biologist is now beginning to understand the importance of communication itself as a human activity. What I hope to show is that proper use of communication has been the chief secret of the success of human societies in the past, and that it will certainly be so in both the immediate and the more distant future. Evidence of this is the fact that very extensive parts of the brain are concerned with speech. We are only beginning to understand, however, how the brain works to produce particular methods of speaking. Societies certainly change their methods of communication through the centuries. In the past fifty years alone, the Western world has developed a whole new set of techniques for the transfer of information. As a result, cooperation among individuals has improved, and better tools and machines have been produced. Men have gradually learned the great advantages that come from being able to convey information fully and exactly. The impact of new techniques of communication is felt in numerous ways. Everyone appreciates that the spread of education transforms society, that education, when allied to science, gives great new powers to a community. In World War II, England owed its survival to the radar-communicating devices that helped to win the Battle of Britain. Modern armies, by making use of their well-trained brains and new equipment, can overwhelm less-developed military organizations. These are only a few examples of the power that comes from utilizing advanced methods of communication.

Much more important, however, are the ways by which large groups of people are knit together. It is only by proper communication that human societies retain the adherence of their members. Perhaps nothing is more important for man's future than to discover the best ways of obtaining knowledge about communication. It may, at present, be used for the interests of particular groups, classes, or countries. These are natural units of communication, and it would be unrealistic to ignore their importance. But we can try to find ways of making as many of them as possible interact for the benefit of mankind as a whole. Whether we like it or not, we can be sure that societies that use to the full the new techniques of communication, by better language and by better machines, will eventually replace those that do not.

BRAIN AND MIND

What I shall discuss, therefore, is how the brain makes communication among humans possible. Here we come up against a difficulty, as there are two ways of thinking about these matters. On the one hand each of us knows that he or she has what seem to be private experiences, sensations, thoughts, pleasures, and pains. These are, in some sense, for each of us, our own. They seem to occur in us, and yet are not part of our physical body. On the other hand, we also think about communication as a physical system—a transmitter (the brain, tongue, and larynx) in one person, and a receiving system (the ears and brain) in another. This is the well-known dualism of mind and matter, which is perhaps the central problem of modern philosophy, religion, and science. No doubt most of us have felt our thinking blocked by the imposed obscurity of the relation between mind and matter. The consideration of this problem by philosophers in recent years has shown how easily we are deceived in the way we use such words as "mind." I propose to show that for the biologist there is perhaps a way of examining this matter that avoids the dilemma altogether.

First, without leaving the topic of the brain we can at least begin to discuss many, perhaps all, human activities. The method I suggest as a working basis is to organize all our examination of human powers and capacities around knowledge of what the brain does. When the philosopher studies the way in which people think, let him consider what activity this represents in the brain: for certainly there is some. When the theologian studies the fact that human beings tend to organize their activities around statements about gods, let him consider the activity that this involves in the brain. When the educationist and the psychologist follow the ways in which the child grows to his mature powers and later perhaps goes astray, let them consider the processes of the development and decay of the activities of the brain.

This is a simple, straightforward way of proceeding, and yet it may seem strange and new. Some people are curiously unwilling to accept and use the obvious idea that everything they do, including the more complicated ones (say, painting a picture), involve activity in the brain.

Indeed, the skeptic may deny what I have just said. "But it's not true that my brain paints the picture—it is *I* who do that. I am not just a mass of whitish stuff inside my skull." But at least he should agree that when a picture is being painted the eye is receiving light and is sending messages to the brain. Then, after appropriate activity, the brain sends other messages back to the hands. "Yes," he may reply, "I agree about that, but what about thinking? It is *all* internal." There, too, I am prepared to say that there are some brain processes at work whenever anyone thinks. Moreover, it is not impossible that these could be detected. Then I could literally read his thoughts. "An unpleasant prospect," he might reply, "but in any case where is all this getting us? What about my pains and pleasures, hopes and fears, all my experience? They still remain mine, don't they? However much I share them with you does not alter the fact that there is an 'I' experiencing them, who is in some way distinct from my body. Surely this experience is, for me, the ultimate reality."

I agree that there is one sense in which we can say that this is so. But it is important to realize how extraordinarily difficult it is going to be to find that sense. As the biologist sees it, the brain is so constituted that man has learned to function in terms of self and otherness. From babyhood onwards he has learned to satisfy his needs by communicating with others and eliciting their cooperation. The brain therefore acts in ways that are effective for this purpose. We soon acquire, for instance, the habit of focusing attention on certain sorts of objects around us and naming them. The brain has remarkable powers of comparing each new object with some familiar one, and this tendency can be seen at work in the growth of the habit of speaking of "I," of oneself, the habit that gives rise to so much of the confusion about the dualism of mind and body. In order to speak about ourselves we use the convention that there is within us an agent who is said to act as we describe other men acting. This habit of postulating active creatures within bodies, the habit of *animism,* is an extremely convenient device for communication. It enables one to speak of the actions of all sorts of things in terms of the actions of other people, which are easily described, and this has become an integral part of our Western system of communication. It is not easy to talk without speaking of some entity, the self, communicating with others. Our brains have become so arranged that we organize nearly all our experience into these forms in order to talk about it. We can say if we like that our experience is our own; but we are so built that we must try to communicate it. To do this we put this so-called raw experience into the form of a something called "me," here, communicating with a something "not me."

I do not propose to pursue the question further here; philosophers can do it far better than I. It did seem essential to raise it at this point, however, difficult though it may be to grasp.

Consider now that man's highest thoughts and aspirations are functions of the brain. This would seem absurd if I did not make it clear that for each of us, in some sense, what is called inner experience is the core function which reveals to man a world outside himself. The world is like that for man because he puts as much as possible of his experience into a form suitable for communication to others. His brain makes him able to communicate by comparing one thing with another. In early stages of human communication man ascribed the actions of all bodies to the powers of spirits. Recently he has learned that it is better not to use this animistic way of conceiving of physical things. Perhaps, therefore, he does not even need to do this when talking about himself, or others. He may ultimately be able to dispense with the concepts of mind altogether.

Science has discovered that it can do without animistic models. Instead it compares whatever human functions it is studying with man-made machines. Further, science has developed other special techniques of communication, such as mathematics. Certainly, we have improved considerably our ways of speaking in recent years so that we come to talk in greater detail about phenomena and hence to control them better. Such improvement has been going on by fits and starts ever since the beginning of human history. Consider how man has improved in this respect. He has gradually given up thinking that the world consists of entities that are moved by capricious spirits. He has reached a state where he can agree with his fellows about the occurrence of marvelous phenomena which were previously not understood or were even wholly unknown. But he remains man; and he is not a superman: He must use the nature and habits he inherits, including those of language. Let us then try to see what the biologist can tell us about man.

THE USE OF ANALOGY IN THOUGHT

This means spending some time examining what has been found out about the nerves and the brain. Such matters are spoken of, as are most things, mainly by comparison. In what ways, for instance, is the brain like a calculating machine? This procedure of finding analogies is a characteristic human method. It suggests, as we shall often see, new ways of looking, which actually lead us to new discoveries. The brain is continually searching for fresh information about the rhythm and regularity of what goes on around it. This is the process that I call doubting, seeking for significant new resemblances. Once they are found, they provide a new system of law, of certainty. We decide that this is what the world is like now and proceed to talk about it in those terms. Then, sooner or later, someone comes along who doubts, someone who tries to make a new comparison; when he is successful, mankind learns to communicate better and to see more.

So the brain makes comparisons, and its mode of doing so is continually modified by the happenings that occur to it. This is the process called learning. Little is known of the actual changes in the brain that learning involves. The child learns its system of certainty, its laws of acting, through a series of operations of doubt. Human society has developed its plan of brain action, which is handed on from generation to generation. For example, early systems of brain action were modified to produce those current in the Middle Ages. These, in turn, gave rise by gradual development to the ways of behaving that we call "scientific." Finally, these early scientific ways themselves became modified and enlarged through a continuation of the same process.

But of course it is no good hoping to learn to understand all the functions of the brain in an article so brief as this. You would not expect me in this time to teach you how to analyze and make a wireless set, or even how to drive a railway engine. The human brain is enormously more complicated than such machines. To understand all the functions of the human brain would require a collection of specialists at least as numerous as all our present-day engineers and a vocabulary at least as esoteric as theirs. At present, there are relatively few people at work on the function of the brain, and so, comparatively little is known. And the reason for that is not just shortsightedness; it is literally that the study of the human brain has seemed so difficult that few have elected to attempt it. Not many people have been able to see even that there could be wide and powerful generalizations made about the brain, much less that there could be practical applications of this knowledge.

Such shortsightedness is not a new phenomenon. In much the same way there were only a few people in the Middle Ages who could see why it was worthwhile to study physical science or astronomy. When they did undertake such study, they found it showed them how to navigate and to do all sorts of other practical things. Man has been gradually learning the possibility of using new techniques of communication ever since his earliest days. The information collected about the brain is now, at last, sufficient to be of some use. Science is beginning already to see the sources of some of our cruder brain disorders. Surgeons can sometimes help patients to overcome epilepsy and other physical difficulties of communication that twenty years ago would have been called purely "mental." Two hundred years ago, these same conditions would have been attributed to possession by evil spirits and perhaps even resulted in execution for witchcraft. But even more fundamental than these practical applications of medical knowledge about the brain is the increased understanding it gives us about ourselves. By further study of these matters, we may be able to see the connection between our doubts, longings, and highest aspirations and the processes that have been going on in animals for hundreds of millions of years, perhaps even a connection with the eternal processes of the stars. These are high aims; but would you expect less from the study of man's outstanding feature—his brain?

ADDITIONAL COMMENTS

The method suggested here for the study of communication is a combination of the techniques of evolutionary biologists and communication engineers. It may make this method clearer to add some further details about how this combination has developed. In every age men speak about themselves and the world around them partly by comparing themselves with the tools that they use. Conversely, they describe the actions of their tools by speaking of them as if they were men. Some of the most powerful of our modern tools are those used for communication: the telegraph, the telephone, the television, and especially the computer; therefore, in recent years biologists have begun to use the language of the communication engineer to describe the behavior of animals and men. This language has been especially useful for those who study the brain, whose functions, in man, are largely concerned with establishing communication between individuals.

Some of the best mathematical brains have recently been devoted to analyzing the processes of control and regulation of machines and the communication of information. They have worked out what system of signs or coding will enable us to convey the greatest possible amount of information in a given time by telegraph, computer, or other means. Norbert Wiener has been especially prominent in this work, and he has attempted to make his results available in his book on cybernetics—the study of governors or steerers. Being a mathematician, however, he explains his findings using a symbolism that can only be understood properly by those whose knowledge of mathematics is considerable. It may be argued that this is inevitable, since the terms engineers use in speaking of this subject are largely mathematical, and it is therefore illogical to bowdlerize them by turning them into ordinary speech. Undoubtedly, mathematics provides a powerful means of saying things exactly and briefly. Being myself a feeble mathematician, I am in no position to say whether the ideas of engineers lose all value without symbolism. However, I have found that emphasis on the significance of communication seems to help a great deal in clearing up even the most persistent difficulties that arise in common speech, for example, the meanings that we attach to the words *mind* and *matter*. The Reith lectures [on which this chapter is based] provide a good opportunity to test whether emphasis on significance in speaking is also useful for others. The lectures were established as a tribute to Lord Reith's pioneer work in developing a new form of communication. It is appropriate that this tribute should take the form of lectures which are more difficult than most people are accustomed to following, and it is particularly suitable that the lectures should be devoted to exploring some of the wider implications of extended communication that Reith has done so much to foster.

Comparison with Tools

There is a continual alternation in the use of words for describing man's own actions and those of the tools that he produces. Men first spoke of fire as a living thing, then having discovered a use for it and invented cooking, people went on to speak of vital fires and vital cookings within them. So, in the development of modern science physicists and engineers first spoke of the tools that they made as using force and doing work, as a human body was said to do. Then, after such terms had been made exact and a mathematical language had been developed for describing events in terms of them, biology was able to borrow them back. The novel tools of the nineteenth and early twentieth centuries were power tools, steam and gas engines and dynamos. Correspondingly, the physiology of that time dealt mainly with the interchange of work and energy in the body. It investigated how much fuel the body needs, and how much oxygen to burn that fuel. There was elaborate analysis of the efficiency with which the muscles work, how much heat they produce, and so on. This knowledge is the classical framework of physiology, based on classical physics and engineering. It uses as its language Newton's dynamics, which assumes that we begin with a system of particles whose state is known and then discover what happens when the system is acted upon by known forces.

The early developments of electrical engineering followed this same classical scheme in that such developments were also concerned with power. More recently, however, there has developed a whole new branch of the subject, sometimes called small-current engineering. This is concerned with using electrical effects not to do the heavy work for man, but to control the machines which do that work and to improve communication among people. These functions of control and communication had originally been performed by man alone. In developing ways of talking about the new machines, the small-current engineers therefore borrowed terms that were previously used to describe human communication, just as their predecessors had borrowed the terms *energy, force,* and *work,* which described human effort. Engineers and laboratory workers very readily borrow terms in this way and use them first as a kind of slang among themselves. The study of the development of language in workshops would be a very rewarding one. It is important when such laboratory slang is found to be used more widely that its origins be recognized and its new content be defined as accurately as possible.

The communication engineer talks a great deal about *information,* a term originally used in an entirely human context to indicate what one person tells another. It is important to be clear about what this term has come to mean to the biologist, who studies the behavior of organisms. He sees every organism as a system continually interchanging with its environment. Every plant and animal, including man, maintains its organization by taking in food, water, and oxygen. With the energy provided by these, it does work of various sorts to keep itself intact. In order that the body do the right thing to achieve this end, it must receive information about the changes that go on in the world around it, and, indeed, also in the different parts of its own body. It is the function of the sense organs, or as they are better called "receptors," to provide this information. Any system —say, the body—is able to receive information if when a change occurs the system is capable of reacting in such a way as to maintain its own stability. Raindrops falling cannot be said to carry information, but raindrops falling on a person's head inform him of how hard it is raining. To speak of a change as giving information implies that there is somewhere a receiver able to react appropriately to the change.

Control Machines

Engineers have produced many machines that are able to receive and react to information and to exert control, for example, by ensuring that some action continues in a steady way. A regulating machine of this sort is said to receive an input of information, from which, after calculation, it produces an output that exerts the control. The output may act in various ways—for instance, by pulling upon wires or chains in automatic steering devices. Special use has been made of machines that are able to keep a vessel on a fixed course, and comparison with these machines is valuable in biology because living things regulate in a similar way in the sense that they maintain a steady state and tend to produce actions that correct any deviation from this state. The essential feature of steering machines that keep on a fixed course is, in engineers' jargon, "feedback." Every deviation of the rudder from the course is noted on a suitably sensitive receiving apparatus; this sends information to correct the deviation. Much attention has been devoted to theory of how such devices can best be made to maintain stability. For example, if there is too strong a feedback and any divergence is too powerfully corrected, there will be an overswing in the opposite direction, and the system then will not maintain a steady course, but will oscillate or zigzag.

Evidently, these steering machines work very much like living things and we can recognize a great number of feedback systems in the body. When a change is reported by one of its receptors, it tends to produce an appropriate action by the body that will keep the life system stable. We draw our hand away when the receptors record a high temperature, when our taste receptors record sweetness we swallow, and so on. Some of the actions are very complicated. It should be possible to use the precise language developed by engineers to improve our understanding of these feedback systems that produce stability in our lives, but physiologists have not been able to go very far with this method yet. The living organism is so complicated that we seldom have enough data to be able to work out exactly what is happening by means of mathematics. Up to the present, the general ideas and terminology used by engineers have been of more value to biologists than have been the detailed application of their mathematical techniques.

One of the chief methods of control that modern man uses to ensure his stability is communication with others. This forms the basis of cooperative social action. The process of communication consists of converting the input of information that an individual receives into an output that also has the character of information because it is directed to another person. This is only a roundabout way of saying that people talk, but speaking in the combined languages of the engineer and the biologist helps to make very much clearer the nature of all speech and writing. It emphasizes that these are but part of the system of control by which the stability of human organization is maintained. This should be obvious enough, but often we forget it. A great increase in clarity results from emphasizing the fact that our words have biological functions.

Information Theory

The information that we convey to other people helps to ensure survival of our race. It is, therefore, an output designed to have some regulating effect. The full sequence of communication involves the sending of information from one individual to another, who then sends back a recognized or expected response which helps to satisfy the need of the original sender. The exchange of information thus becomes reciprocal, and the two or more people concerned form a cooperating system whose final output is the tools, building operations, or the like, that ensure the survival of the race.

In its usually accepted sense, therefore, the word *communication* implies interchange of information among two or more people or animals. We cannot speak of communication between two clouds, because their effects on each other are not interchanges between two self-regulating systems. Certain useful extensions in the use of the word *communication* arise, however, in relation to some of our own products, especially machines and social organizations that are self-regulating. From speaking about these products, we gain words that we use to describe each other. There are many examples of this: In the seventeenth century, man was compared with a clock; in the twentieth, with a computer. Again, I suggest that there are some advantages in speaking of people the way we do larger social organizations, which are also human products. In a sense there is, therefore, communication of information between man and his products.

Human society has long been a self-regulating system, and we can say that it preserves itself by conveying information to its members and receiving information from them. Human tools are also self-regulating, insofar as they convey to us sufficient power or information to ensure that we return to them the power and information needed for their continuance. This is the relationship, for example, between a man and his watch. Many people fear that as our tools become more complicated they will control us, instead of the other way around. There is, indeed, a sense in which tools become more independent as they become more self-regulating and more able to tell us things that are useful. It is perhaps natural for each generation to fear its own products, but surely it is more satisfactory to welcome their independence and the new information that they provide as an aid to the continuation of the whole system.

Communication, Organization, and Change

I have tried to trace the way in which change in communication systems has been a central feature of change in human society. The change is not steadily in the direction of increasing transfer of information, but the biologist and historian alike must recognize that the whole organization of our system today involves much more detailed intercommunication than there was, say, ten thousand years ago. Moreover, there has been an accelerating change in this direction during the last three hundred years, following the adoption of a new system after the Middle Ages and, especially, with the rise of science. Recent years have seen further great advances not only in mechanical aids to communication, but also in relationships among individuals. Comparison with new tools, such as the radio, is bound to produce further big changes in the way we talk about ourselves. The rise of classical physics after the seventeenth century produced in us the habit of speaking about ourselves as "machines having structure and functions." This has brought about enormous improvement in medical science, through which we control our bodies. But classical physics dealt mainly with the *work* that men and machines did and paid little attention to their *organization*. The new physics and engineering differ from the old in that they deal with complicated organizations and the way that these change. When we have learned to speak of our own organization in these terms, our methods of controlling this organization should become much better, just as, in speaking of the body as a power machine, medicine has given us far greater control over it than did animism and astrology in the Middle Ages. The method of classical physics is to postulate a system whose behavior is completely known and whose future can therefore be determined. Physics has recently discovered that the complicated patterns of relationships between ourselves and what we observe cannot be described in this way. We have to start with an initial organization that we can describe only imperfectly and whose future we cannot forecast exactly. We can, however, determine the probability that it will behave in any given way. The new physics is therefore statistical, and it employs a type of mathematics suitable for forecasting probabilities.

This development of methods for describing complicated organizations and forecasting their future brings the techniques of physics closer to those of biology. The biologist also cannot yet exactly control conditions in the system he observes, because he cannot reproduce its past history. He has therefore developed statistical methods for forecasting as nearly as possible what organisms will do. These methods are related to those of the statistical physicist, and the two sciences converge most closely in the study of communication, where neither can do without the other. The two techniques together are gradually providing us with a language in which we can speak in new ways about ourselves. With it, we find that we can avoid some of the puzzles and obscurities that have arisen through the use of words based on older comparisons. The inadequacy of many of our familiar words becomes apparent. We can do better than such terms as *I myself, my mind, soul, consciousness, knowledge,* and *will.* Similarly, the physicist no longer speaks of his surrounding as a world of "matter" or of "force." Finally, there is no sense anymore in speaking of beginnings and endings—or of "creation."

All this may seem disturbing to many people; some will give it a verdict of unnecessary and even silly. We need not be dogmatic or expect sudden changes of practice—but changes are certainly going on as they always do. We probably could not stop them if we tried. The discovery of new tools and new language is altering society, and I have tried to trace some of the directions of these alterations. There is no need to be unduly alarmed about them. Probably they will be fundamentally less radical than they seem in prospect.

Those who are not accustomed to the language of behaviorism are apt to consider it in some way derogatory to human status and values. Certainly, the behaviorist refuses to conduct all his descriptions with reference only to man; he tries to make comparisons between man and other aspects of nature and he holds that this increases rather than decreases our range of vision and, hence, our dignity. A more serious difficulty is the suspicion that in refusing to use such words as *mind, will,* and *pleasure,* the behaviorist wishes to take away the experiences associated with these names altogether and to "reduce man to a mere machine." To make any such attempt would, of course, be ludicrous—we all have the experience of living. The behaviorist is particularly anxious that we should enlarge the scope of our lives. He believes that we can do this best by comparing human life with that of other animals and with other natural phenomena. In particular, he believes that we shall gain, not lose, by close investigation of the words that we use. Such investigation should especially pursue the problem of what we mean when we speak of "experience" and "life." The method demands that we approach these problems as we would others in semantics. For example, when we say that the center of life is the soul, we should ask ourselves exactly what observation we wish to convey to each other. Doing this might lead us to alter our use of the word *soul,* perhaps even to abandon it. But this would only be because we believed that it was possible in some other way to convey *more* than the old word covered. The whole purpose of new words and comparisons is to *enlarge* our experience, not to reduce it.

Behaviorist language is often labeled "materialistic." If a materialist is a person unwilling to talk about indescribable entities, the behaviorist would be proud to accept the label. He believes that we shall gain rather than lose by comparing man to material objects. But this does not mean asserting that we know all about matter and have nothing further to learn about the universe. The scientist is in a better position than anyone else to see that we are beset by mysteries. It is his business to grapple with ghosts every day of his life, and he must refuse to allow them to be laid through the process of labeling them with a primitive nomenclature. The mysteries of the universe are too great to be expressed by such simple comparisons as those implicit in either the word *spirit* or the word *matter.*

On the other hand, the scientist agrees with other sensible men that our system of words must abide by some conventions if it is to be useful and ensure stability. I have felt the way here toward definition of a sure basis for such convention.

The biologist has the advantage of looking at millions of organisms spread over millions of years. He sees two things most clearly: first, that each particular individual or type of organization seldom survives for very long and, second, that living organization is nevertheless one of the most stable things upon the earth. It changes, but only slowly. Its continuity is the best reference point that we have.

REFERENCES AND SUGGESTED READINGS

1. Adrian, E. D., *The Physical Background of Perception.* Oxford: Clarendon, 1947.
2. Beadle, George W., and Muriel Beadle, *Language of Life.* Garden City, N.Y.: Doubleday, Anchor Books, 1966.

3. Bertalanffy, Ludwig von, "The Theory of Open Systems in Physics and Biology," *Science,* Vol. 111, 1950.
4. Bertalanffy, Ludwig von, *Problems of Life.* New York: Wiley, 1952; New York: Harper & Row, Torchbooks, 1960.
5. Bertalanffy, Ludwig von, *General System Theory.* New York: Braziller, 1968.
6. Bloom, Benjamin S., *Stability and Change in Human Characteristics.* New York: Wiley, 1964.
7. Brian, Russell, *The Nature of Experience,* Riddell Memorial Lectures. Oxford: Oxford University Press, 1959.
8. Darlington, C. D., *The Evolution of Genetic Systems,* 2nd. ed., Edinburgh: Oliver and Boyd, 1958.
9. Delgado, Jose M. R., *Physical Control of the Mind.* New York: Harper & Row, 1969.
10. Dubos, René, "Environment Biology," *Bioscience,* Vol. 14, 1964.
11. Dubos, René, *So Human an Animal.* New York: Scribner, 1968.
12. Eccles, J. C., *The Neurophysical Basis of Mind.* Oxford: Clarendon, 1953.
13. Geertz, Clifford, "The Growth of Culture and the Evolution of the Mind," in *Theories of the Mind,* ed. by J. M. Scher. New York: Free Press, 1962.
14. Lashley, *Brain Mechanisms and Intelligence.* New York: Hafner, 1964.
15. Meade, J. E., and A. S. Parkes, eds., *Biological Aspects of Social Problems.* New York: Plenum, 1965.
16. Medawar, P. B., *The Uniqueness of the Individual.* London: Methuen, 1957.
17. Newton, Grant, ed., *Early Experience and Behavior.* Springfield, Ill.: Charles C Thomas, 1966.
18. Penfield, W., *The Excitable Cortex in Conscious Man.* Liverpool: Liverpool University Press, 1958.
19. Roe, A., and S. G. Simpson, eds., *Behavior and Evolution.* New Haven: Yale University Press, 1958.
20. Sluckin, W., *Imprinting and Early Learning.* Chicago: Aldine, 1965.
21. Whitehead, Alfred North, *Science and the Modern World.* Cambridge, England: Cambridge University Press, 1926.
22. Wiener, Norbert, *Cybernetics.* New York: Wiley, 1949.
23. Yorkey, H. P. *et al.,* eds., *Symposium on Information Theory in Biology.* New York: Pergamon Press, 1958.
24. Young, J. Z., *Doubt and Certainty in Science: A Biologist's Reflection on the Brain.* New York: Oxford University Press, 1950.

Dr. Bent Stidsen is Assistant Professor of Marketing at McMaster University, Hamilton, Ontario. He served as Senior Research Assistant at the Marketing Science Institute and Lecturer in Marketing at the Wharton School of Finance and Commerce, University of Pennsylvania. Dr. Stidsen has written numerous articles and papers in marketing, economics, and advertising and is the author of *Personal Selling in a Modern Perspective.*

4

ECONOMICS AND MARKETING: AN APPROACH TO HUMAN COMMUNICATION

BENT STIDSEN

Economics and marketing have roots in the same basic concept. This is the concept of the *market*. In its simplest possible sense, a market is a place or a center to which producers bring their surplus goods or services and from which consumers attempt to fill their needs and wants. An economic and marketing approach to communication focuses upon the market as a zone and as the means of interaction and mutual influence—of communication—between producers and consumers.

There are, then, two rather distinct senses in which economics and marketing are inextricably bound up with the study of human communication. The marketplace, by its very nature, brings people together and facilitates the exchange of information. At another more subtle and yet significant level, economics and marketing are special instances of communication involving a relationship between producer and consumer in which the basic units of human transaction are money, products, and services. These units form a vocabulary for meaningful human interaction as do words and gestures.*

In ancient Greece, for example, the market was a center not just for the exchange of goods and services, but also for the exchange and propagation of news, ideas, and political influence. It was truly a *community* center. The modern concept of the market, though no longer limited to the idea of a place, retains the essentially communicational overtones of the histori-

---

* Compare the foregoing remarks with Alfred G. Smith's discussion of the impact of the introduction of money in a traditional culture in Chapter 1 of this volume.

cal marketplace.[6] The shopping centers, supermarkets, and farmers' markets of today are thus variations on an age-old theme: people getting together to exchange the fruits of their individual and disparate, or specialized, labors in the interest of higher individual and collective standards of living.

In ancient markets people bartered goods and services. Someone with a surplus of wine and a shortage of tools would seek to make an exchange with someone who had a surplus of tools and a shortage of wine. That is the basic prototype of a market exchange, and modern economics and marketing theory and practice (for all their seeming complexity) can be viewed as elaborations upon this basic prototype.[82]

In a community of any size at all, the barter economy is problematic in two important respects: (1) Direct exchanges are difficult to arrange (the toolmaker may not need wine, or the winemaker may not need tools); and (2) establishing the relative values of many disparate products in terms of each other is a tedious process (wine will have one price in terms of tools, another in terms of meat, yet another in terms of cloth, and so on). The merchant emerged to solve the first of these problems, and money came into use as a solution to the second problem. In a wider sense, the first problem is one of distribution, and it is at the core of modern marketing.[66] The second problem is one of allocation of economic goods and services, and it is at the core of modern economics.[53]

ECONOMICS: THE PROBLEM OF ALLOCATION

A basic postulate underlying the economic theory of demand is that the market is cleared by price.[25] That is, it is postulated that there is some specific price at which the total supply of a particular product will be bought or taken off the market by consumers. In the simplest possible case, this price is taken to be determined by the relative quantities of the product supplied and demanded. Figure 4.1 represents the fundamental economic relation between producers and consumers. The price (p_2) fails to clear the market [demand (q_2) is less than supply (q_3)], whereas the price (p_1) equates demand and supply at (q_1).

The demand curve (D) represents consumers' tastes or attitudes and willingness to buy, and the utility of the product involved. The supply curve (S) represents producers' marginal costs for producing various quantities of the product.

If the price (p_1) is to represent the best possible allocation of economic resources to the product involved relative to alternative products, the following assumptions must hold: [47]

1. Prices are perfectly flexible. Neither producers nor consumers possess control over prices.

*

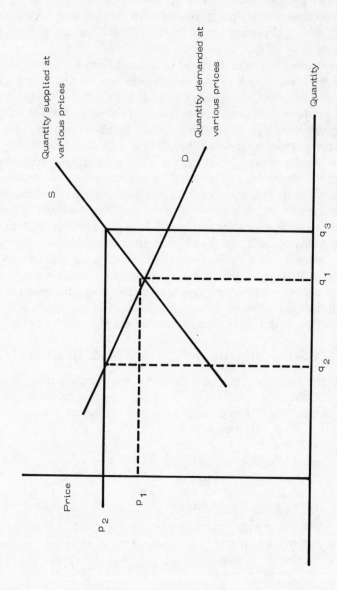

Figure 4.1 Economic relationship between producers and consumers

2. Producers and consumers possess full and perfect knowledge of market conditions.

3. Producers and consumers share a homogeneous value framework, which allows the equation of individual and social value. What is good for the individual is good for society, and vice versa.

4. Prices of all other products are optimal and constant.

If these assumptions hold, it is not difficult to show that the market will tend to force producers to make and sell what consumers want, thus subordinating the production of economic goods and services to the demands of consumers. A producer must sell at whatever price he can obtain (determined by supply relative to demand). Given also that the costs of production are independent of the price the finished product can command on the market (costs determined by the relative scarcity of resources and raw materials), it follows that the producer can maximize his profits only if he markets products which consumers will buy at the highest possible prices relative to costs of production. Thus, under this assumption, whether it is better to have more automobiles than bathtubs, more toothpaste than books, or more television sets than refrigerators, can be taken to depend upon consumer preferences, as expressed through the prices they are willing to pay, relative to the cost of producing these various articles. [9]

Clearly, economists would not insist that the assumptions outlined earlier represent the actual conditions of the market. And the greater part of microeconomic theory and research is devoted to the specification of the consequences of relaxing those assumptions. [37]

If the market is taken to be cleared by price, it follows that producers compete with each other along the dimension of price. If we assume: (1) many firms in an industry, (2) a homogeneous product, (3) freedom of entry and exit to the industry, and (4) no collusion among the firms in an industry, a state of *perfect competition* may be said to exist. Under conditions of perfect competition, no producer has control of the market or of the prices at which his product sells. [62]

It is doubtful that any industry exists in which perfect competition prevails, although certain agricultural products (e.g., wheat, butter, eggs) may come close. Usually, producers are capable of differentiating their products, thereby creating conditions of *monopolistic competition*. [14] In communication terms, perfect competition would correspond to conditions of perfect communication, and monopolistic competition to conditions of imperfect communication.

Why? If one assumes conditions of perfect competition (and communication), then it is not difficult to show that whatever allocation of economic resources obtains must be the best possible one. Under conditions of monopolistic competition (imperfect communication), the problems of allocation and valuation are much less tractable.[59] If neither producers nor consumers possess full knowledge of market conditions, then there is no reason to assume that their decisions represent the best possible choices. Or, if demand is even partly a function of supply (people buy television sets because they are available and they are available because someone knows how to make them), then the sheer fact that all television sets produced are eventually sold at some price cannot be interpreted as an indication of optimum allocation of economic resources. Under conditions of monopolistic competition (by far the most common form of competition), the market cannot be said to be cleared by price, and neither can price be viewed as an adequate representation of the communicational link between producers and consumers.[75]

It should be emphasized that most economists are not primarily concerned with the communicational dimensions of the market. Usually, economists prefer to rest their theories concerning market conditions and market structure on ascertainable flows of money and goods in the market, on the assumption that producers and consumers are each seeking to (and are capable of) rationally maximizing their profits and satisfactions respectively.[45]

A few economists have objected to the traditional emphasis on the formal logic of market behavior. They are usually referred to as "institutional economists," and Karl Marx is perhaps their most famous spokesman. In America, Thorstein Veblen, John R. Commons, and John Maurice Clark are among the best known of the institutional economists. Perhaps the most significant difference between institutional and traditional economists is the refusal of the former group to accept the fiction of rational economic man as a basis for economic theory and research.[90; 17; 15]

Institutional economists are not, however, in the mainstream of modern economics. Modern microeconomics is almost exclusively price theory and comprises attempts at developing a consistent logic of resource allocation and production. Demand theory (or theories of consumer behavior) reached an impasse because of the incomparability of two or more consumer utility curves, but the emergence of game theory and Paul Samuelson's revealed-preference theory seemed to revive it.[25] Both theories were thought to offer operational measures of consumer preferences which would enable an empirical definition of particular demand curves. Samuelson showed, for example, how actual choices could be used to develop an individual's "indifference map," or his preference ordering of all possible combinations of products and combinations of products.[41] But if for no other reason than the sheer complexity of computation, neither game theory nor revealed-preference theory has gone much beyond the theoretical stage.

In sum, while economists possess reasonably complete theoretical models for the market and for its two protagonists (producers and consumers), the problem of empirical measurement has, as yet, prevented any but the most general practical applications. We know in principle how the best allocation of economic resources might be established. But since we do not know how to operationalize that best allocation, we are yet very far from knowing *what* that allocation might be.[31]

THE PROBLEM OF DISTRIBUTION

While economists view the market as a means of accomplishing a rational allocation of economic resources to human needs, marketers view it in a more neutral sense as a zone of influence between sellers and buyers.[76] The marketer assumes that the market is cleared by information, which includes price among other things.[2] But even though marketing as a discipline and as an activity clearly presumes that the assumptions underlying traditional economic theory (as outlined earlier) do *not* hold, the marketer's view generally supports rather than conflicts with the economist's. The essence of the modern marketing concept is still that the consumer is king and that the marketer's obligation is to enable the consumer to maximize his satisfaction and the producer to maximize his profits.[67] In other words, marketers view marketing as a way of actualizing the economist's assumptions, thus viewing themselves as instrumental in the application and realization of the economist's theory of optimal resource allocation and distribution.

As in the case of economics, marketing involves the producer-consumer relation. But since marketers do not assume that people and products are homogeneous entities, the marketer's representation of that relation is more complex than the economist's.

For purposes of discussion, the elements of marketing can be divided into the following five basic categories:

1. Market segmentation and specification—determination of characteristics of the consumers served by the firm;
2. Promotion and selling—the firm's efforts to inform and to influence consumer buying behavior;
3. Product and service development and pricing;
4. Market conditions and structure—the divisions of tasks and the conflicting interests of the various members of the distribution channel through which products pass from producer to consumer;
5. Marketing and its external (legal, economic, and social) constraints and facilitators, and the purpose and value of marketing in light of legal, economic, and social values and criteria.

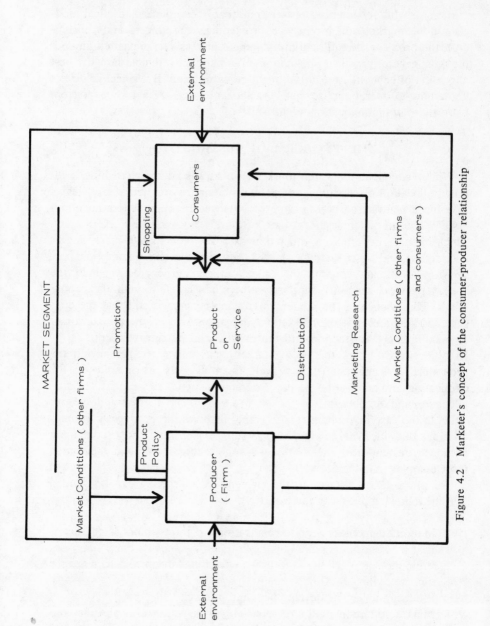

Figure 4.2   Marketer's concept of the consumer-producer relationship

These are the communicational dimensions of modern marketing. Early definitions of marketing, influenced by classical economic theories, emphasized the geographical separations between producers and consumers. Marketing was viewed as a physical-distribution function made necessary because of this separation. Modern marketing, however, emphasizes communication much more heavily than it does the logistics of physical distribution.[36; 21]

Market Segmentation and Specification

Market segmentation is the marketer's term for audience analysis.[87] A large variety of criteria for market segmentation have been developed and tested in recent years. In general, these criteria may be grouped in the following categories:

1. Geographical segmentation—neighborhood, city, rural, region, county, density of population;
2. Segmentation by buying behavior—product usage rate, buying motives, brand loyalty, price sensitivity, advertising sensitivity;
3. Segmentation by personality characteristics—compulsiveness, gregariousness, conservatism, authoritarianism, leadership, ambitiousness;
4. Socioeconomic segementation—age, sex, family size, income, occupation, education, religion, race, social class.

Formal market segmentation, whatever the criterion or combination of criteria used, is aimed at providing a basis for marketing planning and policy formulation for the firm. The problem is thus one of finding criteria for market segmentation which are reasonably operational from a research standpoint, and which are at least correlated with, if not causally related to, the demand for particular products or services.[91]

Rigorous quantitative analysis has been attempted on a variety of market-segmentation criteria. Frank and Massy attempted to measure the effects of price and promotional changes in relation to market segments established on the basis of family-purchase characteristics and characteristics of product bought.[30] Frank and Boyd attempt to relate predilection for private label brands (i.e., distributor's brand as contrasted with manufacturer's brand) to various measurable consumer characteristics.[29]

With particular reference to consumer behavior, Katona has examined the relation between consumer psychology and economic behavior.[46] Lazer and Kelley have emphasized the usefulness of psychological variables such as learning, motivation, perception, and cognition in any attempt at understanding consumer behavior.[51] Bauer and Cunningham have reported several studies designed to test the theory that consumer behavior can be usefully viewed as a consequence of perceived risk.[7; 22] And several researchers have attempted to test Festinger's cognitive dissonance theory in the context of consumer behavior.[40] Green and Carmone have developed a method of multidimensional scaling which they have applied in a number of contexts, as a means of ascertaining the dimensions of consumer attitudes and preferences with respect to particular products.[33]

Similarly, Nicosia has examined and compared a number of theories of consumer behavior and decision making.[70] Tucker and Howard and Sheth have developed independent theories of buyer behavior.[88; 43] Yankelovich has argued that the usual demographic segmentation criteria are outmoded and must be replaced with more subtle value and preference indicators.[92]

While no general conclusions have emerged from market segmentation and from consumer-behavior research, theories, methodologies, and research applications abound.[86] Rigorous generalizations, however, have so far been unsuccessful, and one commentator has gone so far as to suggest that a product policy based on simple variety may be more effective than one based on rigorously identified market segments.[77]

Occasionally, the study of marketing itself has been differentiated in relation to a particular scope of the market or a particular group of buyers. Thus, consumer and industrial marketing have emerged as reasonably distinct approaches to the study of marketing. Consumer marketing involves the distribution of goods and services to final consumers, while industrial marketing refers to the distribution of goods and services to intermediate manufacturers.[55] International marketing is another branch of the study of marketing, which has emerged in response to the increasing importance of cross-cultural trade.[57]

Promotion and Selling

Promotion (advertising, personal selling, and sales promotion) are the marketer's major means of communicating to consumers. The theories and research efforts related to promotion can be categorized loosely as follows:

1. Media-selection models and media-audience studies;
2. Theory and measurement of promotional effectiveness;
3. Personal selling and sales-force management;
4. Management of sales promotion and measurement of the effectiveness of particular promotions (deals, stamps, and contests).

The issues related to the planning and implementation of particular promotional "mixes" are closely related to and dependent upon available ways of segmenting markets.[10] Frank and Massy attempted, with limited results, to relate a brand's price and dealing policies to the characteristics of various market segments. Little and Lodish, among others, have developed a media-planning, or selection, model designed to predict optimum promotional allocation and scheduling in terms of reach (number of people reached), frequency of ads, and periodicity (interval between campaigns).[58] A number of commercial data-collection agencies conduct regular studies on media with respect to reach, exposure, and recall. Dalbey, Gross, and Wind examined the methods of these commercial agencies in the light of an ideal measure of advertising effectiveness.[23] Colley, Lucas, and Britt have discussed the issues of advertising objectives and the measurement of effectiveness, and Kassarjian has attempted to relate Riesman's inner-other-directed theory to the effects of particular ads.[16; 60; 44]

The aim and purpose of promotion is to positively influence the sales and profits of the producer. This pragmatic requirement has led to a continuing controversy between those who would measure promotional effectiveness in terms of sales and those who would use various communication criteria (exposure, recall, attitude changes). Practices range from simply allotting a fixed percentage of a product's price for promotion to conducting elaborate laboratory tests on particular ads to ascertain their attention-getting and persuasive qualities.

Those who advocate communicational criteria in the measurement of promotional effectiveness rest their case on a "hierarchy-of-effects" model of the attention-interest-desire-action (AIDA) type.[72] Those who advocate sales criteria in the measurement of promotional effectiveness argue that attitude changes are neither necessary nor sufficient conditions for action or purchase, and that the ability of an ad to evoke interest in, or desire for, a product may therefore be irrelevant.[89; 73] Festinger has questioned the validity of assuming that behavior is a function of attitude. And Howard and Sheth have formulated attitude and behavior as interdependent concepts.[28; 43]

There are different philosophies on the best way of promoting a product. Since Brink and Kelley made it popular to consider promotion an entity (as contrasted with piecemeal views of promotion), it has become more common to look upon advertising, personal selling, and sales promotion as mutually supportive promotional means.[11] Cash and Crissy have compared advertising and personal selling.[12] And Kuehn has attempted to show that the effectiveness of advertising depends on the quality of other promotional elements.[49]

The literature and research on personal selling roughly divides into the following categories:

1. Sales-territory identification and evaluation in relation to call frequencies, sales expectations, and the logistics and time requirements of travel;

2. Selection and training of salesmen;
3. Selling job or persuasive interpersonal communication;
4. Management and evaluation of and compensation for salesmen.

The question of what makes a good salesman has received a great deal of attention—though with disappointing results.[65] A number of techniques have been developed to select, train, and motivate salesmen, and although none of these techniques has received universal acceptance, each of them has its devoted adherents.[13] A major problem pervading the practice and study of personal selling is its comparatively low prestige, but a number of serious studies of personal selling have begun to emerge.[64]

Ackoff attempted to relate call frequencies to sales in much the same way the frequency of ads has been related to the sales effectiveness of advertising.[1] Evans studied the effect insurance salesmen's personalities have upon their selections of prospects, and their relative abilities in selling insurance to prospects like themselves and prospects unlike themselves.[27] Davis studied the effectiveness of wholesale-drug salesmen.[24] Robinson and Stidsen attempted to develop a communication model for personal selling viewed as an element of the marketing mix.[80] Goodman reports on the state of the art in personal selling and sales-force management. His recent book demonstrates that the discipline has emerged from its "how-to-win-friends" stage and is now the subject of serious study by several researchers.[32]

Sales promotion is a catchall phrase encompassing everything from point-of-purchase displays to "cents-off" deals and the distribution of free samples. Coupons, premiums, trading stamps, contests, and mail promotions are among commonly used sales-promotion devices. Some of these occasional means of promotion have shown themselves more amenable to rigorous quantitative analysis than have advertising and personal selling. Hinkle has examined the characteristics and the effectiveness of price deals.[38] Frank, Kuehn, and Rohloff used mathematical models to develop general methods for predicting the effectiveness of various sales-promotion devices.[79]

The greater part of the theory and research related to promotion and selling takes the viewpoint of the seller or producer. Even the considerable volume of research and commentary on consumer behavior involves the consumer as a means to higher sales, rather than as an end. In other words, however useful consumer-behavior research is to marketers, it is unlikely to be of any use to a consumer who might wish to improve his decision making. With rare exceptions, promotion is studied as a cause-and-effect relationship rather than as a phenomenon.[8] Even critics of advertising prefer to complain about what advertising does *to* people rather than to seriously examine the advantages and disadvantages of the ways it is used *by* people.

Production Development and Pricing

A product is most obviously a physical thing with certain technical specifications. But it is more than that too.[56] From the standpoint of consumption, it can be viewed more realistically as a bundle or package of potential services to be realized by the consumer or user. Product development thus involves the formulation of a suitable package of services which appeals to the consumer and is capable of satisfying the needs and wants he associates with the product. Theories and research in product planning and development fall into the following groups: (1) new-product development, packaging, and testing; (2) demand analysis, sales forecasting, economic analysis, and pricing; and (3) analysis of the product life cycle and product policy formulation.

With the exception of relatively minor modifications on existing products, technical product design is usually viewed as outside the scope of marketing. A few attempts have been made to involve consumers in the product design process, but with discouraging results. The marketing issues of new-product development have been described in some detail by Pessemier.[74] Packaging, branding, and test-marketing are some of the major concepts associated with new-product introduction.[18]

It has been estimated that as many as nine out of ten new products never reach the stage of successful market introduction. In consequence, the process of consumer adoption of a new product and the diffusion process of innovations have received a good deal of attention in marketing.[78] Miracle attempted to develop a method for characterizing or classifying products which could be related to particular marketing strategies.[69] Attempts have also been made to develop techniques for simulating new-product introductions.[5] Nevertheless, bringing a new product to market remains fraught with uncertainties and risks.

Demand analysis involves estimation of a probable demand curve for a product and estimation of the sensitivity of the demand for a product to price and promotion policies. The marketer's demand analysis differs in some respects from demand analysis in economics. Whereas the economist is usually content to establish the relation between demand and various prices, the marketer needs to establish in somewhat more detail the factors that influence consumer buying behavior.[42] A number of econometric techniques have been developed to aid the marketer in forecasting the sales of new and existing products. A variety of marketing research techniques, including data collection and data-processing techniques and models, have also been formulated and tested in recent years. [34]

An important purpose of demand analysis (though by no means the sole purpose) is the establishment of a price for the product. The marketer's concept of pricing is somewhat more complex than that of the economist. Indeed, there are several distinct concepts of pricing in marketing. [61] (1) *Cost-plus* pricing: the producer adds a profit margin to the cost of producing a product and attempts to sell the product at the resulting price. Or, the producer may calculate the cost (plus a profit margin) of producing various quantities of a product and then select the price at which he feels he is most likely to maximize his return. This latter procedure is often referred to as "target pricing," since the producer seeks to price to a predetermined return on an investment goal or target. (2) *Psychological* pricing: consumers often estimate product quality and value from the price of the product. This tendency for consumers to use price as information enables (and occasionally forces) producers to price products significantly above the least possible price (thereby, of course, also limiting the effective demand for the product). Pricing with numbers ending in 9 (e.g., $5.99) is another form of psychological pricing. [84] (3) *Product-line* pricing: often a new product is designed to fit into an existing product line, and its price (and quality) is therefore partly determined by the prices of the established products. In such cases, profitability of the total product line rather than of the individual product may be considered. [71]

Leavitt has attempted to establish the extent to which consumers use price as a means of measuring product quality. [52] Scitovsky has discussed the consequences of this phenomenon on economic theory. The habit of judging quality of price undoubtedly leads directly or indirectly to monopolistic price discrimination. But more importantly, it may indicate a society on the way from valuing products *by* their prices to valuing them *for* their prices. [83]

The concept of a product life cycle has become prominent in marketing literature as a basis for discussions on the producer's product policies. It is empirically evident that most products go through a cycle consisting roughly of four stages: market development, growth, maturity, and decline. Several attempts have been made to formulate specific marketing strategies for each of these stages of the product life cycle. [54]

Market Conditions and Structure

Viewed from a structural standpoint, the market encompasses an intricate web of relationships usually referred to as "channels of distribution." The distribution channel for a particular product is the path taken by that product as it moves from producer to consumer. A typical channel structure is illustrated in Figure 4.3.

The market is characterized by both horizontal and vertical divisions. Horizontal divisions encompass differentiations among industries, individual producers, and middlemen (i.e., divisions among members of the channel occupying the same level). Vertical divisions encompass the functional differentiations of producers, wholesalers, and retailers.[63]

A channel of distribution serves several important functions. At the level of producers, products are usually assorted in relation to technical production criteria (e.g., raw materials employed, production process involved). At the level of retailers, on the other hand, products are usually assorted according to usage patterns (e.g., kitchen appliances, clothing, and accessories). In addition to this assortment function, the channel also serves storage, risk-sharing, financing, and information-dissemination functions related to the anticipation and satisfaction of consumer needs and wants. In the words of one theorist, the channel provides place-and-time utility for consumers by making available products and services where and when they are desired by consumers.[2]

Theories and research related to the structure of markets can be classified as follows:

1. General cost-of-distribution studies;
2. Channel-management studies pertaining to the issues and problems of cooperation and conflict among the various members of the channel;
3. Studies of individual channel institutions and their functions (e.g., retailing, wholesaling, credit, franchising);
4. Studies of the marketing system or institution in general (comparative marketing, marketing viewed as a social institution, and the role of marketing in economic development are some of the approaches taken in this context).

Several studies have concluded that the cost of distribution is approximately 50 percent of the total amount paid for products by the consumer.[20] There is disagreement, however, as to what this means. Some would argue that the cost of marketing is a cost to society, which must be minimized. Others would argue that the cost of marketing is a measure of its value to society, and that marketing does not cost enough.[39] Clearly, the proponents of these two viewpoints employ different communication models. If one accepts the economist's assumption that perfect communication is an ideal, then the cost of marketing can be viewed as a social cost of the absence of the ideal situation. On the other hand, if one assumes that communication is a means of economic and social development, then the cost of marketing might be viewed as one measure of the effort devoted to that end (i.e., the cost of marketing viewed as a value).

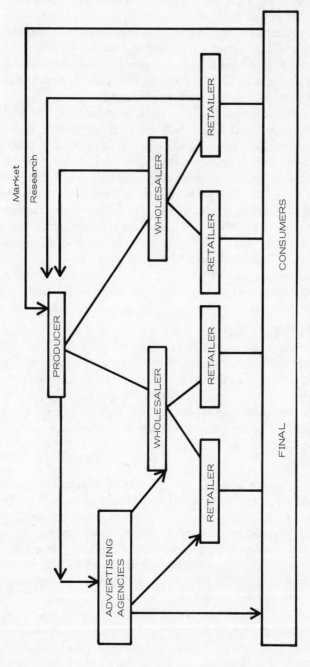

Figure 4.3 Typical channel structure for product distribution

There can be no doubt, however, that the prevailing criterion applied to the management of the channel of distribution is that of efficiency (i.e., marketing viewed as a cost). Given a particular channel structure, marketers will, on the whole, seek to minimize the cost of moving a product through the channel. More often than not, the channel is dominated by the manufacturer.[68] But there are significant examples of retailer domination in certain channels, and some researchers predict greater retailer control in the future. Increasing size of retailing units, combined with a growing interest in private brands (i.e., products marketed under the retailer's brand rather than the manufacturer's), make it increasingly difficult for the manufacturer to control the distribution channel.

Unlike retailers, advertising agencies are, as yet, at the mercy of the manufacturer. A few agencies have shown some signs of independence, but the plethora of agencies and the absence of any direct relation between advertising agency and consumer make it difficult for the agency to acquire the leverage necessary to significantly influence the manufacturer's information-dissemination decisions and practices. Deprived of control over the structure of the communication channel between manufacturer and consumer (outside the tolerance usually accorded creative efforts), the advertising industry is characterized by fads and fashions to an extent quite unknown in retailing.[81]

It may be for these reasons, too, that advertising and advertising agencies are rarely studied as independent institutions in the way that retailing and wholesaling have been studied. Furthermore, even though retailing and wholesaling have been studied as institutions since the turn of the century, it is only recently that such studies have been more generally recognized by their authors as particular cases in social organization and social change.[19]

Of a more recent date and still in the embryonic stage are comparative marketing studies. These studies aim to uncover significant dynamic dimensions in marketing systems by comparing marketing systems of different countries and of countries at different stages of development.[85]

It should be evident, even from this brief outline, that from the ancient marketplace has evolved an exceedingly complex set of intricately related agencies and activities. The modern market, for all its failures and excesses, is a delicately tuned system deeply imbedded in, and deeply suffused by, the cultural and social values and structures of modern society. Contemplate, for example, the importance of shopping as a social activity. Or consider that this system of marketing (including transportation) supplies New York City on an inventory so small that New York would be reduced to starvation within a week of serious disruption of supplies. This degree of efficiency is accomplished in spite of—or perhaps because of—the fact that no one in particular is in charge of this system of marketing.

External Influences on Marketing

The idea of external influences is, to be sure, an abstraction. There is no clear-cut boundary between what is and what is not marketing. Usually, however, economics and marketing are viewed as contained in cultural, social, and political systems which constrain and facilitate the functioning of the marketing system.

Theory and research concerning marketing externalities might be grouped as follows: (1) marketing and government: examinations of the relation between government and marketing and of the consequences of particular legislative interventions in the marketing system; (2) marketing and social responsibility: discussions concerning the relations between marketing activities and social values and social development; and (3) normative models or concepts of marketing: attempts at formulating criteria for strategic decision making in marketing.

Social critics abound who attribute a wide range of social ills and superficialities to marketing activities. Some of their criticisms are undoubtedly well taken, but little serious study has been devoted to the relation between values and ways of producing, distributing, and consuming economic products and services in society.[50] Legislative interventions into the functioning of the economic and marketing systems are often conflicting and are usually aimed at maintaining economic competition among producers. (The exception is legislative quality specifications on certain products such as food, drugs, and textiles).[35]

The revitalization of the consumer-oriented movement promises more vigorous attention to the ecological and social criteria for economic production, distribution, and consumption. Of course, there are among producers and marketers those who would engage in sharp practices, given the opportunity. But they hardly constitute a major policy concern.

The crucial question at this level is, Who or what social group or agency is to be the repository or ultimate referent for social values? [4] If marketers do indeed substantially satisfy consumer needs and wants, then it is not marketers but consumers at whose doors must be laid the criticisms for rampant materialism, inane advertising, and ubiquitous commercialization.

Do marketers and marketing substantially influence the values and decisions of consumers? If they do, the claim that producers and marketers are merely servants facilitating consumption is obviously disingenuous. There is by no means agreement on this point, and there may never be. In the final analysis, marketers are themselves subject to the same cultural ideals and influences as consumers. The question is then not so much whether marketers overemphasize material solutions to human needs, but whether we all do. In some respects, we undoubtedly do overemphasize material possessions—perhaps even to the point of assuming that we are what we possess. And the more complex these possessions, the larger the realm of needs and wants generated by the possessions.

To evaluate the cultural ideals underlying marketing and production in our society, we must compare that society with others. Ours is a culture which emphasizes the relation of man to his physical environment more than it does the relation of man to man. This man-nature emphasis has led to greater mobility, greater power to control our living conditions, and greater opportunity to exercise our productive genius than in other cultures. It has also led to air, water, and noise pollution, a higher need for all kinds of repair functions (e.g., mechanics, psychiatrists, social workers), and perhaps to a greater degree of social alienation than in other cultures. Whether this state of affairs is good or bad clearly depends on one's social philosophy.

SUMMARY AND CONCLUSION

Economics and marketing approaches to communication center on the concept of the market as a zone of mutual influence between producers and consumers. For the economist, the major communicational link between producers and consumers is the price system, which, given certain constraining assumptions, can be viewed as an unambiguous feedback mechanism that enables demand and supply to be equalized at an optimum level of economic welfare.

The marketer's approach to communication with consumers involves the following elements:

1. Market segmentation and consumer-behavior analysis;
2. Promotion and selling;
3. Product development and pricing;
4. Specialization of marketing tasks within distribution and information-dissemination channels;
5. Conceptualization and assessment of the external influences upon marketing.

The basic model guiding most marketers is that of satisfying consumer needs at a profit. Or, as one recent author put it: "Marketing involves the analyzing, organizing, planning and controlling of the firm's customer impinging resources, policies, and activities with a view to satisfying the needs and wants of chosen customer groups at a profit." [48, p. 10]

Marketers frequently view themselves as instrumental in fulfilling the assumptions necessary to validate economic theory. That is, it is usually assumed or implied by marketing writers that if a perfect line of communication were established between producers and consumers then everyone would be better off. Those who build marketing strategies around the consumer, of course, make the same assumption. They usually assume that if consumers only knew exactly what producers know, then consumers would be able to make better decisions. But the issue involved is not quite that simple.

The economics and marketing approach to communication suffers from a substitution of means for ends. This is not a malady unique to economics and marketing. It appears to characterize communication research in general. The means-end substitution is expressed in the belief that if we only knew how to communicate better (e.g., with "truth in advertising"), all would be well. Unfortunately, the things we seem to communicate best (i.e., with least noise) are usually the things that matter least.

Inherent in the buying and selling decisions and activities of the market are the conception, dissemination, acquisition, and utilization of technology to modify the quality and style of human life. And it is a mistake to assume that if only perfect competition and perfect communication could be realized, these technological modifications would automatically work to our advantage. They would not. The phrase "truth in advertising" is deceptively simple. It is not necessary to be an advocate of "untruth" in advertising to sense the naïveté (and danger) in associating advertising with the question of truth at all. True advertising may, for all we know, be more disadvantageous to the quality of human life than "untrue" advertising.

The crucial question for the future is not how but what to communicate. We clearly do not want cars that are unsafe at any speed, but neither do we want cars that are safe at any speed. Or, to put it more generally, any attempt at structuring and regulating the market so as to relieve people of their obligation to exercise personal judgment and responsibility is bound to have ambiguous consequences. It may, of course, be possible to cut the number of highway deaths by a few thousand with mandatory safety devices that operate independently of the driver. But the process would be self-defeating. Where no judgment is required, no judgment will be made. As a result, highway accidents and deaths would be likely to increase rather than decrease.

It is both interesting and important to know *how* people communicate. But the communication student, perhaps more than anyone else, must carry on a constant vigil against answering *what* questions with *how* answers. We possess the most powerful production machine the world has ever known. We know a good deal about how to sell and distribute its output. But do we know what we want?

REFERENCES AND SUGGESTED READINGS

1. Ackoff, Russell L., "Allocation of Sales Effort," in *Proceedings of the Conference on: What is Operations Research Accomplishing for Industry?* Cleveland, Ohio: Case Institute of Technology, April, 1955.
2. Alderson, Wroe, *Dynamic Marketing Behavior.* Homewood, Ill.: Irwin, 1965.
3. Alderson, Wroe, "Factors Governing the Development of Marketing Channels," in *The Marketing Channel,* ed. by Bruce Mallen. New York: Wiley, 1967.
4. Alderson, Wroe, "A Normative Theory of Marketing Systems," in *Theory in Marketing,* ed. by Reavis Cox, Wroe Alderson, and Stanley J. Shapiro. Homewood, Ill.: Irwin, 1964.
5. Balderston, Frederick E. and A. C. Hoggett, "Simulating Market Processes," in *Marketing Models: Quantitative and Behavioral,* ed. by R. E. Day. New York: International Publishers, 1964.
6. Bartels, Robert, *The Development of Marketing Thought.* Homewood, Ill.: Irwin, 1962.
7. Bauer, Raymond A., "Consumer Behavior as Risk Taking," in *AMA Proceedings,* ed. by R. E. Hancock. December, 1960.
8. Bauer, Raymond A., and S. A. Greyser, *Advertising in America: The Consumer View.* Boston: Harvard Business School, 1968.
9. Baumol, William J., *Economic Theory and Operations Analysis.* Englewood Cliffs, N.J.: Prentice-Hall, 1961.
10. Borden, Neil H., "The Concept of the Marketing Mix," in *Science in Marketing,* ed. by George Schwartz, New York: Wiley, 1965.
11. Brink, Edward L., and William Kelley, *The Management of Promotion.* Englewood Cliffs, N.J.: Prentice-Hall, 1963.
12. Cash, Harold C., and William J. Crissy, "Comparison of Advertising and Selling," *The Salesman's Role in Marketing, The Psychology of Selling,* Vol. 1–12, 1965.
13. Cash, Harold C., and William J. E. Crissy, "Comparison of Advertising and Selling," *The Salesman's Role in Marketing, The Psychology of Selling,* Vol. 12, 1965.
14. Chamberlin, Edward H., *The Theory of Monopolistic Competition.* Cambridge, Mass.: Harvard University Press, 1956.
15. Clark, John M., *Alternative to Serfdom.* New York: Knopf, 1948.
16. Colley, Russel H., *Defining Advertising Goals for Measured Advertising Results.* New York: Association of National Advertisers, Inc., 1961.
17. Commons, John R., *The Economics of Collective Action.* New York: Macmillan, 1951.
18. Cook, Victor J., and Thomas F. Schutte, *Brand Policy Determination.* Boston: Allyn and Bacon, 1967.
19. Cox, Reavis, "Consumer Convenience and the Retail Structure of Cities," *Journal of Marketing,* Vol. 23, 1959.
20. Cox, Reavis, Charles C. Goodman, and Thomas C. Fichandler, *Distribution in a High-Level Economy.* Englewood Cliffs, N.J.: Prentice-Hall, 1965.
21. Crane, Edgar, *Marketing Communications: A Behavioral Approach to Men, Messages, and Media.* New York: Wiley, 1965.
22. Cunningham, S., "Perceived Risk as a Factor in the Diffusion of New Product Information," in *Science, Technology, and Marketing,* ed. by R. M. Hass. Chicago: American Marketing Association, 1966.

23. Dalbey, Homer, Irwin Gross, and Yoram Wind, *Advertising Measurement and Decision Making*. Boston: Allyn and Bacon, 1968.
24. Davis, James H., *Increasing Wholesale Drug Salesmen's Effectiveness*. Columbus, Ohio: Bureau of Business Research, Ohio State University, 1948.
25. Dorfman, Robert, *The Price System*. Englewood Cliffs, N.J.: Prentice-Hall, 1964.
26. Ellsberg, D., "Classical and Current Notions of Measurable Utility," *Economic Journal*, Vol. 64, 1954.
27. Evans, R. B., "Selling as a Dyadic Relationship—A New Approach," *American Behavioral Scientist*, Vol. 6, 1963.
28. Festinger, Leon, "Behavioral Support for Opinion Change," *Public Opinion Quarterly*, Vol. 58, 1964.
29. Frank, Ronald E., and Harper W. Boyd, Jr., "Are Private-Brand-Prone Grocery Customers Really Different?" *Journal of Advertising Research*, Vols. 27–35, 1965.
30. Frank, Ronald E., and William F. Massy, "Market Segmentation and the Effectiveness of a Brand's Price and Dealing Policies," *The Journal of Business*, Vol. 38, 1965.
31. Galbraith, J. Kenneth, *The New Industrial State*. Boston: Houghton Mifflin, 1967.
32. Goodman, Charles S., *Management of the Personal Selling Function*. New York: Holt, Rinehart and Winston, 1971.
33. Green, P. E., and F. J. Carmone, *Multidimensional Scaling and Related Techniques for Marketing Analysis*. Boston: Allyn and Bacon, 1970.
34. Green, P. E., and D. S. Tull, *Research for Marketing Decisions*. Englewood Cliffs, N.J.: Prentice-Hall, 1971.
35. Grether, Edwald T., *Marketing and Public Policy*. Englewood Cliffs, N.J.: Prentice Hall, 1966.
36. Halbert, Michael, *The Meaning and Sources of Marketing Theory*. New York: McGraw-Hill, 1965.
37. Henderson, J. N. and R. E. Quandt, *Microeconomic Theory*. New York: McGraw-Hill, 1958.
38. Hinkle, C. L., "The Strategy of Price Deals," *Harvard Business Review*, Vol. 43, 1965.
39. Hollander, Stanley C., "Measuring the Cost and Value of Marketing," *Business Topics*, Vol. 9, 1961.
40. Holloway, Robert J., "An Experiment on Consumer Dissonance," *Journal of Marketing*, Vol. 31, 1967.
41. Houthhakker, Hendrik S., "Revealed Preference and the Utility Function," *Economica*, Vol. 17, 1950.
42. Howard, John A., *Marketing Management: Analysis and Planning*. Homewood, Ill.: Irwin, 1963.
43. Howard, John A., and Jagdish N. Sheth, *The Theory of Buyer Behavior*. New York: Wiley, 1969.
44. Kassarjian, W. M., "A Study of Riesman's Theory of Social Character," *Sociometry*, Vol. 25, 1962.
45. Katona, George C., *Psychological Analysis of Economic Behavior*. New York: McGraw-Hill, 1951.
46. Katona, George C., "Rational Behavior and Economic Behavior," *Psychological Review*, Vol. 60, 1953.

47. Knight, Frank H., *Risk, Uncertainty, and Profit*. Boston: Houghton Mifflin, 1921.
48. Kotler, Phillip, *Marketing Management: Analysis, Planning, and Control*. Englewood Cliffs, N.J.: Prentice-Hall, 1967.
49. Kuehn, A. A., "How Advertising Performance Depends on Other Marketing Factors," *Journal of Advertising Research*, Vol. 2, 1962.
50. Lazer, William, "Marketing's Changing Social Relationships," *Journal of Marketing*, Vol. 33, 1969.
51. Lazer, William, and E. J. Kelley, "Interdisciplinary Horizons in Marketing," *Journal of Marketing*, Vol. 24, 1953.
52. Leavitt, Harold J., "A Note on Some Experimental Findings About the Meaning of Price," *Journal of Business*, Vol. 27, 1954.
53. Leftwich, Richard H., *The Price System and Resource Allocation*. New York: Holt, Rinehart and Winston, 1966.
54. Levitt, Theodore, "Exploit the Product Life Cycle," *Harvard Business Review*, Vol. 43, 1965.
55. Levitt, Theodore, *Industrial Purchasing Behavior*. Cambridge, Mass.: Division of Research, Harvard University, 1965.
56. Levy, Sidney J., "Symbols for Sale," *Harvard Business Review*, Vol. 37, 1959.
57. Liander, Bertil, ed., *Comparative Analysis for International Marketing*. Boston: Allyn and Bacon, 1969.
58. Little, J. D. C., and L. Lodish, "A Media Planning Calculus," *Operations Research*, January–February, 1969.
59. Little, J. M. D., *A Critique of Welfare Economics*. London: Oxford University Press, 1958.
60. Lucas, Darrell B., and S. Henderson Britt, *Measuring Advertising Effectiveness*. New York: McGraw-Hill, 1963.
61. Lynn, Roger A., *Price Policies and Marketing Management*. Homewood, Ill.: Irwin, 1967.
62. Machlup, Fritz, *The Economics of Seller's Competition*. Baltimore, Md.: Johns Hopkins Press, 1952.
63. Mallen, Bruce, "Conflict and Cooperation in Marketing Channels," in *The Marketing Channel*, ed. by Bruce Mallen. New York: Wiley, 1967.
64. Mason, J. L., "The Low Prestige of Personal Selling," *Journal of Marketing*, Vol. 29, 1965.
65. Mayer, D., and H. M. Greenberg, "What Makes a Good Salesman," *Harvard Business Review*, Vol. 42, 1964.
66. McInnes, W. C., "A Conceptual Approach to Marketing," in *Theory in Marketing*, ed. by Reavis Cox, Wroe Alderson, and Stanley J. Shapiro. Homewood, Ill.: Irwin, 1964.
67. McKitterick, J. B., "What is the Marketing Management Concept?" in *Marketing Management and Administrative Action*, ed. by S. Henderson Britt and Harper W. Boyd, Jr. New York: McGraw-Hill, 1963.
68. McVey, P., "Are Channels of Distribution What the Testbooks Say?" in *The Marketing Channel*, ed. by Bruce Mallen. New York: Wiley, 1967.
69. Miracle, Gordon E., "Product Characteristics and Marketing Strategy," *Journal of Marketing*, Vol. 29, 1965.
70. Nicosia, Francesco M., *Consumer Decision Processes: Marketing and Advertising Implications*. Englewood Cliffs, N.J.: Prentice-Hall, 1966.
71. Oxenfeldt, Alfred R., "Product Line Pricing," *Harvard Business Review*, Vol. 44, 1968.

72. Palda, Kristian S., "The Hypothesis of a Hierarchy of Effects: A Partial Evaluation," *Journal of Marketing Research,* Vol. 3, 1966.
73. Palda, Kristian S., "Sales Effects of Advertising: A Review of the Literature," *Journal of Advertising Research,* Vol. 4, 1964.
74. Pessemier, Edgar A., *New Product Decisions: An Analytical Approach.* New York: McGraw Hill, 1966.
75. Polanyi, Karl, *The Great Transformation.* Boston: Beacon Press, 1957.
76. Revzan, David A., "The Holistic Institutional Approach to Marketing Theory," in *Perspectives in Marketing Theory,* ed. by Jerome B. Kernan and Montrose S. Sommers. New York: Appleton-Century-Crofts, 1968.
77. Reynolds, William H., "More Sense about Market Segmentation," *Harvard Business Review,* Vol. 43, 1965.
78. Robertson, T. S., "The Process of Innovation and the Diffusion of Innovation," *Journal of Marketing,* Vol. 31, 1967.
79. Robinson, P. J., ed., *Promotional Decisions Using Mathematical Models.* Boston: Allyn and Bacon, 1967.
80. Robinson, P. J., and B. Stidsen, *Personal Selling in a Modern Perspective.* Boston: Allyn and Bacon, 1967.
81. Rubel, I. W., "Toward Better Advertiser-Agency Relations." *Harvard Business Review,* Vol. 36, 1958.
82. Schumpeter, Joseph A., *The Theory of Economic Development.* New York: Oxford University Press, 1961.
83. Scitovsky, Tibor, "Some Consequences of the Habit of Judging Quality by Price," *The Review of Economic Studies,* Vol. 12, 1944–1945.
84. Shapiro, B. P., "The Psychology of Pricing," *Harvard Business Review,* Vol. 46, 1968.
85. Shapiro, Stanley J., "Comparative Marketing and Economic Development," in *Science in Marketing,* ed. by George Schwartz. New York: Wiley, 1965.
86. Sheth, Jagdish N., "A Review of Buyer Behavior," *Management Science,* Vol. 13, 1969.
87. Smith, W. R., "Product Differentiation and Market Segmentation as Alternative Marketing Strategies," *Journal of Marketing,* 1956.
88. Tucker, William T., *The Social Context of Economic Behavior.* New York: Holt, Rinehart and Winston, 1964.
89. Udell, John G., "Can Attitude Measurement Predict Consumer Behavior?" *Journal of Marketing,* Vol. 29, 1965.
90. Veblen, Thorstein, *The Theory of the Leisure Class.* New York: Macmillan, 1899.
91. Wasson, Chester R., and David H. McConaughy, *Buying and Marketing Decisions.* New York: Appleton-Century-Crofts, 1968.
92. Yankelovich, Daniel, "New Criteria for Market Segmentation," *Harvard Business Review,* Vol. 42, 1964.

Dr. Richard W. Budd is Professor of Communication and Chairman of the Department of Human Communication at Rutgers University. He is the author of two books, the most recent of which is *Content Analysis of Communications,* and co-editor of this volume. He has written a number of book chapters, journal articles, papers, and monographs. His most recent work deals primarily with communication and communication education.

5

ENCOUNTER GROUPS: AN APPROACH TO HUMAN COMMUNICATION

RICHARD W. BUDD

INTRODUCTION

O NE of the most pervasive and controversial social forces of this century has been making rapid strides during the past twenty-five years. Under the names T-groups, sensitivity training, encounter groups, human-relations laboratories—to mention the most common—intensive group experiences have arisen in a variety of environments: industry, college campuses, religious organizations, etc. A burgeoning number of books and articles—both academic and popular—have been published that alternately extol or denounce such experiences. The encounter group has formed the subject matter of several movies, television series, and late-night talk shows. In fact, it is referred to in some manner in no fewer than five of the chapters appearing in this book. The vocabulary of the encounter group has gained common usage in our everyday language and, more recently, has been capitalized upon in a series of "sensitivity greeting cards."

It is difficult to find anyone today who isn't aware of encounter groups and who doesn't hold a fairly emotional opinion concerning them. At the same time, it is infinitely more difficult to find someone who has both studied the theory of such groups and had substantial experiences as a participant. Such ignorance, however, has not prevented a fair number of people from serving as trainers or facilitators for encounter groups, or from being severe critics of the T-group ("T" is for training) as a viable learning experience.

It is not the intent of this piece to set the record straight. In the bibliography at the end of this chapter are included the major, basic works on T-group theory and training, and the record can only be set straight by studying and understanding the basic concepts contained in these works. From that point on, the student must make his own judgments. What this chapter does intend to do is present a synthesis of current encounter-group theory (which at its simplest implies a theory of human communication), look at the process of the basic encounter group (which is where the theory is put into practice), and critically compare the two.

ORIGINS OF THE ENCOUNTER GROUP

The notion of intensive group work as a means of facilitating learning about human relations grew out of a broader search for more viable ways of approaching the human learning experience. Some have credited the psychologist Kurt Lewin with providing the innovative spark that resulted in the first T-group conducted at Bethel, Maine, in 1947.

> This laboratory was designed to try out new methods for re-educating human behavior and social relationships.
> The major method of learning employed is one in which participants are helped to diagnose and experiment with their own behavior in a specially designed environment. (5, p. vii)

This maiden T-group was held under the auspices of the National Training Laboratory in Group Development, a subgroup of the National Education Association. The National Training Laboratory became an independent organization in 1951, and for the most part has concentrated its efforts in the industrial field. NTL coordinates a network of quasi-accredited trainers, which it will recommend to organizations seeking to establish laboratory training programs.

At about the same time Lewin and his associates were laying the groundwork (Lewin died prior to the occurrence of the first T-group) at the Massachusetts Institute of Technology, Carl Rogers and his associates at the Counseling Center of the University of Chicago were also beginning experiments in intensive group experiences for use in training counselors.

> Our staff felt that no amount of cognitive training would prepare them, so we experimented with an intensive group experience in which the trainees met for several hours each day in order better to understand themselves, to become aware of attitudes which might be self-defeating in the counseling relationship, and to relate to each other in ways that would be helpful and could carry over into their counseling work. (19, p. 3)

The NTL approach, which had its beginnings in training in human relations skills, and the Rogers approach, which is aimed more toward personal growth and development, and improvement in interpersonal communication, provided the thrust behind a movement which today has numerous approaches and extensions.* The range of activities many people are willing to pigeonhole under the label "sensitivity training" today extends from workshops on how to be a better PTA president to week-long nude marathon sessions in the Colorado mountains.

ENCOUNTER-GROUP THEORY

It should be clear to the reader that I am using the terms *T-group* and *encounter group* interchangeably. I will also use the term *sensitivity training* to refer to the overall process. Some writers insist upon making clear distinctions between the terms. I find little value in doing so, since in practice the distinction seems meaningless.

As noted earlier, T-group theory is basically a theory of communication. More accurately, it is a set of prescriptions for human communication, designed to lead to improved interpersonal relationships. Bradford, Gibb, and Benne wrote about the encounter group:

> It has its roots in a system of values relative to mature, productive and right relationships among people. It is grounded in assumptions about human nature, human learning, and human change. [5, p. 1]

These assumptions will become clear as we reveal the outcomes expected from an encounter-group experience.

Whatever else it is, the encounter group is designed to be an experience-based learning exercise—the experience from which learning is to occur is that of each individual interacting with others in the encounter group. That experience can be as limited or as broad as the individual participant wishes to make it. It will also help to remember that encounter groups are not therapy groups. The distinction often made by writers in the area is that an encounter group is for "well" people, whereas a therapy group is designed to help persons in need of psychological or psychiatric help. An encounter group does not focus on past behavior, or "why people are the way they are" from a historical perspective. The encounter group is distingushed by its here-and-now focus, dealing only with the interactions among the individuals making up the group at a given time.

---

* Academicians seem to have a penchant for historicizing the development of concepts and movements in a "begatting" sort of fashion. Often such narratives of development are crucial to understanding a concept, sometimes not. In the present case I am not sure, but I am struck with certain similarities between the notions enbodied in T-group operations and those set out by Hanno Hardt in Chapter 17 in this volume, on philosophy, the section on existentialism. Of particular interest is the work of Karl Jaspers [25, pp. 114–140]. Of somewhat lesser value is C. M. Hampden-Turner's "An Existential 'Learning Theory' and the Integration of T-Group Research." [in 12]

A Common Framework

While encounter groups vary in purpose (usually indicated by what they are called) and in superficial design, there is a framework (sometimes referred to as theory) that seems to be common to most T-groups.

Following an initial period of "flailing" and coping with the ambiguity of the situation (during which the leader does not lead and there is no agenda), participants begin to express their feelings about the situation and about themselves with respect to it. Gradually there develops in the group a climate of psychological safety which allows participants to express their immediate feelings and reactions toward other members in the group, thereby tending to reduce defensiveness. Golembiewski and Blumberg observe:

> One of the goals of sensitivity training is to help people examine their typical modes of behavior, in a psychologically safe atmosphere, to permit them to test whether their interaction with others is coming across as intended. (12, p. 6)

Out of the free expression of feelings, both negative and positive, the climate of safety develops into one of mutual trust, displacing defensiveness and paving the way for self-acceptance. The climate thus developed is conducive to personal experimentation with new forms of behavior. Feedback from other members of the group allows the individual to learn something about the impact he is making on others. With this greater freedom and improved communication comes the possibility for changing his behavior and attitudes. Changes made and tested in a supportive climate may have greater potential to become lasting, and are more likely to benefit the participant in his post-encounter-group experiences.

Basic Methodology

Some of the concepts presented in this brief summary of T-group theory need to be expanded somewhat, but that can wait upon a short discussion of the methodology involved in making an encounter group happen. Obviously, the outcomes specified above do not come about magically by declaring a group a T-group. The process has to be carefully facilitated by a trained leader. In spite of what the reader may have read to the contrary —even in books about T-group theory and method—encounter groups *are* run by rules, extremely important rules. The keeper of the rules is the "facilitator" or trainer.

There are conflicting notions about how the trainer should operate within the encounter group. (For detailed discussion on this, see pertinent sections in 5, 19, and 20 under References.) Some writers insist the trainer be more or less invisible, making interventions in participant exchanges only to point up the rules, to seek clarification, or to facilitate the examination of what he thinks is a crucial interchange or behavioral act on the part of participants.

Still another view is that the trainer assume a more active role in the group, but still keep on top of things by not getting personally involved. Here, the trainer is active with a purpose, the purpose being to keep the rules by "modeling" behavior. The idea here is that if the trainer consciously behaves as a model participant, the participants will eventually come to use his method of approach, and the rules will become normative behavior without ever having been explicitly stated.

Carl Rogers offers still another alternative, but one that assumes that the facilitator has himself internalized the rules to the point that he, in a sense by his own behavior, *is* the rules. Rogers explains this role by talking about the qualities he does not like in a facilitator:

> I do not like the facilitator who withholds himself from personal, emotional participation in the group—holding himself aloof as the expert, able to analyze the group process and members' reactions through superior knowledge. This is often seen in individuals who make their living by conducting groups, but seems to show both a defensiveness in themselves and a deep lack of respect for the participants. Such a person denies his own spontaneous feelings and provides a model for the group—that of the overly cool, analytical person who never gets involved—which is the complete antithesis of what I believe in. [19, p. 67]

But to what rules and by what means must the facilitator hold the participants, if the encounter group is to proceed as it should? One, perhaps the most important one, has already been mentioned. The trainer must somehow get the group to accept a here-and-now perspective. This means that participants are expected to react to one another on the basis of what happens in the group. So-called there-and-then information—incidents or feelings generated elsewhere, in some other time—must be ruled out.

Further, norms of openness and honesty are expected to evolve as the primary values in encounter-group communication. Openness and honesty mean not only the participant's expressing his feelings about another participant, but also revealing aspects of himself to other members of the group. This mission of the encounter group is perhaps best summed up in Figure 5.1, the Johari Window, also more properly known as the Johari Awareness Model, developed by Joseph Luft and Harry Ingham.* Quadrant 1 refers to the open feelings and behaviors known to others and known to self. The second area, the blind quadrant, refers to feelings and behaviors that are known to others and not to self. Quadrant 3 represents

---

* A detailed explication of this model appears in Joseph Luft, *Group Processes: An Introduction to Group Dynamics* (Palo Alto, Calif.: National Press, 1963).

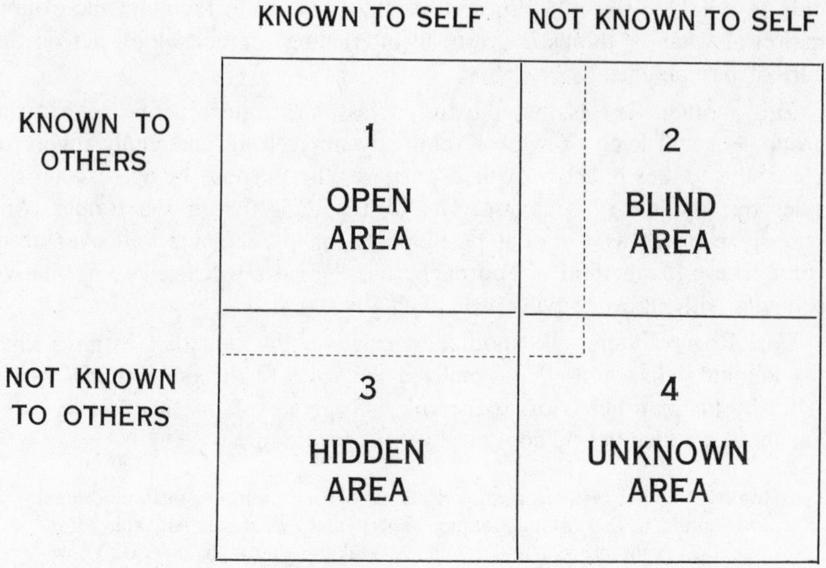

KNOWN TO SELF   NOT KNOWN TO SELF

KNOWN TO OTHERS	1 OPEN AREA	2 BLIND AREA
NOT KNOWN TO OTHERS	3 HIDDEN AREA	4 UNKNOWN AREA

Figure 5.1

those feelings and behaviors that are known to self, but unknown to others. Quadrant 4 represents the feelings and behaviors unknown to self and unknown to others.

The openness and honesty we were talking about earlier becomes an essential ingredient in quadrants 2 and 3 and, indirectly, in quadrant 1. The encounter group is designed to enlarge quadrant 1 by decreasing the size of 2 (by accepting feedback from other participants) and the size of 3 (by revealing self to others).

To accept potentially useful feedback from others (especially when it is negative) requires that the participant be able to hear it, which usually requires the prior step of reducing defensiveness. *Useful* is the key word used in conjunction with feedback, in the context of an encounter group, and to ensure usefulness of feedback, the facilitator must in some way encourage participants to follow a simple set of guidelines:

1. Feedback is descriptive rather than evaluative. By describing his own reaction, it leaves the individual free to use it or not use it as he sees fit. By avoiding evaluative language, it reduces the need for the individual to react defensively.

2. Feedback is specific rather than general. Rather than using labels such as "dominating," it will probably be more useful simply to describe the action and the feeling he had about it.

3. Feedback takes into account the needs of both the receiver and the giver. Feedback can be destructive when it serves only the needs of the initiator.

4. Feedback is directed toward behavior the receiver can do something about. It is not useful to remind someone of a shortcoming over which he has no control.

5. Feedback is solicited, rather than imposed.

6. Feedback is well timed. In general, feedback is most useful at the earliest opportunity after the given behavior.

7. Feedback is checked to ensure clear communication. This is accomplished by the receiver rephrasing what he has heard to see if it corresponds to what the sender had in mind.

8. When feedback is given in a training group, both giver and receiver have the opportunity to check with others in the group the accuracy of the feedback. Is this one man's impression or an impression shared by others? *

The participant's revealing himself to others is a bit different process from feedback, although some of the criteria set out above might be useful. The major issue in opening up the hidden area, however, is another key aspect in the theory of interpersonal growth—the issue of *risk*. Revealing something about himself that he believes others may view as a weakness involves a fair amount of personal risk. So does reaching out to establish a relationship with someone else when he is basically a retiring person unaccustomed to doing so. The crucial question, of course, is, *What is he risking?* The answer comes much harder, especially if he is answering his own question. What is being risked is his personal image, or at least the image he believes others have of him. The risk is in the old childhood fear of being "last chosen," of rejection, of ridicule, or of feeling less human.

Risk has been aptly described by several people as "letting go." Interpersonal risk-taking must be akin to the feeling of apprehensiveness the novice trapeze artist has when he takes his first swing across the bars; he has let go of the first trapeze but hasn't yet gotten a firm grip on the second. It is, of course, more secure to hold fast to the first bar (or perhaps not to go out on the trapeze in the first place); it is uncomfortable and dangerous to be suspended between both; and it must be a great relief to have negotiated successfully to the second. The notion of risk is inextricably bound up with the growing process, whether it be interpersonal or intellectual.

---

* From "Feedback and the Helping Relationship," in *NTL Institute: Reading Book* (Washington, D.C.: NTL Institute for Applied Behavioral Science, 1967).

THE ENCOUNTER-GROUP PROCESS

In this section I would like to take a brief look inside an encounter group, to describe as well as possible in the limited space available how the theory and methods laid out in the previous section are frequently operationalized. Starting with the knowledge that the dynamics of each group encounter vary, sometimes considerably, and that the experience for each individual is different (even at different points in time), it is possible to provide some general description of the T-group process. One should not come away with the impression that the occurrences, as they are observed here, come about in any particular order, or even that certain events must occur in every encounter group in order for it to be successful. What follows is a composite of events I have observed through working in many encounter groups, presented in a way that might contribute to a clearer understanding of the process. At the same time, the limitations of the language and the medium of the written word do not permit re-creation of an experience that is at once so potent, emotional, complex, and engaging at so many levels.

Setting and Format

In the program with which I am familiar, one can only become a participant in an encounter group on a voluntary basis, after completing an application to a laboratory and passing a preliminary screening interview. (*Laboratory* is not used here synonymously with *encounter group*. A laboratory is the setting in which the encounter group is used as the main learning vehicle. The encounter groups making up the laboratory meet regularly as a community for instructional purposes.) The several encounter groups making up the laboratory are formed from the accepted applicants, each group ranging in size from nine to fifteen participants. Many designers of encounter-group laboratories prefer to use an isolated site, such as a camp, conference center, or lodge, away from normal patterns of life that might prove distracting to participants. In such settings, participants eat together and spend most of their waking hours either in group meetings or in informal sessions with other participants in the laboratory.

Encounter-group laboratory sessions extend anywhere from three days to two weeks (the average being about five days). During an average day, participants will spend from six to eight hours in their individual groups and from one to three hours in community sessions, where groups gather for discussions of the interpersonal process, usually led in a more familiar educational pattern by an instructor.

The Group Encounter

The range of reasons participants give for wanting to take part in an encounter group varies widely, from simple curiosity to quite specific statements concerning personal growth and the desire to improve or alter specific aspects of personal behavior. Similarly, the participants arrive for a human-relations laboratory with a variety of feelings. Some are eager to begin, genuinely looking forward to the experience. Others suffer great anxiety about what is going to happen to them personally, quite often triggered by unclear stories they have heard, or by somewhat ambiguous articles in the popular press which often focus on more dramatic aspects of the process or seek to exploit bizarre extremes in the movement. In any case, most labs begin among a conglomeration of tensions.

The first few T-group sessions offer little in the way of reducing tensions. In one way or another (either the trainer mentions it or his behavior implies it), participants discover that they are faced with a considerable amount of freedom and no formal leadership. At the most, participants are told they will have the opportunity, over the next several days, to learn more about themselves, how they impact other people, and how others impact them, and that they will learn these things through their own participation and experiences in the encounter group.

The first session will most likely include periods of extended silence, interrupted by comments such as "How are we supposed to get this thing going?" or "Did we travel all the way out here just to sit and stare at each other?" There may be attempts at humor or suggestions for ways of starting, such as "Why don't we go around and introduce ourselves to each other?" But almost always, there is considerable pressure to fill the vacuum left by the lack of formal leadership.

One participant later described the opening session of his encounter group as a "chicken dance." Carl Rogers aptly describes it as "milling around." [19] This early, superficial chatter means different things to different people. To some, it is a way of forestalling involvement. For others, it may be the only reaction they know of for dealing with a situation which violates their expectations of what a normal learning environment should be.

Quite frequently, some members of the group will attempt to force leadership onto the trainer by directing their questions through him. For many, the early experience is frustrating. Others get angry. Others sit back in silence, and still others decide to lead. While such struggling with feelings and frustrations may seem painful, it begins almost instantly to provide the raw data upon which the group will subsequently begin to act. How rapidly it begins to work depends upon the composition of the group, the facilitator's style of working, the commitment level of individuals in the group, and other factors which differ from group to group.

More and more, however, expressions of feelings by participants will account for an increasing part of the discussion. Often, such self-disclosures will be limited to the relationships and occurrences which have taken place outside the group. A professor tells the group of his own feelings of inadequacy when among his colleagues. A minister talks of his inability to show his care for others, even those quite close to him. Another dwells on his tendency to be a "loner," but adds that he likes it that way. In a sense, these represent feelings participants have, but they also represent talk *about* feelings rather than expressions of *current* feelings for other members of the group. Some facilitators feel that this kind of early there-and-then discussion is necessary, to enable participants to develop pictures of one another before they move more directly into the here and now. Other trainers view this sort of interaction as a clear violation of the here-and-now norm, and insist that participants begin immediately to express their feelings for others in the group. Whichever, these early forays represent the first steps both in building and in testing the level of safety in the group. They do not, however, represent the central work of the group, dealing with here-and-now feelings, reactions, and emotions.

Inevitably, the first expressions of feelings about persons within the group will be made. Quite consistently, these first open expressions are likely to be negative ones, and they are often likely to be directed at the facilitator. Oddly enough, both ways of behaving can be viewed as relatively safe. If a participant makes a negative response to another member of the group, there is a high probability that such a comment will draw a negative response. If one is prepared for a negative reply, it is more easily defended against. The alternative is reaching out in a positive way, but in so doing, one makes oneself vulnerable to rejection and hurt, which to most of us seems much more difficult to cope with. Directing negative expressions at the trainer does not carry with it the same risk as does expressing negative feelings to another participant; after all, it is the trainer who says the agenda for the meeting is an open one. Carl Rogers suggests that early expressions of negative feelings are a way of testing freedom in the group.[19] Of some importance to this discussion is an observation often made by participants: The results of expressing a feeling about another person to that person are usually much less frightening than the consequences anticipated prior to doing so.

As the sessions wear on, participants become increasingly aware that nothing significant will happen in the group unless they themselves make it happen. This realization, coupled with seeing other group members express their feelings without devastating consequences (sometimes, with positive results), helps to reduce for the participant the perceived risk in participating. To reveal himself to the group in any significant way at this stage, however, still represents a personal risk of major proportions.

As the exchanges among those in the group become freer and more specific, there will frequently emerge those who are overly concerned about the consequences for *other* members of the group who reveal their feelings. These members will, as a result, resist the direction of the group in the name of a fellow participant, saying "I don't think Donna should have to respond to that" or "She's already feeling badly; all she's feeling right now is that you should leave her alone." A medical student in a group I once worked with spent the first sessions of the encounter group coming to the aid of participants he felt were being "put on the spot." His resistance became so disruptive to the group that several participants confronted him with the issue. He made clear, after considerable time, that he was expressing his own concern about being "put on the spot" himself.

Well into the encounter, things happen rapidly and sometimes without any reasonable order or explanation. As the issues become more personal and more emotional, the theory and the rules often fail to account for the phenomenon. The rules of feedback are frequently laid aside, and out of context the interchanges are anything but specific or caring and supportive. Rogers suggests that *feedback* is too mild a term to describe such encounters, and he prefers to use the word *confrontation*.[19, p. 31] The following example particularly involves one of the two facilitators in a group and a fairly interpersonally powerful male who had dominated the group for nearly two days.

Tom (fac.): (*jumps to his feet*) Goddammit Barry, I've had it with you. I've held out my hand to you time and time again, and all you've done is spit in it.

Barry: I've spit in it, huh? Tell me Tom, how have I spit. . . .

Tom: You know goddamn well you have. You don't give a damn about me or about this group. The only thing you've done with any success since this group started is to prevent it from learning anything. As far as you're concerned, we're all here just to entertain your passion for emotional binges.

Georgianne: You know Tom's right, Barry. (*Several others in the group nod and vocalize agreement.*) You've done nothing but egg other people on, hoping to see them cry or perform for you.

Barry: How have I spit in your hand, Tom? What's the matter? Are you upset because I'm messing up your plans, because I won't follow your damn rules? To hell with your rules. I'm going to do what I want to in here, and if you don't like it, that's your problem.

Tom: I think the least you could do is listen to what other people here have to say.

Gary (fac.): (*to the group*) How about that?

Diane: What difference does it make? Barry already told us he doesn't care how we feel anyway.

Chuck: You've just closed the door in my face, Barry. You told me I have nothing of value to say to you.

Clearly, there was fairly strong agreement in the group that Barry's behavior was somewhat less than acceptable, but little specific feedback about the problem. On the other hand, Barry was insisting that his nonacceptance by the group was not his, but their problem. Gary, the uninvolved member of the training team, sensing a stalemate, diverted the action elsewhere. On the following morning, still another incident occurred in the same group.

Diane: God, Mary, you *are* a mouse. If anyone ever called me a soppy piece of milquetoast, like Ben just did to you, I'd scream. . . . I'd be madder than hell.

Mary: It didn't bother me that much.

Rich: (*to Mary*) You mean you aren't the least bit upset?

Mary: It really doesn't bother me.

Ben: Good God, girl, you're not even human!

Tom (fac.): Ben, it might be helpful to Mary if you could be more specific about how she comes across to you.

Ben: Hey, you heard her, man, she already knows.

Barry: What you need, Mary, is some backbone. You know what I'd like to see you do right now. I'd like to see you tell Ben to go screw himself. I'd like to see you go around this room and say something negative about everyone in this group.

Georgianne: Come on, Mary, start with me if you'd like.

Gary (fac.): Mary, I guess I'd like to know how you are feeling about what's going on here.

Mary: I don't know, I really can't say. I guess I'd like to know what Tom thinks about me.

Tom: Are you asking me as a person, or me as someone in this group you see as an authority figure?

Mary: No, I really respect you and I want to know what you think of me.

Tom: Okay. I guess I agree with what I've heard others say. I think you're . . . uhmm . . . wishy-washy.

Mary: (*after a pause*) All right. I guess I can't disagree with you, but . . . can you accept me for that?

Tom: (*after a very long pause*) Yes, I can. (*pause*) I think I can.

Almost immediately after this exchange with Mary, and without any apparent provocation, Tom made the following statement to Barry.

Tom: I've been thinking a lot about what I said to you yesterday, Barry, and I think you were right. It was my problem. I have a great deal of trouble relating to people I see as being very powerful. You were a threat to me and to the way I wanted to run this group. For reasons that I still have to work out for myself, I simply could not accept your independence. I guess I was preventing you from learning as much as I thought you were preventing others in the group from learning. I'd like to try it again.

And so the process proceeds, sometimes in a very gentle and supportive way, at other times, in a driving, almost brutal, manner, but always moving in a single direction. This was best expressed by a girl who told another participant in a recent group: "Quit playing the analyst. I don't give a damn how you *view* our relationship in clinical terms. I want to know how you *feel* about me. Please, let me get to know *you*."

In the typical laboratory, there are a number of other means for facilitating learning, used in conjunction with the encounter group. The laboratory community (composed of several encounter groups) attends a series of theory sessions, interspersed with the group sessions. These are either lectures or structured exercises which focus on some communicative tool. While the encounter group as an educational device stresses learning through experience, the theory behind it is that intellectual integration of that experience with others is necessary if participants are to extend their learning beyond the laboratory setting. Schein and Bennis write:

> In order to optimize learning, delegates (participants) attend daily information or theory sessions. The content of these sessions is designed to help them understand the experiences they are having in the T-group by focusing on topics such as the following: what to observe in a group, emotional problems of becoming a member of a new group, decision-making and problem solving in a group, the communication process, styles of emotional expression and presentation of self to others. [20, p. 19]

The nexus intended through coupling of the encounter-group experience with the theory sessions is, of course, behavioral change. As Schein and Bennis further observe,[20, p. 19] "The major learning outcomes, therefore, will be increased awareness, changed attitudes, and greater interpersonal competence."

There are two other methods used in an encounter-group laboratory that I will mention here. They are the so-called helping-pairs and the creation of new encounter groups. Helping-pairs brings together two participants, usually from different encounter groups, who meet periodically for half-hour talks throughout the laboratory. Participants in the pairs are encouraged to share their feelings about what has been happening to them in their respective encounter groups and their general feelings about the total experience. Many participants have credited these two-person encounters with making it easier for them subsequently to bring up a particular problem before their own encounter group. In many cases, participants have pointed out that their partners have given them new insights into things they were having difficulty sorting out for themselves. At any rate, the response to this particular technique indicates that participants see it as a valuable part of their laboratory experience.

The establishment of new encounter groups—usually done near the end of the laboratory—serves a critical function in carrying through the notion of behavioral changes, by giving the participant, while still in the laboratory setting, the opportunity to "try on" his new behavior, to test what he has learned about himself on others with whom he has had little or no prior contact. The new group is designed to provide the first step back into what can turn out to be, by comparison, a chilly real world.

THE ENCOUNTER GROUP AS COMMUNICATION THEORY

It would be a gross oversight not to point out the rather obvious theory and the working model of communication suggested by T-group theory and practice, particularly since that seems to be based upon a rather simplistic, and now outmoded, view of the communication process. The underlying human-communication theory implied by encounter-group theory is that sources do things to receivers through messages in a one-way, cause-and-effect fashion. This conceptualization (see Chapters 13 and 20 in this volume) once widely accepted, now appears inadequate for understanding many complex human-communication phenomena. A misconception about how human communication works is reflected not only in T-group theory, but in practice as well. This is perhaps most clearly seen in the notion of feedback. It is the manner in which feedback is conceived of and used in the encounter group that limits the group's usefulness in communication theory.

Schein and Bennis provide a commonly accepted view of feedback and its functions:

> Practically all of our learning is based on the idea of obtaining information about our performance and then determining how far our progress deviates from some desired goal.
> Feedback serves some covert purposes as well, for example, confirmations and disconfirmations about various realities concerning ourselves, or external events. [20, p. 41]

Perhaps a brief example would help at this point. Marti, a girl in the group, had received a considerable amount of feedback regarding her aloofness from several members. There was general agreement that she was coming across cold and uncaring. Finally, one of the group members provided this feedback.

Ted: I think I know what a large part of the problem is for me Marti. Do you realize that whenever you talk to people in here you hardly ever maintain eye contact with them?
Marti: I don't?
Gina: (*speaking to Marti*) Yeah. I didn't realize what it was about you either until Ted just mentioned it. You talk to me, but your eyes just wander all over the place.
Marti: Yeah? I guess I just didn't think. . . .
Gina: See, you're doing it right now. You started to talk to me and, blooey, you're gone. That makes me feel sort of . . . put off. You know, like you really don't care whether you talk to me or not.
Marti: I guess I never realized I did that; nobody ever told me about it before or said that it bothered them.
Ted: Sure, but that's why we're here, see.
Fac.: We don't know too much about what happened before, Marti, but I hear some people right here and right now saying it bothers them. The question is, does that bother you, Marti, that people react negatively to that?
Marti: Well, yeah. I mean I don't want people turned off by such a small thing.
Fac: Would you like to change that behavior?

This dialogue, I believe, represents fairly the pattern of feedback most frequently assumed in an encounter group. It appears to meet several of the criteria for useful feedback: It is descriptive, specific, timely, and about behavior that can be altered. While this pattern of interaction would appear not to violate T-group theory, it reflects a lack of understanding about the process of human communication.

Let's review the interchange. There are a number of implications growing out of the discussion among the three participants and the facilitator: that there is a reality that exists out there called "aloofness," that it can be objectively identified, that Marti has it, and that it should be purged from her behavior to make her more interpersonally competent. As the transcript from which this dialogue was taken shows, her lack of eye-contact behavior (which, in part, was responsible for her aloofness) was replaced by group-and-facilitator-sanctioned, more-eye-contact behavior. The change met with considerable support from the group, and, indeed, increased acceptance for Marti.

As near as I can determine, feedback in the context of the encounter group means *information*. Such information normally comes after a preamble such as "You make me feel. . . ." suggesting that the cause of the feeling and the responsibility for altering it lie with the receiver of the feedback. The basic problem with this formulation is that nowhere does it acknowledge that the observer (in this example, Ted) had anything to do with the observation. In understanding human communication, one must understand that Marti's behavior (lack of eye contact) and Ted's understanding of that behavior (aloofness) are, in a very real sense, two separate phenomena. And while Marti's behavior was a necessary condition for the interaction, Ted's observation must stand as his own creation, based on what he understood her behavior to mean. The observation does not necessarily have anything to do with what Marti is or is not.

That Ted's observation was supported by Gina does not make the observation more valid, an assumption too frequently made in the encounter group. (One of the guidelines listed earlier suggests that a way to validate feedback is to check it out with other group members.) Gina's observation and Ted's observation must also be viewed as two different ways of understanding, each of which is personal to Ted and to Gina. They can, and unfortunately do, appear to be corroborative, since both were formed from apparently the same raw data, that is, Marti's lack of eye contact.

This customary use of feedback in the encounter group, then, can neither confirm nor disconfirm anything for the receiver of the information. At best, the target of such feedback, regardless of how well it adheres to the guidelines, can learn something about the realities of the source, but relatively little about his own. Ignorance of this simple fact on the part of either the trainer of a group or its members could raise some serious concerns about the nature of the learning and behavioral change that occurs within a group.

Returning to our example, let's pursue some of the consequences for participants when they have not been made aware of this basic issue. In the group most recently referred to, Marti decided to act upon the feedback she received. Such a decision was an easy one, since she received considerable support for making the change from the members of her group. This is not to say that the change in her behavior is necessarily a bad thing, but that the reasons for that change most certainly need to be examined. She may very well have changed her behavior to gain acceptance, to increase her interpersonal skills, both of which—we must add—do very little to increase her understanding of herself. In addition, if she did change her behavior for those reasons, she should know that the acceptance and support of her new behavior, including the judgment that it made her more competent, were conferred only by the participants of the T-group, here and now, and not by a broader population.

Marti should not be permitted to ignore the fact that, whatever else her behavioral change represents, it also represents a way of coping with the pressures she felt in the here-and-now environment of her T-group. I recall one young student who found her first encounter-group experience so fascinating and so helpful to her in her personal relationships after the laboratory that she went to another. All through her second laboratory, and for a considerable while afterward, she was despondent and generally unhappy with herself as a person. She told me that her unhappiness stemmed from the fact that during her most recent T-group she had received a good deal of negative feedback concerning the new behavior she had acquired during her first group. From that she deduced that she wasn't making any progress at all, and she was raising questions within herself regarding her authenticity. Her problem was that no one had told her that the second time around there would be a different T-group, with different people who developed a different set of realities from those in her first group. She was, in a manner of speaking, caught between two different sets of communicational realities, in which there was apparently very little agreement. Marti may very well face that same sort of problem and discomforting concern about herself after her T-group, the first time someone takes her to task for staring at him—another of the realities people can reasonably invent from the raw data of too much eye contact.

I would not like these last several paragraphs to be understood as debunking encounter groups. That would be throwing out the baby with the bath water. But what has been written here should be understood as underscoring the fact that encounter groups and the theory of encounter groups are not yet out of their babyhood. In light of that, I will suggest a recasting of the notion of feedback.

Feedback in the context of the encounter group is, at best, a report on the internal state of the source of the feedback. This further suggests that the most appropriate receiver of feedback in an encounter group is the source of the feedback himself, since it concerns mainly his concept of what is happening, and may only coincidentally have relevance for the receiver. So why have an encounter group? Because, I think, it is useful for others to observe the process by which an individual comes to grips with his ordering and his understanding of the environment. A useful part of that struggle, I believe, is having others around who are willing to participate in his efforts and are committed to doing the same things for themselves. This, of course, means that participants attending a T-group do so with the tacit agreement that they will be *using* each other to achieve this end (as opposed to the commonly accepted notion that what participants are doing in a T-group is building interpersonal relationships with one another). To develop the dynamic to produce the feelings and emotions necessary for this sort of self-examination means, in lieu of any new developments, continuance of the use of the here-and-now norms and feedback, but for different reasons and toward different ends. The most crucial aspect of this reconceptualization is the reeducation of the trainer to understand what feedback represents and how he can maximize its usefulness for (1) the source and (2) the receiver of the feedback.

This approach would alter the normal interaction sequences of the encounter group. In the most recent example, Ted offered feedback to Marti about her lack of eye contact, and the attention of the group and the trainer were focused upon Marti and her problem. To make the T-group a useful exercise for understanding communication, the attention should have been focused upon Ted, and, subsequently, Gina, who supported Ted. The facilitator might, for example, have asked Ted, "What is there in the fact that Marti doesn't maintain eye contact with you when she talks to you that disturbs you?" or "Why is that significant to you?" or "Why must Marti alter her behavior in order for you to accept her?"

Under this kind of guidance, the initiator of the feedback is required to examine *his own ways* of defining and relating to his environment, and perhaps to discover something about his own behavior. What Marti can gain from all this is the addition of yet another concept of how people see and define, thus increasing her own range in understanding the realities of others. Learning in this context, then, is not necessarily manifested by explosive emotional scenes filled with blinding insights, but rather it takes the form of a quiet, internal revolution against old and narrow ways of seeing and understanding. Such learning occurs between and after encounter-group sessions more often than during them.

Given this sort of orientation, what one might logically expect to come from an encounter group is not so much a change in one's own behavior as a change in the ways one understands one's reaction to the behavior of others.

FUTURE DIRECTIONS

Jurgen Ruesch recently told me that the encounter-group phenomenon was dead. Carl Rogers, on the other hand, looks to a future of expanded and increased use of the T-group as a device for interpersonal growth. It is quite likely that the disparity between these two attitudes comes from looking at two different things. Rogers' optimism stems from his long and intensive work with a methodology that appears to produce results consistent with encounter-group theory. Ruesch's pessimism stems from looking at a theory which has become stagnant and is, to a large degree, supplanted by a methodology. These two attitudes may not be disparate but complementary: Encounter groups may simply grow themselves to death.

If I have been at all fair in presenting a picture of current T-groups in the preceding sections, then it is difficult to ignore some of the obvious differences between theory and practice in the T-group setting. The heart of the problem might be that during the past twenty-five years, T-group theory has remained relatively unchanged from its initial formulations, while T-group practitioners have been hard at work developing new techniques for use in encounter-group laboratories. This is witnessed by the numerous exercise handbooks currently available on the market. There has been in all of this, it would seem, a tacit assumption that the methodology of T-groups works in close harmony with its theory. What I suggest is that the preoccupation with techniques has existed at the expense of possible refinement and regeneration of T-group theory.

There are a number of examples of the sort of questions that would have been raised if advocates of the encounter group were actively trying to update their theory. T-group theory, for example, supports an open, relatively unstructured, rule-free environment in which the individual participant must identify and cope with problems for himself as a means of developing his own understanding (awareness) of what goes on around him.

This notion of personal growth and learning developed from a disenchantment with the traditional approach to education—where students are "taught" to view the world through the experiences of the teacher. Inherent in this approach is a high value for learning of truths and of right and wrong ways of understanding things. Of equal importance to personal growth and learning, however, is the notion that there are no right and wrong ways of understanding human phenomena, and that truths about ourselves and others with whom we have relationships are, at best, transient.

Under optimum conditions, to achieve personal growth and learning means providing learners with an environment and a goal. Within this environment, the learners determine how they will organize themselves with respect to each other and with respect to the goal they are to achieve. This sort of environment leaves the participants free to name and to invent strategies for coping with problems that evolve as a result of their natural interaction *en route* to their goal. Such an environment also forces participants to live with the consequences of their behavior. The rationale for such a design is that it permits the learner to create new knowledge and new ways of thinking; he develops a framework for solving problems, rather than being given solutions to problems already named.

Measured against this standard, the ongoing encounter group falls somewhere short of the mark. The core of the dilemma is that in practice the encounter group advocates a particular pattern of communication and human interaction intended to increase interpersonal competence. To ensure that participants learn the appropriate communication patterns and the devices for attaining them, the encounter group must necessarily become more heavily rule-laden, and thus considerably more closed in practice than its philosophy would indicate or perhaps intend.

The participant who says, as Barry did earlier, "I'm not interested in your rules for playing this game. I plan to say and do whatever *I* damn well please in here," quickly learns there are fairly sharp boundaries around his environment's "openness." He is likely to learn that his personal method of experimentation is unacceptable, both through pressure from the trainer and, if the trainer has successfully developed the proper norms in his group, from other participants.

In a very real sense then, the dynamics of the encounter group are such as to provide participants with a single and, therefore, limited way of understanding human problems (defensiveness, lack of spontaneity, low trust level, etc.) and a single and, therefore, limited way of coping with those problems (honesty, openness, trust, etc.). This way of coping interpersonally is embedded in the methodology of all encounter groups. Participants are urged to level with each other, to give their honest reactions to one another, to have enough trust in their fellow group members so that they can openly reveal themselves to them. Without these essential elements, there is no T-group. What this means, of course, is that there is, from the viewpoint of encounter-group theory, a predetermined pathway that leads to "mature, productive, and right relationships among people"—as Bradford and others suggest. It also means that if a participant had a particularly good experience, he could emerge from a T-group believing that he had learned *the right way* to approach his interpersonal relationships. Too frequently, participants have taken from a group the rubrics of openness, honesty, and trust, and run with them, only to butt into the stone wall of deceit, manipulation, and rejection. I am reminded of a friend with considerable T-group experience who cautions, "There is a very thin line between trust and folly."

This is not to say that the encounter group does not provide considerable room for experimentation. It does. My basic quarrel, if it is one at all, is that those in the forefront of T-group theory have not continued to do their homework. I simply do not think those of us involved in the movement have been intellectually honest about what we are doing, either with ourselves or with the participants for whom we have accepted responsibility. We have more or less been content to let our theory evolve loosely from the doing of T-groups. As a result, we have too often sent participants away ill-prepared to cope with what we have insisted they learn for themselves. Perhaps we haven't made enough of the point that the encounter-group experience is only that; its methodology is only one way of understanding interpersonal relationships. And in the state in which encounter-group theory currently finds itself, that way of understanding may not be the most sound one. To the extent that those of us thinking about and doing T-groups do not understand this, the encounter-group movement is indeed dead.

REFERENCES AND SUGGESTED READINGS

1. Allport, Gordon W., *Personality and Social Encounter*. Boston: Beacon Press, 1960.
2. Argyris, Chris, *Interpersonal Competence and Organizational Effectiveness*. Homewood, Ill.: Dorsey-Irwin, 1962.
3. Bennis, Warren, K. Benne, and R. Chin, *The Planning of Change*. New York: Holt, Rinehart and Winston, 1961.
4. Bennis, Warren, E. H. Schein, F. I. Steel, and D. E. Berlew, *Interpersonal Dynamics*. Homewood, Ill.: Dorsey-Irwin, 1968.
5. Bradford, L., J. Gibb, and K. Benne, eds., *T-Group Theory and Laboratory Method,* New York: Wiley, 1964.
6. Budd, Richard W., "The Encounter Group: Some Implications for the Helping Professions," in *Nursing Clinics of North America,* December, 1969.
7. Budd, Richard W., "Communication, Simulation and Education," Institute for Communication Studies, Rutgers University, 1970.
8. Carkhuff, Robert, *Helping and Human Relations I, II*. New York: Holt, Rinehart and Winston, 1969.
9. Egan, Gerard, *Encounter*. Belmont, Calif.: Brooks/Cole, 1970.
10. Goffman, Irving, *Interaction Ritual*. Garden City, N.Y.: Doubleday, Anchor Books, 1967.
11. Goffman, Irving, *Strategic Interaction*. Philadelphia: University of Pennsylvania Press, 1969.
12. Golembiewski, R., and A. Blumberg, *Sensitivity Training and the Laboratory Approach*. Itasca, Ill.: Peacock, 1970.
13. Jourard, Sidney, *Personal Adjustment,* 2nd. ed. New York: Macmillan, 1958.
14. Jourard, Sidney, *The Transparent Self*. New York: Van Nostrand Reinhold, 1964.
15. Jourard, Sidney, *Disclosing Man to Himself*. New York: Van Nostrand Reinhold, 1968.
16. Mann, Richard, with G. Gibbard and J. Hartman, *Interpersonal Styles and Group Development*. New York: Wiley, 1967.
17. Rogers, Carl, *Client-Centered Therapy*. Boston: Houghton Mifflin, 1951.
18. Rogers, Carl, *On Becoming a Person*. Boston: Houghton Mifflin, 1961.
19. Rogers, Carl, *Encounter Groups*. New York: Harper & Row, 1970.
20. Schein, E., and W. Bennis, *Personal and Organizational Change Through Group Methods*. New York: Wiley, 1967.
21. Schutz, William, *Joy*. New York: Grove Press, 1967.
22. Shands, Harley, *Thinking and Psychotherapy*. Cambridge, Mass.: Harvard University Press, 1960.

23. Slater, Phillip, *Microcosm*. New York: Wiley, 1960.
24. Tiger, Lionel, *Men in Groups*. New York: Random House, Vintage Books, 1969.
25. Wallraff, Charles, *Karl Jaspers: An Introduction to his Philosophy*. Princeton: Princeton University Press, 1970.
26. Wassell, B., *Group Analysis*. New York: Citadel Press, 1966.

6

GENERAL SEMANTICS: AN APPROACH TO HUMAN COMMUNICATION

RICHARD W. BUDD

Gᴇɴᴇʀᴀʟ semantics, as an area of study, focuses upon the relationship between the language people use and how they think and behave. The area needs to be differentiated from *semantics,* which deals primarily with words and their meanings, and from *linguistics,* which is concerned with the analysis of language structure. In addition to integrating elements of both semantics and linguistics, general semantics offers a theory of behavior upon which an operational philosophy that is essentially "hygienic" in nature is built. One of the basic tenets of general-semantics theory is that an individual's assumptions, beliefs, and attitudes are a function of the structure of his language, and that his perception and behavior will be affected more or less in direct relationship to his susceptibility to influence by that language structure. In its operational philosophy, general semantics proposes a systematic method and a set of working principles designed to provide the individual with a set of guidelines for personal adjustment. In a very direct sense then, general semantics is, in its entirety, a model of and a prescription for the process of human communication.

FOUNDATIONS OF GENERAL SEMANTICS

Alfred Korzybski, a Polish mathematician and engineer, was the formulator of the principles subsumed under the title "General Semantics." The area of study was so named by Korzybski in his monumental work *Science and Sanity,*[18] first published in 1933. But the foundations of general se-

97

mantics were laid several years earlier by Korzybski in his first major work, entitled *Manhood of Humanity,* published in 1921. It was in this volume that Korzybski offered his observation that man was a "time-binder." * Humans, he wrote, compared with other life forms, have the unique capacity to pass along accumulated knowledge from one generation to the next; each new generation builds upon that knowledge and passes it along to the succeeding one. Korzybski theorized that since man was a time-binder, the progress that he could make from generation to generation should increase exponentially. At the same time, he was distressed by what he considered a sharp difference between the rate of progress in science and technology, each of which seemed to advance at an increasingly rapid pace, and that in areas of human affairs such as politics, philosophy, and education, areas which Korzybski felt had been stifled and were, at best, chaotic in their development.

The crucial link in Korzybski's time-binding notion was language, the human invention which made possible the accumulation, storage, and eventual retrieval of knowledge. He attributed the great disparity between progress in the scientific and nonscientific domains to the differing ways in which people talked about, and thus thought about, problems in both areas. It was his contention that the language of science matched the facts of science. In other words, Korzybski felt the assumptions implicit in the language of science (its structure) to be in close accord with the structure of reality being examined by science, or, as he was fond of analogizing, the "map" (language) fairly well represented the "territory" (empirical facts). He did not find this relationship to hold true in everyday human affairs. To the contrary, Korzybski found most human endeavors beset by unquestioned traditions, routinized habits, and unchallenged beliefs about "human nature" and about causes and effects which, to him, were inconsistent with the laws of nature. Further, Korzybski was concerned that most of mankind were unaware that their lives were governed by these "false-to-fact" doctrines and truths, which he attributed to a faulty relationship between the structure of our language and the structure of reality.

Korzybski summed up the relationship between language and behavior as follows:

> A language, any language, has at its bottom certain metaphysics, which ascribe, consciously or unconsciously, some sort of structure to the world. . . .

---

* Korzybski classified life forms in terms of what they could *do,* as opposed to the classical philosophical categorization by what man *is.* Anatol Rapoport cites this shift as crucial to an operational discipline. Korzybski classified plants as "chemical-binders," because they convert solar energy into organic chemical energy (first dimension of life); animals, while possessing chemical-binding characteristics, move from place to place and are "space-binders" (second dimension of life); man the time-binder possesses chemical- and space-binding characteristics, but language and the capacity to store language permit him to bind time (third dimension of life).

Now these structural assumptions are inside our skin when we accept a language, any language. . . . We do not realize what tremendous power the structure of a language has. It is not an exaggeration to say that it enslaves us through the mechanism of semantic reactions and that the structure which a language exhibits, and impresses upon us unconsciously, is automatically projected upon the world around us. (18, pp. 89–90)

Korzybski maintained that the structure of our language affects the functioning of our nervous system, and he expressed concern that our language was too often "false-to-fact"—that the structure of our language did not adequately represent the structure of empirical reality. In fact, he was convinced that the structure of our language caused us to see and understand things by the names we gave them. This defining before seeing, or "projection," as he called it, was counter to the way the human nervous system ought to operate. As he put it:

To achieve adjustment and sanity and the conditions which follow from them, we must study structural characteristics of this world *first,* and, then only, build languages of similar structure, instead of habitually ascribing to the world the primitive structure of our language. (18, p. 59)

Drawing from his background in mathematics (which Korzybski believed to be the only language with a structure similar to that of the human nervous system) and engineering, and heavily influenced by Einsteinian physics, biology, neurology, psychology, and psychiatry, Korzybski formulated a "corrective theory" and method for developing adequate "language-to-fact" relationships, which he first called human engineering and, later, general semantics.

BASIC PREMISES OF GENERAL SEMANTICS

The whole structure of general semantics has been built upon a single basic assumption: that reality is to be conceived of as a *process.* This basic notion of modern science postulated that the universe is in a constant state of motion, its elements in a perpetual state of change and changing relationships. More than two thousand years ago, Heraclitus stated the concept quite simply: One may not step in the same river twice. Wendell Johnson,* one of Korzybski's major interpreters, further observes:

. . . One may not step in the same river twice, not only because the river flows and changes, but also because the one who steps into it changes too, and is never at any two moments identical. (16, p. 23)

---

* Wendell Johnson was my teacher, colleague, and friend from 1960 until his death in 1965. Much of my understanding of general semantics came from working and teaching with him. Throughout this chapter, I have tried to indicate the material in the text that represents his own thinking and writing. Considerably more than has been footnoted undoubtedly should have been, since I borrowed liberally from his mind during those years.

> For once we grasp clearly what has been "known" for centuries and what is, in fact, the central theme of modern science, that no two things are identical and no one thing is ever twice the same, that everywhere is change, flux, process, we understand that we must live in a world of differences. (16, p. 25)

As was noted earlier, the notion of a process reality, with its consequences of change and differences, occupies a central role in general-semantics theory. At the time these notions were introduced by Korzybski, they represented a major break with tradition. Korzybski underscored this break with the past by referring to his new system as "non-Aristotelian."

Korzybski based his non-Aristotelian system on three basic principles: (1) the principle of *nonidentity* (A is not A); (2) the principle of *nonallness* (A is not all A); and (3) the principle of *self-reflexiveness*. Korzybski's premises were called non-Aristotelian because they were markedly different from the basic assumptions of Aristotle (which Korzybski felt had been internalized by Western society and were largely responsible for false-to-fact evaluations): (1) the law of identity (A is A, or whatever a thing is, it is); (2) the law of noncontradiction (everything is A or not-A); and (3) the law of the excluded middle (nothing is both A and not-A).

The first of these three non-Aristotelian principles, the principle of non-identity, says, to use Korzybski's analogy, "the map is not the territory," the word is not the object it stands for. As Johnson interprets Korzybski:

> . . . the name given to a fact, or any statement made about the fact, is not identical with that fact.
> Since "the word is not the object" is so utterly indisputable, we tend very strongly to develop an illusion of complete understanding. Moreover, we find it most difficult to believe anyone has ever doubted it or has ever believed that the word is not the object.
> The identification of which we speak is that seen, for the most part, in those instances in which people *act as if* the word were the object. (16, p. 172)

As an example of identity, Johnson points out that for many years one did not use the word *syphilis* in conversation. Despite the fact that medical science had developed a means of controlling, and perhaps even eliminating the disease, little was accomplished in bringing syphilis under control because the "taboos" of society operated to prevent discussion, much less public information campaigns.

> People acted toward the word *syphilis* very much as they did toward what it presumably represented. They sought to avoid not only syphilis, but the word *syphilis*. Their behavior was remindful of the primitive word magic, in accordance with which it is naively assumed that by controlling the word, one controls the thing it stands for. (16, p. 172)

The second of Korzybski's premises, the principle of nonallness, supplements and, to a large extent, subsumes the first. It states that the map does not represent all the territory. Anatol Rapoport writes:

> . . . no matter how good a map you make, you cannot represent all of the territory in it. Translated into terms of language, it means that no matter how much you say about some "thing," "'event," "quality," or whatnot, you cannot say *all* about it. (23, pp. 19–20)

The second non-Aristotelian premise suggests that in terms of ordinary human behavior, we become aware, we perceive, through a process of abstracting, which in turn is a process of leaving out details. Our best description of any object or event, for example, at least in everyday life, simply does not include a detailed account of the object's atomical structure, "the mad dance of whirling electrons," or its relationship to other objects in the universe. Since the process of abstracting is central to an understanding of general semantics, the notion will be presented in some detail later in this chapter.

The third premise states, in essence, that we employ language for talking about language, we make statements about statements, we make evaluations about evaluations. Johnson points out that the infinite regress is a case of self-reflexiveness gone wild. "How miserable I am when I think about how miserable I am"; "How worried I am when I think about how worried I am." At the same time, the self-reflexive nature of language, as we shall see later, makes possible the making of abstracts of abstracts, which is at the heart of the development of scientific theory.

THE PROCESS OF ABSTRACTING

The literature of general semantics is shot through with the notion that our everyday language, unlike the language of science, is often false to fact. Much of the criticism leveled at general semantics centers on this very notion. Do general semanticists have a corner on knowing what is fact and what is not? It is perhaps unfortunate that the false-to-fact notion has been expressed the way it has by so many general semanticists, for at first blush it does seem to imply that there is a knowable reality and that what general semantics is all about is fitting our language structure to the structure of reality. Perhaps some of the confusion can be sorted out by understanding how general-semantics theory views fact.

Among the main generators of credibility in modern society are statements something to this effect: "Look at the facts," or "The facts show." Behind such statements lies the assumption (and perhaps a hope of the susceptibility that we will believe) that facts are facts, and, at the least, everyone knows a fact when he meets one.

What we call facts, writes Johnson,[16, p. 93] change "so that yesterday's statistics become today's fairy tales." Every fact appears different, depending upon whether you are labor or management, tenant or landlord, the manipulated or manipulator. Facts, says Johnson, are a matter of social agreement. In summary, writes Johnson,[16, p. 94] any given fact is (1) necessarily incomplete (since it is impossible to know *all* the fact about anything), (2) changeable, (3) a personal affair, and (4) useful to the degree to which others agree with you about it.

Einstein, who had a strong influence on Korzybski's formulations, offers an observation quite consistent with Johnson's:

> The belief in an external world independent of the perceiving subject is the basis of all natural science. Since, however, sense perception only gives information of this external world or of "physical reality" indirectly, we can only grasp the latter by speculative means. It follows from this that our notions of physical reality can never be final. We must always be ready to change these notions. . . . [7, p. 156]

As noted earlier, however, many writers in general semantics, in their efforts to simplify Korzybski's basic notions, do not present a clear picture of the relativity of fact or reality. We have belabored the issue here because it seems crucial to an understanding of the process of abstracting as a viable model of human communication.

The notion of abstracting, as it relates peculiarly to general semantics, was first modeled by Korzybski in *Science and Sanity,* where he called it the "structural differential." Adaptations of this model appear in virtually every major book written about general semantics, among them the "process of abstracting," [16] "the abstracting process," [29] the "abstraction ladder," [13] to name a few. The alterations in drawings or titles have clarified Korzybski's original presentation of the notion but have not impacted the basic concept.

Growing out of Korzybski's three basic, non-Aristotelian principles, the notion of abstracting states simply that there are limitations upon our ability to "see" the world around us, and that our language restricts us even further when we attempt to communicate our observations to others. Following Korzybski's original formulation, most writers have presented the notion in terms of levels of abstraction, with a clear-cut division between the nonverbal and verbal levels. For reasons mentioned earlier, I feel more comfortable using Johnson's adaptation of Korzybski's structural differential than any of the others.

The Nonverbal, Unspeakable World of Not-words

"We live in two worlds, which must not be confused, a world of words, and a world of not-words," wrote Irving Lee.[19, p. 16] His statement simply reiterates one of general semantics' basic themes: The phenomenon of language is different from the nonverbal phenomena we represent by it. The part of the abstracting process with which we deal in this section concerns those "preverbal" levels of our observations and experiences.

As I have pointed out, there are limitations upon what we are able to see, feel, hear, smell, and taste. The facts we are able to observe at the *macroscopic,* neural level are, we know, incomplete—an abstract of a more detailed reality. In order to see beyond the limits of that which we can experience directly, we must use some extension of our neural system (e.g., microscope, telescope, magnifying glass, electronic-sensing equipment) to extend the range of our senses (referred to as the microscopic level). In Figure 6.1, the relationship between these two levels, in terms of abstracting, is shown by the differing number of dots within the two circles. We are able to observe considerably more at the microscopic level, with the aid of instruments, than at the macroscopic level of direct sensing. Our "first-order facts" at the macroscopic level are, then, abstracts of what we are able to observe at the microscopic level. But even at the microscopic level there are limitations (the closed circle on both levels indicates a finite set of possible observations). With the invention of each new and more powerful telescope, for example, scientists find things they were unable to see before.

Beyond the microscopic level lies the *submicroscopic* level. Korzybski called it the "event level." Johnson, in his classes in general semantics, called it the "beable" level—that which *might exist* in a process reality to explain what we are able to observe only partially at the upper two levels. His label "beable" clearly places the submicroscopic world in the inferential class. Johnson uses a quote from Einstein and Infeld's *The Evolution of Physics* [9] in a slightly different context than the one used here, but it aptly addresses itself to the philosophical and epistemological questions embedded in any discussion of reality, be it of the process or any other variety.

> In our endeavor to understand reality we are somewhat like the man trying to understand the mechanism of a closed watch. He sees the face and the moving hands, even hears the ticking, but he has no way of opening the case. If he is ingenious he may form some picture of a mechanism which could be responsible for all the things he observes, but he may never be quite sure his picture is the only one which could explain his observations. He will never be able to compare his picture with the real mechanism and he cannot even imagine the possibility or the meaning of such comparison. But he certainly believes that, as his knowledge increases, his picture of reality will become simpler and simpler and will explain a wider and wider range of his sensuous impressions.

This section of this chapter is under the heading "nonverbal, unspeakable world" simply because such direct experiences as are covered here cannot be transformed into words. You can tell someone *about* your toothache, but all the words in the dictionary will not make him *experience* the toothache. Verbal communications simply describe experiences, they are not the experience being described. Korzybski said, "Whatever you say a thing is, it is not." More likely, when someone describes his toothache to us, what we feel, or perhaps more accurately what we recall, is a toothache we once had.

The World of Words

The core of general-semantics theory and the study of language and behavior lie at the conceptual interface of language and reality—of the "world of words" and the "world of not-words." The greater share of what we know about the world around us—the basis for our beliefs and disbeliefs, for the way we act, comes to us through words. Further, general semantics points out, the greater portion of what others tell us (and we tell others) is not words about facts, but is, rather, words about words. Reports of our direct experience (sensing) account for very little of the intercommunication among most of us. Herein lies the *raison d'être* of general semantics. Commenting on these observations, Johnson writes:

> Nevertheless, firsthand reports of direct experience must form the basis of our entire language structure, unless we are to live in a gravely disordered relationship to the world of non-verbal reality. (16, p. 113)

Most general semanticists do not appear to mean by this, as criticism frequently seems to indicate, that what we say must always have as a referent some immediate experience or object or person that can be offered as tangible evidence to back up our words. What does seem important is that our statements, through a series of interconnected relationships, eventually be tied to "facts" derived from the levels of observation referred to in the preceding section on nonverbal levels. For as Johnson points out:

> Language is never so boring, however, or so ineffectual, as when it is kept on the level of sheer enumeration of first-order facts. In order to say anything significant, one simply has to rise above that level, and the higher above it one can rise, the more significant one's remarks become—provided the steps taken in rising, so to speak, are taken in orderly fashion and can be traced back to the level of factual data. (16, p. 114)

A good example of what is being discussed here is the *atom*. Atoms are not tangible things. There is no direct referent for an atom. An atom is one of those ingenious constructs of which Einstein spoke, a "picture of a mechanism" which *could* be responsible for the things which man has been able to observe. Clearly, however, scientists have been able to trace the concept back to the level of factual data.

Now, general-semantics theory argues that this crucial relationship between language and reality is a *structural* relationship. The heart of Korzybski's thesis is that if we are to achieve personal adjustment and productive social organization, *the structure of a language must correspond to the structure of reality.*[18, p. 58] Korzybski, and those who have written about general semantics since, believe there is ample evidence to the contrary—that the structure of our everyday language does not correspond very well to the structure of reality. The evidence presented in the literature of general semantics is drawn from comparisons of the structure of language with the structure of reality, employing as a criterion for that analysis the basic assumption presented earlier: Reality is to be conceived of as a process. The notion of a process reality implies two basic characteristics of structure: (1) change and (2) differences. The second is the child of the first.

Structural Comparison and Change

As was noted earlier, no two things are alike, and no one thing is ever twice the same. A fact, says Johnson, occurs only once. This, of course, is not true of words in our language. We use the same words over and over again, although we certainly do not always intend for them to mean the same thing each time we use them. And there is the rub. If the structure of language were to match the structure of reality (as reality is here defined), each word, like each fact, would occur only once. As Johnson puts it:

> Reality is process-like; language by comparison is static. The world in which we live and we who live in it change faster than does the language we use to speak about the world and ourselves. So it is words become generalized because the conveyer belt of time brings under their spell a changing inventory of "meanings." [16, p. 117]

This is not to deny that language changes. One need only stay up and watch an old late movie, or curl up for an evening with one of Shakespeare's plays, to understand that it does. But crucial to the point made here is that, at a rather fundamental level, our language is slow to change.

Perhaps the major problem, in a sense, has less to do with the words that are spoken than with those of us who use the words. Because the words we hear others say now seem to be the same as words we have heard before, *we* make the assumption that what we understand is basically the same as that which we have always understood. "There is nothing new under the sun." "What you are saying is basically the same as what I heard So-and-So say." "I would never have believed he could do such a thing. He was always such a nice boy." It is in this same response pattern that we feel comforted when we deal with a company that has been in business "since 1845," while perhaps the only thing about the company that is 180 years old may be the artifacts hanging on the walls. General semanticists believe that an unawareness of the disparity between the relatively slow pace of change in language and the higher rate of change in technology and social life can lead to personal maladjustment and, ultimately, to a state of persistent disillusionment.

> There are maladjusted individuals—and societies—who live as though they looked upon the present as a temporary deviation from the past. Their norm being of yesterday, they treat the here and now as though it were a condition of abnormality.
> The essential forms of our language were devised by ancient men who were remarkably unfamiliar with present-day knowledge. Because they had not been driven to assume the superdynamics of the submicroscopic realm which we accept, the world in its visible aspects seemed far more static to them than it does to us. In devising our language, they created a world of words that implied a relatively static world of not-words. (16, p. 120)

Structural Comparison and Differences

As noted above, change necessarily gives birth to differences. In the preceding section, the major point was that there is a fundamental difference between the structure of language and the structure of reality, because of the static nature of language relative to a process reality. Here we compare most specifically the infinite differentiation inferred to exist in a process reality with the ability of our language to reflect such differentiation. In short, what are some of the problems brought on by having at our disposal a finite language for speaking about an infinite reality or, at the least, for having an infinite number of ways to conceive of that reality?

To begin with, one word may mean many different things, and several different words can often mean the same thing. This particular problem can take two quite different forms. First, it can be confounded by the "Dictionary Dans" of the world, who insist on the "one word, one meaning" approach. Hayakawa writes:

> Everyone, of course, who has ever given any thought to the meanings of words has noticed that they are always shifting and changing in meaning. Usually, people regard this as a misfortune, because it "leads to sloppy thinking" and "mental confusion." To remedy this condition, they are likely to suggest that we should all agree on "one meaning" for each word and use it only with that meaning. (13, p. 60)

While we can all read that quote with some amusement, we cannot read it without reflecting upon the number of quarters we have won—or lost—betting with a friend on what "a word really means," and having resolved that bet by going to the dictionary. This particular problem would perhaps be easier to deal with if we were at least consistent in our responses to words. We are, however, more likely to vigorously defend those words we have internalized with all sorts of intense feelings (e.g., *Communist, Negro, right, wrong*), and show considerable flexibility toward others about which we don't care.

The other form this problem takes (although it may be of the same genre) is that one word is often used to refer to a variety of behaviors or activities or assumed attributes. The basic problem here is that the users of such words are unaware that the words could have any other meanings except the ones they carry around in their own heads. The list of such words is inexhaustible: *beauty, democracy, love, freedom, intelligence, male chauvinism,* and so on. Incredibly enough, such words have consumed an embarrassing number of pages in leading scholarly journals, not to mention the time taken up at PTA, congressional, professional, or neighborhood meetings that would better be spent on crucial human problems.

General-semantics theory attributes these and similar problems to the structural differences between language and reality. Most writers in the field pinpoint the problem as stemming from Aristotle's third law that nothing is both A and not-A. Our language basically tends to be *two-valued,* to take an "either-or" form reflecting two categories: win-lose; for-against; right-wrong; real-fantasy; liberal-conservative; Republican-Democrat; labor-management; love-hate; intelligent-stupid; success-failure. At best, we add a third, "middle-of-the-road" category, which we generally think of as being "unprincipled" or "wishy-washy." The nub of the problem, again, is traced to our attempts to categorize an infinite-valued reality in terms of a two-valued (or three-valued) language structure.

This pattern repeats itself on a slightly higher level of analysis in the disparity between the structures of reality and language, or what Korzybski calls a problem of "ordering," and Johnson refers to as the "organization" of language. The grammar used to classify words in our language, in any language, is also used to organize and classify reality; rules essentially invented for organizing words into classes and syntactical relationships are not necessarily the best rules for organizing reality.

In our grammar, nouns name things (persons or places), adjectives impute qualities, verbs establish relationships between things and the qualities. One of the consequences of this organization is discussed by Ruben:

> In classificational thinking, things (nouns) do things (verbs) to other things (nouns), in a unidirectional, unidimensional fashion. The paradigm is: "This (one) thing caused that (one) thing." Our thinking, our literature, and our vocabularies are replete with examples. It is common, for example, to say, "You made me mad," "Smoking causes cancer," or "You don't understand what I am telling you." In each instance a single factor causes some *thing* to happen. [25, p. 7]

The structure of the language used in Ruben's examples guides us toward (insists upon) the classical cause-and-effect model. Embedded in this kind of language structure is the assumption that things (persons or places) themselves possess the qualities, and that such qualities are, in a manner of speaking, "observer-free." What is more, such "truths" appear to be self-evident from the use of the verb "is," traceable to Aristotle's law of identity (A is A; whatever a thing is, it is). The simple statement, "Marcia is immoral," is often regarded as a fact of nature, rather than being seen as a creation of the speaker; the *is* in the sentence would seem to make it so. *Is* implies that the immorality resides in Marcia. Perhaps she is even "possessed" by it. That the "immorality" could—depending upon the observer—range anywhere from chewing gum or smoking on the street to giving birth to an illegitimate child, seems irrelevant once the is and the label are affixed. The statement about Marcia ignores a very basic point. The "immorality" being talked about does not belong to her alone, but, as R. D. Carmichael [4] has pointed out, is a joint product of the observed and the observer. The evaluation of Marcia tells us as much about the speaker as it does about Marcia, if not more. To paraphrase Wendell Johnson, there is no immorality in nature; immorality is a human invention and is a matter of evaluation. Immorality may only be the difference between what you demand of others and how others behave for themselves.

A number of writers of general-semantics books have taken a great deal of space to punish, as it were, the word *is*. But again, perhaps we should be less concerned with the word as such, and more concerned about its users. The first paragraph of this chapter pointed out that general semantics was basically concerned with one's susceptibility to influence by the language structure. The implication of this particular section is not so much that the structure of the language be altered—although this seems to be one of the less-thought-out goals of general semantics—but that in using language, one develop an awareness of its structural implications for enabling (or disabling) oneself to see the world around one.

The Verbal Levels of Abstracting

In an earlier section we diagramed the nonverbal levels of the process of abstracting. In the past several pages, the discussion has focused upon comparisons between the structure of reality and the structure of language. The nature of this relationship might be better understood by completing the diagram of the process of abstracting.

Figure 6.1 developed three levels of abstracting—macroscopic, microscopic, and submicroscopic—all preverbal. Figure 6.2 adds a fourth level of abstraction, which Johnson called the first-order verbal level of

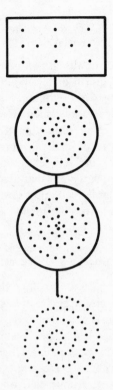

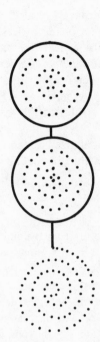

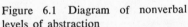

Figure 6.1 Diagram of nonverbal levels of abstraction

Figure 6.2 Diagram of nonverbal levels and first-order verbal level of abstraction

abstraction,[16, p. 127] or, more simply, the level of "labeling" or "description." On this level, our preverbal observations, feelings, and experiences are named or labeled and described. The experience being described *is not* the experience itself. As we move from the nonverbal to the verbal level, we leave out detail, as shown in the diagram by the smaller number of dots in the rectangle. We simply cannot say *all* there is to say about what we have seen or felt, because our observation, made at either the macroscopic or the microscopic level, according to the theory developed earlier, is only an abstract of reality. Descriptions at this level are specific and exhaustive, involving definitions of definitions. Relationships between facts do not occur on this level; relationships between events are "higher-order" abstractions. Writes Johnson:

> It is to be understood, then, that there are certain words which according to their accepted usages, may not be used on the first-order verbal level of abstraction. They do not serve to name or label particular observable

facts. They represent relationships among facts, or they refer to constructs of inferential data. [16, p. 130]

Since the discussion is leading toward the higher levels of abstraction, it will be useful at this point to complete the diagram of the process of abstracting. In Figure 6.3, three more verbal levels, called "inference levels," have been added. Each higher level shows fewer dots than each preceding level, indicating the further omission of detail and the attendant increasing of generalization. At the top of the diagram is an *ETC.* representing the self-reflexive nature of the process of abstracting: every abstraction can be further abstracted.

A simple example drawn from Hayakawa's popularized version of general semantics [14] might help clarify the notion of the abstracting process.

> Bessie is a living organism, constantly changing, constantly ingesting food and air, transforming it, getting rid of it again. Her blood is circulating, her nerves are sending messages. [14, p. 166]

Using Figure 6.3, follow the levels of Bessie the cow from the bottom up. To the physicist, Bessie is the "mad dance of electrons" mentioned earlier. She is a dynamic, ongoing process (submicroscopic level). At the microscopic level, she is a mass of tissue, cells, corpuscles, and the like. Many of the details of the process-cow are left out. At the macroscopic level, where we see and sense the cow, she is shape and movement, color and texture, noise and odor, although, again, much detail from the previous level is left out.

At the descriptive level, the word "Bessie" is the label we give to that which we observe. She is a specific cow, the cow of our experience. But since the word is not the experience itself (they are, in a sense, two different phenomenon), we have, in effect, supplanted the experience, "leaving behind," in a manner of speaking, a great wealth of experiential detail. At the next level, we might talk about "cows," since Bessie has a great deal in common with other animals of similar description (some people might go so far as to say cows are cows; when you've seen one, you've seen them all). Specific characteristics of Bessie, our cow, are left out; we begin to lump together common characteristics—to generalize. At inference$_2$ level we might talk of Bessie as "livestock," and only those characteristics she has in common with other farm animals are included. And so it goes, from livestock to "farm assets" to "assets" to "wealth" to "economic indicators," etc.

We come now to the one remaining aspect of the diagram—perhaps its most crucial aspect—the line and arrow running from the highest inference level to the submicroscopic level. It is important to recall at this juncture that the submicroscopic level, according to Korzybski and others, is the event level, the level of the posited process reality. Figure 6.3

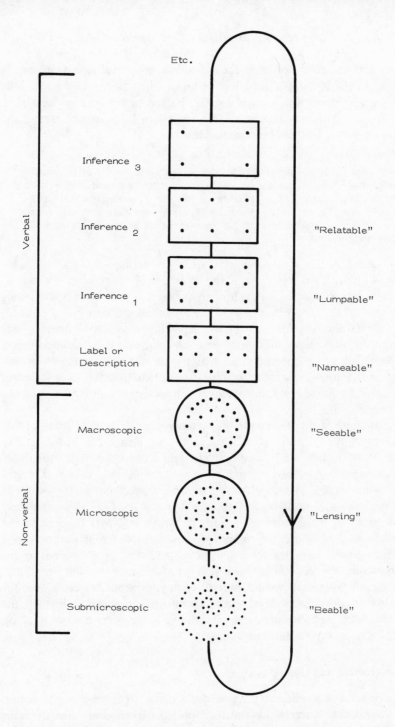

Figure 6.3   Diagram of the process of abstracting
From Wendell Johnson, *People in Quandaries* (New York: Harper, 1946), p. 135.

makes it abundantly clear that the submicroscopic level is, essentially, an extremely *high* level of abstraction. It means that the process reality, the basic premise upon which general-semantics theory is built, is a construct, an inference of the highest order: an assumption. Johnson underscores the circularity of the process of abstracting thusly:

> The statement which each man gives to his highest-order inferences—the way, that is, in which he describes the unobservable aspects of reality, the inferential data—determines his manner of investigating what is observable on the microscopic and macroscopic levels. The particular observations he makes and the particular observations he fails to make are determined mainly by the assumptions on the basis of which he undertakes to make observations. (16, p. 136)

Embedded in this statement of Johnson's is perhaps the real value for coming to more than a superficial understanding of the process of abstracting. He says, in effect, that each of us proceeds on a set of assumptions about reality, and, regardless of how carefully these assumptions are stated, they will be different for each of us, depending upon our purposes, our perspectives, our capabilities, and our competencies. Of equal importance, and perhaps a key anchor point for better understanding human communication, is the notion that what we observe and what we fail to observe are determined by the assumptions under which we operate in making our observations.

Perhaps one of the less subtle understandings to be gained from all this is that whenever we make some observation, we abstract from the totality of the event "to be seen." In so doing, if one accepts the basic premise of abstracting, we must also then leave some things out. It was Kenneth Burke who wrote: "A way of seeing is also a way of not seeing—a focus upon object A involves a neglect of object B." (3, p. 70) The key communicational question, then, has been raised. If Mr. A and Mr. B come to the same event with different assumptions, based on different purposes and different competencies (as we know they will), what promise does an intercommunication encounter hold for them, as their variant "realities" (which each has developed for himself communicationally) come face-to-face? At an operational level, general semantics provides a method for analyzing such problems and, in a prescriptive sense, gives a set of working principles to cope with those problems.

On Abstracting and Coping

For general semanticists, there is decidedly a right way and a wrong way to abstract. Korzybski claimed, as noted earlier, that most of us in our everyday lives do it wrong. Science, on the other hand, does it right, as demonstrated by its comparatively rapid progress. We have already noted that the abstracting process is circular. What is thought to occur on the submicroscopic level (the "beable" level) is inferred from what we can see or experience. That is to say, the atoms and electrons which scientists talk about are objects which have never been seen or touched. From what scientists have been able to observe on the microscopic and macroscopic levels, they have inferred that which they think must exist on the submicroscopic level (the process moves correctly in the direction indicated by the arrow in Figure 6.3). An atom is nothing more than a verbal construct. This is not to say that atoms are fanciful inventions belonging to the same category as good fairies and evil spirits; the survivors of Hiroshima and Nagasaki can tell us differently. The difference is that the verbal construct of an atom, used to explain the behavior of matter on the submicroscopic level, has proved to have a high degree of *predictability*. Until this construct proves to be too imprecise for use in science, and until further observations indicate that the concept of atoms and electrons is more complex than previously imagined and thus requires revision, its acceptance is productive. Fairies and spirits, on the other hand, have little predictability, but are easily blamed for events after the fact.

Our inferences, then, are only as good as our observations, our observations as good as our reality, and our reality as good as our inferences. Proper abstracting, according to general-semantics notions, requires moving up and down the "abstraction ladder": observations first, followed by careful description, followed by inferences. The well-adjusted person, however, understands that his inferences are only assumptions and he will move "back down" to the nonverbal levels to test his inferences through continued observation. Korzybski and his followers describe this "adjusted" behavior pattern as an *extensional* orientation—a predisposition to inspect the territory first and then to build the conceptual maps to correspond with it. A not-so-well-adjusted person—and Korzybski believes that includes most of us to some degree or other—does not tend to see first and then define, but to define first and then see. (Walter Lippmann discusses this and related notions in *Public Opinion*. The statement above is simply a paraphrase of Lippmann's observation.) Korzybski refers to this behavior pattern as an *intensional* orientation. To be intensional in orientation is to become more involved in the map, and the expense of the territory—perhaps, in extreme conditions, to assume that the map (the feelings, thoughts, deep-seated beliefs) *is* the territory.

What general semantics as a method strives toward is, at the least, an *awareness of the process of abstracting* and, at best, an understanding that our realities are temporary, communicationally created assumptions subject to continuous revision. Being aware simply means that the individual is more likely to do the revising himself, rather than have the rug of change snatched without warning from beneath his feet. This notion is made somewhat more clear in Figure 6.4, in the "short-circuited" abstracting process. [16, p. 138] The diagram is intended to represent the individual who fails to recognize that a high-level abstraction such as "Marcia is immoral" is an assumption, but rather assumes it to be a statement of fact. Any observations at the macroscopic or microscopic level are treated as irrelevant. Any abstracting done bypasses the nonverbal levels of abstracting.

> This is the mechanism of the "closed mind," of the old dog that cannot learn new tricks. It is represented in the behavior of the Indian who dances in a particular way in order to make the corn grow well, regardless of the corn crops that have followed his dancing in the past. To him the god who will refuse to make the corn grow if he does not dance is not an assumption to be tested but a fact to be respected. Since, to him, it is not an assumption, the way the corn grows has no bearing on its truth or falsity. [16, p. 140]

While it is always easier to talk about Indians or aboriginal tribes in some distant country, the pattern is readily discernible closer to home. Someone once said "structure is the residue of function." Endless numbers of human organizations continue to follow rules, procedures, and traditions that no longer facilitate their functions. (Schools divided by grades, grades divided by subject matter, universities divided into departments, the President officially elected by the electoral college, are some obvious examples.) On the individual level, we still go through all sorts of interaction rituals which deny us our honesty and our individuality, paying the price in frustration and ulcerated stomachs. But this, some semanticists feel, is the small of it. Wendell Johnson, for example, devotes six chapters of *People in Quandaries* [16] specifically to the more serious problems of schizophrenia, paranoia, hysteria, and other disorders which, general semanticists contend, grow out of and are defined through language. Thus it is that general semantics was earlier labeled a "hygienic" philosophy.

The Working Devices

The working devices of general semantics, organized for the most part by Korzybski in *Science and Sanity,* are more preventative than curative. They are, as we shall see, only reminders—aids to coping. Using the devices is one thing; understanding why one is using them is quite another. Korzybski lists five such extensional devices:

> (1) *Indexes.* The index is designed to expand the language and focus on differences. The function of indexing in language is not unlike the use of serial numbers on automobiles or numbers on the shirts of our football players. While they are all cars or all football players, it becomes useful to be able to tell them apart. So with language, the device love$_1$, love$_2$; or

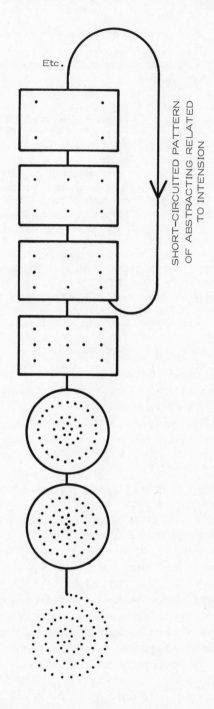

Etc.

SHORT-CIRCUITED PATTERN
OF ABSTRACTING RELATED
TO INTENSION

Figure 6.4   Diagram of "short-circuited" process of abstracting
From Wendell Johnson, *People in Quandaries* (New York: Harper, 1946), p. 139.

peace$_1$, peace$_2$ might well alert us against making unwarranted, perhaps disastrous, generalizations.

(2) *Dates*. Dates are a specialized form of the index; they index time. I$_{1972}$ am not I$_{1954}$ (and remembering that may help prevent me making a fool of myself at some time). And although the "since 1845" business establishment would like us to believe so, The Emporium$_{1972}$ is not The Emporium$_{1845}$.

(3) *Etc.* The good grammarian refuses to accept etc. as a "word." Its use grows from Korzybski's principle of non-allness. Stated simply, it means, "I haven't said all that could be said about X." It can be used effectively in conjunction with item 1 above: beauty$_1$, beauty$_2$, etc.

(4) *Quotation Marks.* Terms are placed in quotes, writes Johnson, to remind both the speaker and the listener that they are to be evaluated with regard to their false-to-fact implications. [16, p. 214] The quote marks permit us to use the language without implying the absoluteness of certain terms. For example, quote marks have been used extensively in this chapter, frequently with the word "reality."

(5) *Hyphen.* The hyphen is used in much the same way as quote marks, to remind us of the systemic nature of "process reality." As Korzybski pointed out, our language permits us to separate things verbally which cannot in reality by separated. Einstein, for example, refers to "space-time," which he considered to be inseparable notions.

There are a number of other devices offered by other writers in general semantics which will not be dealt with here. But, whether or not they would qualify as working devices (or extensional devices, as Korzybski called them), two questions which often cut effectively through "semantic flack" were frequently employed by Johnson: What do you mean? and How do you know?

GENERAL SEMANTICS FROM ANOTHER VIEW

It would be a gross oversight not to spend at least a few pages taking a more global view of general semantics, both as a scholarly pursuit and as a pragmatic social force. If there is one thing general-semantics theory and principles has not been, from *Science and Sanity* on, it is noncontroversial. As an area of study, it has spanned the range of potential responses, from basking in the adulation of those who believe it a panacea for all the ills of all mankind to wincing under the intellectual whips of those who find it a hollow, murky haven for naïve charlatan-scholars.

In a not uncommon pattern, many of the admirers of general semantics have also been the authors of basic general-semantics books, not the least of whom is Korzybski himself. Both *Manhood of Humanity* and *Science and Sanity* are couched in rather imperative tones from which one draws a real sense of urgency. In an effort to interpret and spread Korzybski's notions, a number of his commentators reflect this urgent tone (the last chapter of Johnson's book,[16] for example, is entitled "The Urgency of

Paradise"), bringing on a frequent criticism that general semantics seems more of a religion than a rational approach to the study of language and behavior. Thayer writes in the introduction to his recent reader in general semantics:

> My major criticisms of the present state of general semantics—that it is for many of its central spokesmen more of a religion than an intellectual discipline; that its disciples often exhibit a kind of "intellectual imperialism"; that it is static, closed, and proprietary; that it is myopic and naive—have not changed essentially with the additional contact I have had with it, through its proponents and dissidents, during the development and editing of this book. (28, p. viii)

While this remains, as Thayer notes, a major criticism of general semantics, it hardly seems appropriate to dismiss the entire area of study because of the overzealousness of a few writers who have found it necessary to publish accounts of their personal salvation through general semantics. The misfortune for general semantics is that scholars who have studied it enough to find it lacking, have done very little about it. Criticism of general semantics, like that of a great many other disciplines, tends to be reactive in the sense that it focuses upon what is wrong with the discipline; the critics rarely assume a proactive stance by taking the further step toward reconceptualization of the field.

The subissues raised in Thayer's critique seem to provide a far more central and solid base for mounting criticism of general semantics. General semantics has not progressed markedly or been substantially revised since *Science and Sanity* was first published. For the most part, general semantics$_{1933}$ *is* general semantics$_{1972}$. The irony is that Korzybski himself hoped and publicly called for such revision. At a deeper level of analysis, it can easily be construed as a gross violation of the principles Korzybski himself advocated that the dozen or so major books published since 1933 are highly redundant. It is, for example, difficult to believe that Korzybski said *all* there is to be said about language and behavior, or that forty years have not brought about changes that his conceptualization did not take into account.

It might be useful for the student of general semantics to, at some point, find out how well general semantics might withstand examination by its own principles. The outline for such a test was provided by Korzybski:

> Because of the cumulative and non-elementalistic character of human knowledge, a mere challenge to a "principle" does not carry us far. For expediency, assumptions underlying a system have (1) to be discovered, (2) [to be] tested, (3) [to be] eventually challenged, (4) [to be] eventually rejected, and (5) [finally] a *system,* free from the eventually objectionable postulates, has to be built. (1S, p. lxiii)

Once again we may be jockeying ourselves into the position of blaming general semantics rather than some of those who write and talk about the principles subsumed under that name. In view of that, it seems only fair to point out J. Samuel Bois's definition of general semantics, which has stimulated my final observation. Wrote Bois, "A definition of general semantics can be given in two words: *up-to-date epistemology.*" [1, p. 12] Perhaps one of the most serious deficiencies of most basic general-semantics textbooks is that they are markedly lacking in considerations of epistemology, much less up-to-date ones. One of Thayer's observations was that general semantics is essentially a closed area of study. Those pursuing the discipline might find considerable value in expanding their conceptualization of general semantics to include more of the theories of epistemology, the sociology of knowledge, general systems theory, symbolic interactionism, and a variety of other related areas which have, for the most part, been ignored in classical studies of semantics. (Anatol Rapoport serves as one of the better examples of a scholar who has used much of what general semantics has to offer as a point of departure in his work.)

From another view this and other similar criticisms of general semantics might reasonably be called "shooting fish in a barrel." General semantics may not be a discipline at all; it may simply be an elaborate methodology. If this is true, it would help explain why it appears static and closed; for with a methodology, there is really only one step beyond the mastery of its principles—that is, behaving as if one understood them. From this perspective, perhaps general semantics can only have its intended social impact on an each-one (general semanticist), teach-one (nonsemanticist) basis.

If, indeed, general semantics is a methodology (and this issue should be explored), it should be suggested that general semantics could (or has) become not non-Aristotelian, as Korzybski proclaimed, but rather, neo-Aristotelian.

REFERENCES AND SUGGESTED READINGS

1. Bois, J. Samuel, *The Art of Awareness*. Dubuque, Iowa: Brown, 1966.
2. Boulding, Kenneth, *The Image*. Ann Arbor: University of Michigan Press, 1950.
3. Burke, Kenneth, *Permanence and Change*. New York: The New Republic, 1935.
4. Carmichael, R. D., *The Logic of Discovery*. Chicago: Open Court, 1930.
5. Chase, Stuart, *The Tyranny of Words*. New York: Harcourt, Brace, 1938.
6. Chisholm, Francis P., *Introductory Lectures on General Semantics*. Chicago: Institute of General Semantics, 1944.
7. Einstein, Albert, *The World As I See It*. London: Lane, 1935.
8. Einstein, Albert, "Physics and Reality," *The Journal of the Franklin Institute*, Vol. 221, 1936.

9. Einstein, Albert, and L. Infeld, *The Evolution of Physics*. New York: Simon & Schuster, 1938.
10. Einstein, Albert, *Ideas and Opinions*. New York: Crown, 1954.
11. Hall, William T., *The Silent Language*. New York: Doubleday, 1959.
12. Haney, William V., *Patterns of Communication*. Homewood, Ill.: Irwin, 1960.
13. Hayakawa, S. I., *Language in Thought and Action*. New York: Harcourt, Brace, 1939.
14. Hayakawa, S. I., ed., *Language, Meaning and Maturity*. New York: Harper & Row, 1954.
15. Hayakawa, S. I., ed., *The Use and Misuse of Language*. New York: Fawcett, Premier Books, 1962. (Paper edition of 14.)
16. Johnson, Wendell, *People in Quandaries*. New York: Harper, 1946.
17. Korzybski, Alfred, *Manhood of Humanity: The Art and Science of Human Engineering*. New York: Dutton, 1921.
18. Korzybski, Alfred, *Science and Sanity*, 3rd ed. Lakeville, Conn.: The International Non-Aristotelian Library Publishing Company, 1948. (First Edition, Dutton, 1933.)
19. Lee, Irving J., *Language Habits in Human Affairs*. New York: Harper, 1941.
20. Rapoport, Anatol, *Science and the Goals of Men*. New York: Harper, 1950.
21. Rapoport, Anatol, *Operational Philosophy*. New York: Harper, 1953.
22. Rapoport, Anatol, *Fights, Games, and Debates*. Ann Arbor: University of Michigan Press, 1960.
23. Rapoport, Anatol, "What is Semantics," in *The Use and Misuse of Language,* ed. by S. I. Hayakawa. New York: Fawcett, Premier Books, 1962. (Also in 14.)
24. Rogers, Carl, *On Becoming a Person*. Boston: Houghton Mifflin, 1961.
25. Ruben, Brent D., *A Model of Communication and Human Organization: Toward a Unified Theory of Education*. Iowa City: The University of Iowa, 1970.
26. Ruesch, Jurgen, and Gregory Bateson, *Communication: The Social Matrix of Psychiatry*. New York: Norton, 1951.
27. Ruesch, Jurgen, and Weldon Kees, *Nonverbal Communication*. Berkeley: University of California Press, 1956.
28. Thayer, Lee, ed., *Communication: General Semantics Perspectives*. New York: Spartan Books, 1970.
29. Weinberg, Harry L., *Levels of Knowing and Existence*. New York: Harper & Row, 1959.
30. Weiss, Thomas M., and K. H. Hoover, *Scientific Foundations of Education*. Dubuque, Iowa: Brown, 1960.
31. Whorf, Benjamin L., *Language, Thought, and Reality*, ed. by J. B. Carroll. New York: Wiley, 1956.
32. Young, J. Z., *Doubt and Certainty in Science*. New York: Oxford University Press, 1950.

Dr. Brent D. Ruben is Assistant Professor of Communication and Director of the Institute for Communication Studies at Rutgers University. He is author of two books, several book chapters and scholarly papers, and coeditor of this volume. He also serves as a communication consultant in business, government, and education.

7

GENERAL SYSTEM THEORY: AN APPROACH TO HUMAN COMMUNICATION

BRENT D. RUBEN

FUNDAMENTALLY, general systems is a science of organizing and organization. Since communication is the means through which human organizing and organization occur, it occupies a central role in general system thinking.

Unlike most of the disciplines represented in this book, there are no departments of general systems in present-day colleges. It is not a self-sustaining discipline, but rather a conglomeration of scholars from a diversity of fields, who contribute to and draw upon a growing collection of concepts, propositions, and understandings.

For those interested in human communication, a general system approach has much to offer. It presents a way of thinking about living things—as living systems—and focuses attention on the fundamental life processes that all living things have in common: the metabolism of matter-energy and the metabolism of information.[46, p. 338] From this perspective, communication is basic to the activity of all living things and, therefore, central to the emergence and survival—the total functioning—of human beings, their friendships, families, organizations, and societies.[61, p. 17]

There are a number of interesting inferences that can be drawn from this central framework. Among them is that human communication is not a one-way process, as suggested by sender-message-channel-receiver-oriented models (see Chapter 13), but rather a multidirectional phenomenon with no distinguishable beginning or end.

Another concept that can be generated from system thinking is that what is normally thought of as perfect or effective communication implies

120

the control and manipulation of a receiver of messages by the sender. The more effective is the communication, the more like tape recorders—and one another—become the message recipients. In an educational context— where creativity and diversity are desirable, the best teacher-student relationship turns out to be, therefore, one in which the teacher fails to communicate to the students.

A third notion of relevance for human communication is that the individual and the reality he experiences are codetermining phenomena, such that the way an individual thinks determines what he sees, hears, touches, and so on; and conversely, that what he sees determines how he will think. As a consequence, what we see in, and say about, other people (and things) says far more about us than about them.

But general system theory is not so much a set of neat propositions as it is a way of thinking about things. To make use of it in human communication requires a commitment to spending some time acquiring a framework for understanding its goals, scope, and basic concepts. It is here that we will begin, and because it is useful, we will look first at the background.

Background of General System Theory

General system theory has a rich and lengthy heritage. Aspects of it can be traced to Aristotle, for example, who stated in *Politics* that a state is composed of villages, which are in turn made up of households, which contain families.[32] Conceiving of things in terms of wholes and interrelated parts is a basic concept in the general system framework of today.

This element of general system theory* is also reflected in our daily language and our thought patterns. We use terms such as *universe, society, community,* and *individual* to classify reality into units consisting of parts or components. Dictionary definitions of these terms help to illustrate my point. A common meaning of *universe* is the comprehensive system—the total of all things. The universe is said to consist of, among other things, societies. *Society* refers to groups of related and interdependent people who constitute communities. In most human societies and communities, there are smaller constituent units called families, which are composed of a parent, or parents, and their children—individuals.

Many other trappings of the modern system approach date back little more than twenty or thirty years, to the early work of Ludwig von

---

* Sometimes *general system theory* is referred to as *general systems theory* or *General System(s) Theory* and the three distinguished from less formal terms like, *general system(s) thinking, the system(s) approach, and the system(s) perspective.* This tends to muddy already polluted water; therefore, all are used interchangeably in this chapter.

Bertalanffy,[15, pp. 256-258] Norbert Wiener,[73; 75] Shannon and Weaver,[59] and von Neuman and Morgenstern. Of these, only Bertalanffy was directly concerned with system theory *per se,* but all shared an interdisciplinary orientation and a concern for organization and communication.

General system theory has been greatly influenced by developments in related fields. Particularly significant in this regard were the contributions of Norbert Wiener, whose highly impactful book entitled *Cybernetics* appeared in 1948. Information theory, and in particular, the work of Shannon and Weaver, *The Mathematical Theory of Communication,* published in 1949, also had an important effect upon developments in system thinking. A third major thrust came in the area of game theory from contributions of von Neuman and Morgenstern in 1947, in *Theory of Games and Economic Behavior.*

The more recent history of general system thinking dates back to 1954 and the founding of the Society for General Systems Research, and to 1956, when the society began publishing *General Systems,*[16] the major journal in the field. It was largely in and through the society and its journal that the present form of general system thinking was molded.

In the words of the original statement of the society, its major functions were to:

> (1) investigate the isomorphy of concepts, laws and models in various fields, and to help in useful transfers from one field to another; (2) minimize the duplication of theoretical effort in different fields; (3) encourage the development of adequate theoretical models in fields which lack them; (4) promote the unity of science through improving communication among specialists. [14, p. 15]

Writing for the first volume of *General Systems,* Bertalanffy, credited by his peers as the father of modern general system theory, explains the impetus for the development of a general theory in this way:

> Modern science is characterized by its ever-increasing specialization, necessitated by the enormous amount of data, the complexity of techniques, and a breakdown of science as an integrated realm: The physicist, the biologist, the psychologist, and the social scientist are, so to speak, encapsulated in a private universe, and it is difficult to get a word from one cocoon to the other.
>
> There is, however, another remarkable aspect. If we survey the evolution of modern science, as compared to science a few decades ago, we are impressed by the fact that similar general viewpoints and conceptions have appeared in very diverse fields. Problems of organization, or wholeness, of dynamic interaction, are urgent in modern physics, chemistry, physical chemistry, and technology. The same trend is manifest in gestalt theory and other movements as opposed to classical psychology, as well as in modern conceptions of the social sciences. These parallel developments in the various fields are even more dramatic if we consider the fact that they are mutually independent and largely unaware of each other. [13, p. 1]

Not only were there parallel developments in the fields Bertalanffy mentions, but there were also parallel efforts under way aimed toward cross-disciplinary unification. Commenting upon this trend in *Communication: The Social Matrix of Psychiatry,* an important volume on communication and organization, Ruesch and Bateson point out:

> The convergence of physiology, ecology, and ethology—fields that study the organism's transactions with his physical and social environment—have resulted in the emergence of general systems theories of the biological sciences. The convergence of psychiatry, psychology, sociology, and anthropology—fields that study man's behavior alone and in groups—has led to what is now known as behavioral science. The convergence of administration, social organization, group management, and group therapy—fields that share in common the tendency to steer, organize, or change social behavior—have resulted in a theoretical body of knowledge concerned with social operations. (57, p. vii)

The foregoing was written a number of years ago; in current conception, the scope of general system theory is considerably broader than suggested by Ruesch and Bateson, finding application not only in physiology, ecology, and ethology, but in many other disciplines as well.

Scope

Contrary to what must be a logical inference from much of what has been said thus far, general system theory is not seeking to become a single theory designed to replace all the specialized theories of particular fields. As Boulding points out:

> Such a theory would be almost without content, for we always pay for generality by sacrificing content, and all we can say about practically everything is almost nothing. Somewhere, however, between the specific that has no meaning and the general that has no content there must be, for each purpose and at each level of abstraction, an optimum degree of generality. It is the contention of the General Systems Theorists that this optimum degree of generality in theory is not always reached by the particular sciences. (17, p. 11)

There is no clear-cut agreement among general system writers as to where that optimum level is; likewise, there is no single answer as to how it might be found. Boulding (17, p. 131) has outlined what he considers to be two alternatives. The first proceeds by examining the universe to identify certain general phenomena which are found in various disciplines, and then it seeks to build up generalized theories taking into account these phenomena. The second begins by arranging the various empirical fields in a hierarchy based upon the complexity and level of abstractness of the phenomena with which they deal. Ashby, who shares a similar view, also suggests two ways of proceeding:

> One [method] . . . takes the world as we find it, examines the various systems that occur in it—zoological, physiological, and so on—and then draws up statements about the regularities that have been observed to hold. . . . The second method is to start at the other end. Instead of studying first one system, then a second, then a third, and so on, it goes to the other extreme and considers the set of all conceivable systems and then reduces the set to a more reasonable size. [1, p. 2]

These alternatives circumscribe the range of research approaches utilized in general system theory. For our purposes, what is most important is the set of concepts and the basic framework for conceiving of organizing and organization which have emerged from this research.

What follows is a brief summary of basic system concepts and terminology, included because it is essential to understanding the language and framework of human communication in system perspective. The first section deals with those terms related to system *structures;* the second section considers systems in terms of their *processes.*

SYSTEM STRUCTURES

System

The concept of the *system* is the unifying idea around which revolve the goals and methods of the general system perspective. The term implies wholeness and suggests the presence of parts in relationship.

Roy Grinker, in *Toward a Unified Theory of Human Behavior,* provides the following perspective on the concept of the system:

> The reader may be somewhat bewildered by the use of the term "system" applicable to the biological, psychological, cultural or social aspects of life-in-process. A "system" is considered to be some whole form in structure or operation, concepts or functions, composed of united and integrated parts. [29, p. 370]

In further discussion, he states that "its parts are in continued activity in relation to each other and to the whole. . . ." [29, p. 370]

Bertalanffy [13, p. 3] has defined a system as a set of elements which stand in interaction. With a slightly different emphasis, Churchman [23, p. 11] characterizes the system as made up of sets of components that work together for the overall objective of the whole.

The most illustrative of the various definitions is provided by Hall and Fagen. [30, p. 18] They define a system as "a set of objects together with relationships between the objects and between their attributes." They point out also that their definition implies that "a system has properties, functions or purposes distinct from its constituent objects, relationships and attributes." They use a series of examples to clarify their definitions:

Objects are simply the parts or components of a system, and these parts are unlimited in variety. Most systems in which we are interested consist of physical parts: atoms, stars, switches, masses, springs, wires, bones, neurons, genes, muscles, gases, etc.

Attributes are properties of objects. For example, in the preceding cases, the objects listed have, among others, the following attributes:

atoms—the number of planetary electrons, the energy states of the atoms, the number of atomic particles in the nucleus, the atomic weight.

stars—temperature, distances from other stars, relative velocity.

switches—speed of operation, state.

masses—displacement, moments of inertia, momentum, velocity, kinetic energy, mass.

springs—spring tension, displacement.

wires—tensile strength, electrical resistance, diameter, length.

The *relationships* to which we refer are those that "tie the systems together." It is, in fact, these relationships that make the notion of "system" useful · . . . we take the attitude that the relationship to be considered in the context of a given set of objects depend on the problem at hand. . . . [30, p. 18]

Subsystems or Components

Systems can be divided up conceptually into subsystems or components. In discussing this concept, Churchman [23, p. 64] describes subsystems in terms of the various activities that are performed within a system. Applying this scheme to an educational situation, for example, components would include teachers, classrooms, books in the library, and so on.

According to J. G. Miller,[46, p. 218] "The totality of all the structures in a system which carry out a particular process is a subsystem." Like Churchman, Miller contends that a subsystem or component is identified by the process it performs.

Suprasystem

The components or subsystems of suprasystems are systems. In Miller's terms, "the suprasystem of any living system is the next higher system in which it is a component or subsystem." [46, p. 218] According to this definition, every system has a suprasystem except the universe.

Boundary

Boundaries hold together the components which make up a system. According to Miller,[46, p. 342] where systems are living things, boundaries are regions at the outside edges of a system, which protect them from environmental stresses and exclude or admit various sorts of matter-energy and information.

In discussing boundaries of systems made of living things, Miller offers the following description:

> System boundaries at various levels are quite different. Cells have walls; organs have covering membranes or capsules; organisms have skin, fur, scales, feathers, hair, exoskeletons, and other structures. All these have many gaps in them through which matter-energy and/or information can pass.
>
> When functioning normally, boundaries selectively filter, admitting desired inputs and blocking out excessive, dangerous or unwanted . . . inputs. (46, p. 342)

Environment

Systems are embedded within physical, spatial, temporal, and sometimes symbolic sets of conditions called environments. Environments characteristically affect the systems which interact with them and are, in turn, affected by those systems. Miller says:

> The immediate environment is the suprasystem minus the system itself. The entire environment includes this plus the suprasuprasystem and the systems at all higher levels which contain it. (46, p. 218)

With a slightly different emphasis, Churchman (23, p. 63) describes environment as a set of conditions that are relevant, but not directly under the influence of a system.

An Example

Some of the basic system structure concepts can be meaningfully illustrated by examining briefly a typical living-room stereo system. When we talk about a stereo sound system, we generally take that to imply a whole—a unit consisting of various components, or subsystems, integrated with one another to perform operations that no single component could itself accomplish.

Minimally, such a system would consist of a record changer (or turntable), stylus (or perhaps a cartridge tape player), amplifier, and two speakers (or a set of headphones). In nontechnical terms, the function of the system is to detect sound from a source (record, FM station, or tape, for example), amplify and thereby reproduce it loudly enough so that a human ear can hear it from the speakers or headphones.

Subsystem boundaries are the several wood or metal encasements which protect each component from the environment, while allowing appropriate and necessary transactions between them via wires connected to terminals of each subsystem. To make our example neat, let us say that all of the components are housed in a single console, which could be thought of as

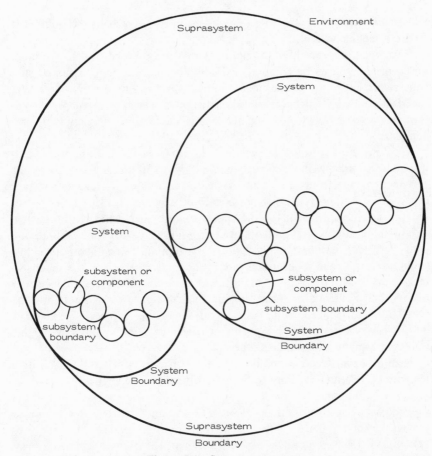

Figure 7.1   System structure

the system boundary. For purposes of this example, we can say that the room in which the stereo operates is the immediate environment of the system.

Level of Analysis

In the foregoing example, we used the term *system* to refer to the sum, or aggregate, of the components—the turntable, amplifier, and so on. It is important to point out that entering at this level of analysis, though common, is arbitrary. That is, we could just as well consider the turntable as the system, and the set of components the suprasystem. If we had done that, we would have described the components or subsystems of the turntable. Or the turntable components might have been referred to as systems, and so on. Several levels down, we might have referred to the automatic record rejection system.

If we want, we can think of suprasystems as composed of systems, composed of subsystems or components, composed of subcomponents or subsubsystems, made up of subsubcomponents, and so on ad infinitum, or we could alternatively conceive of this state of affairs as a *hierarchy of encompassing systems*,[17; 60] ranging in this case from the simple to the complex.

Selecting the appropriate level of analysis from the hierarchy depends upon one's purpose and perspective. That which is usefully viewed as the system or whole from one point of view is useless or irrelevant from another. Since we are frequently not consciously aware of selecting a level of analysis at all, we often make the choice more by accident than by design.

Examples are as abundant as our willingness to think of them. Kim [31, pp. 143-144] illustrates this point by a football game. The perspective and purposes of the quarterback are different from those of the defensive tackle, the coach, the general manager, or the fans. Each has a concept of the football system appropriate to his purposes and based upon how he sees, and is organized with, that system—upon his perspective. There is no single level right for all purposes. Each level of analysis highlights some phenomena and obscures others.

Take an example from another situation: The level of analysis at which a salesman operates is likely to be quite different from that utilized by the president of the same company.

Understanding this about level of analysis can serve to dispel some of the mysticism associated with system thinking. One realizes that the way system, subsystem, boundary, and environment get defined depends mostly upon the level of analysis one selects—and that that decision depends largely upon how one conceived of the situation in the first place. This is an extremely important point—one which draws upon system thinking to explain system thinking. Specifically, it involves the notion of the codeterminacy between the individual's mind and his reality, discussed in an upcoming section entitled "Individual Communication System." Reread this paragraph after having completed that section.

SYSTEM PROCESSES

Living Systems

The distinction between *open* and *closed* systems is extremely valuable in understanding human communication. Living systems are units of living things and are more-or-less open systems. Open systems are so named because they exist only through continual exchanges with the environment.[14, p. 32] They maintain themselves through a continual inflow and outflow, a building up and breaking down of components.[14, p. 39] This process is known as metabolism. J. G. Miller [46, p. 338] has pointed out that there are two types of metabolism basic to the functioning of all living systems: the metabolism of matter-energy* and the metabolism of information. Living systems organize themselves only in and through these two processes. Some processes also involve both together.)

Lee Thayer, an important contributor to the interface of general system thinking and human communication theory, has extended and elaborated upon Miller's basic notion of information metabolism, which Thayer terms *communication:*

> Communication may thus be conceived of as the dynamic process under-lying the existence, growth, change, the behavior of all living systems—in-dividual and organization. Communication can be understood as that indis-pensable function of people and organization through which the organization or the organism relates itself to its environment, and its parts and its processes one to the other.
> Communication is as fundamental to the living system—the individual or the organization—as is ingestion and consumption of "food" and "fuel" to run its physical and physiological machinery. [61, p. 17]

In contrast is the closed-system model, which comes from conventional physics and is directly applicable to things in the physical and mechanical realm. These systems are termed "closed" because they function in isola-tion from their environment. Bertalanffy [14, p. 39] cites as an example of a closed system the domain of physical chemistry, which, he points out, is concerned with reactions, their rates, and the chemical state which eventu-ally comes about in a closed container where several reactants are brought together.

One interesting characteristic of closed systems is that their eventual state is always determinable from the initial conditions.[14, p. 40] In the case of a process involving chemicals in a closed vessel, the final concentrations of the reactants can be calculated from a knowledge of the initial concen-trations. If either the starting conditions or the process is altered, the final state is also changed.[14, p. 40] This is not the case for open systems, where the same final state may be reached from different initial conditions and in different ways. This characteristic of open systems is termed *equifinality*.

This distinction reflects a more basic difference between the two types

---

* "Metabolism involves an interchange of material between living organisms and the environment, by which the body is built up and energy for its vital life process is secured. Within the body of the individual both constructive and destructive proc-esses take place. The incorporation of materials is known as anabolism and the breaking down of these materials for the release of energy contained in them is catabolism." *The Complete Book of Science* (New York: J. J. Little & Ives Co., 1959).

of systems: Closed systems are conceived as behaving according to the second law of thermodynamics, and open systems are not. This law states that in a closed system, a quantity called *entropy* increases to a maximum and eventually stops when the conditions of the system are random, chaotic, and deteriorated, as the system loses organization and structure. The process of a closed system then, is one of continual deterioration.

Open systems work differently. In these systems, an increase in organization and a decrease in entropy is thermodynamically possible, since the systems interact and exchange matter-energy and information with their environments.[14, p. 150]

While the open-system model has obvious relevance for understanding the organization and communication processes of living things, the applicability of a closed-system framework is indirect. Though all living systems are open and interact with their environments, in terms of communication, not all seem to exhibit the same degree of openness. Some, in fact, become more or less isolated from their environments and undergo processes analogous to the loss of organization and structure of chemicals in a closed vessel.[57; 72] Sometimes, this general deterioration even leads to total chaos and a breakdown in the system structure, as in the case of a mental breakdown, divorce, or revolution. The second law of thermodynamics and elements of the closed-system model can provide new ways to think about such phenomena in terms of organization and communication.

Feedback Systems

The classification of systems in terms of feedback is common, due primarily to the widespread application of feedback systems in electronics, biology, and social sciences. Also, the basic elements of the feedback system are the core of the science called cybernetics, originated primarily by Norbert Wiener, and concerned with self-steering and self-regulating devices.[2; 8; 9; 73] Such mechanisms have been essential to the development of the computer, guided missiles, and other "intelligent" and "automatic" machines.

In the context of human communication, feedback has been used to refer to information about the outcome of communicating that is rechanneled back to the source for his use. This is illustrated in the communication models and discussion of feedback presented in the chapters of this volume entitled "Mass Media: An Approach to Human Communication," by Richard F. Hixson, and "Sociology: An Approach to Human Communication," by John W. and Matilda Riley. The notion is that the source can then modify his manner of communicating, based on a knowledge of how effective or successful he has been.

This basic conceptualization has been applied to mass communication as well as to face-to-face interaction. A difference sometimes cited between the two, however, is that feedback in mass-communication situations is often delayed (for example, television ratings or letters to the editor), whereas in interpersonal interaction, feedback may be immediate.

The concept has also been used widely in the context of the encounter group, where it refers to reports a T-group participant receives from others in the group about how he has affected them—"come across." Presumably, once the "feedback" is gotten, an individual can make comparisons between what he intended to communicate and what actually happened. When the two don't match, he can make changes to become more effective interpersonally.

These applications capture the most obvious aspects of the concept of feedback systems, but miss some of the deeper conceptual structure. In a generic sense, feedback refers to a portion of a system's output which is fed back or recycled to the system as input, thereby affecting the functioning of the system such that it is able to regulate itself and reach a preset or adaptive goal.[31, p. 1]

The origins of the concept can be followed back to the sixteenth century.* The more recent history traces to the work of James C. Maxwell on the steam engine governor. The governor works as follows:

> An engine turns at an increasing speed; the arms are mounted on pivots so that they are free to rise by centrifical force as they revolve; the arms operate a valve which admits power to the engine, so that the valve is closed in proportion as the arms rise and the speed grows. [31, p. 18]

Stafford Beer's description [8, p. 29] of the governor reflects the basic propositions implicit in the current conception of the feedback system. The contemporary view utilizes a series of specialized concepts including *input, output, control, goal,* and *deviation* in addition to *feedback.*

Input and output refer to directions of flow to and from a system or subsystem across its boundaries. Goal refers to a desired state of a system which is either present and predetermined, or emerges out of the activity of the system. Control is the consequence of the comparison performed between the actual output level and the desired level or goal. Feedback is the information with which this comparison is made.

Suppose we were going to bake a cake. We would begin by turning the oven temperature control (thermostat) to 375 degrees, and then we would turn the oven on. The 375 degrees represents our desired output state or goal. The oven heating elements turn on and begin to output heat, a portion of which is monitored by the thermostat (as input). The thermostat will keep the elements turned on until the actual output corresponds to the

---

* In discussing the background and basic concepts of feedback and feedback systems I draw heavily upon the work of John Kim.[31]

desired goal. When both equal 375 degrees the oven will temporarily turn off and will remain off until, once again, the thermostat detects a discrepancy or deviation between the oven output temperature and the desired output temperature (375 degrees). When a difference is detected, the oven will be turned back on and remain on until the gap between the present input goal and the oven output has been eliminated.

The thermostat and other cybernetic self-regulating, self-steering, or control systems, as they are variously termed, operate by detecting gaps, differences, *errors,* and *deviations.*[31] Systems which look for deviation, error, or difference which they are designed to counteract, eliminate, or equalize are traditionally termed *negative feedback systems.*

Magorah Maruyama [42] has proposed another conceptualization of system processes which he refers to as "the second cybernetics," since positive rather than negative feedback is involved. (Maruyama prefers not to use the terms *negative* and *positive,* but for our purposes here they serve to clarify the nature of his contribution to cybernetic thinking.) In the excerpt that follows, he provides us not only with a description of his concept, but also with a sense of the scope of application of "the first cybernetics."

> Since its inception, cybernetics was more or less identified as a science of self-regulating . . . systems. Thermostats, physiological regulation of body temperature, automatic steering devices, economic and political processes were studied under a general mathematical model of deviation-counteracting feedback networks.
>
> By focusing on the deviation-counteracting aspects . . . cyberneticians paid less attention to the systems in which the effects are deviation-amplifying. Such systems are ubiquitous: accumulation of capital in industry, evolution of living organisms, the rise of cultures of various types, interpersonal process that are loosely termed as "vicious circles" and "compound interests. . . ." [42, p. 164]

Maruyama [42; 40; 41] termed these deviation-counteracting (negative) feedback processes, *morphostasis.* Deviation-amplifying (positive) feedback processes, he termed *morphogenesis.* These concepts differ from the less complex notions of negative and positive feedback processes in that Maruyama's terms describe relationships which are mutually causal rather than one-way.

This represents a significant modification of the earlier feedback system framework. The classification solved a number of problems associated with the elementary feedback models and thereby provided an alternative to the more mechanistic conceptions of feedback in human processes.[14, p. 191] Such things as play, exploratory behavior, and creativity could now be better accounted for.

In the perspective of the elementary negative feedback system these phenomena were classed as "error" to be corrected out, since they represented a gap or deviation from normative behavior (the desired goal).[65; 55]

Additional refinements were embodied in this new classificational scheme. In the models of the first cybernetics the direction of feedback was understood to be one-way—from output to input; and feedback was presumed to exist and operate within a single system and therefore more or less in isolation from the environment and other systems.[31]

According to the refined framework, feedback is understood to imply at least a two-directional and mutually causal relationship involving two interconnected systems. Kim,[31, p. 31] after Ashby, proposed that feedback could appropriately be conceived to exist "when two or more interacting systems are mutually related to each other through input and output." One system's input is another's output, and vice versa; and the model becomes, in Maruyama's terms, one of multilateral mutual causality.

This conception is useful in several ways for thinking about human communication. In the first place, the model can be understood to indicate that communication always implies a relationship between two or more interacting systems. It suggests further that these communication relationships are mutually causal and multilateral, and that such mutually causal communication relationships involve mutual control and manipulation of the two components in relationship, each by the other.

Traditional feedback-oriented communication models viewed the process of human communication as one-way, cause-effect relationships—where sources (or initiators or senders) create messages, which they transmit over one of various channels, and cause a variety of effects in the receiver. Feedback was conceived of as that information which the source used to monitor his effect.

In contrast to this view, a mutually causal framework calls attention to the fact that it is logically sound, and probably more useful operationally, to say that it is the receiver who causes messages to have their meaning and significance and it is therefore the receiver who causes communication to have effects upon him.

From this perspective, it also becomes clear that defining communication effectiveness from the point of view of the sender often leads in paradoxical directions. In the case of the student-teacher communication pattern, for example, effective communication from the source's point of view is having the students learn exactly what a teacher intends. The perfect solution for this communication problem is a classroom filled with tape recorders—or students who act like them. Whether we intend it or not, an attendant consequence of perfect communication is homogenization. Ironically, creativity can therefore be thought of as a consequence and instance of ineffective communication.[65; 55]

But one need not take quite such an extreme position to find value in the concept of human communication as multilateral, mutually causal systems. One need only recall a typical argument between two individuals, each bantering with the other, and in so doing, perpetuating and perhaps intensifying the argument in a spiraling cause-and-effect fashion.[72, pp. 96-98]

It is interesting to note that the notion of feedback is not crucial to the mutually causal system perspective since, as you may recall, the concept of feedback implied a one-way process and suggested a source-oriented view of communication. What is feed*back* to the source is feed-*forward* to the receiver. A letter to the editor, for example, is feedback from the point of view of the newspaper, but feed-forward from the perspective of the audience member writing the piece.

HUMAN COMMUNICATION SYSTEMS

Up to this point, we have reviewed general system thinking. We looked briefly at the background, goals, and scope of general system theory, reviewed basic concepts related to system structure, and discussed several classifications of system processes. In the remaining pages, we will turn our attention to human communication systems, drawing upon those aspects of general system thinking which seem most generic in their relevance to human communication.

Information and Communication Systems

To begin with, we need to distinguish between *information systems* and *communication systems*. Lee Thayer provides a view that is well suited to our purposes. His differentiation is between communication systems on the one hand, and data systems (termed "information systems" here) on the other:

> There are at least two useful distinctions to be made. . . . Data systems [information systems] map the flow of *data* to and from humans or machines from the point at which that data is generated or disseminated, to the point of its intended destination. Data systems [information systems] are rational systems designed by people, deduced from some set of rational criteria of system efficacy.
>
> *Communication systems,* by contrast, are defined by the data acquisition —consumption practices (rational or not) of the consumers of the output of that system, whether by intention or accident. [61, p. 116]

Thayer makes a further distinction between the nature of the two sorts of systems, which helps to clarify his notion of each:

> . . . people may be *informed* by the data systems [information systems] which serve them. But people are *in-formed* within their communication systems. [61, p. 117]

The stereo system discussed earlier in this chapter was a good example of an information system. The structure and process of that system was discussed primarily in terms of the flow of data and messages from one component to another. The general goal was the detection and amplification of sound that is loud enough to be detected by the human ear. If we add to that system a human being—a listener—the system would move closer to the definition of a communication system. However, as long as the primary focus is upon the mechanical flow of messages—even with a listener included as one of the components—it would still be termed an information system. Only when the significances, competencies, purposes, functions, and desires which the listener brings to the situation were defined as a crucial aspect of the system, would it meet the definition of communication system.

Where an important question for examining an information system is, "How does it work?" the question of importance for the communication system is, "How are people using it?" It follows that the most effective information system might be an extremely ineffective communication system. The finest reproduction of classical music, for example, is worthless to the listener who enjoys only folk rock.

Many people who study human communication focus their attention upon information systems—upon the flow of messages from one place or one person to another. Unfortunately, this perspective misses much that is relevant for understanding human communication in system perspective. No amount of study of the postal system, linguistics, or cross-cultural communication—message flows—is likely to provide an adequate understanding of the significance that a letter from a boy in Princeton, New Jersey, to an intimate friend in London, England, will have for the two of them.

Communication System Framework

While most authors writing about human communication are drawing increasingly upon the terminology of system theory, the applications are often shallow, and are not accompanied by the use of an internally consistent system thinking framework. Of the growing number of basic human communication books, I am familiar with only two, *Communication and Communication Systems* [61] and *Pragmatics of Human Communication*, [72] which utilize an integrated system framework as an approach to human communication.

What follows is a skeleton model of a human communication-system framework, which builds upon and reflects many of the ideas presented in those two volumes.

To begin with, we propose conceiving of the totality of human enterprise as a suprasystem—a complex and interrelated hierarchy of systems and their components—organized and organizing itself and its parts one with the other. The systems making up the suprasystem—individuals, friendships, marriages, business organizations, people riding an elevator together, fraternities, strangers passing on a street, universities, or societies —are continually in process and thereby maintain and modify previous patterns of organization within and among one another.

This suprasystem, together with the environment, can be thought of as an ecosystem (ecological system), since the individual systems and components within depend for their survival, growth, and change upon their ability to fit themselves with one another and with the environment. The ecosystem notion implies that there are two fundamental life systems through which all organization and organizing occur: matter-energy systems and communication systems. The complexity and intricacy of pathways and interconnections necessary to even maintain these systems are impossible to enumerate, and difficult even to conceive of. In *The Origin of the Species,* Darwin examined the relationship between red clover and the bumblebees which pollinate it, in an attempt to suggest the intricacy and elaborateness of such ecological systems. Farb refers to the story as an "ecological classic."

> Darwin discovered that bumblebees, because of their long tongues, are the only insects which can effectively pollinate the deep red clover flowers. From this he argued that the success of red clover in England can be attributed to the fact that bumblebees are so prevalent there. He then went on to quote an authority who had found that there were more bumblebees' nests in the vicinity of villages and towns than elsewhere because field mice, which eat bumblebee combs and larvae, are scarce around towns. And why are field mice scarce? Because towns usually harbor large numbers of cats which prey upon the field mice and keep the population down. Here a German scientist took up the argument: cats, he said, were thus proved responsible for the prevalence of red clover in England; red clover, a staple food of British cattle, could be ecologically linked to the British navy, whose staple diet was bully beef; hence cats could be given ultimate credit for Britain's dominance as a world power. Thomas Huxley then went even one step further: he suggested, half humorously, that since old maids were well known to be the principal protectors of cats throughout England, the fact that Britannia ruled the waves might logically—and ecologically—be traced right back to the cat-loving tendencies of her many spinsters. (25, pp. 35–36)

As Farb points out, the "cat-and-clover" story is obviously overdrawn and implies a one-way cause-and-effect relationship, but the interconnections discussed serve to illustrate the far-reaching ecological interrelationships and interdeterminancies that inextricably bind together systems and subsystems within the ecosuprasystem.

The story also indirectly makes the point that biological and social existence depends upon living systems organizing themselves metabolically and informationally with their environments and with the other living systems in it. For man, this is a particularly complex phenomenon, because unlike lower organisms whose relationships with their environment and other living things are largely determined genetically, man can and literally must organize himself through participation in communication systems.

To understand how this occurs, we need to consider two different levels of analysis of human communication systems, and the manner in which systems at these two levels relate to each other. The first we can call the individual communication system. The second is the multiperson communication system.

Individual Communication System

Man can and must invent whatever significances he attaches to himself, his environment, and the people in it. It is this capacity of communication, and the consequent, wide-ranging potential for individual uniqueness, that most clearly distinguishes man from other living things.

Human individuals have no way to experience their milieu other than in and through participation in communication systems. This participation is mandatory. It is in becoming organized through participation that man comes to comprehend and give significance and meaning to his experiences. Human sensory receptors are sensitive to light, sound, and pressure —and not to reality. One hears and sees those things which one has become organized to experience, in the same manner as one can eat and metabolize those foods that one is biologically organized to accommodate. Thayer's description of this parallel is a good one:

> Looking is a matter of registering light waves; perceiving a matter of having translated those light waves into an idea or image, into something manipulable not by the eye but by the mind. Listening is a matter of registering sound waves; hearing is a matter of having translated those sound waves into a meaningful pattern or an image, into something, again, manipulable not by the mechanics of the ear, but by the mind.
>
> Information is not something which inheres in the objects and events of man's world. Information is what a man endows those objects and events with. Man literally in-forms himself. He may be constrained or even destroyed by his environment. But its meaning . . . its significance . . . its utility for him . . . these are ultimately properties of him. Information is thus the lifeblood of his awareness, his consciousness, his knowledge of his environment, in the same way that the highly refined and translated products of metabolic process are the lifeblood of his body. An indigestible or undigested herb is either as useless or as troublesome to man as is being unaware or unable to inform himself adequately of some event in his environment which might have vital consequence for him. (66)

The process of becoming organized has multilateral mutually causal consequences, since how man becomes organized determines what he sees, hears, believes, comes to know—his sense of what reality is, which in turn determines how he can become organized. And it is in this way that we get what we see.

Man creates the reality and environment he knows and at the same time, probably, the mind by which he knows it and therefore himself. While there is certainly a great deal more to be learned about the way the mind develops,[33, p. 6] it appears that it organizes itself in and through participation in the individual communication system, as the child, and later the adult, seeks to make sense of his life encounters. As Delgado explains:

> The newborn baby is not capable of speech, symbolic understanding or directing skillful mobility. It has no ideas, words, or concepts, no tools for communication, no significant sensory experience, no culture. The newborn baby never smiles. He is unable to comprehend the loving phrases of his mother or to be aware of the environment. We must conclude that there are no detectable signs of mental activity at birth and that *human beings are born without minds.**

Pertinent also is Delgado's further point that the mind can best be defined as the *"intracerebral elaboration of extracerebral information,"* implying the interrelatedness and codeterminacy of mind and experienced reality. Both can therefore be viewed as structural residues of participation in the processes of the individual human communication system, as can beliefs, attitudes, and personality.

Vickers captures the essence of this point:

> Insofar as I can be regarded as human, it is because I was claimed at birth as a member by a communicative network, which programmed me for participation in itself.**

Multiperson Communication Systems

At a different level of analysis are communication systems involving more than one person. The most obvious examples that come to mind are families, clubs, fraternities, universities, societies, and the like; however, a group of people riding an elevator or two strangers passing on the street are also examples of multiperson communication systems. Wherever organization between two or more persons exists, there is an instance of multiperson human communication systems.

Organization in these systems occurs through interaction between indi-

---

* José M. R. Delgado, *Physical Control of the Mind* (New York: Harper & Row, 1969), p. 45. See also the chapter of this volume by Delgado entitled, "Neurophysiology: An Approach to Human Communication."

** Geoffrey Vickers, "The Multivalued Choice," in *Communication Concepts and Perspectives,* ed. by Lee Thayer (New York: Spartan Books, 1967).

viduals whereby significances are created and maintained. The exchanges may involve words, money, gestures, eye glances, flags, or automobiles. Participation in multiperson communication systems is mandatory. At a given time each of us is a participant in a multitude of such systems.

The basic unit of the multiperson communication system is two or more individuals organized with one another, intentionally or by accident. Elaborations of this basic structural relationship indicate a variety of configurations in terms of level of complexity and the degree of organization. At one extreme is the simple and minimally organized system composed of several individuals riding together on an elevator. At a more complex and organized level is the multiperson relationship involved when one individual negotiates past another on a sidewalk. At a still more complex and intricately organized level is a system like friendship, and at an extreme in terms of complexity and intricacy of interrelationship is a multiperson system like society.

Peter Berger's view of society provides a good example:

> Every individual biography is an episode within the history of society, which both precedes and survives it. Society was there before the individual was born and it will be there after he has died. What is more, it is within society, and as a result of social processes, that the individual becomes a person, that he attains and holds on to an identity, and that he carries out the various projects that constitute his life. Man cannot exist apart from society.*

This description not only suggests something of the nature of society viewed as a multiperson communication system, but also raises the question of the relationship between society and the individual. For our purposes here, the generic issue is a larger one, having to do with the relationship of the individual not only to society, but to all other human, multiperson communication systems as well.

Like the relationship of mind and the reality it experiences, the relationship between the individual and the multiperson communication system is mutually causal. The raw data with which the human individual organizes himself (and in the process, develops a mind and a concept of reality) are products and consequences of the various multiperson communication systems which he encounters. Each has a reality of its own and its own tokens of significance, with which the individual comes to organize himself. Not only does each multiperson system have a part in the creation or positing of reality, but each also plays an important role in setting the agenda for the individual's encounter with nature as well.

For example, we do not experience trees or rivers at random. They are encountered in social context. Trees are for parking strollers under or for

---

* Peter Berger, *The Sacred Canopy* (Garden City, N.Y.: Doubleday, 1969), p. 1.

taking rides through in the fall or for climbing; rivers are for swimming or for fishing or for boating—or if they are spanned by bridges, for crossing in cars.

The other side of the coin is that while the individual is organizing himself to participate in various multiperson systems, he is helping to sustain them by contributing to the production of the raw data with respect to which other individuals must organize themselves.

It is in this sense that the input to the individual system is the output of the multiperson system, and, conversely, the output of the individual system is the input to the multiperson system. The relationship between the two is also codetermining in the sense that the individual mind is both a producer and a consumer of multiperson reality.

CONCLUSION

We could—and perhaps we ought to—spend years exploring the implications of this fundamental notion about the nature of human organization. We are victimized by our ignorance of these matters, whether we understand that it is happening or not. How often, for example, do we involve ourselves in the age-old activity of consulting with our closest friends, relatives, peers—those with whom we have become most closely organized—to assess the propriety of our actions and to validate our thoughts? In a literal sense, when we do this we are talking to ourselves.

Or how often do we search for failure to communicate in the person who is speaking rather than in the listener? If you do not understand this chapter is it *I* that have failed? How often do we find ourselves blaming others for the way we comprehend reality?

The fundamental nature of this mutually causal communication suprasystem of which we are all a part is so basic and complex as to defy mastery by generations of men who have sought to institutionalize—through churches, schools, prisons—the balance or "match" between the individual and the multiperson system. Our vocabularies would be greatly restricted if suddenly we had to eliminate words like "criminal," "sociopath," "pervert," "genius," "creative," and "insane" that we use to refer to "mismatches." We never have figured out what to do about diversity.

And as our youth are anxious to point out, most of our institutions reflect a morphostatic perspective—they are designed to eliminate and counteract mismatch, rather than to tolerate or amplify differences between individuals. It remains to be seen, however, whether those who clamor the loudest for deviation-amplifying or tolerating relationships can resist the temptation to replace old morphostatic institutions with new ones when an opportunity for change presents itself.

We are desperately in need of better ways to conceive of and cope with these sorts of issues. We need to look again and with a new scrutiny at ourselves and what we are about. And if we believe it a worthy goal, to strive to make a difference in the course of human affairs. And if we attempt to make that difference as a consequence of planning, then we can ill afford the luxury of having at our disposal any less than the most powerful ways for conceiving of man and the processes of human communication.

I think that general system thinking can provide such a tool.

REFERENCES AND SUGGESTED READINGS

1. Ashby, W. Ross, "General Systems Theory as a New Discipline," *General Systems,* Vol. 3, 1958.
2. Ashby, W. Ross, *An Introduction to Cybernetics.* London: Chapman, 1961.
3. Bahm, Archie J., "Systems Theory," *General Systems,* Vol. 14, 1969.
4. Bakke, E. Wight, "Concept of the Social Organization," in *Modern Organization Theory,* ed. by Mason Haire. New York: Wiley, 1959.
5. Bateson, Gregory, "Cybernetic Explanation," *The American Behavioral Scientist,* Vol. 10, 1967.
6. Bateson, Gregory, "Pathologies of Epistemology," paper prepared under Career Development Award (K2–21, 931) of the National Institute of Mental Health, Oceanic Institute, Hawaii.
7. Beer, Stafford, "Below the Twilight Arch," *General Systems,* Vol. 5, 1960.
8. Beer, Stafford, *Cybernetics and Management.* New York: Wiley, 1959.
9. Beer, Stafford, *Decision and Control.* New York: Wiley, 1966.
10. Bennis, Warren G., "Towards a 'Truly' Scientific Management," *General Systems,* Vol. 7, 1962.
11. Berrien, F. Kenneth, *General and Social Systems.* New Brunswick, N.J.: Rutgers University Press, 1969.
12. Bertalanffy, Ludwig von, "General System Theory—A Critical Review," *General Systems,* Vol. 7, 1962.
13. Bertalanffy, Ludwig von, "General System Theory," *General Systems,* Vol. 1, 1956.
14. Bertalanffy, Ludwig von, *General Systems Theory, Foundations, Developments, Applications.* New York: Braziller, 1968.
15. Bertalanffy, Ludwig von, "An Outline of General System Theory," *British Journal of Philosophical Science,* Vol. 1, 1950.
16. Bertalanffy, Ludwig von, and A. Rapoport, eds., *General Systems.* Washington, D.C.: The Society for General Systems Research, 13 vols., since 1956.
17. Boulding, Kenneth E., "General Systems Theory—The Skeleton of Science," *Management Science,* Vol. 2, 1956.
18. Boulding, Kenneth E., "Political Implications of General Systems Research," *General Systems,* Vol. 6, 1961.
19. Boulding, Kenneth E., "Toward a General Theory of Growth," *The Canadian Journal of Economics and Political Science,* Vol. 19, 1953.
20. Buckley, Walter, *Modern Systems Research for the Behavioral Scientist.* Chicago.: Aldine, 1967.
21. Buckley, Walter, *Sociology and Modern Systems Theory.* Englewood Cliffs, N.J.: Prentice-Hall, 1967.

22. Caws, Peter, "Science and System," *General Systems,* Vol. 13, 1968.

23. Churchman, C. West, *The Systems Approach.* New York: Dell, 1968.

24. Emery, R. E., ed., *Systems Thinking.* Baltimore, Md.: Penguin, 1969.

25. Farb, Peter, *Ecology.* New York: Time-Life, 1963.

26. Gardner, John W., *Self-Renewal.* New York: Harper & Row, 1965.

27. Gerard, R. W., "A Biologist's View of Society," *General Systems,* Vol. 1, 1956.

28. Gray, William, Frederick J. Duhl, and Nicholas D. Rizzo, *General Systems Theory and Psychiatry.* Boston: Little, Brown, 1969.

29. Grinker, R. R., Sr., ed., *Toward a Unified Theory of Human Behavior,* 2nd ed. New York: Basic Books, 1967.

30. Hall, A. D., and R. W. Fagen, "Definition of System," *General Systems,* Vol. 1, 1956.

31. Kim, John Y., "Feedback and Human Communication," unpublished doctoral dissertation, University of Iowa, 1971.

32. Kim, John Y., "A Thought on Systems," Institute for Communication Studies, University of Iowa, 1969. (Mimeographed.)

33. Laszlo, Ervin, *System, Structure, and Experience.* New York: Gordon and Breach, 1969.

34. Laszlo, Ervin, ed., *The Relevance of General Systems Theory.* New York: Braziller, 1972.

35. Lawson, Chester A., "Language, Communication, and Biological Organization," *General Systems,* Vol. 8, 1963.

36. Lektorsky, V. A., and V. N. Sadovsky, "On Principles of System Research," *General Systems,* Vol. 5, 1960. "O Printsipakh Issledovania Sistem," trans. by A. Rapoport from *Voprosy Filosofii,* No. 8, 1960.

37. Lysloff, George O., "Semantic Categories and Hierarchy of Systems," *General Systems,* Vol. 14, 1969.

38. MacKay, Donald M., *Information, Mechanism and Meaning.* Cambridge, Mass.: M.I.T. Press, 1969.

39. Maruyama, Magorah, "Metaorganization of Information," *Cybernetica,* No. 4, 1965.

40. Maruyama, Magorah, "Morphogenesis and Morphostasis," *Methodos: Language and Cybernetics,* Vol. 12, No. 48, 1960.

41. Maruyama, Magorah, "A Postscript to 'The Second Cybernetics,'" *American Scientist,* Vol. 51, 1963.

42. Maruyama, Magorah, "The Second Cybernetics," *American Scientist,* Vol. 51, 1963.

43. McClelland, Charles A., "Systems and History in International Relations," *General Systems,* Vol 3, 1958.

44. Meadow, Charles T., "The Analysis of Information Systems," in *Dimensions in Communication,* 2nd ed., ed. by J. H. Campbell and H. W. Hepler. Belmont, Calif.: Wadsworth, 1970.

45. Mesarovic, M. D., *Views on General System Theory,* New York: Wiley, 1964.

46. Miller, James G., "Living Systems: Basic Concepts; Living Systems: Structure and Process; Living Systems: Cross-Level Hypotheses," *Behavioral Science,* Vol. 10, 1965.

47. Milsum, J. H., "Technosphere, Biosphere, and Sociosphere," *General Systems,* Vol. 13, 1968.

48. Monane, Joseph H., *A Sociology of Human Systems.* New York: Appleton-Century-Crofts, 1967.

49. Platt, John, "Hierarchical Restructuring," *General Systems,* Vol. 15, 1970.

50. Pringle, J. W. S., "On the Parallel Between Learning and Evolution," *Behavior,* Vol. 3, 1951.

51. Ramsoy, Odd, *Social Group as System and Subsystem.* New York: Free Press, 1963.

52. Rapoport, Anatol, "Methodology in the Physical, Biological and Social Sciences," *General Systems,* Vol. 14, 1969.

53. Rapoport, Anatol, "Modern Systems Theory," *General Systems,* Vol. 15, 1970.

54. Rice, Charles E., "A Model for the Empirical Study of a Large Social Organization," *General Systems,* Vol. 6, 1961.

55. Ruben, Brent D., and Albert D. Talbott, "Communication, Information and Education Systems," a paper presented to the 17th Annual Conference of the National Society for the Study of Communication, Cleveland, Ohio.

56. Ruesch, Jurgen, Epilogue to the 2nd edition of R. R. Grinker, ed., *Toward a Unified Theory of Human Behavior,* 2nd ed., New York: Basic Books, 1967.

57. Ruesch, Jurgen, and Gregory Bateson, *Communication, the Social Matrix of Psychiatry.* New York: Norton, 1951, 1968.

58. Schroder, Harold M., Michael J. Driver, and Siegfried Streufert, *Human Information Processing.* New York: Holt, Rinehart and Winston, 1967.

59. Shannon, Claude E., and Warren Weaver, *The Mathematical Theory of Communication.* Urbana: University of Illinois Press, 1949.

60. Simon, Herbert A., "The Architecture of Complexity," *Proceedings of the American Philosophical Society,* Vol. 106, No. 6, 1962.

61. Thayer, Lee, *Communication and Communication Systems.* Homewood, Ill.: Irwin, 1968.

62. Thayer, Lee, "Communication and Organization Theory," in *Human Communication Theory,* ed. by Frank E. X. Dance. New York: Holt, Rinehart and Winston, 1967.

63. Thayer, Lee, "Communication: Sine Qua Non of the Behavioral Sciences," in *Vistas in Science,* ed. by D. L. Arm. Albuquerque: University of New Mexico Press, 1968.

64. Thayer, Lee, "Communication Systems," in *The Relevance of General Systems Theory,* ed. by E. Laszlo. New York: Braziller, 1972.

65. Thayer, Lee, "On Communication and Change," *Systematics,* Vol. 6, No. 3, 1968.

66. Thayer, Lee, "On Human Communication and Social Development," a paper presented at the first World Conference on Social Communication for Development, Mexico City, March, 1970.

67. Thompson, John W., "Mental Science, Meteorology, and General System Theory," *General Systems,* Vol. 5, 1960.

68. Vickers, Geoffrey, "A Classification of Systems," *General Systems,* Vol. 15, 1970.

69. Vickers, Geoffrey, "Control, Stability and Choice," *General Systems,* Vol. 2, 1957.

70. Vickers, Geoffrey, "Is Adaptability Enough?," *Behavioral Science,* Vol. 4, 1959.

71. Vickers, Geoffrey, *Value Systems and Social Process.* New York: Basic Books, 1968.

72. Watzlawick, Paul, Janet H. Beavin, and Don D. Jackson, *Pragmatics of Human Communication.* New York: Norton, 1967.

73. Wiener, N., *Cybernetics.* New York: Wiley, 1948.

74. Wiener, N., "Cybernetics and Society," in *The Human Dialogue,* ed. by Floyd W. Matson and Ashley Montagu. New York: Free Press, 1967.

75. Wiener, N., *The Human Use of Human Beings*. New York: Avon, 1950.
76. Wilson, Donna, "Forms of Hierarchy," *General Systems,* Vol. 14, 1969.
77. Wisdom, J. O., "The Hypothesis of Cybernetics," *The British Journal for the Philosophy of Sciences,* Vol. 2, 1951.
78. Young, O. R., "The Impact of General Systems on Political Science," *General Systems,* Vol. 8, 1963.
79. Young, O. R., "A Survey of General Systems Theory," *General Systems,* Vol. 8, 1963.

Dr. Hanno Hardt is Associate Professor of Journalism at the University of Iowa. Professor Hardt studied law at Kiel and Heidelberg universities in Germany. He has contributed numerous articles and papers in both the United States and Germany. His most recent contributions include a chapter in *International Communication,* by Heinz-Dietrich Fischer and John C. Merrill, and one in *Communication: General Semantics Perspectives,* by Lee Thayer. He is currently completing a book about ethics and social communication.

8

HISTORY: AN APPROACH TO HUMAN COMMUNICATION

HANNO HARDT

COMMUNICATION AND HISTORY: THE DIMENSIONS OF MAN'S REALITY

MAN lives within the bounds of history. He faces the inexplicable and the unknown in the wake of constant changes in his own existence and in his immediate world. He seeks comfort and security in contemporary ideologies of order and stability not unlike ancient man, for whom mythology provided reassurance and promise of definite purpose and direction in life. Prehistoric man created a reality that merged past and present into a timeless world, thus creating the opposite of what can be called "history." As Philip Rahv observed, "Myth is reassuring in its stability, whereas history is that powerhouse of change which destroys custom and tradition in producing the future." [31, p. 205] Communication, and its perfection through the development of language, led to the discovery of the mind or, to borrow from Bruno Snell, to "scientific thinking" and to attempts to understand not only the laws of nature and the workings of the physical world, but also the impact of man's social and political behavior upon the shaping of his contemporary and future enterprises. In this sense *epos* and *logos* evolved out of *mythos,* as Rahv suggested. [31, p. 206]

Curiosity, Complexity, Dialogue

The increasing sophistication of communication also marked the beginning of a conscious effort to collect, preserve, and expand man's knowl-

145

edge of the past. History became a way of solving social problems, and it has retained its importance as a humanistic approach to the study of man's concept of reality, most closely related to sociology and the sociology of knowledge. The evolution from mythical thought to logic, already accomplished at the time of the Greeks, emphasized the shift from man's passive reliance on myths to his search for truth and the resultant expansion of his scientific knowledge. The curiosity of the learner, the activity of the mind in the discovery of the unknown, underlay man's desire not only to understand the physical environment, but also to explore the realms of his own social and political nature. Man's complexity, the characteristics of his objective-subjective world of meanings, the traditional ties of his ethicoreligious beliefs and his communal or societal identity, offered a demanding challenge to his ingenuity and intuition as an inventor of philosophical and scientific theories about himself and society. Henri Marrou once said that history is the response to a question which the curiosity, concern, and existential anxiety of the historian collectively asks of the mysterious past.[26, p. 63] Marrou reflected upon the role of the historian as a problem solver who senses the magnitude of his task and whose attitudes toward understanding man are basic to an understanding of history.

Marrou's statement also suggests that inherent in the discussion of purpose and meaning in history is the concept of communication, the idea of a dialogue between the historian and his environment as sources and resources of historical knowledge. Language and communication, as necessary elements for the maintenance, transmission, and perpetuation of human culture, are not only important indices of the sociocultural conditions of society, but are also the means of discovering, interpreting, and manipulating their effects in explaining contemporary theories of man's condition. Since both history and communication are necessary components for the construction of man's reality, an understanding of their relationship may be an important prerequisite for the development of theories on man and society. Specifically, this chapter is an attempt to outline some ideas about a humanistic theory of history and communication.

Experience, Knowledge, and History

Although problems of historical explanation were not extensively argued until the nineteenth century, signs of a modern approach to history can be detected as early as the seventeenth century, when Giambattista Vico developed historical studies into a special field of scholarly inquiry. Prior to this time a number of writers whose interests in history had led them to speculation about its nature and importance in the realm of human knowledge had followed St. Augustine's philosophical lead. *The City of God* had rejected theories of the cyclical nature of history and stressed a philosophy of Christian salvation based upon the Scriptures and centered upon God. Vico's work, on the other hand, reflects a search for an empirical base in history, one knowable by man. In *The New Science,* his most influential book, Vico recognized the importance of studying the creations of man's mind and imagination, his laws and customs, his language, his mythologies and religions, to help determine the existence of a universal law of history. Explaining his philological method, Vico argued that etymologies of language will

> tell us the histories of the things signified by the words, beginning with their original and proper meanings and pursuing the natural progress of their metaphors according to the order of the ideas, on which the history of languages must proceed. (35, p. 94)

In addition, his solution to the problem of understanding, that the "mental vocabulary of human social things, which are the same in substance as felt by all nations, but diversely expressed in language according to their diverse manifestations" (35, p. 94) supplies the historian with an argument for the generality of human thinking and experience that enables man to discover those elements of the past that were created by other men. More specifically, in his principle of *verum factum,* Vico stated: "The world of civil society has certainly been made by men, and that its principles are therefore to be found within the modifications of our own human mind. . . . Since men had made it [the civil world], men could hope to know. . . ." (35, p. 85)

Vico's observations were a reaction to René Descartes' criticism of historical explanations, which reflected the preoccupation of Cartesian thinkers with problems of science and mathematics. Vico, on the other hand, was convinced that a system of universal principles could be developed from what had been created by men, and from what could be found within the limits of the human mind. He shifted his attention from the exploration of natural or physical phenomena in the world to a quest for a comprehensive understanding of man as a symbol user and creator of the true and knowable in the world. Underlying his recognition of a unifying character of social change and of the simultaneous development of nations was a philosophy of history that outlined the duality of language, or words, as exterior and interior realities of man.

Disagreements about the nature and purpose of history became more obvious in the methodological and theoretical disputes of the nineteenth and twentieth centuries. While the positivists emphasized the appropriateness of a universal, scientific approach to all areas of human knowledge, the idealists disagreed with them over the nature of historical understanding and claimed that historical explanations needed a frame of reference different from that of natural phenomena. This dualism found its appropriate expression in the words *Naturwissenschaften* and *Geisteswissenschaften,* which became synonymous with the categorization of scientific and historical thinking.(2; 3; 13; 14; 18; 23; 36; 37) At the center of the controversy lie problems of historical understanding, questions of historical facts, and notions of objectivity in historical explanations which are also crucial considerations in the development of a critical theory of history and communication.

Communication and History

Communication is a basic life function. Man, in his communication with others, engages in the processing of data and information, which are needed for the maintenance of his physical and spiritual conditions. (34, pp. 28–30) History represents man's concern with the interior and exterior condition of his being; it is limited by his ability to communicate, and it provides a bridge between the nowness of his experience and past and future actions. Man therefore engages in the processing of historical matter upon which he must rely for everyday information about his physical and social environment. Based upon his understanding of communication with others, man forms a concept of his *Umwelt* that will affect his present and future position in the community.

In making judgments and in formulating decisions about his own needs and those of his environment, man is restricted by the verbal and nonverbal symbol systems of his social and cultural habitat. History consists of the interpretation of objects and events and the description of their existence in terms of their spatial and temporal relationships to the interpreter. Interpretation and description, however, occur in the present, because man is in the present. As Frederick Jackson Turner stated, the aim of history is "to know the elements of the present day by understanding what came into the present from the past." (33, p. 200)

History has also been described in a more dramatic way as the sole product of the historian. Michael Oakeshott claimed that "history is the historian's experience. It is 'made' by nobody save the historian: to write history is the only way of making it." (28, p. 99) This implies not only that the historian's sphere of communication provides the dimensions for historical analysis, but that man's experience is the key to history and that only man can make history. In this respect, his theory of history is related to "inside" and "outside" events, as used by R. G. Collingwood to distinguish man's external movements from his internal thoughts or ideas. Collingwood acknowledged that the historian is "never concerned with either of these to the exclusion of the other." (10, p. 213) He failed to realize, however, that through the process of internalization, thoughts and external actions merge into historical interpretations in a spatial sense, by becoming inside events for the historian, and in a temporal sense, by being reduced to explanatory statements. Thus even the outside of an event is composed of these external and internal conditions (e.g., individuals, groups, or societies and their organizations) and the respective social and cultural disposition of the historian.

While the former aspects compose the raw material or data of historical explanations, the uses made by the latter of this data constitute the historical information offered by a historian. Although both are closely related, in a manner not unlike that of data and information in a communication system, they fulfill specific roles: historical data are the unorganized matter needed for the processing of historical information in the decision-making process of man as a historical being. In this sense, words and other symbolic languages, for instance, can be organized into information that constitutes a meaningful interpretation of a historical event. Both historical data and historical information merge in the process of communication, to form a historical explanation that is the function of the historian and those external conditions that help shape his point of view.

This means, in effect, that the development of a philosophy of history is based not upon what really happened, to use von Ranke's phrase, but upon the historian's interpretation of what happened. Subjective aspects of reality were described by Ortega y Gasset, who observed that reality is synonymous with the "point of view to which each of us has been inescapably assigned in the universe." On another occasion he said, "Each man has a mission of truth. My eye has its unique place: the part of reality that my eye sees is seen by no other eye." [24, p. 113] Although Ortega's argument suggests the generally acceptable idea of an impossible state of perfect communication, it neglects to discuss communication as a social phenomenon based upon a common symbol system and defined in terms of process and change.

History and the Nature of Man

Historical understanding rests partly upon the historian's concept of reality, but also upon the extent to which symbols and their meanings are commonly shared. Communication as a social process and history as a social and cultural experience are shared by individuals in their respective communities: they are both forms of social expression; they are interpretations of life as these evolve from social interaction of men; and they are neither conceived nor perpetuated *in vacuo,* but come about through reactions with and to others. It is this closeness of history to the existence of man and his engagement in the historical process that are central to Wilhelm Dilthey's philosophy of history. William Kluback, in discussing Dilthey's thought, says:

Man, by nature, had to express himself. Those expressions that were recorded, formed the universal historical stream. This stream became man's cultural environment, and it helped to shape his further thoughts. Life expression thus not only determined the future course of history, but was in turn molded by the past course of history. Man engaged, then, in a continual process of taking from the stream of history, refining the contents in terms of his own interests, and giving the refined product back to the stream. In the process he developed his own nature more fully; he also gradually moved history in the direction of the realization of his own nature. History was thus slowly evolving toward a self-realization. (22, p. 57)

According to Kluback, Dilthey's method for studying the history of ideas is as follows:

First of all, the student had to enter into a like mind in the past by a process of intuition. He had to re-create in his imagination, by a 'reflective creative act,' the life situation which gave rise to the specific ideas and expressions of the laws of the human mind. Universal knowledge of past history was, therefore, possible. (22, p. 69)

It is also important to consider in this connection that the communication of ideas throughout history, once it has been removed from its sources and returned to what Dilthey called the historical stream, has become an independent force that enters the social and cultural realm of society through processes of interaction described by Berger and Luckman as externalization, objectivation, and internalization. (4, p. 129) Dilthey also spoke of the "objective mind," a concept used earlier by Hegel, as a form in which commonly held ideas have objectified themselves and have become the basis for understanding oneself and others. He said that "the past is a permanently enduring present for us," (16, p. 120) and emphasized an empathic approach to historical understanding by pointing out that "every significant conversation demands that the expression of the speaker should be placed into an inner context which is not given in his words." (16, pp. 77–78) Man as a historical being is "determined by his place in time and space and his position in the interaction of cultural systems and commmunities." (16, p. 79) To give a true account of societal or individual history, the historian must "understand the whole life of an individual as it expresses itself at a certain time and place." (16, p. 79) Since life, experience of life, and *Geisteswissenschaft* are related, Dilthey argues that the latter must be based upon the "becoming aware of a mental state in its totality and the rediscovering of it by empathy." (16, p. 79)

Marrou made a similar point when he asked:

How can we understand unless we have that attitude of mind which makes us connatural with others? It is this that enables us to feel their passions and re-conceive their ideas in the very light in which they were experienced —in short, it permits us to commune with them. Even the word 'sympathy' is insufficient in this respect. Between the historian and his object a friend-ship must be formed, or how else can the historian understand? [26, p. 105]

He also points out that "critical spirit and sympathy are not inherently contradictory." And he describes the contribution of both aspects as a "collective effort" in which sympathy becomes the "source and condition of understanding," while criticism "demolishes the provisional edifice of imperfect knowledge." [26, p. 105]

History and Empathy

The existence of empathy and its usefulness in historical research has been widely recognized. As a representative of positivism, Carl Hempel, [17, p. 121] for example, speaks of empathy as "essentially a heuris-tic device" and not an explanation in itself, and he argues that "what counts, is the soundness of the general hypotheses involved, no matter whether they were suggested by empathy, or by a strictly behavioristic procedure." The empathic quality of historical inquiries may, indeed, be considered consistent with a humanistic discipline that develops general propositions to aid man in the construction of his reality. In this sense, the dialogical approach of the historian, provided by the presence of historical data and his existential curiosity, requires an attitude of intense interest in and compassion for an object that may well yield an explanation of the contemporary dilemma of man.

History per se is the involvement of man in his social and cultural com-munity; in a way, he can be sympathetic or empathic only in the explana-tion of his own existence. Hence, the construction of a historical frame-work that fits the requirements of his subjective reality always rests upon the identification and selection of relevant or significant historical factors; in other words, man's perception of historical data and their organization into historical information occurs in the context of other social and cul-tural constructs, which help define relevancy or significance of facts.

Concepts of Historical Selection

The process of selection was emphasized by Lewis Namier, who de-scribed the function of the historian as:

akin to that of the painter and not of the photographic camera: to dis-cover and set forth, to single out and stress that which is of the nature of the thing, and not to reproduce indiscriminately all that meets the eye. . . . History is therefore necessarily subjective and individual, conditioned by the interest and vision of the historian. [33, p. 379]

His suggestions of subjectivity raise the question of the nature of historical facts or data, since these concepts have the ring of stability and reliance that are ordinarily associated with the world of objective scientific study. When Carl Becker observed some years ago that the "facts of history come in the end to seem something solid, something substantial like physical mattter . . . something possessing definite shape, and clear persistent outline . . . ," [32, p. 42] he related the ease with which historians and others have come to think of facts since the rise of scientific and technological thinking in the nineteenth century. Since then society has begun to share and perpetuate the image of solid and permanent fact in the Western world.

The questionable practice of worshiping facts has been described from the point of view of a professional communicator in Claud Cockburn's autobiography.

> To hear people talking about the facts you would think that they lay about like pieces of gold ore in the Yukon days, waiting to be picked up—arduously, it is true, but still definitely and visible—by the strenuous prospectors whose subsequent problem was only how to get them to market. Such a view is dangerously naive. There are no such facts. Or if there are, they are meaningless and entirely ineffective; might in fact just as well not be lying about at all until the prospector—the journalist—puts them into relation with other facts, presents them, in fact, and then they become as much a part of a pattern created by him as if he were writing a novel. In that sense, all stories are written backward—they are supposed to begin with the facts and develop from there, but in reality they begin with a journalist's point of view, a conception, and it is the point of view from which the facts are subsequently organized. [6, p. 252]

In a similar vein, Edward H. Carr spoke of the impossibility for facts to "exist in a pure form: they are always refracted through the mind of the recorder," [5, p. 24] and Becker pointed out that the historian can only deal directly with "a statement about the event. He deals, in short, not with the event, but with a statement which affirms the fact that the event occurred." [32, p. 47] In the final analysis, the historian always deals with an affirmation: "an affirmation of the fact that something is true." [32, p. 47]

Historical Assumptions

These observations and similar ones found throughout historical literature are quite correct in assuming the subjective character of man's perception of his existence (his point of view), but they do not adequately explain that man's reality is also objective. Man did not create the historical facts or data upon which he builds his world, but adopted, inherited, or learned them through processes of socialization; they function without his presence, without his using them; they are, in this case, external phenomena. It is the process of communication that reveals the subjective nature of historical explanation, and the idea of change that affects perception of the relevance or significance of historical facts. Collingwood observed that the "actual object of historical thinking is an object which is not 'given' but perpetually in process of being given." [9, p. 44] A philosophy of history can "only be a philosophical reflection on the historian's effort to attain truth, not on a truth which has not been attained." [9, p. 44]

In this context, the problem of historical facts raises the question of historical judgment, which is not more and not less than the question of demonstrating historical truth. As David Fischer remarked, the historian is really faced with the dilemma that "every true statement must be thrice true. It must be true to its evidence, true to itself, and true to other historical truths with which it is colligated." [19, p. 40] The historian must establish a logical consistency not only in terms of the historical explanation, but also in terms of its relation to other explanations, despite the fact that man cannot know the historical world any more than he can know the present without bias, prejudice, or human error. To attain historical truth means to conceptualize and to articulate historical information that will be able to stand the test of its assumptions. It involves historical judgment, which is defined as the skill of the historian to verbalize his insights or knowledge about past events, to create a kind of self-awareness, and to add to the understanding of the present.

Historical judgment, then, is not a scientific method for testing the actual, but a skillful attempt to communicate about the possible and about what seems relevant to an explanation of man's condition. The result is a short-lived truth, time bound and subject to the process of social and cultural changes. In this respect, history must be written continuously, as it becomes the basis for the creation of man's subjective-objective reality. Raymond Aron summarized the idea by saying that

> at a given moment in time, an individual reflects upon his adventure, a collectivity upon its past, humanity upon its evolution: thus are born respectively autobiography, individual history, universal history. [26, p. 214]

All of them, one must add, are states of becoming.

In summary, history, as a study of man, does not determine the relationship of history to man, but presupposes that the relationship exists; communication, as the study of an existential phenomenon, defines the relationship. Both history and communication, as humanistic approaches to the study of man, contribute to the understanding of historical facts and the construction of reality—as functions of the subjective-objective quality of historical information or events. The methodology of historical explanation—not unlike the range of communication theories—varies from a position of idealism, with its foundation in the *Geisteswissenschaften,* to a scientific position based on the *Naturwissenschaften,* with a single logic of explanation for historical and natural phenomena.

Historical inquiries are evaluations of content and form in human communication, within the limitations of contemporary symbol systems. Historians as collectors, translators, and interpreters of historical facts are restricted in their judgments by assumptions based on the availability and accessibility of *objets d'histoire.* They also lack knowledge of the motives and purposes of the individuals and societies who ultimately become history makers. Historians are also necessarily removed from an understanding of the limitations of the form and content of the historical statements with which they have to work, and at times fail to reflect the subjective nature of their own historical reconstructions. History and communication define the limits of man's reality; they also contribute to an understanding of his existential condition.

REFERENCES AND SUGGESTED READINGS

1. Aron, Raymond, *Introduction to the Philosophy of History.* Boston: Beacon Press, 1961.
2. Berdyaev, Nikolai, *Destiny of Man.* London: Centenary, 1937.
3. Berdyaev, Nikolai, *Meaning of History.* London: Centenary, 1936.
4. Berger, Peter L., and Thomas Luckmann, *The Social Construction of Reality.* New York: Doubleday, 1966.
5. Carr, Edward H., *What is History?* New York: Knopf, 1964.
6. Cockburn, Claud, *A Discord of Trumpets.* New York: Simon & Schuster, 1956.
7. Cohen, Morris R., *Reason and Nature.* New York: Harcourt, Brace, 1931.
8. Collingwood, Robin G., *An Essay on Metaphysics.* Oxford: Clarendon, 1940.
9. Collingwood, Robin G., *Essays in the Philosophy of History,* ed. by William Debbins. Austin: University of Texas Press, 1965.
10. Collingwood, Robin G., *The Idea of History.* Oxford: Clarendon, 1946.
11. Croce, Benedetto, *History as the Story of Liberty.* London: Allen and Unwin, 1941.
12. Croce, Benedetto, *History—Its Theory and Practice.* New York: Russell and Russell, 1921.
13. Dante, Arthur, *Analytical Philosophy of History.* Cambridge, England: Cambridge University Press, 1965.
14. D'Arcy, M. C., *The Meaning and Matter of History.* New York: Farrar and Straus, 1959.
15. Dilthey, Wilhelm, *The Essence of Philosophy.* Chapel Hill: University of North Carolina Press, 1954.
16. Dilthey, Wilhelm, *Meaning in History: W. Dilthey's Thought on History and Society,* ed. by H. P. Rickman. London: Allen and Unwin, 1961.
17. Dray, William H., *Laws and Explanations in History.* London: Oxford University Press, 1957.
18. Dray, William H., *Philosophy of History.* Englewood Cliffs, N.J.: Prentice-Hall, 1964.
19. Fischer, David H., *Historian's Fallacies.* New York: Harper & Row, 1970.

20. Hempel, Carl G., "Explanation in Science and in History," in *Frontiers of Science and Philosophy,* ed. by R. G. Colodny. Pittsburgh: University of Pittsburgh Press, 1962.

21. Hempel, Carl G., "The Function of General Laws in History," in *Theories of History,* ed. by P. Gardiner. New York: Free Press, 1959.

22. Kluback, William, *Wilhelm Dilthey's Philosophy of History.* New York: Columbia University Press, 1956.

23. Löwith, Karl, *The Meaning of History.* Chicago: University of Chicago Press, 1949.

24. Lukacs, John, *Historical Consciousness or the Remembered Past.* New York: Harper & Row, 1968.

25. Mandelbaum, Maurice, *The Problem of Historical Knowledge.* New York: Harper & Row, 1967.

26. Marrou, Henri-Irénée, *The Meaning of History.* Baltimore: Helicon, 1966.

27. Nash, Ronald H., *Ideas of History,* 2 vols. New York: Dutton, 1969.

28. Oakeshott, Michael, *Experience and Its Modes.* Cambridge, England: Cambridge University Press, 1933.

29. Popper, Karl, *The Logic of Scientific Discovery.* New York: Basic Books, 1959.

30. Popper, Karl, *The Poverty of Historicism.* Boston: Beacon Press, 1957.

31. Rahv, Philip, *Literature and the Sixth Sense.* Boston: Houghton Mifflin, 1969.

32. Snyder, Phil L., *Detachment and the Writing of History: Essays and Letters of Carl L. Becker.* Ithaca, N.Y.: Cornell University Press, 1958.

33. Stern, Fritz, ed., *The Varieties of History.* New York: Meridian Books, 1956.

34. Thayer, Lee, *Communication and Communication Systems.* Homewood, Ill.: Irwin, 1968.

35. Vico, Giambattista, *The New Science of Giambattista Vico,* trans. by Thomas G. Bergin and Max H. Fisch. Ithaca, N.Y.: Cornell University Press, 1948.

36. Walsh, W. H., *An Introduction to the Philosophy of History.* London: Hutchinson, 1958.

37. White, M. G., *Foundations of Historical Knowledge.* New York: Harper & Row, 1965.

Dr. Donald K. Darnell is Professor of Communication and Theatre at the University of Colorado. He has authored numerous articles and papers on communication and information theory. The most recent of those is a chapter, "Information Theory," in *Communication Concepts and Processes,* edited by Joseph A. DeVito.

9

INFORMATION THEORY: AN APPROACH TO HUMAN COMMUNICATION

DONALD K. DARNELL

INFORMATION theory began in several places at different times. Samuel F. B. Morse, for instance, met and solved some of the problems of signal transmission. He recognized that there is more than one way to transmit a message and that some ways are more efficient than others. The story goes that he counted pieces of type in a printer's type box (which, of course, was an index of the relative frequency of use of the different letters) and assigned short signals to frequent letters and longer signals to less frequent ones. The coding system which he thus devised proved to be a satisfactory approximation of the ideal coding system.[7, p. 25]

Mathematicians from around the world were involved at one time and another with the problems of telegraphic communication and contributed to the development of information theory. But the credits for full formalization usually are assigned to Norbert Wiener [11] and Claude E. Shannon.[8] Both men were stimulated by technical problems and requirements for communication that arose during World War II, which accounts for their simultaneous publications. Although Wiener and Shannon solved essentially the same problems (from slightly different points of view),[7, p. 42] it is most commonly Shannon's work that is referred to by the term *information theory*. It is the one I am most familiar with, and it is Shannon's paper, later published in a book by the same title with an explanatory paper by Warren Weaver,[9] that is the primary source for what follows.

It is important to keep in mind that Shannon, an engineer, conceived of a communication system in mechanistic terms. He says that a communication system consists of essentially five parts: an *information source,* a

156

transmitter, a *channel,* a *receiver,* and a *destination.*[9, pp. 4-6] In discussing these, he quietly introduced four additional components of the system: a message, the transmitted signal, the received signal, and a noise source. The information source is that which "produces a message or sequence of messages to be communicated to the receiving terminal." The transmitter is that which "operates on the message in some way to produce a signal suitable for transmission over the channel." The channel is "merely the medium used to transmit the signal from transmitter to receiver." (It is in contrast to this definition that McLuhan's assertion "the medium is the message" takes on its great significance.) [6, pp. 23ff.] "The receiver ordinarily performs the inverse operation of that done by the transmitter, reconstructing the message from the signal. "The destination is the person (or thing) for whom the message is intended." The important thing to remember about the message is that it represents a choice or sequence of choices made by the source. Although the message may take any form, it is always, from Shannon's point of view, a thing chosen from a set or ensemble of things, and it is from that proposition that the information-theory concept of information derives. Information contained in a signal is a function of the ensemble from which it was chosen and the freedom of choice of the chooser. This very fundamental idea can be encoded in quite a different way.

> What one does is only one
> Of the several things he might have done.
> One must know the things rejected
> To appreciate the one selected.

The transmitted signal may take a form different from that of the original message, and often does. What is critical here is that for the system to operate effectively, the transmitter must be able to construct within the limits of the channel as many *different* signals as the source has *potential* messages to transmit. For efficient operation, the transmitter must use short (i.e., inexpensive) signals for the frequent messages, and may use longer (i.e., expensive) ones for infrequent messages.

The received signal does not always correspond to the transmitted signal, due to the operation of a *noise source.* A noise source is, simply, anything that affects the signal in transit which prevents the received signal from being identical with the transmitted signal. It is important, of course, that the destination be able to reconstruct the message formulated by the information source. If it is unable to reconstruct the message, to designate which alternative has been chosen by the source due to inadequate operation of the transmitter, channel, or receiver, or due to the interference of a noise source then the system fails outright or there is equivocation—

uncertainty about the message sent even though the message received is known.

The central concern of information theory can now be specified. It is: how to send a message through a communication system having a source with certain characteristics and a channel with certain characteristics, doing this with maximum efficiency and a tolerable level of error or equivocation in the presence of noise.

The problems suggested by the statement above were solved. Shannon demonstrated that it is possible to encode messages in such a way as to make the probability of error or the amount of equivocation arbitrarily small, even in the presence of noise, and to obtain optimal efficiency for a given level of noise and a given level of tolerable error. In one sense then, the theory is obsolete, for the technical transmission problem it has solved no longer exists. In another sense, the theory was never quite applicable to human communication systems, since it made some assumptions that are not exactly tenable for human systems. It also seems that people have a rather high tolerance for error in ordinary day-to-day communication, and little concern for efficiency. So, there is some legitimacy to the point of view that information theory is not "where it's at"—is not the central concern of today's study of communication. I would even be inclined to say that the mechanistic view of communication suggested so far by this description has caused two problems for every one it has solved. But there is more to it than that. Information theory, in spite of its mechanistic view and mathematical precision, contains some highly creative ideas and provides a foundation from which a creative person can leap to new insights about human communication.

INFORMATION

One common misunderstanding about information theory is related to the fact that it is not concerned with information at all—in the ordinary sense. Information theory is directly concerned with only the technical problem of getting symbols or signals from one place to another without distortion. It does not relate directly to the interpretation of those symbols. This has been a severe disappointment to many people and may be the primary reason for the sneers that sometimes appear when information theory is mentioned. This is not to say, however, that the technical concept of information is useless to the nonengineer. The technical, mathematical concept of information corresponds to *surprise* and *uncertainty*. It is a mathematical function of the number of things a system (an information source, for instance) can do and of the probabilities of occurrence of those different possibilities. It is the inverse of *predictability*. It is the freedom of choice of the source. Information is what you *don't* know about what is going to happen next.

To be more precise, the information value of a particular signal is the logarithm of the reciprocal of the probability of that signal's occurrence (log $1/p$). (The reciprocal is used simply to make the value positive, as the logarithm of a fraction is negative.) To describe the output of a particular source, the mean or average information value of its output signals is used. That is, if one computes the information value of each of the different things a source could do, multiplies each of those values by the probability that it will be transmitted, and adds the products together, that sum is the average information value of a particular source's output. The ordinary way of expressing these operations mathematically is $-\Sigma p_i$ log p_i. (By using the minus sign in front of the formula one gets rid of that pesky reciprocal.)

Even more precisely, information theory uses the logarithm to the base two which serves to define the unit of measurement. If there are two things a source can do, and they are equally probable, that source will transmit each time and on the average one *bit* of information per transmission. *Bit,* incidentally, is short for *binary digit.* If a source is restricted to the use of binary digits, the maximum information it can transmit is one bit per symbol. If a source is capable of transmitting N messages, but the transmitter or channel is limited to the use of binary digits (or on-off states), $\log_2 N$ digits will be sufficient to transmit each of those messages. So, the use of the base 2 logarithm and the technical term bit, though confusing to those not familiar with them, is not arbitrary. It fits right into a computer's or an electrical engineer's way of thinking. It will fit right into your thinking, too, if you will think of communication as a game of twenty questions and consider how many yes-no questions you would have to ask in order to identify the unknown object. Say, for example, you are trying to guess which numbers a friend is thinking of between 1 and 10. If your friend is just as likely to be thinking of one number as another and if you are careful to ask the optimal question (one that divides the remaining possibilities in half), you will require, on the average, $\log_2$ 10 or 3.322 questions to find out what he is thinking. Or, for example, if you are turning over cards one by one from a shuffled deck of ordinary playing cards, the first card transmits 5.7 bits ($\log_2$ 52) of information. The next card gives a little less information (because there are fewer things that can happen). The twenty-first card gives you 5 bits ($\log_2$ of the 32 remaining possibilities), and the last card gives you zero information, for you know what it must be before it has been turned. For any set of alternatives, whatever their probabilities, the general formula given above specifies the average information revealed (transmitted) by each outcome of the system.

This technical concept of information was crucial to the solution of the technical problems of symbol transmission through noisy channels. It might have attracted more general interest had it been called a measure of *interest,* which it more nearly is. But, Shannon assumed that an information source makes choices from a set of alternatives and that the destination knows in advance the alternatives and the restraints under which the source makes its choices. From that he reasoned that the uncertainty of the receiver-destination is equal to the freedom-of-choice of the source, that the receipt of the message in an ideal system informs the destination of the source's choice and eliminates the destination's uncertainty; and therefore, the information contained in the message is equal to the freedom-of-choice of the source and the uncertainty of the destination. The assumption seems reasonable for electronic communication systems, and the logic is impeccable. A human destination, though, almost never knows exactly the choice available to a human source (in terms of the alternatives from which he chooses and the restraints under which he operates), so the three values are not equal for human communication systems. Furthermore, human beings place on messages values related to another large set of variables—messages mean more to human beings than their mere occurrance. Nevertheless, the technical concept—if we can avoid getting burned by the short circuit between two kinds of information—can be very stimulating in the analysis of human behavior.

For example, I submit that human sources do make choices when they transmit messages. Human destinations attribute choices to others, and they respond to just those choices. I suggest that one can respond appropriately to another's message only if the choice(s) attributed approximates the choice(s) actually made. (Now reread the little jingle on page 157 and see if it makes a different kind of sense.) This point of view suggests that entirely too much emphasis has been placed on the form and style of messages (the outputs of communication systems) and not enough on the very human choices involved in the production of those messages; not enough on the alternatives that might have occurred, but did not; and not enough on the process of attributing choices to others, given their output and limited information about the restraints under which they operate. At this moment, I would even go so far as to say that the meaning of a message to its originator *is* the choice(s) he makes in constructing it, and the meaning of that message to another *is* the choice(s) he attributes to its originator. Communication occurs, therefore, to the extent that the attributed choice approximates the actual choice. (If that suggestion gets past your critical judgment, we have just succeeded in putting Humpty Dumpty [information] together again.)

The mathematical expression for information also seems to make precise a number of vague concepts that are commonly used in the description and analysis of human behavior. It has already been suggested that the mathematical expression may be used to define uncertainty. When one is attempting to predict the outcome of any system, his uncertainty approaches zero as the probability of a single outcome approaches unity. His uncertainty increases as a function of the number of different things that could happen, and reaches a maximum for any particular number of alternatives when any one is just as likely as any other to occur. These conditions are implied by the mathematical expression for information. The precision of such a definition should facilitate the manipulation of uncertainty in various contexts and the investigation of possible differences in one person's response, compared to another's, to different degrees of uncertainty. Ability to cope with uncertainty may well be the variable that separates men from boys, stable personalities from unstable personalities, officers from enlisted men, scholars from students, and executives from laborers; but I am uncertain as to which half of each dichotomy has the higher tolerance or the greater ability.

I have also suggested here that the mathematical expression for information defines the interest value of a stimulus. Man's very survival depends on paying attention to aspects of the environment that change. Constants can be ignored (if they are constant and they haven't killed us yet, they won't). I maintain that this explains why people are the most interesting beings on earth. They are capable of so many different kinds of behavior and they change from one to another with charming capriciousness.

The mathematical expression for information has been applied to the definition of *cognitive conflict*. By substituting relative response strength for *p* in the information formula, Berlyne [2] obtains a definition of conflict which significantly reduces the vagueness of his whole theoretical formulation. The same expression may also be used to measure decision difficulty or complexity of a choice. Since the very essence of being human seems to involve the ability to make choices among sets of alternatives (words, ice creams, potential mates, etc.), to be interested in some things and not in others, and to resolve conflict, this formula which seems so mathematical, so precise, so cold, may after all be one of the keys to man's understanding himself—if he only turns it the right way.

I want to discuss at some length two further applications of information. One involves a method of measuring language proficiency which has worked rather well. The other involves the American system of law, which could work better. These two examples will, hopefully, provide some support for the generalization I have just made.

An Application to Language Testing

Another common name for information uncertainty is *entropy*. The word is borrowed from thermodynamics and is used in information theory because of mathematical similarities between the two theories. As far as information theory is concerned, *entropy* is just another synonym for unpredictability. The testing procedure I am about to describe is called *cloz-entropy* (pronounced klo-zin'-tro-py, with the accent on "zin"). It is a combination of "cloze procedure" (a fill-in-the-blanks type of test instrument) [10] and information (entropy) analysis. The name is supposed to remind one of these antecedents. [4]

To construct a cloze test, one selects a sample of prose (or poetry) and replaces every nth word with a blank. A cloze item might look like this: I am describing a ———— of language proficiency. One then asks a number of people to fill in the missing word. In this case, one might get *test, measure, definition,* or other responses. Originally, for purposes of measuring the readability of the prose passage, a respondent was given a point for replacing the word that had been deleted, and nothing for any other response. For an entropy analysis, one counts up the frequency of each different response, divides that number by the total number of responses, and substitutes that relative frequency for p in the formula for information $(-\Sigma p_i \log_2 p_i)$. The value obtained reflects the number of different responses and their relative frequency of occurrence. The value may be called "the entropy of the blank," or a measure of the freedom of choice permitted by the context. Following this, one computes the difference between this entropy value (it is an average, you will recall) and the information value of each different response $(\log_2 1/p$ or $-\log_2 p)$ by subtracting the latter from the former. This difference value may be called a "compatibility score," as it is a measure of the degree to which a particular response stands out or fits into the array of responses obtained from the group.

For example, suppose the sample item, "I am describing a ———— of language proficiency," has been given to 100 people and 50 *test* responses, 25 *measure* responses, 20 *definition* responses, and 5 unique, or one-of-a-kind responses have been obtained. The average entropy value for the blank is approximately 1.80. A summary of the results might look like this:

Response	p	Information Value	Difference (D)
Test	.50	1.00	.80
Measure	.25	2.00	−.20
Definition	.20	2.32	−.52
Description	.01	6.64	−4.84
Thing	.01	6.64	−4.84
Something	.01	6.64	−4.84
View	.01	6.64	−4.84
Notion	.01	6.64	−4.84

One need not be concerned with the computations in detail. It is enough to point out that the D values reflect the strangeness of each response in relation to the total array of responses. The perfect correlation between the p values and the D values may bring up the question why the p values only were not used. The fact is that the D values would change for a particular p, if the array were to change. For example, if there were only two responses each with a p of .50, the D value would be zero for both, indicating that neither was any more unusual than the other.

Suppose now that one wanted to know if the one-hundred-and-first person fitted into this group. He would be given the same test item. If he gives any of the responses obtained from the criterion group, he would have a D score. If he gives a response that differs from any of these he would be assigned the same score as the unique responses (-4.84), which would suggest that he fits only as well as five members of the group in the example above. Across a number of such items, an individual would have to give a high-frequency answer rather consistently to accumulate a positive score. The magnitude and sign of his score would reflect how well he fits into the criterion group in relation to the linguistic choices reflected in the test.

This procedure was applied to groups whose native language was English, and a two-hundred-item test proved sensitive enough to detect differences between the language patterns of graduate and undergraduate students and between engineering and nonengineering students. The test was also given to 48 foreign students and showed that they, as a group, were significantly different from the 200 English-speaking students in their word choices, although a few of them accumulated positive scores across the two hundred items. (One of these turned out to be a Canadian whose native language was also English.)

A comparison of the results on the clozentropy test and the Test of English as a Foreign Language (TOEFL) showed the two to be quite comparable in reliability (both coefficients rounded out to .86); and the two correlated quite highly (.838) for the total group of foreign students. These results suggest that the two tests are measuring largely the same things, one about as well as the other, although their logical bases are quite different. The result seems reasonable if we assume that the English-speakers, who were all college students, had internalized the rules of language on which the TOEFL is based.

Theoretically, the clozentropy procedure could be used to assess the ability of a native English speaker to pass himself off as a foreign student speaking English, the ability of a White Anglo-Saxon Protestant to speak the argot of the black ghetto, or the ability of an English teacher to speak like an uneducated laborer, while the more traditional type of test, such as TOEFL, could assess only a person's ability to follow the rules of some prescriptive model of the language. The clozentropy procedure could be used to assess an individual's ability to adapt his language to different groups with whom he wants to communicate. The more traditional type of test assumes that such adaptation is not only unnecessary, but undesirable.

The conceptual heart of clozentropy procedure, both aspects of it, is derived from information theory. Cloze procedure amounts to introducing noise (by deletion) into a communication channel, and then determining the ability of a destination to reconstruct the message. The entropy analysis directly utilizes the mathematics of information theory to compute the degree of consensus among a group of destinations reconstructing the same noisy message, and the acceptability (compatibility) of an individual's reconstruction with that of the group. I am assuming, of course, that an individual who wants to communicate with a person or group through language would be advised to make choices that fall within the latitude of freedom of choice exercised by that person or group. Perhaps that assumption needs confirmation; but it is obviously true in extreme cases and would seem to be acceptable generally.

The mathematics of entropy analysis, as I have described it, would seem to be applicable to the analysis of any kind of normative behavior. It implies, for instance, that if one should walk into a group and observe that one-third of them have their hands over their ears, one-third have their hands over their mouths, and one-third have their hands over their eyes, one can assume that it is reasonably safe in this group to do any one of these things. However, if one keeps his hands in his pockets or waves them around, it is almost certain to attract the attention and the possible censure of the group. This model is also a good way of predicting the latitude of permissible variation in hair and dress style in specific groups or on specific occasions.

An Application to Decision-making Systems

The following application of information theory is quite beyond the scope of the original theory. It is purely hypothetical—that is, there are no empirical data to support the claims I am about to make and no precedents to cite. It simply illustrates that if one starts from a different point of view in analyzing a situation, one is likely to come up with a different conclusion. Not being a lawyer I am not inhibited by conventional notions of legality and justice. I choose to write about the legal system because it is a decision-making system that is reasonably familiar to almost anyone. Because the decisions made are often life-and-death decisions, they should be of concern to everyone, especially since less than half the people involved in these decisions are lawyers and judges.

A decision-making system (hereafter called a DMS) is established whenever and wherever there is an intolerable amount of uncertainty. A DMS is an uncertainty absorber, a means of establishing a single outcome when two or more outcomes are logically possible. If one is undecided about whether to spend his last dollar for beer or ice cream, he may flip a coin to absorb his uncertainty. If society is undecided about who should have custody of a child, or whether an individual is guilty or innocent of murder, the case may be consigned to a court of law which will act to absorb the uncertainty and render a more-or-less satisfactory decision. If we are undecided about who is the best man to run the country, we decide that issue through an election.

What is common to all these situations is that there are two or more options, and it is important that these be reduced to one so that we can act. The process of reducing alternatives to one is the process of making choices or decisions; information theory is a theory of choice making. It equates freedom of choice, information, and uncertainty with an ideal communication system. In these terms, with only a slight twist in logic, it can now be asserted that if a DMS's freedom of choice is less than the quantity of uncertainty to be absorbed in the situation to which it is assigned (due to bias or other extraneous influences or to the construction of the DMS), it cannot transmit a sufficient amount of information, cannot effectively absorb the uncertainty of the situation, although it may actually render a decision. For example, if one is trying to decide between three equally desirable alternatives (beer, ice cream, or chocolate), one cannot satisfactorily do so with a single flip of a coin, because the situation contains 1.57 bits of uncertainty and the coin is capable of transmitting only 1.00 bits of information per flip.

If one were able to obtain independent measures of the DMS's freedom of choice and the uncertainty of the situation, one could determine whether or not a particular DMS has the *capacity* to make a satisfactory decision in that situation. I cannot think of a method for measuring directly the freedom of choice of any DMS more realistic than the coin-flip example. We can, however, and do take a negative approach to the problem. When there is evidence that a particular DMS is biased, has a "vested interest" in the decision, is subject to political or economic pressure, we readily infer that it is incapable of making some decisions.

In spite of the methodological limitation, it still seems important that one of the necessary qualifications of a decision-making system is its capability to transmit information equal to (sufficient to absorb) the uncertainty in the situation in which it is expected to function.

Given that formulation, one can assess the qualification of a DMS in terms of limitations on information-transmission capacity. Before I go into that, however, I shall discuss justice in these mathematical terms. It can be said that a DMS capable of rendering justice must be capable of transmitting, on the average, maximum information. That means that for a just system, in every case, the a priori expected information value is at least $\log_2 N$ (where N is the number of alternatives from which the choice is made in each case). For binary decisions, such as are typically found in formal debate and in courts of law, this formulation implies that a just system must be able to transmit at least one bit of information with each decision.

There are two conditions that would cause an information source to transmit at less than the theoretical maximum average rate and, hence, two limitations on the adequacy of a DMS that should be considered. (1) If the probabilities of the alternatives from which the choice is to be made are not in any case equal (i.e., the decision maker is biased in favor of one of the alternatives prior to examination of the relevant evidence) or (2) if sequential choices are not independent, then a source (or DMS) must necessarily transmit information at a rate less than $\log_2 N$. If the capacity of a particular DMS is suspect because of either of these two limiting factors, a satisfactory DMS may be constructed by combining two or more decision-making components so as to create a system with an information-transmission capacity equal to, or greater than, $\log_2 N$ (e.g., the use of multiple sources, multiple judges, or a jury to increase the transmission rate). However, in such a case, if the k components do not operate independently, the system must necessarily transmit at a rate less than $k \log_2 N$. That is, if the behavior of the second component is in any way dependent upon the behavior of the first component, then the information transmitted by the second is to some extent redundant to that transmitted by the first, and the whole is less than the sum of the parts. Intercomponent dependency, then, is a third possible limitation on the adequacy of a DMS. If, because of bias, sequential dependency, or dependency among components of the system, or any combination of these, the total information capacity of a DMS is less than the amount of uncertainty in the situation, then the system is incapable of rendering a satisfactory decision. If the total capacity of a DMS is, on the average, less than $\log_2 N$, then that system is incapable of rendering justice in the long run.

According to this formulation, the ideal judge (DMS) (1) would have no vested interest in the particular decision and would be unaware of the past records of the advocates; (2) would be unencumbered by his past decisions (e.g., not be compelled to meet any quota of positive and negative decisions); and (3) would be uninfluenced by any other judgments rendered in the particular case (e.g., by the popular press). In courts of law, this ideal may be approximated. In other, less rigorous, systems, it probably is not.

This information-theory formulation seems to have led to some common-sense conclusions. Where then is its advantage? I see it this way. In situations where the ideal is unavailable or unattainable (i.e., at least one of the presumptions is untenable in absolute form), this mathematical formulation would make it possible to calculate the relative adequacy of a particular DMS and to choose the better of a set of alternative systems, though admittedly all are imperfect. Such computations should also make it possible to show that a given DMS is entirely adequate for a given decision task, although it is composed of imperfect components. The procedure of such a demonstration would involve the computation of information-transmission-absorption capacity for the DMS, given whatever estimates of bias and dependency seem plausible. If that value is greater than the maximum uncertainty of the decision situation, then that DMS is generally adequate. If the DMS's capacity is less than the potential maximum uncertainty of the situation, then that capacity figure indicates the level of uncertainty that must be achieved by other means (e.g., through argument) for that DMS to render a satisfactory decision.

From a consideration of the information transmitted by each of the possible decisions of a DMS, it would be possible to conclude that certain decision outcomes would satisfactorily resolve the uncertainty of the situation, but others would not. For example, a judge who renders a decision counter to his presumed bias might expect the rightness of his decision to go unquestioned, but a decision which parallels the presumed bias of the DMS might be entirely unconvincing. It is this same principle, I contend, that lends greater credence to testimony from a "reluctant witness" than to the same testimony from one whose own ends are obviously served by it.

I have mentioned before the possibility of constructing an adequate DMS out of imperfect components. I now contend that this is precisely the intent of the American jury-trial system. Given that judges (although trained in law and well-practiced in objectivity) are nevertheless human, and may not therefore be capable of rendering justice in all instances, our system provides for an alternative DMS. This system, which was presumably designed without the benefits of information theory, allows for a large margin of error. That is, the typical decision between guilty and not-guilty would require a one-bit absorption capacity for satisfactory decisions to be made. A twelve-man jury would, theoretically, be capable of transmitting twelve bits of information with a unanimous decision—a considerable safety factor. Given that advocates for the defense and prosecution are allowed to challenge and eliminate jurors suspected of bias, and that jurors are typically not called upon to make a succession of related judgments, the system should be entirely adequate. However, in the American jury-trial system, jurors do not make their judgments independently, but are permitted to arrive at their collective decision through group deliberation. Given, for instance, the effects of interpersonal influence investigated by Asch, there is reason to believe that some juries are less capable of rendering a satisfactory decision than a single, qualified judge. Given, for instance, a jury composed of one severely biased and articulate juror and eleven acquiescent others, one could expect to obtain less than one bit of information from even a unanimous decision of such a group. The general finding by Asch and others that the majority effect grows stronger as the clarity of the situation diminishes, suggests that when judgments are rendered dependently, a jury has less decision capacity (provides less information) as the decision grows more difficult. Although an 1100 percent safety factor would seem to be ample, there are at least some situations in which it is not sufficient. (Recently, the charges against the leader of the Black Panthers were dismissed on exactly those grounds—that a jury adequate to decide the case could not be constituted.) If jurors were required to render their decisions independently, a smaller number, or a less-than-unanimous decision would (according to this view) be more satisfactory in every case than the present system. The principle that independent data units provide more information than dependent data units is clearly recognized in statistics. It is apparently not recognized in the American legal system, or is considered of less significance than the other distorting influences.

CONCLUSIONS

In this chapter it was not my intention to popularize information theory —to explain its postulates, theorems, and conceptual structure in ordinary language. I may have done that accidentally, but I suggest that *Symbols, Signals and Noise,*[7] two earlier attempts of mine,[3, 5] or any of a half-dozen other discourses on the subject be read for a more thorough understanding. What I have attempted to do here is point out some limitations of information theory as it applies to human communication; to give some justification for the feeling of disappointment that many feel toward it; and to express my excitement at the potential I see in some of the concepts of information theory when they are "creatively misapplied."

The tentative conclusion I have reached from my study of information theory and my observation of men communicating, for what it's worth, may be expressed as follows:

What Am I Doing?

No form, no style, no rule
Can determine the behavior of any but a fool,
For all men have access to choice
And wise men use it.
What fool I, then, to look for
Rules and tools to manipulate fools
I will choose to ignore dogmatic voices;
There is more to be learned from wise men's choices.

REFERENCES AND SUGGESTED READINGS

1. Asch, S. E., "Effects of Group Pressure upon the Modification and Distortion of Judgments," in *Dimensions in Communication,* ed. by James H. Campbell and Hal W. Hepler. Belmont, Calif.: Wadsworth, 1965.
2. Berlyne, D. E., *Conflict, Arousal and Curiosity.* New York: McGraw-Hill, 1960.
3. Broadhurst, Allan R., and Donald K. Darnell, "Introduction to Cybernetics and Information Theory," *Quarterly Journal of Speech,* Vol. 51, 1965.
4. Darnell, Donald K., "Clozentropy: A Procedure for Testing English Language Proficiency of Foreign Students," *Speech Monographs,* Vol. 37, 1970.
5. Darnell, Donald K., "Information Theory," in *Communication Concepts and Processes,* ed. by Joseph A. DeVito. Englewood Cliffs, N.J.: Prentice-Hall, 1971.
6. McLuhan, Marshall, *Understanding Media: The Extensions of Man.* New York: McGraw-Hill, 1964.
7. Pierce, J. R., *Symbols, Signals, and Noise.* New York: Harper & Row, Torchbooks, 1961.
8. Shannon, Claude E., "The Mathematical Theory of Communication," *Bell System Technical Journal,* 1948.
9. Shannon, Claude E., and Warren Weaver, *The Mathematical Theory of Communication.* Urbana: University of Illinois Press, 1949.
10. Taylor, Wilson L., " 'Cloze Procedure': A New Tool for Measuring Readability," *Journalism Quarterly,* Vol. 30, 1954.
11. Wiener, Norbert, *Cybernetics.* New York: Wiley, 1948.

Dr. James W. Markham, prior to his untimely death, was
Professor of International Communication at the University of
Iowa. He has contributed widely in the area of international
communication, participating in symposia in South America,
Sweden, and Yugoslavia, and has authored numerous journal
articles, monographs, and books. Dr. Markham's most recent
major works include *Voices of the Red Giants,* which was
awarded the Kappa Tau Alpha national literary prize, and
International Communication as a Field of Study.

10

INTERNATIONAL BEHAVIOR: AN APPROACH TO HUMAN COMMUNICATION

JAMES W. MARKHAM

INTRODUCTION

THE STUDY of international relations goes back only about fifty years.
The newer behavioral-science approach to the study of international problems is a development of the past ten or fifteen years. The notion that
communication has something to do with international politics and cultural
relationships is also comparatively new, and not many scholars have specialized in communication processes at the international and cross-cultural
level. This chapter will (1) examine concepts of and approaches to the
study of international communication; (2) analyze aspects of international
behavior from a communication point of view; and (3) relate 1 and
2 above to research in international, cross-cultural, and comparative
communication.

THE STUDY OF INTERNATIONAL BEHAVIOR

When one considers that almost all political and social behavior involves communication of some sort,[30; 77, p. 11] it is surprising that the
communication process as a factor in international behavior has only recently received attention. Still, progress has been made, and today there
are a number of approaches to the study of international and comparative
communication, each of which provides a unique perspective. One approach focuses on the role and uses of communication in the new diplomacy, stressing communication as influence exerted by individuals, groups,

and governments on public opinion and on the foreign-policy decisions of nations. Another approach is the study of international political communication, which is closely related to public diplomacy. Unlike the diplomatic approach, political communication focuses on the professional techniques of international persuasion or on interpersonal and mass communication as factors facilitating change in transitional and underdeveloped societies that seek to develop political participation and identity. Another perspective is provided by the behavioral approach of the social psychologist, who seeks to understand international relations in terms of a theory of individual and group behavior. There is also the communication and mass-communication approach developed in journalism—communication and speech which emphasizes the viewpoint of the professional writer, journalist, and broadcaster and offers an integration of the frameworks of the other approaches. [44, p. iv] This approach draws heavily upon the humanities and the social sciences in an effort to explain international activity.

A Communication Approach

A communication and mass-communication approach requires a knowledge of the structures and functions performed by human communication and the mass media. It sees mass communication as a new force in the world, possessing potential for man's intellectual, moral, and material advancement, and for improved relations among nations and peoples.

Communication has been described as the web of human society and has come to be looked upon as a major cohesive element in the international behavior of states. Students of international politics once defined foreign policy as primarily the response of a state to external events and conditions. Because of revolutionary changes in the way nations relate to each other since World War II, scholars now see foreign-policy behavior as a reaction to both internal and external stimuli, and there is a widespread recognition that communication plays a major role in this process. From this perspective, communication is viewed as a mediator, and in some instances a primary determinant in international behavior. It should also be clear that mass communication, as it relates to public-opinion formation and public diplomacy, occupies an important place in the communication perspective.

INTERNATIONAL COMMUNICATION

Definitions

International communication may be defined as any kind of communication between or among private individuals, groups, or government officials of more than one nation-state, across any recognized geographic-political boundary. The meaning of *international* in this sense is the common one. Communication is the exchanging of information or the sharing of thoughts with others. Communication may be said to exist when these minimum specifications are met: a source (and transmitter), a message, and a receiver. Since two-way communication is usually implied in examples of the communication process, this proposition may be reversed, the original receiver becoming a source to convey a responsive message to the original source, who then becomes the receiver.[44]

Cross-cultural communication may be either international or intranational. It is normally differentiated from international only when the messages are confined within the boundaries of a single nation-state; when they cross those boundaries, the term *cross-cultural* may be used as a synonym for international. Communication among two or more clearly defined cultural or subcultural groups within a single state is properly referred to as "cross-cultural communication."

Comparative communication differs from international communication in that, instead of dealing with communication between states and across national boundaries, it is generally concerned with the study, by the comparative method of analysis, of internal communication systems of two or more states or cultures. Comparative studies are not generally focused on communication transmission across national boundaries, although occasionally the difference is tenuous. A comparative study of international news communication to audiences in different countries should serve as an example of both. However, comparative research is generally thought of as including some comparison of the characteristics of national or subnational systems and behavior in two or more states or cultures.

In its simplest form, international communication may be described as "peoples speaking to peoples," and "governments speaking to governments." This definintion assumes that "governments" refers to the legitimate national governments of individual states considered actors in the international system because they engage in various transactions with other actor-members of the system. By "peoples" is meant, collectively, the nationals (but usually the elites) of a given country who are not members of the government. The term also may be used in the sense of individuals or groups speaking in their private or public capacities across national boundaries. Peoples as nationals or elite groups may register their communication as vox populi, or public opinion.

In order to identify the strategic points in the international communication process most crucial to international interaction, a model of the processes and flows of international communication—internal and external—requires at least six sets of specifications.

1. International communication, as distinguished from national, inter-

nal, or domestic communication, is a communication between at least two persons of different nationalities, thus involving in the interaction a minimum of two actors of different nations. Of necessity, subnational or internal subsystems of communication become a link in the chain of other communication systems because of their interdependence in the international communication system. Once a message has been received from nation A by a principal actor of nation B, it may be fed into the domestic communication system for transmittal to others. Internal communication subsystems then serve as relays for conveying information received from outside, and in this way become a part of the national (internal or domestic) dialogue, private and public. The process may be reversed when a message originates in nation B for transmission to nation A.

2. Communication, as distinguished from mass communication, is personal, private, and informal. Mass communication is formal, public, and comparatively impersonal. Domestic, national, mass-media institutions, agencies, and channels are important subsystems in the international system. Without the national subsystems, international mass-communication message flows from the outside could not reach internal audiences (except through private sources). The international system is a composite of national political systems steered by national actors. National-systems communication inputs, outputs, and exchanges are produced and transmitted by employing professional communicators who owe allegiance to the respective nation-states.

3. Two principal senders (sources) and receivers of international communication messages, both private and public, are (*a*) the national governments and (*b*) people, public, or elite, of the nation-states. Governments may be viewed as the national political decision system, the policy of which has an impact at the international level. People as international communicators may consist of individuals, elites, organized groups, or associations not formally part of the domestic decision-making system. Governments engage in diplomatic negotiations and bargaining, exchanging a great daily volume of official messages, most of which are private. People participate in international communication transactions of many kinds, through international trade, travel, and mail and through participation in international and cross-cultural organizations. In the process, people also communicate with their governments, and governments with people.

4. Although not a principal actor in international communication behavior in the same sense as government decision makers and elite groups, the international mass-communication elites are actors of no small consequence and must not be dismissed simply as channels or public carriers. The organized mass-communication system that collects and disseminates ideas, information, and opinion within and between countries per-

forms a crucial gatekeeping function, selecting the information to which its audience will be exposed. As such, mass-communication elites serve as receivers, originators, and sources as well as senders. It is interesting to note that the body of information at the disposal of the mass-communication elite is considerably smaller than that of the political decision makers. Generally, mass communicators are limited to that information which is made public.

5. Government decision systems possess both private and public information in their own spheres of activity, and exercise varying degrees of control on mass-communication messages. They select from their private lives that information which will be made public, discarded, or stored. In so doing, they exercise a gatekeeper function over information and opinion to be made public via the mass-media channels. The press and public may in some instances expose that which the government or some private party wishes to keep secret. Actors representing the governments and the people thus influence the nature, quality, volume, timing, and strategy of message inputs into the stream of public mass knowledge. Additionally, both governments and elites exercise ultimate control over information through their decisions as mass-communication receivers and consumers.

6. Since, by definition, communication implies a two-way exchange, actors of all nationalities may contribute to, select from, use, respond to, or store, as they wish, the common flow or pool of public international mass communication.

CONCEPTS OF THE INTERNATIONAL SYSTEM

The Nation-State Concept

As an aid in locating and defining the communication element in the international system, it is appropriate to begin by examining certain aspects of international behavior at a generic level. The system today appears to be based on a loose bipolar concept of relations among sovereign nation-states. The nation-state is a peculiar fifteenth-century western-European institution. The international system consists of nation-states whose governments conceive of themselves as autonomous and sovereign in their relations with each other. Today, the system also includes the United Nations and other international organizations, some of which may be classified as governmental and public, some as nongovernmental and private.

Since the concept of a nation-state carries the assumption of sovereignty and autonomy, it follows that the government of a nation-state becomes the supreme political power in domestic affairs. The degree of supremacy it enjoys in international affairs depends upon the international hierarchy of nations. A state's position in the pecking order at a particular time depends chiefly and ultimately upon its military and economic resources. An autonomous system, or a subsystem in the case of a hierarchy of nation-states, is one whose responses are not totally predictable, even with a most thorough knowledge of the environment. Sovereignty is seen from the outside as an incisive type of autonomy. The popular viewpoint seems to be that in most cases political leaders enjoy a rather wide choice of alternatives in making decisions in both internal and external affairs, as would be in keeping with their sovereign positions. This view is erroneous. National decision and policy makers today find their range of options more and more limited by environmental circumstances and by other factors, internal and external, latent and overt, some of which we shall examine.

Government Information Systems

One major consideration is the adequacy of the national decision maker's own information systems. Two of the decision maker's principal information channels are the formal intragovernmental systems of intelligence on the one hand, and diplomacy on the other. Unfortunately for the decision maker, codes of patriotism and secrecy by which intelligence and espionage services operate tend to work against the reporting of uncolored facts. Also, protocol and hierarchy in diplomatic upper circles generally tend to isolate key decision makers from practical matters. Another difficulty is that officials who wish to move up in the establishment may be conditioned to color facts according to what they think their superiors want to hear.

Another source of government information is the public mass media, whose external sources are fewer and generally no more reliable than those of intelligence and diplomacy. Mass communication serves international decision-making processes through the regular gathering, reporting, and analysis of world public information or news. Mass-media correspondent appraisals of international situations are sometimes shown to be more useful as a basis for international decision making than are the best appraisals of public officials. On the other hand, because of the secrecy which cloaks international political transactions, particularly the more delicate ones, press analyses tend, for the most part, to represent only the surface of issues and events. Journalists are often forced to resort to speculation where hard facts cannot be obtained because of official secrecy.

Government information systems today function more effectively than they did at one time. It is not clear, however, in this age of computerized knowledge, rapid transmission of words and images, and increasing knowledge of the science of communication, why they continue to fall short of expectations.

INTERNATIONAL DYNAMICS

As previously stated, in the international system, those who conduct foreign and international affairs are the top decision makers or the principal actors. Various agencies, such as the state department, military, intelligence, and government agencies of international trade, commerce, banking, and the like, contribute to and participate in the dynamics of the system. National policy making is a primary factor in this regard. Among the forces which affect policy making are international images, public and private communication, public opinion, personal pressures, and external and internal events. Characteristically, the international decision process, which in the past has functioned largely on a combination of folk (or intuitive) knowledge and literary knowledge, rather than empirical knowledge, is fraught with risk and uncertainty.

Types of Process

There is general agreement that actions in the international systems are usually of three types: threat, exchange, and integration. Threat is a method used in reaching objectives which are competitively pursued by two or more nations, and which are perceived by each as necessary to its own self-interest or security.[57] Stated another way, threat activity involves those aspects of power and influence in which each nation tends to operate to maximize rewards and minimize punishments from its point of view.[53; 1; 37] A threat type of activity, for example, may involve responses to the perception by nation A, that nation B is threatening its goals or capabilities. Such perceptions are frequently related to military security and defense, or to political and economic objectives.[48]

Exchange activity does not refer to cultural exchange, but rather to political negotiation and bargaining usually conducted at the diplomatic level. Modern technology, nuclear deterrence, and a host of other factors have limited the traditional range of options for resolving differences between nations by threat activity. As a consequence, exchange activity has increased in importance. Morgenthau [52] states that the traditional alternatives are diplomacy, war, and renunciation. Since there is no longer safety in renunciation (a response to threat), nor necessarily victory in war (use of force as a threat), diplomatic-negotiation exchange has become the primary means of settlement.

A third form of international activity, integration, consists of supranational cooperation in economic, political, education, scientific, and cultural matters. Action of this type takes place in many areas and on various levels, and sometimes overlaps the realm of diplomatic exchange. Recent examples are the international geophysical year, the communication satellites, and other scientific, technological, and educational ventures at the multinational level. The ultimate success of integrative planning and programs will perhaps take the form of political cooperation among existing sovereign states, as is the case with the Council of Europe, the development of political communities,[24] or supranational unification.[27]

Communication and interaction appear to be the essence of such forms of cooperation. There is a popular belief that the jet airplane, electronic communication, the rise of literacy and education, and other factors are breaking down nationalism, ethnocentrism, xenophobia, and other barriers to multinational cooperation. As a consequence, it is said that modern life tends to be more international and supranational now than in the past. Studies by Deutsch,[24] however, produced no clear-cut evidence to support this view. McClelland [48] likewise finds no empirically derived support for the proposition that increased communication or integration activity between cultures and societies always leads to the kind of understanding which results in resolution of international differences. All that can be said is that no systematic relationship has been found between communication and the resolution of international conflict. The effect and, indeed, the entire role and process of human and mass communication in the areas of international exchange and integration need to be studied much more.

Some progress in the area of improved international understanding has been achieved. Communication developments in the diplomatic areas, for example, include the growth and expansion of mass media and the rise of cross-national opinion polling, both of which have the potential to affect international decision making. In the area of integration, one should mention the significant efforts to establish a supranational news agency, the conferences and treaties to control the use of communication satellites, the universal copyright convention and other United Nations declarations, codes, and conventions affecting communication, the growth of world broadcasting networks, and the rise of international advertising and public relations.

Maintenance Costs

The cost of the international system is so large as to keep nations impoverished. By far the greatest part of the total outlay goes not to support education, communications, or cooperation, but to finance the threat segment of international action. In 1965, military and defense budgets were estimated at between $130 billion and $150 billion a year. They total substantially more than that today. The other two types of activity negotiation and bargaining exchange (diplomacy) and integration, cost only a fraction of the amount spent for the threat system. In 1965, the total budget of the

United Nations was about one-third of half-a-billion dollars or only .3 percent of the world war industry.

The Decision System in International Policy

We return briefly to the role of the decision maker in the dynamics of the international system. Earlier in this chapter, it was suggested that his role today provides a somewhat limited range of choices. These limitations are of three sorts: those that arise from latent processes, those that arise from random internal or external events, and those that arise from actions of other nations. The first two forces appear to be largely beyond the control of the decision maker of a single state, and unpredictable. The third, actions of other nations, may be anticipated or not, depending upon information.[5; 22] However, even a foreseeable war, as Vietnam has shown, becomes a process of its own and eventually moves beyond controlled calculation.

Latent processes may be economic or population growth-rate changes, and are sometimes the unforeseen outcome of prior decisions and policies. The impact of unpredictable events and processes, both latent and overt, on the international decision system has increased in modern times. Perhaps mass communication, with its rapid diffusion of news of events, has contributed to the effect. The result is that the international system in the postwar years is usually steered by what might be termed "crisis" decisions. In such cases, the final—and often a less-than-best-possible—decision is forced by emergency and the demand for immediate action.

Another variable which plays an important part in the function of the international decision process is the decision makers' own frames of reference.[22] International decisions are made, we are told

> in the light of some kind of image of the world and particularly some kind of image of the international system. The decision maker will have an image of his own nation and his responsibilities towards it and also an image of other nations with which he has relations. These images have no obligation to be consistent. . . . [4]

Images, indeed the entire personalities of decision makers—their motives, goals, and values—constitute a variable of great importance, and one closely related to communication, mass communication, and education. Also important in this regard are aspects of role and related influences on the nature of the decision process.[64; 22; 37]

THE STUDY OF COMMUNICATION IN INTERNATIONAL BEHAVIOR

Because reasonably reliable and complete information is a prerequisite for effective political decision and policy, the study of international behavior focuses on the process of decision making itself. Location of, and access to, the central decision system of a state becomes then the first major problem in the study of communication in international behavior. Part of the problem is that, in general, most international decision centers are located within states. Assuming that major power decisions tend to bypass the United Nations, no decision center exists outside a state's boundaries —a center, that is, from which decisions inside could be studied and predicted. Major multipower decisions in the United Nations are related primarily to peace keeping, and provide a central external "showcase" for analysis; but usually the negotiations leading to decision and policy are made privately and internally in London, Paris, Moscow, Bonn, or Washington.

Another problem we face in studying international communication has to do with the general climate of international negotiation and bargaining. Frequently, both occur in a closed and often restrictive setting. Such interpersonal and group-communication situations are clearly not conducive to empirical investigation and calm scientific analysis. Curiously enough, these same conditions affect access to information by the mass media and the public as well.

Considerations of secrecy and privacy present added difficulties. Often, the researcher must wait many years before documents are made available to him, thus depriving him of any opportunity to observe the decision process in action. Primary sources eventually appear in the form of documents and correspondence, complemented by reminiscences, memoirs, diaries, biographical and autobiographical records, and writings of retired statesmen, but by this time the crucial issues affecting the course of nations have become history. The most unfortunate aspect of this situation is that such useful insight comes along after conditions have changed, and science is deprived of its opportunity to provide empirical knowledge of the kind that could improve the processes and possibly the outcomes of international decision making.

Boundaries

Another perplexing problem is that of national boundaries. A state attempts to separate into distinct categories its domestic and international affairs, but static lines of demarcation tend to blur. In the modern world what are deemed "domestic matters" refuse to remain domestic, and foreign interests often insert themselves into the internal scene. Southern African apartheid, some would argue, is a matter of international concern; yet others classify it under the doctrine of self-determination, as a purely domestic matter with which outsiders should not meddle.

The ambiguous character of boundaries contributes to the steadily eroding principle of national sovereignty and autonomy. Jurisdictional disputes, not only over conceptual boundaries, but also over territorial boundaries between states, are as frequently the subject of debate among political leaders as among scientists attempting to define them. Boundaries need to be recognized as man-made, and they may not accurately reflect cultural, ethnic, religious, geographical, or ideological realities. Supranational organizations and communities based on multiple interdependence and common interests, such as the European Economic Community, international communism, or Roman Catholicism, are examples of international structures existing across political boundaries. [22; 20; 5]

Deutsch separates external from internal by indicating a point at which there can be distinguished "marked discontinuities in the frequency of transactions and . . . responses." [22] While the definition is useful only to those who can measure the frequencies, it serves to illustrate the complexity of the problem.

Despite the difficulties it presents, the study of international behavior has received increasing scholarly attention. Published research from various social- and behavioral-science disciplines reflects a vigorous search for models and theoretical formulations leading toward the development of the ephemeral "general theory." [5; 37]

Research in International Communication

There has been a strong effort to identify and define the salient problems related to conflict and diplomacy in terms that can be researched by empirical methods. [39; 48] Scholarly work in the field has increased greatly in volume and sophistication. Trends have been generally in the following directions: from micro to macro levels and back to micro levels; from historical, descriptive analysis to sample-survey, attitude, and experimental research; from case-and-content analysis to systems analysis, gaming, and simulation. Using a systems approach, relationships are sought in data from international- and cross-cultural-image, value, political-communication, and public-opinion studies. Subjects also include the strategy of conflict and cooperation; arms and disarmament problems; strategy in bargaining, and negotiation; international exchanges; education, and persuasion; international policy decision making; the communication factor in international transactions; and the effects of institutional class, influence, and value structures.

The evolution of a model called "international systems theory," based on recent theoretical insights, has been mentioned by a number of writers. [35; 53] Boulding [5] describes the model as (1) a systems approach taking a universalistic view that each nation's behavior is dependent on the behavior of all, rather than an internal, environmental view of any single nation; (2) a parametric theory implying mutual interaction of a great many variables; (3) a dynamic theory recognizing the dynamic processes of interaction; (4) an institutional theory recognizing the importance of institutions and organizational structures, including channels of communication and political and legal systems; (5) a transactional approach stressing the characteristics of the actors themselves, as well as the relations and transactions among them; and (6) an aggregative theory looking for methods of reducing and indexing huge bodies of information into simple quantitative indices of the system's essential characteristics, and seeking to discern regular, systematic, and persistent patterns and processes and to describe them by stochastic or probabilist models. Such behavioral models can be applied to the study of communication in the international system.

Process-and-Effects Studies

Model and theory building are needed to help us determine the role of mass communication in national and international decisions, and research in this area is of a high priority. Additionally, studies are needed to explore the relationships involved in, and effects of, specific patterns of interpersonal and mass communication upon decision making and international behavior.

A question of primary importance for further theoretical development has to do with the effects of communication. Is communication an effective method of settling disputes, of relieving tensions, or of resolving conflict? As was previously pointed out, it has not been demonstrated empirically that any systematic relationship exists between communication and tension reduction. Some evidence tends to support the theory that certain kinds of communication are of value in improving human relations. There is also evidence to the contrary—that communication and mass communication of specified kinds can aggravate declining relations and, indeed, can become causative factors in the rise and frequency of disputes, aggression, violence, and war.[48]

Indications of some degree of relationships between controlled communication and conflict resolution has been suggested by John W. Burton [7; 9] of the Center for the Analysis of Conflict at University College, London. In a series of case experiments, Burton and his associates called together official decision makers (or their representatives) of countries currently engaged in a dispute to meet with nonpartisan social scientists from neutral countries, for discussions analyzing international issues, motivations, and alternatives. Decisions in the direction of resolution tended to emerge from the talks.

Additionally, more empirical knowledge about primary, secondary, and cumulative (or long-range) effects and effectiveness of mass communications should be sought. Primary effects are more direct, and derive from the international decision maker's exposure to contact with, and utilization of, mass-media content. Perhaps more difficult to investigate are the secondary effects. These are the real or imagined effects of the mass media. For example, the presence of television cameras and lights, the presence of newsmen and correspondents all have an important psychological impact on the behavior of decision makers, both during and after contact.

Also presumed to be of significant influence on national and international decision systems, and therefore worthy of further study, is the force of internal and external public opinion. If it can be demonstrated empirically that public opinion is a product, at least in part, of mass communication then the link between this kind of communication effect and the decision system can be explored meaningfully. The reverse of this kind of effect has probably been studied more frequently. That is, the effect on public opinion exerted by a charismatic political leader who uses mass communication to mobilize acceptance of his leadership and support for his policies. A theoretical formulation to help us understand more about this three-way relationship and its effect on international behavior is needed. [12; 61; 64; 11]

The relationships and processes involved in mass-communication effects on public opinion and international decisions at the internal or national level are difficult to study when external dimensions are introduced. Yet external mass communication and opinion appear to be increasingly important factors in the behavior of states. For example, Japanese and British public reaction to atmospheric testing of atomic devices was said to be instrumental in the decision of the United States and the Soviet Union to ban such tests.

Another potentially productive area for communication research in international behavior appears to be the effect of unpredictable or latent events on the decision system. Several cases suggest themselves in this respect. The decision of the French and Chinese governments to develop atomic arsenals and the change of leadership in the Soviet Union following the death of Stalin were latent events that are probably still affecting international behavior.

More systematic and comparative examinations of large-scale mass-produced message systems are also needed. Such studies can provide clues to the public perspectives, values, images, and ideas that different types of mass-communication systems tend to cultivate. [32] Perspectives conveyed and cultivated on a long-term basis through private and public communication are closely related to social behavior and the political process. Analysis of mass-communication message systems at the national and comparative level can provide insight into patterns of national dialogues understood by the people of the countries involved. The common experiences of collective history, habits of reasoning, aspirations, beliefs, values, and loyalties—when reinforced by mass communication—become internalized in the individual and determine the interpretation of reality by which he acts. Thus these national perspectives constitute reality as understood and agreed upon by the people who share the common experience. Analysis of their national message systems should, therefore, provide essential clues to understanding the formation of national policy and relations with other nations.

Future Directions

International communication is assuming the characteristics of a specialized area of inquiry upon which a number of social-science disciplines converge. At the forefront is the sociopsychological approach, which seeks clues to understanding international behavior from knowledge of human behavior. Human behavior, both individual and social, cannot be studied without examining man's behavior over time, his institutional systems, his environment past and present, his learning and adaptive processes, and his violent conflicts with his fellowman. Hence, the field has attracted the contributions of political scientists, historians, legal scholars, sociologists, economists, geographers, anthropologists, mathematicians, and military strategists. Kelman [39] concludes that a key characteristic of behavioral study of international relations is that it cannot possibly be linked to a single discipline.

Depending upon the viewpoint, the new profession has been variously labeled the science of foreign-policy analysis, the social psychology of international relations, the science of international politics, the new profession of communication analysis, or simple social and political communication.

Advances in our knowledge about communication behavior in the international system depend upon two developments: first, the emergence of theoretical insights identifying the essential variables of the system; and second, the relating of those variables in a systematic manner to that model. The model should be capable of continual modification to reflect the results of new observations. The problems appear so formidable that theory testing may have to await the development of a new mathematics of systems and relationships.

If these two goals are achieved, the future of international communication points to the following: (1) we shall be able to predict more precisely from the outside, internal distribution of communication message flows from the point of input; (2) we shall be able to predict in more precise terms the effects and effectiveness of communication in all aspects of international behavior. This means that we shall have to know a great deal more than we do at present about the interactive processes at work in the relations between governments and peoples, about image formation and change as it relates to the knowledge process, about the cumulative effects of mass public communication and public opinion, about the content of public and private message systems, and about the role of communication in international power, influence, policy, and decision among nations; and (3) finally, we shall hopefully be able to use our knowledge of communication as a tool not only for further international and supranational integration and cooperation, but also for resolution of international conflict.

SUMMARY

While study of the international system itself is more advanced than that of communication in the international dimension, it, too, is in the early stage of development. Social-science approaches hold the promise for mankind's acute dissatisfaction with the management of international affairs that in time, through an improved understanding of the process of human communication, some elements of control and foresight can be introduced into the hazardous realm of international decision making and the relations between the peoples of the world.

REFERENCES AND SUGGESTED READINGS

1. Bachrach, Peter, and Morton S. Baratz, "Decisions and Non-Decisions: An Analytical Framework," *American Political Review*, Vol. 57, 1963, p. 633.
2. Bienen, H., *Violence and Social Change: A Review of Current Literature.* Chicago: University of Chicago Press, 1968.
3. Boulding, Kenneth, *Conflict and Defense: A General Theory.* New York: Harper, 1962.
4. Boulding, Kenneth, *The Image: Knowledge in Life and Society.* Ann Arbor: The University of Michigan Press, 1961.
5. Boulding, Kenneth, *The Impact of the Social Sciences.* New Brunswick, N.J.: Rutgers University Press, 1966, pp. 53–74.
6. Brown, Dennis, "Trust in International Relations: A Mass Media Perspective," *Journalism Quarterly*, Vol. 46, 1969, pp. 777–783.
7. Burton, John W., *Conflict and Communication: The Use of Controlled Communications in International Relations.* London: Macmillan, 1969.
8. Burton, John W., *International Relations: A General Theory.* Cambridge, England: Cambridge University Press, 1965.
9. Burton, John W., *Systems, States, Diplomacy and Rules.* New York: Free Press–Macmillan, 1968.
10. Cantril, Hadley, *The Human Dimension: Experiences in Policy Research.* New Brunswick, N.J.: Rutgers University Press, 1967.
11. Cantril, Hadley, *The Pattern of Human Concerns.* New Brunswick, N.J.: Rutgers University Press, 1965, pp. 301–326.

12. Cohen, Bernard C., *The Press and Foreign Policy*. Princeton, N.J.: Princeton University Press, 1963, pp. 208–218.
13. Coser, L., *Continuities in the Study of Social Conflict*. New York: Free Press, 1967.
14. Coser, L., *The Functions of Social Conflict*. New York: Free Press, 1956.
15. Davison, W. Phillips, *International Political Communication*. New York: Praeger, 1965.
16. De Fleur, Melvin, *Theories of Mass Communication*, 2nd ed. New York: McKay, 1970.
17. Delaney, Robert F., "Introduction," in *International Communication and the New Diplomacy*, ed. by Arthur S. Hoffman. Bloomington: Indiana University Press, 1968, pp. 3–6.
18. De Rivera, J., *The Psychological Dimensions of Foreign Policy*. New York: Merrill, 1968.
19. Deutsch, Karl W., *The Analysis of International Relations*. Englewood Cliffs, N.J.: Prentice-Hall, 1968, pp. 102–135.
20. Deutsch, Karl W., "Autonomy and Boundaries According to Communication Theory," *Toward a Unified Theory of Human Behavior: An Introduction to General Systems Theory*, 2nd ed., ed. by Roy R. Grinker, Sr. New York: Basic Books, 1956, pp. 278–297.
21. Deutsch, Karl W., *The Nerves of Government: Models of Political Communication and Control*. New York: Free Press–Macmillan, 1963.
22. Deutsch, Karl W., "External Influences on the Internal Behavior of States," in *Approaches to International and Comparative Politics*, ed. by R. Barry Farrell. Evanston, Ill.: Northwestern University Press, 1966, pp. 5–26.
23. Deutsch, Karl W., and Richard L. Merritt, "Effects of Events on National and International Images," in *International Behavior*, ed. by Herbert C. Kelman. New York: Holt, Rinehart and Winston, 1965, pp. 132–187.
24. Deutsch, Karl W. *et al.*, *Political Community and the North Atlantic Area*. Princeton, N.J.: Princeton University Press, 1957, pp. 4–7.
25. Deutsch, Morton, "Cooperation and Trust: Some Theoretical Notes," in *Nebraska Symposium on Motivation*, Vol. I. Lincoln: University of Nebraska Press, 1964, pp. 275–319.
26. Dietrich-Fischer, Heinz, and John C. Merrill, eds., *International Communication: Media, Channels, Functions*. New York: Hastings House, 1970.
27. Etzioni, Amitai, "The Dialects of Supranational Unification," *American Political Science Review*, Vol. 56, 1962, pp. 927–936.
28. Etzioni, Amitai, *Political Unification: A Comparative Study of Leaders and Forces*. New York: Holt, Rinehart and Winston, 1965.
29. Eulau, Heinz, *The Behavioral Persuasion in Politics*. New York: Random House, 1963.
30. Fagen, Richard, *Politics and Communication*. Boston: Little, Brown, 1966, pp. 17–18.
31. Free, Lloyd A., "Public Opinion Research," in *International Communication and the New Diplomacy*, ed. by Arthur S. Hoffman. Bloomington: Indiana University Press, 1968, pp. 48–63.
32. Gerbner, George, "An Institutional Approach to Mass Communication Research," in *Communication Theory and Research*, ed. by Lee Thayer. Springfield, Ill.: Charles C Thomas, 1967, pp. 436–437.
33. Hachten, William A., *Muffled Drums: The News Media in Africa*. Ames, Iowa: Iowa State University Press, 1971.

34. Halle, Louis J., *Men and Nations*. Princeton, N.J.: Princeton University Press, 1962.
35. Hoffman, Arthur S., ed., *International Communication and the New Diplomacy*. Bloomington: Indiana University Press, 1968.
36. Janis, Irving L., and M. Brewster Smith, "Effects of Education and Persuasion on National and International Images," in *International Behavior*, ed. by Herbert C. Kelman. New York: Holt, Rinehart and Winston, 1965, pp. 190–325.
37. Kaplan, Morton A., *Systems and Process in International Politics*. New York: Wiley, 1964, pp. 3–88, 113–148, 245–252.
38. Kelman, Herbert C., ed., *International Behavior: A Social-Psychological Analysis*. New York: Holt, Rinehart and Winston, 1965.
39. Kelman, Herbert C., "Social-Psychological Approaches to the Study of International Relations: Definition of Scope," in *International Behavior*, ed. by Herbert C. Kelman. New York: Holt, Rinehart and Winston, 1965, pp. 3–49.
40. Kohn, Hans, *The Age of Nationalism*. New York: Harper, 1962.
41. Lee, John, *Diplomatic Persuaders: New Role of the Mass Media in International Relations*. New York: Wiley, 1968.
42. Lent, John A., *The Asian Newspapers' Reluctant Revolution*. Ames: Iowa State University Press, 1971.
43. Lerner, Daniel, *The Passing of Traditional Society: Modernizing the Middle East*. New York: Free Press, 1958.
44. Markham, James W., ed., *International Communication as a Field of Study*. Iowa City, Iowa: International Communication Division, Association for Education in Journalism, 1970, pp. iv, vii–viii.
45. Markham, James W., *International Images and Mass Communication Behavior: A Five-Year Study*. Iowa City: The School of Journalism, University of Iowa, 1967.
46. Markham, James W., "Investigating the Mass Communication Factor in International Behavior," in *Mass Media and International Understanding Symposium*. Ljubljana, Yugoslavia: School of Political Science, Sociology and Journalism, 1969, pp. 124–137.
47. Markham, James W., *Voices of the Red Giants: Communications in Russia and China*. Ames: Iowa State University Press, 1967.
48. McClelland, Charles A., *Theory and the International System*. New York: Macmillan, 1966, pp. 1–32, 76–77, 114–115, 119–120.
49. Merrill, John C., *The Elite Press: Great Newspapers of the World*. New York: Pitman, 1968.
50. Merrill, John C., Carter R. Bryan, and Marvin Alisky, eds., *The Foreign Press*. Baton Rouge: Louisiana State University Press, 1964, 1970.
51. Morgenthau, Hans, "The Art of Diplomatic Negotiation," in *The State of the Social Sciences*, ed. by Leonard D. White. Chicago: University of Chicago Press, 1956, pp. 404–414.
52. Morgenthau, Hans, *Politics Among Nations*, 4th ed. New York: Knopf, 1967, pp. 49–91, 410–411.
53. North, Robert C. *et al.*, *Content Analysis: A Handbook with Applications for the Study of International Crisis*. Evanston, Ill.: Northwestern University Press, 1963, pp. 147–182.
54. Olson, Kenneth E., *The History Makers: The Press of Europe from Its Beginning Through 1965*. Baton Rouge: Louisiana State University Press, 1966.
55. Osgood, Charles E., *Studies on the Generality of Effective Meaning Systems*. Urbana, Ill.: Institute of Communication Research, 1961.

56. Osgood, Charles E., J. Succi, and Percy H. Tannenbaum, *The Measurement of Meaning*. Urbana: University of Illinois Press, 1957.
57. Pruitt, Dean G., "Definition of the Situation as a Determinant of International Action," in *International Behavior: A Socio-Psychological Analysis,* ed. by Herbert C. Kelman. New York: Holt, Rinehart and Winston, 1965, pp. 394–396.
58. Pye, Lucien, ed., *Communications and Political Development*. Princeton, N.J.: Princeton University Press, 1963.
59. Rao, Nagaluppi Baskara, "Controlled Mass Communication in International Conflict: Analysis of Editorials in Indian and Pakistani Newspapers" unpublished doctoral dissertation, University of Iowa, 1970.
60. Rao, Y. V. Lakshmana, *Communication and Development: A Study of Two Indian Villages*. Minneapolis: University of Minnesota Press, 1966.
61. Rivers, William L., *The Opinion Makers*. Boston: Beacon Press, 1965, pp. 90–91.
62. Rogers, Everett M., *Modernization Among Peasants: The Impact of Communication*. New York: Holt, Rinehart and Winston, 1969.
63. Rosecrance, R. V., *Action and Reaction in World Politics*. Boston: Little, Brown, 1963.
64. Rosenau, James N., *Public Opinion and Foreign Policy*. New York: Random House, 1961, pp. 3–26.
65. Sawyer, Jack, and Harold Guetzkow, "Bargaining and Negotiation in International Relations," in *International Behavior,* ed. by Herbert C. Kelman. New York: Holt, Rinehart and Winston, 1965, pp. 466–532.
66. Schelling, Thomas C., *Arms and Influence*. New Haven, Conn.: Yale University Press, 1966.
67. Schiller, Herbert I., *Mass Communication and American Empire*. New York: Augustus M. Kelley, 1969.
68. Schramm, Wilbur, *Mass Media and National Development*. Stanford, Calif.: Stanford University Press, 1964.
69. Scott, William A., "Psychological and Social Correlates of International Images," in *International Behavior,* ed. by Herbert C. Kelman. New York: Holt, Rinehart and Winston, 1965, pp. 71–103.
70. Singer, J. David, "The Level of Analysis Program in International Relations," in *The International System: Theoretical Essays,* ed. by Klaus Knorr and Sidney Verba. Princeton, N.J.: Princeton University Press, 1961, p. 420.
71. Snyder, Richard C., H. W. Bruck, and Burton Sapin, "Decision-Making as an Approach to the Study of International Politics," in *Foreign Policy Decision-Making,* ed. by Richard C. Snyder *et al.* New York: Free Press, 1962, pp. 14–185.
72. Sprout, Harold, and Margaret Sprout, *Foundations of International Politics*. Princeton, N.J.: Van Nostrand, 1962, p. 139.
73. Stagner, Ross, *Psychological Aspects of International Conflict*. Belmont, Calif.: Brooks/Cole, 1967.
74. Symposium: *The Mass Media and International Conflict*. Ljubljana, Yugoslavia: School of Political Science, Sociology and Journalism, 1969.
75. Tanter, R., "Dimensions of Conflict Behavior Within and Between Nations, 1958–60." *Journal of Conflict Resolution,* Vol. 10, 1966.
76. Van Dyke, Vernon, *Human Rights, The United States, and World Community*. New York: Oxford University Press, 1970.
77. Wright, Charles R., *Mass Communication: A Sociological Perspective*. New York: Random House, 1959, p. 11.

78. Wright, Quincy, *Problems of Stability and Progress in International Relations.* Berkeley, Calif.: University of California Press, 1954.
79. Wright, Quincy, William M. Evan, and Morton Deutsch, *Preventing World War III: Some Proposals.* New York: Simon & Schuster, 1962.
80. Zawodny, J. K., *Man and International Relations: Contributions of the Social Sciences to the Study of Conflict and Integration.* San Francisco: Chandler, n.d.

Dr. Lee M. Brown is Associate Professor of Journalism at the University of Maryland. He was for five years a newsman in Southern California and served last as Metropolitan Editor of the Long Beach *Independent Press-Telegram*. Dr. Brown has written an intensive study of the right-wing press in America, and an investigation of press performance in self-criticism. He is coauthor of *Intermedia*.

11

JOURNALISM: AN APPROACH TO HUMAN COMMUNICATION

LEE M. BROWN

That which is most essential in journalism is not a knowledge of history. Not a knowledge of men. Not the ability to catch a point quickly, nor the art of presenting facts properly, nor the skill to display the news appealingly in the headlines. It is the love, the worship of truth. The journalist has but one ancestor—Diogenes.

And, like Diogenes, he goes everywhere, with his lantern in his hand, searching for the truth.

Sometimes he thinks he has found it, but discovers he has been mistaken. This means the work must be started over again.

The most important attribute of a journalist is good faith. Men or women of bad faith are unworthy to be journalists.

Stephane Lauzanne, *Le Matin* *

Journalism is, above all, a pragmatic profession. Its standards are based on practical values and consequences. Lauzanne's notions, couched as they are in soaring prose, may seem more an expression of romance from the romantic profession of a more innocent epoch. Even so, two closely related, practical concepts underpinning modern journalism are precisely named: (1) the journalist is involved with the telling of truth or truths and (2) the journalist must keep good faith with the reader, listener, or viewer.

Telling the truth and keeping good faith with the reader could be taken as one and the same, on the premise that the one defines the other. Yet, a more complete discussion is possible when they are treated separately.

---

* Quoted from H. F. Harrington and T. T. Frankenberg, *Essentials in Journalism* (Boston, The Athenaeum Press, 1924), p. v.

189

LEVELS OF TRUTH

The journalist's mission of "telling it like it is," is confounded by several convergent factors. Truth, it seems, exists at several levels. There is what may be expressed as The Truth, which exists unchanging and immutable, through time and space and which may be applied only to certain physical laws and physical properties.

At a second level, there is Truth which may be described as fixed values and set beliefs existing within persons. At the same level, but in a different dimension, is the Truth which we take to be history.

Most journalists operate at a third level: the seeking of things that are true. Discovering and faithfully telling of a true event or occurrence is no mean task. It is the basis of the journalist's day-to-day challenge, and he approaches it from the standpoint of accuracy and with facts. Since the journalist is also supposed to be fair and unbiased in what he does, remaining accurate and factual is a sufficient challenge for the wisest member of the Washington Press Corps, as well as for a beginning writer assigned to obituaries on the smallest and most obscure newspaper. One journalism professor, J. Edward Gerald, once declared that the best remedy for bias is information. Seeking information and, thus, facts, and constraining personal biases of which he is aware, are the central chores to which the reporter addresses himself.

Another complication in the reporting of even minor truths is their plurality. Truth seems to change with time, place, and identity. The Japanese legend of Rashomon illustrates the point neatly. A samurai warrior was sent to dispense justice and punishment after a venal crime had been committed in a distant province. He interviewed several witnesses who confounded his purpose by giving several honest but contradictory accounts of the crime. The reporter covering the most minor "fender-bender" has the same problem. If two drivers are involved in the collision, so are two "truths."

The notion of a plurality of truths in reporting was discussed by Tom Wicker of the *New York Times* in his keynote speech at the Robert F. Kennedy Awards ceremony in 1971:

> . . . the press of America is not an adjunct of politics or an appendage of the government, but an estate of its own, with its own commitments. . . . If reporters don't know that truth is plural, they ought to be lawyers.
>
> Those who want us to report "good news" or "what is right about America" are simply those who are afraid we might do our real work of looking for the truth and setting down what we find, harsh and beautiful, on the page and on the screen.*

---

* From the *Washington Post* (April 29, 1971), p. F-1.

Wicker's remark that "truth is plural" expresses an old idea that is too often forgotten in the flurry of the newsroom and the demands of deadlines. In 1922, Walter Lippmann expressed the same idea in *Public Opinion,* when he wrote about "the world outside and the pictures in our heads."

Another factor, time, complicates the performance of the reported who approaches his practice with the objective of reporting the truth. Newscasts are broadcast and newspapers published with a reverence for the day, the hour, and the minute; and the concern for timeliness frequently contravenes the concern for factual, accurate reporting. It is an ongoing problem, but rarely an unresolvable one. John Hohenberg's analysis of the problem also is an apt description of it. He wrote:

> No journalist can wait until he thinks he has attained perfection. There comes a time when he must adhere to the old deadline rule: "Go with what you've got." . . . And, if when that moment of truth arrives, there is some material that is not sufficiently developed for use, another old newsroom saying still applies: "When in doubt, leave out until you check the facts." For facts reported without understanding can betray the truth. . . .
> (15, p. 6)

Under any circumstances, "going with what you've got" is a risky, if necessary, practice. Reporting the truth about something or someone is difficult under any circumstances, and some of the difficulties have already been discussed. Even so, the reporter approaches his task pragmatically, with the knowledge that if his story doesn't make this edition or this newscast, it may never be told at all. Reporters report to be read, heard, or seen; otherwise, their efforts would have little meaning.

Most reporters are familiar with Milton's dictum: "Let Truth and Error grapple. Who ever knew Truth to be put to flight in a free and open encounter?" If most reporters know it, however, few believe it. Many see themselves as willing and necessary allies of truth in whatever they encounter, and they conduct their professional activities not only to inform the people, but also to make it a matter of record or to set straight the record.

Finally, the serious reporter has some concept of this high trust placed in him by the public. If he stops to think about it, he knows the thing he is doing may become what Philip Graham, the late publisher of the *Washington Post,* used to term "the first rough draft of history."

KEEPING GOOD FAITH

Good faith is the second major aspect of the journalist's approach to his calling. So closely related is good faith to truthfulness that the Canons of

Journalism, adopted in 1924 by the American Society of Newspaper Editors, includes both under a single heading:

IV. *Sincerity, Truthfulness, Accuracy.* Good faith with the reader is the foundation of all journalism worthy of the name.

1. By every consideration of good faith a newspaper is constrained to be truthful. It is not to be excused for lack of thoroughness or accuracy within its control or failure to obtain command of these essential qualities.

Similar statements that define keeping good faith with the consumer appear in the Code of Broadcast Ethics adopted by the Radio Television News Directors Association in 1966, and in the Basic Statement of Principles adopted in 1949 by the National Conference of Editorial Writers. In sum, the several statements define the heart of journalism: a devotion to truth and a resolve to keep faith with the public.

In 1960, while he was managing editor of the *New York Times,* Clifton Daniel made a speech in which he said:

I could simply say that the responsibility of reporters is to get the facts straight and spell the names right. And the responsibility of editors is to fire them if they don't. That is really not a bad creed for newspapermen, but there is more to it than that.

Stripped to essentials, the responsibility of the reporter and editor is simply to serve the public—not the profession of journalism, not a particular newspaper, not a political party, not the government, but the public. (19, pp. 116–121)

The aim of the journalist, his *raison d'être,* is thus to serve the public in good faith by accurately reporting what truth he can. To a great extent this defines the journalist's approach to communication or, more appropriately, an approach to communicating. If communication is a phenomenon that thus far has been spared a final, total definition, few if any journalists are in the field pursuing that definition. Many may be satisfied with the notion that communication is something that occurs when a meaning is shared, but this is not what the journalist is about. He is a sharer first, a receiver second. While he receives and gathers information, he does so with the goal of sharing it with the public. He functions in the afferent dimension as a news gatherer, but that function can have meaning only when he functions in the efferent dimension as a news sharer.

The journalist's need to share the news with the public is illustrated by the press's battle with the federal government in the summer of 1971 over publication of the controversial Pentagon Papers. A government consultant had turned over to the *New York Times* a multivolume, highly classified report revealing much that had not previously been known by the public about the United States' involvement in the Vietnam conflict. The case was finally decided by the Supreme Court in favor of the press (several other newspapers followed the *Times* in printing excerpts and analyses of reports), and the federal government thereby failed in its attempts to prevent publication of the documents. A. M. Rosenthal, managing editor of the *Times,* later defended his paper's decision to print classified material in spite of the vigorous opposition of the Justice Department.

> How could the *New York Times* not have published these documents; how could it sit on a treasure trove of historical material and say to its readers we know what it is, but you can't know it? *

The focus of the sharing, as the *Times* case indicates, is on the event, not the audience. The first-order question of both reporter and editor is "What actually happened, and does this story represent it fairly?" How to make an event understandable is a matter of great concern, but it is a problem of the second order. The journalist is communicating about something with an audience he cannot see or personally experience at the moment. What is important is that he is communicating *about* something, for example, a news event. His professional integrity rests with the fidelity of his reporting relative *to the event,* not relative to the audience. Reporting is thus an event-centered experience for the journalist, even though his writing is for the audience. Sharing what truths he knows about the event, with what mastery he has of the language, is his service to the public. It means that an accurate representation of an event has a higher priority for the journalist than does a mass understanding of the event. In a complex, difficult story, the newsman is constrained to stick to the facts as he knows them, even if the event is so complex that many readers will abandon his story before reaching its end.

It is important to remember that it is inaccurate to lump together all journalists as if they were a single person with a single outlook—as are all such generalizations. At the same time, the concepts of basic involvement with the telling of truths and keeping good faith with the public are so basic to journalism that most serious, competent journalists are likely to agree to such a generalization without question or quibble. Unfortunately, journalism, like any other calling, has its share of frauds, incompetents, sycophants, and hacks. Yet without ideals and an ethical base for behavior, the journalist is a mere nuisance, nipping at the heels of other persons and other endeavors that at least claim morality. To discuss journalistic approaches and practice is also to discuss ethics and ideals.

Among the ideals supporting the practice of journalism are these:

- The first is the never-ending search for the truth.
- The second is to push ahead to meet changing times instead of waiting to be overtaken by them.

---

* Reported in *Editor and Publisher* (July 24, 1971), p. 5.

- The third is to perform services of some consequence and significance to mankind.
- The fourth, and by all odds the most important, is to maintain a steadfast independence. (15, p. 4)

Serious journalists are concerned about these ideals and about the ethics of their profession, but a casual visitor to a newsroom might not be able to observe either individual or collective expression of that concern. "Newsmen do talk about ethics, objectivity, and the relative worth of various papers, but not when there is news to get. News comes first, and there is always news to get," is the way one sociologist described, in part, his view of newsroom behavior.* In a similar vein, but with a more dramatic flair, is this vignette by a one-time editor of the *Chicago Daily News* of a city editor setting in motion a large staff at deadline time, minutes after a nearby federal building has been bombed:

> His mind is ablaze with enterprises and pierced with apprehensions. . . . He is at bay, fighting an invincible alliance of enemies: The clock, his rivals, the tangle of things to do, his own rebellious nerves, the nerve reactions of everybody else. He calls upon his uttermost reserve. He is four men in one. He is enraged at life—but he is deliriously happy. . . . (A wan joke), which goes unspoken, is extinguished by a wave of perception, vaguer than these words, but suggesting to him that society is a brutal and turbulent thing, and bringing to him, like a passing flash of the cinema, a picture of the federal building portico in ruins, and the bodies lying there. (27, p. 14)

The "invincible alliance of enemies" is comprised of a larger array than this passage suggests. The enemies may be encountered at every step of the elaborate news gathering, editing, and disseminating process. In sum, they compose much of the fabric of a newsman's life, shaping not only his approach to communication and communicating, but also regulating and modulating his behavior relative to the tasks he performs.

The battle with the clock has become largely an internal matter for the print media, since it is impossible to compete with radio and television at being first with breaking news stories. Deadlines remain uncompromising, and they remain a matter of internal concern only. They exist to expedite the flow of news through the labyrinthine printing process and to integrate the diverse activities of the process with a minimum of waste. While most systems can absorb some tardiness at some point along the line, a deadline violation serves to embarrass reporters and editors, and to infuriate general managers and production superintendents.

Rivals, particularly among newspapers, are nearly extinct. An honest "extra" edition is a rare occurrence, although many editors continue to re-

---

* See Warren Breed's article, "Social Control in the Newsroom," *Social Forces* (May, 1955), pp. 326–335.

make and treat each regular edition with an almost quixotic fervor, suggesting that every issue is an extra.

Confluence of economic pressures through increased production and materials costs; monopoly newspaper growth in cities that once were served by competitive media; and, where there are competitive newspapers, the division of cities by afternoon and morning papers, instead of by street corner, also have led to the demise of the "scoop." When a scoop occurs now, it usually is the result of careful, independent research and reporting involving dozens, or even hundreds, of man-hours. Of course, newspapers with vast daily circulations have earlier deadlines than newspapers with shorter press runs. Larger newspapers are consequently scooped frequently, but usually on stories of lesser importance. In any case, television and radio are capable of such rapid news reporting that only the longer, slower, detailed, and more complete accounts of the news are left to newspapers.

The "tangle of things to do" when a major newsbreak occurs remains immense for an editor. He must notify the rest of the staff, including those who are printers, pressmen, and circulators, of imminent production delays; he must assign reporters and photographers to the scene of the event—perhaps to hospitals and morgues, to law-enforcement agencies; in effect, he must spread a net of reporters to seine a broad stream of human and institutional activity for pertinent news. The editor may cause rewrite men to pour through clippings relative to the event while they are waiting for the first phone calls from the men at the scene. Meanwhile, if there are not pages to be planned anew, there are the other diverse stories and enterprises either awaiting decisions or in the process of completion.

Similarly, a radio or television news director must notify his own staff of reporters, cameramen, air men, and station executives when there is a major news crisis. He may quickly arrange for on-the-spot recording or photography and, at the same time, begin analyzing the programming schedule for bulletin announcements of breaking developments.

The pressure to succeed when there is little time, many persons to guide, and facts to winnow from fiction, and the often-herculean effort which is required to adjust a large and complex organization to a systemic crisis, do take their toll on nerves. But, as the description of the city editor suggests, there is a joy in accepting the challenge and something akin to elation in meeting it, particularly when success is a personal index of professionalism. Reporting and editing have evolved into essentially cognitive activities. The brawling, crime-solving, "rock-'em, sock-'em" newsmen portrayed in a generation of bad movies and television melodramas are gradually being replaced by "eggheads," fortunately some hard-boiled ones.

The "invincible alliance of enemies" takes different shapes for those assigned differing tasks in the news-gathering process. The routine operations performed by a reporter are: preliminary checking for background information; witnessing an event; interviewing or taking information from official records; reflecting and considering the meaning of events; planning the story; and writing the story.

Cliché or not, it may be said that each of these steps "is fraught with peril." Earlier stories found in clippings may contain inaccuracies a reporter could unknowingly incorporate into his own. In witnessing an event, the reporter must be aware of his own biases—of his symbolic as well as his literal points of view. Otherwise, his story could easily contain more than tolerable distortion. Those same biases, unnoticed, are enemies in the interview, as is the all-too-eager subject or the openly hostile or evasive one. Similarly, aimless, off-the-cuff questions can lead the reporter and his subject down a false semantic path, at worst inaccurate and at best soporific.

In approaching the task of writing, the reporter must mull over the meaning of what has occurred and what, if any, social significance his story is likely to have. It is a challenge to his intellect, his news judgment, and his values; certainly, it is a challenge to his ethics, particularly in the suspension of personal values.

A newsroom shibboleth correctly admonishes: "Blessed is he who hath vocabulary." There are about 450,000 words defined in the largest unabridged dictionary of the English language. The reporter who has done his homework and performed with purpose in the field should then be able to use the language to write his story in a meaningful way. Even the most experienced newsmen occasionally discover after they are well into a story that they have no particular reason for being exactly where they are, and that they are telling it poorly.

When the story leaves the hands of the reporter, it enters the hands of a series of editors who examine it for accuracy, sense, literacy, logic, and style. Space is reserved for the story in a newspaper or magazine; time is reserved for it on radio or television newscasts. A headline is ordered to size and space on a print medium. A bulletin is often written for the electronic media. The story passes through the gatekeepers, those who literally regulate the flow of news stories: on newspapers, the city and news editors, and in the electronic media, the news director. A headline or bulletin is written and checked for accuracy against the story, often with a blather of debate over language.

Ultimately, the story is submitted to the uncertainties of machines that set words into type, or it is stacked preparatory to releasing it to the vagaries of the airwaves. The "invincible alliance of enemies" thus relaxes after each edition or after each newscast, only to reassemble as the next begins to take shape. Part of the alliance is seen to be built into the system, but the greater part endures outside the mass-communication systems, invincible only in the sense that it does endure, and unfailingly challenges newsmen who probe its complexities and duplicities in the interest of fact-seeking and public service.

MEETING THE BASIC IDEALS

There is a high degree of agreement among journalists on the basic journalistic ideals of seeking truth and keeping faith with the public, but less agreement on how these ideals are best pursued. During the excess of the 1890s, when sensationalism was rampant, "blood, sex, and money" was a popular formula for successfully attracting readers. It still works, but, as John Zug, a former city editor of the *Des Moines Register,* complained, a major "weakness of our profession [is] that we are suckers for violence and intrusion." Similarly, at least one critic has referred to the contemporary daily press as the "daily chamber of horrors." The eventual reaction of the public was predictable, although not predicted. According to Wallace Allen, managing editor of the *Minneapolis Tribune:* "Public criticism of newspapers is the shrillest and most widespread I have seen in eighteen years. The public mood is uneasy, querulous, fearful." *

Newsmen cannot depend on a steadfast, believing public simply because something appears in print or is heard over television or radio. Giving the reader or viewer merely what he will take has proved inadequate, but the proof apparently came too late to prevent a major credibility gap between consumer and mass medium. Public confidence declined as the mass media achieved standards of performance and levels of social responsibility hitherto unattained. Certainly since the end of World War II, the "blood-sex-money" approach has fallen into increasing disrepute among serious journalists. An increasingly pluralistic society and a much better educated one, the advent of television, a diminishing world brought about by the development of jet- and rocket-propulsion systems, the technological-electronic revolution, the paperback boom, the cold war, and the resulting public tension—all of these have caused society's demands upon its institutions, including the press, to increase more rapidly than have the institutions' capabilities for keeping abreast. If there was a time when journalists were not sharply critical of their own performances and the standards of the media they represented, it has passed, and the criticism by journalists of journalism has grown apace.

Every journalism student, at one time or another, has been exposed to "who, what, why, when, where, and how" as necessary components of a

---

* From "Judging the Fourth Estate," reported in *Time* magazine (September 5, 1968), p. 38.

news story. For newsmen seeking to improve their performances, and using the same devices for self-examination, it is the last word—*how*—that raises the most searching questions and continues to generate some of the enduring issues in contemporary journalistic dialogue. The answers greatly influence the journalist's approach to his work. While the questions may begin in workaday situations with "How shall we handle this story?" and "How shall we cover that development?" they end by impacting the essential posture of individual newsmen and the profession itself.

One of the unresolved questions is that of objectivity versus interpretation in news reporting. Two principal views on the question are stark and uncompromising. Ralph McGill, the late editor of *Atlanta Constitution,* represented one view.

> I think that . . . we have not done the mass job of informing the people of the United States on matters about which they should have been informed, for the simple reason that we have been taught to worship a word—objectivity. . . . I want truth and not objectivity, for the simple reason there isn't any such thing as objectivity, and cannot be any such thing. Not only that, there shouldn't be. Objectivity is a phantom.*

Wes Gallagher, general manager of the Associated Press, takes the opposite position.

> The concept of objectivity in the news, and the reporter being a non-combatant and an observer rather than a partisan, is relatively new in journalism. It is this striving for objectivity that places the journalist apart from society today . . . to the true newsman, partisanship is the original sin, the apple in the journalistic Eden.**

Since facts out of context are meaningless, and since interpreted context without facts seems worthless, it is likely that neither mode appears in a pristine state. Many newspapers are as careful to label interpretive articles as "news analysis" as television commentators are to identify commentaries as separate from "straight news."

Another issue of lasting importance which has failed to gain a consensus among newsmen is that of reporting "good news" as well as "bad news." James Reston, of the *New York Times,* explained his views thus:

> I have occasionally flirted with the idea that every responsible paper should have one competent editor in charge of nothing but good news. I am not talking about silly Pollyanna drivel, but about hard factual news, about the accomplishments and decencies of our people, which all too often get buried under the daily torrent of gloom.†

---

* Cal M. Logue, "The Distinction Between Truth and Objectivity," *Nieman Reports* (December, 1968), p. 14.
** Wes Gallagher, "The Newsman: Society's Lonesome End," *Nieman Reports* (March, 1968), p. 15.
† James Reston, "The Press in the Changing World," *Quill* (June, 1966), p. 33.

Walter Cronkite, of the Columbia Broadcasting System, once viewed the reporting of good news as, "Having to report all the cats that aren't lost that day [or] all the cats that didn't get up the tree." He said on a CBS special broadcast: "It is difficult to tell the good news because the good news is the norm. Thank goodness . . . that these things that we report, which are news . . . are rare." *

Whether "good news" is good or bad, and whether or not enough good news is included in the daily news fare generally offered the public, are questions likely to remain unresolved. However, the questions go hand-in-hand with the assertion that overemphasis on disaster, threat, crime, and calamity will contribute to eventual anomie, an assertion frequently linked to charges that the press, in print and electronic form, is obsessed with violence of any kind, and grossly overreports its occurrences.

The advent of the underground press has led to another question about the nature of journalism. Since the underground press is underground in name only, particularly near campuses, it is not altogether surprising that it has been quickly able to capture a significant following, particularly among high school-age and college-age readers. It has carried into the arena of dispute the issue of advocacy journalism, an issue quite separate from the question of interpretation. Advocacy journalism, at least by popular definition, begins with a basic posture that something is either good or bad, and approaches its news reporting with a related end or solution as its goal. It might also be called "activist" journalism. While the establishment press generally rejects as mere pamphleteering the often onesided practices of advocacy journalism, its emergence has impacted the mainstream of journalistic dialogue because it has raised serious questions about objectivity, the role of the press in a changing society, and the value of a rich journalistic tradition in suspending judgments in news reporting.

There are other enduring issues among practicing newsmen. The preceding three are more representative than singular in nature or importance. Newsmen argue about the decline of self-discipline and resulting inaccuracies in reporting as the principal causes of the credibility gap between consumer and medium. There is the question of the role of the press, including the electronic media: What is it in a society as complex as this one seems to be? Should the press attempt to be the "fourth branch of government"? Should it operate as a public trust, or at least in that spirit? Is the press failing in its attempts to report urban crises? Does its news balance fairly represent all segments of society? Does it overrepresent them? Underrepresent them? Is the press stuffy, stodgy, and tradition-bound—unwilling or unable to welcome innovation? Should newspaper and broadcast news be written for a mass audience or for an elite audi-

---

* CBS Special Report (December 2, 1969).

ence? Or for both? And if the last, how? Are we telling our viewers or readers what they really need to know to understand and survive in the world today? Is it unfair to print the names of juveniles accused or convicted of crimes? Is it possible to write any kind of pretrial story without prejudicing potential jury members?

The questions go on at different levels and in different milieux, but the ones which cut to the core of journalism, and the problems with which serious journalists are concerned, are those that touch upon the thesis proposed in the opening lines of this chapter: The journalist is concerned with the seeking and telling of the truth, and is thus concerned with keeping good faith with the people.

REFERENCES AND SUGGESTED READINGS

1. Ault, Phillip H., and Edwin Emery, *Reporting the News.* New York: Dodd, Mead, 1959.
2. Baker, Robert K., and Sandra J. Ball, *Mass Media and Violence: A Report to the National Commission on the Causes and Prevention of Violence.* Washington, D.C., United States Printing Office, 1969.
3. Bernstein, Theodore M., *Watch Your Language.* New York: Channel, 1958.
4. Boyd, Malcolm, *Crisis in Communication.* Garden City, N.Y.: Doubleday, 1957.
5. Bush, Chilton R., *Newswriting and Reporting Public Affairs.* Philadelphia: Chilton, 1970.
6. Casty, Alan, ed., *Mass Media and Mass Man.* New York: Holt, Rinehart and Winston, 1968.
7. Cater, Douglas, *The Fourth Branch of Government.* Boston: Houghton Mifflin, 1958.
8. Charnley, Mitchell, *Reporting.* New York: Dryden–Holt, Rinehart and Winston, 1966.
9. Chenery, William L., *Freedom of the Press.* New York: Harcourt, Brace, 1955.
10. Edwards, Verne E., Jr., *Journalism in a Free Society.* Dubuque, Iowa: Brown, 1970.
11. Farrar, Ronald T., and John D. Stevens, *Mass Media and the National Experience.* New York: Harper & Row, 1971.
12. Gross, Gerald, ed., *The Responsibility of the Press.* New York: Simon & Schuster, 1969.
13. Harrington, H. F., and T. T. Frankenberg, *Essentials in Journalism.* Boston: Athenaeum Press, 1924.
14. Harriss, Julian, and Stanley Johnson, *The Complete Reporter.* New York: Macmillan, 1967.
15. Hohenberg, John, *The Professional Journalist: A Guide to the Practices and Principles of the News Media.* New York: Holt, Rinehart and Winston, 1969.
16. Hutchins, Robert M., *A Free and Responsible Press.* Chicago: University of Chicago Press, 1947.
17. Krieghbaum, Hillier, *Facts in Perspective.* Englewood Cliffs, N.J.: Prentice-Hall, 1956.
18. Lee, Richard W., ed., *Politics and the Press.* Washington: Acropolis, 1970.

19. Lyons, Louis M., ed., *Reporting the News*. New York: Atheneum, 1968.
20. MacDougall, Curtis D., *Interpretive Reporting*. New York: Macmillan, 1957.
21. Midura, Edmund, ed., *Why Aren't We Getting Through?: The Crisis in Urban Communication*. Washington: Acropolis, 1971.
22. Peterson, T., *Magazines in the Twentieth Century*. Urbana: University of Illinois Press, 1956.
23. Rivers, William, *The Opinion Makers*. Boston: Beacon Press, 1967.
24. Rivers, William, Theodore Peterson, and Jay W. Jensen, *The Mass Media and Modern Society*. San Francisco: Rinehart Press, 1971.
25. Schramm, Wilbur, ed., *Mass Communications*. Urbana: University of Illinois Press, 1960.
26. Siebert, F. S., Theodore Peterson, and Wilbur Schramm, *Four Theories of the Press*. Urbana: University of Illinois Press, 1956.
27. Smith, Henry Justin, *Deadlines*. New York: Harcourt, Brace, 1922.
28. Wright, Charles R., *Mass Communication*. New York: Random House, 1960.

Dr. Duane D. Pettersen is Assistant Professor of Speech Communication at the University of Montana. Dr. Pettersen's central area of study is language in behavior and information processing. Much of his work in this area has been presented to the International Communication Association. Dr. Pettersen is also a member of the permanent staff of the Agency for International Development Communication Seminars, U.S. Department of State.

12

LINGUISTICS: AN APPROACH TO HUMAN COMMUNICATION

DUANE D. PETTERSEN

A PERSPECTIVE FOR LINGUISTIC COMMUNICATION

In 1964, anthropologist Dell Hymes made the following prediction:

> The salient trait of Linguistics, in the first half of the twentieth century, from the standpoint of anthropology, has been its quest for *autonomy*. Its noted accomplishments have been in the analysis of self-contained *structure*. In the second half of the century, the salient trait will be a quest for *integration*, and the noted accomplishments will concern the engaging of linguistic structures in social contexts—in short, the analysis of *function*. (29, p. 92)

Although Hymes's prediction may be slightly overstated in light of some recent contributions in linguistic theory (notably Chomsky),[15] to date his predictions apparently are being realized. And not only are they being realized in linguistics and anthropology, but the functional approach is having even greater impact in the area of communication.

The generative linguists have clearly and purposely brought linguistics back into the social sciences.[35; 51; 52] During the early forties and fifties, linguistics stood to lose this position. However, the linguistics that has returned is not the mechanistic, behavioristic, physicalistic, or logical-positivistic variety to which most social scientists had become accustomed.

Up to 1960 American linguists had been concerned with describing language in absolutely neutral terms. That is, descriptions of a linguistic code were made out of context or independent of use in the language. Linguistics was engaged in the discovery of the structure inherent in speech samples. The aim was for completely objective, automatic, and rigorous procedures

202

that would, when correctly applied, yield a correct portrayal of these structures. This would be the grammatical analysis, and it would be correct and independent of extralinguistic suppositions. Thus Bloomfield wrote:

> We have learned . . . that we can pursue the study of language without reference to any psychological doctrine, and that to do so safeguards our results and makes them more significant to workers in related fields. [8, p. vii]

Leading questions emerging from Bloomfield's linguistics were how to best describe the system that constitutes a particular language and how to identify and explain the uniformities and differences of internal structure among languages. With the advent of generative-transformationalists (see Appendix for a listing of basic assumptions of the transformationalists and structuralists), greater concern has been with questions such as how to best describe the workings of a language in a particular social context and how to identify and explain the uniformities and differences between languages in social function. Thus, such interdisciplinary terms as *ethnolinguistics, metalinguistics, anthropological linguistics, sociolinguistics, psycholinguistics,* and more recently *interaction ethology,* have developed—attesting to the attention given to social context, or to the function of language in use.

More recent developments in linguistics aim to describe the specialized form of knowledge we use in the comprehension and production of sentences. Thus the generative (*generative* and *transformational* are used interchangeably; however, the former seems to be supplanting the latter) linguists, contrary to structural linguists, assume that whatever we know, we know by some psychological process. Strong psychological assumptions are made in this linguistic approach, and thus it occupies common ground with psychology and other social-science disciplines. Recent developments in generative grammar can be followed in Bach and Harms. [2]

> Linguists call the systematic characterizations of linguistic knowledge grammars. It is important to realize that these grammars are psychological theories. They strive to portray certain facts about the mind, that is, they are supposed to be psychologically correct, and they stand or fall accordingly. [35]

A grammar is not a theory about behavior—the actual encoding and decoding of speech. Rather, a grammar is a theory of competence [14]— what an individual consciously and unconsciously knows about his language. Grammar is a theory about what an individual can potentially say, but not what he actually says. The actual production of sentences—performance—is made possible by one's competence, or grammar.

Chomsky posited that linguistics could well be a part of psychology— theoretical psychology. A generative grammar is rule-governed, that is, it attempts to use a small (finite) set of rules to account for an infinite body of speech. This set of rules will generate all possible utterances of a language (the grammatical ones), and none of the impossible utterances (ungrammatical ones). It is a description of the tacit competence of the speaker-hearer that underlies his actual performance in production and perception (understanding) of speech.

Linguistics, in order to gain interesting insights from the available data, must be mentalistic.[35] Further, the goal of linguistics must not be to emulate the methodology of the physical sciences. The goal of most social sciences in the past twenty years has been to emulate the physical sciences, rather than to handle subject matter so as to obtain interesting insights into the data.[52] Another point which Chomsky addresses is the notion of universals of language: specifically, the investigation of the conditions (mainly neurophysiological) governing the acquisition of language in children, as well as the underlying structures that are common to most languages—that is, a set of elements that would comprise a universal grammar.[14] Finally, linguistics must ask how speakers come to acquire the knowledge to communicate fluently in a natural language. That is, what innate dispositions and developmental processes are responsible for transforming a nonverbal infant into a fluent speaker.[35]

Some basic assumptions of a generative grammar are:

1. A native speaker tacitly knows a system of rules.
2. Each speaker of a language has the same set of rules. An abstract system of rules for an idealized grammar (which may be universal) is the basis for particular language grammars.
3. Communication (total) is possible only when the same set of rules is used.
4. Rules in a generative grammar are exhaustive, systematic, and economical, that is, they are explicit, automatic, and limited.
5. The rules we write reflect a speaker's competence, and this reflects performance (idealized). Factors interfering with the degree to which performance reflects competence include memory span, noise, coding and decoding abilities, perception, and the like.
6. A native speaker has a tacit or intrinsic knowledge of his rules. What a speaker knows and what he reports must be distinguished.
7. Although basically concerned with competence, generative grammar must look at performance, that is, the oral speech of man is the linguist's raw data, which is used for inferences as to the nature of the underlying abstract language system.
8. The propensity for language acquisition appears to be innate, and which speech community one is exposed to determines which language one will learn. An innate propensity for language learning is what differ-

entiates man from animal and is proposed as an explanation of the rapid and early development of complex language behavior on the part of the young child.

An emphasis or focal point of generative grammar concerns the central fact that any linguistic theory must account for the creative ability of a speaker to produce a previously unheard utterance and for another speaker to immediately understand that utterance. It is this creative aspect which previous grammars have failed to come to grips with. They have failed to appreciate the degree of internal organization and the intricacy of the system of abstract structures that have been mastered by the learner, and that are brought to bear in understanding, or even identifying, utterances.

What, if not words and phrases and sentences, do we learn when we learn a language? Obviously, what we learn is a sentence-making mechanism of some sort. The number of possible sentences for any language is, if not infinite, at least near infinite. Thus what we acquire when we obtain a language is the power to generate sentences. The mechanism that enables us to do this is called grammar. From the random sentences that we hear, we build a sentence-making system, going through some process of theory construction. As Chomsky [14] points out, this process is relatively complete at a very early age—say around five or six years. The process goes on whether we are acquiring English, Chinese, or any other language and apparently, regardless of intelligence.

The transformationalists argue that a grammar consists of three components—the syntactic, the phonological, and the semantic. The syntactic component precedes the other two and is generated by sets of phrase-structure rules and transformational rules. Phrase-structure rules generate what is called "deep structure" and transformational rules generate what is called "surface structure." Sentences quite similar in surface structure may yet be quite different in deep structure, as the examples "John is eager to please" and "John is easy to please" suggest. In the first, John is the pleaser, but in the second he is the one to be pleased.

The semantic component of the grammar relates to the deep structure, and it is the deep structure that provides the basic meaning of a given sentence.

The phonological component of the grammar relates to the surface structure and concerns the way in which the elements of the structure are pronounced.

A theory of performance is designed to explain just how the information represented by a grammar, such as that described above, is realized in actual acts of speaking and hearing. [44] Performance is linguistic behavior, either encoding or decoding speech. A theory of performance would clearly be a psychological theory, and thus such a theory would provide the important link between linguistics and communication. At the present time, however, there are no theories of linguistic performance. In part, the lack of such a theory reflects the inadequacy of past theories of grammar. With the advent of the generative grammarians,[15] knowledge of the relevant parameters of a theory of performance is taking form, and the problem is one that now inspires considerable interest among psychologists, sociologists, anthropologists, and communicologists. A number of recent studies can be regarded as bearing on a linguistic performance theory.[44; 45; 42; 60; 57; 9]

In order that the reader better understand the relevance of aspects of grammar to communicative behavior, some of the psycholinguistic research is reviewed below. Generally in such research, the independent variables are the manipulations of formal linguistic variables, and behavioral consequences are measured. Thus the psycholinguistic work not only provides support for a theory of grammar (competence), but also provides insights into a theory of speech (performance).

George Miller has provided the main impetus for psycholinguistic research. In addition to his own work and research with other psychologists, he has jointly written articles with Chomsky which provide further conceptual clarification of the relevance of a generative grammar to communicative behavior. Miller [44] has said that we can't understand a sentence until we can assign a constituent, or deep structure, for it (e.g., "They are flying planes" may be interpreted as "They are doing something with an object called a 'flying plane'" or "They are flying something called a 'plane.'" The surface structure is the same for both interpretations; however, it is the deep structure that helps one to assign meaning to the surface structure. See Figure 12.2 for an example of deep structure). He further argues that in ordinary conversation the functional unit of speech is usually larger than a single word and more nearly the size and shape of a syntactic constituent.

One of the advantages of a generative grammar is that it provides rules for understanding the relationships among types of sentences, rather than individual explanations for each. Miller [44] found that the more complicated a grammatical transformation is, the longer it will take people to process it. (A transformation is a rule that operates on deep structure and transforms it into a surface, or observable, structure [e.g., changing a simple active sentence into a passive structure by means of the "passive" transformational rule].) If individuals are required to match sentences with transformations with those without (simple active), more time is required as more transformations are made on the simple active sentences. His results [44] suggest the following relationships shown in Figure 12.1 among sentences where the kernel (simple active) sentence is the most easily

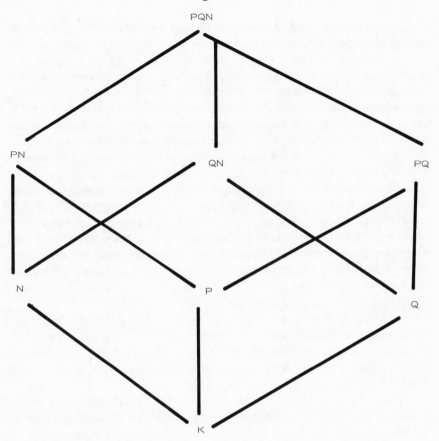

Figure 12.1   K = kernel; N = negative; P = passive; Q = question.

processed and the passive-negative-question is the most difficult to process. Examples of a kernel sentence and its passive-negative-question counterpart are: "The lightning struck the school" and "Was the school struck by lightning?"

Savin and Perchonock [57] obtained similar results when they presented eleven types of sentences, each followed by a list of eight words. They predicted that a kernel sentence would take up the least amount of memory, and therefore, more of the eight words would also be recalled. Likewise, a passive-negative-question sentence would take up the most amount of memory space, and therefore, the fewest words would be recalled. All predictions were borne out. A further explanation of these data might come from Miller's [43] notion of "chunking" or "the magical number 7 plus or minus 2." With the larger number of transformations, an extra unit, or chunk, is taken up, thereby allowing less memory storage for re-calling individual words.

Mandler and Mandler [40] found that on the second presentation of a sentence like: "Five laughing children built beautiful large ships," children learned the words "children built ships" with much greater frequency than any of the other words. This response is the basic kernel sentence with-out any transformations or "embedded" units, thereby supporting the no-tion of a deep and a surface structure in one's grammatical competence.

The clearest evidence for a psychological unit corresponding to an indi-vidual's encoding rules, phrase-structure rules, or deep-structure rules, is given by Johnson [32] in a series of experiments in paired-associate learn-ing. He found that in a sentence such as the one diagramed in Figure 12.2, the probability of a transitional error, or TE (i.e., given one word correct in a paired-associate learning task, what is the probability of get-ting the next word correct?), is much greater on *inter*phrase transitions, but reflects the *intra*phrase structure as well. That is, the greatest probability of a TE occurred between "boy" and "saved"; next between "the" and "tall" and "saved" and "the"; and so on.

This study provides clear evidence for behavioral correlates of phrase-structure rules. The substantial correlates (.60 to .95) between the proba-bility of making a TE and the "linguistic depth" of a transition suggest that a theory of verbal behavior that utilizes a hierarchical conception of language organization may be quite realistic.

Another study being conducted in psycholinguistic research concerns the psychological reality of a language segment and the prepositional phrase, and the hypothesis that latency of coding (i.e., the amount of time it takes to process a given phrase) will occur when the elements of the phrase are out of sequence. Students were asked to read aloud, as quickly as possible, a list of sixty phrases of such nature as "of the dog," "on the mountain," and the like. Some read "the dog of," "the mountain on," and so forth, suggesting that when a preposition leads the phrase, there is a greater proportionate reduction of latency for elements which follow than is the case when another grammatical category leads.

The authors Weaver and Garrison conclude that the small, frequent words in language, the highly redundant elements, "perform a program-ming or planning function which has to do with the retrieval and storage of lexical elements." [65, p. 198]

Michael Johnson [33] has recently provided evidence that syntactic usage and meaning reflect the same distributional properties of English, that is, that grammar is not independent of meaning. He found that a word used in the subject position of a passive sentence has a different meaning, as measured by Osgood's Semantic Differential Scales, [48] than the same word in the object position of its active kernel. For instance, the meaning as-

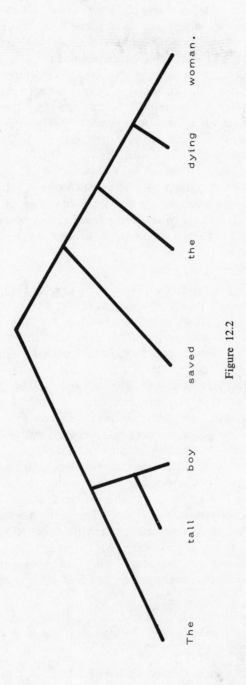

Figure 12.2

signed to "school" in the sentence "The school was struck by lightning" is different from the meaning assigned to "school" in the sentence "Lightning struck the school." Johnson's study is one of the few which begin to study the interaction effects of syntactic and semantic units.

The work of the linguist and psycholinguist in defining what our language system is like and what aspects of the language system are significant in terms of other behavioral correlates is a significant prerequisite to fully understanding the information processing of a message. That is, an understanding of what is learned, perceived, and used—the linguistic phenomena—and the consequences which are observed in human behavior, is vital to the total ethnographic effort. Specifically, it is a necessary prerequisite to studies of the language of the disadvantaged, and the language and its consequences for thought processes in education. It is this approach which is important for studying the information processing of individuals —that is, what is processed and learned, in what ways it is learned, and who is learning it.

LINGUISTICS AND THE SOCIAL SCIENCES

The interface of linguistics and the social sciences in the development of a theory of performance, or language in use, would seem to be at the focus of communicative behaviors, or, more specifically, linguistic communication. Linguistic communication may be defined simply as a concern for language processes in communication contexts. To paraphrase Dell Hymes,[29, p. 93] we might say that whereas it is the task of linguistics to coordinate knowledge about language from the viewpoint of language, it is the communicologist's task to coordinate knowledge about language from the viewpoint of the development of human relationships.

Hymes discusses a number of questions relevant to an ethnography of communication, or the study of linguistic structures in social context. He focuses upon (1) the place of speaking within the total available verbal and nonverbal communication system, (2) the relationship of linguistic habits to perception of the sociocultural environment, (3) the relationship of speech forms to social structure, (4) attitudes toward language, and (5) language behavior and language change. In other words, Hymes has outlined ethnography of communication as a field of inquiry that

> must call attention to the need for fresh kinds of data, to the need to investigate the use of language in contexts of situation and discern patterns proper to speech activities. . . . [It] must take as context a community, investigating its communicative habits as a whole. . . . [29, pp. 2-3]

so that any given use of channel and code takes its place as but part of the resources upon which the members of the community draw. For an ethnography of communication, the aim must be not to divorce message form from context, but to keep the multiple hierarchy of relations between messages and contexts in view.

In regard to theoretical orientations, there must be changes of emphasis and primacy with respect to a number of traits of thought about language: (1) speech over code; (2) function over structure; (3) content over message; (4) the ethnographically appropriate over the ethnologically arbitrary; and (5) the crucial interrelationships of all of these.

Such awareness of societal, group, and individual differences between people, plus the advances in communication theory and technology, have created an increased awareness of and attention to problems of processing messages. That is, a greater effort is made in understanding what aspects of what messages are processed by what kinds of people, in what forms, and with what consequences.

This chapter suggests an ethnographic approach to the study of human communicative behavior—as behavior influenced by all those phenomena which affect the selection, processing, and transmission of messages. The focus is one of emphasizing that any communicative event must be judged *first* in relation to its place in the unique structure of the culture (society, group, etc.) in which the event occurs. All too often, whether the study is of language behavior or of other communicative behaviors, message characteristics are studied independently of the individual and the social structure in which he lives, or behavioral phenomena are studied independently of the linguistic code. And of greater concern, the critical relationship between the two sets of variables is neglected.

In what follows, these views are spelled out more specifically in terms of a conceptual approach to the study of linguistic communication. Although the main concern is with that subset of communicative behaviors which concern information processing of linguistic or verbal (oral or written) messages, the procedures and views (those syntactic, semantic, and pragmatic features of a communicative process) are generalized into message transactions in other code forms which are used by individuals for purposes of communication.

Three conceptual and methodological concerns felt necessary for the study of communicative behaviors are ethnography, verbal learning, and individual differences in verbal behavior. The first of these suggests an approach to studying all communicative behaviors and provides the setting for focusing upon individual communicative events and messages. The second and third consider individual differences in verbal behavior and factors influencing language development and learning. Hopefully, when the reader is finished, he will recognize the significance of linguistics to the total psychological and intellectual growth of the individual as well as its significance in social interaction—communication.

ETHNOGRAPHY OF COMMUNICATION

Ethnography, as studied by anthropologists and similar-minded individuals, is basically a descriptive, but largely theoretical, approach to the functional analysis of existing societies as integrated systems. It is the study of social structure, that is, the study of all those elements, relationships, and functions which influence the particular phenomena to be studied. Conklin [16, p. 119] has stated that "an adequate ethnographic description of the culture of a particular society presupposes a detailed analysis of the communications system and of the culturally defined situations in which all relevant distinctions in that system occur."

Most of the uniquely human forms of social behavior are dependent upon shared language, so that the structure of language used in society may be related to societal functioning in unique ways. For this reason, we will use the example of an ethnography of communication as a means of explicating this approach.

An ethnography of communication takes as its context the entire community, investigating its communicative habits as a whole. The approach makes the assumption that any behavior may be communicative, but whether or not a message is communicative, and what function that message may play for an individual, group, or society, are taken to be problematic. "Any discriminatory response to a stimulus" is not necessarily communication, and what is a message for one may not be a message for another. (Household furniture, for instance, may be arranged in order to create particular attitudes—informally, or to set the stage for particular kinds of interaction.) This approach also assumes that the components in a communication system may, and likely do, have differential roles, differential abilities as senders and receivers, and differential competence with various channels and codes of communication. In other words, it is *not* the case that anyone can say anything to anyone in any form by any channel in any code in any setting of time or place.

Communication ethnographers are basically concerned with five questions: (1) What are the communicative events and their components in a community? (2) What can be symbolized and what are the components of communication involved? (3) What are the relationships among them? (4) What capabilities and states do they have—in general and in particular events? (This implies differential competence and performance of the components in relation to one another; it also implies differential functions of messages and differential purposes for entering into communication.) (5) How do they work? (This is a concern with determining the system's activity, individually and as a whole.)

Let us look at one aspect of the Sapir-Whorf hypothesis as an example of an ethnographic approach to the study of communication. It is frequently assumed that differences between languages—say Hopi and English—condition, or are associated with, differences in world view and communicative behavior. However, this assumes that the languages on one hand, and world view and behavior on the other, have the same functional relation. That is, that the differences between speakers of each community are attributed to differences *in* their respective languages; the function *of* language in both cases is assumed to be the same. An ethnographic perspective, however, considers what role any particular language plays within the "communicative economy" of a society to be problematic.

Once we take into account that language enters into socialization processes differently across and within societies,[27; 28] and that it also enters differently into adult activities with respect to frequency and context of use, then "it becomes an empirical matter . . . as to what role a language may play in sharing one's *Weltanschauung* [world view] in a given community."[30, p. 16; 50] Language represents the world of the possible, the totality of options, and the attendant rules for doing things with words syntactically, lexically, and phonetically.

Speech, on the other hand, is constrained by the circumstances of the moment, by the dictates of a relationship, and so symbolizes not what can be done, but what is done with different degrees of frequency. Speech indicates which options, at the structural and vocabulary levels, are taken up. Between language in the sense defined and speech is *social structure*. The particular form a social relationship takes acts selectively on what is said.[6; 7]

As Hymes states:

> Peoples do not all, everywhere, use language to the same degree, in the same situations, or for the same situations, or for the same things; some peoples focus upon language more than others. Such differences in the place of a language in the communication system of a people cannot be assumed to be without influence on the depth of a language's influences on such things as world view. [29, p. 20]

Hymes also states:

> It is not that linguistics does not have a vital role. Well-analyzed linguistic materials are indispensable, and the logic of linguistic methodology is a principal influence in the ethnographic perspective of the approach. It is rather that it is not linguistics, but ethnography—not language, but communication—which must provide the frame of reference within which the place of language in culture and society is to be described. [29, p. 3]

The situations in which language is used, and the importance of language in those situations, differ in different groups. In some societies, language acts as the central medium of adult roles and skills, while in others, situations of training contain little or no explicit verbal instruction. As Hymes summarizes:

When structural description is extended outward via the referential function of language, it leads from analysis of linguistic form into analysis of patterns of use in contexts of situation. [29, p. 99]

The linguistic relativity which Whorf associated with the content of language becomes secondary to the function of language. It becomes necessary to study the communicative system of an individual and of a society; the relationships and patterns of communicative events in the system; the differential competence and performance of the components of the system in relation to each other; and the functions which messages serve for them, including the purposes for entering into communication. Finally, we must consider the activity of the system, its modification, its monitoring, its capacity and feedback, and the like.

We can see the significance of such an ethnographic approach in cross-cultural research. In mass-media research, we must ask about the use or function of the mode for the individual consumer.[23] For instance, quite different results might be obtained in comparing the effects of television on a social group that employs the medium for its news value with those on a social group that uses television for entertainment or as a "babysitter." It seems superficial from this perspective to speak of the effects of mass media without considering what aspects of what kinds of mass media.

INDIVIDUAL DIFFERENCES

The importance of the ethnographic viewpoint for the study of the individual communicator is also considerable. Significance of the approach for the individual communicator has been given impetus by the amount of attention and research on handicapped and minority-group children during the past years. Studies on the black child, the American Indian child, the aphasic child, and the gifted child have given us much information concerning individual differences and the importance of types of messages and kinds of environments. Shuy,[59] Labov,[36] and others have been keenly aware of problems in education and methods of instruction; Nunnally [47] and many more have been concerned with problems of individual differences in verbal behavior, learning, and word frequency and usage, and the effects of these differences upon learning, perception, personality, and communication behaviors.

Bruner's insight into the educational process (information processing behaviors) and his proposals for a theory of instruction are very much in agreement with an ethnographic point of view in that an identification and specification of the relevant characteristics of the educational and cultural environment are necessary for such a theory. Bruner builds his notions around differences in individuals' social and intellectual rates of development, and thus believes in learning units designed to accommodate those differences in both structure and sequencing.

Bruner suggests that "a theory of instruction, which must be at the heart of educational psychology, is principally concerned with how to *arrange environments* to optimize learning according to various criteria" (italics added). [13, p. 37] He offers four major features of a theory of instruction, that is, a theory which "is concerned with how what one wishes to teach can best be learned." First, Bruner states that such a theory must specify the particular experiences which are most apt to create predispositions toward learning. Second, the theory must specify ways in which a body of knowledge can be structured, recognizing that individuals differ as to their status, their needs, and their abilities—that the optimal structure for any given unit is problematic. Third, Bruner proposes that the material to be learned must be sequenced in the way that will be most effective. And finally, he suggests that the nature or the pacing of rewards and punishments must be specified in the process of learning and teaching.

Jim Nunnally's article [47] on individual differences in word usage represents another research discipline which recognizes an ethnographic methodology. His basic hypothesis, for which he has obtained theoretical as well as experimental support, is:

> if general norms for frequency of word usage are important for predicting group trends in learning, perception, and personality, then it may be that individual differences in frequency of usage of words of particular kinds correlate with individual differences in learning, perception, and personality. [47, p. 331]

It is not enough to say that individual differences are important; the dimensions of these differences must be specified and studied in order to establish a more complete analysis of the nature of individual learning, perception, and personality differences. The area of individual differences in word usage is, of course, a crucial area of study in the implementation of Bruner's ideas on a theory of instruction. Bruner himself discusses the general question of how language affects the cognitive processes. It is concern with the consequences of language for thought that causes Bruner to place "language at the center of the state in considering the nature of intellectual development." [13, p. 20]

Language is also the central focus in studies of the ghetto child by Shuy and others. In a significant study of Detroit dialects, Shuy [59] found a lack of understanding on the part of teachers of ghetto children about the nature of the child's communicative problem. Teachers frequently blamed the home environment, which was assumed to exhibit a lack of sufficient communication; or they said the ghetto child had limited experiences and thus exhibited poor performance in the classroom. The notion of a "different vocabulary" and of a restricted language code [5]—that is, individual differences in language use, in the function of language, and in different physical, social, and psychological experiences—was not considered by many of the teachers. Of the teachers interviewed, 80 percent gave no indication that they thought the home environment might produce a different vocabulary than the school environment demanded. No recognition was given to the fact that the lack of "school vocabulary" might not necessarily mean a lack of overall vocabulary.

Views expressed here concerning an ethnography of communication, individual differences in word usage, and a theory of instruction, as suggested by Bruner, are all extremely important in the education of the disadvantaged student—as the ghetto child has been labeled. These views of language lead us in a full circle and back to a basic understanding of the linguistic system (grammar) and linguistic communication (language as used in human interactions).

FINAL COMMENT

A perspective for linguistic communication was written for a number of reasons. First, to try to show the relevance and necessity of understanding the basic linguistic code systems which underlie much of our communication. Second, to provide a methodology or a conceptual framework in which to explore language and communicative behaviors. I believe that an ethnographic or systems approach provides a needed focus for looking at the motivation for, power of, and implications of, studying human relationships in an environment in which numerous other kinds of behavior are taking place simultaneously.

Communicologists armed not only with a greater understanding of the abstract linguistic code system, but also with a sensitivity to individual differences in learning and teaching, will be more equipped to contribute significantly to further communicative research and theory construction, and to apply that information to solving social problems. It is the study of a communicative event or message within the individual, social, and cultural context which is needed. It is this approach, an interdisciplinary effort on the part of all social scientists and humanists, which is needed for understanding this highly significant aspect of human behavior—linguistic communicative behavior.

APPENDIX *

I. Basic assumptions of American linguistics for twenty-five years following the publication of Leonard Bloomfield's *Language* in 1933, frequently referred to as structural linguistics:

---

* These lists or subsets thereof are found in numerous sources. However, this particular list came from *A Linguistics Reader,* ed. by Graham Wilson (New York: Harper & Row, 1967), pp. 192–193.

1. The description of a language must be based upon a corpus: for instance, the Fries collection of telephone conversations.

2. Any utterance of a native speaker of a language that appears in the corpus must be described and is, therefore, in a sense grammatical. As Smith says, "Every linguistic event is data to be described and analyzed."

3. Faust and Smith indicate—and many contemporary textbooks of grammar show—that a grammar is a description of three sets of patterns in the corpus: phonological, morphological, and syntactic.

4. The description of a language involves dealing in succession with the phonology, the morphology, and the syntax. There is an additional assumption that one must not mix levels; for example, the syntax must not be called in to help describe the phonology. This assumption, however, is understood and discussed in varying ways.

5. There is (or it is possible to develop) a mechanical procedure for revealing the grammar of a language, such as Smith's use of superfixes to define structures and some of the parts of speech.

6. The importance of a structure may be judged by the frequency with which it occurs.

7. Language is binary. Any structure is divisible into two immediate constituents, as Smith points out. This assumption is also understood and discussed in a variety of ways.

8. There is no reason to consider that some structures are basic and some derived; that, for instance, the active voice underlies the passive.

II. Basic assumptions of generative-transformational linguistics following the publication in 1957 of Noam Chomsky's *Syntactic Structures:*

1. The native speaker of English is a fertile source of examples of his own language. To limit him to a corpus other than himself is to sacrifice a chance for much valuable information. Every grammarian knows this, whether his theory suggests it or not.

2. Our frequent inability to manipulate properly any but the simplest English structures shows that we are not invariably grammatical in any meaningful sense of the word.

3. If we stop our analysis after describing the phonology, morphology, and syntax, we have perhaps organized our materials; but we have not produced a grammar. A grammar must specify the sentences in a language.

4. The sentence, rather than the sound, is the natural and proper place to begin work on a grammar.

5. Methodology, far from being a machine for discovering truth, is only a tentative way of looking for it. The scientist finds truth by hy-

pothesis and deduction, and frequently cannot even describe the steps by which he has arrived at it.

6. No one has ever shown any statistical correlation between frequency of occurrence and grammatical importance. Fortunately, few of us ever use such simple-minded sentences as "Dogs bark." These can be found in beginning language texts, and grammatically they are of great importance because they are usually kernel sentences around which elaborate statements are built.

7. Language can be considered binary only at certain levels.

8. The attraction of economy suggests that we think of "A dollar was found by him" as being structurally related to "He found a dollar."

REFERENCES AND SUGGESTED READINGS

1. Bach, E., *An Introduction to Transformational Grammars.* New York: Holt, Rinehart and Winston, 1964.
2. Bach, E., and R. T. Harms, eds., *Universals in Linguistic Theory.* New York: Holt, Rinehart, and Winston, 1968.
3. Bales, R. F., and E. F. Borgatta, "A Study of Group Size: Size of a Group as a Factor in the Interaction Profile," in *Small Groups,* ed. by Paul Hare, E. F. Borgatta, and R. F. Bales. New York: Knopf, 1955.
4. Bateson, Gregory, "Exchange of Information about Patterns of Human Behavior," in *Information Storage and Neural Control,* ed. by William Fields and Walter Abbott. Springfield: Charles C Thomas, 1963.
5. Bernstein, Basil B., "Elaborated and Restricted Codes: Their Social Origins and Some Consequences," *The Ethnography of Communication, American Anthropologist,* 1964.
6. Bernstein, Basil B., "Social Class, Linguistic Codes, and Grammatical Elements," *Language and Speech,* Vol. 66, part 2, 1962.
7. Bernstein, Basil, and D. Henderson, "Social Class Differences in the Relevance of Language to Socialization," *Sociology,* Vol. 3, 1969.
8. Bloomfield, Leonard, *Language.* New York: Holt, Rinehart and Winston, 1933.
9. Blumenthal, A. L., *Language and Psychology: Historical Aspects of Psycholinguistics.* New York: Wiley, 1970.
10. Blumenthal, A. L., "Prompted Recall of Segments," *Journal of Verbal Learning and Verbal Behavior,* Vol. 6, 1967.
11. Boas, Franz, Introduction to *Handbook of American Indian Languages,* ed. by Franz Boas. Washington, D.C.: Smithsonian Institution, 1911.
12. Bruner, Jerome S., *The Process of Education.* New York: Random House, Vintage Books, 1960.
13. Bruner, Jerome S., *Toward a Theory of Instruction.* Cambridge, Mass.: Belknap Press of Harvard University Press, 1966.
14. Chomsky, Noam, *Aspects of the Theory of Syntax.* Cambridge, Mass.: M.I.T. Press, 1965.
15. Chomsky, Noam, *Syntactic Structures.* The Hague: Mouton, 1957.
16. Conklin, Harold C., "Lexicographical Treatment of Folk Taxonomies," *Problems of Lexicography,* ed. by Fred W. Householder and Sol Saporta, Supplement to *International Journal of American Linguistics,* Part IV, Vol. 28, No. 2, 1962.

17. Deese, James, *Psycholinguistics.* Boston: Allyn and Bacon, 1970.
18. DeVito, Joseph, *The Psychology of Speech and Language: An Introduction to Psycholinguistics.* New York: Random House, 1970.
19. Dinneen, Francis P., *An Introduction to General Linguistics.* New York: Holt, Rinehart and Winston, 1967.
20. Fodor, J. A., and J. J. Katz, *The Structure of Language: Readings in the Philosophy of Language.* Englewood Cliffs. N.J.: Prentice-Hall, 1964.
21. Gleason, Henry A., *Workbook in Descriptive Linguistics.* New York: Holt, Rinehart and Winston, 1955.
22. Gleason, Henry A., *An Introduction to Descriptive Linguistics,* rev. ed. New York: Holt, Rinehart and Winston, 1961.
23. Greenberg, Bradley S., and Brenda Dervin, *Use of the Mass Media by the Urban Poor: Findings of Three Research Projects,* with an annotated bibliography. New York: Praeger, 1970.
24. Greenberg, J. H., *Language Universals.* The Hague: Mouton, 1966.
25. Harris, Thomas A., *I'm OK—You're OK: A Practical Guide to Transactional Analysis.* New York: Harper & Row, 1969.
26. Hockett, Charles F., *A Course in Modern Linguistics.* New York: Macmillan, 1958.
27. Hymes, Dell, "Functions of Speech: An Evolutionary Approach," in *Anthropology and Education,* ed. by Fred C. Gruber. Philadelphia: University of Pennsylvania Press, 1961.
28. Hymes, Dell, "The Ethnography of Speaking," in *Anthropology and Human Behavior,* ed. by Thomas Galdwim and William C. Sturtevant. Washington, D.C.: Anthropological Society of Washington, 1962.
29. Hymes, Dell, "Introduction: Toward Ethnographies of Communication," *American Anthropologist,* special publication, *The Ethnography of Communication,* ed. by John Gumperz and Dell Hymes, 1964.
30. Hymes, Dell, "The Anthropology of Communication," in *Human Communication Theory: Original Essays,* ed. by Frank E. X. Dance. New York: Holt, Rinehart and Winston, 1967.
31. Jakobovits, Leon A., and Murray S. Miron, eds., *Readings in the Psychology of Language.* Englewood Cliffs, N.J.: Prentice-Hall, 1967.
32. Johnson, Neal, "Linguistic Models and Functional Units of Language Behavior," in *Directions of Psycholinguistics.* New York: Macmillan, 1965.
33. Johnson, Michael, "Syntactic Position and Rated Meaning," *Readings in the Psychology of Language.* Englewood Cliffs, N.J.: Prentice-Hall, 1967.
34. Kaplan, Abraham, *The Conduct of Inquiry.* San Francisco: Chandler, 1964.
35. Katz, Jerrold J., "Mentalism in Linguistics," *Language,* Vol. 40, 1964.
36. Labov, W., "Stages in the Acquisition of Standard English," in *Social Dialects and Language Learning.* Champaign-Urbana: National Council of Teachers of English, 1965.
37. Lahoff, George, *On the Nature of Syntactic Irregularity,* Harvard University Computation Laboratory Report No. NSF-16, 1965.
38. Langacker, Ronald W., *Language and Its Structure: Some Fundamental Linguistic Concepts.* New York: Harcourt, Brace, 1967.
39. Lenneberg, E. H., *The Biological Foundations of Language.* New York: Wiley, 1967.
40. Mandler, G., and J. Mandler, "Serial Position Effects in Sentences," *Journal of Verbal Learning and Verbal Behavior,* Vol. 3, 1964.

41. McNeill, David, *The Acquisition of Language: The Study of Developmental Psycholinguistics.* New York: Harper & Row, 1970.
42. Mehler, J., "Some Effects of Grammatical Transformations on the Recall of English Sentences," *Journal of Verbal Learning and Verbal Behavior,* Vol. 2, 1963.
43. Miller, George A., "The Magical Number Seven Plus or Minus Two: Some Limits on Our Capacity for Processing Information," *Psychological Review,* Vol. 63, 1956, pp. 81–99.
44. Miller, George A., "Some Psychological Studies of Grammar," *American Psychologist,* Vol. 17, 1962.
45. Miller, George A., and S. Isard, "Free Recall of Self-Embedded English Sentences," *Information and Control,* 1964.
46. Miller, George A., and F. Smith, eds., *The Genesis of Language.* Cambridge, Mass.: M.I.T. Press, 1966.
47. Nunnally, Jim C., "Individual Differences in Word Usage," *Directions in Psycholinguistics.* New York: Macmillan, 1965.
48. Osgood, C. E., George J. Suci, and Percy H. Tannenbaum, *The Measurement of Meaning.* Urbana: University of Illinois Press, 1957.
49. Osgood, Charles E. *et al., Psycholinguistics: A Survey of Theory and Research,* ed. by Charles E. Osgood and Thomas Sebeok, with a survey of psycholinguistic research, 1954–1965, by A. Richard Diebold, Jr., Indiana University Studies in the History and Theory of Linguistics. Bloomington: Indiana University Press, 1966.
50. Pettersen, Duane D., "A Sociolinguistic Study of Elaborated and Restricted Code Systems," unpublished dissertation, Michigan State University, 1970.
51. Postal, Paul M., "Underlying and Superficial Linguistic Structure." *Harvard Educational Review,* Vol. 34, 1964.
52. Postal, Paul M., "Review Articles of Andre Martinet, Elements of General Linguistics," *Foundations of Language,* Vol. 2, 1966.
53. Rosenberg, Sheldon, ed., *Directions in Psycholinguistics.* New York: Macmillan, 1965.
54. Sapir, Edward, *Language.* New York: Harcourt, Brace, 1921.
55. Sapir, Edward, "Communication," in *Encyclopedia of the Social Sciences.* New York: Macmillan, 1931.
56. de Saussure, F., *Course in General Linguistics,* trans. by W. Baskin. New York: Philosophical Library, 1959.
57. Savin, H., and E. Perchonock, "Grammatical Structure and the Immediate Recall of English Sentence," *Journal of Verbal Learning and Verbal Behavior,* Vol. 4, 1965.
58. Schroder, Harold M., Michael J. Driver, and Siefried Streufert, *Human Information Processing: Individuals and Groups Functioning in Complex Social Situations.* New York: Holt, Rinehart and Winston, 1967.
59. Shuy, Roger W., Walter Wolfram, and William Riley, *Linguistic Correlates of Social Stratification in Detroit Speech,* the Cooperative Research Program of the Office of Education, U.S. Department of Health, Education and Welfare, Michigan State University, East Lansing, Michigan, 1967.
60. Slobin, D. I., "Grammatical Development in Russian-Speaking Children," *The Development of Language Functions,* University of Michigan Language Development Program Report, No. 8, 1965.
61. Slobin, D. I., *Psycholinguistics,* Basic Psychological Concepts series. Glenview, Ill.: Scott, Foresman, 1971.

62. Sturtevant, Edgar H., *An Introduction to Linguistic Science*. New Haven, Conn.: Yale University Press, 1947.
63. Terwilliger, Robert, *Meaning and Mind: A Study in the Psychology of Language*. New York: Oxford University Press, 1968.
64. Warner, H. E., "On Remembering, Forgetting, and Understanding Sentences: A Study of the Deep Structure Hypothesis," unpublished doctoral dissertation, Harvard University, 1968.
65. Weaver, W., and N. Garrison, "The Coding of Phrases: An Experimental Study," *The Journal of Communication*, Vol. 16, 1966.
66. Wepman, J., L. Jones, and R. Bock, "Studies in Aphasia: Background and Theoretical Formulations," in *Readings in the Psychology of Language*. Englewood Cliffs, N.J.: Prentice-Hall, 1967.
67. Wilson, Graham, ed., *A Linguistics Reader*. New York: Harper & Row, 1967.

Richard F. Hixson is Professor of Communication at Rutgers University. His primary interest area is the mass media in the history of the United States. He has authored numerous book chapters and journal articles in addition to his own books: *Introduction to Journalism, Isaac Collins: A Quaker Printer in 18th Century America,* and *Heralds of Independence: The Activist Press in Colonial America.*

13

MASS MEDIA: AN APPROACH TO HUMAN COMMUNICATION

RICHARD F. HIXSON

AMONG man's fundamental needs is the need to communicate with his fellow human beings. At this basic level, communication is the transmission of information, ideas, and attitudes from one person to another. However, through the centuries man has constructed with the help of science and technology, intricate communication machinery known as mass media. Also known as "common carriers" because of their pervasiveness and utility, the media serve as channels to the public of intelligence, entertainment, relaxation, and merchandising information. To clarify further, it helps to consider *communication* as the *process* of communicating and *communications* as the *means* of communicating. The mass media of communication are *both* the process and the means.

PROCESS OF COMMUNICATION

In the *Rhetoric,* Aristotle set down the basic principles of human communication thusly:

> Since rhetoric exists to affect the giving of decisions . . . the *orator* must not only try to make the *argument* of his speech demonstrative and worthy of belief, he must also make his *own character* look right and put his *hearers,* who are to decide, into the right frame of mind. [Italics added.]

These words have since become the foundation for the study and use of the communication process, relative to the character and function of twentieth-century mass media. Aristotle identified the ingredients: (1) the person who speaks, (2) the speech that he proposes to give, (3) the personality of the speaker, and (4) the person who listens. However, although he may have been the first "scientist" to direct our attention to the elements of systematic persuasion, it was not until the second quarter of the present century that social scientists began to apply these notions toward the creation of hypotheses, or models, relevant to modern society. [26, p. 14]

One of the first contemporary models, developed by Shannon and Weaver, further identified the ingredients in communication: (1) a source, (2) a transmitter, (3) a signal, (4) a receiver, and (5) a destination. Translated into Aristotelian terms, the source becomes the speaker, the signal the speech, and the destination the listener. Shannon and Weaver, [32] who were talking about electronic, and not human, communication, added the transmitter to send out the message and a receiver to catch the message for the destination.

Schramm, another pioneer in the field, adapted the Shannon-Weaver model to human communication. He maintained that communication always requires at least three elements: the source, the message, and the destination. A source, according to Schramm, [28] may be an individual or an organization. The message may be in the form of ink on paper, sound waves, electric impulses, or any other signal that can be interpreted. The destination may be an individual reading, listening, or watching, or the member of a group such as a lecture audience, a football crowd, or a mob. The destination may also be a member of the mass audience reading newspapers or watching television programs.

Expanding upon his basic triad, Schramm focused upon two supplementary notions: encoding and decoding. As he points out: "the pictures in our head" cannot be transmitted until they have been encoded into a "language" common to both sender and receiver (spoken words, pictures, films). [28, p. 4] How the message is encoded will influence factors such as its speed of transmission, its durability, its understandability, and so forth. According to Schramm, in order for the act of communication to be completed, the message must also be decoded. The receiver will understand the message in terms of his own background and experience, his knowledge of the subject matter, and his attitudes toward both the subject matter and the sender.

In terms of Schramm's model, each of us, then, is at once an encoder, an interpreter, and a decoder. Schramm writes:

> You are constantly decoding signs from your environment, interpreting these signs, and encoding something as a result. In fact, it is misleading to think of the communication process as starting somewhere and ending somewhere. It is really endless. [28, p. 8]

In light of this formulation, Schramm presents an augmented version of the model shown in Figure 13.1. Figure 13.2 diagrams two people in con-

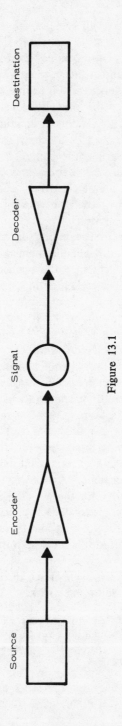

Figure 13.1

versation (although it could be applied equally well to groups). If the conversation is a normal one, part of what is embedded in the return messages is what is frequently called "feedback." In the main, feedback in human communication is that part of the message (although it may be in nonverbal behavior such as a scowl or a nod) which tells us whether or not our message is being decoded and interpreted as we intended it to be. An adroit communicator takes advantage of feedback to modify his message to better suit his audience.

Another hypotheses, formulated by Lasswell,[17] proposed the following simple question as a convenient way to describe the act of communication: *Who* says *what* in *which channel* to *whom* with *what effect?*

The "who" in Lasswell's model is the communicator. Research in this area studies the various kinds of mass communicators in terms of their training, prestige, social and personality characteristics, and their method of presentation. The question is simply, What can the source do to make his communication more effective? Mass media are particularly concerned about hiring reporters, announcers, editors, and salesmen who will be effective communicators.[27; 25; 13]

The "what" is the message. Systematic content analysis of messages contributes to their improvement in terms of style, length, readability, and the like. Research methods include counting the themes of symbols and analyzing the rhetorical devices and their underlying popular appeals. For example, in a 1940s study of magazine fiction, Berelson and Salter found that popular stories, while espousing the doctrine of racial and religious equality, actually tended to reflect the contemporary stereotypes of minorities.[5; 22; 7]

Research on "channels" has included numerous analyses of the coverage by mass media: the number of radio and television outlets and receiving sets, newspaper and magazine circulations, film production and distribution, theater seating capacities, and the like. Most studies, however, extend into the relationship between the channels of communication and the audience. Several years ago, Lazarsfeld and Kendall advanced the all-or-none principle that there is a tendency for a person who is above average in exposure to one medium to be above average in exposure to all media. A person who regularly reads one magazine, for example, probably reads several. Similarly, regular book readers frequent the cinema more often than other people [18; 31]

The "whom" in Lasswell's model is, of course, the audience—studies of whom underlie all communications research. Communicators require knowledge of the public's tastes, opinions, behavior, and size, in order for their messages to be more effective. In an economic sense, the media construe what the public buys as what the public wants. Consequently, mass communicators keep an eye on the public market. The overall goal of au-

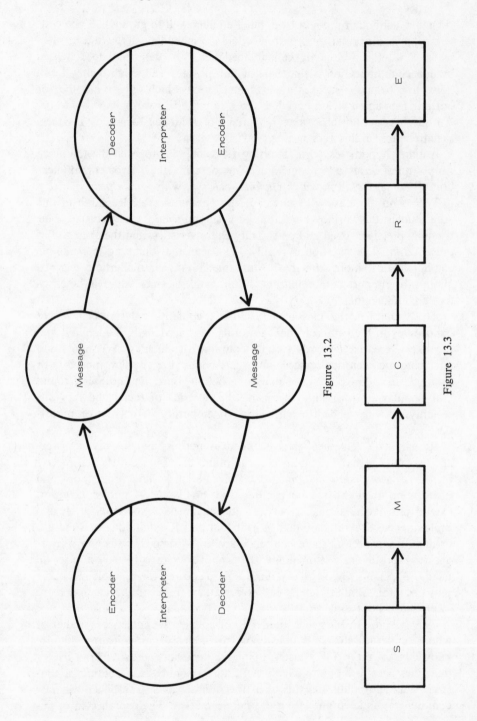

Figure 13.2

Figure 13.3

dience research is to learn how and to what degree human behavior and attitudes are affected by messages.[34]

The "effects" are the main reason for all other communication studies. What does a given message do to people? By what persons, under what conditions, is it likely to be listened to? By whom is it likely to be understood? What attitudes, opinions, or actions will it lead to? One of the earliest of these studies was on the panic that followed Orson Welles's radio dramatization of H. G. Wells's *War of the Worlds*.[8]

There are two prominent theories about the effects of mass communication. One is that they are exceedingly powerful: that mass communication enhances the possibility of mass persuasion, which in turn may lead to mass control of opinions and beliefs. The other theory, which is not concerned with power, is the theory that mass media are by nature conservative and opposed to sudden change. As Lazarsfeld and Merton pointed out several years ago: "Propaganda will not produce the expected response unless its content corresponds to the psychological wants of the audience." [23, p. 519] Berelson later explanded on this point:

> Effects upon the audience do not follow directly from and in correspondence with the intent of the communicator or the content of the communication. The predispositions of the reader or listener are deeply involved in the situation, and may operate to block or modify the intended effect or even to set up a boomerang effect. [4, p. 542]

Integral to the study of the process has been the development of the hypothesis known as the two-step flow of communication. Lazarsfeld, Berelson, and Gaudet discovered, while studying the decision-making process in an election campaign, that the flow of communication may be less direct than had been commonly supposed. They proposed that influences stemming from the media first reach opinion leaders, who, in turn, pass on what they read and hear to their associates down the line. They wrote that "ideas often flow from radio and print to the opinion leaders and from them to the less active sections of the population." [19, p. 151]

The model may be restated as follows: (1) Messages (information) flow from impersonal sources (media) to the opinion leaders—the first step; and (2) the opinion leaders influence the nonleaders (who are less affected by the impersonal sources) by means of word of mouth—the second step.

This hypothesis, which suggests a limited one-way flow of information and influence, has been challenged in recent years (All the models described here have, in fact, been subject to almost continuous reexamination.) While the two-step flow model caused researchers to focus more attention on the role played by interpersonal communication in the transmission of ideas, modifications have suggested, among other things, that the media themselves have a direct impact on people. Multiflow propositions, as well as the one-step flow, have been employed to explain data more adequately.[35; 15; 14; 11]

In a study of decision making in the marketing of a new product, Arndt found that opinion leaders, who are more influenced by impersonal sources, tend to buy new products with or without exposure of word of mouth, thus supporting the notion of the first-step flow of influence. But when it came to the second step, data indicated that word-of-mouth communication was more characterized by opinion sharing than opinion seeking. "In other words, when discussing the new product, the leaders and nonleaders often exchanged transmitter and receiver roles." [15]

Lin, in a test of the diffusion process in a mass-immunization campaign in Honduras, was able to distinguish *information* flow from *influence* flow.

> If the decision period is defined as the period which begins when a person is initially exposed to information about an issue and terminates when he makes a psychological commitment about the issue, information flow concerns the initial point of the decision period and influence flow concerns the terminal point. [20]

With this approach, time becomes a crucial variable, as do a number of other cultural, social, and psychological factors.

All these models help us to understand the communication process that takes place between the birth of an idea and its ultimate acceptance or rejection by the public. Such analyses also help us to understand the role of the communicator in our society and to examine the mass media, the subject of the second part of this chapter.

MEANS OF COMMUNICATION

For purposes of simple identification, the mass media may be divided into two broad categories: print and electronic. The print media—newspapers, magazines, books—are the oldest and are designed for the human sense of sight. Readers turn to newspapers for news and opinion, entertainment, and advertisements. In the United States alone, there are some 14,000 newspapers, of which more than 1,760 are dailies and the rest weeklies, semiweeklies, and monthlies. More than 7,000 different magazines are circulated in the United States each year, most of which appeal to special-interest audiences. By appealing to special interests, magazines tend to be more penetrating than newspapers in their coverage of current affairs. Books offer a longer-range and even more detailed examination of events and subjects. The surge in school and college enrollment, plus the so-called paperback revolution, have contributed greatly to the tremendous growth in the book-publishing industry.

Prominent among the electronic media are radio, television, and films. Radio delivers its messages through sound, and television relays impulses to both the eyes and ears, as does the motion picture. At one point, radio seemed doomed to be replaced by television, but by the early 1960s more than four thousand stations were operating, with an income of more than $700 million annually. Radio now concentrates on local community affairs, leaving the regional and national scene to television. The film industry, like radio, has made a substantial comeback following the appearance of television, and it is certain to remain a major medium of creative expression.

Indispensable adjuncts to the media are the many service agencies that supply the media with news, opinions, and entertainment. These include wire services such as the Associated Press and United Press International, and the many news services and feature syndicates. Usually, advertising agencies and public-relations firms are liaisons between the industries and institutions that they serve and the media. There are also the research individuals and groups, and the free-lance writers and reporters, whose material is transmitted through the media.

As a business, the media are larger collectively than most of the manufacturing industries in the United States. The daily newspaper business, for example, is the nation's fifth-largest employer, according to the U.S. Department of Commerce. Production of newspapers alone constitutes 1.53 percent of the Federal Reserve Board's Index of Industrial Production. By comparison, the automobile industry represents 1.82 percent and the manufacture of television sets less than .50 percent. Television's advertising volume went from $561 million in 1949 to about $1.6 billion in 1962, and to $3.6 billion in 1969. To say that the mass media are big business is surely to beg the question. How they got that way, however, is not an accident of history.

As early as the 1830s, newspapers began to change their content to appeal to large audiences. The growth of the cities made possible the "penny press," hawked on the street corners by newsboys. Papers gave more and more attention to the things that interested the public; they printed more news, crusaded for social change, championed the people, and served up large portions of human interest, sensation, sex, scandal, and gossip.

Technological advances made large circulations possible. Of primary importance and concern today is that the historical transition from simple journalism to complex mass communications has tended to decrease the number of newspapers and the number of newspaper owners. By the 1950s, consolidation into chains, groups, or conglomerates had so diminished their numbers that there were hardly more than one hundred cities in the United States with competing daily newspapers. The main reasons given for this trend have been skyrocketing costs of production and the rigorous competition for mass audiences. These, in turn, have forced standardization among newspapers, which, in turn, has encouraged the concentration of ownership. What this suggests, however, is that fewer newspapers seem to be serving a larger number of people, because while the number of papers remains constant, the total circulation of papers is at an all-time high of more than 62 million.

A more recent development than the modern newspaper is the modern magazine, which emerged in the final years of the nineteenth century. In contrast to earlier types, this modern magazine became known for its low price and popular appeal. The revolution in magazine publishing began when publishers decided to try to appeal to a great number of people by reducing the cost of their magazines below their costs for producing them. What they lost from the sale of copies, they would more than make up from advertising revenue. With the development of faster presses and better transportation facilities, magazines quickly became a national medium.

Popular content and the low prices attracted tens of thousands of readers, whom advertisers paid large sums to reach. Over the years, however, magazines have tended more and more toward special-interest audiences, forced largely into this position by the encroachment of television into the general-interest area. Since magazines are designed to appeal to different audiences at various levels of society, it is comparatively easy to enter the magazine field. Survival is another matter, however, for competition is keen, and readers are fickle.

Because the broadcasting media are much more recent developments than the print media, they have been large and expensive from the beginning. Their technical nature and economic support dictate much of their philosophy and content. Commercial broadcasting, from its inception, aimed at a mass audience. Bagdikian makes the following observation:

> In 1927 a young Mormon, Philo T. Farnsworth, working in a darkened San Francisco apartment, transmitted television images without wires. Perhaps it was symbolic that Farnsworth used the dollar sign as a test pattern and that police raided his apartment under the impression that he was distilling intoxicants. Forty years later, television was still being used primarily as a collector of advertising dollars by selling entertainment. (2, p. ix)

Radio in the 1930s wooed listerners with dramatic programs and variety and comedy shows. Radio was more than democratic, it *was* America. When television replaced it as the family entertainer, individual radio stations turned to music, news, and sports in an effort to find a new identity with the public. By the mid-1960s, the country had more than 5,000 radio stations and nearly 900 television outlets. Big-time radio and television, like big-time newspaper and magazine publishing, is conducive to concentration of ownership. It is illustrative of network domination that in 1963 four radio networks had more than 1,350 station affiliates, and three television networks had more than 600.

Even though small, independent producers have entered the industry in recent years, the medium of film communication is still characterized by bigness, standardization, mass appeal, and consolidation. Unlike the other mass media, however, it is not aligned directly with the marketing system. Box office receipts, rather than advertising, pay the freight. In 1963, the film industry represented investments of $142 million in studios, $24 million in distribution, and $2.5 billion in theaters. The movie *Cleopatra* cost about $40 million to produce.

The film industry depends on foreign markets for a substantial portion of its total receipts. Yet, while economic control of the big companies has been shifted from Hollywood to Wall Street, and in spite of the current fervor over films, the industry as a whole is in serious financial trouble. In 1970, the Associated Press reported that more than thirteen thousand behind-the-camera workers were unemployed, and that five major companies suffered combined losses of more than $113 million. Part of the reason for this revenue decline is that films are increasingly being made in foreign countries, where production costs are lower.

Book publishing is the least egalitarian of the media, reaching perhaps less than 35 percent of the adult population. Fewer than a dozen of the more than 1,760 daily newspapers carry regular book-review supplements. There are only about 4,500 bookstores across the country. One book historian has noted that from the very beginning printing in Europe meant books; in America, it meant newspapers.

Nevertheless, book publishers have sought larger audiences, helped along by school sales and the ubiquitous paperback, with its low price, portability, enormous range of subject matter, and availability. American publishers issue in all about thirty-five thousand titles a year and have become increasingly business-minded. Like their counterparts in other media, they are merging, exploring new marketing ideas, expanding, and diversifying. Symbolic of a trend is McGraw-Hill, one of the giants, which recently dropped the word *Publishing* from its name to indicate more accurately the firm's growing range of products and services.

FUNCTIONS OF THE MASS MEDIA

Through the diffusion of information, the mass communicator influences many aspects of society. Our political, social, economic, and cultural lives are shaped and sustained by and through the media. Schramm identifies the three functions which the mass media of communication perform for society as watcher, forum, and teacher. According to Lasswell they are:

1. *Surveillance* of the environment, disclosing threats and opportunities affecting the value position of the community and of the component parts within it. For much of mass communication, this is reporting and commenting on everything from the town council meeting to political tension in the Middle East; in short, the *watcher* of society;
2. *Correlation* of the components of society in making a response to the environment. As the media reveal the social fabric of the nation, so the nation, as a theoretical democracy, is kept operating by what is called "public opinion," the result of the debate carried on through the mass communications system, the *forum* function;
3. *Transmission* of the social inheritance. The mass media pass on our heritage from one generation to the next. This, the *teacher* task, is an institutional function comparable to the socialization functions of the church, the home, and the school. (17)

Lasswell concludes:

In society, the communication process reveals special characteristics when the ruling element is afraid of the internal as well as the external environment. In gauging the efficiency of communication in any given context, it is necessary to take into account the values at stake, and the identity of the group whose position is being examined. In democratic societies, rational choices depend on enlightenment, which in turn depends upon communication; and especially upon the equivalent of attention among leaders, experts, and rank and file. (17, p. 130)

Some observers fear that the public depends too much on the media as watcher, forum, and teacher. "Americans have become spectators in discussion, just as they have become spectators in sports," goes one criticism. Furthermore, although the media have become highly specialized in coverage of certain journalistic events and issues, much of what the public receives is in generalized or stereotyped form. As a result of the media's pervasiveness, they are thought to blanket much of the public in false reality. And since they tend to be dominated by prevailing institutions and ideas, the media thus contribute to society's general standardization and stagnation. Pictures imprinted on men's minds become what Lippmann (21) many years ago identified as "stereotypes," created not out of real situations, but out of old images perpetuated, if not created, by the media.

To paraphrase Lasswell and Schramm, communication systems generally provide for social control, social stability, and social change. In helping to build the political fabric of a democracy, the media provide political leaders with channels to reach millions of people at one time. Conversely, officials hear through the media what the public thinks and desires (for example, through the Gallup or Harris polls and the Roper survey). The media's political-education roles reach down to the local, grass-roots level as well.

Governance by publicity may, unfortunately, grow out of excessive political use of the political process. When the public, for instance, cannot depend completely on its public officials for unrestricted government information, it depends upon media journalists to uncover the complete story. *Watchdog* is the word most often used in this connection. Clearly, the media in a democracy provide the marketplace for political ideas and goals. Public opinion on government affairs, as well as on other aspects of society, is shaped through the mass media.

Of increasing concern is the extent to which the media control access to the only channels that can reach a complex modern society. Thus, some members of both the legal and journalistic professions urge the adoption of a new first amendment, which would provide full access to the media so that every voice could be heard.[3]

Mass media also play a major role in business life in a capitalist society. This occurs mainly through advertisements in newspapers and magazines, and commercials on radio and television. The high degree of industrial development and cohesion parallels the interwoven system of advertising and marketing, indicating the interrelationship between the media and the rest of society. As with the content in other media, advertising attempts to inform, influence, and convince the public.

So firmly integrated are the media with the economic well-being and growth of the nation, that the survival of the free-enterprise system is almost unthinkable without advertising. Broadly speaking, advertising may be divided nationally and locally. National advertising informs a nationwide or a large regional audience, wherein large corporations proclaim the advantages of their products. At the same time, they may attempt to convey a friendly corporate image by speaking of matters of general economic and social interest. Corporate reaction to the public's drive against air and water pollution is a good example. Local advertising is limited more to the use of community merchants to increase direct sales. Other advertising devices include the classified sections of newspapers, which bring together prospective employees and employers, buyers and sellers. The public forms attitudes on matters of national and local economic policy from reading and listening to business news. Public opinion on such matters is thus formulated in the same manner as are opinions in the political marketplace.

We have seen the mass media of communications in two of its major roles as: (1) a channel for informing people and stimulating and reporting public opinion, and (2) a channel for advertising that contributes to the expansion of the national economy. But the media also serve society by reporting and reflecting on cultural matters and events. They report and reflect on the way human beings behave, their tastes, their work habits, their religious beliefs, their sports, their customs, and their music. The media try to satisfy the public's desire for human interest, the insatiable curiosity humans have about each other. The media are also confronted

with the problem of possible moral or educational aspects of news, opinion, and entertainment. Answers to this problem often are found in the
kind of audience which an individual medium serves, or, in some cases,
exploits. Sometimes the media seek a lower-than-average common denominator in audience intelligence.

The interpretation of society is another social function of the media, il-
luminating the significance of the passing scene through editorials, nationally syndicated columns, and television commentaries. By reflecting the
values and interests of society, the media function as an institution of social control and social change. Contemporary forms of society probably
would not have developed to their present state without the provocation of
the mass media.

More needs to be said about media control. As businesses, the media
form what has been called the "cultural arm of American industry." By
constrast, media in the Soviet Union are more the arm of the political system, which is not to suggest that one is more desirable than the other. By
serving the industrial order, American media tend to preserve the economic system that industry desires and, therefore, produce responses from
the public which are beneficial to industry. With public opinion representing a kind of democratic Holy Grail, social institutions are more inclined
to promulgate existing beliefs than to change them. In this context, the
media have, historically, been reluctant to work toward fundamental
changes in society. Assuming that society is dependent upon the media,
the fear has been that democracy might be stifled by majority views at the
expense of individualism.

The great debate in judging the effects of the mass media evolves from
the question of how much influence the media have on men's minds, their
values, and their beliefs. Whatever the specific effects, the media have a
growing importance, dangerous or not, in contemporary society. The American form of democracy provides the media with their greatest strengths:
independence, competition, and private enterprise. But although the Constitution guarantees these strengths, it does not spell out the responsibilities that accompany them. There are few laws prescribed for either the
media or the public in the realm of information, opinion, and entertainment. Democratic freedom, therefore, magnifies the media's responsibility,
for integrity of the media depends largely on the ethical and moral standards of the people who own and manage them. Self-control, critics say, is a
lot to expect of any institution in our complex society.

REFERENCES AND SUGGESTED READINGS

1. Arndt, Johan, "A Test of the Two-Step Flow in Diffusion of a New Product,"
   Journalism Quarterly, Vol. 45, 1968.

2. Bagdikian, Ben H., *The Information Machines: The Impact on Men and the Media,* New York: Harper & Row, 1971.
3. Barron, Jerome, "Access to the Press—A New First Amendment Right," *Harvard Law Review,* Vol. 8, 1967.
4. Berelson, Bernard, "Communications and Public Opinion," in *Mass Communications,* ed. by Wilbur Schramm. Urbana: University of Illinois Press, 1960.
5. Berelson, Bernard, *Content Analysis in Communication Research.* New York: Free Press, 1952.
6. Berlo, David K., *The Process of Communication.* New York: Holt, Rinehart and Winston, 1960.
7. Budd, Richard W., Robert K. Thorp, and Lewis Donohew, *Content Analysis of Communication.* New York: Macmillan, 1967.
8. Cantril, Hadley *et al., The Invasion from Mars.* Princeton: Princeton University Press, 1940.
9. Casty, Alan, *Mass Media & Mass Man.* New York: Holt, Rinehart and Winston, 1968.
10. De Fleur, Melvin L., *Theories of Mass Communication.* New York: McKay, 1966.
11. Dexter, L. A., and D. M. White, *People, Society and Mass Communication.* New York: Free Press, 1964.
12. Emery, Edwin, Phillip H. Ault, and Warren K. Agee, *Introduction to Mass Communications,* 3rd ed., New York: Dodd, Mead, 1970.
13. Hovland, Carl I., Irving L. Janis, and Harold H. Kelley, *Communication and Persuasion.* New Haven: Yale University Press, 1953.
14. Katz, Elihu, "The Two-Step Flow of Communication: An Up to Date Report on an Hypothesis," *Public Opinion Quarterly,* Vol. 19, 1955.
15. Katz, Elihu, and Herbert Menzel, "Social Relations and Innovation in the Medical Profession—The Epidemiology of a New Drug," *Public Opinion Quarterly,* Vol. 19, 1955.
16. Katz, Elihu, and Paul F. Lazarsfeld, *Personal Influence.* New York: Free Press, 1960.
17. Lasswell, Harold D., "The Structure and Function of Communication in Society," in *The Communication of Ideas,* ed. by Bryson Lyman. Institute for Religion and Social Studies, 1948.
18. Lazarsfeld, Paul F., and Patricia Kendall, "The Communication Behavior of the Average American," in *Mass Communications,* ed. by Wilbur Schramm. Urbana: University of Illinois Press, 1960.
19. Lazarsfeld, Paul F., Bernard Berelson, and Hazel Gaudet, *The People's Choice,* 2nd ed. New York: Columbia University Press, 1948.
20. Lin, Nan, "Information Flow, Influence Flow and the Decision-Making Process," *Journalism Quarterly,* Vol. 48, 1971.
21. Lippmann, Walter, *Public Opinion.* New York: Macmillan, 1922.
22. Merritt, Richard L., "Public Opinion in Colonial America: Content-Analyzing the Colonial Press," *Public Opinion Quarterly,* Vol. 27, 1963.
23. Merton, Robert K., *Social Theory and Social Structure,* rev. ed. New York: Free Press, 1957.
24. Rivers, William L., Theodore Peterson, and Jay W. Jensen, *The Mass Media and Modern Society,* 2nd ed., San Francisco: Rinehart Press, 1971.
25. Rivers, William, *The Opinionmakers.* Boston: Beacon Press, 1965.
26. Roberts, W. Rhys, "Rhetorica," in *The Works of Aristotle,* Vol. XI, ed. by W. D. Ross. New York: Oxford University Press, 1946.

27. Rosten, Leo C., *The Washington Correspondents*. New York: Harcourt, Brace, 1937.

28. Schramm, Wilbur, "How Communication Works," in *The Process and Effects of Mass Communication,* ed. by Wilbur Schramm. Urbana: University of Illinois Press, 1954.

29. Schramm, Wilbur, ed., *Mass Communications*. Urbana: University of Illinois Press, 1960.

30. Schramm, Wilbur, ed., *The Process and Effects of Mass Communication*. Urbana: University of Illinois Press, 1955.

31. Schramm, Wilbur, and David M. White, "Age, Education, and Economic Status as Factors in Newspaper Reading," in *Mass Communications,* ed. by Wilbur Schramm. Urbana: University of Illinois Press, 1960.

32. Shannon, Claude, and Warren Weaver, *The Mathematical Theory of Communication*. Urbana: University of Illinois Press, 1949.

33. Steinberg, Charles, *Mass Media and Communication*. New York: Hastings House, 1966.

34. Steiner, Gary A., *The People Look at Television: A Study of Audience Attitudes*. New York: Knopf, 1963.

35. Troldahl, Verling C, "A Field Test of a Modified Two-Step Flow of Communication Model," *Public Opinion Quarterly,* Vol. 30, 1966.

36. Wright, Charles R., *Mass Communication: A Sociological Perspective*. New York: Random House, 1959.

37. Yu, Frederick T. C., *Behavioral Science and the Mass Media*. New York: Russell Sage Foundation, 1968.

Dr. José M. R. Delgado is Professor of Physiology at Yale University. His current work is in the area of electrical and chemical stimulation of the brain. Dr. Delgado has published over two hundred scholarly articles and papers in neurophysiology. His most recent book is *Physical Control of the Mind.*

14

NEUROPHYSIOLOGY: AN APPROACH TO HUMAN COMMUNICATION

JOSÉ M. R. DELGADO

In Plato's works, Socrates is presented as a kind of intellectual midwife who extracted from the person he questioned knowledge that already existed. According to the doctrine of recollection, learning is only the remembering of knowledge possessed in a former life. In the *Phaedo*, the second argument for the survival of the soul is that knowledge is recollection, and therefore the soul must have existed before birth.

Aristotle rejected the theory of inborn ideas, and proposed the metaphorical tabula rasa, which was subsequently accepted in the seventeenth and eighteenth centuries by empirical physiologists including Locke and Helvétius. The newborn mind was considered a blank tablet on which experience would write messages, and the dissimilarities between individuals were attributed solely to differences in education.

The Aristotelian principle, *"Nihil est in intellectu quod no prius suent in sensu,"* repeated among others by Leonardo da Vinci, expressed the still prevalent idea that "nothing is in the intellect which was not first in the senses." Some authors, including Epicurus and the sensualists, stressed to the limit the importance of sensory inputs, proposing that the intellect is only *what* is in our senses.

WHEN AND HOW THE MIND IS FORMED

Between the extremes of considering the mind either sophisticated or naïve at birth, contemporary opinion holds that both genetic and experiential components are essential, although their functions and relative importance remain controversial. According to several child psychiatrists, heredity and experience are equipotent.[40; 52] Piaget has already emphasized

237

that while the human brain is an almost entirely hereditary regulatory organ, it has practically "no hereditary programming of these regulations, quite unlike the case of so many instincts in birds or fishes. . . ." [45] Intelligence combines two cognitive systems: experience and endogenous regulations. The latter system is a source of intellectual operations. By prolonging the feedbacks and correcting the mistakes, it transforms them into instruments of precognition.

The genetic determination of mental functions has been supported by Rainer, who believes that the fertilized ovum contains "the primordia of what we later call mind," and that "the newborn infant is already as much of an individual 'mentally' as he is physiognomically." [47] According to the evolutionary theories of William James:

the new forms of being that make their appearance are really nothing more than results of the redistribution of the original and unchanging materials . . . the evolution of the brains, if understood, would be simply the account of how the atoms came to be so caught and jammed. In this story no new *natures,* no factors not present at the beginning, are introduced at any later stage. [26]

In agreement with these ideas, Sherrington writes:

Mind as attaching to any unicellular life would seem to me unrecognizable to observation; but I would not feel that permits me to affirm it is not there. Indeed, I would think that since mind appears in the developing soma, that amounts to showing that it is potential in the ovum (and sperm) from which the soma sprang. The appearance of recognizable mind in the soma would then be not a creation *de nova* but a development of mind from unrecognizable into recognizable. [49]

Prenatal Factors in the Development of the Mind

The importance of the prenatal period as a determinant of future behavior crystallized in the concept of "ontogenetic zero," [21] has been accepted by most child psychologists. [7] At the moment of fertilization, the life of a unique individual is initiated (at birth, a child is already nine months old); and some experts have suggested that its beginning should be traced back through evolution of the parental reproductive cells, or even through previous generations.

These theories have the merit of stressing the role of genetics in the formation of the mind, but they give the false impression that genetic factors alone are able to create a mind, or that in some mysterious way, a minute, undeveloped mind already exists in the cells. At the core of this discussion is the meaning of "potentiality," which is a convenient concept provided that we understand its limitations. If we say "a block of marble is potentially a piece of sculpture," we mean that marble is an element which can be shaped into a symbolic pattern with chisels and hammers and with appropriate skills. We may say that all shapes and artistic creations exist potentially in the marble, but the reality is that the piece of stone per se lacks the essential elements to become a work of art in the absence of a sculptor. It would be incorrect to think that tools or skills are hidden within the block of marble, or that if we waited long enough, a statue would emerge spontaneously from the block. This type of incorrect reasoning has been called the "error of potentiality." [30] It has infiltrated the field of embryology and has influenced analyses of the origin and evolution of mental functions by assuming that at a certain stage of development properties exist which are present only at a later stage, and which depend on a series of essential conditions neither present in, nor determined by, the stage under consideration.

If we say that the mind is in the sperm, we can also say that each man has one million children, that a newborn baby will be the inventor of spaceships, or that a worm may evolve into a monkey. These statements may be potentially valid, but their fulfillment is contingent upon a constellation of factors which are not present in the original material. A man, in spite of his genes and his potentials, cannot create a single child without the collaboration of a woman; and a baby will not invent rockets unless he is exposed to a highly sophisticated level of physics. We believe that worms have evolved into more complex forms of life, and that potentially, they may produce dinosaurs, supermen, or inhabitants of the moon; but before we allow our imaginations to wander among the limitless possibilities of nature, it is preferable to identify the factors responsible for the observed reality among an infinite number of theoretical potentials.

According to early theories of preformism, the germinal cell—the ovum —held a miniature organism with microscopic eyes, arms, legs, and other parts of the body, which eventually would grow. The ovaries of Eve had potentially the bodies—and minds—of all mankind. Through scientific embryology it became evident that the germinal cell did not contain a compressed homunculus, but only a plan which required the interaction of other elements in order to develop into a human being.

A relatively small group of organization centers (the genes), with the collaboration of molecules supplied from the outside (the mother), produce another series of organizers (enzymes, hormones, and other active substances) which will arrange patterns of molecules for the construction of cells, tissues, and organs and will also produce a new series of organizers to direct the interaction of these new elements. The organizers are not completely stereotyped in performance, but are influenced by their medium. A particular gene may have different phenotypic effects in different environments, and "genes control the 'reaction norm' of the organism to the environmental conditions." [8] Blood vessels, muscles, and the various organs are differentiated; neurons appear, their interconnections are established, and the brain evolves. Chromosomes have neither heart nor brain —only a set of architectonic plans which under suitable conditions will evolve into a complete organism. These plans are unfulfilled for millions of sexual cells and for countless embryos that are casualties in spontaneous abortions. The possibilities of evolution are far from accomplished realities.

If we accept these ideas, we may also state that the fecundated germinal cell does not talk, understand, or think, and that the resulting embryo has no mental functions before the medullary plate rolls up to form the neural tube. When can we detect the first signs of a functioning mind? How are they correlated with the anatomical development of the central nervous system? The study of these questions may be simplified if we first examine the initial signs of a functioning brain, as revealed by behavioral expression in lower animals. Motor neurons are already growing out to establish neural contacts with muscles before they develop. The order of growth is a "progressive individualism within a totally integrated matrix, and not a progressive integration of primarily individuated units." [10] Motions, therefore, are basically a part of a total pattern, and their relative individualization is only a secondary acquisition. Some efferent motor pathways appear before any afferent fiber enters the cerebrum. Initially, the cerebral association system develops toward the motor system, and the peripheral sensory fibers grow toward the receptor field. Significant conclusions from these facts are that "the individual acts on its environment before it reacts to its environment," [9] that efferent nerves must be stimulated by products of the organism's metabolism, and that "behavior in response to such stimulation is spontaneous in the sense that it is the expression of the intrinsic dynamics of the organism as a whole." [12] Total behavior is not made up of reflexes; rather, "the mechanism of the total pattern is an essential component of the performance of the part, that is, the reflex," and behavior therefore "cannot be fully expressed in terms of S-R (Stimulus-Response)." [12] It is significant that, in man, vestibular connections develop before vestibular sense organs, because this reveals that "the cerebral growth determines the attitude of the individual to its environment before that individual is able to receive any sensory impression of its environment. Hence, the initiative is within the organism." [11]

Some of these findings have been confirmed in the toadfish and the cunner. [54] On the first day that the cunner larva swim around freely, they do not respond to external stimuli. Thus, under natural conditions, this species moves about without an effective exteroceptive mechanism, evidently propelled by a mechanism of motility activated from within. The afferent sensory system grows gradually until it finally captures the primitive motor system. The conclusion is that behavior has two components: "endogenous activity, the fundamental motility conditioned by the inner physiological adjustments of the organism; and exogenous activity, the oriented activity by which endogenous activity is so modified as to render response to external stimuli possible." [15]

This information emphasizes the importance of genetic determination and indicates that some mechanisms for behavioral performance are organized in the absence of environmental inputs. It is generally accepted that development of the nervous system is basic for the onset and elaboration of mammalian behavior, but it is not clear whether any factor can be singled out as decisive. Without synaptic conduction, impulses obviously cannot be transmitted: Thus the functional maturity of synapsis must be essential. [56; 49; 36; 24] Objections have been raised about the acceptance of synaptic permeability as the main reason for onset of behavior, [32] and other factors may be equally important. Activity of peripheral nerve fibers is considered essential for the differentiation and specificity of behavioral performance, [16; 17] and the anatomical development of neurofibrillae may be specifically related to the onset of behavior. [29] These and other studies have provided important information, but its interpretation has often been biased by methodological distortions.

It is a common error in behavioral embryology, and in science generally, to try to simplify the observed phenomena and to reduce causality to a single factor, excluding all other variables. This is the *fallacy of the single cause*, [27] or failure to understand that a biological phenomena is always the product of a complex situation, not of a single determinant. With this pitfall in mind, we must face the task of identifying the several elements essential for the development of any given phenomenon—and both conduction and synaptic mechanisms are certainly basic for the onset of behavior.

Myelin is a substance with insulating properties, covering the nerves. Its appearance in neuronal sheaths has often been associated with the onset and differentiation of behavior by neuroanatomists. A correlation perhaps exists for some specific behavior patterns in the cat and the opossum, [31; 53] but most authors today agree that the myelogenetic law cannot be generalized. In the newborn rat, myelination does not take place for several days, although the fetus starts moving many days before birth, and some discrete reflexes and inhibitory activity in higher centers can be observed in a rat fetus nineteen days after conception. [2] Myelination, therefore, cannot be interpreted as necessary for the conduction of impulses or for functional insulation.

Differences in anatomical and behavioral evolution certainly exist between mammals and lower life forms. In the guinea pig, for example, limbs are well formed in the embryo before the appearance of the first behavioral response, while in the salamander, motor behavior is initiated before morphological differentiation of the limbs. Evidently, embryologic studies of man cannot be as extensive and as well controlled as those of amphibia, but valuable information on this subject already exists.[7] Inside the uterus, the human embryo has a comfortable and sheltered life, without facing responsibilities or making choices. Cells multiply automatically, and organs take shape while the growing fetus floats weightless in the silent night of amniotic fluid. Food and oxygen are provided, and wastes are removed continuously and effortlessly by the maternal placenta. As the fetus grows, many organs perform something like a dress rehearsal before their functions are really required. This is usually referred to as the principle of anticipatory morphological maturation. The heart starts to beat when there is no blood to pump; the gastrointestinal tract shows peristaltic movements and begins to secrete juices in the absence of food; the eyelids open and close in the eternal darkness of the uterus; the arms and legs move, giving the mother the indescribable joy of feeling a new life inside herself; even breathing movements appear several weeks before birth, when there is no air to breathe.[1]

Some extensive information about human fetal behavior has been obtained from pregnant women by indirect methods, while other findings were obtained directly from fetuses removed surgically for medical reasions.[25; 39; 44] The first movement observed in a 4-millimeter-long, three-week-old fetus is the heartbeat, which has intrinsic determinants because it starts before the organ has received any nervous connections. The neural elements needed for a reflex act can be demonstrated in the spinal cord at the second month of embryonic life, and at that time, cutaneous stimulation may induce motor responses. A fourteen-week fetus shows most of the responses which can be observed in the neonate, with the exception of vocalization, the tonic grasping reflex, and respiration. With fetal growth, spontaneous motility increases inside the mother's womb, and it is well known that responses from the fetus may be elicited by tapping the mother's abdominal wall.

Sensory Perception of the Developing Fetus

Sensory perception in the fetus has been investigated in detail by several scientists.[55; 57] Cutaneous reception is well developed long before birth, and mechanical or thermal stimulation of the skin elicits motor activity appropriately related to the stimulated area. The existence of pain perception is doubtful. Proprioceptors of the muscles (the spindles) develop at the fourth month of fetal life, and the labyrinth is evident even earlier. Both organs are active during fetal life; they are capable of postural adjustments and may be partially responsible for fetal motility in the uterus.

The possibility of fetal perception of gastrointestinal movements, hunger, thirst, suffocation, and other types of organic experience, has been debated, and it is generally accepted that internal stimuli may activate skeletal musculature. Distinction of sweet from other tastes, and of unpleasant odors such as asafetida, have been demonstrated in premature babies, showing that these receptor mechanisms are already developed. It is doubtful, however, that with the nose and mouth immersed in amniotic fluid, the fetus could have gustatory or olfactory experiences before birth.

The auditory apparatus is well developed at birth, but the general consensus is that the infant is deaf until the liquid of the fetal middle ear is drained through the Eustachian tube by breathing, crying, and perhaps yawning. Loud noises, however, might be perceived, and some cases of presumed fetal hearing have been reported.[18]

The optic apparatus is sufficiently developed in the newborn infant to permit perception of light and darkness, but the optic nerve is not yet fully developed, and its evolution continues after birth and is probably influenced by sensory perception.[46] It is highly improbable that the fetus has any visual experience during its uterine life.

In summary, it is unlikely that before the moment of birth the baby has had any significant visual, auditory, olfactory, or gustatory experience, and it is probable that it has received only a very limited amount of tactile, organic, and proprioceptive information. The newborn has an elaborated system of reflexes; and coughing, sneezing, sucking, swallowing, grasping, and other actions may be evoked by the appropriate sensory stimulation. In an experimental study of seventeen behavioral responses, their intercorrelations proved to be zero, indicating that "there is no mental integration in the newborn child." [19] This integration usually takes place during the first postnatal month.

Whether or not the fetus is capable of conscious experience was a classic philosophical and psychological problem debated at length with a flourish of words and speculations, but with little factual support.[13; 28; 37; 43] It is difficult to understand the basis for this controversy, since there is no evidence that the fetus has visual, auditory, olfactory, or gustatory stimulation. In the absence of the main sensory faculties, the possibility of fetal awareness is therefore reduced to a limited input of organic sensations of proprioception and touch. Whether or not these phenomena can by themselves create consciousness is mainly a question of definition and arbitrary agreement, but it may be stated that they cannot produce manifestations comparable to those of consciousness in children or adults, which are mainly based on visual and auditory perception and experience. The mystery is perhaps insoluble, due to the impossibility of establishing verbal communication with the newborn.

Anticipatory morphological maturation is present in various mechanisms which remain quiescent in the fetus, ready to perform with physiological efficiency as soon as they are needed. Their necessary links are established before birth and are triggered by appropriate stimulation. These functions, which include oral suction, respiration, kidney secretion, and gastrointestinal activity, are able to act several weeks before an expected delivery, in case the baby is born prematurely.

INFORMATION PROCESSING AND THE MIND

No comparable provisions exist for mental functions. The newborn brain is not capable of speech, symbolic understanding, or of directing skillful motility. It has no ideas, words, or concepts, no tools for communication, no significant sensory experience, no culture. The newborn baby never smiles. He is unable to comprehend the loving phrases of his mother or to be aware of the environment. We must conclude that there are no detectable signs of mental activity at birth, and *that human beings are born without minds.* This statement may seem startling, but it should not be rejected. Potentiality should not be confused with reality. A project is not an accomplished fact, especially when essential elements are lacking in the original design. Naturally, a baby lacks experience, but by recognizing this fact, we are accepting the essentiality of extracerebral elements which originate in the outside world and are independent of both the organism and its genetic endowment. As Cantril and Livingston [6] have said, organisms are in a constant transaction, in a process of becoming, constantly changing into something different from what they were before. Early in life, an infant is attracted to sources of comfort and repelled by sources of distress. These experiences lead to the intelligent recognition of objects and persons associated with positive or negative reinforcement, and they will determine selective patterns of behavioral response. "It is at this point, we think, that 'mind' is born." [6]

The concept of the mindless newborn brain is useful because it clarifies our search for the origin of the mind. If this origin depended on genetic endowment, then mental functions should appear in the absence of other external elements (as respiratory functions do). If genetic determination alone is not sufficient, then we must investigate the source and characteristics of the extracerebral elements responsible for the appearance of the mind as the baby matures.

Sensory Dependence of the Adult Mind

Even if reception of sensory information is accepted as totally essential for the onset and development of mental functions, it is more or less explicitly assumed that an adult has a well-established mental capacity which functions with relative independence from the environment. Individuality, initiative, and free will are expressed in the ability to accept or reject ideas and select behavioral responses. A man can isolate himself, meditate, and explore the depths of his own thoughts. To a great extent, education, especially in Occidental cultures, is based on the belief that individual personality is a self-contained and relatively independent entity with its own destiny, well differentiated from its surroundings and able to function by itself even when isolated from earth and traveling in an orbiting capsule.

A more detailed analysis of reality, however, shows that cerebral activity is essentially dependent on sensory inputs from the environment, not only at birth, but also throughout life. Normal mental functions cannot be preserved in the absence of a stream of information coming from the outside world. The mature brain, with all its wealth of past experience and acquired skills, is not capable of maintaining the thinking process, or even normal awareness and reactivity, in a vacuum of sensory deprivation: *The individual mind is not self-sufficient.*

Support for this statement derives from neurophysiological and psychological experimentation. In mammals, the central organization of motor activity is localized in special regions of the cerebral cortex where muscles and ideokinetic formulas are represented. The motor pathways descend through the spinal cord and emerge through the central roots to form plexus and motor nerves. As should be expected, experimental destruction of the ventral roots in animals or pathological damage of these in man produces complete motor paralysis, because the cerebral impulses cannot reach the muscle target. Considering the input side, we know that all sensory information from the periphery, including proprioceptive impulses from the muscles, is carried by the dorsal roots of the spinal cord. As anticipated, destruction of all dorsal roots produces a loss of sensation, but, in addition, there is a paralysis of the musculature as pronounced as when the motor roots are interrupted. These experiments show that in the absence of sensory information, motor activity is totally disrupted. The brain and motor pathways are not sufficient in themselves; and for proper motor behavior, sensory inputs are absolutely necessary.

The studies of Sprague and others [5] of the cat confirmed the importance of incoming information for normal functioning of the brain. These scientists destroyed the lateral portion of the upper midbrain, including the main sensory pathways, and they observed that, in addition to the expected, marked sensory deficit, the cats exhibited a lack of affect, aggression, and pleasurable responses, and did not solicit petting. The animals remained mute, expressionless, and showed minimal autonomic responses; but in spite of this passivity, they showed hyperexploratory activity with incessant stereotyped wandering, sniffing, and searching, as if hallucinating.

Without a patterned afferent input to the forebrain via the lemnisci, the remaining portions of the central nervous system . . . seem incapable of elaborating a large part of the animal's repertoire of adaptive behavior. [50]

Psychological data also confirm the essential importance of continuous reception of inputs. Experiments on sensory deprivation in animals and man have shown that maintenance of normal mental activity is difficult or impossible when sensory information is reduced and, moreover, that monotonous sensation is aversive. Animals and humans require novelty and continual and varied stimulation from their surroundings.

MAN'S NEED FOR CHANGING ENVIRONMENT

Perception of the environment has positive reinforcing properties. When monkeys were confined in a cage, they would press levers and perform other instrumental responses for the reward of opening a little window and looking at the outside world. Curiosity derives from expectancy of novel sensory stimulation and motivates exploratory behavior in both animals and man, while boredom has negative reinforcing properties and is related to the absence of novel sensory inputs. [3; 22] To be entertained means to be provided with new and changing sensations, mainly visual and auditory. Primitive man probably derived pleasure from looking at the changing beauty of nature, which retains its fascination to the present day. Civilization has provided the technical means for a far greater choice of inputs, and a major portion of our time, effort, mental activity, and economic resources are now devoted to entertainment through books, theaters, radio, television, museums, and other cultural media.

Symbolically, we may speak about "psychic energy" as the level of intracerebral activity which could perhaps be identified in neurophysiological terms by electrical and chemical processes located at specific neuronal fields. This psychic energy may be considered a main determinant of the quantity of intellectual and behavioral manifestations. While this energy obviously depends on cerebral physiology (and indirectly on the health of the whole body), its actual source is extracerebral, because mental activity is not a property of neurons, but is contingent on the received information which activates stored information and past experiences, creating emotions and ideas.

To be alone with our own mind is not enough. Even if all past experiences are included, the exclusion of new perceptions creates serious functional difficulties. This has been shown, for instance, in the studies by Hebb and his group [4] in which college students were asked to lie comfortably on beds in soundproof, lighted cubicles, wearing translucent goggles to minimize optic sensation and gloves with cardboard cuffs to limit tactual perception. The purpose of this isolation experiment was not to cut out all sensory stimulation, but only to remove patterns and symbolic information. Most of the subjects expected to spend their idle time alone, reviewing their studies, planning term papers, or organizing ideas for lectures. The surprising result—for the investigators as well as for the participants—was that the students "were unable to think clearly about anything for any length of time, and their thought process seemed to be affected in other ways." After several hours of isolation, many of them began to see images, such as "a rock shaded by a tree," "a procession of squirrels," or "prehistoric animals walking about in a jungle." Initially, the subjects were surprised and amused, but after a while their hallucinations became disturbing and vivid enough to interfere with sleep. The students had little control over these phenomena, which, in some cases, included acoustic as well as optic perceptions, such as people talking, a music box playing, or a choir singing in full stereophonic sound. Some subjects reported sensations of movement or touch, or feelings of "otherness," or that another body was lying beside them on the bed. Isolation also tended to increase the belief in supernatural phenomena, and several of the students reported that for a few days after their isolation experiment, they were afraid that they were going to see ghosts. The conclusion was that "a changing sensory environment seems essential for human beings. Without it, the brain ceases to function in an adequate way, and abnormalities of behavior develop." [23]

In patients with long-term hospital confinements in beds or in iron lungs or body casts, psychoticlike symptoms including anxiety, delusions, and hallucinations have appeared which did not respond to standard medical or psychiatric treatment, but were easily alleviated by social contact or by sensory stimulation from a radio or television. [33]

In our century, the classic punishment of solitary confinement has been combined with sleep deprivation and used in psychological warfare. Exhaustion and decreased sensory inputs are known to cause mental disturbances and reduce defense mechanisms, and they have been effectively manipulated during brainwashing or "thought-reform" procedures to indoctrinate prisoners. [35; 57]

The literature on sensory deprivation is voluminous [48] and shows conclusively that the cerebral cortex requires a stream of stimulation for the preservation of behavioral and mental normality. We should realize, therefore, that our cerebral and mental functions rely on the umbilical cord of sensory inputs and become disrupted if isolated from the environment. This fact has been recognized by philosophers, and is reflected in the words of Ortega y Gasset who wrote: "Man has no nature; what he has is a history. . . . I am I and my circumstance." [41] The recognition of environmental inputs as a part of personal identity is one of the important contributions of Ortega y Gasset. This idea is presented in *Meditations on Quixote,* [42] when one of the characters states that "circumstantial reality forms the other half of my person. . . . reabsorption of circumstances is the specific destiny of man." A similar thought is expressed in Tennyson's poem "Ulysses," when Ulysses says, "I am a part of all that I have met."

Ortega y Gasset's position is important to philosophical thinking, but we should probably go further and question the existence of that half of personal identity thought not to originate in the environment. If we could erase all individual history, all circumstances and experiences, would there be anything left of our personality? The brain would remain, and neuronal nets would perhaps continue their spiking activity; but devoid of history —of past experiences and knowledge—there could be no mental activity, and the mind would, in fact, be an Aristotelian tabula rasa. Let us remember with Dobzhansky that "genes determine not 'characters' or 'traits' but reactions or response." [14] Our frame of reference and the building blocks of our personality are the materials received from the outside. The role of cerebral mechanisms, which to a great extent are also determined by previous experience, is to receive, bias, combine, and store the received information, but *not to create it*. Originality is the discovery of novel associations between previously received information. We must realize that the anatomical structure of man's brain has not evolved perceptibly in the past several millenniums; what has changed is the amount of information received by the brain and the training to deal with it. The major differences between a caveman and a modern scientist are not genetic but environmental and cultural.

For centuries, philosophical tradition has accepted the existence of the "I," soul, or ego. This more or less metaphysical entity is relatively independent of the environment (and perhaps even of the genes), and is the essence that endows individual man with his unique personal identity and characteristics. Later this essence may be threatened or disallowed by the social medium.

The concept of this "I" is so strong that it has permeated the thinking of authors as original and revolutionary as Marcuse. In *One Dimensional Man,* he distinguishes between true and false needs, declaring:

> False are those who are superimposed upon the individual by particular social interest in his repression. . . . Most of the prevailing needs to relax, to have fun, to behave and consume in accordance with the advertisements, to love and hate what others love and hate, belong to the category of false needs . . . which are determined by external forces over which the individual has no control. . . . The only needs that have an unqualified claim for satisfaction are the vital ones—nourishment, clothing, lodging. [38]

According to Marcuse, inner freedom "designates the private space in which man may become and remain 'himself.' . . . Today the private space has been invaded and whittled down by technological reality."

The basic questions are obviously, Who is this "himself," and What is the origin of his structural elements? Is there any way to provide the experience which will form a baby's mind except by means of the "external powers" of parents, teachers, and culture over which the baby has no control? Are we then going to classify a child's needs as false because they were inculcated? Where is the inner man?

Marcuse's pleas for "intellectual freedom" and his criticism of "material and intellectual needs that perpetuate obsolete forms of the struggle for existence" are certainly valid, but a state of unqualified liberty cannot be supposed to exist for the infant, who is totally dependent physically and psychologically on his surroundings. Freedom must be taught and created.

The mutual dependence of the individual and the "psychic environment" or "noosphere" has been elaborated by Teilhard de Chardin, who wrote that the Universal and Personal "grow in the same direction and culminate simultaneously in each other," the "Hyper-Personal" consciousness at the "Omega point." [51] While it is true that each of us personally receives, interprets, and feels the world around us, why should our individual half be opposed by the noospheric half? Teilhard de Chardin, like Ortega y Gasset and most other philosophers, accepts the existence of the quasi-mystical, inviolable self, an entity somehow identified with the individual mind, ego, or personality, related to the environment, but with a relatively independent existence.

Recent neurophysiological and psychological studies discussed here reveal that this is not the case. The origin of memories, emotional reactivity, motor skills, words, ideas, and behavioral patterns which constitute our personal self can be traced to the environment outside of the individual. Each person is a transitory composite of materials borrowed from the environment, and his mind is the intracerebral elaboration of extracerebral information. The "personal half" is a regrouping of elements of the environment. For the final result, which is manifested as individual reactivity and behavioral responses, the building blocks from culture are more decisive than the individual substratum within which the regrouping is performed.

It is impressive that this is actually the philosophy, as described by Levi-Strauss, [34] of the Bororo Indians, a very primitive tribe living by the Vermelho River in the Amazon jungles of Brazil. For the Bororo, a man is not an individual, but a part of a sociological universe. Their villages exist "for all eternity," forming part of the physical universe along with other animate beings, celestial bodies, and meteorological phenomena. Human shape is transitory, midway between that of the fish and the arara. Human life is merely a department of culture. Death is both natural and anticultural, and whenever a native dies, damage is inflicted not only on his relatives, but on society as a whole. Nature is blamed, and Nature must pay the debt; therefore, a collective hunt is organized to kill some sizable animal, if possible a jaguar, in order to bring home its skin, teeth, and nails, which will constitute the dead man's *mori*, his everlasting personal value.

The conclusion that human beings are part of culture does not deny the fact that individuals have individual reactions and that their brains are unique combinations of elements, but simply points to the source and quality of the factors of personal identity. The cerebral mechanisms which allow us to receive, interpret, feel, and react, as well as the extracerebral sources of stimuli, can and should be investigated experimentally. Then we shall gain a new awareness of the structure of the individual and his relations with the surrounding noosphere.

REFERENCES AND SUGGESTED READINGS

1. Ahfeld, J. F., "Beiträge zur Lehre vom Uebergange der instrauterinen Athmung zur extrauterinen," in *Beiträge zur Physiologie, Festschrift zu Carl Ludwig, zu seinem 20. Geburtstage gewidmet von seinen Schülern.* Leipzig: Vogel, 1890.
2. Angulo Y. Gonzalez, A. W., "Is Myelinogeny an Absolute Index of Behavioral Capability?" *Journal of Comparative Neurology,* Vol. 48, 1929.
3. Berlyne, D. E., *Conflict, Arousal, and Curiosity.* New York: McGraw-Hill, 1960.
4. Bexton, W. H., W. Heron, and T. H. Scott, "Effects of Decreased Variation in the Sensory Environment," *Canadian Journal of Psychology,* Vol. 8, 1954.
5. Canestrini, S., "Uber das Sinnesleben des Neugeborenen," *Monographien aus dem Gesamtgebiete der Neurologie und Psychiatrie,* No. 5, Berlin: Springer, 1913.
6. Cantril, Hadley, and W. K. Livingston, "The Concept of Transaction in Psychology and Neurology," *Journal of Individual Psychology,* Vol. 19, 1963.
7. Carmichael, L., "The Onset and Early Development of Behavior," in *Manual of Child Psychology,* 3rd. ed., ed. by L. Carmichael. New York: Wiley, 1960, pp. 60–185.
8. Caspari, E., "Genetic Basis of Behavior," in *Behavior and Evolution,* ed. by A. Role and G. G. Simpson. New Haven, Conn.: Yale University Press, 1958, pp. 103–127.
9. Coghill, G. E., "Correlated Anatomical and Physiological Studies of the Growth of the Nervous System and Amphibia: The Mechanism of Association of Amblystoma Punctatum," *Journal of Comparative Neurology,* Vol. 51, 1930.
10. Coghill, G. E., "The Mechanism of Integration in Amblystoma Punctatum," *Journal of Comparative Neurology,* Vol. 41, 1926.
11. Coghill, G. E., "The Structural Basis of the Integration of Behavior," *Proceedings of the National Academy of Sciences,* Vol. 16, 1930.
12. Coghill, G. E., "Correlaries of the Anatomical and Physiological Study of Amblystoma from the Age of Earliest Movement to Swimming," *Journal of Comparative Neurology,* Vol. 53, 1931.
13. Cole, L. C., "Can The World Be Saved?" *BioScience,* Vol. 18, 1968.
14. Dobzhansky, T., "Genetics, Society and Evolution," *Bulletin of the New York Academy of Medicine,* Vol. 38, 1862.

15. Dunbar, F., *Emotions and Bodily Changes. A Survey of Literature on Psychosomatic Interrelationships 1910–1953,* 4th ed. New York: Columbia University Press, 1954.

16. Erlanger, J. E., and H. S. Gasser, *Electrical Signs of Nervous Activity.* Philadelphia: University of Pennsylvania Press, 1937.

17. Forbes, A., "The Interpretation of Spinal Reflexes in Terms of Present Knowledge of Nerve Conduction," *Physiology Revue,* Vol. 3, 1922.

18. Forbes, H. S., and H. B. Forbes, "Fetal Sense Reaction: Hearing," *Journal of Comparative Psychology,* Vol. 7, 1927.

19. Furfey, P. H., M. A. Bonham, and M. K. Sargent, "The Mental Organization of the Newborn," *Child Development,* Vol. 1, 1930.

20. Genzmer, A., *Untersuchungen über die Sinneswahrnehmungen des Neugeborenen Menschen,* dissertation, 1873. Halle: Niemeyer, 1882.

21. Gesell, A. L., *Infancy and Human Growth.* New York: Macmillan, 1928.

22. Harlow, H. F., M. K. Harlow, and D. R. Meyer, "Learning Motivated by a Manipulation Drive," *Journal of Experimental Psychology,* Vol. 40, 1950.

23. Heron, W., "The Pathology of Boredom," *Scientific American,* Vol. 196, 1957.

24. Herrick, C. H., *Neurological Foundations of Animal Behavior.* New York: Hafner, 1962.

25. Hooker, D., "Fetal Behavior," *Association for Research in Nervous and Mental Disease Research Publications,* Vol. 19, 1939.

26. James, W., *Principles of Psychology,* Vols. I and II. New York: Dover, 1950.

27. Jennings, H. S., *The Biological Basis of Human Nature.* New York: Norton, 1930.

28. Kussmaul, A., *Untersuchungen über das Seelenleben des Neugeborenen Menschen,* Leipzig, 1859.

29. Lane, H. H., "The Correlation Between Structure and Function in the Development of the Special Senses of the White Rat," *University of Oklahoma Bulletin,* N.S. No. 140, 1917.

30. Lange, F. A., *History of Materialism.* New York: Harcourt, Brace, 1925.

31. Langworthy, O. R., "A Correlated Study of the Development of Reflex Activity in Fetal and Young Kittens and the Myelinization of Tracts in the Nervous System," *Contributions to Embryology,* Carnegie Institute, Washington, 20, No. 114, 1929.

32. Lashley, K. S., "Studies of Cerebral Function in Learning: VI. The Theory That Synaptic Resistance is Reduced by the Passage of the Nerve Impulse," *Psychology Revue,* Vol. 31, 1924.

33. Leiderman, P. H., J. H. Mendelson, D. Wexler, and P. Solomon, "Sensory Deprivation: Clinical Aspects," *Archives of Internal Medicine,* Vol. 101, 1958.

34. Levi-Strauss, C., *A World of the Wane,* trans. by J. Russell, London: Hutchinson, 1961.

35. Lifton, R. J., *Thought Reform and the Psychology of Totalism: A Study of "Brainwashing" in China.* New York: Norton, 1961.

36. Lillie, R. S., *Protoplasmic Action and Nervous System,* 2nd ed. Chicago: University of Chicago Press, 1932.

37. Locke, J., *Essays Concerning Human Understanding.* Cambridge, Mass.: Harvard University Press, 1931.

38. Marcuse, Herbert, *One Dimensional Man.* Boston: Beacon Press, 1964.

39. Minkowski, M., "Sur Les Mouvements, Les Réflexes, et Les Réactions Musculaieres du Foetus Humain de 2 à 5 Mois et Leur Rélations Avec le Système Nerveux Foetal," *Revue of Embryology,* Vol. 37, 1921.

40. Mittleman, B., "Motility in Infants, Children, and Adults: Patterning and Psychodynamics," *Psychoanalytical Study of the Child*, Vol. 9, 1954.
41. Ortega y Gasset, José, *History as a System*. New York: Norton, 1961.
42. Ortega y Gasset, José, *Meditations on Quixote*, trans. by E. Rugg and D. Marin, with notes and introduction by J. Marias. New York: Norton, 1961.
43. Peterson, F., and L. H. Rainey, "The Beginnings of Mind in the Newborn," *Bulletin of Lying-in Hospital*, New York, Vol. 7, 1910.
44. Pflüger, E., "Die Lebensfähigkeit des menschlichen Foetus," *Pflüger Archiv für die gesamte Physiologie*, Vol. 14, 1877.
45. Piaget, Jean, *The Origins of Intelligence in Children*, trans. by Margaret Cook. New York: International Universities, 1952.
46. Pratt, K. C., A. K. Nelson, and K. H. Sun, "The Behavior of the Newborn Infant," *Ohio State University Studies, Contributions in Psychology*, No. 19, 1930.
47. Rainer, J. D., "The Concept of Mind in the Framework of Genetics," in *Theories of the Mind*, ed. by J. M. Scher. New York: Free Press, 1962, pp. 65–79.
48. Schultz, D. P., *Sensory Restriction, Effects on Behavior*. New York: Academic Press, 1965.
49. Sherrington, C. S., *The Integrative Action of the Nervous System*. New York: Cambridge University Press, 2nd ed., 1947.
50. Sprague, J. M., W. W. Chambers, and E. Stellar, "Attentive, Affective, and Adaptive Behavior in the Cat," *Science*, Vol. 133, 1961.
51. Teilhard de Chardin, P., *The Phenomenon of Man*. New York: Harper & Row, 1959.
52. Thomas, A., and S. Chess, "An Approach to the Study of Sources of Individual Differences in Child Behavior," *Journal of Clinical Experimental Psychopathology*, Vol. 19, 1957.
53. Tilney, F., and L. Casamajor, "Myelinogeny as Applied to the Study of Behavior," *Archives of Neurological Psychiatry*, Vol. 12, 1924.
54. Tracy, H. C., "The Development of Motility and Behavior Reactions in the Toadfish (Opsanus Tau)," *Journal of Comparative Neurology*, Vol. 40, 1926.
55. Weiss, A. P., "The Measurement of Infant Behavior," *Psychology Revue*, Vol. 36, 1929.
56. Weiss, P., "Self-differentiation of the Basic Patterns of Coordination," *Comparative Psychology Monographs*, Vol. 17, 1941.
57. West, L. J., "Psychiatry, 'Brainwashing,' and the American Character," *American Journal of Psychiatry*, Vol. 120, 1964.

Dr. Randall P. Harrison is Associate Professor of Communication at Michigan State University. He has written numerous articles and papers in the area of nonverbal behavior and has contributed chapters to *Dimensions in Communication,* edited by J. Campbell and H. Hepler, and *Education Media: Theory and Practice,* edited by W. Meierhenry and R. Wiman. Dr. Harrison has just completed a year in residence at the Institute for Studies in Nonverbal Behavior, San Francisco, and is currently preparing a comprehensive volume on nonverbal communication.

15

NONVERBAL BEHAVIOR: AN APPROACH TO HUMAN COMMUNICATION

RANDALL P. HARRISON

NONVERBAL communication, unlike the other approaches in this book, is not a traditional discipline, or an intellectual fraternity of like-minded scholars. Rather, it is itself one corner of that edifice we call "communication." It, too, has been visited by psychologists, artists, sociologists, ethologists, psychiatrists, anthropologists. Each of these visitors has left his mark, and for a time, nonverbal communication looked like an old storeroom, cluttered with amusing anecdotes and assorted intellectual junk that didn't fit into the properly arranged rooms of "real" communication study.

Recently, however, changes have taken place. The early visitors to nonverbal communication brought back such interesting intellectual artifacts that others began to suspect there was more in that dusty corner than they first supposed. Some even suggested that with diligent excavation, it might be discovered that under the edifice "communication" was another whole room, or even another building—or a city.

So over the past two decades, various search parties have set out—from anthropology, from psychology, from sociology. They have dug in various spots, and the more they have dug, the more it has seemed that they were on to something big. At first, of course, they could each dig separately, not worrying about what someone else was finding.

Very recently, however, some of these explorers have begun to "bump into each other," to compare their findings and even their digging methods. In addition, some of these explorers have been in the field so long, they have begun to think of nonverbal communication as their home.

They mutter that maybe there should be a discipline of nonverbal communication. And the really radical fringe mumbles: "Actually, we're the *real* communication; that verbal stuff is just the tip of the iceberg."

DEFINING *NONVERBAL*

As it has evolved, the phrase "nonverbal communication" cuts a broad swath. It has been applied by writers to many things: ESP, attempted communication with life on other planets, self-awareness, perfumery, the touch of love, the fist of anger, the TV commercial, the street demonstration, the braless girl and the topless dancer.

As nonverbal researchers begin to talk more about what they are doing, they become more self-conscious about the way they use terminology. While there is still no consensus on some key terms, the boundaries are becoming better articulated.

The liberal wing tends to apply "nonverbal communication" to almost everything: any stimulus that impinges on man, animal, plant, or machine. Raindrops on one's head, sunshine on the petals, and electrical impulse in a circuit are all nonverbal communication to the liberal. The study of *human* nonverbal communication is a narrower field. Here, one group points out that all behavior done in the presence of another has communication value, or, as Watzlawick and his associates observe, "You can't not communicate." [50] Even silence and rigid inactivity may tell your partner that you're angry, annoyed, depressed, or fearful.

A middle-of-the-road position suggests that it would be useful to introduce constructs such as "signs" or "codes" to distinguish nonverbal communication from a host of other experiences. In other words, not all stimuli are signs; the latter refers to a special subset of stimuli which can be used to represent other potential stimuli, just as the word *cow* stands for that four-legged creature in the pasture. Similarly, *code* suggests that there is a set of signs, with rules for combining these stimuli, that is, a syntax and an agreement as to what these signs and combinations mean.

Finally, some theorists would restrict nonverbal communication further by imposing qualifications such as *intentionality*. In other words, there might be nonverbal behaviors, such as gestures or facial expressions, which are informative to an observer; but unless these are done with the intent of communicating, they would be ruled outside the borders of nonverbal communication. Similarly, various restrictions can be placed on the complexity or universality of the code employed. If, for instance, you tie a string around your finger to remind yourself of something, and if no one else in your culture does that, or knows what it means, you have a limited, one-symbol code system with no shared meaning. Some researchers would just as soon drop such simple systems from consideration.

While this suggests possible outer boundaries for nonverbal communication, it does not as yet deal with the inner boundary, that gray area between verbal and nonverbal communication. The simplest solution is to define verbal communication as anything that uses written or spoken words, with nonverbal picking up any other kind of symbol. There is, however, an area called "paralanguage," which is vocal, but not strictly verbal. This includes stress, inflection, juncture, and nonword vocalizations such as "umm" and "ah." Sometimes this area is ceded to verbal communication, with nonverbal picking up other vocalizations such as grunts, laughter, sighs, coughs, burps, and so forth.

REDEFINING *COMMUNICATION*

As more and more of the nonverbal domain is unearthed, researchers argue that traditional definitions of communication are too limited. It is increasingly obvious, these researchers suggest, that definitions which emphasize verbal stimuli miss important dimensions of the communication process. Similarly, there has been some discontent with definitions which restrict communication to the intentional or purposeful. Some nonverbal cues operate at a very low level of awareness; while everyone in a culture seems to know how the system works, few can articulate what is going on, nor will they admit to purposely doing what they are obviously doing. All normal people, for instance, are quite capable of regulating a conversation with eye contact and head nods. Yet most people are quite surprised when they are told what they are doing and how they are doing it.

Two quite different approaches to defining communication are taken by Ray L. Birdwhistell, an anthropologist, and Paul Ekman, a psychologist. Birdwhistell, who stimulated much of the recent interest in nonverbal communication, now does not use *nonverbal* and *communication* together. He argues that when communication is properly understood, it is a multichannel phenomenon which must incorporate nonverbal as well as verbal activity. To him, nonverbal communication is like "noncardiac physiology"—a meaningless category.

Ekman, meanwhile, distinguishes between "communicative" and "informative" nonverbal behavior. The former is characterized by intent; the latter includes those activities which may be meaningful to an observer, for example, a trained psychiarist, but which are not done with the intent of communicating. This obviously leaves a third category of nonverbal behavior which is neither communicative nor informative. Some writers seem to imply that scratching or stretching is communication, because it feels good and is therefore meaningful to the person doing it. To Ekman, if these behaviors were unintended and unobserved, they would be neither communicative nor informative.

Still a third approach to defining communication is taken by Christopher Brannigan and David Humphries,[7] two British scientists who come to nonverbal communication from ethology, that is, the study of animal behavior. They say an act of communication occurs any time certain attributes of one individual are capable of altering the future behavior of a second individual. They, of course, are intrigued to note that certain behaviors and responses in humans can also be noted in lower animals. These patterns of interaction apparently had survival value for other species, and have been carried over to undergird human interaction.

A fourth and final approach to defining communication can be seen in the work of Paul Watzlawick and his associates.[50] Working in psychotherapy, and drawing on general systems theory, these researchers define communication as virtually any behavior performed in the presence of another. They distinguish, however, between two dimensions: content and relationship. The former is what is being talked about; the latter refers to those messages which articulate the relationship between communicators —who is superior, how intimate or distant the relationship is, and the like. Similarly, these "metacommunicational" messages reveal the communicator's relationship to the content: how he feels about it, how he evaluates it, what he intends to do about it.

While nonverbal researchers do not agree on a single definition of communication, the work in nonverbal has led to a new perspective on communication: (1) definitions which emphasize only verbal stimuli are seen as clearly inadequate; (2) previous defining characteristics, such as intentionality, purposefulness, and awareness, are being reexamined in a new light; and (3) new attention is being directed to other dimensions of communication, for example, to the emotional as well as the cognitive, to the innate as well as the learned, and to messages about relationship as well as messages about content.

DIMENSIONS IN THE NONVERBAL APPROACH

Although the nonverbal field is becoming increasingly interdisciplinary, it is still possible to identify within it the various disciplines that have explored the area; the anthropological-linguistic school as opposed to the psychological, or the sociological, or the psychotherapeutic, or the ethological. Since this whole book deals with the contributions of these traditions, it may be redundant to reiterate the dimensions highlighted by each discipline. In general, what can be said about communication as a whole applies to the subarea of nonverbal.

An alternate approach is to spotlight two major dimensions: (1) attempts to articulate or "break" the nonverbal codes, and (2) attempts to explicate the functions of nonverbal communication. While these two dimensions are intertwined, they emphasize two distinct problems for the nonverbal researcher.

In the first area, researchers have asked: What nonverbal codes are available to the communicator? What are the code elements, the basic nonverbal signs? And what are the semantics, that is, what do the codes mean and how do they come to have those meanings?

Meanwhile, the functional question is: What do nonverbal signs do in communication systems? What role do they play? While, in part, this is a semantic question, it is not answered by giving the meaning of a nonverbal sign or a whole set of signs. It is a broader question: What things can be communicated nonverbally?

Breaking the Nonverbal Codes

The most obvious nonverbal code stems from the use of the body: facial expression, gesture, body position, and movement. This area of study is known as kinesics. A second major area is the vocal but nonverbal, the area called paralanguage or "extralinguistic." A third area which has been chalked out is "proxemics"—the use of space in communication. While additional areas have been labeled, these three are the primary regions typically mentioned as nonverbal communication.

In their discussion of kinesic and nonverbal research, Larry Barker and Nancy Collins [2] identify eighteen areas of nonverbal study, including animal and insect communication, the media, machines, physiological aspects, music, and time. Meanwhile, Mark Knapp [31] organizes his book around seven major areas: (1) body motion of kinesics, (2) physical characteristics, (3) touching behavior, (4) paralanguage, (5) proxemics, (6) artifacts, and (7) environment.

A fairly comprehensive classification can be obtained by labeling four major sets of codes: (1) performance codes—those nonverbal signs which originate in bodily action, such as facial expression, eye movement, gestures, body posture, tactile contact, and olfaction (included here also are those signs which emanate from nonverbal vocalization such as yawns, laughter, grunts); (2) artifactual codes—those nonverbal signs which arise through the manipulation of cosmetics, dress, furnishings, art objects, status symbols, architecture, and the like; (3) mediational codes—nonverbal signs which emerge in the selections, arrangements, and inventions within the media; for example, the editor, the film director, or the TV producer can recode events by selecting color or black-and-white, photography or cartoon, close-up or long-shot; and (4) contextual codes—nonverbal symbols which arise in the use of time and space, crucial cues which set the tone and the pace of a communication system.

Within each of these areas may be several codes, ranging from the very simple, such as the string on the finger mentioned earlier, to very complex systems with large vocabularies of nonverbal signs and intricate, multileveled syntactic organizations. To date, most work has been done on the very simple, which serve as interesting anecdotes, or on those which are complex, but closely parallel verbal language, for example, Indian sign language or those kinesic areas most similar to paralanguage.

Functions of Nonverbal

When communication scholars first began to look at the nonverbal area, they tended to see it as an adjunct to verbal communication. On occasion, it seemed that facial expression or gestures or pictures could embellish what man was saying verbally, providing helpful redundancy or emphasis, or even saying the same thing more efficiently, like the proverbial picture worth a thousand words.

With the probing of anthropologists, psychologists, and ethologists, however, a somewhat different picture has begun to emerge. Both in the evolution of the species and in the development of individual humans, nonverbal communication appears to precede verbal communication. Thus, some now argue that we learn first to communicate nonverbally, and these basic patterns of interaction remain relatively fixed, with only minor shifts and elaborations when the verbal embellishment is added. To understand fundamental patterns of human interaction then, one must start with the nonverbal rather than the verbal.

Similarly, a concern with nonverbal cues shifts attention to the way communication systems are maintained and regulated; the smile, the nod, the eye contact, the posture may or may not communicate content, but these slight messages may be vital to the initiation, continuation, or termination of interaction.

In general, nonverbal signs appear to operate at three levels. First, they define, condition, and constrain the communication system. For instance, the time of day, or allotted time, the setting, and the arrangement of props may cue the participants on who is in the system, what the pattern of interaction will be, and what is appropriate or inappropriate conversational fare. Secondly, nonverbal cues help to regulate the communication system. They signal status hierarchies, indicate who is to speak next, provide feedback about evaluations and intentions. Finally, nonverbal signs communicate content. Sometimes, the nonverbal code is more efficient; for example, relationships are more easily preserved in an analogic code, such as a map, a blueprint, a picture, a model. Sometimes, the nonverbal code is more effective, perhaps because it uses an additional modality such as touch, or odor, or even taste. And sometimes, the nonverbal code increases efficiency and effectiveness because it provides useful redundancy, another way of saying the same thing.

RESEARCH STRATEGIES

Starkey Duncan,[12] in his review of nonverbal communication, distinguishes two major research strategies: (1) the structural approach, and (2) the external-variable approach. The first tends to look for the structure or rules among nonverbal behaviors. It assumes that nonverbal codes are like language and that methods which have been so fruitful in linguistics will also be useful in breaking the nonverbal codes. The second approach tends to isolate promising nonverbal behaviors and then to examine their relationships to other variables, such as the personality or emotional state of the performer, the interaction situation, or the judgments of an observer.

While Duncan's dichotomy oversimplifies some of the current trends, it does serve to highlight two major streams in nonverbal research. In large part, these streams reflect two major traditions in the study of nonverbal: the anthropological-linguistic and the psychological.

Psychologists such as Paul Ekman or Ralph Exline tend to focus on one type of nonverbal behavior at a time, for example, facial expression, or hand gesture, or eye behavior. Ray Birdwhistell, in the anthropological-linguistic tradition, or Albert Scheflen, in the psychiatric frame, want to look at all that is going on in a given communication system; they argue against one particular type of behavior, or looking at the individual in isolation.

Another distinguishing characteristic of the two approaches is methodology. The psychological or external-variable approach tends to use more statistics and experimental manipulations. Meanwhile, the anthropological approach tends to depend more on linguistic methodologies or the natural-history approach. (See for instance, the chapters in this text by Ralph Exline, Duane Pettersen, and Alfred Smith.)

A middle ground is taken by social psychologists such as Howard Rosenfeld [38; 39] or Albert Mehrabian.[35] These researchers tend to look at nonverbal behavior in an interaction setting, but typically with some experimental manipulation. They might, for instance, program one participant to behave in a particular way and then observe the effects of this behavior on the other participant. For example, Rosenfeld instructed one member of a dyad to seek or avoid the approval of his partner; the partner was a confederate who was instructed to act the same no matter what the other individual did. Rosenfeld then recorded changes in head nods, smiling, gesticulation, and self-manipulations in the approval-seeking and the approval-avoiding conditions.

In contrast to these three strategies, the ethologists have now arrived on the scene, with methodologies carried over from studies of animal behavior. Researchers such as Brannigan, Humphries,[7] and E. C. Grant [23] like to observe nonverbal behavior in naturalistic settings. They have, for instance, observed children at play in a nursery school. For the human ethologist, behavior patterns are recorded and then classified according to those having (1) the same consequences, (2) the same function, (3) the same situation, or (4) the same cause. Differences and similarities may then be seen between, say, an angry brow and a clenched fist.

While these four approaches—the anthropological-linguistic, the psychological, the social-psychological, and the ethological—seem fairly distinct in pure form, researchers in nonverbal communication are moving toward a common center. Increasingly, it is difficult to label researchers with a tag from one discipline. And while basic disagreements exist, the question seems to be primarily one of priorities: Which techniques will move us more rapidly to an understanding of nonverbal communication?

MAJOR NONVERBAL RESEARCHERS

For those interested in history, the study of nonverbal communication can be traced back at least to the time of Aristotle, and perhaps to the time of Moses. Similarly in the East, very early studies were made of pictographic writing, of statuary and design, and of astrological symbols.

The modern era of scientific study, however, is perhaps best begun with Charles Darwin,[8] who penned a tome entitled *The Expression of Emotions in Man and Animals,* after completing his great work on evolution. Darwin was a very good scientist indeed, and he carefully observed and experimented, he compared human expressions with animal expressions, and he wrote to scientist friends around the world to gather data about other animals and other races. A key thrust of Darwin's work was that human expressions are at least in part innate, surviving from evolutionary forces in lower animals. The smile, for instance, might be linked to the pleasant experience of baring the teeth in anticipation of biting into a juicy victim.

While Darwin had a strong influence on psychology in Europe, he was pretty well rejected in America until the past decade. Here, facial expressions were thought to be strictly learned, social habits. However, Paul Ekman has recently summed up the evidence for innate, or at least panhuman, facial expressions of emotion. On the basis of extensive cross-cultural research by Ekman and others, it now appears that Darwin was indeed right—a century ago.

Early psychologists focused on the possible validity of reading man's character, or even his fate, from his facial features—physiognomy. Studies indicated that many popular stereotypes were not very accurate, for example, close-set eyes did not mean a "criminal type," a low forehead did not necessarily indicate low intelligence, a small chin did not mean a weak character, and so on. Psychologists did. find, however, strong agreement among judges about these stereotypes, even if they were inaccurate. This then became an interesting problem for the social psychologist, and it launched some of the early studies in the area now known as "person perception."

While psychologists were able to dispose fairly easily of physiognomy, facial expressions indicating emotion proved to be a more difficult problem. What is the relation of expression to emotion? Can people accurately read expressions of emotion? How many emotions are there? Are there a few major dimensions of emotion? What are the facial cues for each emotion? These are questions which bothered—and defeated—some of the best researchers of this century.

In a recent book, Paul Ekman, Wallace Friesen, and Phoebe Ellsworth [16] reexamined studies in this area. They found that most of the great names in psychology experimented in this field at one time or another. And many of them committed fundamental mistakes in trying to unravel this slippery problem.

Ekman's own research now indicates that there is a set of facially expressed emotions which can be decoded with great accuracy by most people. Building on Silvan Tomkin's theory of emotion, Ekman and his associates have distinguished unique cues for happiness, surprise, anger, sadness, contempt-disgust, fear, and pain. The researchers have also explored what are known as "micro-momentary" expressions—fleeting and sometimes partial facial displays which occur, for instance, in conversation. They find that people differ in their ability to pick up and decode these super-rapid expressions, and that some individuals "block" on one or more affects; that is, they will do significantly less well in catching, say, anger or contempt. Similarly, under the effects of alcohol or marijuana, the same individuals may differ in their sensitivity to certain expressions, such as contempt or happiness. Finally, Ekman and his associates have made the startling discovery that facial expressions of emotion while watching television relate to later aggressive behavior; little boys who look happy during violence on TV later aggress more against other children.

While several perennial questions on facial communication now appear to be on their way to resolution, other questions in the nonverbal spectrum are not. Next to the face, gestures—and body movement in general—have received the most research, and have been the hardest to crack.

The Nazis propounded a theory of the master race. One tenet was that certain peoples—in this case, the Jews—were inherently inferior. According to Nazi propaganda you could tell this by their odd, non-Aryan gestures.

Franz Boas, the great anthropologist, set out to find scientific evidence for this issue. He encouraged one of his students, David Efron, to study the gestural pattern of immigrant Jews and Italians from New York's lower east side, to see, first, if there really were differences in gesture, and, if so, whether these patterns changed over time or from generation to generation.

Efron made an exhaustive study and concluded that, indeed, you could tell the difference between Jewish and Italian gestural patterns. But he also found that in second-generation youngsters these distinctive patterns seemed to fade away, with Jewish youngsters picking up the gestures of their Italian playmates and vice versa. Efron's research was a major breakthrough in the study of gestural communication. Unfortunately, with the onset of World War II, Efron returned to his native Argentina, and for thirty years no one followed up his interesting lead. Recently, however, his book [13] has been republished, and researchers such as Paul Ekman and Wallace Friesen have begun to use the constructs Efron proposed three decades ago.

Kinesics

During World War II and in the difficult postwar years, Americans became increasingly aware of other cultures and the problems of cross-cultural communication. Frequently, there were bizarre breakdowns in such communications, not only because of misunderstanding over what was said, but also over the way they were said—and done. For example, an American might make an "A-OK" sign with his hand in polite European company. In many cultures, that same sign is an obscene gesture representing the female genitalia. To a young woman, it is, in effect, a proposition; to a man, it is an accusation of homosexuality. Needless to say, the consequences of such a gesture were frequently far from "A-OK." In another instance an American might offer food with his left hand. This is considered a grievous insult in certain parts of the world where the left hand is reserved for cleansing the body. Or, an American might become furious when left waiting far past what to him was an appropriate waiting time. Or he might feel distinctly uncomfortable when a foreigner encroached upon his "personal space." These are just a few of the problems Americans confronted when they set out to communicate in other cultures.

Naturally, anthropologists had a great deal of experience in studying other cultures, and their expertise was brought to bear on this problem. Anthropologists such as Birdwhistell and Hall have done some of their early work for the Foreign Service Institute.

Birdwhistell, who is reported to have worked at one time as a vaudeville dancer, brought to his study a keen eye for detail and an amazing ability to mimic expressions and gesture. Well-trained in linguistics, Birdwhistell has concluded that body movements might well be a gestural language not unlike verbal language. This approach, which he calls kinesics, has sought to break the gestural code, just as a linguist would go about breaking an unknown verbal language.

At a very basic level, the linguist isolates rudimentary sounds, which are called "phones." Similarly, Birdwhistell attempts to isolate rudimentary movements, or "kines." Phones which are interchangeable are grouped into a "phoneme." The *t* sound in *team* and *butter* might be distinguishably different to the well-trained ear, but in American English, those two phones belong to the same phoneme. In some other language, however, that difference might be as important as the difference between our *p* and *b,* or our *r* and *l* (two sounds which are merely interchangeable phones in many Oriental languages). Analogously, the kinesicist looks for interchangeable kines which make up a "kineme" in a particular culture. After extensive research, Birdwhistell reports some thirty-two such kinemes in the face and head area.

Unfortunately, there are many problems in kinesic research. Birdwhistell has found, for instance, that the informant technique, so fundamental in linguistic study, is very difficult in gestural studies. In this technique, the linguist presents the native informant—a person who knows the language —with two very similar words, for example, *pin* and *bin*. If the informant points to two different objects, obviously the *p* and *b* sounds are not the same—they are probably different phonemes. However, getting an informant to perform, or discriminate between, two body movements is very difficult.

Another problem in the kinesic approach is the assumption that all body movement is culturally learned and therefore open to research in the same way as in language. To the extent that certain patterns are innate, or at least uniformly learned in the species, there are aspects of behavior which may not follow the language model. The mounting evidence on the universality of facial expressions of emotion suggests that there is at least one area which should be extracted and analyzed separately.

Proxemics

Just as Birdwhistell has applied the linguistic model to body movement, Hall has adopted this analogy for dealing with all the primary message systems, a host of cultural facets which Hall sees as communication. Where the linguist analyzes language into phonemes, morphemes, and syntax, Hall uses comparable constructs which he calls "isolates," "sets," and "patterns."

In his two major works, *The Silent Language* [24] and *The Hidden*

Dimension,[25] Hall makes an extensive analysis of the use of time and space, and the implications of this use for communication. Early in his work, he notes that other cultures make different use of space; in some countries, people stand very close when they converse, in other countries, each individual maintains a sizable space around his person, which is not easily violated. Similarly, some cultures divide up time very precisely and use it very efficiently; other cultures think such a use of time is inhuman and ridiculous.

In the American culture, Hall notes four different zones for different types of interaction. He describes them as the intimate, personal, social, and public zones, and he suggests that different types of communication are appropriate for each. Among other things, a different range of nonverbal signs becomes available or unavailable in kinesthetic, thermal, olfactory, visual, and oral-aural modalities.

Psychotherapy

While cross-cultural communication was gaining attention, the nonverbal dimension was also cropping up in quite a different arena: the interaction of the psychotherapist and his patient. Frequently, the psychiatrist found that the patient was saying one thing verbally, but feeling something quite different—perhaps without even realizing it. The patient might profess to love his wife, but at the same time remove his wedding ring each time his wife's name came up. Such gestures could be very revealing to the therapist and could be used to tap feelings the patient himself did not know he had.

Jurgen Ruesch and Weldon Kees [40] were among the first to use nonverbal communication as the title for a major book. In their volume, Ruesch elaborates on some of the constructs he developed earlier in the psychiatric literature, and he probes the everyday world, the nonverbal facets which might contribute to, or detract from, good mental health.

Ruesch is particularly concerned with the difference between analogic and digital codes, noting that certain ideas, feelings, and messages can be dealt with more effectively in analogic, nonverbal modes. Primarily, the book is a summary of insights and a call for research into nonverbal communication. But it symbolizes a concern which has matured in the research efforts of such men as Joel Davitz, Allen Dittmann, Paul Ekman, and Albert Scheflen.

Interaction

As more has been learned about the nonverbal area, and about communication generally, research has, of course, spread to other areas: healthy interaction as well as the clinical interview; the mass media, particularly television; instructional media, especially the new technology; and a wide range of other fields. While it is not possible to explore all these areas, the bibliography at the end of this chapter provides a sampling of research in many areas. In particular, new books devoted to nonverbal communication provide broader surveys of research and more extensive bibliographies.

One of these volumes may be of special note, *Silent Messages* by Albert Mehrabian. Written in a very popular vein, the book summarizes much of Mehrabian's own research, and it provides a somewhat different tack from the other approaches discussed here.

Very briefly, Mehrabian sees three dimensions to any communication system, and a range of nonverbal signs for dealing with these dimensions. First, there is the problem of "immediacy"—questions of liking-disliking. Second, there is the problem of "power"—who will be dominant and who will be submissive? Finally, there is the problem of what he calls "living things"—how responsive or unresponsive is each participant? Examining physical proximity and a host of facial and gestural cues, Mehrabian makes a variety of predictions about human interaction.

On the basis of his research, Mehrabian comes up with a flat, quantitative evaluation for verbal and nonverbal communication: the verbal contributes 7 percent; vocal (paralinguistic) cues contribute 38 percent; and facial expression provides 55 percent. While these figures come out of a rather specific set of experiments, Mehrabian appears willing to generalize these ratios quite broadly.

FUTURE TRENDS

The field of nonverbal communication has moved so fast in the past decade, it seems dangerous to make predictions for the immediate future. But a few obvious trends are building.

First, those early pioneers who thought there was something worth digging for appear to be right. Much has been uncovered, and these leads in turn have stimulated new interest and new research efforts. Whereas the field was once lonely, with a few scattered explorers who seldom spoke, there is now a growing legion of researchers who constatly share findings and methodologies. There even appears to be some growing agreement about what to look for—what units of analysis will most pay off. At least, there are now several clearly articulated positions and systems.

The inflow of new theoretic fuel, such as the recent addition of ethology, has kept the intellectual arguments burning. But it has also forged some sharp new tools for slicing into the nonverbal domain. Similarly, new technology has replaced the primitive picks and shovels used by early explorers. High fidelity, low-cost video-tape equipment has supplemented the still photo and the intrusive, temperamental motion-picture camera. And computer installations have facilitated the processing and retrieval of video-tape records.

Finally, the ore that is being mined in the nonverbal field appears to be very useful. It provides new purchase on some of man's oldest communication problems.

REFERENCES AND SUGGESTED READINGS

1. Argyle, Michael, *Social Interaction.* New York: Atherton, 1969.
2. Barker, L. L., and N. B. Collins, "Nonverbal and Kinesic Research," in *Methods of Research in Communication,* ed. by P. Emmert and W. D. Brooks. Boston: Houghton Mifflin, 1970.
3. Birdwhistell, Ray L., "Communication," in *International Encyclopedia of Social Science,* Vol. 3, ed. by D. L. Sills. New York: Macmillan, 1968.
4. Birdwhistell, Ray L., "Kinesics," in *International Encyclopedia of Social Science,* Vol. 8, ed. by D. L. Sills. New York: Macmillan, 1968.
5. Birdwhistell, Ray L., *Kinesics and Context.* Philadelphia: University of Pennsylvania Press, 1970.
6. Bosmajian, H., ed., *The Rhetoric of Nonverbal Communication.* Glenview, Ill.: Scott, Foresman, 1971.
7. Brannigan, C. R., and D. A. Humphries, "Human Non-Verbal Behavior: A Means of Communication," in *Ethological Studies of Infant Behavior.* Cambridge, England: Cambridge University Press, 1971.
8. Darwin, Charles, *The Expression of Emotions in Man and Animals.* London: Murray, 1872. (Republished, Chicago: University of Chicago Press, 1965.)
9. Davitz, Joel R., ed., *The Communication of Emotional Meaning.* New York: McGraw-Hill, 1964.
10. Davitz, Joel R., *The Language of Emotion.* New York: Academic Press, 1969.
11. DeVito, J. A., ed., *Communication Concepts and Processes.* Englewood Cliffs, N.J.: Prentice-Hall, 1971.
12. Duncan, S., "Nonverbal Communication," *Psychological Bulletin,* Vol. 72, 1969, pp. 118–137.
13. Efron, D., *Gesture and Environment.* New York: King's Crown, 1941. (Republished as *Gesture, Race and Culture.* The Hague: Mouton, 1971.)
14. Ekman, P., "Universals and Cultural Differences in Facial Expression of Emotion," *Nebraska Symposium on Motivation: 1971.* Lincoln: University of Nebraska Press, 1972.
15. Ekman, P., and W. V. Friesen, "The Repertoire of Nonverbal Behavior: Categories, Origins, Usage, and Coding," *Semiotica,* Vol. 1, 1969.
16. Ekman, P., W. V. Friesen, and P. Ellsworth, *Emotion in the Human Face: Guidelines for Research and an Integration of Findings.* New York: Pergamon Press, 1971.
17. Exline, Ralph, J. Thibaut, C. B. Hickey, and P. Gumpert, "Visual Interaction in Relation to Machiavellianism and an Unethical Act," in *Studies in Machiavellianism,* ed. by P. Christie and F. Geis. New York: Academic Press, 1970.
18. Fast, Julian, *Body Language.* New York: M. Evans, 1970.
19. Frijda, N. H., "Recognition of Emotion," in *Advances in Experimental Social Psychology,* Vol. 4, ed. by L. Berkowitz. New York: Academic Press, 1969.

20. Geldhard, F. A., "Body English," *Psychology Today,* Vol. 2, 1968.
21. Goffman, Erving, *The Presentation of Self in Everyday Life.* Garden City, N.Y.: Doubleday, 1959.
22. Goffman, Erving, *Behavior in Public Places.* New York: Free Press, 1963.
23. Grant, E. C., "Human Facial Expression," *Man,* Vol. 4, 1969.
24. Hall, Edward T., *The Silent Language.* Garden City, N.Y.: Doubleday, 1959.
25. Hall, Edward T., *The Hidden Dimension.* Garden City, N.Y.: Doubleday, 1966.
26. Harrison, Randall P., "Nonverbal Communication," in *Communications Handbook,* ed. by I. de Sola Pool, W. Schramm, N. Maccoby, and E. Parker. Chicago: Rand McNally, 1972.
27. Harrison, Randall P., *Nonverbal Communication.* Englewood Cliffs, N.J.: Prentice-Hall, 1973.
28. Hess, E. H., "Attitude and Pupil Size," *Scientific American,* Vol. 212, 1965.
29. Hewes, G. T., "The Anthropology of Posture," *Scientific American,* Vol. 196, 1957.
30. Jourard, Sidney, and R. Friedman, "Experimenter-Subject 'Distance' and Self-Disclosure," *Journal of Personality and Social Psychology,* Vol. 15, 1970.
31. Knapp, M. L., *Nonverbal Communication in Human Interaction.* New York: Holt, Rinehart and Winston, 1972.
32. Knapp, P. H., ed., *Expression of the Emotions in Man.* New York: International Universities, 1963.
33. LaBarre, W., "Paralinguistics, Kinesics, and Cultural Anthropology," in *Approaches to Semiotics,* ed. by T. A. Sebeok, A. S. Hayes, and M. C. Bateson. The Hague: Mouton, 1964.
34. Mahl, G. L., and G. Schulze, "Psychological Research in the Extra-Linguistic Area," in *Approaches to Semiotics,* ed. by T. A. Sebeok, A. S. Hayes, and M. C. Bateson. The Hague: Mouton, 1964.
35. Mehrabian, A., "Nonverbal Communication," *Nebraska Symposium on Motivation: 1971.* Lincoln: Nebraska University Press, 1972.
36. Osgood, Charles, "The Cross-Cultural Generality of Visual-Verbal Synesthetic Tendencies," *Behavioral Science,* Vol. 5, 1959, pp. 146–169.
37. Osgood, Charles, "Dimensionality of the Semantic Space for Communication Via Facial Expressions," *Scandinavian Journal of Psychology,* Vol. 7, 1966.
38. Rosenfeld, H., "Instrumental Affiliative Functions of Facial and Gestural Expressions," *Journal of Personality and Social Psychology,* Vol. 4, 1966.
39. Rosenfeld, H., "Nonverbal Reciprocation of Approval: An Experimental Analysis," *Journal of Experimental Social Psychology,* Vol. 3, 1967.
40. Ruesch, Jurgen, and W. Kees, *Nonverbal Communication.* Berkeley: University of California Press, 1956.
41. Scheflen, Albert E., "The Significance of Posture in Communication Systems," *Psychiatry,* Vol. 27, 1964.
42. Scheflen, Albert E., "Quasi-Courtship Behavior in Psychotherapy," *Psychiatry,* Vol. 28, 1965.
43. Sebeok, Thomas A., ed., *Animal Communication.* Bloomington: Indiana University Press, 1968.
44. Sebeok, Thomas A., S. Hayes, and M. C. Bateson, eds., *Approaches to Semiotics.* The Hague: Mouton, 1964.
45. Sommer, R., *Personal Space.* Englewood Cliffs, N.J.: Prentice-Hall, 1969.
46. Tagiuri, "Person Perception," in *The Handbook of Social Psychology,* Vol. 3, 2nd ed., ed. by G. Lindzey and E. Aronson. Reading, Mass: Addison-Wesley, 1969.

47. Tomkins, S. S., *Affect, Imagery, Consciousness,* 2 Vols. New York: Springer, 1962, 1963.
48. Vine, I., "Communication by Facial-Visual Signals," in *Social Behavior in Birds and Mammals: Essays on the Social Ethology of Animal and Man,* ed. by J. H. Crook. New York: Academic Press, 1970.
49. Watson, O. M., *Proxemic Behavior: A Cross-Cultural Study.* The Hague: Mouton, 1970.
50. Watzlawick, Paul, Janet H. Beavin, and Don D. Jackson, *Pragmatics of Human Communication.* New York: Norton, 1967.
51. Worth, S., "The Development of a Semiotic of Film," *Semiotica,* Vol. 1, 1969.

Dr. Ronald L. Smith is Professor and Chairman of the Department of Communication and Organizational Behavior at the General Motors Institute and is currently President of the International Communication Association. He has authored numerous articles and papers in the area of communication and organizational behavior. His most recent contribution, "Theories and Models of Communication," appears in *Speech Communication Behavior,* edited by Larry Barker and Robert Kibler.

Dr. Gary M. Richetto is Assistant Professor of Communication in the Department of Communication and Organizational Behavior at GMI. His articles and research abstracts have appeared in *Personnel, Personnel Journal,* and *Industrial Supervisor.* Dr. Richetto teaches courses in Organizational Behavior, Organizational Communication, and Persuasion and Attitude Change and conducts a variety of management development and leadership training seminars both within and without the General Motors Corporation.

Dr. Joseph P. Zima is an Associate Professor of Communication, Department of Communication and Organizational Behavior, GMI. He has written extensively for such journals as *Personnel Journal, Personnel, The Speech Teacher, The Maryland Teacher, Central States Speech Journal, Michigan Speech Association Journal,* and *School and Society.* An essay on interviewing is in press.

16

ORGANIZATIONAL BEHAVIOR: AN APPROACH TO HUMAN COMMUNICATION

RONALD L. SMITH, GARY M. RICHETTO, AND JOSEPH P. ZIMA

INTRODUCTION

Like all living systems, organizations establish and maintain themselves through communication with their environments and amongst their parts. [38]

THIS INSIGHTFUL comment from Lee Thayer's *Communication and Communication Systems* provides a viable approach to organizational communication: the concept of communication as (1) the primary means by which organizations select, control, and coordinate the activities of human and material resources *internally,* and (2) the primary means by which organizations respond and adapt to the *external* environment within which they function.

Considering the implications of so broad a perspective in organizational communication, one may conclude that there are few aspects of an organization's development which are not related in some way to its systems of communication. An organization's communication systems determine so much of its function that the organization and the systems are often difficult to separate. It is as difficult to imagine an organization without communication as it is to imagine communication without organization—of people, of relationships, of groups, of structures.

Chester Barnard, the noted management and organization theorist, recognized this fact in his classic text, *The Functions of the Executive:*

> . . . in an exhaustive theory of organization, communication would occupy
> a central place, because the structure, extensiveness, and scope of organiza-
> tion are almost entirely determined by communication techniques. (2, p. 9)

It appears axiomatic from this that research in organizational communication be conducted by scholars from numerous disciplines. The field is sufficiently broad that all the approaches to the study of communication presented in this volume could be brought to bear on its investigation. Many have been.

The breadth of organizational-communication research is, however, a mixed blessing. On one hand, it provides a large body of knowledge, rich in diversity, and an arena for the exchange of theories and research findings from a variety of disciplines. On the other, it makes a definitive answer to the query "What is organization communication?" almost impossible. Many of those involved in research in that field would, in fact, be reluctant to call organizational communication a "discipline" in the sense that chemistry, physics, mathematics, or perhaps even behavioral sciences like psychology or sociology, are disciplines. Rather, organizational communication is conceived of as a composite of other disciplines, as a general area of empirical research conducted by scholars from a number of fields, all of whom are concerned with the way in which people communicate within their organizations.

Downs provides as valid a statement as any about the state of the art:

> Organizational communication today is in a position comparable to that of
> group dynamics several years ago, with many short research studies, lim-
> ited in scope, with no one to synthesize the results. (14, p. 1)

Implicit in Downs's comment, however, seems to be the idea that if synthesis can be achieved, a concrete discipline may emerge. From our vantage point—exposed daily to communication-related studies from both academic and industrial sources, it seems doubtful that research relevant to organizational communication can be synthesized into a single, integrated body of literature. Doubtful—and in our estimation—relatively unimportant. What is important is that a growing number of behavioral and social scientists, mathematicians, engineers, and the like, are concerning themselves with describing and analyzing the process of human communication within organizational structures. Perhaps they are finally recognizing that to break up and compartmentalize knowledge and research into finite and independent packages is no longer a viable avenue to learning. Perhaps they have come to realize that a "systems approach"—a drawing of relevant information from any and all sources available—is the only rational way of investigating behavioral phenomena in complex organizations.

In essence, this chapter is concerned with introducing the reader to the broad field of research called "organizational communication." While the breadth of this area makes difficult a definition which would satisfy the myriad of scholars investigating it, there does appear to be a framework which can be identified. Our objective will be to provide that framework— first, to describe areas of research, and second, to describe some of the methodologies employed by scholars conducting this research. Third, we will summarize a few important studies in organizational communication. This summary will obviously not be exhaustive, but it will provide the reader with greater insight into the kinds of variables with which organizational communication researchers have been concerned, and with some of their findings. Fourth, we will describe a few of the prominent, ongoing programs in organizational communication in such institutions as the National Aeronautics and Space Administration (NASA), Boeing Aircraft, General Electric, and the Chrysler Corporation. These programs are particularly relevant to this discussion, because they represent the combined efforts of academic research and organizational practice. They reflect one of the unique qualities of organizational communication—its synergy—resulting from the constant interaction of theorists and practitioners.

Finally, we will discuss the future of organizational communication as a field of empirical research. It is a future being shaped, in fact, by the pooling of academic and organizational talents. It is a future marked by the increasingly important role of organizational-communication research in the areas of organizational change and development.

DIMENSIONS OF ORGANIZATIONAL COMMUNICATION

Most writers on human communication in complex organizations have organized and studied communication phenomena from two aspects: *for-*

mal and *informal* communication channels. Basically, formal channels are official, and informal channels are unofficial.

Formal Communication Channels

Formal channels are those emanating from official sources and carrying official sanctions. These channels typically connect the boxes on organization charts. Formal messages usually flow through these channels, thus acquiring legitimacy and authenticity. Formal channels include three dimensions: (1) downward communication—instructions, policies, commands, employee information, and so forth; (2) upward communication—inquiries, requests, reports, complaints, and the like; and (3) horizontal communication—such as reporting, advising, gathering data, solving problems, coordinating effort.

Downward communication has been the most frequently studied dimension of formal channels. Authority, tradition, and prestige are implemented through downward communication. Those at the top of the organization are naturally concerned with the communication effectiveness of their downward-directed messages to employees. Downward-directed communication studies answer the question: To what extent do messages directed downward in the organizational structure obtain the kinds of responses desired by the managerial message sender? Downward communication sets the tone and establishes the atmosphere for effective upward communication.

Upward communication serves as feedback for management, giving clues regarding the relative success of a given message. In addition to revealing the degree to which downward-directed information and ideas are accepted or distorted, upward communication can stimulate employees to participate in formulating operating policies for their department or organization. The subordinate, in communicating upward, must explain himself and gain acceptance from those having positions of greater status and authority. Compounding this problem is the probability that the subordinate may be less fluent and less persuasive than those who communicate downward. For managers who are receptive and responsive, upward communication may help improve departmental and organizational efficiency.

Horizontal communication is indispensable to coordination and essential to the proper functioning of vertical-communication flow. As a business grows in size and complexity, specialized departments emerge for engineering, accounting, marketing, and research. Members play a leading role in communication far beyond the assigned roles of their departments. In many instances, communication is their primary activity. They perform such functions as gathering data, issuing reports, preparing directives, coordinating activities, and advising management. Specialized units are usually quite active in cross-communication with other internal groups, because their activities usually affect several chains of command rather than one.

Informal Communication Channels

Informal communication channels are not specified rationally. They develop through accidents of spatial arrangement, through friendships, and through the varying levels of ability in the organization's "boxes." Informal channels are like the shortcuts or paths students take in getting to classes. Sometimes the sidewalks (formal channels) are not as easily accessible, or perhaps the paths are just more expedient. Informal communication channels carry the so-called grapevine, or rumor messages. The term *grapevine* arose during the Civil War. In those days, intelligence telegraph lines were strung loosely from tree to tree in the manner of a grapevine, and the message was often garbled; thus, any rumor was said to be "from the grapevine." [9, p. 222] Today, the term applies to all informal communication, oral or written. Because the grapevine is somewhat of an unknown and cannot be held responsible for errors, managers sometimes wish it would go away. However, if suppressed in one place, it usually emerges in another.

Before we leave this discussion of channels, another channel should be mentioned which has become increasingly important in recent years. This channel we will call "external." External channels carry messages from the organization to customers, suppliers, and the various other "publics" (government, consumer groups, environmental-action groups) that may threaten the security or existence of the business or corporation. Some may call this channel public relations, but this is too limited a term. More than ever before, business and other organizations are keenly aware of the need for promoting and maintaining felicitous public relations with all their "publics."

Essential Dimensions of Message Effects

Redding [32, pp. 99–112] has elaborated a system of studying the essential dimensions of message effects in the typical complex organization:

1. What kinds of message-initiation and message-diffusion are taking place in the organization, under what conditions and with what consequences for what members?

a. Who initiates what messages (and what messages fail to be initiated at all)?

b. What structural channels (i.e., organizational relationships) are employed in specified message activity? (For example, one could examine messages from superior to subordinate, from subordinate to superior, from peer to peer, in different units and at different levels of the organizational hierarchy).

c. What kinds of topics, or kinds of functions—and accompanied by what kinds of rewards or sanctions—are differentially initiated, by different members in different positions, and in different networks or informational systems?

d. How, and by whom, are these messages received in the organization —i.e., through what channels and what media? The following subdimensions could be studied:

I. Upward initiative (from subordinate to superior)
II. Upward permissiveness (by superior toward messages initiated by subordinates)
III. Downward initiative (from superior to subordinate)
IV. Downward receptiveness (by subordinate toward messages initiated "from above")
V. Lateral initiative (degree to which a specified peer will initiate messages to another peer, or peers)
VI. Lateral receptiveness (degree to which a specified peer is willing to receive messages from another peer).

2. What kinds of feedback activity occur in the organization?

a. To what degree, and under what circumstances, do specified superiors demonstrate "feedback receptiveness"—i.e., do superiors welcome the reception of feedback information from others, especially subordinates, in the organization?

b. To what degree, and under what circumstances, do specified superiors demonstrate "feedback responsiveness"—i.e., do they readily give feedback to incoming messages, especially from subordinates?

3. What kinds of response are apparently correlated with specified messages? Responses (including comprehension, acceptance, liking, etc.) can be examined on the part of message-senders as well as receivers in terms of hierarchical structuring and direction.

4. What kinds, and degree, of "communication satisfaction" exist, on the part of which members of the organization, and with reference to what kinds of communication phenomena? (Communication satisfaction refers to the reported degree to which a specified respondent is satisfied with specified message-sending and message-receiving behaviors or activities.) (32, pp. 108–110)

Redding also suggests some other aspects of organizational communication systems that could be studied:

1. The *efficiency* of communication phenomena (in terms of material human costs, relative to organizational outputs).

2. *Objective validity* (the degree to which messages are judged, according to stated criteria, to be congruent with physical, psychological, or logical premises).

3. *Ethical acceptability* (the degree to which messages, or communication techniques, are judged to be congruent with stated "moral" and "ethical" premises). (32, p. 110)

Organizational-Communication Research Methods

What methodologies are used in studying organizational communication? The methodologies can be classified according to: (1) the type of data collected, (2) the locale where the data is collected, and (3) the techniques used in data collection. [14]

The type of data being collected is both quantitative and qualitative. Homans' statement on the relative value of the two types of data is still appropriate:

> We are told . . . that our data . . . should be quantitative . . . and of course they should. But good observation ought not to be discarded just because it is not numerical. . . . Data are not nobler because they are quantitative, nor thinking more logical because mathematical. . . . Let us make the important quantitative, not the quantitative important. [17, p. 22]

Organizational-communication research has included laboratory and field experiments, surveys, and descriptive field studies. However, there has always been some question about the degree of application of the results of laboratory studies to real-life organizations, for they are typically conducted without organizational constraints such as large size, hierarchy, technology, geographical dispersion, and so forth. Simulations which can be performed with computers or in controlled laboratory experiments are becoming popular and hold tremendous potential for understanding and predicting organizational communication.

The locale of most organizational communication studies has been the field—real-life organization settings. Field studies may be quantitative or qualitative, experimental or descriptive, and may or may not test formally stated hypotheses. The more common types of field studies include the survey and in-depth case studies. Surveys attempt to gather the same kind of information from many organizations, while the case study describes, analyzes, or evaluates a particular situation. Field experiments also offer a great possibility for increasing understanding of communication. However, there have not been many of these because experiments (used here in the sense that manipulation and control of behavior are required) are extremely difficult to arrange in real-life organizations, particularly those with profit requirements.

The most common techniques used in empirical research in organizational communication are direct observation, interviews, and questionnaires. A special type of questionnaire which has enjoyed popularity is the semantic differential: connotative meanings are measured from judgments marked about a specified concept on a seven-point continuum between bipolar adjectives. In order to trace informal chains of communication in the organization, a technique called ECCO analysis (Episodic Communication Channels in Organizations) has been developed. Organization members are asked whether they knew specified information by a specified time, and how and from whom the message was received. The Critical Incident Technique asks organization members to report on important communication behaviors which they have observed directly, and which they can classify as either effective or ineffective in defined situations on the job. Content analysis is used to analyze written messages or responses to open-ended questions from a specified number of respondents. For example, one could examine the most prevalent themes in a union or management newsletter, or the content of written or tape-recorded messages sent through other formal or informal channels.

ORGANIZATIONAL-COMMUNICATION RESEARCH

A Historical Perspective

The famous Hawthorne studies [36] provided the initial impetus for the field of organizational communication. Although not concerned with communication per se, they did emphasize its role in organizational effectiveness. Conducting in-depth interviews with 21,000 employees, a Harvard Business School research team (directed by Roethlisberger) launched what might be termed the first scientific analysis of human communication behavior in a complex organization.

Following the Hawthorne research, a second significant thrust for the field was provided in the writings of management practitioner and theorist Chester Barnard. In *The Functions of the Executive,* Barnard contended that the first function of the executive was to "establish and maintain a system of communication." [2, p. 221]

The next major influence in the field of organizational communication was Alexander Heron. In *Sharing Information With Employees,* published in 1942, [16] Heron advanced a philosophy of communication which viewed the concept as one of sharing, rather than persuasion or propaganda. His philosophy of communication had significant impact on later writings and thought and, in fact, played a major role in the "human relations" movement of the 1940s. It was in this era that works like Paul Pigors' *Effective Communication in Industry* [30] began to stress the reciprocal, "two-way" nature of organizational communication.

By the 1950s communication had received such attention in the business world that its inevitable "packaging" had begun. In 1950, a series of articles by William H. Whyte, Jr., appeared in *Fortune,* launching a scathing attack against those aspects of organizational communication which had become gimmicky and manipulative. [43]

At about the same time, Irving J. Lee, a noted general semanticist from Northwestern University, had become interested in the field. After visiting the Harvard group which had conducted the Hawthorne research, he encouraged his students and colleagues to become active in organizational communication.

One such colleague, P. E. Lull, established the Communication Research Center at Purdue University. The center, now under the directorship of W. Charles Redding, was perhaps the first research institute focusing specifically on the study of communication in organizations.

A Sampling of Research

This discussion of significant research in organizational communication is not an exhaustive review of the literature. I have selected a small, hopefully representative, sample from the volume of work in this area. Extensive reviews of organizational communication research literature have been published by Redding [33] and Tompkins. [39]

We shall approach our review through the framework described earlier: formal channels (focusing on downward, upward, and horizontal channels) and informal channels (focusing on rumor transmission and grapevine communication systems).

At the end of each section, we have attempted to crystallize the overriding implications which have emerged from research in that particular area.

FORMAL COMMUNICATION CHANNELS

Downward Communication   Some of the variables or concepts dealt with in this area have been the filtering of messages from higher to lower organizational levels, trust and the acceptance of messages, communication and morale, and downward-directed media.

A 1963 study by the Opinion Research Corporation revealed that surprisingly large amounts of information generated at the top of an organization did not filter down to its working levels. Studying a large metals-producing company, they found that while 91 percent of the top-level executives possessed information on their products' declining profit margin, only 5 percent of the front-line supervisors were aware of the same information. Similarly, Odiorne [27] found that managers' estimates of amounts of information disseminated to lower levels were significantly higher than the amounts of information actually reaching those levels.

Studies of this type have consistently indicated that each level of management to complex organizations can act as an obstacle, or barrier, to the flow of downward-directed communication.

Research into the area of interpersonal trust, like that of Mellinger, [25] has indicated that the communication behavior of employees is evasive, compliant, and aggressive under conditions of low trust in supervisors.

Contradictory findings have emerged from the investigation of communication and employee morale. Browne and Nietzel,[5] studying communication in a Michigan utilities company, found a significant relationship between satisfaction with communication systems and morale. Similarly, a study by Cohen [7] found that employees who received unclear or inconsistent messages became frustrated and anxious.

In contrast to these findings, Perry and Mahoney [29] found no correlation between employee morale (liking for their company) and employee knowledge about their company. Likewise, Level's [21] study of an urban bank yielded no relationship between communication and morale.

The area of downward-directed media has frequently been investigated. Basically, the research in this area has revealed the superiority of multimedia approaches to disseminating information. Surveying opinions among presidents of the one hundred largest firms in the United States, Lull, Funk, and Piersol [22] reported that the majority of these leaders communicated their most important messages orally, or in combination with written communications.

In perhaps the best-controlled experimental research in downward-directed communication, Dahle [8] proved the efficacy of using oral and written media together. His findings indicate the following order of effectiveness (from most to least effective): (1) combined oral and written, (2) oral only, (3) written only, (4) bulletin board, and (5) grapevine.

Dee's study [12] of a local union yielded similar findings. He found written channels to be inadequate and oral methods (primarily union meetings) poorly planned, publicized, organized, and attended.

Implications of Downward-Communication Research Research conducted thus far seems to indicate that most downward channels in organizations studied enjoy only minimal effectiveness. Findings further indicate that attempts at disseminating information downward in organizations should not depend on a single medium or channel.

Upward Communication A few of the dimensions dealt with in this area are: superior-subordinate relationships, upward-mobility aspirations, and status as determinants of communication behavior.

Studying superior-subordinate relationships, Maier, Read, and Hooven [24] interviewed thirty-five supervisor-subordinate pairs in four companies. Their findings revealed agreement among pairs on the content (responsibilities) of subordinates' jobs, but significant disagreement among pairs when ranking the importance of these responsibilities.

In a similar study, Maier, Hoffman, and Read [23] found that having held a subordinate's job was not a factor in a supervisor's receptivity to upward communication.

Recent research by Zima [45] comparing factory and nonfactory supervisory "counseling communication" revealed that nonfactory subordinates had significantly higher levels of "counseling-communication satisfaction" than did factory subordinates.

In the area of upward-mobility aspirations, an interesting study by Read [31] supported the hypothesis that highly mobile or ambitious employees often withheld or distorted upward-directed information. Ambitious employees were often found to withhold information from their bosses, except under conditions of high interpersonal trust.

Upward-mobility aspirations have proved to be an important variable in informal communication systems as well. Richetto, [35] in studying some two hundred government scientists and technicians, found that informal leaders in work groups evidenced higher aspiration levels than did their peers.

The area of status has been researched by Jackson, [18] among others. His findings reveal the tendency for organization members to direct communications toward those they perceive as having greater status than themselves. By the same token, he found a tendency for organization members to avoid communicating with those perceived to have lower status than themselves.

Implications of Upward-Communication Research   A review of this area reveals a paucity of research. Historically, management's attitude toward upward-communication channels has been one of manipulation or control. Research would suggest that a preoccupation with downward-directed communication has often inhibited the establishment of effective upward-communication systems.

Horizontal Communication   Some of the concepts dealt with in this area are: problems in communication between highly specialized departments, reward structures of horizontal channels, and lateral communication in coordinating work flow.

Opinion Research Corporation [28] compiled considerable evidence that specialization of functions in large organizations significantly impairs communication between departments.

Walton [41] investigates the area of horizontal-communication reward structures—that is, the degree to which organization members are encouraged or rewarded for communicating laterally with other work groups. He concluded that horizontal communication does not typically lead to rewards. In contrast, communicating vertically does. Walton contends that management is directly responsible for this fact, serving as what he calls the "chief dispenser" of rewards.

Smith [37] investigated relationships between interpersonal sensitivity and communication attitudes, behavior, and effectiveness among peer-group supervisors. No strong, stable relationships were found to exist between interpersonal sensitivity and communication. The most plausible explanation for the lack of significant differences among peers, that people probably are selective in choosing others to whom they will be sensitive, seems to support Walton's research. In the organizational setting, there may be greater reward for vertical sensitivity than for horizontal sensitivity. Organizational "payoff" may result from sensitivity to superiors and subordinates rather than to peers.

Implications of Horizontal-Communication Research   Generally speaking, research in this area has been limited in scope. There is simply not much known about horizontal communication. As more and more organizations move toward the project-management or systems models of organization, however, more studies like that of Casey,[6] which investigates lateral communication in decision making, should emerge.

Informal Communication Channels   The bulk of studies in this area have dealt with rumor transmission and the grapevine. Thus far, most such research has been descriptive in nature, focusing on how the informal system operates.

Keith Davis [10; 11] used ECCO analysis (*Episodic Communication Channels in Organizations*) to study the informal network of the Jason Leathergoods Company. He discovered four specific patterns or networks through which rumors flowed. Of these four, the "cluster" network (A tells B, C, and D; D tells E and F, etc.) was found to be most typical in that organization.

A number of studies—Jacobsen and Seashore,[19] and Walton [41]—have identified key liaison or central or linking individuals who serve as gatekeepers for subgroups, thus circulating rumors throughout the informal organizational structure.

Combining this concept with that of source credibility, Richetto [35] developed a model of organizational communication which depicts the dynamics of information flow within the informal organization.

APPLYING ORGANIZATIONAL-COMMUNICATION CONCEPTS TO ONGOING ORGANIZATIONS

The pooling of academic and practitioner talents in organizational-communication research has resulted in the development of a number of comprehensive programs in a variety of organizations. The following is a brief discussion of four such efforts in this area.

One of the most energetic programs of organizational communication was developed by Walter Wiesman,[44, pp. 35–40] Internal Communication

Coordinator for NASA's Marshall Space Flight Center. Wiesman's "wall-to-wall" communication program represents one of the most carefully planned and well-organized efforts with which we are familiar. Developing the program in five-year increments, Wiesman launched a systematic analysis of downward, upward, and lateral channels, and internal and external "communication contributors" (functions), and encouraged the personal involvement of top-level NASA executives at the center. At the core of this program is (1) the use of an annual summer communication consultant (providing a review of the program in light of recent research), and (2) the utilization of doctoral candidates in organizational communication to conduct field-study dissertations at the Marshall Center. Wiesman, now a private consultant, is aiding other organizations in establishing similar OC programs.

James Douglas has recently described the communication program at the Boeing Company in Seattle, Washington. Defining the company's view of communication as "a way of life," Douglas says the program has three prime objectives:

1. A coordination of activities with related functions. We want engineering, manufacturing, personnel, material, to be talking to one another.

2. The proper assignment of people.

3. The motivation of the work force, with there being an understanding of the target and goals of the company, its divisions, and of the work group. (13, p. 27)

To achieve these goals, the Boeing program uses what Douglas terms "total" communication—employing "organization" communication, "instructional" communication, and "attitude" communication at appropriate times and through appropriate media.

One of the best descriptions of the Chrysler Corporation's program in internal communication is provided by Lynn Townsend. The current program is based upon findings in Chrysler's earlier "Operation Better Communication"(OBC). Townsend describes OBC as:

. . . a comprehensive internal communication effort involving oral, visual and written communication channels, continuing research measurement techniques, a headquarters, Communication Department and approximately 25 plant-level Communication Coordinators. (40, p. 209)

The current effort at Chrysler is based upon eight "requirements for effective internal communication":

1. Internal communication must be recognized as an essential tool of good management.

2. Employees must be well informed concerning their mutual interests in company success.

3. Individual managers must actively support the corporate communication effort.
4. Substantially greater emphasis must be put on communication planning and measurement.
5. Top management must establish a good communication climate.
6. A long-term investment in professional talent and communication programming must be made.
7. Management must recognize its responsibility to listen as well as to speak.
8. Managers must recognize the desire of employees to help their company, and the power of communication to tap this great potential. (40, pp. 208–215)

General Electric's Willard V. Merrihue, manager of community and business relations, helped develop a corporate and community-wide communication program. Particular emphasis was placed on the use of communication in managing employee, community, and union relations. GE's program was one of the first to recognize the need for long-range communication planning. GE identified three distinct kinds of communication objectives:

1. To build mutual respect and confidence between employees and managers,
2. To reconcile management and employee attitudes on major economic, social and political issues, and
3. To gain deserved employee support for specific management actions. (26, p. 292)

NEW DIRECTIONS FOR ORGANIZATIONAL COMMUNICATIONS

There have been at least two significant shifts of focus since behavioral scientists began to study communication in organizations. These new perspectives in OC have generally followed and paralleled similar changes in the more inclusive area now called "organizational behavior."

An early attempt to study communication in an organization might be compared with a patron's examination of a large painting in an art museum. At first, he approaches to within a foot of the work of art, closes one eye, and begins to analyze the colors. Finding this of limited value, he moves back until he can see the entire painting, opens his other eye, and begins to examine the system of lines, colors, shading, and other pictorial elements. Like the art patron, the OC specialist has stepped back, gained a new perspective, and realized that OC principles obtain in all types of organizations, not just business, industry, and the military, which sponsored early research. And after initially opening one eye toward achieving organizational objectives, he gradually opens the other eye to create a more balanced focus between goals of organizations and the needs of individuals who work in these organizations.

Earlier, academicians offered courses with titles such as "Industrial Psychology" and "Business and Industrial Communication." The early body of knowledge sprang from business, industry, and military organizations. These groups could afford, and were willing to sponsor, behavioral research. They employed professionals who could apply concepts from psychology, sociology, and other behavioral sciences. Baritz [1] has provided an excellent history of this activity. Then, in the 1960s, many other types of organizations began to feel the impact of behavioral research. Government, education, and religious bureaucracies now faced pressures similar to earlier pressures on business, industry, and the military for technological change. Researchers began to investigate organizations with a greater variety of goals, products, and services. Key variables such as motivation, morale, leadership, and communication emerged across organizations as targets for greater understanding. Renaming industrial psychology as "Organizational Psychology," and business and industrial communication as "Organizational Communication" reflects a more enlightened systems approach to the study of behavior in interrelated bureaucratic organizations. Even with only one eye open, we have a better perspective now that we have stepped back to look at the whole picture of human organizations.

The second change of focus in organizational communication has been more dramatic and is still in process. It has enlarged the area of concern from task-oriented organizational goals (managerial concerns) to the more crucial interaction between individual needs and organizational goals.

The pressure for OC specialists to open both eyes is a product of the times—of pressure for a social revolution with potentially greater consequences than the industrial revolution of a century ago. Yet we cannot lose sight of the fact that the first revolution has made the second one possible.

In their book *The Year 2000*, [20] Kahn and Wiener talk about changes in the kinds of work people are doing. Work can be classified in three categories: (1) primary work—extracting natural resources from our environment: fishing, forestry, hunting, agriculture, mining; (2) secondary work—producing goods from these resources: building better Buicks, longer bridges, and "hotter" hot pants; (3) tertiary work—providing people services: operating hospitals and teaching in schools, providing legal and spiritual services, caring for the aged and the poor—all these are part of the so-called helping professions. Recently, the United States became the first country in history in which technology made it possible for the tertiary work force—the helping professions—to outnumber the primary and secondary work forces combined. Soon we will be followed by Japan, Canada, Scandinavia, France, and West Germany; and by the year 2000, whole continents will be able to claim this statistic. And the skill basic to this new, tertiary work force, and critical to the administration of our primary and secondary work forces, is *communication*.

The pre-"human-revolution" applications of behavioral sciences in organizations had a strictly managerial flavor. Baritz, in his denunciation of these early applications, has drawn our attention to the need for a "both-eyes-open" approach:

> Many industrial social scientists have put themselves on auction. The power elites of America, especially the industrial elite, have bought their services —which, when applied to areas of relative power, have restricted the freedom of millions of workers. Time was when a man knew that his freedoms were being curtailed. Social scientists, however, are too sophisticated for that. The fires of pressure and control on a man are now kindled in his own thinking. Control need no longer be imposed. It can be encouraged to come from within. . . . A major characteristic of twentieth-century manipulation has been that it blinds the victim to the fact of manipulation. Because so many industrial social scientists have been willing to serve power instead of mind, they have been themselves a case study in manipulation by consent. (1, pp. 209–210)

Some may disagree with Baritz' charge of sins in the past, but few will take issue with the need for a different approach to the study of organizational behavior, and particularly organizational communication, in the future.

We predict that in the future, the study of organizational communication will focus more and more on the process of organizational change. Changes in our larger societal system have already precipitated slow but perceptible changes in managerial behavior. Bennis points out three new managerial concepts:

> 1. A new concept of *man* based on increased knowledge of his complex and shifting needs, which replaces an oversimplified, innocent, pushbutton idea of man.
>
> 2. A new concept of *power,* based on collaboration and reason, which replaces a model of power based on coercion and threat.
>
> 3. A new concept of *organizational values,* based on humanistic-democratic ideals, which replaces the depersonalized, mechanistic value system of bureaucracy. (4, p. 22)

These concepts, if implemented, will make it necessary for people in organizations to cope with an almost unbelievable amount of change.

Regardless of the method of implementing change, new levels of skill in interpersonal communication and new concepts of design in organizational communication will be called for. Greiner has categorized approaches to organizational change under three alternative uses of power. Communication is basic to all three:

1. Unilateral Power:

   a. *The Decree Approach.* A "one-way" announcement originating with a person with high formal authority and passed on to those in lower positions.

   b. *The Replacement Approach.* Individuals in one or more key organizational positions are replaced by other individuals. The basic assumption is that organizational changes are a function of a key man's ability.

   c. *The Structural Approach.* Instead of decreeing or injecting new blood into work relationships, management changes the required relationships of subordinates working in the situation. By changing the structure of organizational relationships, organizational behavior is also presumably affected.

2. Shared Power:

   d. *The Group Decision Approach.* Here we have participation by group members in selecting from several alternative solutions specified in advance by superiors. This approach involves neither problem identification nor problem solving, but emphasizes the obtaining of group agreement to a particular course of action.

   e. *The Group Problem-Solving Approach.* Problem identification and problem solving through group discussion. Here the group has wide latitude, not only over choosing the problems to be discussed, but then in developing solutions to these problems.

3. Delegated Power:

   f. *The Data Discussion Approach.* Presentation and feedback of relevant data to the client system either by a change catalyst or by change agents within the company. Organizational members are encouraged to develop their own analyses of the data, presented in the form of case materials, survey findings, or data reports.

   g. *The Sensitivity Training Approach.* Managers are trained in small discussion groups to be more sensitive to the underlying processes of individual and group behavior. Changes in work patterns and relationships are assumed to follow from changes in interpersonal relationships. Sensitivity approaches focus upon interpersonal relationships first, then hope for, or work toward, improvements in work performance. (15, pp. 3–4)

The new concepts of man, power, and organizational values make inadequate our present ways of thinking about and measuring organizational communication. Bennis illustrated this inadequacy in his analysis of the classic networks research:

> The basic flaw in the present effectiveness criteria is their inattention to the problem of adapting to change. To illuminate some of the consequences of this omission, let us turn to one rather simple example. The example is drawn from an area of research, started at the Massachusetts Institute of Technology about 1949, on the effects of certain organizational patterns (communication networks) on problem solving by groups. Two of these networks, the Wheel and the Circle, are shown in [Figure 16.1]
> The results of these experiments showed that an organization with a structure like the Wheel can solve simple tasks (e.g., identification of the color of a marble that is common to all five group members) more rapidly,

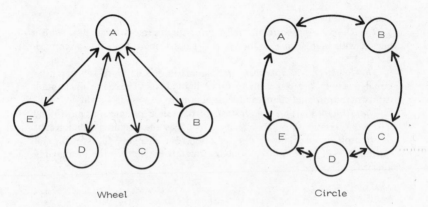

Wheel   Circle

Figure 16.1   Two types of communication networks for problem solving by a group of five persons

more clearly, and more efficiently than an organization with a structure like the Circle. Thus the Wheel arrangement is plainly superior in terms of the usual criteria employed to evaluate effectiveness. However, if we consider two other criteria of organizational effectiveness that are relevant to the concern with change flexibility and creativity, we discover two interesting phenomena. First, the rapid acceptance of a new idea is more likely in the Circle than in the Wheel. The man in the middle of the Wheel is apt to discard an idea on the grounds that he is too busy or the idea is impractical. Second, when the task is changed, for example, by going from "pure-color" marbles to unusually colored marbles (such as ginger-ale color or blue-green), the Circle organization is better able to adapt to this change by developing a new code. [3, pp. 42–43]

We predict the new focus on change will affect the nature and purpose of organizational-communication research. There may be less emphasis on laboratory research (as exemplified by network studies) and field-experimental research (as exemplified by the Dahle study). We predict an increase in action research, using what Greiner earlier cited as the data-discussion approach.

At the University of Michigan, the Institute for Social Research has established a Center for Research on Utilization of Scientific Knowledge (CRUSK) to promote action research. The mission of CRUSK is to study the processes of science utilization, the spread of new knowledge, ways of training practitioners to apply research findings effectively in their respective fields, and the value and ethical issues in the use of scientific knowledge. This mission requires that the new center be concerned with both application and research. The members of this center not only observe, but frequently intervene in the processes required to move new facts from research through development to general use. They also record and measure changes along this chain of events. One of the basic premises underlying the work of this center is that careful and systematic research on knowledge utilization will lead to better ways of making the most appropriate use of our knowledge.

The new center has brought together a group of social scientists and professionals with skills and competencies in both change and measurement. These are men and women from widely different fields of specialization and practice. They work together in teams, using a cross-disciplinary approach that is problem centered and that draws heavily on the behavioral sciences for its content and methodology and on practicing professionals for its clinical and social-action skills. Substantively, these people are concerned with the conceptualization and measurement of communication and influence processes, with the change-agent skills needed for either meeting resistance or handling overenthusiasm and premature acceptance of innovations without feasibility testing. CRUSK appears to be a prototype organization for action research.

Warren Bennis summed up the intense need and opportunity for organizational approaches to communication when he wrote:

> Change is the biggest story in the world today, and we are not coping with it adequately: change in the size of and movement of people; change in the nature, location, and availability of jobs; changing relations between whites and blacks, between students and professors, between workers and employers, between generations, and violent change at that; violent change in the cities; change in relations between village and town, town and city, city and nation, and, of course, change in the relations between the empires that are falling and the empires that are rising. [4, pp. 1-2]

REFERENCES AND SUGGESTED READINGS

1. Baritz, L., *The Servants of Power: A History of the Use of Social Science in American Industry.* Middletown, Conn.: Wesleyan University Press, 1960.
2. Barnard, C., *The Functions of the Executive.* Cambridge, Mass.: Harvard University Press, 1938.
3. Bennis, Warren G., *Changing Organizations: Essays on the Development and Evolution of Human Organization.* New York: McGraw-Hill, 1966.
4. Bennis, Warren G., *Organization Development: Its Nature, Origins, and Prospects.* Reading, Mass.: Addison-Wesley, 1969.
5. Browne, C. G., and B. J. Nietzel, "Communication, Supervision and Morale," *Journal of Applied Psychology,* Vol. 36, 1952.
6. Casey, G., "A Case Study of Technical Decision-Making in an Aerospace Organization," Ph.D. dissertation, Purdue University, in process.
7. Cohen, A., "Situational Structure, Self-Esteem, and Threat-Oriented Reactions to Power," in *Studies in Social Power,* ed. by D. Cartwright. Ann Arbor, University of Michigan Press, 1959.
8. Dahle, T. L., "An Objective and Comparative Study of Five Methods of Trans-

mitting Information to Business and Industrial Employees," Ph.D. dissertation, Purdue University, 1953.

9. Davis, Keith, *Human Relations At Work,* 3rd. ed. New York: McGraw-Hill, 1967.

10. Davis, Keith, "Management Communication and the Grapevine," *Harvard Business Review,* Vol. 31, 1953.

11. Davis, Keith, "A Method of Studying Communication Patterns in Organizations," *Personnel Psychology,* Vol. 6, 1953.

12. Dee, J. P., "Written Communications in the Trade Union Local," *Journal of Communication,* Vol. 9, 1959.

13. Douglas, James R., "A Large Industry Looks at Communication," in *Conference on Organizational Communication,* ed. by G. M. Richetto, monograph, NASA, George C. Marshall Space Flight Center, Huntsville, Alabama.

14. Downs, C. W., "Research Methods in Organizational Communication: A Review in Proposals," a paper presented at the Speech Communication Association Convention, December, 1969.

15. Greiner, L. E., "Patterns of Organization Change," *Harvard Business Review,* May–June, 1967.

16. Heron, A., *Sharing Information with Employees,* Stanford, Calif.: Stanford University Press, 1942.

17. Homans, G. C., *The Human Group.* New York: Harcourt, Brace, 1950.

18. Jackson, J. M., "Analysis of Interpersonal Relations in a Formal Organization," Ph.D. dissertation, University of Michigan, 1953.

19. Jacobsen, E., and S. E. Seashore, "Communication Practices in Complex Organizations," *Journal of Social Issues,* Vol. 7, 1951.

20. Kahn, H., and A. J. Wiener, *The Year 2000: A Framework for Speculation on the Next Thirty-Three Years.* New York: Macmillan, 1967.

21. Level, D. A., Jr., "A Case Study of Human Communications in an Urban Bank," Ph.D. dissertation, Purdue University, 1959.

22. Lull, P. E., F. E. Funk, and D. T. Piersol, *Business and Industrial Communication from the Viewpoint of the Corporation President,* monograph published by the Department of Speech, Purdue University, June, 1954.

23. Maier, N. R. F., L. R. Hoffman, and W. H. Read, "Superior-Subordinate Communication: The Relative Effectiveness of Managers Who Held Their Subordinates' Position," *Personnel Psychology,* Vol. 26, 1963.

24. Maier, N. R. F., W. H. Read, and J. Hooven, "Breakdown in Boss-Subordinate Communication," in *Communication in Organizations: Some New Research Findings,* monograph, Foundation for Research on Human Behavior, Ann Arbor, 1959.

25. Mellinger, G. D., "Interpersonal Trust as a Factor in Communication," *Journal of Abnormal and Social Psychology,* Vol. 52, 1956.

26. Merrihue, Willard V., *Managing by Communication.* New York: McGraw-Hill, 1960.

27. Odiorne, G. S., "An Application of the Communication Audit," *Personnel Psychology,* Vol. 7, 1954.

28. Opinion Research Corporation, "Avoiding Failures in Management Communication," research report of *The Public Opinion Index for Industry,* January, 1963.

29. Perry, D., and T. A. Mahoney, "In-plant Communication and Employee Morale," *Personnel Psychology,* Vol. 8, 1955.

30. Pigors, P., *Effective Communication in Industry*. New York: National Association of Manufacturers, 1949.

31. Read, W. H., "Upward Communication in Industrial Hierarchies," *Human Relation*, Vol. 15, 1962.

32. Redding, W. Charles, "Human Communication Behavior in Complex Organizations: Some Fallacies Revisited," in *Perspectives on Communication*, ed. by C. E. Larson and F. E. X. Dance. Milwaukee: University of Wisconsin, Speech Communication Center.

33. Redding, W. Charles, "The Empirical Study of Human Communication in Business and Industry," in *The Frontiers in Experimental Speech-Communication Research*, ed. by P. E. Reid. Syracuse: Syracuse University Press, 1966.

34. Redding, W. Charles, and G. A. Sanborn, "Historical Highlights," in *Business and Industrial Communication*. New York: Harper & Row, 1964.

35. Richetto, Gary M., "Source Credibility and Personal Influence in Three Contexts: A Study of Dyadic Communication in a Complex Aerospace Organization," Ph.D. dissertation, Department of Communication, Purdue University, January, 1969.

36. Roethlisberger, F. J., and W. J. Dickson, *Management and the Worker*. Cambridge, Mass.: Harvard University Press, 1939; see also E. Mayo, *The Human Problems of an Industrial Civilization*. New York: Macmillan, 1933; T. N. Whitehead, *The Industrial Worker*, 2 vols., Cambridge, England: Cambridge University Press, 1938.

37. Smith, Ronald L., "Communication Correlates of Interpersonal Sensitivity Among Industrial Supervisors," Ph. D. dissertation, Department of Communication, Purdue University, August, 1967.

38. Thayer, Lee, *Communication and Communication Systems*. Homewood, Ill.: Irwin, 1968.

39. Tompkins, P. K., "Organizational Communication: A State of the Art Review," in *Conference on Organizational Communication*, ed. by G. M. Richetto, monograph, NASA, George C. Marshall Space Flight Center, Huntsville, Alabama, 1967.

40. Townsend, Lynn A., "A Corporate President's View of the Internal Communication Function," *The Journal of Communication*, Vol. 15, 1965.

41. Walton, E., *A Magnetic Theory of Organizational Communication*, monograph, U.S. Naval Ordinance Test Station, China Lake, California, 1962.

42. Walton, E., "Motivation to Communicate," *Personnel Administration*, Vol. 25, 1962.

43. Whyte, W. H., Jr., and Editors of *Fortune, Is Anybody Listening?* New York: Simon & Schuster, 1952.

44. Wiesman, Walter F., "A Government Agency Looks at Communication," in *Conference on Organizational Communication*, ed. by G. M. Richetto, monograph, NASA, George C. Marshall Space Flight Center, Huntsville, Alabama. (See especially pp. 35–40.)

45. Zima, Joseph P., "The Counseling Communication of Supervisors in a Large Manufacturing Company," Ph. D. dissertation, Department of Communication, Purdue University, August, 1967.

17

PHILOSOPHY: AN APPROACH TO HUMAN COMMUNICATION

HANNO HARDT

TOWARD A THEORY OF ACTION

As EACH AGE has pondered philosophical questions about the scope and nature of human knowledge, it has also produced its own particular explanations for understanding knowledge, for the process of verification, and for the meaning of truth. In modern times, Western thought has been shaped by the writings of philosophers such as René Descartes, John Locke, David Hume, and Immanuel Kant. Their contributions to epistemology range from Descartes' proposition that man does not know through his senses or imagination, but through reason, to Locke's rejection of a theory of innate ideas and his emphasis upon experience as a source of knowledge, Hume's definition that knowledge consists of perceptions and is based upon experiences, and Kant's idea of knowledge as an active function of man that embraces a priori perceptions and sensory impressions.

Since the end of the nineteenth century, philosophical discussions of knowledge have shifted from general descriptions of the phenomenon to questions of understanding and meaning and, in particular, to aspects of language and communication. Susanne Langer characterizes the importance of the study of symbolization in modern philosophy as a "keynote of all humanistic problems," and suggests:

> If it is indeed a generative idea, it will beget tangible methods of its own, to free the deadlocked paradoxes of mind and body, reason and impulse, autonomy and law, and will overcome the checkmated arguments of an earlier age by discarding their very idiom and shaping their equivalents in a more significant phrase. (26, p. 25)

Langer also speculates that the philosophical study of symbols may hold the "seed of a new intellectual harvest, to be reaped in the next season of the human understanding."

These problems of meaning and meaningful or intelligent human communication have received considerable attention from a number of influential philosophical schools of thought, among them pragmatism, logical positivism, and existentialism. In this context, this chapter is an attempt to provide an introduction to the philosophical study of language and communication; it should be considered a tentative statement about the scope and direction of these philosophies, and by no means an exhaustive treatment or a complete history.

The nineteenth century and the emerging theories of Charles Darwin provided the stage for a revolution in all fields of thought. Darwinism, as the foundation of a new social theory, helped accelerate the growing interest in science, and the natural sciences in particular. In addition, it created an atmosphere of intellectual and philosophical development that sought a reconciliation between science and traditional moral values, by calling for a type of "radical empiricism" that would allow for new ways of understanding the nature of man and man's role in nature.

Chronology of Philosophers

René Descartes: 1596–1650
John Locke: 1632–1704
Gottfried Wilhelm von Leibniz: 1646–1716
David Hume: 1711–1776
Immanuel Kant: 1724–1804
Charles Darwin: 1809–1882
Sören Kierkegaard: 1813–1855
Charles S. Peirce: 1839–1914
William James: 1842–1910
Josiah Royce: 1855–1916

John Dewey: 1859–1952
Moritz Schlick: 1882–1936
Karl Jaspers: 1883–1969
C. D. Broad: 1887–
Ludwig Wittgenstein: 1889–1951
Martin Heidegger: 1889–
Rudolf Carnap: 1891–
Susanne K. Langer: 1895–
Jean-Paul Sartre: 1905–
A. J. Ayer: 1910–

PRAGMATISM

In the spirit of a developing philosophy of pragmatism that was described as a method of "making our ideas clear" [30, pp. 286–302] or as a "new name for some old ways of thinking," [22] a number of American philosophers sought to establish a theory of logic and a principle of ethical analysis that stressed the consequences of human action as crucial for a definition of meaning and communication. According to John Dewey, the important question was, "Does it end in conclusions which, when they are referred back to ordinary life-experience and its predicaments, render them more significant, more luminous to us, and make our dealings with them more fruitful?" [11, p. 7] Thus pragmatism as an American philosophy began to make its impact upon science and society. The emphasis of pragmatic thinkers like Charles S. Peirce, William James, and Dewey, was at least in part placed upon constructing a logic of procedure or methodology that would allow for speculation about the nature of scientific theories, the structure of beliefs, and the significance of inquiry as a communication process.

The Contributions of Charles S. Peirce

In his extensive phenomenology of human thought, Peirce formulated a pragmatic maxim which recognized the clarity of meanings in communication processes as a necessary condition for a concept of reality based upon a process of inquiry. He proposed, in effect, a method of philosophizing, and suggested that, while pragmatism does not solve real problems, it at least "shows that supposed problems are not real problems." (30, par. 8.259) This defined, in a way, his specific interest in pragmatism as a theory of meaning. Underlying all his philosophical work was the ambition to develop a philosophy "so comprehensive that for a long time to come the entire work of human reason, in philosophy of every school and kind, in mathematics, in psychology, in physical science, in history, in sociology, and in whatever other departments there be, shall appear as the freeing up of details." (30, par. 1.1) Although commonly identified as the originator of pragmatism, Peirce was too diverse and original a thinker to be placed within the boundaries of any particular philosophical school. Alfred North Whitehead described Peirce as a "very great man, with a variety of interests in each of which he made original contributions. The essence of his thought was originality in every subject that he taught. For this reason, none of the conventional labels apply to him. He conceived every topic in his own original way." (40, p. 276)

According to Peirce, the construction of man's reality is based upon the settlement of opinions and interpretations of perception, which take place in the realm of communication and in the community of interpreters. He argued that the "reality of that which is real does depend on the real fact that investigation is destined to lead, at least, if continued long enough, to a belief in it." (30, par. 5.408) His original definition of pragmatism is rather unclear. "Consider what effects, that might conceivably have practical bearings, we conceive the object of our conceptions to have. Then, our conception of these effects is the whole of our conception of the object." (30, par. 5.402)

To Peirce, meanings of words and intellectual concepts are bound up in a process of inference, from which understanding arises. The judgment of evidence, upon which a theory of reality is based, consists of an interdependence of man and his symbols. According to Peirce:

> Man makes the word, and the word means nothing which the man has not made it mean, and that only to some man. But since man can think only by means of words or other external symbols, these might turn round and say: "You mean nothing which we have not taught you, and then only so

far as you address some word as the interpretant of your thought." In fact, therefore, men and words reciprocally educate each other; each increase of a man's information involves and is involved by, a corresponding increase of a word's information. (30, par. 5.313)

The solutions to problems of information, truth, and reality lie inside man and his ability to make judgments in the process of communication.

All human thought and opinion contains an arbitrary, accidental element, dependent on the limitations in circumstances, power, and bent of the individual; an element of error, in short. But human opinion universally tends in the long run to a definite form, which is the truth. Let any human being have enough information and exert enough thought upon any question, and the result will be that he will arrive at a certain definite conclusion, which is the same that any other mind will reach under sufficiently favorable circumstances. (30, par. 8.12)

Peirce's pragmatic philosophy, then, evolved from a theory of signs or instruments of communication, which, although never completed, represents a highly complex and far-reaching attempt to build a communication theory for the solution of philosophical problems. Rejecting the Cartesian method of introspection, which proceeds from the consciousness of man to his environment, Peirce emphasized the relation of the ideas of truth and meaning to the environment; in other words, man's experience becomes his source of knowledge. Speaking about a concept of reality that is symbolic, Peirce acknowledged the importance of any and all sensory perception in the search for truth; *Nihil est in intellectu quod non prius juerit in sensu* (30, par. 5.181) describes his position that sense perception is a necessary, but not sufficient condition for the accumulation of knowledge.

The matter of sensation is altogether accidental; precisely the same information, practically, being capable of communication through different senses. And the catholic consent which constitutes the truth is by no means to be limited to men in this earthly life or to the human race, but extends to the whole communion of minds to which we belong, including some probably whose senses are very different from ours, so that in that consent no predication of a sensible quality can enter, except as an admission that so certain sorts of senses are affected. (30, par. 8.13)

Underlying this suggestion is the notion that signs consisting of words, concepts, and other types of human behavior presuppose interpretation; thus, the interpretation of sense data is the basis for establishing meaning and truth.

In his theory of signs, Peirce differentiated among three kinds of signs: icons, indices, and symbols. The icon:

. . . may serve as a sign simply because it happens to resemble its object. This resemblance will, then, constitute its internal meaning. But it cannot be said to have any external meaning, since it does not profess to represent anything; for if it did, that would be a manner of signifying its object, not consisting in merely resembling it. (30, par. 8.119)

The importance of the concept of internal meaning, which is iconic, was pointed out by Peirce on another occasion.

> The only way of directly communicating an idea is by means of an icon; and every indirect method of communicating an idea must depend for its establishment upon the use of an icon. Hence, every assertion must contain an icon or a set of icons, or must contain signs whose only meaning is explicable by icons. (30, par. 2.278)

About the second kind of sign, which is of an indexical nature, Peirce remarked:

> There are other signs which become such by virtue of being really connected with their objects. Such is a symptom of disease, or the letters attached to parts of a diagram. The external meaning of such a sign is its most prominent feature. (30, par. 8.119)

Peirce described symbols as signs of a totally different order, not by virtue of any character of their own, nor by virtue of any real connections with their objects, but simply by virtue of being represented as signs. He characterized their meaning as not only internal or external, but as of a third sort that "consists in the character of the interpretant signs which they determine. This is their principal meaning." (30, par. 8.119)

For an understanding of the meaning of signs, Peirce insisted that propositions must consist of signs, that is, of icons, indices, and symbols whose irreducible, triadic sign-object-effect relationship produces an interpretant. He also suggested that the meaning of words or propositions is of a purposive nature and must be defined by its effect on the receiver or interpreter. Since clarity of language and communication, that is, interpretation, also involve the reliance upon habits (which are produced by beliefs), the question of meaning is also related to his claim that the "ultimate" logical interpretant of a sign is a habit. (30, par. 5.491) In his article, "How to Make Our Ideas Clear," Peirce presented his principle of meaning as an introductory remark to his pragmatic axiom.

> From all these sophisms we shall be perfectly safe so long as we reflect that the whole function of thought is to produce habits of action; and that whatever there is connected with a thought, but irrelevant to its purpose, is an accretion to it, but no part of it. . . . To develop its meaning, we have, therefore, simply to determine what habits it produces, for what a thing means is simply what habits it involves. Now, the identity of a habit depends on how it might lead us to act, not merely under such circumstances as are likely to arise, but under such as might possibly occur, no matter how improbable they may be. What the habit is depends on *when* and *how*

it causes us to act. As for the *when,* every stimulus to action is derived from perception; as for the *how,* every purpose of action is to produce some sensible result. Thus, we come down to what is tangible and conceivably practical, as the root of every real distinction of thought, no matter how subtle it may *be;* and there is no distinction of meaning so fine as to consist in anything but a possible difference of practice. (30, par. 5.400)

His interest in a theory of meaning led Peirce to the development of communication based upon a sign-object-interpreter relationship that creates effects necessary for comprehension of meanings of signs. Or, as H. S. Thayer stated:

> what is important for Peirce is that signs are socially standardized ways in which one thing (a thought, word, gesture, or object as *sign*) refers *us* (a community) to something else (the interpretant, the significant effect or translation of the sign, being itself another sign). Thus signs presuppose minds in communication with other minds, which in turn presupposes a community (or interpreters) and a system of communication. (36, p. 83)

The Contributions of William James

James popularized the notion of pragmatism in ways that led Peirce to reject it as the correct philosophical concept, in favor of what he called "pragmaticism." James's interest in man, and his humanistic approach to the philosophy of pragmatism, may be responsible for the overall popularity of the philosophy, but they had little to do with Peirce's original intention to develop a philosophical system. Ralph Barton Perry states that "the modern movement known as pragmatism is largely the result of James's misunderstanding of Peirce." (31, Vol. II, p. 409)

The differences between James and Peirce have been described by Peirce in a letter. He states that James "has almost lost the power of regarding matters from the logical point of view, in defining pragmatism, speaks of it as referring ideas to *experiences,* meaning evidently the sensational side of experience, while I regard *concepts* as affairs of habit or disposition, and of how we should react." (25, p. 718) What James had in mind was the establishment of a method of inquiry that would permit the investigator to establish practical differences; the pragmatic method "is primarily a method of settling metaphysical disputes that otherwise might be interminable." (20, p. 142) Attacking the use of concepts or names in metaphysics, he declared that by following the pragmatic method, one "must bring out of each word its practical cash-value, set it at work within the stream of your experience. It appears less as a solution, then, than as a program for more work, and more particularly as an indication of the ways in which existing realities may be *changed.*" (20, p. 145)

As a result, James concentrated on the development of a theory of truth, which he also saw as operating within the definition of pragmatism.

"Such then would be the scope of pragmatism—first, a method; and second, a genetic theory of what is meant by truth." [20, p. 151] He introduced the idea of mind as a teleological mechanism, saying "It is a transformer of the world of our impressions into a totally different world, the world of our conception; and the transformation is effected in the interests of our volitional nature, and for no other purpose whatsoever." [23, p. 117] Inherent in this statement and in his line of reasoning is the notion of truth as a process.

Communication, that is, the exchange of ideas and the agreement upon words, concepts, and opinions, lies at the center of James's conception of truth. It makes agreement important, and leads to "consistency, stability and flowing human intercourse"; [20, p. 167] and pragmatism defines agreeing to mean "certain ways of 'working,' be they actual or potential." [21, p. 218] The social aspects of the concept of truth or agreement and the underlying presupposition of communication as the process of verification and validation, have been described by James as follows:

> All human thinking gets discursified; we exchange ideas; we lend and borrow verification, get them from one another by means of social intercourse. All truth thus gets verbally built out, stored up, and made available for every one. Hence, we must *talk* consistently just as we must *think* consistently: for both in talk and thought we deal with kinds. Names are arbitrary, but once understood they must be kept to. We mustn't now call Abel 'Cain' and Cain 'Abel.' If we do, we ungear ourselves from the whole book of Genesis, and from all its connexions with the universe of speech and fact down to the present time. We throw ourselves out of whatever truth that entire system of speech and fact may embody. [20, p. 166]

Recognizing the differences of time and place which limit the realization of truth, James suggested a relativity of true ideas:

> we have to live today by what truth we can get today, and be ready tomorrow to call it falsehood. . . . The present sheds a backward light on the world's previous processes. They may have been truth-processes for the actors in them. They are not so for one who knows the later revelations of the story. [20, pp. 170–171]

The interpretation of ideas and opinions, then, the definitions of false or true, are relative not only to the situation, but also to the effectiveness or ineffectiveness of the proposition as defined by the communication process in society or among men; only in this sense are "true ideas . . . those that we can *assimilate, validate, corroborate* and *verify*." [20, p. 160] In a way, James argued for a commitment to life and its uncertainties; he dismissed the meaningless questions of metaphysics and urged that "the whole function of philosophy ought to be to find out what definite difference it will make to you and to me at definite instants of our life. . . ." [22, p. 50]

James's philosophizing reflects the risks of these uncertainties and the spirit of inquiry that can lead to the discovery of what makes a difference.

The Contributions of John Dewey

Dewey elaborated on the writings of Peirce and James; he called his theory of thought "instrumentalism," and labeled it "an attempt to constitute a precise logical theory of concepts, of judgments and inferences in their various forms, by considering primarily how thought functions in the experimental determination of future consequences." [10, p. 26] Communication emerged as a central concept of man and society in Dewey's philosophy. Accordingly, he argued that "To learn to be human is to develop through the give-and-take of communication an effectiveness of being an individually distinctive member of a community." [32, p. 389] Implicit in this statement is the concept of the social as the inclusive philosophical idea. [10, p. 77] Dewey discussed the importance of inquiry in the context of environment as a process of settling doubts and attaining beliefs. He defined inquiry as "the controlled or directed transformation of an indeterminate situation into one that is so determinate in its constituent distinctions and relations as to convert the elements of the original situation into a unified whole." [12, pp. 104–105]

Embedded in the notion of inquiry is the principle of continuity, whose meaning he defined as "the growth and development of any living organism from seed to maturity." [12, p. 23] Also, the contextual framework for growth was provided by Dewey, who stressed the publicness of the communication when he said:

> Knowledge cooped up in a private consciousness is a myth, and knowledge of social phenomena is peculiarly dependent upon dissemination, for only by distribution can such knowledge be either obtained or tested. [32, p. 394]

The social consequences of Dewey's philosophical view are evident in education and in social institutions that man has established to help direct his capacity for growth. Dewey's intense interest in social and political theories, and his theory of education reflect his concern with the changes in modern society. He realized the importance of communication for the survival of community and society, noting that society exists not only *by* but also *in* communication. [9, p. 5] Stressing the experience of shared beliefs, aspirations, and knowledges, he argued that only communication which produces similar emotional and intellectual dispositions can bring about a common understanding. [9, p. 5] He said:

> To be a recipient of a communication is to have an enlarged and changed experience. One shares in what another has thought and felt and in so far,

meagerly or amply, has his own attitude modified. Nor is the one who communicates unaffected. (9, p. 6)

The idea of the community of inquirers (Peirce) and the Great Community (Josiah Royce) are merged in Dewey's concept of democracy, which is "a name for a life of free and enriching communion. . . . It will have its consummation when free social inquiry is indissolubly wedded to the art of full and moving communication." (13, p. 184)

The same attitude was expressed by Dewey on another occasion:

> Of all affairs, communication is the most wonderful. That things should be able to pass from the plane of external pushing and pulling to that of revealing themselves to man, and thereby to themselves; and that the fruit of communication should be participation, sharing, is a wonder by the side of which transubstantiation pales. When communication occurs, all natural events are subject to reconsideration and revision; they are readapted to meet the requirements of conversation, whether it be public discourse or that preliminary discourse termed thinking. (5, p. 133)

More than any other philosophy, Dewey's instrumentalism represented the social, cultural, and political concerns needed for understanding the rise of technology in a growing and maturing nation and for realigning old attitudes and beliefs with the spirit of progress.

LOGICAL POSITIVISM

The Contributions of Ludwig Wittgenstein

The trend away from metaphysical questions and toward a critical and analytical philosophy has continued with more vigor and persistence throughout the twentieth century in Europe and the United States. This new attitude toward philosophy has been described by C. D. Broad, who said: "the most fundamental task of Philosophy is to take the concepts that we daily use in common life and science, to analyse them, and thus to determine their precise meanings and their mutual relations." (7, p. 16) This notion is similar to Ludwig Wittgenstein's consideration of philosophy as not a theory, but an activity of clarification. According to Wittgenstein, "without philosophy thoughts are, as it were cloudy and indistinct: its task is to make them clear and to give them sharp boundaries." (42, par. 4.112)

Wittgenstein's concern with the use and limits of language, specifically, the concern with propositions as pictures of reality, is the main theme of his *Tractatus Logico-Philosophicus*. He described language as an important device for the stating of facts, which consist of sentences, which, in turn, contain words that correspond to objects in reality. Truth, then, becomes a function of the mapping of words and objects and is restricted to propositions that deal with facts verifiable by the senses—that is, facts verifiable within the framework of the natural sciences. This concept brought Wittgenstein to the conclusion that "the totality of true propositions is the whole of natural science (or the whole corpus of the natural sciences)." (42, par. 4.11) As a result, propositions of metaphysics and philosophy (including his own), although important, are nonsense, since they go beyond the limits of language. As he explained, "anyone who understands me eventually recognizes them [propositions] as nonsensical, when he has used them—as steps—to climb up beyond them. . . . What we cannot speak about we must consign to silence." (42, par. 6.54) During his later period, however, Wittgenstein returned to a more flexible and, in a way, pragmatic, view of language and communication.

The limits of languages, as stated in Wittgenstein's *Philosophical Investigations,* are described by the rules of language games, which de-emphasize the importance of the ideal language suggested earlier, calling such an ideal a valuable but artificial attempt. The diversity of rules and of meanings of concepts in the language game is illustrated by his example of a toolbox: "there is a hammer, pliers, a saw, a screw-driver, a rule, a gluepot, nails and screws. The functions of words are as diverse as the functions of these objects." (41, p. 11) Wittgenstein suggested that it is important to identify meaning with use, that questions about the employment of a word will tell us about the operation of the word in the game, and how a word is used will reveal the rules or procedures of the expressions in the specific language game. Thus, the limits of the language and the limits of communication are defined only by the rules of the language games.

His desire to develop a philosophy of language based on the notion of use in a specific situation, real or imagined (since thinking necessarily involves the use of language), is reminiscent of Peirce's theory of meaning and communication. The mastery of a language, according to Wittgenstein, is "part of a form of life," (41, par. 19.23) and the task of philosophy is "a battle against the bewitchment of our intelligence by means of language, (41, par. 109) [since] the problems arising through a misinterpretation of our forms of language have the character of *depth.* They are deep disquietudes; their roots are as deep in us as the forms of our language and their significance is as great as the importance of our language." (41, par. 111) The writings of Wittgenstein influenced two important philosophical movements of this century: logical positivism and ordinary language analysis. (The question of ordinary language analysis will not be discussed in this chapter; however, the center of philosophical activity in this field is at Cambridge, England, where contemporary philosophers have become interested in questions of ethical language and in the analysis of religious language, coupled with a renewed interest in metaphysics.)

The Contributions of Rudolf Carnap

The logical positivists of the Vienna Circle (for further discussion see *The Vienna Circle* by Victor Kraft) and Rudolf Carnap, in particular, advocated the elimination of metaphysics from philosophy, describing metaphysics as a "pseudo statement" and maintaining that philosophy can only be a method of semantic analysis. Carnap suggested that the problem of communication could not be solved by metaphysical conceptualizations, and he followed the view that a scientific approach to language should result in the formulation of a unified language of science. Underlying his theory of, language is a verification principle, earlier developed by Wittgenstein, that "the meaning of a proposition consists in its method of verification." (15, p. 839) This notion was also expressed by Moritz Schlick, the founder of the Vienna Circle, who maintained that meaning can only mean "verifiable meaning." (3, p. 95) In terms of communication, a proposition is understandable only by "what it communicates, and a meaning is communicable only if it is verifiable. Since propositions are nothing but vehicles for communication we can include in their meanings only what they can communicate." (3, p. 95)

In other words, to arrive at a logical and meaningful system of communication, man is restricted in his use of symbols to those that have a logical and mathematical base or that contain empirical concepts. Carnap, for instance, advocated the replacement of ordinary language with a formalized language system, which would provide a basis for the intersubjectivity needed for the understanding of scientific methods and expressions. This idea is also present in his distinction between the material mode of language, which consists of discussions of things, facts, and the real world, and the formal mode of language, which stresses the verifiability and testability of sentences and expressions and their meanings. Through this latter process, his argument goes, the problems of metaphysics will disappear, drop out, since metaphysics deals with knowledge that is not within the parameters of empirical verifiability. Carnap argued that "the sentences of metaphysics are pseudo sentences which on logical analysis are proved to be either empty phrases or phrases which violate the rules of syntax." (8, p. 8)

The Contributions of A. J. Ayer

A. J. Ayer, on the other hand, recognized the possibility of common understanding and communication of experiences among individuals, although he defined meaning in terms of empirical verifiability in sense experiences. While Carnap suggested that experiences are private and, therefore, incommunicable, Ayer outlined the possibilities for the communicability of man's experiences:

> each of us has good reason to suppose that the other people understand him, and that he understands them, because he observes that his utterances have the effect on their actions which he regards as appropriate, and that they also regard as appropriate the effect which their utterances have on his actions; and mutual understanding is defined in terms of such harmony of behavior. (2, pp. 207–208)

What Ayer proposed, then, was that although there are private experiences, man can and does describe them to others; *ergo,* nothing is incommunicable, and all language is in this sense, public. Ayer elaborated on the point of communication in a later essay, in which he described the range of communication and his particular interest in the possible methods of communication. He said, "We communicate information, but also knowledge, error, opinions, thoughts, ideas, experiences, wishes, orders, emotions, feelings, moods. Heat and motion can be communicated. So can strength and weakness and disease." (4, p. 19) But he confessed to viewing communication essentially as:

> transference of information, in a very broad sense of this term, which may be taken to include not merely the imparting of news, in a factual sense, but also the expression of feelings, wishes, commands, desires, or whatever it may be. It covers all deliberate uses of language by human beings as well as voluntary and involuntary exclamations, movements, gestures, singing, crying, laughing, dancing, in so far as they are informative. (4, p. 21)

Ayer acknowledged, in other words, methods of communication other than the use of language, and he rejected Carnap's concept of physicalism as an unnecessary, if not erroneous, explanation of public language.

Although the Vienna Circle was disbanded in the 1930s, its members continued to exert a significant influence upon the thinking of philosophers in England and the United States. In the United States especially, logical positivism found its followers among contemporary philosophers.

EXISTENTIALISM

The Contributions of Karl Jaspers

In existentialist thought, communication represents a source of self-realization and provides man with a direct way for understanding his existential self. This role has been acknowledged by a number of existentialist philosophers, including Karl Jaspers, Jean-Paul Sartre, and Martin Heidegger. Sören Kierkegaard, as an early representative of existentialism, gave considerable thought to the problem of communication. As early as 1847, he had developed a model for communication.

Jaspers' philosophy is based upon the argument that the objective world of science, which man can observe and communicate about through his experiences, is not the complete or ideal state of objectivity. Instead, there is an area of feelings, sensations, and intuitions beyond the realm of public knowledge that is also part of the comprehensive world in which the individual exists. Man, although himself an entity, can only come to reality through communication with others. In describing the difficulties of reaching this stage of existential communication, Jaspers said:

> The struggle involved is that of an individual for *Existenz*—at once that of the other and of the self. While at the level of empirical existence any weapon at all is acceptable, the use of cunning and deception is unavoidable, and the opponent is to be treated as an enemy on all fours with the entirely alien physical nature that resists all our efforts, the struggle for *Existenz* is infinitely different. It involves complete openness, unqualified renunciation of the uses of power and advantage, and concerns the other's self-realization as fully as one's own. In this struggle, both dare to dispense with concealment, to be completely themselves, and to submit to probing questions. (39, p. 135)

Jaspers argued that communication is the result of individuals participating in the task of finding the truth. He called it the loving struggle of communication.

The Contributions of Jean-Paul Sartre

Similarly, Sartre compared the problems of love to those of communication; in both instances, "a subjectivity experiences itself as an object for the other." (33, p. 372) Sartre agreed with Heidegger that "I am what I say," and he continued that "Language is not an instinct of the constituted human creature, nor is it an invention of our subjectivity. . . . It forms part of the human condition." (33, p. 373) In his essay "What Is Writing," Sartre distinguished between the poet and the prose writer: "the poet has withdrawn from language-instrument in a single movement. Once and for all, he has chosen the poetic attitude which considers words as things and not as signs. . . . The man who talks is beyond words and near the object, whereas the poet is on this side of them." (34, p. 308) The writer, however, who uses the words, needs the Other to discover meaning, since he never knows exactly whether he has signified what he wished to signify. "The Other is always there, present and experienced as the one who gives to language its meaning." (33, pp. 373–374)

Sartre emphasized the importance of the communicator-audience relationship in yet another way, when he concluded that the writer must understand that

> no prose-writer is *quite* capable of expressing what he wants to say; he says too much or not enough; each phrase is a wager, a risk assumed. . . .

Thus, each word is used simultaneously for its clear and social meaning and for certain obscure resonances. . . . The reader, too, is sensitive to this. At once we are no longer on the level of concerted communication, but on that of grace and chance. (34, p. 316)

The Contributions of Martin Heidegger

Heidegger, who views communication as an ontological problem, argued that it could only be understood in the context of *Dasein* (a translation of *Dasein* causes problems, and it has been proposed to leave this key term in German, as a *terminus technicus heideggerianus*), and the study of Being as a basic and irreducible concept. This view of communication suggests an intimate relationship between *Dasein* and communication; it also suggests that the study of the whole man is the *sine qua non* in understanding any aspect of human communication.

Western philosophers since Aristotle have viewed man as being in the world under the assumption that he is conscious of his environment and that he can objectively relate his *Umwelt*. The impossibility of such detachment, or posture of objectivity, has been demonstrated by Heidegger, in whose opinion *Dasein* and world merge. Since they cannot exist independently of each other, Being-in-the-world becomes an a priori mode of *Dasein*. If one accepts this philosophical framework, it follows that man can become himself only through his familiarity with the world, or, expressed differently, Being is always Being-in-the-world. Included in this conceptualization is the aspect of shared experience. In Heidegger's terms, that world of *Dasein* is a "with-world" (*Mitwelt*), and "Being-with" means Being-with-others (*Mitdasein*).(16, p. 149)

This approach is essential to a better understanding of man's existential condition and his relationship to others and the world around him. First, the all-inclusiveness of *Dasein* gives new meaning to discussions of man's isolation and alienation from society, and stresses the use of empathic skills in communication. If one accepts Being-with-others as a basic structure of man's self in the sense of "I-myself-with-others," problems of empathy and understanding of others become part of Being; that is to say, embedded in the irreducible with-structure of man is an understanding of others and the world.(17, p. 108) Second, it also reflects upon the concepts of individual freedom and responsibility and, therefore, responsible communication. No man can escape from being responsible for actions (or words) of others if he chooses to exist in this world—if he chooses to exist in this world because of the with-worldishness of the concept. And if he exists fully conscious of his world-relatedness and aware of the consequences of his communicational behavior, he may begin to grasp the meaning of his own existence.

As was recognized very early in Western philosophy, the interpretation of things and events in man's environment, including his relationships with others, is based on language, and, more specifically, on talk and hearing. But the basis of human communication lies in the discourse of Being, which is needed to translate the silent words of Being into human words. According to Heidegger, thinking brings the unvocalized words of Being into language.[19, p. 45] He describes language as the house of Being. This phrase implies the standing of man within the world, and, as Vincent Vycinas suggests,[38] it does not stress the subordination of Being to man, since man is "applied by Being for the establishing of a house of Being-for establishing the language." Hearing, in the Heidegger sense, must be considered the existential openness of *Dasein;* man hears and understands others because he is in the same world. He hears because he understands. The German poet Hölderlin expressed the same thought when he said: "Much has man learnt. Many of the heavenly ones he has named, since we have been in conversation and have been able to hear from one another."[18, p. 300] Only in and through language does man possess anything.

Discourse and hearing in these specific senses are elements of authentic communication. They reveal glimpses of the authentic existence of man, a central idea in contemporary existentialist thought and one that has gained contemporary social importance because the far-reaching scientific and technological developments of this age have had profound effects upon man and his desire for the attainment of an "authentic" life. "Subjective man of today does not know of his original position within the world, but creates a picture of the world in his mind and confronts it. He is not in unity with the world, but torn from it; an isolated, worldless I."[37, p. 41]

Human communication reflects this state of isolation amidst the triumph of science and technology. In discussing this development, Heidegger maintained that some time ago "*Dasein* began to slide into a world without depth . . . all things were reduced to one level, resembling a blank mirror, in which nothing appears, nothing reflects."[17, p. 35] Thus, communication in contemporary society, at the level of the spoken word, never transcends its inauthentic form to become discourse and hearing in their authentic meaning. Instead, communication becomes chatter (*Gerede*) and curiosity (*Neugier*), which conceal or lie about the truth of *Dasein* and lead to a never-ending pursuit of the ever-changing, sensational, unheard-of, and, therefore, "desirable" facets of life.

The results of these changes are evident in the performances of the mass media (e.g., definitions of newsworthiness and truth and objectivity, the process of simplifying issues and recognizing social problems); the form and content of interpersonal communication (e.g., matter-of-fact appeals, communicational concerns for control); and, generally, the social behavior of groups and individuals in contemporary society (e.g., hippie cultures, religious sects, and encounter groups). The particular dangers of this situation lie in the ambiguity of the everyday *Dasein,* which creates an atmosphere in which chatter and curiosity reign supreme, making everything appear quite clear and recognizable, when, in fact, nothing is actually understood.

Chatter, curiosity, and ambiguity are the major characteristics of the inauthentic level of Being, according to Heidegger, when *Dasein* is cut off from itself. They also describe the state of modern man in mass society, in which individuals are prepared to lead average and secure lives, without major decisions, undisturbed and even protected by society in return for specific services and functions that are also predetermined by the managers of mass society. The everyday *Dasein* depends on what Heidegger called the neutral and anonymous forces of "they" (*das Man*).(16, pp. 164–165) Since "they" are responsible for everything, nobody feels a sense of responsibility, and it becomes impossible to be oneself. This is a distortion of the only meaningful way of existence, because it denies individuals a free choice within the limits of their own range of possibilities, their own finiteness. Instead, social status, economic position, and accomplishments in society are measured by what others are or have, and an understanding of oneself no longer rests in oneself, but can be reached only by measuring economic or social distances between others and oneself.

The phenomenon of "keeping up with the Joneses" has long since turned into being like the Joneses, with the result of increased standardization of buying habits and forms of living that characterize mass society. Freedom of choice in private or public matters has been reduced to a conceptual construct of one's attempt to be like the rest of society.

In a sense also, this brings to mind Leibniz's concern, expressed long ago, that with the invention of printing and the subsequent production of enormous quantities of books that will not be read, man faces a breakdown in the dissemination of knowledge that may lead to a kind of barbarism perpetrated by mass-media representatives. The quantity and quality of the information flow in advanced technological societies may very well be determined by intellectual elites and bureaucracies, whose words will rise to the level of "truth" or social or political "reality" and influence man's perception of what he knows or needs. As Heidegger described the channeling of literary and intellectual interests: "We take pleasure and enjoy ourselves as they take pleasure, we read, see and judge about literature and art as they see and judge . . . we find shocking what they find shocking." (16, p. 164)

Jaspers made a similar observation when he said:

In man's naive, unquestioning existence in community his individual consciousness coincides with the general consciousness of his neighbors. He does not ask about his being; the very question would open the rift. However sure the instincts that tell him how to pursue his advantage, the basis of his sense of existence is still the entirety of common bonds and common knowledge. The substance of communal life, the world and the thinking of the people he belongs to—these are not other things subject to inquiry and proof and confronting a particular individual self-awareness. In naive existence I do what everyone else does, I believe what everyone else believes, I think as everyone else thinks. Opinions, goals, fears, and joys are imperceptibly transferred from person to person because of an original, unquestioning identification of all. (39, p. 48)

Thus, in the everyday Being-in-the-world, it is no longer man who is there, it is the anonymous "they" who become the center of man's concern; he is among them, yielding to the pressures of mediocrity and the processes of leveling that dominate his existence. Seduced by words and pictures, man has accepted a practical definition of communication; almost blind and deaf, he may never sense the lack of communication and may continue without the experience of *Daseinskommunikation,* which alone would allow him to fathom the depths of his existence and the meaning of life.

CONCLUDING REMARKS

In summary, language and communication are recognized as basic phenomena of human life. Throughout recent history, man the communicator has stimulated philosophical thought and analysis; the discussions of the uses of language and of the methods of communication lead to considerations of meaning, understanding, and the concept of man.

Pragmatists have expressed a particular interest in questions of the functions of language and communication and the consequences of these functions; knowledge becomes a guide for action and actions have consequences. In this context, language functions as an instrument: Its uses and purposes for the achievement of goals are revealed in communication. Pragmatism has developed into a theory of human action, a plan for directing social conditions and for assimilating moral and scientific knowledge.

Analytic philosophers of the Vienna school have argued that language and communication reveal the knowledge of man—of himself and of others. Metaphysics, as far as it represented what could not be said—that is, what did not correspond to facts—has been denounced as operating beyond the possible realm of experience. The analytic model of communication, consisting of content and structure, with only the latter communicable through appropriate signs, has led to a theory that has denied the communication of experiences, since these are unverifiable, and has stressed observable behavior as the only element of successful communication. The inadequacy of this position has encouraged the development of alternate theories.

Existentialist philosophers have regarded man's concrete situation in the world as the starting point of their investigations. Language and communication are key elements in the reconstruction of man's existence; they reflect the pragmatic impact of existentialism, which considers the ends as the measure of attitudinal and existential change. Representing a movement against the spread of scientism, existentialism emphasizes the freedom of man to inquire into his own being and to structure his own experiences through language and communication.

OUTLINE OF SELECTED PHILOSOPHICAL APPROACHES

PRAGMATISM

General

Ayer, Alfred J., *The Origins of Pragmatism*. Baltimore, 1968.
Dewey, John, "The Development of American Pragmatism," Chapter 2, *Philosophy and Civilization*. New York, 1931.
Hook, Sidney, *The Metaphysics of Pragmatism*. Chicago, 1927.
Konvitz, Milton, and Gail Kennedy, eds. *The American Pragmatists*. New York, 1967.
Moore, Edward C., *American Pragmatism: Peirce, James, Dewey*. New York, 1961.
Thayer, H. S., *The Logic of Pragmatism*. New York, 1952.
Wiener, Philip P., *Evolution and the Founders of Pragmatism*. Cambridge, Mass., 1949.

Charles S. Peirce

Alston, William, "Pragmatism and the Theory of Signs in Peirce," *Philosophy and Phenomenological Research*, Vol. 17, 1956–1957, pp. 79–88.
Barnes, H. F. Winston, "Peirce on How to Make our Ideas Clear," in *Studies in the Philosophy of Charles S. Peirce*, ed. by Philip P. Wiener and F. H. Young. Cambridge, Mass., 1952, pp. 53–60.
Buchler, Justus, *Charles Peirce's Empiricism*. New York, 1935.
Burks, Arthur, "Icon, Index and Symbol," *Philosophy and Phenomenological Research*, Vol. 9, 1949, pp. 673–689.
Burks, Arthur W., and Paul Weiss, "Peirce's Sixty-six Signs," *Journal of Philosophy*, Vol. 42, 1945, pp. 383–388.
Cohen, Morris R., "Charles S. Peirce and a Tentative Bibliography of His Published Works," *Journal of Philosophy*, Vol. 13, 1916, pp. 726–737.
Dewey, John, "Peirce's Theory of Linguistic Signs, Thought and Meaning," *Journal of Philosophy*, Vol. 43, 1946, pp. 85–95.
Dewey, John, "The Pragmatism of Peirce," *Journal of Philosophy*, Vol. 13, 1916, pp. 709–715.
Feibleman, James K., *An Introduction to the Philosophy of Charles S. Peirce*. Cambridge, Mass., 1970.

Fitzgerald, John J., *Peirce's Theory of Signs as Foundation for Pragmatism.* The Hague, 1966.

Gallier, W. B., *Peirce and Pragmatism.* Harmondsworth, 1952.

Murphey, Murray G., *The Development of Peirce's Philosophy.* Cambridge, Mass., 1961.

Peirce, Charles S., *Collected Papers,* Vols. 1–6, ed. by C. Hartshorne and Paul Weiss; Vols. 7–8 ed. by Arthur Burks. Cambridge, Mass., 1931–1935.

Weiss, Paul, "The Essence of Peirce's System," *Journal of Philosophy,* Vol. 37, 1940, pp. 253–564.

Wennerberg, Hjalmar, *The Pragmatism of Peirce.* Copenhagen, 1962.

William James

Castell, Alburey, ed., *Essays in Pragmatism by William James.* New York, 1948.

James, William, *Collected Essays and Reviews.* New York, 1920.

James, William, *Essays in Pragmatism.* New York, 1948.

James, William, *The Meaning of Truth.* New York, 1909.

James, William, *Pragmatism: A New Name for Some Old Ways of Thinking.* New York, 1907.

McDermott, John J., ed., *The Writings of William James: A Comprehensive Edition.* New York, 1967.

Mead, George Herbert, "The Philosophies of Royce, James and Dewey in their American Setting," *International Journal of Ethics,* Vol. 40, 1930 and reprinted in *John Dewey: The Man and His Philosophy,* ed. by Henry W. Holmes. Cambridge, Mass., 1930, p. 75.

Perry, Ralph Benton, *Annotated Bibliography of the Writings of William James.* New York, 1920.

Perry, Ralph Benton, *The Thought and Character of William James,* 2 vols. Boston, 1935.

Reck, Andrew J., *Introduction to William James.* Bloomington, 1967.

Schiller, F. C. S., "William James and the Making of Pragmatism," *The Personalist,* Vol. 8, 1927.

Wild, John, *The Radical Empiricism of William James.* Garden City, 1969.

John Dewey

Bernstein, Richard J., *John Dewey.* New York, 1966.

Dewey, John, *Art as Experience.* New York, 1934.

Dewey, John, *Democracy and Education.* New York, 1916.

Dewey, John, *Freedom and Culture.* New York, 1939.

Dewey, John, *Philosophy and Civilization.* New York, 1931.

Dewey, John, "What Does Pragmatism Mean by Practical," *Journal of Philosophy,* Vol. 5, 1908.

Edman, Irwin, ed., *John Dewey: His Contribution to the American Tradition.* New York, 1955.

Geiger, George R., *John Dewey in Perspective.* New York, 1958.

Hook, Sidney, *John Dewey, An Intellectual Portrait.* New York, 1939.

Nathanson, Jerome, *John Dewey: The Reconstruction of the Democratic Life.* New York, 1951.

Ratner, Joseph, ed., *Characters and Events: Popular Essays in Social and Political Philosophy*, 2 vols. New York, 1929.
Roth, Robert J., *John Dewey and Self Realization*. Englewood Cliffs, 1962.
Schilpp, P. A., ed., *The Philosophy of John Dewey*. Chicago, 1939.
Thomas, M. H., ed., *John Dewey, A Centennial Bibliography*. Chicago, 1962.
White, Morton G., *The Origin of Dewey's Instrumentalism*. New York, 1943.

LOGICAL POSITIVISM

General

Ayer, A. J., *Logical Positivism*. Glencoe, 1959, with extensive bibliography.
Ayer, A. J., *The Revolution in Philosophy*. London, 1956.
Bergmann, Gustav, *The Metaphysics of Logical Positivism*. New York, 1954.
Black, Max, *The Labyrinth of Language*. New York, 1968.
Black, Max, *Language and Philosophy*. Ithaca, 1949.
Joergenson, Joergen, *The Development of Logical Empiricism*. Chicago, 1951.
Kraft, Viktor, *The Vienna Circle*. New York, 1953.
Linsky, Leonard, *Semantics and the Philosophy of Language*. Urbana, 1952.
von Mises, Richard, *Positivism: A Study of Human Understanding*. New York, 1956.
Morris, Charles W., *Logical Positivism, Pragmatism and Scientific Empiricism*. Paris, 1937.
Reichenbach, Hans, *The Rise of Scientific Philosophy*. Berkeley, 1953.
Weinberg, J. K., *An Examination of Logical Positivism*. London, 1936.

Rudolf Carnap

Philosophy and Logical Syntax. London, 1935.
Logical Syntax of Language. London, 1937.
Introduction to Semantics. Cambridge, 1942.
Formalization of Logic. Cambridge, 1943.
Meaning and Necessity. Chicago, 1947.
Introduction to Symbolic Logic. New York, 1958.
Schilpp, Paul A., ed., *The Philosophy of Rudolf Carnap*. La Salle, 1964.

Alfred J. Ayer

Language, Truth and Logic. London, 1936, 1946.
The Foundation of Empirical Knowledge. London, 1940.
Thinking and Meaning. London, 1947.
The Problem of Knowledge. London, 1956.
The Concept of a Person and Other Essays. London, 1963.

Ludwig Wittgenstein

Tractatus Logico-Philosophicus. London, 1922.
Philosophical Investigations. New York, 1953.

The Blue and the Brown Books. New York, 1958.
Copi, Irving M., and Robert W. Beard, eds., *Essays on Wittgenstein's Tractatus.* London, 1961.
Fann, K. T., ed. *Ludwig Wittgenstein, The Man and His Philosophy.* New York, 1967.
Pitcher, George, ed., *Wittgenstein, The Philosophical Investigations.* New York, 1966.

EXISTENTIALISM

General

Blackham, Harold J., *Six Existentialist Thinkers.* London, 1951.
Collins, James, *The Existentialists: A Critical Study,* Chicago, 1952.
Grene, Marjorie, *Introduction to Existentialism.* Chicago, 1959.
Grimsley, Ronald, *Existentialist Thought.* Cardiff, 1967.
Wild, John, *The Challenge of Existentialism.* Bloomington, 1955.

Jean-Paul Sartre

Existentialism. New York, 1947.
The Psychology of the Imagination. New York, 1948.
Being and Nothingness. New York, 1956.
The Emotions: Outlines of a Theory. New York, 1956.
Cranston, Maurice, *Sartre.* London, 1962.
Manser, Anthony, *Sartre, A Philosophic Study.* London, 1966.
Murdoch, Iris, *Sartre: Romantic Rationalist.* Cambridge, 1953.
Natanson, Maurice, *A Critique of Jean-Paul Sartre's Ontology.* Lincoln, 1951.

Karl Jaspers

The Way to Wisdom. New Haven, Conn., 1951.
Man in the Modern Age. New York, 1957.
Reason and Existenz. New York, 1957.
The Future of Mankind. Chicago, 1961.
Philosophy, 3 vols. Chicago, 1970.
Allen, E., *The Self and Its Hazards: A Guide to the Thought of Karl Jaspers.* New York, 1951.
Schilpp. Paul A., ed., *The Philosophy of Karl Jaspers.* New York, 1957.
Wallraff, Charles F., *Karl Jaspers, An Introduction to His Philosophy.* Princeton, N.J., 1970.

Martin Heidegger

What Is Philosophy. London, 1956.
The Question of Being. London, 1958.
An Introduction to Metaphysics. New Haven, Conn., 1959.
Being and Time. New York, 1962.

Discourse on Thinking. New York, 1966.

Frings, Manfred S., ed., *Heidegger and the Quest for Truth.* Chicago, 1968.

Grene, Marjorie, *Martin Heidegger.* New York, 1957.

Langan, Thomas, *The Meaning of Heidegger.* New York, 1959.

Richardson, William J., *Heidegger: Through Phenomenology to Thought.* The Hague, 1963.

Vycinas, V., *Earth and Gods.* The Hague, 1961.

REFERENCES AND SUGGESTED READINGS

1. Ayer, Alfred J., *The Concept of a Person and Other Essays.* London: Macmillan, 1963.

2. Ayer, Alfred J., *Language, Truth and Logic.* London: Gollancz, 1938.

3. Ayer, Alfred J., ed., *Logical Positivism.* Glencoe, New York: Free Press, 1959.

4. Ayer, Alfred J., *Metaphysics and Common Sense.* New York: Macmillan, 1969.

5. Bernstein, Richard J., *John Dewey.* New York: Washington Square Press, 1966.

6. Bock, Irmgard, *Heideggers Sprackdenden.* Meisenheim/Glan: Anton Hain, 1966.

7. Broad, C. D., *Scientific Thought.* London: Kegan Paul, 1923.

8. Carnap, Rudolf, *The Logical Syntax of Language.* New York: Humanities Press, 1951.

9. Dewey, John, *Democracy and Education.* New York: Macmillan, 1916.

10. Dewey, John, "The Development of American Pragmatism," reprinted in *Philosophy and Civilization.* New York: Minton, Balch, 1931.

11. Dewey, John, *Experience and Nature.* Chicago: Open Court, 1925.

12. Dewey, John, *Logic: The Theory of Inquiry.* New York: Holt, Rinehart and Winston, 1938.

13. Dewey, John, *The Public and Its Problems.* New York: Henry Holt, 1927.

14. Fitzgerald, John J., *Peirce's Theory of Signs as Foundation for Pragmatism.* The Hague: Mouton, 1966.

15. Gilson, Etienne, Thomas Langan, and Armand A. Maurer, *Recent Philosophy.* New York: Random House, 1966.

16. Heidegger, Martin, *Being and Time.* New York: Harper & Row, 1962.

17. Heidegger, Martin, *Einführung in die Metaphysik.* Tübingen: Max Niemeyer Verlag, 1953.

18. Heidegger, Martin, *Existence and Being.* London: Vision Press, 1956.

19. Heidegger, Martin, *Uber den Humanismus.* Frankfurt: V. Klostermann, 1947.

20. James, William, *Essays in Pragmatism,* ed. by Alburey Castell. New York: Hafner, 1948.

21. James, William, *The Meaning of Truth.* London: Longmans, Green, 1909.

22. James, William, *Pragmatism: A New Name for Some Old Ways of Thinking.* London: Longmans, Green, 1907.

23. James, William, *The Will to Belief and Other Essays in Popular Philosophy.* London: Longmans, Green, 1897.

24. Kraft, Viktor, *The Vienna Circle.* New York: Philosophical Library, 1953.

25. Ladd-Franklin, Christine, "Charles S. Peirce at the Johns Hopkins," *Journal of Philosophy, Psychology and Scientific Methods,* Peirce commemorative issue, 1916.

26. Langer, Susanne K., *Philosophy in a New Key.* Cambridge, Mass.: Harvard University Press, 1942.

27. Lieb, Irwin C., ed., *Letters to Lady Welby*. New Haven, Conn.: Whitlock's, 1953.
28. Morris, Charles, *Signs, Language and Behavior*. New York, Braziller, 1946.
29. Ogden, C. K., and I. A. Richards, *The Meaning of Meaning*. New York: Harcourt, Brace, 1956.
30. Peirce, Charles S., "How to Make Our Ideas Clear," *Popular Science Monthly*, 1878; reprinted in the *Collected Papers of Charles Sanders Peirce*, ed. by Charles Hartshorne and Paul Weiss. Cambridge, Mass.: Harvard University Press, 1931–1935.
31. Perry, Ralph Barton, *The Thought and Character of William James*. Boston: Little, Brown, 1935.
32. Ratner, Joseph, ed., *Intelligence in the Modern World: John Dewey's Philosophy*. New York: Random House, 1939.
33. Sartre, Jean-Paul, *Being and Nothingness*. New York: Philosophical Library, 1956.
34. Sartre, Jean-Paul, *The Philosophy of Existentialism*, ed. by Wade Baskin. New York: Philosophical Library, 1965.
35. Stenius, Erik, *Wittgenstein's Tractatus*. Oxford, Blackwell, 1960.
36. Thayer, H. S., *Meaning and Action: A Critical History of Pragmatism*. Indianapolis: Bobbs-Merrill, 1968.
37. Vietta, Egon, *Die Seinsfrage bei Martin Heidegger*. Stuttgart: Curt E. Schwab, 1940.
38. Vycinas, Vincent, *Earth and Gods: An Introduction to the Philosophy of Martin Heidegger*. The Hague: Martinus Nijhoff, 1961.
39. Wallraff, Charles F., *Karl Jaspers: An Introduction to His Philosophy*. Princeton, N.J.: Princeton University Press, 1970.
40. Wiener, Philip P., and Frederic H. Young, eds., *Studies in the Philosophy of Charles Sanders Peirce*. Cambridge, Mass.: Harvard University Press, 1952.
41. Wittgenstein, Ludwig, *Philosophical Investigations*, trans. by G. E. M. Anscombe. New York: Macmillan, 1953.
42. Wittgenstein, Ludwig, *Tractatus Logico-Philosophicus*, trans. by C. D. Ogden. London: Kegan Paul, 1922.

Dr. Richard L. Merritt is Professor of Political Science and
Research Professor in Communications at the University of
Illinois. He is the author of over fifty books, articles, and
monographs in the area of political behavior and communica-
tion. Among his more recent volumes are *The Student Political
Scientist's Handbook*, *Systematic Approaches to Comparative
Politics*, *Nationalism and National Development*, *Symbols of
American Community, 1735–1775*, and *Communication in
International Politics*.

18

POLITICAL SCIENCE: AN APPROACH TO HUMAN COMMUNICATION

RICHARD L. MERRITT

T HE term *political* conjures up a variety of images: Party nominating
conventions and elections, "deals" with City Hall, the appointment of a
superintendent of schools, the enactment by Congress of a new draft law,
a presidential message over nationwide television announcing price and
wage controls, an agreement regulating the status of Berlin, a dramatic
confrontation between nuclear giants.

However diverse in form, all these events share some common elements.
They are, first of all, social phenomena—patterns of interaction among
human beings. Second, they imply that people have conflicting notions of
both what things are important in life and how a society should distribute
its valued resources. Some people value affection, others wealth, still others enlightenment or respect or power. A third element is that, to avoid
anarchy, people will create and submit to informal and formal processes
seeking to accommodate the conflicts of values in a way that the group
considers "just." A government is such a formalized set of institutions that
makes decisions about the distribution of values among a larger group of
people. Governments are effective if they can implement their decisions,
authoritative if the people accept these decisions, and legitimate if the decisions accord with commonly accepted notions of justice.

In their specifically political aspect, the events mentioned above entail
what Karl W. Deutsch calls the control of human behavior through a combination of enforcement and voluntary compliance.[10] They are thus

"who-whom" relationships based on probabilities: the probability that A, albeit at some cost to himself, can change the behavior of B to a given extent with respect to given realms of action. Such power relationships are at the core of politics. It is nonetheless clear that other values affect them and hence are also germane to the study of politics. To the extent that they are acting consciously, as Harold D. Lasswell has pointed out, people seek to use their values at hand to maximize the probability of achieving their valued goals.[15] A millionaire may spend his wealth to attain a position in which he has relatively more power in a system. Or a popular movie actor may parlay his public affection, respect, and skill into a gubernatorial post from which he can exercise power over a large number of people. It is the relevance of these other values to the distribution of power in a system that makes such instances interesting to political analysts.

Politics rests upon communication processes transmitting values among humans. We usually think of communication transactions in terms of messages comprising signs, signals, and symbols, but they may include also the transmission from one actor to another of concrete objects or goods (such as gold, which symbolizes the value of wealth). Assuming communication effectiveness, or relatively noise-free transmission, messages of either type contain information that redistributes values between source and recipient.[20] Political communication thus implies those transactions that affect the distribution of power in a human action system.

The very pervasiveness of communication in the political process has led political scientists to focus upon many of its facets. Some of these— public opinion, mass media, trade, bargaining, international communication—are discussed extensively in other chapters of this volume, and therefore need little elaboration here. This chapter, instead of trying to be exhaustive, will concentrate upon three broad but crucial areas of concern in the study of political communication. First is the practical and highly visible dimension of public policy: To what extent do political considerations govern the operation of a communication system in a society? Second, an area that has received considerable attention is what we may call microcommunication: the purposes, processes, and effects of interpersonal communication in the political arena. Third, a relatively new field of study is macrocommunication. It deals with the effects of a society's communication system upon social mobilization, political development, internal violence, and other societal parameters.

THE POLICY DIMENSION

The dilemma of human freedom has puzzled philosophers since early times. We prize the modality of spontaneity. The image of man unfettered by laws dances about tantalizingly in our heads, even though we know that this "ideal" state of man in nature could all too quickly become one in which, to use the words of Thomas Hobbes, "every man is enemy to every man," and life is "solitary, poore, nasty, brutish, and short." Hence we stress simultaneously the principle of responsibility: Man must exercise restraint, or society must impose constraints upon him, to ensure that his actions do not damage the society of which he is a member. Translating our cognitions about freedom into practical terms poses immense problems. What is the proper mixture of spontaneity and responsibility in a society? To whom is the individual responsible? It is this basic dilemma about the nature and implications of freedom that underlies the raging debate on the "freedom of communication" in today's world. Even more significantly, it goes to the very heart of the question of the principles according to which we want to be governed.

Governmental Controls

Since the beginnings over five centuries ago of modern techniques for mass communication, there has doubtless been not a single government that has not sought to exert some measure of control over their use. We think of such government controls as part and parcel of authoritarian regimes. But they also exist in countries like the United States, which prides themselves on their "free" press. "Congress shall make no law," states the First Amendment to the Constitution, "abridging the freedom of speech, or of the press." In fact, of course, all three branches of the American government have done just that, usually with the announced intent to protect the population or to safeguard the existence of alternative sources of information.

The Principle of Protection   Governments are increasingly disinclined to tolerate libertarian notions of communications freedom that prove harmful to individuals or to society as a whole. Perhaps the least disputed among a country's arsenal of control measures are its libel laws, which seek to inhibit the public circulation of malicious defamations. Second, and more controversial, are laws aimed at protecting public safety. Through its Food and Drug Administration and the Federal Communications Commission, the American government has the authority to ban deleterious products, prevent manufacturers from making false claims about their products, and even exclude from the airwaves advertisements for products that may be dangerous to health. A third concern is the protection of public morality. Thus obscenity laws restrict the production and distribution of materials which the average citizen is thought to find offensive. Fourth, some control measures seek to protect a society's political system. Examples include censorship in time of war and the prohibition of anticonstitutional parties in time of peace.

With respect to each of these modes of regulation, it is in the large gray area between absolute license and rigid governmental control that public policies must be made. What federal agencies find too dangerous to be advertised, such as cigarettes, is not always viewed as dangerous by manufacturers.[13] Indeed, tobacco growers spend large sums trying to counteract what they view as the federal government's unreasonable hostile attitude and intervention into the free-market economy. In a similar way, what is art for some people is pornography for others. Because of the near impossibility of finding a generally accepted definition of obscenity that will stand up in court, and because of the inconclusiveness of evidence purporting to show any causal relationship between the consumption of "pornography" and deviate sexual behavior or criminal acts, a presidential commission recommended in 1970 the repeal of obscenity laws currently in force and the appropriation of more funds for sex education. That the country's top political leadership sharply rejected the commission's recommendations suggests that the debate will continue.

Of particular concern is the extremely thin line separating measures aimed at protecting the political system from measures seeking to suppress enemies of a particular regime. In some countries opponents of the government end up in jail or worse. And even in pluralist democracies like the United States, officials have been known to keep politically damaging documents from the public eye. Their exposé by a journalist or newspaper —whatever the motive, be it an acute sense of the national interest, partisan sniping, a muckraking spirit, or simply financial gain—can embarrass the government in power and invite its retaliation.

The Principle of Equity   Governments usually maintain that communication media must be responsive to the people they serve. Who "the people" are is, not unexpectedly, often left undefined. In some cases, such as radio and television broadcasting in western Europe, this means government ownership and control by a board of officials appointed by and responsible to the government. In the United States, by contrast, private ownership is assumed to provide access for a plurality of interests. But ensuring this requires some government regulation. The task of the Federal Communications Commission, according to its director in 1970, Dean Burch, "is to keep broadcasting an 'open' medium of expression, to supply the framework within which the industry can—and must—present a diverse fare of information and views on significant public issues." Careful licensing and distribution of adequate spectrum space have been the traditional means to prevent too much concentration of control or uniformity of content. New developments, however, such as community antenna television, subscription television, and expansion in the UHF portion of the television spectrum, make it likely that the scope of the FCC's task will grow in coming years. And, of course, not a few Americans, some of them in high political office, are appalled by what they see as the abuses and one-sidedness of the media, and are calling for even greater governmental controls.

Information Policy In the modern state the government is one of the primary producers of information. This is not only true in countries like the Soviet Union, where the government uses a wide variety of techniques to communicate its messages to the public—preferably to the exclusion of messages from other sources.[4] In the United States, too, government messages flood the communication channels. Congressmen and elected officials hold press conferences virtually whenever they think anyone may listen to them. The executive branch, particularly in the person of the President, has privileged access to the media at prime time for the purposes of announcements, press conferences, interviews, and fireside chats. The Associated Press estimated in the late 1960s that the executive branch spends about $400 million annually for public information and public relations. It provides services ranging from the publication of pamphlets on peach canning to the dissemination of presidential papers, demonstrations of technical equipment, and air shows. Of particular concern to opponents of America's involvement in Vietnam is what Senator William J. Fulbright has termed the "Pentagon propaganda machine." [14] A television program by the Columbia Broadcasting System in late 1970 exposing the techniques and sums spent in the "selling of the Pentagon" brought public cries of outrage and even a congressional investigation—the latter aimed not at the public-relations expenditures of the Department of Defense but rather at CBS itself! President Nixon subsequently ordered federal agencies to trim "self-serving" public-relations activities from $164 million in the fiscal year 1971 to $48 million in 1972.

When journalists are unwilling to take the initiative or are unable to conduct their own investigations, the information fed into the media by governmental sources may well dominate the interpretation of events. This happens when officials deny journalists access to documents or knowledgeable personnel; and the ingenious reporter who breaks through these barriers of official secrecy not infrequently incurs the wrath of officialdom. The publication by the West German news magazine, *Der Spiegel,* of classified information about the German army's miserable showing in its 1962 maneuvers even led to later indictments for treason (which did not hold up in court) and a nationwide scandal. Something similar occurs when newspapers and television companies, short of personnel, accept government stories without carefully checking them out first. In the early 1950s, as Susan Welch has demonstrated, news reports and editorials on the Indochina war appearing in major American newspapers relied almost completely upon governmental news sources. The reliance did not prepare the American people for the shock they received in later years when more independent reporters in Vietnam began sending back articles sharply at odds with the official view.

The issue is thus both quantitative and qualitative. By the sheer bulk of information that a government feeds into all levels of a national communication system, it can virtually drown out competitive voices. Further, officials with something to hide or a special line to peddle can use their ability to "manage" information for their own ends. Both aspects pose severe tests of a country's freedom of communication.

The Continuum of Controls   The general use by governments of direct and indirect controls over the operation and content of communication media suggests that freedom of communication is indeed a relative matter. The serious questions focus on the magnitude of inadvertent as well as intended controls, their scope, and the degree to which governments actually implement them. "Totalitarian" governments lay claim to complete control, but the costs of making good this claim mean varying degrees of enforcement. The success of the controls in molding the images and attitudes of their populations is yet another question. "Liberal democracies" aim, at least in principle, at minimal controls. The practice is frequently rather different, although rarely can we get government officials and media spokesmen to agree on what is in fact the situation, and how the balance between spontaneity—the freedom to know, to tell, and to find out [26]— and responsibility should be set.

What Western writers are just beginning to notice, however, is that, in focusing primarily upon the putative governmental threat to freedom of communication, they have all but ignored a critical point. The way in which a society is organized, that is, the structure of both its dominant values and dominant groups, provides the basis for defining the role and nature of communications in the first place.

Social Controls

"Pluralism" is the governing ideal of American politics. It postulates equal access for all citizens to the centers of decision making, a marketplace of ideas in which the better ones ultimately survive, a combination of cooperation and competition that furthers the general welfare, and withal government regulation to protect those less well able to take care of themselves. It does not require a very radical perspective to realize that this American dream has not fulfilled its promise.

Access to the Public Forum Mass communication systems are costly. Not since the days of Guttenberg has the average literate individual had the technical means at his disposal to compete with organized interests in communicating to others on a mass basis. The capital required to enter the communications industry has skyrocketed. And with these rising costs has come a greater concentration in the media: The number of daily newspapers in the United States, estimated at 2,442 in 1914 (or about one for every 40,000 inhabitants) dropped to 1,652 in late 1969 (or about one for every 120,000 inhabitants); most of America's large cities no longer have directly competitive newspapers; and three national networks account for the bulk of the programs beamed to American television viewers.[27] Compounding this pattern is the emergence of a new form of economic organization, the conglomerate. It avoids the threat of antitrust suits by diversifying its investments rather than seeking monopolistic control in any single sector. A conglomerate that controls a television network may also have branches publishing books or magazines, distributing records, or manufacturing chemicals. A firm with overseas operations, such as a movie company or an advertising agency, has even more opportunities to direct the production and distribution of media products.

Added to growing concentration in various forms is the fact of communication saturation. The individual is barraged with media and messages competing for his attention. A new message alone is usually insufficient to break into his established attention patterns in a meaningful way. To do this requires the mediation of firms or networks with an impact extensive enough to overcome the barriers of habit and overload, and this in turn is costly. The point is not that the maverick or tough-minded individual cannot make his message heard above the din of well-financed competition, or even that a clique of gigantic corporations is conspiring to control the communications industry; rather, the scale and costs of the industry make it exceedingly difficult for the newcomer to go it alone.[2] His best bet, if he is interested in surviving, may be to join established Goliaths, not to set himself up as a Davidlike competitor.

Unconscious Self-limitation But more than the economics of scale limits the access of individuals to the mass communication arena; also important is the social framework within which the media operate. As a general rule, organizations such as governments and political systems have a conservative bias; they favor norms and procedures that maintain the organization with only marginal changes. Rarely will they tolerate radical change that alters the structure of the organization or threatens the incumbents of leading roles. And, as a general rule, communication media assist in the maintenance of the system. Even the tradition of the American press, from the muckrakers at the beginning of the century to the publication by

The *New York Times* of the "Pentagon Papers," has stressed reform rather than overthrow of the political status quo.

So internalized in the population and the communication industry itself is this system-maintaining norm that radical voices find it difficult to make themselves heard. Sometimes this is due to conscious decisions made by newspaper publishers or network owners who find distasteful what radicals of the right or left have to say. More frequently, however, it is a matter of unconscious but nonetheless systematic suppression. Media analysis and plain common sense give the media operator a good idea of his audience's range of opinion. Moreover, arguments and interpretations outside this broad spectrum of tolerated opinion often rest upon a set of perspectives and a logic that those in the mainstream cannot readily grasp. To pay too much attention to such views is risky. The regular audience might not understand them, and hence lengthy explanations would be needed, or else it might reject the entire publication or program as frivolous. Besides, the media operator may conclude, the flow of ample information from "respectable" channels hardly makes the risk worthwhile.

The consequence is a stifling, self-regenerative cycle of "acceptable" messages. This may be system maintaining in the short run, but in the long run it almost always damages the organization's self-steering (or governing) capabilities. Gadflies can be troublesome: They are sometimes garrulous, repetitive, self-righteous, and downright silly. But to ignore them systematically is to court disaster. A major task of politics, then, turns out to be to find ways of encouraging the open expression and evaluation of radical critiques of the political system's premises, values, and procedures.

Ties of Interaction Limiting the possibility for the infusion of new perspectives into the social consciousness are the level and type of interaction between the media on the one hand and, on the other, government and business. The traditionally accepted norm, William L. Rivers has pointed out, views them as adversaries.[25] But is this view anything more than a cliché? Certainly it is true that the press and other media are not infrequently vicious critics of the business community and government. And certainly we can reject as inadequate the claim that America is governed by a handful of men who comprise a tightly interlocked business-government-communication elite—despite some evidence that leaders in all three social sectors come from roughly the same social class and interact frequently with one other. Even so, a nagging doubt remains that Robert Cirino may have more than a kernel of truth when he charges that the media bias, distort, and censor their reports in serving the profit-making and political interests of the "corporate establishment." [6]

Beyond the fact, already suggested earlier, that leaders in many sectors of society have a concrete interest in maintaining the existing political system, with marginal improvements to be sure, is the possibility of co-optation. The communication media rely on government and business and, overt demonstrations of "objective" opposition notwithstanding, may bend themselves unconsciously to their purposes. Government provides information to the media, on both a routine and a privileged basis. It is the latter that makes for the scoops and television specials that enhance the prestige of the media scoring the coups. The threat by stung executive-branch officials to cut off a newspaper's "pipeline to the White House" can be a serious one indeed. Or White House reporters, getting accustomed to the perquisites of their job, are reluctant to jeopardize it. Or editors kill stories on the request of high-level administration officials—as the *New York Times* did at the time of the Bay of Pigs invasion. Or, more simply, they accept the government's position without question.

The media rely upon business for advertising revenues and other forms of economic support. Critical editorials or controversial television programs sometimes lead firms to withdraw this backing. Despite some blatant examples to the contrary,[26] such genteel blackmail is evidently rarely threatened or spoken aloud. It is nonetheless an ever-present possibility that without question colors the editorial framework within which decisions about content and policy are made. If media operators were inclined—which I have suggested they are not—persistently to present information or views damaging to the political status quo, of which the government and business community are substantial pillars, such pressure could be very intimidating.

There is also some degree of mobility among these three social sectors. Publishers like Walter H. Annenberg secure top-level positions, in this case that of American ambassador to the Court of St. James. Media experts like Edward R. Murrow and Carl Rowan assume leadership of the United States Information Agency. Journalists like Walter Lippmann become intimates of Presidents and senators. General David Sarnoff spanned all three social sectors. And flocks of reporters move in and out of lower-level government positions both nationally and locally. This type of interchangeability and interaction can serve only to weaken the "adversary" conditions thought to prevail.

Nowhere, Herbert I. Schiller has argued, is this basic community of interest among communication, business, and government leaders more plain than in America's international communications policy.[29] At a time when federal agencies were removing cigarette advertisements from domestic television, other federal agencies were working with media experts to increase tobacco exports to other countries. Communication executives have long advised the government on its overseas propaganda and information programs. And, in 1962, the three sectors joined forces in the Communication Satellite Corporation (Comsat), thereby improving markedly the prospects for each in the race that would develop to dominate the international telecommunication system.

To date, political analysts have only scratched the surface of this very deep-seated issue: the latent influence on communication policy exerted by complex networks of social relationships and values. The writing in this area, frequently exploratory, passionate, and hortatory, has by and large left much to be desired in terms of rigorous scientific analysis. It has nonetheless pressed upon political analysts a new perspective on communication policy and broader areas of social life—a perspective that will force them to rethink the traditional wisdom about "freedom of communication," what it means, what its costs are, and how to further it in more than a formal sense. To some extent new research is needed to test empirically the propositions offered by this radical critique. More significant in the short run, however, is the need to reevaluate existing findings on communication in the political process to see what new light they can shed.

COMMUNICATION IN THE POLITICAL PROCESS

The study of microcommunication processes focuses upon direct and mediated interpersonal communication. This implies most immediately face-to-face communication: a husband and wife over the breakfast table, a discussion in a small group, transactions in supermarkets or real estate offices, correspondence with loved ones far away. In larger communication systems there may be a mediator between source and recipient. In some circumstances local opinion leaders "interpret" world events for their clientele; we learn about what happens in a distant city, such as Hollywood or Saigon, not through personal observation but from reports in the newspapers or magazines we read or the newscasts we watch. Microcommunication processes of particular importance in political analysis include socialization (or how we acquire the values, information, and techniques we need to operate in a social setting), the mobilization of mass support for political parties and policies, and the way people, especially national leaders, make decisions.

Political Socialization

People learn values and techniques.[8] We do not inherit them; they must somehow be communicated to us. As the child progresses from his mother's knee into a series of schools and finally becomes an adult, he encounters a variety of socializing agents: individuals such as his parents, playmates, teachers, employers, co-workers, and friends; and organizations such as the clubs he joins and the mass media. All these, by both what they communicate and the way in which they do it, can potentially influence his views toward life and politics. If we want to understand a person's political behavior, therefore, we must go beyond the dissection of his current value system into a reconstruction of its origins.

Political analysts have approached this task in many ways. One approach looks at the individual. If sufficient information about a person's background is available—with whom and with what ideas and events he came into contact, and how he pieced these socializing experiences together—then it is in principle possible to write what Lewis J. Edinger has called a developmental biography. In practice this is difficult, however, because of the paucity of information helping the analyst get inside the subject's psyche. Furthermore, the amount of time required for research on an adequate developmental biography means that few will be written, and these will deal with the great figures in history rather than with the common man. An alternative is to use interviews of a more or less psychoanalytic character to investigate the origins of political value systems in more accessible persons who are hopefully typical of their society.

Another approach examines the influence of experiences common to all people or large aggregates of people. The age of a child makes a difference in terms of the content and complexity of his political imagery. And so do the socioeconomic and cultural conditions in which he grows up. Research on how such existential circumstances shape life experiences—or, more accurately stated, how individuals interpret and respond to these circumstances—generally correlates data on the social background of the elite or the masses with indicators of their current political values. The result is a set of probability statements, more accurate for describing and predicting the perspectives of a class of people than those of any single member of that class.

Still other studies look at what is communicated to people. The partly conscious, partly unconscious use of words, images, and other stylistic elements in textbooks, television programs, and other forms of communication is presumed to influence the recipient's perspectives. But do achievement-oriented children's stories lead to an achieving society, textbooks stressing the hierarchical organization of society to authoritarian thinking, violence on television to violent behavior by viewers? The cause-and-effect sequences are far from simple. Available research suggests merely that the answers to such questions are positive if and only if intervening factors (such as social support) are also pushing the recipients in the predicted direction. *How much* of which intervening factors remains unanswered. But this research problem is not unique to studies of socialization: It is prominent in the mind of anyone seeking to mobilize support or influence the perspectives of others.

Mobilizing Support for Partisan Purposes

To pursue any political aim requires mobilizing support. This is true regardless of whether we are speaking about "totalitarian" countries,[4] which are far from the monoliths we sometimes picture them to be, or "democratic" countries with open elections and relatively uncontrolled communication media; developed countries with sharply differentiated social structures, or developing countries trying to build a sense of nationalism to supersede local loyalties.

Electioneering   Certainly the most frequently studied type of effort to mobilize political support is the partisan election. It is crucial for those seeking to garner support for candidates and parties to know what the predispositions of the electorate are, and what appeals to them are likely to have any effect. This need contributed to the development of rather sophisticated techniques, derived for the most part from an earlier concern with consumer behavior, for analyzing and predicting electoral behavior. By now, too, the findings of this research are sufficiently sophisticated that campaign managers must possess not only the traditional political savvy, but also expertise in the communication techniques that have so effectively changed the public context within which elections take place.[19] One such finding is that the importance of local opinion leaders is declining as mass media assume an ever greater role in people's lives. Hence how a candidate is "packaged" and "sold" to the public via the mass media makes a world of difference in the electoral outcome.[18; 21] Even so, issues remain important in voters' minds; and we can anticipate the further development of techniques, possibly computer-based, enabling candidates and parties to deal with the subtle distinctions made by issue-oriented citizens.

Support for Policy   Elected politicians and appointees face the task of realizing their policy goals. Since new policies imply a redistribution of society's resources, they inevitably engender opposition from individuals and groups holding different value priorities. What ensues is a complex process of bargaining among those most affected by the proposed redistribution or most able to influence the ultimate decision. To line up support for a policy, its proponents may use a variety of techniques, ranging from simple efforts at persuasive communication, such as personal telephone calls from the President to key congressmen, all the way to "logrolling" and even cruder forms of political horse-trading. In some cases policy advocates may see the need for public support. Thus in 1919 Woodrow Wilson undertook an ill-fated speaking tour of the nation to marshal support for America's entry into the League of Nations; Harry S. Truman, to secure backing for his program to aid countries he saw threatened by communism, adopted the scare tactic of painting a grim picture of the consequences for America should the aid measure not be adopted; and, as the "Pentagon Papers" have revealed, subsequent national leaders were not averse to presenting the public with only part of the truth if this would gain support for their policies. Such techniques may backfire, of course. The public can weary of a public figure who oversells his message, or become suspicious—the famous "credibility gap"—about the veracity of someone whose versions of policy needs are not borne out by independent observers or later events.

National Interests   Even when leading policy makers are convinced that some program is nonpartisan and vital to the survival of the nation-state, they may have trouble enlisting support. This was the case in France in 1940 after the Nazi invasion. And defining continued American involvement in Vietnam or a freeze on wages and prices as policies of national interest failed to prevent the growth of opposition to them. The problem is that there are varying interpretations of what the national interest is and how it can best be served. Appeals to nationalism may enhance an existing or emerging consensus. But wrapping too many policies in the American flag may merely deaden the population's susceptibility to such appeals, or alternatively stir up a xenophobic jingoism that makes more difficult America's future relations with foreign countries.

Developing countries have a special problem in this respect. Beyond their need to create political institutions and economic well-being, they must frequently face the task of forging a sense of national identity out of local and sometimes conflicting loyalties. Such a nationalism rests to an extraordinary degree, as Deutsch has argued, upon the growth of common habits of and facilities for communication.[9] It is not to be wondered, therefore, that revolutionary leaders and postindependence elites stress the development and control of such facilities. And many new nations, including the United States in its first years, filter through the bottleneck of nationalism both their foreign policies and the resolution of many social conflicts at home.

Decision Making

Implicit in all these attempts to mobilize support for partisan or national purposes is a model of the policy-making process. Who the participants are and how they interact to make and implement decisions are crucial questions in political analysis. Few questions have engendered more controversy than these.

The participants in governmental decision making are astonishingly many. Earlier studies tended to stress individual national leaders (or the "gray eminences" behind the throne), and more recently some writers have seen a "power elite" of a handful of individuals well-placed in various sectors of the society making the most important decisions. Actually, individual citizens, spokesmen for interest groups, political party officials, journalists and editorial writers, newscasters, businessmen, congressmen, State Department employees, cabinet members, the President—all these and many others shape the way in which the decision situation is framed, the range of acceptable policy alternatives, the choice among these alternatives, and their implementation. What is more difficult to specify are the extent to which and the ways in which they make their contribution. Empirical studies reveal, for instance, that State Department officials concede public opinion to be an important desideratum in formulating policy; but what these officials mean is less mass attitudes as reflected in public opinion polls than the views of prominent congressmen and such "prestige" publications as the *New York Times*.[7; 11] Similarly, these State Department officials are more willing than either newsmen or interest-group spokesmen to approve the manipulation of information for policy purposes.[5]

In analytic terms, Deutsch points out, what flows through a decision-making system is information.[10; 32] An event occurs in the system's environment. Information about it is selectively perceived and reported by various actors in the system, who interpret it as a situation calling for closer attention. The proximate decision makers, to use Charles E. Lindblom's term, may search for additional information—either about the event itself, or about the state of the environment, or the state of the decision-making system (such as public opinion)—before assembling a collection of possible responses they could make.[17] They then narrow down the range of choices, possibly sending up trial balloons to see what the reaction to particular policies would be in other sectors of the system, before selecting one to implement.

Such a formulation, however intuitively interesting, poses serious practical and analytic problems. Is this in fact the way in which decision makers in government go about their task? To answer this question we need considerable information about those who make more than a marginal contribution to the decision-making process, the degree to which they could specify the important values in play, whom they consult or pay attention to, the exhaustiveness with which they search for possible strategies, the extent to which they seek to optimize their values rather than "satisfice," and the ways in which they get feedback about the effects of the policies they seek to implement. Second, can we spell out these procedures in more operational terms that will permit us to formulate and test empirically propositions about them? And, third, can we use findings from such empirical investigations to construct a satisfactory theory of decision making? Political analysts already have a wealth of case-study material to work with, isolated findings on information flows and negotiation processes in government, and a small bundle of promising theoretic frameworks with which to view political decision making. What they lack is a fully elaborated theory purporting to explain the decision-making process itself. On this topic as well as other microcommunication processes social scientists, although they have learned much to date, have a great deal more to learn.

COMMUNICATION SYSTEMS AND POLITICAL OUTCOMES

The need for data and theory is even more glaring in the study of political macrocommunication, which deals with the effect of a communication subsystem upon systemic outputs. In an earlier section of this chapter, concerned with the policy dimension, we examined the influence of governmental systems and policies upon a society's communication subsystem. Fred S. Siebert, Theodore B. Peterson, and Wilbur Schramm have delineated quite nicely the communication consequences of authoritarian, libertarian, Soviet Communist, and social-responsibility theories of political life.[31] The question here is the obverse: What function does a nation-state's communication subsystem perform in its total social system and its foreign relations?

Functional Approaches

In seeking to answer this question, analysts have proposed varying but converging ideas about the communication subsystem's functions in society. Robert E. Park wrote in 1939 that communication's function "seems to be to maintain the unity and integrity of the social group in its two dimensions—space and time." Lasswell spoke of it as "(1) the surveillance of the environment, (2) the correlation of the parts of society in responding to the environment, (3) the transmission of the social heritage from one generation to the next." To these Schramm and others have added the function of entertainment. Charles R. Wright has presented a convenient formula outlining the basic communication activities in society: [33]

	(1) manifest	(3) functions	
What are the	and	and	of mass communicated
	(2) latent	(4) dysfunctions	

(5) surveillance (news)	for the (9) society
(6) correlation (editorial activity)	(10) subgroups
(7) cultural transmission	(11) individual
(8) entertainment	(12) cultural system?

Such an inventory raises politically relevant questions similar to those touched upon in the second part of this chapter: What difference does it make in terms of citizens' later loyalties if their main political socialization (which transfers culture) takes place in state-operated rather than private or parochial schools? What difference do varying types of editorial selection, interpretation, and prescription in the mass media (Lasswell's "correlation") make in terms of electoral outcomes? How does the rapidity with which a state's communication system gathers, processes, and disseminates news (surveillance) affect the state's decision making? As suggested earlier, such questions are the traditional stuff of political microcommunication analysis.

But such a functionalist approach also enables us to ask broader, macroanalytic questions: Do levels of communication freedom in societies give us any clues about the political stability of these societies, the operation of their party systems, or their propensity to get involved in foreign wars? What effect do socialization patterns have upon levels of cohesion or anomie in societies? How does communications development affect an emerging country's political development? Daniel Lerner, writing about the passing of traditional society in the Middle East, noted that mass media of communication broaden the empathic abilities of their recipients, that is, the probability that they can imagine themselves in someone else's shoes.[16] This in turn increases the likelihood that they will make greater demands upon the political system: Once people can imagine themselves leading a different and presumably better life, they may begin questioning why they cannot have this life for themselves. Lerner's view, in brief, is that urbanization leads to increases in educational and literacy levels; the latter set the stage for the expansion of communication habits and facilities, which in turn is the condition in which democratic political development occurs. Ithiel de Sola Pool, in seconding Lerner's view, also stressed the importance of the media in shoring up the "modernizing" political leaders and the values they are trying to promote.[24; 30] We are learning, however, that all too frequently this means ensconcing in power that portion of the traditional elite that understands the winds of change sufficiently to bend them to its own purposes. This, then, takes us back to the question, asked at the outset, about the principles according to which we or any other group want to be governed.

A somewhat different functionalist approach has been proposed by Gabriel A. Almond.[1] Instead of asking what functions communication systems perform in society, he reversed the question to ask, first, what functions are performed in every political system and, second, what portion of these functions is performed by structures that we traditionally term communications. In his earlier work he identified four *input* functions (political socialization and recruitment, interest articulation, interest aggregation, and political communication) and three *output* functions (rule making, rule application, and rule adjudication). Political communication is the means by which the other input and output functions are performed; and it can be characterized in terms of the homogeneity, mobility, volume, and direction of flow of information. Almond later reformulated his views to concentrate upon three major systemic functions: capabilities, conversion, and maintenance and adaptation (which includes the earlier socialization and recruitment). In this revised statement the communication function is one of six comprising the conversion process. But, besides merely transforming inputs into outputs (the conversion function), communication is also important for a system's capabilities and maintenance and adaptation functions. In short, although Almond's starting point is different (and raises some serious conceptual questions about the meaning of the term *function:* Is it merely an activity of a political system, or is it a *necessary* activity of that system?), the questions he asks are not dissimilar to those posed by Lasswell, Wright, and others.

Answering the macroanalytic questions in any scientifically satisfactory manner is a task at once difficult and challenging. What is needed are empirical propositions, or assertions that can be proved true or false by the systematic test of objective, replicable, impersonal, and preferably quantitative data gathered from the observable world. This need has led not a few political analysts to develop potentially relevant social indicators of the communication process.

Social Indicators in Communications Research

The search for social indicators of the communication process stems in large part from the work of Karl W. Deutsch. In his studies of nationalism and large-scale political integration,[9] he realized that it was possible to develop quantitative indicators of significant aspects of social mobilization: exposure to modern life, exposure to mass media, residential mobility, literacy, and so forth. These in turn enabled him to reformulate his ideas into a quantitative model of social mobilization. Subsequent researchers have built up extensive collections of data on politics, including some communication variables. The latter include facets of domestic communication systems, such as book production, broadcasting time, cinema attendance, language groups, news services, newspaper circulation, press freedom, radio and television ownership, road density, telegraph and telephone usage, and traffic density; interactions across national boundaries, such as air transportation, mail flow, migration, and trade; and a whole host of variables on international perceptions and diplomatic exchanges.

Social scientists have made some promising analytic beginnings. Bruce M. Russett and his associates, for instance, found that some of the domestic communication variables listed above were highly intercorrelated for close to a hundred countries, and were associated generally with high levels of economic development.[28] Proceeding in part from an Almondian framework, Arthur S. Banks and Robert B. Textor attempted among other things to see what difference the degree of freedom of the press implied for political systems.[3] They categorized 115 countries on 57 variables, which were then correlated with each other in bivariate analyses. The 43 countries in which there was "no censorship or government control of either domestic press or foreign correspondents" turned out to be those with constitutional regimes that tended to have "conventional" ideological orientations, competitive electoral systems, a "nonmobilizational" style of system operation, tolerated and fully autonomous interest groups, parties that were neither class-oriented nor multi-ideological, a nonelitist political leadership, effective legislatures, neutral participation in politics by the military, and an insignificant role for political police. (Raymond B. Nixon's replication of this study, using a more elaborate indicator of press freedom, corroborated the main findings listed above, but suggested an even stronger relationship between press freedom and legislative effectiveness.) [22] A subsequent factor analysis by Phillip M. Gregg and Banks of these (largely judgmental) data revealed that freedom of the press correlated highly with other variables in an attribute dimension labeled "degree of access to political channels," which in turn was not associated with violent or diplomatic foreign conflict.

Data Requirements

Such findings, however interesting, are clearly limited in scope and tell us little about the impact of variations in communication subsystems upon systemic outputs. They reveal the need for considerable conceptualizing and data gathering in the study of macrocommunication. To date researchers have used, often with great effectiveness, the statistics on communication readily available in international handbooks, or have made shrewd guesses about such phenomena as freedom of the press. But these data have their limitations. It is no great exaggeration to note that they have not been able to produce any truly significant, verified response of even a partial nature to the sorts of questions asked earlier about the difference given structures or activity levels of communication systems make in terms of political outcomes.

To move beyond trivial research will require a delineation of both what we want to know about this interaction and how we intend to find it out. The testable propositions we derive from current theory must be cumulative so as to contribute to the reformulation of the theory. Examples might be: The openness of the communication system varies inversely with the degree of concentration of ownership; the probability of anomic outbursts within a society varies directly with the openness of the communication system; the degree of concentration of ownership varies directly with the level of a society's economic development. But to list such propositions poses new problems. How can we operationalize such variables as "openness of a communication system" (e.g.; Ref. 23) or "anomic outbursts"? What data will provide reliable indicators of them?

Without attempting to answer such questions fully here, it may nonetheless be useful to specify some types of variables on which data are in principle available:

1. Openness of the communication system: degree of governmental control, range of acceptable opinion, plurality of information sources, government share of information output, concentration in media ownership, probability that particular categories of information will get into given media, linkages among different media in terms of both interaction and the content of what they transmit [12]

2. Domain of the communication system: potential versus actual audience, the acceptance (internalization) of various categories of information by different audiences

3. Quantity of information in the communication system: information output, channel and network capacity, ratio of loads to capacity, rapidity of information flow in various portions of the system

4. Quality of information in the communication system: amount of noise or false signals in the system, accuracy of transmission throughout system, completeness of information transmitted.

The mere enumeration of these potential variables, together with a recognition of the difficulties entailed in gathering appropriate data for over a hundred independent countries, should suffice to indicate how far the study of political macrocommunication has yet to go. It is nonetheless a promising path if we want to learn something substantial about the relationship between communication and political systems.

REFERENCES AND SUGGESTED READINGS

1. Almond, Gabriel A., and G. Bingham Powell, Jr., *Comparative Politics: A Developmental Approach.* Boston: Little, Brown, 1966.
2. Aronson, James, *The Press and the Cold War.* Indianapolis: Bobbs-Merrill, 1970.
3. Banks, Arthur S., and Robert B. Textor, *A Cross-Polity Survey.* Cambridge, Mass.: M.I.T. Press, 1963.
4. Barghoorn, Frederick C., *Politics in the USSR.* Boston: Little, Brown, 1966.

5. Chittick, William O., *State Department, Press, and Pressure Groups: A Role Analysis.* New York: Wiley-Interscience, 1970.
6. Cirino, Robert, *Don't Blame the People: How the News Media Use Bias, Distortion and Censorship to Manipulate Public Opinion.* Los Angeles: Diversity Press, 1971.
7. Cohen, Bernard C., "The Relationship Between Public Opinion and Foreign Policy Maker," in *Public Opinion and Historians: Interdisciplinary Perspectives,* ed. by Melvin Small. Detroit: Wayne State University Press, 1970.
8. Dawson, Richard E., and Kenneth Prewitt, *Political Socialization.* Boston: Little, Brown, 1969.
9. Deutsch, Karl W., *Nationalism and Social Communication: An Inquiry into the Foundations of Nationality,* rev. ed., Cambridge, Mass.: M.I.T. Press, 1966.
10. Deutsch, Karl W., *The Nerves of Government: Models of Political Communication and Control,* rev. ed. New York: Free Press, 1966.
11. Dunn, Delmer D., *Public Officials and the Press.* Reading, Mass.,: Addison-Wesley, 1969.
12. Fagen, Richard R., *Politics and Communication.* Boston: Little, Brown, 1966.
13. Fritschler, A. Lee, *Smoking and Politics: Policymaking and the Federal Bureaucracy.* New York: Appleton-Century-Crofts, 1969.
14. Fulbright, J. William, *The Pentagon Propaganda Machine.* New York: Liveright, 1970.
15. Lasswell, Harold D., and Abraham Kaplan, *Power and Society: A Framework for Political Inquiry.* New Haven: Yale University Press, 1950.
16. Lerner, Daniel, with the collaboration of Lucille W. Pevsner, *The Passing of Traditional Society: Modernizing the Middle East.* New York: Free Press, 1958.
17. Lindblom, Charles E., *The Policy-Making Process.* Englewood Cliffs, N.J.: Prentice-Hall, 1968.
18. McGinniss, Joe, *The Selling of the President 1968.* New York: Trident Press, 1969.
19. Mendelsohn, Harold, and Irving Crespi, *Polls, Television, and the New Politics.* San Francisco: Chandler, 1970.
20. Merritt, Richard L., "Transmission of Values Across National Boundaries," in *Communication in International Politics,* ed. by Richard L. Merritt. Urbana: University of Illinois Press, 1972.
21. Nimmo, Dan, *The Political Persuaders: The Techniques of Modern Election Campaigns.* Englewood Cliffs, N.J.: Prentice-Hall, 1970.
22. Nixon, Raymond B., "Freedom in the World's Press: A Fresh Appraisal with New Data," *Journalism Quarterly,* Vol. 42, 1965.
23. Nixon, Raymond B., and Tae-youl Hahn, "Concentration of Press Ownership: A Comparison of 32 Countries," *Journalism Quarterly,* Vol. 48, 1971.
24. Sola Pool, Ithiel de, "The Mass Media and Politics in the Modernization Process," in *Communication and Political Development,* ed. by Lucian W. Pye. Princeton: Princeton University Press, 1963.
25. Rivers, William L., *The Adversaries: Politics and the Press.* Boston: Beacon Press, 1970.
26. Rivers, William L., and Wilbur Schramm, *Responsibility in Mass Communication,* rev. ed. New York: Harper & Row, 1969.
27. Rucker, Bryce W., *The First Freedom.* Carbondale and Edwardsville: Southern Illinois University Press, 1968.

28. Russett, Bruce M., Hayward R. Alker, Jr., Karl W. Deutsch, and Harold D. Lasswell, *World Handbook of Political and Social Indicators*. New Haven: Yale University Press, 1964.
29. Schiller, Herbert I., *Mass Communications and American Empire*. New York: Augustus M. Kelley, 1969.
30. Schramm, Wilbur, *Mass Media and National Development: The Role of Information in Developing Countries*. Stanford: Stanford University Press, 1964.
31. Siebert, Fredrick S., Theodore Peterson, and Wilbur Schramm, *Four Theories of the Press*. Urbana: University of Illinois Press, 1956.
32. Snyder, Richard C., H. W. Bruck, and Burton Sapin, eds., *Foreign Policy Decision-Making: An Approach to the Study of International Politics*. New York: Free Press, 1962.
33. Wright, Charles R., "Functional Analysis and Mass Communication," *The Public Opinion Quarterly*, Vol. 24, 1960.

Dr. Ralph V. Exline is Professor of Psychology at the University of Delaware. Professor Exline has written numerous journal articles, papers, and monographs in the area of social psychology and group dynamics. His work in visual interaction is referred to in the recent best seller, *Body Language*. Among other recent contributions is a chapter in *Studies in Machiavellianism*.

19

PSYCHOLOGY: AN APPROACH TO HUMAN COMMUNICATION

RALPH V. EXLINE

It would be misleading to speak of the psychological approach to the study of communication, for, as Alfred Smith [117] has shown, psychologists have been active in all three of the major divisions held to constitute the field. Psychologists have been active, that is, in the study of syntactics (the interrelations of signs), semantics (the meanings attributed to signs), and pragmatics (the human reactions to signs).

Neither should the title of this chapter lead the reader to assume that he is to be treated to an all-encompassing review of psychology's contributions to the field of communication. The author is a social psychologist, and will limit himself to a consideration of social-psychological approaches to communication phenomena.

Finally, this chapter will constitute a suggestive rather than an exhaustive review of the work of social psychologists. Beginning with a brief indication of why social psychologists are concerned with communication, it will cite studies which, hopefully, will represent the nature of the contributions which social psychologists have made to each of the three aspects of communication mentioned earlier, and will conclude with a somewhat more detailed description of the author's own work.

The research to be discussed in the last section of this chapter represents one small segment of a relatively recent but rapidly intensifying interest of psychologists in nonword aspects of social communication, a topic which is more thoroughly developed by Harrison in another chapter of this book.

COMMUNICATION PHENOMENA IN THE HISTORY OF SOCIAL PSYCHOLOGY

In 1908, McDougall published one of the first books to contain "social psychology" in its title. In it he speaks of suggestion as "a process of communication resulting in the acceptance with conviction of the communicated proposition in the absence of logically adequate grounds for its acceptance." [93, p. 100] Today McDougall's statement would be concerned with what Smith [117] has described as the pragmatics of communication, and the term "process of communication" would be depicted in more general terms. [27] Nevertheless, it demonstrates that communication and social psychology have been linked from the start.

Gordon Allport [2] suggests that long before social psychology emerged as a topic area, social theorists linked communication with social-psychological variables. In his discussion of "simple and sovereign" theories, Allport refers to Hobbes's proposition that power holders are motivated to corrupt communication to create an ideology favorable to themselves.

In more recent times the importance of the study of verbal communication to social psychologists has been stated by Cartwright as follows:

> When one stops to think of it, it is really surprising how much of the subject matter of social psychology is in the form of verbal behavior. The formation and transmission of group standards, values, attitudes and skills are accomplished largely by means of verbal communication. Education in the schools, in the home, in business, in the neighborhood, and through mass media is brought about by the transmission of information and by the exercise of controls which are largely mediated through written and spoken words. If one is concerned with problems of social organization the situation is similar. Supervision, management, coordination, and the exertion of influence are principally matters of verbal interaction. . . . The work of the world, and its entertainment, too, is in no small measure mediated by verbal and other symbolic behavior. [20, p. 422]

Though Cartwright places his major stress on verbal communication, the phrasing of the last sentence quoted above anticipates the recent growth of interest in the study of nonverbal-communication phenomena.

Communication as a topic figures prominently in the latest edition of *The Handbook of Social Psychology,* appearing in all five volumes of this comprehensive work. [82] Though no specific treatment of nonverbal-communication phenomena is included in the handbook, two reviews of research and theory concerning such phenomena have been published recently in the *Psychological Bulletin.* [29; 96]

Before moving on to a consideration of psychological research relevant to the three aspects of communication suggested by Smith, [117] let us consider how psychologists generally define the term *communication.* Elsewhere in this book, Harrison points to definitions of the term ranging from any behavior performed in the presence of another [122] to definitions requiring that the term be reserved for purposive communication acts, that is, actions intended to produce specific effects upon another person or persons. [14; 86] Ekman and Friesen would seem to represent the latter position in making a distinction between *communicative* (intended) and *indicative* (nonintended) nonverbal behavior, as does Hebb, who writes that:

> The essence of purposive communication is that the sender remains sensitive to the receiver's responses during sending, and by modification of his sending shows that his behavior is, in fact, guided by the intention (expectancy) of achieving a particular behavioral effect in the receiver. [66, p. 739]

Hebb, however, is willing to include "reflexive" acts (e.g., the startle response, rapid eye blinking) as communicative, but considers such behavior as being at a lower psychological level than "true" (purposive) communication. Hebb, moreover, would seem to be against limiting the term to verbal behavior marked by intentionality, for he argues that too much attention has been given to man's special vocal behavior—"in sign language and gesture, man's distinctiveness is equally clear." [66, p. 739]

In establishing my own position I was impressed by a remark made by Jonathan Miller, the British actor, director, producer, who once told me it was his belief that "a word existed only in the context of its performance." Thus, when two people interact, a message may be coded with purposive intent by a sender, but in the transmission, indicative or informative actions may accompany the purposive message. If these "metamessages" affect the receiver's interpretation of and response to the purposive message, and if the sensitive sender uses the receiver's responses to modify his own sending, then can we not, after Hebb's own formulation, call the unintended metamessages communicative? Thus, in agreement with Birdwhistell, [12] I view communication as a multichannel phenomena in which metamessages combine with purposive intent to affect the receiver.

Communication, then, involves a sender, a message which is encoded by the sender, channels through which messages and metamessages flow to a receiver, who decodes the message, a referant, and a shared code used by both sender and receiver. To conceptualize information as flowing simultaneously through several channels permits us to study a number of interesting problems concerned with the simultaneous transmission of congruent and/or incongruent information. Research relevant to such problems will be touched upon later in this chapter.

SYNTACTICS

Smith [117] has suggested that from a social-psychological point of view, it is appropriate to view syntactics as the study of relations between messages as well as the relations between signs. Space is one such relation between messages, and space is organized into communication networks. Bavelas [6; 7] and Leavitt [80] pioneered in the systematic study of the effects of different communication networks or structures. According to the arrangement of positions in space, networks have been labeled as wheels, chains, circles, Ys,[80] kites, slashes, and barred circles, each of which work independently, and comcon (in which all channels open to each other).[113] When restricted to various arrangements of one-way channels, alpha, beta, and pinwheel networks have been created.[113] Positions in such networks can be identified as to distance, and as to centrality or peripherality,[6; 80] and outcomes are discussed in terms of differences among networks and between different positions within a network. Put another way, results show how position in the network determines individual behavior, and how the nature of the network determines group productivity and individual satisfaction. Thus, we learn that people tend to be happier in a group when they occupy a central rather than a peripheral position in the group; [80; 111; 113; 53] that peripheral members tend to provide more creative ideas than central members, as Leavitt pointed out; and that conflicting results have been found concerning the relative speed and accuracy with which problems are solved in the various networks. With respect to the latter point, Leavitt [80] found the wheel to be speedier than the circle, while Shaw [111] found the reverse; Bavelas [7] found the chain to result in greater accuracy than the circle, while Macy, Christie, and Luce [84] found the reverse to be true.

Also related to the question of position and structure is the work of Kelley,[77] who has shown how the significance of position in a status hierarchy determines the rate and direction of communication. People generally prefer to communicate upwards in the hierarchy, a tendency Kelley views as a vicarious form of social mobility.

Though Smith suggested that psychological space organized into communication networks forms a relation between messages, it would seem to me that such network relations could be equally well described as relations between positions (roles). Depending on his position in the particular network, an occupant is likely to conceptualize his role as being primarily that of a sender, a transmitter, or a receiver, or any combination of the roles. In a five-person unidirectional chain, for example, there would be one initiator, one transmitter, and three receivers. In a four-person unidirectional wheel there would be three initiator-receivers and one initiator-transmitter-receiver; in a three-person concom there would be three initiator-transmitter-receivers.

There is evidence to suggest that one's role affects the cognitive set he brings to the communication task. Zajonc [124] and Cohen [22] have conducted experiments which demonstrate that the transmitter role has systematically different effects upon the activation of an occupant's cognitive structures than does the transmitter role. According to Zajonc,[124] complex, unified, differentiated, and organized structures are more likely to be activated by the transmitter than by the receiver role. Cohen [22] suggests that transmission requires a tight, bounded cognitive package which can be readily communicated to others, whereas the set of a receiver requires one to maintain a more flexible cognitive structure, which inhibits tendencies toward the quick polarization characteristic of the transmitter role.

Position in the structure also affects expectations as to who will play a leadership role. The early work of Leavitt [80] showed that the occupant of a central position in chain, circle, wheel, and Y networks would be more likely to be nominated as leader than would the occupant of a peripheral position. These results were replicated by Gilchrist, Shaw, and Walker [53] with the wheel network, by Goldberg [58] with chain, wheel, and Y networks, and extended by Shaw [111] with circle, wheel, and slash networks.

Many variables other than those discussed above have been studied, with later researchers introducing such factors as the nature of the task,[23] distribution of information,[112] personality of group members,[8] opportunity to organize,[60] to name but a few. Relationships between task complexity, task efficiency, and centralization of networks have also been discussed. For a more thorough treatment of the literature on communication networks, the reader should see excellent reviews by Glanzer and Glaser,[54] Shaw,[113] and Collins and Raven.[24]

SEMANTICS

The question of the meaning of a communication involves language codes (whether verbal or nonverbal) and encoding and decoding processes. Unless sender and receiver share a common code, the meaning intended by the sender cannot be apprehended by the receiver. Sharing of a common code, however, does not necessarily guarantee that the message as intended by the sender will be apprehended by the receiver. Encoding and decoding abilities of sender and receiver come into play here, as do factors concerned with the congruity of information content transmitted simultaneously through multiple communication channels. Implied in the foregoing discussion is the distinction which psycholinguists have made between speech and language. Miller and McNeill,[99] for example, argue that psycholinguists must address themselves on the one hand to the construction of a therory concerning the way that "this competence is reflected, or actualized, in the acts of speaking and hearing speech." [99, p. 671] The organization to be followed in discussing social-psychological contributions to the semantic aspect of communication will be to focus first on the question of codes in general, then to review research concerned with the process of encoding and decoding.

Coding

Technically a code is "an agreed transformation . . . by which messages may be converted from one set of signs to another." [21, p. 8] The Morse code is an example. In this paper, however, the term is used more in the sense of a language code, that is, an organically developed code with guiding rules concerning generally accepted meanings. These shared meanings enable people to associate with one another via understood communications.

While psycholinguists are concerned with the distinction between reference and meaning in language codes, this paper will be restricted to considerations of meaning. Osgood [101] addressed himself to the question as follows: "In simplist terms, therefore, the question is: Under what conditions does something which is not an object become a sign of that object?" [101, pp. 200-201] He then reviews several theories of meaning, before fixing upon the mediation hypothesis, that is, the "presence or absence of a representational mediation process in association with the stimulus," [101, p. 203] as the most fruitful approach. Osgood and his associates [103] have, by combining associational and scaling procedures, developed an empirical technique of measuring meaning of words which they have called the Semantic Differential. This technique has been used by psychologists (including this author) in a great variety of studies. Snider and Osgood [118] provide an excellent review of the theory underlying the technique, as well as a review of the literature representing the ways in which it has been used. Miller and McNeill [99] suggest that the technique taps the emotional connotations, as distinct from the logical connotations, of words. This may explain the ubiquity with which the three factors of evaluation, potency, and activity appear when the technique is applied to respondents from a wide variety of cultures.

Osgood and other psycholinguistically oriented psychologists, for example, Miller, [98] Brown, [16] and Carroll, [19] to name but a few, have focused on the study of meaning in verbal languages. There is another group of researchers interested in the semantics of nonverbal languages. The growth of this interest has been rapid in recent years. One reason for such growth is suggested by Mehrabian's claim [97] that only 7 percent of the variance in interpersonal communication is explained by verbal phenomena. He argues that the remaining 93 percent is explained by paralinguistic cues (38 percent) and facial expressions (55 percent). The work of a few members of this group will be mentioned only to suggest the rich variety of semantic studies.

Harrison, in an earlier chapter, suggests that research on breaking the nonverbal codes can be classified in the three or four types of codes: (1) performance, (2) artifactual, (3) mediational, and (4) contextual. With respect to performance codes Ekman and his associates,[33; 35; 36; 37] Izard,[72] and Frijda [52] have been active in studying facial expression of emotion. Birdwhistell,[11; 13] Scheflen,[109] Mehrabian,[96; 97] and Efron [32] have addressed themselves to the study of posture, gesture, and body motion in general. Argyle and Dean,[3] Exline,[41; 42; 43; 44; 50] Hess,[68] Kendon,[79] and Ellsworth [38] have investigated eye movements and other aspects of eye engagement.

Sommer's work on space use in architecture,[119] though also concerned with space as a contextual code, is relevant to the artifactual code. McLuhan's [95] writings call attention to the importance of mediational codes, while both Sommer's [119] work on personal space and Hall's investigations of Proxemics, that is, studies of man's use of time and space, are concerned with assessing meaning within a contextual code. Hall's two books, *The Silent Language* [61] and *The Hidden Dimension* [62] provide fascinating insights into the different meanings attributed to space use and time in a variety of cultures. Finally the insightful analyses of Erving Goffman integrate concepts relevant to all four of the areas mentioned above, as he attempts to discover the normative behavioral order underlying the interaction of people in both private and public places.[55; 56; 57]

Cultural versus Pancultural Codes   Codes are learned symbol systems, the meanings of which are shared by the members of a communicating group. Certain of these systems, whether language or gesture, are shared only by members of a particular culture. Efron [32] demonstrated subcultural differences in gestures when he studied the behavior of first-generation immigrant members of two ethnic groups living in New York City. The fact that members of both groups interacted with one another under the umbrella of the larger culture resulted in a blending of the gesture patterns of the two groups in the second generation.

Evidence of the existence of pancultural codes with respect to certain aspects of human communication behavior has recently been developed by Paul Ekman and his associates.[33; 36; 37] This research group has exhaustively studied facial expression in a number of cultural groups and has demonstrated that basic emotional expressive displays, such as happiness, sadness, or disgust, will be elicited by appropriate stimuli in such fashion that they can be accurately judged by members of many cultures. Ekman calls his theory "neurocultural" to emphasize that there is a neurological relationship between the firing of certain facial muscles and particular emotions, which creates universally elicited and cross-culturally read displays, while other determinants are learned and culture-specific. Examples of the latter are rules concerning control of the appearance of emotion, events eliciting the emotion, and consequences of emotional arousal.

Ekman's work is more thoroughly discussed in the chapter on nonverbal communication and is mentioned here only to suggest that the meaning read into emotional displays can in some instances be universal across cultures, while in other instances meaning must be referred to the specific cultural code.

Encoding

Encoding is concerned with the dependencies of message events upon psychological processes in the message sender.[102] Given such a definition, the number and varieties of variables which can be and have been studied are legion. Holsti,[70] in a recent treatment of the field of content analysis, identifies the study of the encoding process as one of three major classifications used in the application of content analysis. Thus content analysis is employed to discover "lawful relations between events in messages and processes transpiring in the individuals who produce . . . them." [102, p. 36]

It follows, then, that personal documents ranging from diaries and intimate letters through autobiographies to speeches before large audiences permit the investigator to draw inferences concerning the personality values and intentions of the originator.[1]

One interesting example of such research is that carried out by Osgood and Walker [104] in which they demonstrated that systematic differences could be predictably discovered in the analysis of true and faked suicide notes. Other examples of the use of such materials have been provided by Shneidman [114; 115] in his study of rhetoric employed by Kennedy, Nixon, and Khrushchev; and by various investigators who have analyzed the writings of literary figures to infer key psychological traits of the authors, for example, D. H. Lawrence,[92] Dostoevsky,[76] and Shakespeare.[91]

Materials other than personal documents have been used to study the encoding process. Exline [40] used Thurstone scaling techniques to weight, for intent to control others, messages written in a group-decision task. He later replicated the study, asking new subjects to select one of a set of the weighted messages to serve as the first message they wished to send to the other members of the group. Subjects high in number of affiliation were found to pick significantly less controlling messages than those low in number of affiliation. Exline inferred that high affiliators more or less consciously meant to communicate their lack of desire to control others. Gottheil, Thornton, and Exline [59] used still photographs of schizophrenic and normal men who were instructed to show how they communicated happiness, anger, fear, sorrow, and surprise without using words. Their results indicated that normal persons were no better than schizophrenics in their ability to encode the nonverbal signs of the various affects. Background affects of anger, sadness, and fear, however, were found to be more characteristic of the encoding actions of schizophrenic males, while normal males encoded more happiness along with the other appropriate affect sign. Sound recordings of therapeutic interviews have also been used to study the encoding process in schizophrenia.[73]

Societal as well as individual differences have been inferred from differences in encoding of communications. Lewin [81] found that German youth literature placed significantly more emphasis on national loyalty, identification, and determination than did American literature, which stressed altruism, creativity, and religion. McClelland and his associates [89; 90] have also studied the literature of various countries at various times to determine the extent to which achievement imagery characterized the encoding of thematic materials. Cross-national studies of movie plots, television programming, folktales, sermons, and magazine photographs indicate the variety of ways in which the encoding process has been studied.

Decoding

Decoding has been defined as concern with "dependencies of events in listeners and readers (their meanings, emotions, attitudes, and the like) upon the content and structure of messages." [102, p. 36] It is clear that the decoding process is the complement of the encoding process and that without a shared language code the intent and purpose of the sender cannot be apprehended by the receiver.

This latter point is well illustrated in the work of Bernstein,[9; 10] who argues that different linguistic codes are generated by the life experiences of individuals in different social strata. A middle-class child is likely to develop an "elaborated" code in which vocabulary and structure are drawn from a wide range of possibilities, are complexly organized, and communication does not rely heavily on extraverbal channels. A "restricted" code on the other hand, characterizes the communication style of the lower-class child. The "restricted" code draws its vocabulary and structure from a narrow range of possibilities, is simply organized, and depends heavily on extraverbal channels of communication. Bernstein characterizes speech patterns based on elaborated codes as "formal" and that based on a restricted code as "public." Compared to the former, public speech is marked by shorter, grammatically simpler, and unfinished sentences; by a more limited use of adjectives, more personal pronouns, and categorical statements (e.g., imperatives) which limit the range of responses of their targets. It is clear that one brought up in a restricted-code (public language) community will not find it easy to decode the messages sent by a communicator versed in usage of the elaborated (formal) code, and vice versa.

It has already been suggested that language codes are not restricted to words alone, and also that psychologists are increasingly interested in extraverbal codes. Events in listeners are dependent upon the structure of extraverbal as well as verbal messages, and Bernstein's work suggests that communication difficulties across class lines are in part due to encoding and decoding habits with respect to extraverbal phenomena. One of the reasons that blacks find whites to be cold and lacking in "Soul" (to the dismay of the liberal, intellectual white man) may be that blacks are more likely to learn the restricted language code with its greater stress on the use of extraverbal channels of communication.

It is difficult to discuss studies of the decoding process without getting into pragmatics, for to know what impact a message has on a receiver we must know how he decodes it. Before turning to a discussion of pragmatics, however, I would like to suggest a reason why most of the studies of the decoding process have been undertaken in terms of the analysis of the verbal content of messages. To study decoding processes in face-to-face interaction requires a methodology which permits the study of how one decodes messages simultaneously flowing through several nonverbal transmission channels. This is a difficult task at best, and one which can be approached only if one has sophisticated recording, storage, and retrieval apparatus. In any event, this is most easily accomplished by studying how people react to signs; therefore, studies of decoding in face-to-face situations would fall under the heading of pragmatic studies of communication.

PRAGMATICS

In his book *Communication and Culture,* Alfred Smith [117] lists empirical studies of pragmatics under the two subheadings of mass communication and intercultural communication. Rather than duplicate Smith's treatment, or the treatment provided by those who conceptualize communication in terms of propaganda and persuasion [71; 106] or attitude change in general,[94] the treatment of pragmatics in this chapter will be limited to interpersonal communication. Furthermore, the major focus of attention will be upon studies of person perception, and upon the author's own work with extraverbal variables.

Person Perception

The term *person perception* identifies a major emphasis in the social psychologist's study of the impact of person-generated signs upon the receiver. Original research in this area was mainly concerned with the accuracy of our perceptions of the other's emotions and personality traits.[51; 123] Later research focused on how we form impressions of another.[4; 5; 18] Most recently, psychologists have attempted to analyze the inference of dispositional properties of another by observing his actions in social situations. This latter approach was stimulated by Heider's theory of the perception of causality—either within the actor or within the environment,[67] and has been explicated by Jones and Davis [75] and Kelley,[78] as "attribution theory," which traces a communication from intent through acts to effects and attributions. The reader's attention is called to an excellent discussion of the history and development of research on person perception in a recent monograph by Hastorf, Schneider, and Polefka.[65] Their summary statement argues that "person perception has shifted in interest from . . . the accuracy with which (stimuli) are recorded to the ways that perceivers actively process . . . stimuli to create interpersonal meaning." [65, p. 91] Thus semantics cannot be separated from pragmatics in this approach to the study of human communication.

The Pragmatics of Eye Engagement

The study of eye engagement illustrates the complex interweaving of semantic and pragmatic factors in human communication. Though poets and novelists speak of the "language of the eyes," [85] it is a language that is at least ambiguous, and one which is difficult to decode without additional knowledge of the context or "frame" in which the interaction takes place.

Literary usage of the term implies that eye engagement serves several functions. Poets, novelists, and philosophers refer to it in terms of the communication of emotional expression,[100] as an indication of momentary involvements [15] or more lasting communion,[116] of enmity toward [87; 88] or dominance over another person.[107; 87] There is even a rather amusing suggestion that nightclub strippers can take off their clothes convincingly and with style only if they look steadily into the eyes of one solitary male sitting in the audience watching the routine.[83] E. T. Hall, the anthropologist who coined the term *proxemics* to describe the study of man's use of space and time in interpersonal relations, would seem to agree with the above categorization when he suggests that the eyes are used to communicate "dominance vs. submission, involvement vs. detachment, and positive vs. negative attitude." [63, p. 140]

The author's own research illustrates the complexity involved in decoding the meaning and assessing the affects of visual interaction. Figure 19.1 represents an early study of mutual glances exchanged in interpersonal interaction. From this study we can see that personality attributes and sex-role considerations interact with situational contexts to determine the extent to which participants in a decision-making task exchange mutual glances. The data show that women exchange more mutual glances than do men, but that affiliative persons of both sexes show reduced mutual glances when the situation requires a relatively more competitive orientation.

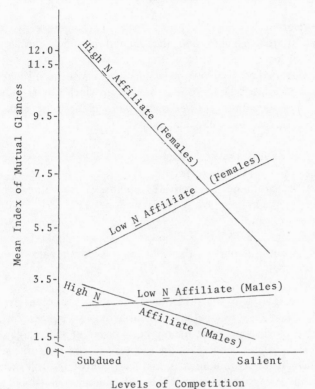

Figure 19.1   Mean percentage of time each sex spends in mutual visual interaction for each of two levels of *n* (number of) affiliation at two levels of competition. (R. V. Exline, "Explorations in the Process of Person Perception: Visual Interaction in Relation to Competition, Sex and the Need for Affiliation." By permission
from *Journal of Personality*. Copyright © 1963 by Duke University Press.)

Further work on personality attributes indicates that the sex differences
in mutual glances (a difference which shows up whenever we use sex as a
variable) is probably related to a greater willingness to describe oneself as
open to giving and seeking affection in relationships with others.[42] Thus,
to engage in mutual glances would seem to be a sign that, in contexts
where dominance issues are not salient, a person is relatively open to affiliative involvement with other persons.

Relevant to the above point are findings from studies in which dominance or competitive relations were not relevant but where preference for
or aversion to another person were experimentally manipulated. There is
evidence from these studies [43] to indicate that one decreases the amount
to which he will engage in mutual glances with one who denigrates him, and
increases his engagement with that one of a pair of persons for whom he

develops a preference. Rubin,[107] found a significant and positive relationship between mutual glances and the degree to which dating couples claimed to be in love.

We have also studied the ways in which the eyes are used when questions of dominance are salient. An experiment in which power differentials in legitimate and illegitimate power dyads were induced by experimental maniputation produced the following results:

1. Persons with less power looked at those with more power significantly more than was the reverse.
2. Subjects in legitimate power dyads monitored each other more than did subjects in illegitimate power dyads.
3. The previous finding was due mainly to the behavior of the low-power person in the illegitimate power dyad who looked significantly less at his high-power partner than did the low-power partner in the legitimate dyad.[50]

Though more than one interpretation of the above findings is possible (for example, the high-power person's visual-avoidance behavior may have been motivated by discomfort at having been given an advantage over the others), the data suggest that even in a transient experimental situation, one way in which one communicates his definition of his role in a situation of different interpersonal power is by the manner in which he gives visual attention to the other. Brown [17] has postulated that status is inversely related to the desire to become involved with another; power-position differences in visual monitoring reported above would seem to support Brown's contention. In addition, the finding that the greatest amount of visual monitoring of the other was recorded in the case of the low-power person in the legitimate power dyad brings to mind our stereotype of the behavior of the organizational "yes" man.

Relevant to the above argument are two other studies in which personality traits akin to dominance-submission affected (1) the visual behavior of the subjects and (2) impressions formed by more and less dominant subjects of the personality of a looking and a nonlooking listener.

In the first study [44] controlling, less affiliative subjects gave significantly less visual attention to an experimental confederate who provided the subject with little social reinforcement than did noncontrolling affiliation-oriented subjects. In the second study [47] control-oriented subjects rated a confederate who looked over a subject's head whenever the subject spoke, as significantly more potent than they did a confederate who gave the speaker his entire visual attention. The reverse tended to be true for less controlling subjects.

Other investigators have confirmed the powerful impact of the stare.

Edleman, Omark, and Freedman [31] have shown that elementary school boys who win staring contests are perceived as "tough," while Strongman and Champness [120] and Thayer,[121] in their studies of college-age males, have shown a positive relationship between dominance and winning a staring contest. Ellsworth [39] carried out an interesting study in which she demonstrated that motorists accelerated faster across an intersection if, while they were waiting for a traffic signal to change, they were stared at by a pedestrian who stood on the sidewalk next to the car. At the University of Delaware we have carried out an experiment which indicates that pedestrians on a campus will veer farther away from an occupied bench if the occupant stares steadily at the approaching pedestrian than if he ignores the passerby. These findings are consistent with results of a questionnaire in which Exline and Snadowski [49] found that both British and American men and women of college age state that a silent steady stare from a person of their own age, or a generation older, is the most uncomfortable of all possible looking-listening-speaking combinations in face-to-face interaction.

Ethological studies of primates suggest that the powerful impact of the mutual glance is not limited to man alone. There is considerable evidence to support the view that the mutual glance between male primates "triggers off" threat displays which reaffirm or reorder one's place in the dominance hierarchy. Such behavior has been reported for baboons,[64] gorillas,[112] langurs,[74] and macaques.[69] Diebold [28] has suggested that such behaviors are part of a shared primate ethogram, and we have demonstrated [45] that humans can elicit and inhibit threatening displays on the part of rhesus macaques merely by initiating and breaking off eye contact. Table 19.1 demonstrates the nature of the displays and the incidence of threat and attack behavior in the presence of a steady stare (challenge) and a stare followed by a downcast look (deference).

The primate stare would thus seem to be a powerful communicative signal, whether exchanged within or across general boundaries.

Degree of eye contact can signal motives to become more or less involved with other persons on bases other than love or dominance. Exline and Winters [43] demonstrated that mutual glances between a speaker and a visually attentive listener were inversely related to the cognitive difficulty of the discussion topic. Exline, Thibaut, Carole, and Gumpert [46] have shown that low Machiavellian test scorers avoid, whereas high scorers increase, mutual glances with one who has accused them of cheating. Exline and Greenberg [48] manipulated the authenticity of a speaker's communication and found tendencies in women (men were not studied) to avoid eye contact with the others when repeating false as opposed to true impressions of them.

It should be noted that there are those who would deny that eye en-

TABLE 19.1

PERCENT RHESUS MACAQUE RESPONSES CODED AS ATTACK-
ING, THREATENING, OR NONAGGRESSIVE TO DIRECT (CHAL-
LENGING) AND DIRECT-DOWN (DEFERENT) EYE ENGAGE-
MENTS BY *HOMO SAPIENS* MALE (N = 60 PER STIMULUS
GLANCE PER MONKEY) [a]

Monkey No.	Stimulus Look	Response Category		
		Attack	Threaten	Non-aggressive
1	Direct (challenge)	35	15	50
	Down (deferent)	18	4	78
2	Direct	25	48	27
	Down	22	20	58
3	Direct	97	0	3
	Down	54	0	46
4	Direct	23	55	22
	Down	25	25	50
Total response X look	Direct	47	29	24
	Down	28	12	60

[a] R. V. Exline, "The Glances of Power and Preference," in J. K. Cole, ed., *Nebraska Symposium on Motivation,* Vol. 19, 1971. By permission from the University of Nebraska Press, Copyright © 1972.

gagement, as described in many of the above studies, represents communicative activity. They would prefer to view eye engagements described in the preceding paragraph, for example, as indicators of the state of the sender rather than communicative acts.[33] Those who take this position would cite a study by Kendon [79] as an example of eye engagement as a communicative act. Kendon took movies of a conversation between two men, and through a careful frame-by-frame analysis demonstrated that a systematic pattern of the speaker's visual activity coincided with the end of a speech unit. Just before a speaker neared the end of his comment he would break eye contact with the listener—looking back just as he fell silent. Kendon programmed his own behavior according to this observation, and demonstrated that, by varying the pattern, he could control the speed with which the other would take over the floor.* My own position is that such

---

* Duncan [30] has since shown that eye engagements are but one of a set of extra-verbal indicators of floor turnovers.

behaviors, supplemented by other extraverbal phenomena, make available information which persons in a communicative interchange use to more or less unconsciously qualify (i.e., confirm or disconfirm) the verbal content in the interchange. In addition, such information is often used to draw inferences about the nature of the relationship existing or developing between the interactants.[122] Any study of the pragmatics of interpersonal communication, it seems to me, must take such phenomena into account.

Before closing this admittedly selective account of psychological approaches to communication, I would like to mention recent developments in the use of small-group methods to improve communication skills. Proponents of sensitivity training, "T-groups," encounter groups, and the like, often speak of the group experience as a means of getting in touch with oneself and improving communication with others. The methods, though varied, have in common the fact that they provide considerable feedback and commentary on the behavior of members of the group. The purpose of this feedback is to confront participants with "a constant stream of information about their own behavior [on the assumption] that becoming aware of how others perceive them will enable them to control those behaviors which tend to antagonize and alienate [others]." [105, p. 19]

Thus the sensitivity-training group has the structure of a concom network and would seem to operate under a set of norms which encourage public articulation of decoding processes in order to assist group members in the creation of a common language code. By continuously informing each other of the impact of their behaviors, members can assess the extent to which their own encoding processes facilitate or interfere with their ability to communicate with others. By the same token, decoding processes can be tested to ascertain whether events within the receiver systematically distort or promote clear reception of the intended and metacommunicational messages of the sender.

This chapter has attempted to call attention to the variety of ways in which social psychologists have approached the study of communication. Attention was earlier drawn to Cartwright's statement of surprise concerning the extent to which verbal behavior comprises the subject matter of social psychology. It is the hope of the author that the reader will agree that Cartwright's statement should be amended to read "communication behavior."

REFERENCES AND SUGGESTED READINGS

1. Allport, Gordon W., "The Historical Background of Social Psychology," in *The Handbook of Social Psychology*, Vol. 1, ed. by G. Lindzey and E. Aronson. Reading, Mass.: Addison-Wesley, 1968.
2. Allport, Gordon W., *The Use of Personal Documentary in Psychological Science*, Social Science Research Council Bulletin No. 49, 1942.

3. Argyle, Michael, and Janet Dean, "Eye Contact, Distance and Affiliation," *Sociometry*, Vol. 28, 1965.

4. Asch, Solomon E., "Forming Impressions of Personality," *Journal of Abnormal and Social Psychology*, Vol. 41, 1946.

5. Asch, Solomon E., *Social Psychology*. Englewood Cliffs, N.J.: Prentice-Hall, 1952.

6. Bavelas, A., "A Mathematical Model for Group Structure," *Applied Anthropology*, Vol. 7, 1948.

7. Bavelas, A., "Communication Patterns in Task-Oriented Groups," *Journal of the Acoustical Society of America*, Vol. 22, 1950.

8. Berkowitz, Leonard, "Group Norms Among Bomber Crews: Patterns of Perceived Crew Attitudes, 'Actual' Crew Attitudes, and Crew Liking Related to Air-Crew Effectiveness in Far Eastern Combat," *Sociometry*, Vol. 19, 1956.

9. Bernstein, B., "A Public Language: Some Sociological Implications of Linguistic Form," *British Journal of Sociology*, Vol. 10, 1959.

10. Bernstein, B., "Social Class and Linguistic Development: A Theory of Social Learning," in *Education, Economy and Society*, ed. by A. H. Halsey, J. Floud, and A. Anderson. New York: Free Press, 1961.

11. Birdwhistell, Ray L., "The Kinesic Level in the Investigation of the Emotions," in *Expression of the Emotions in Man*, ed. by P. H. Knapp. New York: International Universities, 1963.

12. Birdwhistell, Ray L., "Communication," in *International Encyclopedia of Social Sciences*, Vol. 3, ed. by D. Sills. New York: Macmillan, 1968.

13. Birdwhistell, Ray L., *Kinesics and Context*. Philadelphia: University of Pennsylvania Press, 1970.

14. Birens de Haan, J. A., "Animal Language in Relation to that of Man," *Biological Review*, Vol. 4, 1929.

15. Broch, Herman, *The Sleepwalkers, A Trilogy*. New York: Pantheon Books, 1964.

16. Brown, Roger W., *Words and Things*. New York: Free Press, 1958.

17. Brown, Roger W., *Social Psychology*. New York: Free Press, 1965.

18. Bruner, Jerome S., D. Shapiro, and Renato Tagiuri, "The Meaning of Traits in Isolation and Combination," in *Person Perception and Interpersonal Behavior*, ed. by Renato Tagiuri and L. Petrullo. Stanford, Calif.: Stanford University Press, 1958.

19. Carroll, John B., *Language and Thought*. Englewood Cliffs, N.J.: Prentice-Hall, 1964.

20. Cartwright, Dorwin P., "Analysis of Qualitative Material," in *Research Methods in the Behavioral Sciences*, ed. by L. Festinger and D. Katz. New York: Holt, Rinehart and Winston, 1953.

21. Cherry, Colin, *On Human Communication*, rev. ed. Cambridge, Mass.: M.I.T. Press, 1966.

22. Cohen, Arthur R., "Cognitive Tuning as a Factor Affecting Impression Formation," *Journal of Personality*, Vol. 29, 1961.

23. Collins, Barry E., and H. Guetzkow, *A Social Psychology of Group Processes for Decision Making*. New York: Wiley, 1964.

24. Collins, Barry E., and B. H. Raven, "Group Structure: Attractions, Coalitions, Communication, and Power," in *The Handbook of Social Psychology*, Vol. IV, ed. by G. Lindzey and E. Aronson. Reading, Mass.: Addison-Wesley, 1969.

25. Davitz, Joel R., ed., *The Communication of Emotional Meaning*. New York: McGraw-Hill, 1964.
26. Davitz, Joel R., *The Language of Emotion*. New York: Academic Press, 1969.
27. Deutsch, M. "Field Theory in Social Psychology," in *The Handbook of Social Psychology*, Vol. 1, ed. by G. Lindzey and E. Aronson. Reading, Mass.: Addison-Wesley, 1968.
28. Diebold, A. Richard, "Anthropology and the Comparative Psychology of Communication Behavior," in *Animal Communication: Techniques of Study and Results of Research*, ed. by T. A. Sebeok. Bloomington: University of Indiana Press, 1968.
29. Duncan, S., "Nonverbal Communication," *Psychological Bulletin*, Vol. 72, 1969.
30. Duncan, S., "Floor Appointment in a Dyad," paper presented at the 78th Annual Meeting of the American Psychological Association, Miami, Fla., September 3–8, 1970.
31. Edleman, M. S., D. R. Omark, and D. G. Freedman, "Dominance Hierarchies in Children," unpublished manuscript, Committee on Human Development, University of Chicago, 1971.
32. Efron, David, *Gesture and Environment*. New York: King's Crown Press, 1941.
33. Ekman, P., and W. V. Friesen, "Nonverbal Behavior in Psychotherapy Research," in *Research in Psychotherapy*, Vol. 3, ed. by J. Shlien. Washington, D.C.: American Psychological Association, 1968.
34. Ekman, P., E. R. Sorenson, and W. V. Friesen, "Pancultural Elements in Facial Displays of Emotion," *Science*, Vol. 164, 1969.
35. Ekman, P., and W. V. Friesen, "The Repertoire of Nonverbal Behavior: Categories, Origins, Usage and Coding," *Semiotica*, Vol. 1, 1969.
36. Ekman, P., W. V. Friesen, and Phoebe C. Ellsworth, *Emotion in the Human Face: Guidelines for Research and an Integration of Findings*. New York: Pergamon Press, 1971.
37. Ekman, P., "Universals and Cultural Differences in Facial Expression of Emotion," in *Nebraska Symposium on Motivation: 1971*, Vol. 19, ed. by J. K. Cole. Lincoln: University of Nebraska Press, 1972, in press.
38. Ellsworth, Phoebe C., and M. Carlsmith, "Effects of Eye Contact and Verbal Content on Affective Response to a Dyadic Interaction," *Journal of Personality and Social Psychology*, Vol. 10, 1968.
39. Ellsworth, Phoebe C., M. Carlsmith, and A. Henson, "The Stare as a Stimulus to Flight in Human Subjects: A Series of Field Experiments," *Journal of Personality and Social Psychology*, Vol. 19, 1971.
40. Exline, Ralph V., "Effects of Need for Affiliation, Sex and the Right of Others Upon Initial Communications in Problem-solving Groups," *Journal of Personality*, Vol. 30, 1962.
41. Exline, Ralph V., "Explorations in the Process of Person Perception: Visual Interaction in Relation to Competition, Sex, and Need for Affiliation," *Journal of Personality*, Vol. 34, 1963.
42. Exline, Ralph V., D. Gray, and D. Schutte, "Visual Behavior in a Dyad as Affected by Interview Content and Sex of Respondent," *Journal of Personality and Social Psychology*, Vol. 1, 1965.
43. Exline, Ralph V., and L. C. Winters, "Affective Relations and Mutual Glances in Dyads," in *Affect, Cognition, and Personality*, ed. by S. Tomkins and C. Izard. New York: Springer, 1965.

44. Exline, Ralph V., and D. Messick, "The Effects of Dependency and Social Reinforcement Upon Visual Behavior During an Interview," *British Journal of Social and Clinical Psychology*, Vol. 6, 1967.

45. Exline, Ralph V., and A. Yellin, "Eye Contact as a Sign Between Man and Monkey," in nonverbal communication. Symposium presented at the XIXth International Congress of Psychology, M. Argyle, chairman, London, July 27–August 2, 1969.

46. Exline, Ralph V., J. Hickey Thibaut, B. Carole, and P. Gumpert, "Visual Interaction in Relation to Machiavellianism and an Unethical Act," in *Studies in Machiavellianism,* ed. by R. Christie and Florence Geis. New York: Academic Press, 1970.

47. Exline, Ralph V., B. Fairweather, J. Hine, and M. Argyle, "Impression of a Listener as Affected by His Direction of Gaze During Conversation," unpublished manuscript, Psychology Department, University of Delaware, 1971.

48. Exline, Ralph V., and E. Greenberg, "Visual Behavior in Relation to the Authenticity of a Message in a Dyad," unpublished manuscript, Psychology Department, University of Delaware, 1971.

49. Exline, Ralph V., and A. Snadowski, "Anticipations of Comfort with Various Age and Sex Partners According to Visual Behavior During Speech and Silence," unpublished manuscript, Psychology Department, University of Delaware, 1971.

50. Exline, Ralph V., "The Glances of Power and Preference," in *The Nebraska Symposium on Motivation,* Vol. 19, ed. by J. K. Cole. Lincoln: University of Nebraska Press, 1971.

51. Feleky, Antoinette M., "The Expression of the Emotions," *Psychological Review,* Vol. 14, 1914.

52. Frijda, N., "Recognition of Emotion," in *Advances in Experimental Social Psychology,* Vol. 4, ed. by L. Berkowitz. New York: Academic Press, 1969.

53. Gilchrist, J. C., M. E. Shaw, and L. C. Walker, "Some Effects of Unequal Distribution of Information in a Wheel Group Structure," *Journal of Abnormal and Social Psychology,* Vol. 49, 1954.

54. Glanzer, Murray, and Robert Glaser, "Techniques for the Study of Group Structure and Behavior: II, Empirical Studies of the Effects of Structure in Small Groups," *Psychological Bulletin,* Vol. 58, 1961.

55. Goffman, Erving, "On Face Work: An Analysis of Ritual Elements in Social Interaction," *Psychiatry,* Vol. 18, 1955.

56. Goffman, Erving, *The Presentation of Self in Everyday Life.* Garden City, N.Y.: Doubleday, 1957.

57. Goffman, Erving, *Behavior in Public Places.* New York: Free Press, 1963.

58. Goldberg, Solomon, "Influence and Leadership as a Function of Group Structure," *Journal of Abnormal and Social Psychology,* Vol. 51, 1955.

59. Gottheil, E., C. C. Thornton, and Ralph V. Exline, "Appropriate and Background Affect in Posed Photographs of Normal and Schizophrenic Males," unpublished manuscript, Department of Psychiatry, Jefferson Medical College, Philadelphia, 1971.

60. Guetzkow, Harold, and H. A. Simon, "The Impact of Certain Communication Nets Upon Organization and Performance in Task-oriented Groups," *Management Science,* Vol. 1, 1955.

61. Hall, Edward, T., *The Silent Language.* Garden City, N.Y.: Doubleday, 1959.

62. Hall, Edward T., *The Hidden Dimension.* Garden City, N.Y.: Doubleday, 1966.

63. Hall, Edward T., "Silent Speech," *Playboy,* June, 1971.
64. Hall, K. R. L., and I. Devore, "Baboon Social Behavior," in *Primate Behavior: Field Studies of Monkeys and Apes,* ed. by I. Devore. New York: Holt, Rinehart and Winston, 1965.
65. Hastorf, Albert H., David J. Schneider, and Judith Polefka, *Person Perception.* Reading, Mass.: Addison-Wesley, 1970.
66. Hebb, Donald O., "The Social Significance of Animal Studies," in *The Handbook of Social Psychology,* Vol. 2, ed. by G. Lindzey and E. Aronson. Reading, Mass.: Addison-Wesley, 1968.
67. Heider, Fritz, *The Psychology of Interpersonal Relations.* New York: Wiley, 1958.
68. Hess, E. H., "Attitude and Pupil Size," *Scientific American,* Vol. 212, 1965.
69. Hinde, R. A., and T. E. Rowell, "Communication by Posture and Facial Expressions in the Rhesus Monkey (Macaca Mulatta)," *Proceedings of the Zoological Society of London,* Vol. 138, 1962.
70. Holsti, Ole R., "Content Analysis," in *The Handbook of Social Psychology,* Vol. 2, ed. by G. Lindzey and E. Aronson. Reading, Mass.: Addison-Wesley, 1968.
71. Hovland, Carl I., Irving L. Janis, and Harold H. Kelley, *Communication and Persuasion.* New Haven: Yale University Press, 1953.
72. Izard, Carroll E., *Face of Emotion.* New York: Appleton-Century-Crofts, 1971.
73. Jaffe, Joseph, "Computer Analysis of Verbal Behavior in Psychiatric Interviews," in *Disorders of Communication,* ed. by D. M. Rioch and E. A. Weinstein. Research Publications of Association for Research on Nervous and Mental Disorders, No. 42, 1964.
74. Jay, Phyllis, "Field Studies," in *Behavior of Nonhuman Primates: Research Trends,* ed. by A. Schrier, H. F. Harlow, and F. Stollnitz. New York: Academic Press, 1965.
75. Jones, Edward E., and K. E. Davis, "From Acts to Dispositions: The Attribution Process in Person Perception," in *Advances in Experimental Social Psychology,* Vol. 2, ed. by L. Berkowitz. New York: Academic Press, 1965.
76. Kanzer, M., "Dostoevsky's Matricidal Impulses," *Psychoanalytic Review,* Vol. 35, 1948.
77. Kelley, Harold H., "Communication in Experimentally Created Hierarchies," *Human Relations,* Vol. 4, 1951.
78. Kelley, Harold H., "Attribution Theory in Social Psychology," in *Nebraska Symposium on Motivation,* Vol. 15, ed. by D. Levine. Lincoln: University of Nebraska Press, 1967.
79. Kendon, A., "Some Functions of Gaze-Direction in Social Interaction," *Acta Psychologica,* Vol. 26, 1967.
80. Leavitt, Harold J., "Some Effects of Certain Communication Patterns on Group Performance," *Journal of Abnormal and Social Psychology,* Vol. 46, 1951.
81. Lewin, H. S., "Hitler Youth and the Boy Scouts of America: A Comparison of Aims," *Human Relations,* Vol. 1, 1947.
82. Lindzey, Gardner, and Elliot Aronson, eds., *The Handbook of Social Psychology,* 5 vols. Reading, Mass.: Addison-Wesley, 1968–1969.
83. Loren, Sophia, "When Stripping Look into a Man's Eyes," *Life,* Vol. 56, 1964.
84. Macy, J., Jr., L. S. Christie, and R. D. Luce, "Coding Noise in a Task-oriented Group," *Journal of Social and Abnormal Psychology,* Vol. 48, 1953.

85. Magnus, Hugo F., *Die Sprache Der Augen*. Wiesbaden: Wur Burg, 1885.
86. Maier, Norman R. F., and T. C. Schneirla, *Principles of Animal Psychology*. New York: McGraw-Hill, 1935.
87. Mailer, Norman, *The Armies of the Night*. New York: New American Library, Signet Books, 1968.
88. Marsh, Ngaio, *Spinsters in Jeopardy*. Boston: Little, Brown, 1953.
89. McClelland, David C., and G. A. Griedman, "A Cross-cultural Study of the Relationship Between Child-Rearing Practices and Achievement Motivation Appearing in Folk Tales," in *Readings in Social Psychology*, 2nd ed., ed. by G. E. Swanson, T. M. Newcomb, and E. L. Hartley. New York: Henry Holt, 1952.
90. McClelland, David C., "The Use of Measures of Human Motivation in the Study of Society," in *Motives in Fantasy, Action and Society*, ed. by J. W. Atkinson. Princeton: Van Nostrand, 1958.
91. McCurdy, Harold G., *The Personality of Shakespeare: A Venture in Psychological Method*. New Haven: Yale University Press, 1953.
92. McCurdy, Harold G., "Literature and Personality: Analysis of the Novels of D. H. Lawrence," *Character and Personality*, Vol. 8, 1959.
93. McDougall, William, *Introduction to Social Psychology*. London: Methuen, 1908.
94. McGuire, William J., "The Nature of Attitudes and Attitude Change," in *The Handbook of Social Psychology*, Vol. 3, ed. by G. Lindzey and E. Aronson. Reading, Mass.: Addison-Wesley, 1969.
95. McLuhan, Herbert M., *Understanding Media: The Extensions of Man*. New York: McGraw-Hill, 1964.
96. Mehrabian, Albert, "Significance of Posture and Position in the Communication of Attitude and Status Relationships," *Psychological Bulletin*, Vol. 71, 1969.
97. Mehrabian, Albert, "Nonverbal Communication," in *Nebraska Symposium on Motivation: 1971*, ed. by J. K. Cole. Lincoln: University of Nebraska Press, 1972, in press.
98. Miller, George A., *Language and Communication*. New York: McGraw-Hill, 1951.
99. Miller, George A., and D. McNeill, "Psycholinguistics," in *The Handbook of Social Psychology*, Vol. 3, ed. by G. Lindzey and E. Aronson. Reading, Mass.: Addison-Wesley, 1969.
100. Ogden, A., "Looks and Glances," *Harper's Bazaar*, Vol. 84, 1961.
101. Osgood, Charles E., "The Nature and Measurement of Meaning," *Psychological Bulletin*, Vol. 49, 1952.
102. Osgood, Charles E., "The Representational Model and Relevant Research Methods," in *Trends in Content Analysis*, ed. by I. de Sola Pool. Urbana: University of Illinois Press, 1959.
103. Osgood, Charles E., George Suci, and Percy H. Tannenbaum, *The Measurement of Meaning*. Urbana: University of Illinois Press, 1957.
104. Osgood, Charles E., and Evelyn G. Walker, "Motivation and Language Behavior: Content Analysis of Suicide Notes," *Journal of Abnormal and Social Psychology*, Vol. 59, 1959.
105. Phillips, Gerald M., and Eugene C. Erickson, *Interpersonal Dynamics in the Small Group*. New York: Random House, 1970.
106. Rosnow, Ralph L., and Edward J. Robinson, eds., *Experiments in Persuasion*. New York: Academic Press, 1967.

107. Rubin, Z., "Measurement of Romantic Love," *Journal of Personality and Social Psychology*, Vol. 16, 1970.

108. Sartre, Jean-Paul, *Being and Nothingness*. London: Methuen, 1957.

109. Scheflen, A., "The Significance of Posture in Communication Systems," *Psychiatry*, Vol. 27, 1964.

110. Shaller, G., *The Mountain Gorilla: Ecology and Behavior*. Chicago: University of Chicago Press, 1963.

111. Shaw, Marvin E., "Some Effects of Unequal Distribution of Information Upon Group Performance in Various Communication Nets," *Journal of Abnormal and Social Psychology*, Vol. 49, 1954.

112. Shaw, Marvin E., "Random Versus Systematic Distribution of Information in Communication Nets," *Journal of Personality*, Vol. 25, 1956.

113. Shaw, Marvin E., "Communication Networks," in *Advances in Experimental Social Psychology*, Vol. 1, ed. by L. Berkowitz. New York: Academic Press, 1964.

114. Shneidman, E. S., "A Psychological Analysis of Political Thinking: The Kennedy-Nixon 'Great Debates' and the Kennedy-Khrushchev 'Grim Debates,' " unpublished manuscript, Harvard University, 1961.

115. Shneidman, E. S., "Plan 11. The Logic of Politics," in *Television and Human Behavior*, ed. by L. Arons and M. A. May. New York: Appleton-Century-Crofts, 1963.

116. Simmel, George, "Sociology of the Senses," in *Introduction to the Science of Sociology*, ed. by R. E. Park and E. W. Burgess. Chicago: University of Chicago Press, 1969.

117. Smith, Alfred G., *Communication and Culture*. New York: Holt, Rinehart and Winston, 1966.

118. Snider, James G., and Charles E. Osgood, eds., *Semantic Differential Technique*. Chicago: Aldine, 1969.

119. Sommer, Robert, *Personal Space: The Behavioral Basis of Design*. Englewood Cliffs, N.J.: Prentice-Hall, 1969.

120. Strongman, K. T., and B. G. Champness, "Dominance Hierarchies and Conflict in Eye Contact," *Acta Psychologica*, Vol. 28, 1968.

121. Thayer, S., "The Effect of Interpersonal Looking Duration on Dominance Judgments," *Journal of Social Psychology*, Vol. 79, 1969.

122. Watzlawick, Paul, Janet H. Beavin, and Don C. Jackson, *Pragmatics of Human Communication*. New York: Norton, 1967.

123. Woodworth, Robert S., *Experimental Psychology*. New York: Holt, Rinehart and Winston, 1938.

124. Zajonc, Robert B., "The Process of Tuning in Communication," *Journal of Abnormal and Social Psychology*, Vol. 61, 1960.

Matilda White Riley is Professor of Sociology at Rutgers University. She is a continuing contributor to numerous sociological journals and is coauthor of *New Product Research* and *Sociological Studies in Scale Analysis* and author of *Sociological Research*, Volumes 1 and 2, and *Aging and Society*, Volume 1.

Dr. John W. Riley, Jr. is currently Vice-President and Director of Social Research at The Equitable Life Assurance Society of the United States. Formerly a Professor of Sociology at Harvard University, Dr. Riley has authored many book chapters and articles, including *The Student Looks at His Teacher, The Reds Take a City,* and *Sociological Studies of Scale Analysis.*

20

SOCIOLOGY: AN APPROACH TO HUMAN COMMUNICATION

JOHN W. RILEY, JR. AND
MATILDA WHITE RILEY

EDITORS' PREFACE

SOCIOLOGISTS study an immense variety of topics employing diverse methodologies, and frequently express quite different opinions about the same social phenomenon. Any single definition of what sociology *is* would, indeed, fail to accurately reflect the richness to be found in the heterogeneity of the discipline. At the same time, to deny that the central focus of sociological study can be defined is to deny the legitimacy of it.

The Sociology Panel of the recent Behavioral and Social Sciences Survey Committee wrote that the "mission of sociology is the scientific study of all that is social in the human condition." [49]

> The subject matter of sociology, then, is found in the demographic-ecological, social-psychological, collective, structural, and cultural aspects of social life. The sociological enterprise is to explain regularities, variations, and interdependencies among these aspects. [49, p. 32]

The eminent American sociologist Talcott Parsons [35] says simply that sociology is concerned with the analysis of social systems, "with special but by no means exclusive reference to the type of social system we call society." Berger stresses concern with discipline:

> The sociologist, then, is someone concerned with understanding society in a disciplined way. The nature of discipline is scientific. This means that

what the sociologist finds and says about social phenomena he studies occurs within a certain rather strictly defined frame of reference.(6, p. 16)

The charge of this chapter is to provide a sociological approach to communication. In one sense, sociologists have not dealt very directly with the
generic processes of human communication. Where sociology has been
concerned with communication, it has typically been through work in mass
communication, symbolic interactionism (such as Blumer's chapter in this
volume), and less directly in organizational sociology and in sociology of
small groups. Work in the area of human communication is frequently
considered on the fringes of sociology, and scholars who so direct their efforts have themselves expressed feelings of being isolated from the mainstream of sociology. As Hugh Duncan has observed:,

> American sociologists of the present (third) generation have no theory
> of symbolic action. In American sociology, communication is now studied
> as "mass communication," and this is not a study of interaction as a sym-
> bolic act, but as a mechanical process. (13, p. 149)

Duncan points out that *Sociology Today,* a major work on sociology
written in 1957 under the auspices of the American Sociological Society,
"contains *no* index reference to symbols, and only two references to 'communication.' " We might also note that a second major and more recent
compendium, *American Sociology,* published in 1968, indexes four references to symbols and two to communication.

In quite another sense, and from certain communication-theory viewpoints, sociology in its basic and traditional thrust almost always deals
with communication. Highly consistent with what many communication
scholars find central in their work is Parsons' notion that sociology is concerned with integration, with

> . . . the structures and processes by which the relations among the parts of
> a social system—persons in roles, collectivities, and normative pattern com-
> ponents—either become so ordered as to promote harmonious functioning
> in their respective involvements with each other in the system, or in spe-
> cific and understandable ways fail to do so. (35, p. 322)

Communication, argue many communication theorists, is the indispensable
ingredient to all interaction processes and social relationships.

In this chapter, with a specially edited version of a piece published
earlier in *Sociology Today,* John and Matilda Riley set forth a sociological
view of communication. In doing so, they quite naturally focus upon mass
communication as a means of presenting their notions concerning the influence of reference groups in the communicative act. The Rileys formulate a working model which organizes strands of ongoing research and related theory, focusing upon both the communicator and the recipient in
the communication process.

A SOCIOLOGICAL APPROACH TO MASS COMMUNICATION

A great deal has been written about the millions of messages directed to mass audiences by advertisers, educators, government officials, preachers, entertainers, and propagandists. Yet only some of the answers have been found to such questions as: Does mass communication serve to change basic values and beliefs, or does it dictate only minor decisions of thought and deed? And, whatever its effects, how does it achieve them? What is the process whereby a mass communication may in some way arouse, persuade, or change? This chapter sets forth a sociological view of mass communication, fitting together the many messages and the manifold individual reactions to them within an integrated social structure and process. It is formulated as a working model which identifies some of the available pieces of substantive knowledge and suggests how they may be organized in terms of relevant theories of social systems.

Our sociological approach takes its start from the traditional approach that centers in Lasswell's much-quoted formulation: "Who says what in which channel to whom with what effect?" [23, p. 37] This traditional view does not fully take into account, however, those ongoing processes of social interaction of which the single communicative act is merely one component. Hence we shall outline, step by step, the gradually emerging sociological extensions of this view. We shall deal in turn with the recipient of the mass-communicated message, the communicator, and finally with their mutual relationship within an overall social system; and we shall indicate how such an approach may explain the mass-communications process more adequately and may predict its outcome more accurately.

THE COMMUNICATION RECIPIENT AND HIS PRIMARY GROUPS

As a first extension of the traditional view, a person's relationship to various groups in the society affects his tendencies to perceive a message selectively, to distort it, to accept or reject it, and to act upon it. For example, early experiments conducted by Sherif [46] and Asch [1] point to certain possible connections between perception and the perceiver's relationship to the social structure. These experiments show that individuals asked to make judgments severally in a group (about the apparent movement of a spot of light or the relative length of fairly equal lines) tend to agree with the judgments of the others in the group, whether or not they are objectively right. The group consensus may provide a standard òr frame of reference for the individual judgments.

But the others in the group need not be on the scene to guide or to reinforce the individual's perception. Indeed, his perceptions of a message and his responses to it are often strikingly similar to those of his family, his friends, and the members of other groups which are significant to him —quite apart from whether the members of these groups receive the message together with him or have a chance to discuss it with one another or with him. This agreement occurs in large part because of the continuing interplay between the individual and these significant groups. He shares many of his experiences with them. He has learned from them many of his basic ideas and beliefs about what is true or aesthetically appropriate or morally right. And these very experiences and values tend to govern what he perceives and how he perceives it. Thus it appears that mass communications tend to reach the target individual as a member of various groups which are important to him.

Reference-Group Theory

A considerable store of theory, often summarized under the heading of reference-group theory, is at hand to describe the communication recipient as a member of a group. As set down by such scholars as Sherif, Newcomb, Merton, and others [45, pp. 41–42] this theory "centers on the processes through which men relate themselves to groups and refer their behavior to the values of these groups." [30, pp. 41–42] Not only do the groups provide a standard against which the individual may evaluate himself and others; more importantly, the individual's family, his community, his workmates—all of his significant "primary" groups—teach him their values and shape his values in line with theirs. During the course of his lifetime, he incorporates many of the central values of these others; the others come to constitute for him, in Mead's term, an "inner forum" before which he privately debates alternatives. Moreover, in the course of daily interaction, whenever he conforms in his acts or expressions of opinion to the values of his associates, these others are likely to approve and reward; and when he fails to conform, they may disapprove, bringing negative sanctions to bear. Hence, he often conforms in order to win approval or (in Veblen's telling irony) to gain "an increment of good repute."

Selected Applications

Such theories are usefully applied to problems of mass communication. The traditional approach has long found it fruitful to classify individuals in terms of their location in different parts of the country or different types of communities or in terms of their socioeconomic status within the larger society. In addition to this, if the recipient's values are indeed shaped in part by the primary groups to which he belongs or aspires, his perception of a message and his response to it may be better understood in terms of his relationship to these groups and to their values. As part of the Yale program of research, Kelley and Volkart set up an experiment in which an outside adult speaker at several Boy Scout meetings criticized the Scout emphasis on the values of camping and woodcraft and advocated various urban activities instead. Attitude tests conducted among the boys before and after this speech suggest that the boys who were most strongly motivated to retain their membership in the Boy Scouts were the most resistant to a communication which ran counter to the standards of the group.[21] In another study, Festinger, Riecken, and Schachter observed the members of a religious sect at a time when they expected that the earth would be destroyed and only "believers" would be saved. Even though the prophesied event failed to occur, those who received support from others of the faithful (unlike members who faced the crisis alone) tended to regard the failure merely as a slight miscalculation and not as disconfirmation of their essential belief.[15]

Some Rutgers research illustrates an application of reference-group theory to the receipt of quite another kind of message—one which, made up of fiction or fantasy, is not explicitly designed to persuade, although it may nevertheless exert considerable influence. An exploratory study of children's mass-media preferences suggests that the individual's integration into a significant group may affect both his choice of materials to read or listen to and his interpretation of media content. In this study, children who were not disposed to talk extensively with friends—and who doubtless felt the strain of exclusion from the peer group—were found to express relatively high interest in stories which foster fantasies of aggression or escape. They were more apt than high communicators to like radio and television programs characterized by action and violence. Even when the excluded child and the integrated child are exposed to the same media material, the content may have a different function for each. In describing a program such as "The Lone Ranger," the low communicators typically used terms like "scary," "creepy," "hard to get out of your mind when you go to sleep"; the high communicators tended to couple exposure to this program with "playing guns" with their friends subsequently.[38; 39]

Another piece of related research develops the hypothesis that media preferences may be associated, not only with the individual's disposition to communicate with the members of the group (parents, in this instance), but also with his agreement with their values. A sample of adolescent boys in New Jersey high schools were asked which of a list of topics they "like best to read about or listen to" in the mass media. The first step in the analysis again compared high and low communicators. The proportion of boys who named "news" as a desired topic was as follows:

Degree of communication with parents

	Low	High
Percent who like to read or listen to news	50	65
Total respondents = 100%	(755)	(357)

This finding is consistent with the notion that the boys' media behavior tends to conform to the expectations of their middle-class parents, even when these significant others are not immediately present to exert control.

Moreover, when the boys were subdivided according to the degree to which their own aspirations (classified in terms of their responses to a series of vignettes embodying selected values of concern to adolescents) conformed to the expectations of parents or peers, the results were as follows:

	Degree of communication with parents			
	Low		High	
Predominant agreement with	Peers	Parents	Peers	Parents
Percent who like to read or listen to news	47	55	58	70
Total respondents = 100%	(433)	(322)	(155)	(202)

Thus it appears that a boy's selection of media materials in line with probable parental expectations is related to his predominant agreement with parental values, as well as to his disposition to interact with his parents as persons.

Consequences for Primary Group Structure

One outcome of individual tendencies to adopt a group as a source of guidance and orientation is the development of a considerable degree of homogeneity in attitudes and values among the group members. (The implementation of these values is often differentiated, of course, according to some "division of labor" among the individual roles.) Newcomb, starting from sociological theory and the work of Heider has developed a theory to account for such homogeneity, explaining how group members, as they interact and talk among themselves, feel rewarded when their attitudes coincide, and thus tend to influence one another to arrive at similar attitudes.[33] And Festinger states a set of hypotheses, developed from a wide variety of empirical experiments in the Lewinian tradition, which indicate in some detail how discrepancies in group opinion lead to pressures toward uniformity—or, failing this, toward extrusion of dissident members from the group. He suggests, for example, that the amount of change in an individual's opinion resulting from the attempts of the other members to persuade him will

—increase as the pressure toward uniformity in the group increases;
—increase as the strength of the resultant force to remain in the group increases for the recipient;
—decrease in the degree to which the opinions and attitudes involved are anchored in other group memberships or serve important need-satisfying functions for the person.[14]

Conflicting Reference Groups

This mention of "other group memberships" leads to the highly important point that the individual belongs and refers, not just to one group, but to many. The expectations of such groups may reinforce one another, so that he uses them jointly as a reference. If their values conflict, however, he is in a "role conflict," or under "cross-pressure."

Toward a Sociological View

These few examples suggest how the social structure underlies and tends to integrate the great diversity of individual perceptions of and responses to the mass-communicated message. It becomes apparent that the consumer faced with a baffling array of brands, the voter choosing between political courses with unknown consequences, or the entertainment seeker with untold possibilities on his television dial makes choices which are not based primarily on the inherent merits of the object chosen—no matter how persuasively these merits may have been advertised. It appears that these choices are widely affected, not alone by the choice object itself or by advertising and propaganda about it, but also by other people. The individual often decides to purchase or to vote or to look at television programs *with* trusted other people, rather than *for* a particular brand or candidate or program. Thus his reactions are not random relative to the reactions of these others. His perceptions and his responses form part of a pattern of interactions and mutual orientations among all the members of the group.

By focusing on the recipient's place within such a pattern, reference-group theory points the way toward an extension of the traditional approach in the direction of a larger sociological view. Figure 20.1 begins to suggest the nature of this emerging view. The arrow from *C* (the communicator) to *R* (the recipient) indicates the traditional focus. The sociological approach makes its first contribution to the model by taking into account the connections between *R* and the many primary groups with which he interacts, which shape his values, sanction his behavior, and, accordingly, impinge upon his role as a recipient in relation to *C*.

Some Further Problems

The use of this reference-group concept in research raises a number of fairly clear-cut questions for further study. Merton, in his detailed analysis of work on reference groups and social structure, has done a great deal to clarify the general problems at hand.[29; 30] With specific reference to the field of mass communications, we can identify some of the types of questions that seem to require attention at this time, such as: How is the recipient's reaction to a mass communication related to his membership (or coveted membership) in a *single* primary group? How does this reaction vary, on the one hand, with his positive or negative feelings toward the members of this group and, on the other hand, with his agreement or disagreement with their values? How does it vary with his status in the group and the particular role he is expected to perform? How does his reference group seem to affect his reactions to different types of communication—those intended to inform, persuade, and commit him to action, and those intended merely to entertain and provide him with food for fantasy? Moreover (a far more complicated question), how does he respond when he must react to a message in multiple roles as a member of conflicting reference groups? How does his reaction vary with the relative significance of these groups to him, with the relative degree of his positive or negative feelings toward them?

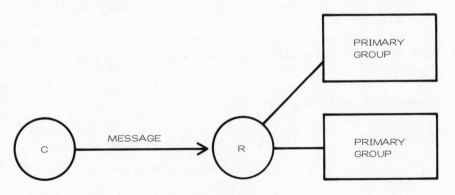

Figure 20.1

Answers to such questions should go far toward locating the recipient in the social structure, but they will serve primarily to locate him in relation only to his diverse primary groups.* They cannot in themselves fully describe the structure within which mass-communicated messages are received, for, just as the audience is not composed of discrete individuals, neither is it composed of discrete primary groups. These smaller, solidary groupings must also be viewed in a more inclusive system. By analogy, the economist does not (cannot) account for depressions merely by studying the personal inefficiency of given individuals or the reduced incentives for wage-earning in given families. Nor did Durkheim account for social differences in the suicide rate as exclusively a function of personal motivation or of family integration. In both instances, the relevant theory also invokes wider structures and longer-term changes which include and also transcend the individual or the primary group as such.

THE RECIPIENT AND THE LARGER SOCIAL STRUCTURE

Concomitant with such studies of the individual recipient and his primary groups, a quite different and less-developed line of research explores the more inclusive structure of social organizations and institutions which surrounds the recipient. For, if the recipient's role is affected by the values and goals of his diverse primary groups, how do these groups themselves derive such values and goals? How are the primary groups related to one another? How are they integrated within the more embracing social structure and process?

Because this larger structure transcends both the individual and his primary groups, many of the pertinent studies have their major focus, not on the recipient (as in most reference-group research), but on the structure itself. That is, they do not start with the individual recipient and work outward through his primary groups, hoping thereby to piece together the complex network within which these groups are intertwined and interdependent. Instead, they start with the larger structure, examining first the relationships of the primary groups to the larger structure and to one another, and finally seeking the recipient's place within the whole. (Ultimately, these two complementary approaches should dovetail.)

Studies of Formal Organizations

A number of studies in other fields illustrate the fruitfulness of this focus on the structure itself. The classic Western Electric investigations,

---

* The reference-group approach is not by definition limited to primary groups; it applies also to larger, more distant social groupings, as the next section indicates. As effective reference groups, however, the primary groups, with which the individual is most closely associated, seem to have the most compelling hold upon him.

for example, deal with the industrial plant as a social system made up of interrelated parts. This system is composed of a technical organization and a human organization, each of which affects the other. The human organization, in turn, is subdivided into formal and informal social organizations. Within such a system, research observations indicate the processes through which the informal groupings of friends and co-workers may function either to support or to detract from the formal organization's goal of efficient productivity.[40] In a somewhat similar fashion, studies of the combat behavior of American troops in World War II examine the formal organization which achieves its goals by ordering men to fight, and within this the informal organizations of friends which, because of the common threat, shared ideals of manliness, and the like, reinforce the goals of the formal system. As Williams and Smith conclude, "Affective ties binding the group together were important in keeping men in combat because, among other reasons, the group through its formal organization was inextricably committed to the fight; anything that tied the individual to the group therefore kept him in combat." [53, p. 100]

A Study of Propaganda

The prototype of studies of this type in the mass-communication field is perhaps the evaluation by Shils and Janowitz [48] of the impact of propaganda by the Western Allies on the fighting effectiveness of the German Army in World War II. Contrary to earlier views of propaganda as a panacea, their findings did not reveal that the invocation of adverse political, ideological, and cultural symbols produced any sweeping disaffection or collapse in military morale. Nor did they reveal that the extraordinary tenacity of the *Wehrmacht* was due primarily to the political convictions of the German soldier—to his direct attachment to the Nazi system itself as a reference group. They showed, rather, that his resistance to Allied propaganda and his sustained motivation to fight rested upon the persistence of the primary-group structure of the component units of the army. These analysts concluded that only when the primary groups themselves start to dissolve does propaganda (and then only certain kinds of propaganda) facilitate disintegration.

This study merits careful attention, since it seems to illustrate an important, but little exploited, approach to the study of the social structure within which communications are received. In order to account for the stability of the army and its resistance to propaganda against its norms, Shils and Janowitz began with an investigation of the basic military organization and its relationship to the system of primary groups. They examined the process by which the goals of the larger bureaucratic structure were met by the functioning of smaller groups of friends, suggesting a number of linkages between the army and these smaller groups. For example, membership in the informal social group was seen to coincide roughly with membership in the military squad. Both the larger structure and the primary group are exposed to the same external danger and share the same ideal of soldierly honor. The small but hard core of Nazis, as well as the paternally protective noncommissioned officers and junior officers, served as mediators, or linking persons, between the primary group and the army. Moreover, the larger system was observed to exercise various controls over the smaller. Not only did the *Wehrmacht* exert authority through its officers, it also deliberately manipulated various factors affecting small-group solidarity. For example, it maintained in the same units men who had gone through a victory together and who shared the same recollections. It warned deserters of severe sanctions. It prevented family groups from weakening the hold of the army on the men by issuing strict injunctions against references to family deprivations in letters to the front. At the same time, it encouraged letters which would reduce the men's anxieties about their families and give the supplementary affection which the army unit could not provide.

Within this social structure and ongoing social process, Shils and Janowitz examined the ties between the individual soldier and his group of friends and analyzed the fundamental indifference of the troops to the millions of Allied leaflets and the continuous Allied broadcasts. Small wonder that the German soldier, bound to his fellows by spatial proximity, intimate association, and the military organization itself, paid little heed to Allied propaganda (even when he believed it) which exhorted him to desert his friends or abandon their goals. It is in this sense that the recipient's response may be understood—first, in terms of his primary groups, and second, in terms of the larger organizations in which these groups are implanted.

Primary and Secondary Reference Groups

Studies with this structural focus ultimately lead back, of course, to the individual recipient of the message and his reference groups. (They deal with the same problem as reference-group studies, merely approaching it from another level.) In general, the relevant studies of the recipient tend to distinguish between his relationships to the larger, secondary system and to his primary groups. Thus the worker's productivity is viewed as the outcome of his relationships both to the formal structure of the plant and to his fellow workers. The individual soldier's willingness to fight is explainable both through his relationship to the army and through his affectional ties to his buddies and his unwillingness to let them down. (Of course, this is merely a reemphasis of an old insight; as early as the first century after Christ, Tacitus, in the *Germania,* explained the bravery of the barbarian hordes through the presence of their families with them on the battlefield.)

The findings of such studies seem to converge in emphasizing the great importance of the primary reference group within the larger reference system. A study of the reasons given by refugees for fleeing the Communist regime in North Korea reports, for example, that "the ideological repugnance to communism . . . runs a poor second to the more impelling consideration that the system has marked a member of the family for liquidation or imprisonment." [37, p. 277] Accordingly, it seems that the recipient of a communication is rarely reached directly in his role as an anonymous and isolated member of a bureaucracy or of a mass society. His receipt of this message is, rather, "mediated" through the close, informal groupings to which he also belongs.

Studies of Election Campaigns

If studies like the one by Shils and Janowitz seem to be successful in dealing with this important problem of the relations between the recipient and the environing social structure as it bears upon his role in the mass-communication process, their success is doubtless due in part to their use of a type of social structure which is manageable in research. The military structure, as well as the structure of the industrial plant, has a clearly specified formal organization which affords a firm framework within which primary groups may be located and communications traced. Moreover, an army or a factory, although it may be large, is by no means so unwieldy for the researcher as a whole society. How, indeed, is the researcher to cope with larger, less explicitly formulated social structures, or with the whole society?

Some work on the voter—the recipient of the political campaign message—might suggest the general character of a sociological approach to the political structure. In the noteworthy last chapter of *Voting,* Berelson, Lazarsfeld, and McPhee write:

> After examining the detailed data on how individuals misperceive political reality or respond to irrelevant social influences, one wonders how a democracy ever solves its political problems. But when one considers the data in a broader perspective—how huge segments of the society adapt to political conditions affecting them or how the political system adjusts itself to changing conditions over long periods of time—he cannot fail to be impressed with the total result. . . . This suggests that . . . what are undervalued are certain collective properties that reside in the electorate as a whole and in the political and social system in which it functions.
> (5, pp. 311–312)

A clearer model of the larger system is developed, within which primary groups are organized and the individual voter responds to campaigns. This would appear to have important further implications for an understanding of mass communication. The voting studies show, for example, that exposure to election campaigns through the mass media not only seems to heighten the interest of voters but also strengthens the relative importance of political, as compared with social, factors in this interest.[5, p. 34, 252] Thus the influence of a campaign (reinforced by the influence of the opinion leaders) is to line voters up behind one candidate or the other and at the same time to inhibit any concern over the specific and particularistic demands of their smaller social groupings; the apparent effect, that is, is toward two-party integration of the political system in this country, rather than toward a fragmentation along primary-group lines.

Toward a Sociological View

Such scattered empirical findings, together with such developing theory, begin to specify the place in the working model of the individual recipient, as he is attached to primary groups which are, in turn, systematically related to the larger structure ("by diverse patterns of ties," as Shils [47, p. 135] put it). The processes which occur among individuals within primary groups contribute to the functioning of the more inclusive process; and conversely, the individual's actions tend to be channeled not only by his relationship to his significant reference groups but also by the alignments of these reference groups within the larger structure. Thus, it appears that mass-communicated messages reach individuals whose group members and group references themselves have determinate interrelationships. In Figure 20.2, which shows this further elaboration of the developing sociological view, the circle represents the larger social structure within which the recipient's smaller groupings tend to be integrated and patterned with reference to one another.

Some Unanswered Questions

For the present, however, a great many challenging and basic questions remain to be answered. If the "collective properties of the electorate" have been isolated and formulated as a theoretical model, can similar models be formulated of the larger structures within which the consumer responds to advertising, or the student to teaching? How can such models be clarified through further theoretical analysis and tested through further research? If it has been demonstrated that much can be learned by observing the effects of mass communication within a formal structure, would not similar structures lend themselves to observation and experiment in order to test,

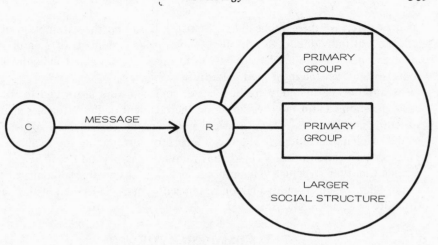

Figure 20.2

revise, and supplement the earlier findings? Or, returning to the individual receiver, what more can be learned about his relationship to his primary groups as contrasted with his relationship to the larger structure? Under what conditions does the primary group appear to be the more effective of the two in guiding his responses?

In order to answer such questions, further advances in available research methods seem also to be required. The major research unit, in studies of a social system, may be either the system or the individual within it. Using a system approach, the Western Electric investigations indicate the feasibility of experimentation in the study of corporate structures; the *Wehrmacht* analysis shows the advantages of focusing on a system which is at a critical point of rapid process or change. Yet this focusing of major research on the system often presents difficulties. Shils and Janowitz solved these problems by supplementing the data obtained from individuals with "captured enemy documents, statements of recaptured Allied military personnel, and the reports of combat observers." [48, p. 282] In view of the patent value of documents and the testimony of "experts" in system analysis, the development of rigorous procedures for the use of such materials would appear highly desirable.

The alternative method consists of collecting and fitting together data about individual members within the structure. But such a method often requires that established procedures of sampling individuals give way to the study of *all* the individuals within the group in order to uncover the crucial bonds in the network of interrelationships. Moreover, once the individual data have been obtained, they cannot merely be aggregated. Here the usual group measures using the mean and variance of individual responses may lose their applicability. Statistics based on the assumption of independent individual data are often inappropriate. Methods of measurement and analysis are needed which will fit together data about individuals so as to represent the integrated pattern for the group.

As appropriate methods are developed, some answers are found to the basic questions about the pressure upon the recipient of the ambient social structure and process. These answers point to the inadequacies of any model of communication, of the social structure surrounding the recipient. The communication process clearly has ramifications beyond the individual recipient and his structure. This process includes, of course, the communicator, who, whether individual or organized group, is located within a structure of social relationships.

THE COMMUNICATOR

A vast literature deals with the relationship between the communicator and his social environment. Countless analyses of the creative writer or artist treat him as the product of his historical epoch or of his family setting. Treatises from Milton's *Areopagitica* to Schramm's *Responsibility in Mass Communication* [12] have discussed such topics as formal censorship versus self-regulation, the monopoly of channels by groups in selected economic positions, and the social pressures toward the commercialization of mass-produced art. Like the recipient, the communicator has a cognitive structure through which he screens his perceptions and choices; he too has personal friends and reference groups; he too is part of a larger social structure made up of business concerns or manufacturers' associations or labor or farm or veterans' groups.

The Social Structure Surrounding the Communicator

A model of the social structure as it affects the initiator of mass communications is implied within the venerable tradition of the sociology of knowledge. This field of inquiry, which deals with "the entire gamut of cultural products (ideas, ideologies, juristic and ethical beliefs, philosophy, science, technology)" seeks: "the social determinants of the intellectual's [the communicator's] perspectives, how he came to hold his ideas. . . . The student of mass communications, on the other hand, has almost from the beginning been concerned primarily with the *impact* of the mass media *upon* the audiences. . . . The one centers on the source, the other on the result." [29, pp. 439–456] In his paradigm for the classification of the many findings already existent in this field, Merton's list of the "social bases for mental productions" might well be used to indicate the major group affiliations and structural contexts which affect the behavior of the professional communicator.

Although Merton's own studies in the sociology of science illustrate the fruitfulness of this approach, which has the special asset of reaching back into the historical past, there have been few explicit attempts to utilize in systematic field research such a model of the communicator's place within the social structure. A few case studies, such as those of the movie makers by Rosten,[41] tie output to the communicator's place in a social system, but work, on the whole, has been scattered.

Of possible relevance for an understanding of the mass communicator are various studies dealing with communicative behavior as a form of control in groups. Williams,[52] for example, in a summary of research on disaster, describes the process by which the larger system of a community, confronted by a flood or a tornado, fails to communicate to the populace the information needed for proper control. No adequate communication processes or channels exist in the crisis to control the unprecedented flow of supplies and manpower, to prevent traffic congestion, to distribute patients to hospitals, and the like. At the same time, as private citizens rush in to rescue relatives and friends, primary-group communications tend to increase. Urgent personal messages are relayed, not merely by word of mouth, but also through emergency private use of the community's communications channels. Although this may prove functional for the immediate rescue and welfare task, it interferes with communication at the community level, resulting in confusion. Thus the private communicator seems temporarily to usurp the role of the large-system communicator. In this way, Williams locates this large-system communicator within a social structure, much as Shils and Janowitz locate the recipient within the cohesive organization of the *Wehrmacht*.

Feedback to the Communicator

To be sure, community communications of the sort investigated by Williams are not limited to mass communications; a good deal of direct response from the recipient, of feedback, is possible in such situations. Yet the very emphasis of the findings upon the importance of the flow of communications, *to* as well as *from* the communicator, underscores the significance of the restrictions on feedback within the mass-communication process. Williams' analysis, for example, building on the work of Homans [18, pp. 461–462] and on "communication theory," stresses the need of the community system itself for feedback information about the outcome of its previous messages, which would indicate what its next steps should be in attempting to control the environment. Thus, one of the major impairments wrought in the communication system by disaster is the cutting off of the communicator's own source of information.

Observations of much smaller groups, such as a street corner gang or a problem-solving group in a laboratory, seem also to imply that the function of the chief communicator or leader is not only to initiate but also to receive a large share of the interpersonal communication. Bales, for example, has found that, as the size of the task group increases from three to eight men, the top man tends to initiate a larger and larger share of the total communication, and also to address more and more of his remarks to the group as a whole rather than to specific individuals. Thus one might say that the largest of his small groups begins to approximate an audience being addressed by a mass communicator. Interestingly enough, Bales concludes:

> If the situation is one in which *inter*-action is expected by the participators, however, there would seem to be a ceiling on the amount of participation for the top man. . . . Even if the top man is initiating most of the action, he still has to expect that he will receive a "feed-back of reactions," of both a positive and a negative sort, that will tend to equal the amount of action he initiates. (3, p. 155)

In the study of mass communications, however, relatively little explicit attention has been paid to this element of feedback to the communicator. Yet even here, a degree of feedback clearly tends to exist—scant, indirect, and obscure though it may be. Some kind of reciprocal channel is needed if the communicator is to learn whether and how his message was received, if he is to have any basis for sending further messages. Perhaps the mass response may consist merely of increased listening to the program, or increased purchase of the product advertised, or reduction of the enemy's will to fight in line with a psychological-warfare message. To be sure, advertisers give careful scrutiny to resultant sales, just as actors, editors, and Presidents pay strict heed to their fan mail; but more research seems needed on the impact of such scrutiny upon the communicator. For, as the Hartleys (17, p. 31) point out, "If the communication is at all successful, the audience responds in some way, and its response affects future communications."

Toward a Sociological View

Thus the communicator emerges as part of a larger pattern, sending his messages in accordance with the expectations and actions of other persons and groups within the same system. As a political communicator, he may act with reference to the other members of his party and the other citizens in his community; as a copywriter, he may act as an employee of an advertising agency sponsored by a particular manufacturing client. Figure 20.3 adds to the developing sociological model by suggesting schematically the social structure within which the communicator, as well as the recipient, is placed. Moreover, the two-directional arrows connecting *C*'s struc-

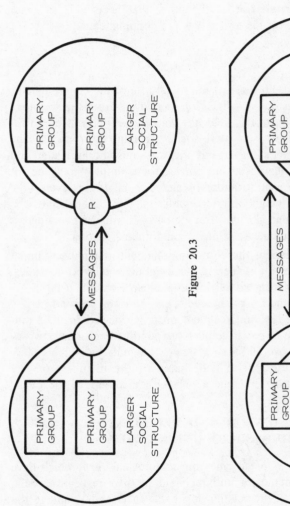

Figure 20.3

Figure 20.4

ture with *R*'s indicate that the communicator is always acting (with more or less conscious intent) in relation to the recipient and to the recipient's probable response. In Mead's words, the effective speaker "assumes the attitude of the other individual as well as calling it out in the other. He himself is in the role of the other person whom he is so exciting and influencing. It is through taking this role of the other that he is able to come back on himself and so direct his own process of communication." [27, p. 254]

Some Further Problems

Further study is needed, however, if the social role of the communicator is to be thoroughly understood. Codification of findings from the sociology of knowledge in application to this field has scarcely begun. Few empirical studies attempt to explicate the total social structure surrounding the sender, in line with Blumer's suggestions that the outstanding leader and top-level propagandist (in a social movement, for example) must be located in relation to "the vast structure of agitation on lower levels—the community agitators, the neighborhood organizers, the local officials, the zealots among the rank and file, the average party member discussing his view with friends, acquaintances, relatives, and fellow workers." [7, p. 148]

Moreover, this discussion of the communicator, with its implication of the interactive character of even the mass-communication process, underscores the impossibility of conceptualizing any single element in the process apart from all the others. As the recipient tends to respond to the communicator, communicator and recipient must be viewed in their mutual relationship. And the larger structures surrounding each one now appear as subsystems of an overall social system, with some individuals playing parts in both structures,* and with many of the members of one structure intercommunicating and interacting with members of the other.

COMMUNICATOR AND RECIPIENT:
TOWARD A SOCIOLOGICAL VIEW

The foregoing discussions of an emerging sociological view, which have located both mass communicator and recipient in their respective social groupings, lead us back to the relationship between C and R and to the process of mass communication itself. The traditional Lasswellian view of this relationship tends to atomize the audience and to isolate the communicated message from the social process as a whole. If we reexamine this

---

* Of course, in extreme cases, the two structures may be relatively unconnected, as when the communicator belongs to the state department of one country and broadcasts to citizens of a foreign and alien country.

relationship in light of the developing sociological model, several further aspects seem to emerge clearly.

First, communicator and recipient are now seen as interdependent; their relationship no longer fits the one-way, who-to-whom notion.

Second, with rare exceptions, this relationship does not consist of a single communication which potentially elicits only a single reply. Any given communication is, rather, one link in a chain of communications which extends over time. This chain, of course, is by no means limited to a simple personal relationship between C and R exclusively, in which C beams his message to R and R replies directly. When the communication is sent by a publishing house, a film studio, or a broadcasting network, there is, as Schramm puts it, "very little *direct* feedback from the receiver to the sender. The destination . . . will very seldom talk back to the radio network or write a letter to the editor." Much of the C-R relationship, is, rather, indirect, proliferating through the other members and groups to which C and R belong, so that the message is transmitted from individuals in C's groups to individuals in R's groups who in turn reply.

Third, each of these individuals has a definite position in the social structure. This does not mean merely that C's role in the process, as well as R's, tends to be affected by its social context. Beyond this, these several positions are related to one another within the social system. Thus the several communications which flow from one individual or group to another appear no longer as random or unrelated acts but as elements in a total pattern of ongoing interaction.

Specification of the Model

A good deal of theory and a number of research approaches are available for use in filling in the further details of such a model of the indirect, interactive, proliferated relationship between mass communicator and audience. Parsons, for example, lays the groundwork on which a communication theory might be built in both the economic and the political fields. Within his schemes of interchange between firms and household, and between political parties and public, communication—often in the form of mass communication—undoubtedly enters wherever persuasion seems necessary. Thus there are attempts on the part of firms to persuade households to purchase goods and to provide labor services, while members of households directly or indirectly attempt to persuade firms to pay higher wages or to produce more desirable goods. Similarly, representatives of political parties exhort the public to support their leaders and their specific decisions, while members of the public put pressure behind certain policies and demand more effective leadership.

This initiation of communication by the public to the policy makers (as distinct from mere feedback) has been explicated in an article by Cohen, among others. Consistent with our emphasis on the systemic character of the social environment surrounding the recipient (who in turn acts as communicator), he says: "The kinds of political behavior engaged in by specific groups among the articulate public seem to be partly traceable to some rather stable factors which are internal to such groups, and which are mostly unaffected by kaleidoscopic changes in policy issue or political alignment." [9, pp. 27–38] Thus, whereas homogeneous groups can agree rather easily on the measures to be advocated in messages to congressmen or to the President, more heterogeneous groups are slower to come to any operational consensus and so impose restrictions on the communications addressed by their spokesmen.

Another approach to the C-R relationship utilizes the content of communication in order to make inferences about the nature of the ongoing interaction. Here again, small-group research uncovers findings about interpersonal communication which have possible relevance for the mass-communication system. (It often seems instructive to use the small group as a basis for comparison in studying the larger system, with its complex structure and its restrictions on reciprocal action. In this way, it may be possible to discover how mass communication differs from face-to-face conversation, or to specify the conditions under which these differences may be functional or dysfunctional for the system. Moreover, since the small group lends itself as a system to observation, its study suggests modes and procedures of analysis which may be adaptable to large-system research.)

In a relevant set of small-group studies, Bales has developed a distinction between "instrumental" communication, in which instructions are given or information conveyed, and "expressive" communication, through which tensions are released and group solidarity restored. He suggests that the process of interpersonal communication consists of instrumental acts, through which the group may pursue its goals but which place strains upon its members, alternating with expressive acts, which ease such strains and tend to reestablish the equilibrium. A proper balance between instrumental and expressive activity seems necessary to the maintenance of the system. Bales also has found that two kinds of "leaders" are likely to emerge in each small task group to take care of these two functions: a so-cial-emotional, expressive leader, or "popular" man, and an instrumental leader, who guides the group and provides ideas for it. [2]

Sutton and his associates deal with this same problem of intercommunication in a study of the American business creed, which illustrates another approach at the level of the large system and a quite different method of content analysis. The public messages issued by business leaders are seen, on the one hand, to form a "patterned reaction to the patterned strains of a social role" [51, p. 307]—to emanate from C as a member of business and other groups. On the other hand, those businessmen who receive these messages use them as a guide to action. The ideology, as the authors point out,[51, p. 383] serves to promote solidarity among the divergent elements of the business community. Presumably R, receiving the messages as a member of his groups, demands (perhaps even participates in) further communication of a similar sort. Thus the given set of messages under study appears as merely one link in a chain of continuing interactions. This example typifies the adaptation of content analysis to the tracing of the broader processes of interactive communication—as the ideas of some people influence other people, who in turn exert further influence, through the course of time.

The Recipient as Active Participant

Research might be done on the individual roles of C and R in communication conceived as an interactive process. Communication in general is ordinarily defined by sociologists as a form of interaction between two or more persons. According to Davis, for example, one person first infers from the behavior of another the idea or feeling that the other is trying to convey. He then responds, not to the behavior as such, but to the inferred idea or feeling. The other person in turn reacts to this response in terms of the idea or feeling—the meaning—behind it.

In line with this general definition of communication, our earlier discussion of C has indicated that the flow of communication to the mass communicator (as well as from him) may be functional for the process. Does the model also require that the recipient send messages as well as accept them? Are there any indications, for example, that his active participation may likewise contribute to the effectiveness of the process? A number of loosely related studies seem to provide certain clues. There is some experimental evidence, for example, that the recipient is more apt to be influenced by a message when he is given a role as an active communicator. Lewin has demonstrated that group discussion may be more effective than one-way lectures in changing food habits.[25, pp. 207-381] Coch and French [8] found higher production rates and less quitting and aggression among factory employees when job and rate changes were discussed through group participation rather than announced through lectures. Hovland reports a finding which might be interpreted to mean that persuasion is enhanced when the recipient participates, even indirectly, by handing on the message: As the researchers say, "When exposure . . . is held constant, individuals who are required to verbalize the communication aloud to others will tend to be more influenced than those who are passively exposed." [19, p. 278]

It may also be that the receiver responds more readily to a mass communication if he is given even the illusion of participation. In Aristotle's view of Greek tragedy, the actors, through their "imitation of the universal," allow the spectators to identify directly with the interaction on the stage. In this sense, the basis for catharsis becomes a kind of pseudoparticipation by spectators. Merton's analysis of Kate Smith's remarkable success in selling war bonds perhaps implies that the listener perceives the radio performance as a mutual relationship in which, as it were, "Kate is wearing herself out in this marathon broadcast because she expects me to purchase —if I fail to buy bonds, she will be disappointed—but if I do buy, she'll see the sales figures mounting and will express her pleasure over the radio— her pleasure, in turn, will make me feel that I did the right thing."

The Paths of Communication

Still another approach to the mass-communication process traces the course along which information or influence flows from one person and group to another. Dodd [12] developed the basic model for studying the successive steps in the process whereby the original recipients of a mass-communication message, or "knowers," might be expected to tell others, who in turn become "knowers" and tell still others, and so on. During the past several years, a number of such "diffusion" studies have shed considerable light on this process. In general, these studies have shown that the diffusion of information follows a fairly standard pattern or curve, the shape of which appears to be controlled mainly by the importance of the event.

Of central importance here is the series of studies conducted by Lazarsfeld and his associates which traces the flow of influence (on voting behavior, purchasing, movie selection, and the like) through the social structure within which the recipient is imbedded. [24: 5] Katz, for example, speaks of the "networks of interconnected individuals through which mass communications are channeled," thus replacing the traditional image of the audience as "a mass of disconnected individuals hooked up to the media but not to each other." [20, p. 61] These studies investigate a "two-step flow of influence" from the mass communicator through the "opinion leader" to the other members of the group. Merton elaborates this notion of opinion leaders as recipients, comparing the mass-media exposure of "local influentials," who are the center of the web of primary-group relationships within the community, and "cosmopolitan influentials," who serve as the connecting links between the community and the outside world.[28, pp. 180-219] Such studies point to the ultimate sociological view of the mass-media audience as a composite of recipients who are related to one another, and whose responses are patterned in terms of these relationships.[32, pp. 262-265]

A study of this kind typically deals with a particular content as it flows along the path from communicator to opinion leader to any given other individual (R) who is at the receiving end—and here the study ends. Presumably this same path ultimately winds back, however indirectly, to the original communicator. To trace this return path would mean shifting the research focus, since this path undoubtedly carries different content—a positive or negative response, for example, or a question, as in the small-group studies. It is to be hoped that future research on the paths of communication will examine these two-directional aspects further. Such research would come close to utilizing the full dynamic sociological model of the intercommunication between members of C's groupings and of R's.

Figure 20.4 shows the two interdependent structures of C and R as aspects of the same wide society and the same secular trend, which is represented by the oval boundary that encompasses them both.* The arrows indicate the flow of communication back and forth among the several members of these interdependent structures. Within such an all-embracing system, the mass-communications process is now seen as a component of the larger social process, both affecting it and being in turn affected by it.

The Need for a Working Model

An understanding of the sociological processes through which mass communications take effect thus seems to require the formulation of a working model, based on codification of the empirical findings available in several fields, and on application of the relevant theory. In light of such a model, the problems still at hand may be defined. Further studies of these problems may then progress concurrently, so as to throw light on different aspects and from different points of view. Each finding from further research, although in itself partial and incomplete, should have its proper place within the unified scheme of the model. Ultimately, insofar as the several findings fit together, mass communication may indeed be viewed as an integral part of the social system.

---

* Cf. Mead's early statement that: "The process of communication cannot be set up as something that exists by itself, or as a presupposition of the social process. On the contrary, the social process is presupposed in order to render thought and communication possible" (27, p. 260). Cooley defines communication as the "mechanism through which human relations exist" (Charles H. Cooley, *Social Organization,* Scribner's, 1937, p. 61). And Park speaks of it as spinning "a web of custom and mutual expectations which binds together social entities" (Robert E. Park, "Reflections on Communication and Culture," *Amer. J. Sociol.,* 44 [1939], 191).

380   *Approaches to Human Communication*

REFERENCES AND SUGGESTED READINGS

1. Asch, S. E., "A Study of Some Social Factors in Perception," *Archives of Psychology*, No. 187, 1935.
2. Bales, Robert F., "The Equilibrium Problem in Small Groups," in *Working Papers in the Theory of Action*, ed. by Talcott Parsons, Robert F. Bales, and Edward A. Shils. New York: Free Press, 1953.
3. Bales, Robert F., "Some Uniformities of Behavior in Small Social Systems," in *Readings in Social Psychology*, ed. by Guy E. Swanson, Theodore M. Newcomb, and Eugene L. Hartley. New York: Henry Holt, 1952.
4. Berelson, Bernard R., *Content Analysis in Communication Research*. New York: Free Press, 1952.
5. Berelson, Bernard R., Paul F. Lazarsfeld, and William N. McPhee, *Voting: A Study of Opinion Formation in a Presidential Campaign*. Chicago: University of Chicago Press, 1954.
6. Berger, Peter, *Invitation to Sociology*. Garden City, N.Y.: Doubleday, Anchor Books, 1963.
7. Blumer, Herbert, "Collective Behavior," in *Review of Sociology*, ed. by Joseph B. Gittler. New York: Wiley, 1957.
8. Coch, Lester, and John R. P. French, Jr., "Overcoming Resistance to Change," *Human Relations*, Vol. 1, 1948.
9. Cohen, Bernard C., "Political Communication on the Japanese Peace Settlement," *Public Opinion Quarterly*, Vol. 20, 1956.
10. Davis, Kingsley, *Human Society*. New York: Macmillan, 1949.
11. DeFleur, Melvin L., and Otto N. Larsen, *The Flow of Information: An Experiment in Mass Communication*. New York: Harper, 1958.
12. Dodd, Stuart C., "Diffusion is Predictable," *American Sociological Review*, Vol. 20, 1955.
13. Duncan, Hugh D., *Communication and Social Order*. New York: Oxford University Press, 1962.
14. Festinger, Leon, "Informal Social Communication," *Psychological Review*, Vol. 57, 1950.
15. Festinger, Leon, Henry W. Riecken, and Stanley Schachter, *When Prophecy Fails*. Minneapolis: University of Minnesota Press, 1956.
16. Foote, Nelson S., and L. S. Cottrell, Jr., *Indentity and Interpersonal Competence*. Chicago: University of Chicago Press.
17. Hartley, Eugene L., and Ruth E. Hartley, *Fundamentals of Social Psychology*. New York: Knopf, 1952.
18. Homans, George C., *The Human Group*. New York: Harcourt, Brace, 1950.
19. Hovland, Carl I., Irving Janis, and Harold Kelley, *Communication and Persuasion*. New Haven: Yale University Press, 1953.
20. Katz, Elihu, "The Two-Step Flow of Communication: An Up-to-date Report on an Hypothesis," *Public Opinion Quarterly*, Vol. 21, 1957.
21. Kelley, Harold H., and Edmund H. Volkart, "The Resistance to Change of Group-Anchored Attitudes," *American Sociological Review*, Vol. 17, 1952.
22. Larsen, Otto N., and Richard J. Hill, "Mass Media and Interpersonal Communication in the Diffusion of a News Event," *American Sociological Review*, Vol. 19, 1954.
23. Lasswell, Harold, "The Structure and Function of Communication in Society," in *The Communication of Ideas*, ed. by Lyman Bryson. Institute for Religious and Social Studies, 1948.

24. Lazarsfeld, Paul, Bernard Berelson, and Hazel Gaudet, *The People's Choice,* 2nd ed. New York: Columbia University Press, 1948.
25. Lewin, Kurt, "Studies in Group Decision," in *Group Dynamics: Research and Theory,* ed. by Dorwin Cartwright and Alvin Zander. New York: Harper, 1953.
26. Lundberg, George A., and Margaret Lawsing, "The Sociography of Some Community Relations," *American Sociological Review,* Vol. 2, 1937.
27. Mead, George H., *Self and Society.* Chicago: University of Chicago Press, 1934.
28. Merton, Robert K., "Patterns of Influence: A Study of Interpersonal Influence and Communications Behavior in a Local Community," in *Communication Research,* ed. by P. Lazarsfeld and R. Stanton. New York: Harper, 1948–1949.
29. Merton, Robert K., "Social Theory and Social Structure," in *Sociology Today,* ed. by R. K. Merton, L. Broom, and L. S. Cottrell. New York: Basic Books, 1959.
30. Merton, Robert K., and Alice S. Kitt, "Contributions to the Theory of Reference Group Behavior," in *Continuities on Social Research: Studies in the Scope and Methods of "The American Soldier,"* ed. by Robert K. Merton and Paul F. Lazarsfeld. New York: Free Press, 1950.
31. Miller, Delbert C., "A Research Note on Mass Communication," *American Sociological Review,* Vol. 10, 1945.
32. Moreno, J. L., *Who Shall Survive?* Nervous and Mental Disease Publishing Company, 1934.
33. Newcomb, Theodore M., "An Approach to the Study of Communicative Acts," *Psychological Review,* Vol. 60, 1935.
34. Newcomb, Theodore M., *Social Psychology.* New York: Dryden, 1950.
35. Parsons, Talcott, ed., *American Sociology.* New York: Basic Books, 1968.
36. Parsons, Talcott, and Neil J. Smelser, *Economy and Society, A Study in the Integration of Economic and Social Theory.* New York: Free Press, 1956.
37. Riley, John W., Jr., Wilbur Schramm, and Frederick W. Williams, "Flight from Communism: A Report on Korean Refugees," *Public Opinion Quarterly,* Vol. 15, 1951.
38. Riley, Matilda White, and Samuel H. Flowerman, "Group Relations as a Variable in Communications Research," *American Sociology Review,* Vol. 16, 1951.
39. Riley, Matilda White, and John W. Riley, Jr., "A Sociological Approach to Communications Research," *Public Opinion Quarterly,* Vol. 15, 1951.
40. Roethlisberger, F. J., and William J. Dickson, *Management and the Worker.* Cambridge, Mass.: Harvard University Press, 1940.
41. Rosten, Leo C., *Hollywood: the Movie Colony, the Movie Makers.* New York: Harcourt, Brace, 1941.
42. Schramm, Wilbur, *Responsibility in Mass Communication.* New York: Harper, 1957.
43. Schramm, Wilbur, *The Process and Effects of Mass Communication.* Urbana: University of Illinois Press, 1954.
44. Shannon, Claude, and Warren Weaver, *The Mathematical Theory of Communication.* Urbana: University of Illinois Press, 1949.
45. Sherif, Muzafer, *An Outline of Social Psychology.* New York: Harper, 1948.
46. Sherif, Muzafer, "A Study of Some Social Factors in Perception," *Archives of Psychology,* No. 187, 1935.
47. Shils, Edward A., "Primordial, Personal, Sacred and Civil Ties," *British Journal of Sociology,* Vol. 8, 1957.

48. Shils, Edward A., and Morris Janowitz, "Cohesion and Disintegration in the Wehrmacht in World War II," *Public Opinion Quarterly*, Vol. 12, 1948.
49. Smelser, Neil J., and James A. Davis, *Sociology*. Englewood Cliffs, N.J.: Prentice-Hall, 1969.
50. Sussmann, Leila, "FDR and the White House Mail," *Public Opinion Quarterly*, Vol. 20, 1956.
51. Sutton, Francis X., Seymour E. Harris, Carl Kayser, and James Tobin, *The American Business Creed*. Cambridge, Mass.: Harvard University Press, 1956.
52. Williams, Harry B., "Communication and Control in Disaster: An Interpretation," paper delivered at the annual meeting of the American Sociological Society, 1957.
53. Williams, Robin M., Jr., and Brewster M. Smith, "General Characteristics of Ground Combat," in *The American Soldier, Studies in Social Psychology in World War II*, Vol. II, ed. by Samuel A. Stouffer *et al.* Princeton: Princeton University Press, 1949.

Dr. Gerald R. Miller is Professor of Communication at Michigan State University. He has published widely in the area of speech communication and in 1967 was a recipient of a Speech Association of America Golden Anniversary Award for outstanding scholarly publication. In addition to six book chapters and more than fifty articles, Dr. Miller authored *Speech Communication: A Behavioral Approach* and *Perspectives on Argumentation*.

21

SPEECH: AN APPROACH TO HUMAN COMMUNICATION

GERALD R. MILLER

AUTHORING this chapter has occasioned a mild attack of schizophrenia, an attack resulting from the curious dual status of speech as an area of scholarly inquiry. On the one hand, the study of speech has a long, dignified history firmly grounded in antiquity. Still, after scrutinizing events of the last decades, it becomes apparent that students of speech have entered the behavioral arena with halting, unsure steps. Their hesitancy has hindered both theoretical and empirical progress; it has severely restricted the original scientific contributions of speech scholars to the study of human communication. Smith nicely contrasts the intellectual plentitude of the ancients with the theoretical poverty of contemporary students of speech:

> Speech, the modern term for rhetoric, though grounded in the sound scholarship of the classical rhetorical tradition, lacks the rich theoretical development characterizing other modern behavioral sciences. Perhaps its royal heritage somehow stunted its growth. Whatever the reason, as a discipline it has proved singularly sterile in generating new research theory. . . . Except for classical rhetoric, little exists within the province of speech theory proper. [40, p. 1]

To say speech has made few recent theoretical contributions to the study of human communication does not imply that speech researchers have been hard pressed to find theories. Rather, students of speech have repeatedly violated the first portion of Shakespeare's injunction, "Neither a borrower nor a lender be." Theories developed in anthropology, engineering, linguistics, and social psychology—here let the reader consult the contents of this volume to augment the list—have provided grist for the hy-

383

pothesis-generating mill. The report of the recent New Orleans Conference on Research and Instructional Development specifically noted the catholicity of the discipline, stating "In an educational context increasingly dominated by narrow specialization, speech-communication characteristically builds on accumulated knowledge and creative thinking available in these related disciplines." [25, p. 6] Thus, whether this universality is an asset, as the conference report implies, or a liability, as Smith's remarks suggest, it must be granted that speech cannot stake sovereign claim to a body of contemporary communication theory.

Nor is the field of speech characterized by a distinctive methodology. Unlike the anthropologist, utilizing his natural-history approach, or the linguist, employing his analyses of deep and surface structure, the speech researcher has resorted to rummaging through the methodological toolboxes of other disciplines. By far the most frequently used tool has been the laboratory study, particularly the experiment. While laboratory experimentation has produced some intriguing findings, its hegemony among members of the speech community is far from an unqualified blessing, as I have emphasized elsewhere:

> The more humanistically-oriented [speech] researchers sometimes accuse their scientific colleagues of devoting considerable time and energy to verifying trivial propositions. While there are ready retorts to this accusation, it is a rare individual who, at one time or another, has not admitted that this charge comes dangerously close to the mark. This concern with trivia stems partially from a desire to predict correctly the outcomes of experiments. *For since so little is known about the complex behaviors being studied, accurate prediction depends upon selecting rather simple, self-evident notions to begin with.* [30, p. 61]

Simply stated, my argument goes as follows: since speech has not developed its own distinctive methodology, it must borrow from other fields. In its zeal to achieve scientific respectability, it has relied heavily on one of science's most revered techniques, the experiment. *But* the value of experimentation is directly proportional to the level of theoretical and empirical sophistication of a field. Since the level of sophistication in speech is relatively low, experiments often center on mundane hypotheses, for as Bakan has cogently pointed out, the phrase, "well-designed experiment," implies that "the outcomes of the experiment have been completely anticipated, and that one will not allow the experience of conducting the experiment to lead one to consider alternatives outside of the ones already thought of beforehand." [5, p. xiii] That speech researchers have sometimes succumbed to the trivial hypothesis is indisputable. In their defense, it must be added that investigators in fields with relatively distinctive methodologies are not immune to this same malady.

Some writers would disagree with my contention that speech lacks a distinctive methodology. Oliver,[34] for instance, argues that the chosen methodology of speech is essentially rhetorical. Nowhere in his essay, however, do I encounter a clear statement of how one applies rhetorical method to communication problem solving; in fact, Oliver also alludes to the extensive theoretical and methodological borrowing by speech from other disciplines. Moreover, I seriously question whether the concept of a rhetorical methodology is viable. Whereas such labels as "historiography" and "experiment" denote particular methodologies, the terms "rhetoric" and "rhetorical" refer to a distinctly human process: *a process lending itself to investigation by means of numerous methodologies.*

At this point, many readers may feel that the picture is bleak. After all, if a field is largely devoid of original theoretical contributions and lacks a distinctive approach to inquiry, why assign it a place in this volume? My answer to this plausible query is twofold: First, and least satisfactorily, the absence of original theory and distinctive methodology is not unique to the field of speech; second, and more positively, speech scholars have contributed valuable research insights to many of the problem areas of concern to students of human communication. This chapter focuses on some of these contributions.

THREE PROBLEM AREAS

My major aim is to discuss critically three problem areas that have witnessed the active involvement of speech researchers. For each area, I shall sketch some of the origins of interest in the problem, present an overview of previous research (and, coincidentally, a sample of active researchers in the field), and, perhaps most importantly, indicate some of the thorny theoretical and procedural problems to be faced by tomorrow's researchers. Obviously, spatial limitations preclude exhaustiveness. The areas chosen represent only three of many possible selections, and even the treatments accorded these three problem areas might best be characterized as intellectual vignettes. For readers seeking a reasonably complete compendium of studies conducted by speech researchers, a recent work by Thompson [41] is excellent. For readers concerned with a particular problem area, literature reviews such as those of Andersen and Clevenger,[2] Higbee,[22] McCroskey,[27] and Miller [31; 32] furnish the most complete sources of information.

From Ethos to Credibility

"There are three things which inspire confidence in the orator's own character—the three, namely, that induce us to believe a thing apart from any proof of it: good sense, good moral character, and goodwill." [3, p. 91]

With these words, Aristotle signaled the importance of *ethos,* or the speaker's ethical proof, as a determinant of persuasive effectiveness. So important was ethos, in Aristotle's opinion, that he included it with *logos,* or logical proof, and *pathos,* or emotional proof, as *the* three types of proof crucial to the potential persuader's success.

Concern with the role of ethos in the persuasive communication process has continued to the present day. While the contemporary label "credibility" has largely replaced the original Greek term, the key assumption remains the same: *Who the speaker is makes a difference in how his message is received.* For their part, speech researchers have examined numerous questions related to credibility. Does credibility make a difference in speaking effectiveness? If so, what are the dimensions of credibility which influence persuasive outcomes? What strategies give rise to positive audience perceptions of speaker credibility? Let us consider each of these questions briefly.

Several early studies, both in speech and in other disciplines, tested the relationship of the differences in perceived credibility to subsequent persuasive effectiveness. Save for minor variations, these studies share a common design: In one condition, a speaker is introduced so as to foster favorable audience perceptions of his credibility, while in the other, the introduction is structured to induce negative audience reactions. Persons in both conditions then hear the same speech, after which they report their attitudes toward the issue discussed by the speaker and their perceptions of his credibility.

Not surprisingly, most of these studies report a direct relationship between the perceived credibility of the speaker and the magnitude of his influence on the target audience. Andersen and Clevenger sum up the results in these words:

> The finding is almost universal that the ethos of the source is related in some way to the impact of the message. This generalization applies not only to political, social, religious, and economic issues but also to matters of aesthetic judgment and personal taste. Some evidence even shows that "prestige-suggestion" can affect the appetite for certain foods and can influence performances of perceptual and psychomotor tasks. (2, p. 77)

Obviously, the credibility construct is multidimensional; for instance, consider Aristotle's specification of the three possible dimensions of good sense, good moral character, and goodwill. What dimensions do audience members employ when evaluating a speaker? This question has received considerable empirical attention from speech researchers.

The advent of high-speed computers has enabled investigators to examine the credibility construct by using a technique called factor analysis. While an explanation of this technique must necessarily be oversimplified, the procedure is essentially as follows. A large sample of persons rate numerous speakers on a series of scales (see Figure 21.1 for an abbreviated example of a rating instrument). After the ratings are obtained, the items (scales) are subjected to a correlational routine known as factor analysis. This analysis groups the scales into subsets which "go together"; that is, it identifies subsets of scales that elicit similar responses from an individual. Each subset constitutes a factorial dimension of credibility. By examining the bipolar adjectives bounding a particular subset, the investigator can assign a name to that dimension of speaker credibility.

Investigations by Andersen,[1] Berlo, Lemert, and Mertz,[8] and McCroskey [26] have yielded encouragingly similar results, particularly when differences in factor-rotation methods are taken into account. One factor that consistently emerges—a factor indexed by such scales as trained-untrained, intelligent-stupid, and wise-foolish—concerns the

We are interested in determining how individuals respond to particular speakers. Below you will find a list of speakers, each followed by a series of scales. For each speaker, place a check on the interval of *each* scale that best describes your opinion of that speaker. For instance, if you thought Speaker X was *very wise,* you would mark the scale as follows:

wise : √ :___:___:___:___:___:___: foolish
      +3   +2   +1   0   −1   −2   −3

Generally, think of plus 3 and minus 3 as "very," plus 2 and minus 2 as average or unqualified, and plus 1 or minus 1 as "somewhat." If you don't know, have no opinion, or feel a particular scale is irrelevant to a speaker, check the zero, or neutral point. Work rapidly and record your first impressions. DO NOT OMIT ANY OF THE SCALES.

Gerald Miller

stupid :___:___:___:___:___:___:___: intelligent

bold :___:___:___:___:___:___:___: timid

cruel :___:___:___:___:___:___:___: kind

trained :___:___:___:___:___:___:___: untrained

honest :___:___:___:___:___:___:___: dishonest

introverted :___:___:___:___:___:___:___: extroverted

Figure 21.1   An abbreviated instrument for measuring dimensions of credibility

speaker's expertise, or competence. A second, reflected by such scales as honest-dishonest, kind-cruel, and friendly-unfriendly, centers on the speaker's safety, or trustworthiness. Finally, scales such as bold-timid, extroverted-introverted, and enthusiastic-unenthusiastic seem to encompass a dynamism, or general energy factor. Thus, *at least in terms of the operational procedures used for these studies,* the credibility construct embraces the relatively independent dimensions of competence, trustworthiness, and dynamism.

The reader will likely note the similarity of these three dimensions to the three components of ethos posited by Aristotle. Given such close conceptual harmony, the methodological sound and fury associated with large-scale research endeavors may seem superfluous: would it not be simpler to turn such questions over to a good mind in an armchair? My response to this question recognizes both the value of creative armchair thinking and the necessity of empirical verification. For while I would agree that it is essential for good minds to engage in the conceptualization process, I would also argue that their ideas must be checked empirically, that Aristotle's perceptions of the dimensions of credibility must be compared with those of the average audience member. Only then can speech researchers know how people in general respond to a speaker's attributes.

Let me stress that, as yet, little research has sought to determine if audience members respond to these dimensions independently in actual speaking situations. The reader will recall that in a preceding paragraph the phrase, "at least in terms of the operational procedures used for these studies," was given emphasis. This was done advisedly, for the circumstances involved in rating such well-known speakers as former President Kennedy on a series of seven-interval scales differ markedly from those involved in sizing up a previously unknown speaker who seeks your commitment to his cause. In the former case, prior knowledge, as well as the nature of the task itself, may facilitate discrimination between the various dimensions of credibility; in the latter, strong positive or negative perceptions on one dimension—say dynamism—may produce a generalized "halo effect" which influences judgments of the other dimensions. Certainly, future researchers should delve into this possibility.

Credibility Formation

Thus far, discussion has centered on the effects of previously established speaker credibility and on the various dimensions of the credibility construct. In many situations, however, the speaker is initially unknown; in such cases, the primary issue is one of *credibility formation,* of behaving in ways calculated to engender positive audience perceptions of the speaker. These situations are of considerable import to the speech researcher, since the most important determinant of audience response will usually be the speaker's communicative behaviors: his organizational and stylistic strategies and his manner of presentation. Invariably, we judge unknown communicators largely on grounds of the way they communicate.

Numerous studies have examined the influence of organizational and presentational factors on audience perceptions of speaker credibility. Miller and Hewgill [33] and Sereno and Hawkins [38] found that quantity of nonfluency is inversely related to audience judgments of an unknown speaker's competence and dynamism, but not his trustworthiness. Moreover, this effect was more pronounced for a repetition nonfluency than for a vocalized pause. In an early study, Flemming [18] reported a direct relationship between vocal pleasantness and 30 of the 45 desirable speaker traits considered in the study, though it should be noted that his statistical procedures were not clearly specified. A study by Bettinghaus [9] revealed that effective delivery not only enhanced the credibility of an unknown speaker, but also heightened his persuasive impact. Finally, in unpublished research, Addington found that mispronunciation does not significantly influence ratings of speaking effectiveness, but that it does affect judgments of an unknown speaker's credibility.

Two studies dealing with aspects of organization have yielded interesting outcomes. Sharp and McClung [39] reported that students exposed to a disorganized speech lowered their postcommunication ratings of the speaker's credibility, while precommunication and postcommunication ratings of students who heard an organized address remained relatively stable. Rather than varying the organizational quality of the speech, Baker [6] manipulated speaker cues denoting disorganization—for example, "Let's see now, where was I?" or "Oh, yes, I almost forgot. . . ." Those persons hearing the version containing disorganization cues did not differ in their precommunication and postcommunication credibility judgments. By contrast, auditors exposed to the speech devoid of disorganization cues reported significantly more favorable postcommunication judgments of credibility. Thus, while the presence of disorganization cues did not reduce speaker credibility, the absence of such cues bolstered the relatively unknown speaker's ethos.

This enumeration of studies may cause the reader to assume that the question of the role of communicative behavior in credibility formation has received adequate attention. Actually, the surface has only been scratched. A myriad of verbal and nonverbal behaviors undoubtedly influence perceptions of speaker credibility. Moreover, many stylistic and content strategies await investigation. And perhaps the greatest challenge lies in integrating these diffuse research findings into a coherent theory of credibility formation, for such a theoretical framework is essential to our understanding of the process.

Other problems confront the researcher interested in speaker credibility. For example, audiences often perceive particular speakers unfavorably. In such cases, the speaker derives little solace from knowing that if his credibility were high, he would be more effective. What he needs are strategies enabling him to reduce the impact of his low credibility; unfortunately, there is a paucity of research dealing with this problem. A series of studies by Greenberg and Miller [21] affords one exception. Their research revealed that if a low-credibility speaker can delay his identification until he has presented his message, his persuasiveness will be enhanced. Obviously, this strategy has limited applicability, for in most speaking situations, it is impossible for the person to remain anonymous until he has finished speaking. Beyond this finding, the literature contains few strategic guidelines for relatively low-credibility speakers.

Future research should also investigate whether credibility functions primarily as a dichotomous threshold variable or as a continuous linear factor. Stated differently, credibility may be viewed as an "either you've got it, or you haven't" phenomenon (the threshold notion) or as a "the more the merrier" phenomenon (the linear notion). The former view implies that once a certain level of credibility is achieved, further increments are unnecessary; the latter posits a direct functional relationship between level of credibility and magnitude of subsequent persuasive influence.

Finally, a potentially serious flaw in previous research on speaker credibility should be underscored. Current writers agree that credibility is in the mind of the listener, that audiences *confer* credibility on speakers. Such a conceptual stance views credibility as a relational, dyadic variable. Still, most researchers have operationalized credibility unidirectionally and monadically; they have defined credibility as a single element in the persuasive situation, specifically, as an audience evaluation of a persuasive speaker. Mertz, whose study represents a single attempt to treat credibility relationally, argues cogently for the dyadic approach:

> In contrast to the singular focus of monadic approaches to the variable, one can conceptualize credibility by stressing the *source-receiver relationship* which is implied by credibility judgments. This conceptualization asserts a source's influence potential to be a joint function of (1) receiver evaluations of the message source, and (2) receiver self-evaluations. Under this approach, a source's acceptability as a source of information and opinion in a given message situation is determined by a series of self-source comparisons on specific judgmental dimensions. To the extent that the receiver rates the source as *higher than self* on these dimensions—whatever his absolute rating—he will tend to accept the proffered influence. On the other hand, when the receiver judges the message source *lower than self* on these dimensions, he will reject the source's influence attempts. Thus, a source's "credibility" and subsequent influence potential are seen to depend, not on his absolute rating, but on his evaluative standing relative to receiver self-evaluation. [29, pp. 12–13]

While not conclusive, Mertz' results suggest the dyadic approach's predictive superiority over traditional monadic procedures. Certainly, a great deal more research employing relational measures of credibility should be conducted.

The problems raised above are not intended to minimize the previous efforts of researchers interested in speaker credibility. They do, however, emphasize that tomorrow's speech researchers must attend closely to their methods, for while superficially it may seem as if a great deal is known about the credibility variable, most of the important questions remain unanswered. Indeed, one might facetiously observe that our own scientific credibility in regard to the credibility area is not as high as one would ideally desire.

The Problem of Stage Fright

Since students of speech have traditionally expressed deep concern for pedagogical questions, it is not surprising that the problem of stage fright, or speaker anxiety, has received a large share of attention from speech researchers. This does not imply that the problem lacks theoretical significance, but even if it did, its place as the first concern of beginning speech students would ensure it a fair and extensive research hearing. The magnitude of student concern is reflected by figures compiled by Menchofer,[28] who found that 90 percent of a group of 240 college students in a beginning speech course listed their first objective as overcoming nervousness. Obviously most of the students surveyed took a speech class in order to become more confident speakers.

Perhaps the best place to begin our excursion into the realm of stage fright is with the perplexing question: What is stage fright? On the surface, the answer to this query probably seems self-evident; in fact, each reader probably has a firmly established meaning for the term. But for the researcher, the solution is not so simple. Because stage fright, or anxiety, occurs within the speaker (i.e., it is what the behavioral scientist calls an *intervening variable*), its existence must be inferred from some overt, public measure. Given the existence of several measurement alternatives, the researcher strives to select the most useful one. His problem would be less acute if the various measures were highly correlated, but as I shall indicate later, available evidence suggests that this is not the case.

Speaker self-reports constitute one index of stage fright. Persons are asked to complete a series of items reflecting feelings of confidence or fear about speaking. One such instrument is Gilkinson's [19] Personal Report of Confidence as a Speaker (PRCS). If the respondent checks numerous fear-oriented responses, the researcher infers a severe case of stage fright;

if the respondent's answers reflect confidence, his speech anxiety is assumed to be minimal.

Rather than asking the speaker himself, a measure of stage fright may be obtained from observer ratings of the speaker. This technique, used by such researchers as Clevenger and King,[14] Dickens, Gibson, and Prall,[17] and Holtzman,[23] most closely approximates the typical speaking situation, for our inferences about speakers' anxiety are usually based on observations of their overt communication behaviors.

A third alternative consists of measuring various physiological changes which occur during speaking. Changes on such measures as galvanic skin response, palmar sweat, pulse rate, and blood pressure supposedly index increased anxiety resulting from the speaking situation. For example, Dickens and Parker [16] found that the normal pulse- and blood-pressure rates in over 90 percent of their subjects were measurably affected by the speaking situation, and Bode and Brutten [11] reported that speakers who thought they were communicating to an audience, even though the audience was not actually present, showed a measurable increase in palmar sweating.

Although each of these three measures seems like a reasonable index of stage fright, they are not highly correlated. Clevenger,[13] after examining the results of 27 studies on stage fright, concludes that self-reports, observer ratings, and physiological indicants are only moderately related. While this does not mean one of the measures is more valid than the others, it does indicate that the three indices are measuring somewhat dissimilar phenomena and/or that the three types of responses are controlled by different antecedent conditions.

Several possible explanations for the low correlation of the three speech-anxiety measures can be offered. Speaker self-reports risk contamination resulting from social desirability factors. Respondents may be reluctant to choose responses indicating high anxiety, even though those responses most accurately reflect their attitudes about speaking. To the extent that this occurs, a low correlation of self-reports with observer ratings or physiological indices would be expected.

Physiological measures are difficult to interpret, for as yet the optimum level of anxiety for a speaker is unknown. To say that extremely high anxiety inhibits speech performance in no way implies that extremely low anxiety leads to effective speaking; rather, the relationship between anxiety arousal and speaking effectiveness probably is curvilinear. Thus, changes in physiological indices occurring in a speaking situation may sometimes reflect movement from low to moderate anxiety. In such cases, these changes might not be reflected by other measures of stage fright.

The preceding remarks suggest an extensive program for future research. Before the dynamics of stage fright can be grasped, it is necessary to arrive at a better understanding of what is happening in the speaking situation. In particular, basic research should aim at establishing the functional relationship between level of anxiety arousal and speaking effectiveness.

Previous researchers have also examined the influence of various individual-difference variables on susceptibility to stage fright. Chenoweth [12] found that confident speakers had continuous and varied speech experiences and speech training from early childhood through high school, while those persons who feared speaking did not. Gilkinson [20] reported that when compared with confident speakers, fearful speakers had less formal speech training and fewer speaking experiences, expressed low preference for occupations involving public speaking, and manifested greater anxiety about themselves and their social relations. After summarizing a number of studies dealing with correlates of speech fright, Thompson concludes that "stage fright is the most acute in those who have general feelings of social inadequacy and in those whose speech experiences have been limited." [41, p. 171]

While many of these correlational studies yield interesting findings, they do not explain the onset and subsequent development of stage fright. Probably, the seeds of stage fright are sown when early childhood attempts to communicate are punished by parents. Such negative responses not only cause withdrawal from interaction situations, they also contribute to a low self-concept. If the child learns to withdraw from speaking situations, it ensures that when he is trapped in circumstances requiring communication he will experience high anxiety and perform poorly. His poor performance elicits more negative feedback, and the vicious process becomes self-perpetuating.

Restoring a Speaker's Confidence

How is the process to be arrested and the speaker's confidence restored? Teachers of speech believe training and practice in speaking accomplishes this worthy objective. Still, given traditional classroom procedures, one wonders if this is really the case. In most instances, speech is still taught for credit. Where credit is involved, the grade serves as the primary reinforcer. Thus, students with a long history of speech failure are placed in a situation where they are competing for grades with confident students. The end result is almost inevitable: The confident students receive high grades, while the anxious students are assigned low marks. The net effect is to further convince the anxious student he cannot communicate orally. While admittedly speculative, the preceding argument points to future research needed on the problem of reducing speech fright.

Some innovative classroom attempts are being made to combat speaker anxiety. At Florida State University, partial success has been realized through hypnosis. At Michigan State University, researchers such as McCroskey,[7] Ralph,[7; 36] and Goss [36] have achieved excellent results by using a technique known as systematic desensitization. Students participate in a number of training sessions in which they perform relaxation exercises and are forced to cope with their speaking fears.

While some inroads have been made, the causes and cure of stage fright remain problems for future investigation. It is to the credit of speech researchers that they continue to pursue research in this area diligently, for they realize that any advances made will contribute to the objective of a society composed of happier, better-adjusted oral communicators.

The Effects of Evidence and Logic

Most writers in speech emphasize the importance of rational, reasoned discourse. Few would quarrel with the *value* of training speakers who strive to win others to their causes by formulating logical, well-reasoned arguments. But actually, how important are sound reasoning and valid supporting materials to the persuader? Does rationality make a difference in the persuasive process, and if so, under what circumstances does it play an important role? Research on evidence and logic deals with these questions.

McCroskey, the most active researcher in the evidence area, defines *evidence* as *"factual statements originating from a source other than the speaker, objects not created by the speaker, and opinions of persons other than the speaker that are offered in support of the speaker's claims."* [27, p. 170] Even though his definition specifies several types of supporting materials, McCroskey himself underscores a problem for future research when he asserts we know very little about the relative impact of each type. "Some researchers have investigated this area, but too many uncontrolled factors were in their designs to make interpretation of the results possible." [27, p. 176]

Speaker credibility, a variable discussed earlier in this chapter, seems to be the most significant determinant of the persuasive importance of evidence. Based on a series of well-conceived studies, McCroskey [27] draws the following conclusion: If the source's initial credibility is high, a speech containing evidence produces no more immediate attitude change than a no-evidence message; if his initial credibility is moderate to low, a speech using evidence results in greater immediate attitude change and more favorable postcommunication perceptions of credibility than an evidence-free communication. Thus, given high credibility, inclusion of evidence may not be worth the bother; given questionable credibility, the inclusion of evidence enhances both credibility and immediate persuasive impact.

The preceding conclusion is tempered by the fact that audiences in all of McCroskey's studies heard only a single speech by the highly credible communicator. Perhaps an attractive speaker's failure to use evidence on a single occasion will not affect his persuasiveness. But what if he engages in several communication transactions where evidence is not employed? Might not the continued omission of evidence from his speeches eventually have negative effects on both his credibility and his effectiveness? To raise this question does not detract from McCroskey's previous research; rather, it emphasizes the need for future studies examining the influence of many of these variables across a series of speeches.

A second reservation concerning the apparent unimportance of evidence to the highly credible source should also be noted. In several studies, McCroskey has obtained measures of attitude change for periods up to seven weeks after the speech. *Even though measures taken immediately following the speech reveal no differences between evidence and no-evidence messages, his delayed measures indicate that evidence enhances the amount of attitude change retained over time.* While reasons for this finding are unclear, the sleeper effect posited by Hovland and Weiss [24] may be operating: Over time, listeners may forget the message source but retain the message content. If so, the inclusion of evidence may make the content more compelling and persuasive, thus accounting for the greater magnitude of sustained change. Since persuaders often aim for long-range effects, this finding is particularly intriguing and merits future investigation.

Other variables mediate the importance of evidence in the persuasive equation. Arnold and McCroskey [4] found that when a speech is delivered effectively, evidence heightens its persuasive impact; however, when delivery is poor, inclusion of evidence does not result in greater attitude change. Prior audience knowledge of the evidence employed is also a determinant of its effectiveness. Not surprisingly, fresh, unfamiliar evidence facilitates audience attitude change, while evidence familiar to the audience appears to exert little influence.

Logic and Persuasion

Let us now turn to the literature dealing with the effects of sound logic on persuasive speaking. In general, prior research suggests that audiences are not perceptive about the logical soundness of arguments, nor do the studies indicate that logical arguments are more persuasive than other types of appeals. In fact, Ruechelle [37] found that persons were incapable of reliably classifying logical versus emotional arguments. Moreover, Paulson, [35] after summarizing the outcomes of seven experiments, concludes they provide no support for the assumption that sound logic is more effective than emotional appeals.

What does seem to enhance persuasive impact are message cues underscoring the importance of being logical. Bettinghaus [10] reported that a speech containing periodic reminders of the values of being logical produced greater attitude change than a message devoid of these reminders. His finding is consistent with social norms stressing the desirability of logical thought.

Why do individuals find it difficult to make judgments of logical validity? A substantial body of research, which I have summarized elsewhere, [31] indicates that the impact of other variables weighs heavily on the judgmental process. Thus, if a person agrees with the content of an argument, he is more likely to endorse its logical soundness. Likewise, if an argument is attributed to a highly credible source, persons err in the direction of judging logically invalid arguments as valid; if the argument is paired with a low-credibility source, the opposite error occurs. Finally, personal characteristics such as critical ability, tolerance for ambiguity, and dogmatism exert an influence on people's ability to judge logical soundness.

Several reservations about these previous studies should be underscored. First, the logical form used most frequently is the syllogism. Obviously, few speeches consist of fully formalized syllogisms. Moreover, the logical certainty of the syllogistic conclusion does not parallel the probabilistic contentions found in persuasive speeches. Thus, future researchers face the conceptual problem of developing logical tests suitable to the structure of spoken discourse. As I have previously stated:

> Obviously, oral argument is enthymematic and does not easily lend itself to adequate description by traditional systems of logic. What is needed first is a taxonomy and a set of formal relationships for describing oral argument. If such a system can be developed—and the task is admittedly horrendous —the communication scientist should have an easier time developing useful statements about the variables influencing judgments of logical soundness. [31, p. 286]

Closely related to this point is the fact that most prior studies have used written arguments. When judging written arguments, the respondent has the benefit of visual and spatial cues not present for the auditory channel. In fact, the two processes differ markedly, so much so that it is difficult to generalize extant findings to the spoken word with any degree of confidence. Certainly, tomorrow's speech researchers should systematically investigate possible differences between the two channels, for only after such research will a basis exist for comparing written and spoken arguments.

A final note of caution: Some readers may feel that in light of the research discussed above, the speech teacher's concern with sound reasoning and evidence makes little sense. Such a conclusion is not warranted, for even if persons have difficulty judging the soundness of evidence and the logical validity of arguments, the value of trying to teach these skills is not negated. After all, not many students become really good mathematicians, yet few argue against the wisdom of mathematics instruction. In fact, one of the tasks facing speech researchers is the development of better techniques for teaching reasoning skills. If decisions are to be made on rational grounds, people must be capable of assessing the relative soundness of the many competing oral messages with which they are barraged.

LOOKING FORWARD

Yesterday's research is history; tomorrow's is adventure. The preceding pages have afforded the reader a fleeting, fragmentary glimpse of the history of speech research. My concluding observations will focus on possible *future* speech research trends.

Tomorrow's speech researcher will devote considerably more energy to studying situational contexts other than the public speech. The prevailing tendency to use public-speaking situations for hypothesis testing stems largely from historical concerns of the discipline. But when one reflects on the oral-communication transactions of most persons, it becomes clear that only a small percentage of them consist of lengthy periods of uninterrupted discourse directed at sizable target audiences. In the give-and-take of dyadic dialogue, the communication flow of the small group—for that matter, the reception of messages from the mass media—one finds most of the communication action. Moreover, students of speech are increasingly sensitive to this fact, as witnessed by the recent spate of textbooks dealing with interpersonal communication. If our understanding of the factors influencing spoken discourse is to expand markedly, our research scholars must follow the lead of our textbook writers. I believe they will.

Closely related to the preceding point is the need to devote more research attention to characteristics of the message. The reader has likely observed that two of the problem areas discussed in this chapter concern the speaker, while only one deals with the message. To be sure, other problem areas might have been chosen: areas such as language intensity or message bias. But even when these areas are scrutinized, one is struck by the rather primitive state of our techniques for analyzing and describing messages. If one is hard put to describe what goes into a message, he lacks any clear basis for interpreting the outcomes resulting from it.

Future research will also focus more heavily on communication functions other than the persuasive, or compliance, function. Most of the studies cited herein deal with variables influencing persuasive communication. Perhaps our emphasis on speaking which aims at inducing others to comply with speaker demands reflects our client-centered approach to inquiry. After all, most societal institutions that have consented to finance communication research have done so because of their desire to construct more persuasive messages. Obviously, however, speech serves other vital functions: It is essential to the exchange of information, the resolution of conflict, and the development of self-concept. While existing literature provides few insights concerning the variables affecting these functions, I expect this shortcoming to be eradicated by future studies.

Finally, with all its attendant perils and promises, I look for more research which seeks to contribute solutions to immediate social, political, and economic problems. As Cronkhite [15] has contended, we need to emerge from our ivory towers on occasion and look closely at the "real world" in which we live. Such a position does not demean the importance of basic research and theory building; it merely recognizes the social responsibility of the communication scientist. Recommendation 32 of the New Orleans Conference on Research and Instructional Development captures the essence of my argument: "Although the conference participants stress the need for basic research, they encourage attempts to extend the generalizations from speech-communication research to pressing social and intercultural problems." [25, p. 36] If speech researchers can achieve this healthy blend of social concern and zest for understanding, the intellectual future of the discipline will be in good hands.

REFERENCES AND SUGGESTED READINGS

1. Andersen, Kenneth E., "An Experimental Study of the Interaction of Artistic and Nonartistic Ethos in Persuasion," doctoral dissertation, University of Wisconsin, 1961.
2. Andersen, Kenneth E., and Theodore Clevenger, Jr., "A Summary of Experimental Research in Ethos," *Speech Monographs*, Vol. 30, 1963.
3. Aristotle, *Rhetoric*, trans. by W. R. Roberts. New York: Modern Library, 1954.
4. Arnold, William E., and James C. McCroskey, "The Credibility of Reluctant Testimony," *Central States Speech Journal*, Vol. 18, 1967.
5. Bakan, David, *On Method: Toward a Reconstruction of Psychological Investigation*. San Francisco: Jossey-Bass, 1967.
6. Baker, Eldon E., "The Immediate Effects of Perceived Speaker Disorganization on Speaker Credibility, and Audience-Attitude Change in Persuasive Speaking," *Western Speech*, Vol. 29, 1965.
7. Barrick, James E., James C. McCroskey, and David C. Ralph, "The Effects of Systematic Desensitization on Speech and Test Anxiety," paper presented at Speech Association of America convention, 1968.
8. Berlo, David K., James B. Lemert, and Robert J. Mertz, "Dimensions for Evaluating the Acceptability of Message Sources," *Public Opinion Quarterly*, Vol. 33, 1970.
9. Bettinghaus, Erwin P., "The Operation of Congruity in an Oral Communication Situation," *Speech Monographs*, Vol. 28, 1961.

10. Bettinghaus, Erwin P., *Persuasive Communication*. New York: Holt, Rinehart and Winston, 1968.

11. Bode, D. L., and Eugene J. Brutten, "A Palmar Sweat Investigation of the Effect of Audience Variation upon Speech Fright," *Speech Monographs*, Vol. 30, 1963.

12. Chenoweth, Eugene C., "The Adjustment of College Freshmen to the Speaking Situation," *Quarterly Journal of Speech*, Vol. 26, 1940.

13. Clevenger, Theodore, Jr., "A Synthesis of Experimental Research in Stage Fright," *Quarterly Journal of Speech*, Vol. 45, 1959.

14. Clevenger, Theodore, Jr., and Thomas R. King, "A Factor Analysis of the Visible Symptoms of Speech Fright," *Speech Monographs*, Vol. 28, 1961.

15. Cronkhite, Gary L., "Out of the Ivory Palaces: A Proposal for Useful Research in Communication and Decision," in *Conceptual Frontiers in Speech-Communication*, ed. by R. J. Kibler and L. L. Barker. New York: Speech Association of America, 1969.

16. Dickens, Milton, and W. R. Parker, "An Experimental Study of Certain Physiological, Introspective and Rating-Scale Techniques for the Measurement of Stage Fright," *Speech Monographs*, Vol. 18, 1951.

17. Dickens, Milton, Francis Gibson, and Caleb Prall, "An Experimental Study of the Overt Manifestations of Stage Fright," *Speech Monographs*, Vol. 17, 1950.

18. Flemming, E. G., "Pleasant Voice," *Quarterly Journal of Speech*, Vol. 20, 1934.

19. Gilkinson, Howard, "Social Fears as Reported by Students in College Speech Classes," *Speech Monographs*, Vol. 9, 1942.

20. Gilkinson, Howard, "A Questionnaire Study of the Causes of Social Fears Among College Speech Students," *Speech Monographs*, Vol. 10, 1943.

21. Greenberg, Bradley S., and Gerald R. Miller, "The Effects of Low-Credible Sources on Message Acceptance," *Speech Monographs*, Vol. 33, 1966.

22. Higbee, Kenneth L., "Fifteen Years of Fear Arousal: Research on Threat Appeals: 1953–1968," *Psychological Bulletin*, Vol. 72, 1969.

23. Holtzman, Paul D., "An Experimental Study of Some Relationships Among Several Indices of Stage Fright and Personality," *Speech Monographs*, Vol. 18, 1951.

24. Hovland, Carl I., and Walter Weiss, "The Influence of Source Credibility on Communication Effectiveness," *Public Opinion Quarterly*, Vol. 15, 1951.

25. Kibler, Robert J., and Larry L. Barker, eds. *Conceptual Frontiers in Speech-Communication: Report on the New Orleans Conference on Research and Instructional Development*. New York: Speech Association of America, 1969.

26. McCroskey, James C., "Scales for the Measurement of Ethos," *Speech Monographs*, Vol. 33, 1966.

27. McCroskey, James C., "A Summary of Experimental Research on the Effects of Evidence in Persuasive Communication," *Quarterly Journal of Speech*, Vol. 55, 1969.

28. Menchofer, J. D., "Cause and Cure of Stage Fright," *Western Speech*, Vol. 3, 1938.

29. Mertz, Robert J., "Acceptance of Persuasive Influence as Related to Three Dimensions of Source Evaluation," doctoral dissertation, Michigan State University, 1966.

30. Miller, Gerald R., "Human Information Processing: Some Research Guidelines," in *Conceptual Frontiers in Speech-Communication*, ed. by Robert J. Kibler and Larry L. Barker. New York: Speech Association of America, 1969.

31. Miller, Gerald R., "Some Factors Influencing Judgments of the Logical Validity of Arguments: A Research Review," *Quarterly Journal of Speech,* Vol. 55, 1969.
32. Miller, Gerald R., "Counterattitudinal Advocacy: A Current Appraisal," in *Advances in Communication Research,* ed. by C. David Mortensen and Kenneth K. Sereno. New York: Harper & Row, in press.
33. Miller, Gerald R., and Murray A. Hewgill, "The Effect of Variations in Nonfluency on Audience Ratings of Source Credibility," *Quarterly Journal of Speech,* Vol. 50, 1964.
34. Oliver, Robert T., "Contributions of the Speech Profession to the Study of Human Communication," in *Human Communication Theory,* ed. by Frank E. X. Dance. New York: Holt, Rinehart and Winston, 1967.
35. Paulson, Stanley F., "Social Values and Experimental Research in Speech," *Western Speech,* Vol. 26, 1962.
36. Ralph, David C., and Blaine Goss, "Implementing a Systematic Desensitization Laboratory," paper presented at Speech Communication Association convention, 1970.
37. Ruechelle, Randall C., "An Experimental Study of Audience Recognition of Emotional and Intellectual Appeals in Persuasion," *Speech Monographs.* Vol. 15, 1958.
38. Sereno, Kenneth K., and Gary J. Hawkins, "The Effects of Variations in Speakers' Nonfluency upon Audience Ratings of Attitude Toward the Speech Topic and Speakers' Credibility," *Speech Monographs,* Vol. 34, 1967.
39. Sharp, Harry, Jr., and Thomas McClung, "Effects of Organization on the Speaker's Ethos," *Speech Monographs,* Vol. 33, 1966.
40. Smith, Raymond G., *Speech-Communication: Theory and Models.* New York: Harper & Row, 1970.
41. Thompson, Wayne N., *Quantitative Research in Public Address and Communication.* New York: Random House, 1967.

Dr. Herbert Blumer is Professor and Chairman of the Department of Sociology at the University of California at Berkeley. He has published widely in the area of sociology, with emphasis on symbolic interaction. Dr. Blumer has been President of the American Sociological Association and Vice-President of the International Sociological Association. His most recent book is entitled *Symbolic Interactionism: Perspective and Method.*

22

SYMBOLIC INTERACTION: AN APPROACH TO HUMAN COMMUNICATION

HERBERT BLUMER

SYMBOLIC INTERACTIONISM

SYMBOLIC interactionism rests, in the last analysis, on three simple premises. The first premise is that human beings act toward things on the basis of the meanings that the things have for them. Such things include everything that the human being may note in his world—physical objects, such as trees or chairs; other human beings, such as a mother or a store clerk; categories of human beings, such as friends or enemies; institutions, such as a school or a government; guiding ideals, such as individual independence or honesty; activities of others, such as their commands or requests; and such situations as an individual encounters in his daily life. The second premise is that the meaning of such things is derived from, or arises out of, the social interaction that one has with one's fellows. The third premise is that these meanings are handled in, and modified through, an interpretative process used by the person in dealing with the things he encounters. I wish to discuss briefly each of these three fundamental premises.

It would seem that few scholars would see anything wrong with the first premise—that human beings act toward things on the basis of the meanings which these things have for them. Yet, oddly enough, this simple view is ignored or played down in practically all of the thought and work in contemporary social science and psychological science. Meaning is either taken for granted and thus pushed aside as unimportant or it is regarded as a mere neutral link between the factors responsible for human behavior

401

and this behavior as the product of such factors. We can see this clearly in the predominant posture of psychological and social science today. Common to both of these fields is the tendency to treat human behavior as the product of various factors that play upon human beings; concern is with the behavior and with the factors regarded as producing them. Thus, psychologists turn to such factors as stimuli, attitudes, conscious or unconscious motives, various kinds of psychological inputs, perception and cognition, and various features of personal organization to account for given forms or instances of human conduct. In a similar fashion sociologists rely on such factors as social position, status demands, social roles, cultural prescriptions, norms and values, social pressures, and group affiliation to provide such explanations. In both such typical psychological and sociological explanations the meanings of things for the human beings who are acting are either bypassed or swallowed up in the factors used to account for their behavior. If one declares that the given kinds of behavior are the result of the particular factors regarded as producing them, there is no need to concern oneself with the meaning of the things toward which human beings act; one merely identifies the initiating factors and the resulting behavior. Or one may, if pressed, seek to accommodate the element of meaning by lodging it in the initiating factors or by regarding it as a neutral link intervening between the initiating factors and the behavior they are alleged to produce. In the first of these latter cases the meaning disappears by being merged into the initiating or causative factors; in the second case meaning becomes a mere transmission link that can be ignored in favor of the initiating factors.

The position of symbolic interactionism, in contrast, is that the meanings that things have for human beings are central in their own right. To ignore the meaning of the things toward which people act is seen as falsifying the behavior under study. To bypass the meaning in favor of factors alleged to produce the behavior is seen as a grievous neglect of the role of meaning in the formation of behavior.

The simple premise that human beings act toward things on the basis of the meaning of such things is much too simple in itself to differentiate symbolic interactionism—there are several other approaches that share this premise. A major line of difference between them and symbolic interactionism is set by the second premise, which refers to the source of meaning. There are two well-known traditional ways of accounting for the origin of meaning. One of them is to regard meaning as being intrinsic, as being a natural part of the objective makeup of the thing. Thus, a chair is clearly a chair in itself, a cow a cow, a cloud a cloud, a rebellion a rebellion, and so forth. Being inherent, meaning needs merely to be disengaged by observing the objective thing that has the meaning. Since the meaning emanates, so to speak, from the thing, there is no process involved in its formation; all that is necessary is to recognize it. It should be immediately apparent that this view reflects the traditional position of "realism" in philosophy—a position that is widely held and deeply entrenched in the social and psychological sciences. The other major traditional view regards "meaning" as a psychical accretion brought to the thing by the person for whom the thing has meaning. This psychical accretion is treated as being an expression of constituent elements of the person's psyche, mind, or psychological organization. The constituent elements are such things as sensations, feelings, ideas, memories, motives, and attitudes. The meaning of a thing is but the expression of the given psychological elements that are brought into play in connection with the perception of the thing; thus one seeks to explain the meaning of a thing by isolating the particular psychological elements that produce the meaning. One sees this in the somewhat ancient and classical psychological practice of analyzing the meaning of an object by identifying the sensations that enter into perception of that object; or in the contemporary practice of tracing the meaning of a thing, such as let us say prostitution, to the attitude of the person who views it. This lodging of the meaning of things in psychological elements limits the processes of the formation of meaning to whatever processes are involved in arousing and bringing together the given psychological elements that produce the meaning. Such processes are psychological in nature, and include perception, cognition, repression, transfer of feelings, and association of ideas.

Symbolic interactionism views meaning as having a different source than those held by the two dominant views just considered. It does not regard meaning as emanating from the intrinsic makeup of the thing that has meaning, nor does it see meaning as arising through a coalescence of psychological elements in the person. Instead, it sees meaning as arising in the process of interaction between people. The meaning of a thing for a person grows out of the ways in which other persons act toward the person with regard to the thing. Their actions operate to define the thing for the person. Thus, symbolic interactionism sees meanings as social products, as creations that are formed in and through the defining activities of people as they interact. This point of view gives symbolic interactionism a very distinctive position, with profound implications that will be discussed later.

The third premise mentioned above further differentiates symbolic interactionism. While the meaning of things is formed in the context of social interaction and is derived by the person from that interaction, it is a mistake to think that the use of meaning by a person is but an application of the meaning so derived. This mistake seriously mars the work of many scholars who otherwise follow the symbolic-interactionist approach. They fail to see that the use of meanings by a person in his action involves an interpretative process. In this respect they are similar to the adherents of the two dominant views spoken of above—to those who lodge meaning in the objective makeup of the thing that has it and those who regard it as an expression of psychological elements. All three are alike in viewing the use of meaning by the human being in his action as being no more than an arousing and application of already established meanings. As a result, all three fail to see that the use of meanings by the actor occurs through a *process of interpretation*. This process has two distinct steps. First, the actor indicates to himself the things toward which he is acting; he has to point out to himself the things that have meaning. The making of such indications is an internalized social process in that the actor is interacting with himself. This interaction with himself is something other than an interplay of psychological elements; it is an instance of the person engaging in a process of communication with himself. Second, by virtue of this process of communicating with himself, interpretation becomes a matter of handling meanings. The actor selects, checks, suspends, regroups, and transforms the meanings in the light of the situation in which he is placed and the direction of his action. Accordingly, interpretation should not be regarded as a mere automatic application of established meanings, but as a formative process in which meanings are used and revised as instruments for the guidance and formation of action. It is necessary to see that meanings play their part in action through a process of self-interaction.

It is not my purpose to discuss at this point the merits of the three views that lodge meaning respectively in the thing, in the psyche, and in social action, nor to elaborate on the contention that meanings are handled flexibly by the actor in the course of forming his action. Instead, I wish merely to note that by being based on these three premises, symbolic interaction is necessarily led to develop an analytical scheme of human society and human conduct that is quite distinctive. It is this scheme that I now propose to outline.

Symbolic interactionism is grounded on a number of basic ideas, or "root images," as I prefer to call them. These root images refer to and depict the nature of the following matters: human groups or societies, social interaction, objects, the human being as an actor, human action, and the interconnection of the lines of action. Taken together, these root images represent the way in which symbolic interactionism views human society and conduct. They constitute the framework of study and analysis. Let me describe briefly each of these root images.

NATURE OF HUMAN SOCIETY

Human groups are seen as consisting of human beings who are engaging in action. The action consists of the multitudinous activities that the individuals perform in their life as they encounter one another and as they deal with the succession of situations confronting them. The individuals may act singly, they may act collectively, and they may act as representatives of some organization or group. The activities belong to the acting individuals and are carried on by them always with regard to the situations in which they have to act. The import of this simple and essentially redundant characterization is that fundamentally human groups or society *exists in action* and must be seen in terms of action. This picture of human society as action must be the starting point (and the point of return) for any scheme that purports to treat and analyze human society empirically. Conceptual schemes that depict society in some other fashion can only be derivations from the complex of ongoing activity that constitutes group life. This is true of the two dominant conceptions of society in contemporary sociology—that of culture and that of social structure. Culture as a conception, whether defined as custom, tradition, norm, value, rules, or the like, is clearly derived from what people do. Similarly, social structure in any of its aspects, as represented by such terms as social position, status, role, authority, and prestige, refers to relationships derived from how people act toward one another. The life of any human society consists necessarily of an ongoing process of fitting together the activities of its members. It is this complex of ongoing activity that establishes and portrays structure or organization. A cardinal principle of symbolic interactionism is that any empirically oriented scheme of human society, however derived, must respect the fact that in the first and last instances human society consists of people engaging in action. To be empirically valid the scheme must be consistent with the nature of the social action of human beings.

Nature of Social Interaction

Group life necessarily presupposes interaction between the group members; or, put otherwise, a society consists of individuals interacting with one another. The activities of the members occur predominantly in response to one another or in relation to one another. Even though this is recognized almost universally in definitions of human society, social interaction is usually taken for granted and treated as having little, if any, significance in its own right. This is evident in typical sociological and psychological schemes—they treat social interaction as merely a medium through which the determinants of behavior pass to produce the behavior. Thus, the typical sociological scheme ascribes behavior to such factors as status position, cultural prescriptions, norms, values, sanctions, role demands, and social-system requirements; explanation in terms of such factors suffices without paying attention to the social interaction that their play necessarily presupposes. Similarly, in the typical psychological scheme such factors as motives, attitudes, hidden complexes, elements of psychological organization, and psychological processes are used to account for behavior, without any need of considering social interaction. One jumps from such causative factors to the behavior they are supposed to produce. Social interaction becomes a mere forum through which sociological or psychological determinants move to bring about given forms of human behavior. I may add that this ignoring of social interaction is not corrected by speaking of an interaction of societal elements (as when a sociologist speaks of an interaction of social roles or an interaction between the components of a social system) or an interaction of psychological elements (as when a psychologist speaks of an interaction between the attitudes held by different people). Social interaction is an interaction between actors and not between factors imputed to them.

Symbolic interactionism does not merely give a ceremonious nod to social interaction. It recognizes social interaction as being of vital importance in its own right. This importance lies in the fact that social interaction is a process that forms human conduct instead of being merely a means or a setting for the expression or release of human conduct. Put simply, human beings in interacting with one another have to take account of what the other is doing or is about to do; they are forced to direct their own conduct or handle their situations in terms of what they take into account. Thus, the activities of others enter as positive factors in the formation of their own conduct; in the face of the actions of others one may abandon an intention or purpose, revise it, check or suspend it, intensify it, or replace it. The actions of others enter to set what one plans to do, may oppose or prevent such plans, may require a revision of such plans, and may demand a very different set of such plans. One has to fit one's own line of activity in some manner to the actions of others. The actions of others have to be taken into account and cannot be regarded as merely an arena for the expression of what one is disposed to do or sets out to do.

We are indebted to George Herbert Mead for the most penetrating analysis of social interaction—an analysis that squares with the realistic account just given. Mead identifies two forms or levels of social interaction in human society. He refers to them respectively as "the conversation of gestures" and "the use of significant symbols"; I shall term them respectively "nonsymbolic interaction" and "symbolic interaction." Nonsymbolic interaction takes place when one responds directly to the action of another without interpreting that action; symbolic interaction involves interpretation of the action. Nonsymbolic interaction is most readily apparent in reflex responses, as in the case of a boxer who automatically raises his arm to parry a blow. However, if the boxer were reflectively to identify the forthcoming blow from his opponent as a feint designed to trap him, he would be engaging in symbolic interaction. In this case, he would endeavor to ascertain the meaning of the blow—that is, what the blow signifies as to his opponent's plan. In their association human beings engage plentifully in nonsymbolic interaction as they respond immediately and unreflectively to each other's bodily movements, expressions, and tones of voice, but their characteristic mode of interaction is on the symbolic level, as they seek to understand the meaning of one another's action.

Mead's analysis of symbolic interaction is highly important. He sees it as a presentation of gestures and a response to the meaning of those gestures. A gesture is any part or aspect of an ongoing action that signifies the larger act of which it is a part—for example, the shaking of a fist as an indication of a possible attack, or the declaration of war by a nation as an indication of a posture and line of action of that nation. Such things as requests, orders, commands, cues, and declarations are gestures that convey to the person who recognizes them an idea of the intention and plan of forthcoming action of the individual who presents them. The person who responds organizes his response on the basis of what the gestures mean to him; the person who presents the gestures advances them as indications or signs of what he is planning to do, as well as of what he wants the respondent to do or understand. Thus, the gesture has meaning both for the person who makes it and for the person to whom it is directed. When the gesture has the same meaning for both, the two parties understand each other. From this brief account it can be seen that the meaning of the gesture flows out along three lines (Mead's triadic nature of meaning): It signifies what the person to whom it is directed is to do; it signifies what the person who is making the gesture plans to do; and it signifies the joint action that is to arise by the articulation of the acts of both. Thus, for illustration, a robber's command to his victim to put up his hands is (1) an indication of what the victim is to do; (2) an indication of what the robber plans to do, that is, relieve the victim of his money; and (3) an indication of the joint act being formed, in this case a holdup. If there is confusion or misunderstanding along any one of these three lines of meaning, communication is ineffective, interaction is impeded, and the formation of joint action is blocked.

One additional feature should be added to round out Mead's analysis of symbolic interaction, namely, that the parties to such interaction must necessarily take each other's roles. To indicate to another what he is to do, one has to make the indication from the standpoint of that other; to order the victim to put up his hands the robber has to see this response in terms of the victim making it. Correspondingly, the victim has to see the command from the standpoint of the robber who gives the command; he has to grasp the intention and forthcoming action of the robber. Such mutual role taking is the *sine qua non* of communication and effective symbolic interaction.

The central place and importance of symbolic interaction in human group life and conduct should be apparent. A human society or group consists of people in association. Such association exists necessarily in the form of people acting toward one another and thus engaging in social interaction. Such interaction in human society is characteristically and predominantly on the symbolic level; as individuals acting individually, collectively, or as agents of some organization encounter one another they are necessarily required to take account of the actions of one another as they form their own action. They do this by a dual process of indicating to others how to act and of interpreting the indications made by others. Human group life is a vast process of such defining to others what to do and of interpreting their definitions; through this process people come to fit their activities to one another and to form their own individual conduct. Both such joint activity and individual conduct are formed *in* and *through* this ongoing process; they are not mere expressions or products of what people bring to their interaction or of conditions that are antecedent to their interaction. The failure to accommodate to this vital point constitutes the fundamental deficiency of schemes that seek to account for human society in terms of social organization or psychological factors, or of any combination of the two. By virtue of symbolic interaction, human group life is necessarily a formative process and not a mere arena for the expression of preexisting factors.

Nature of Objects

The position of symbolic interactionism is that the "worlds" that exist for human beings and for their groups are composed of "objects" and that these objects are the product of symbolic interaction. An object is anything that can be indicated, anything that is pointed to or referred to—a cloud, a book, a legislature, a banker, a religious doctrine, a ghost, and so forth. For purposes of convenience one can classify objects in three categories: (1) physical objects, such as chairs, trees, or bicycles; (2) social objects, such as students, priests, a president, a mother, or a friend; and (3) abstract objects, such as moral principles, philosophical doctrines, or ideas such as justice, exploitation, or compassion. I repeat that an object is anything that can be indicated or referred to. The nature of an object —of any and every object—consists of the meaning that it has for the person for whom it is an object. This meaning sets the way in which he sees the object, the way in which he is prepared to act toward it, and the way in which he is ready to talk about it. An object may have a different meaning for different individuals: A tree will be a different object to a botanist, a lumberman, a poet, and a home gardener; the President of the United States can be a very different object to a devoted member of his political party than to a member of the opposition; the members of an ethnic group may be seen as a different kind of object by members of other groups. The meaning of objects for a person arises fundamentally out of the way they are defined to him by others with whom he interacts. Thus, we come to learn through the indications of others that a chair is a chair, that doctors are a certain kind of professional, that the United States Constitution is a given kind of legal document, and so forth. Out of a process of mutual indications, common objects emerge—objects that have the same meaning for a given set of people and are seen in the same manner by them.

Several noteworthy consequences follow from the foregoing discussion of objects. First, it gives us a different picture of the environment or milieu of human beings. From their standpoint the environment consists *only* of the objects that the given human beings recognize and know. The nature of this environment is set by the meaning that the objects composing it have for those human beings. Individuals, also groups, occupying or living in the same spatial location may have, accordingly, very different environments; as we say, people may be living side by side yet be living in different worlds. Indeed, the term *world* is more suitable than the word *environment* to designate the setting, the surroundings, and the texture of things that confront them. It is the world of their objects with which people have to deal and toward which they develop their actions. It follows that in order to understand the action of people it is necessary to identify their world of objects—an important point that will be elaborated later.

Second, objects (in the sense of their meaning) must be seen as social creations—as being formed in and arising out of the process of definition and interpretation as this process takes place in the interaction of people. The meaning of anything and everything has to be formed, learned, and transmitted through a process of indication—a process that is necessarily a social process. Human group life on the level of symbolic interaction is a vast process in which people are forming, sustaining, and transforming the objects of their world as they come to give meaning to objects. Objects have no fixed status except as their meaning is sustained through indications and definitions that people make of the objects. Nothing is more apparent than that objects in all categories can undergo change in their meaning. A star in the sky is a very different object to a modern astrophysicist than it was to a sheepherder of biblical times; marriage was a different object to later Romans than to earlier Romans; the president of a nation who fails to act successfully through critical times may become a very different object to the citizens of his land. In short, from the standpoint of symbolic interactionism human group life is a process in which objects are being created, affirmed, transformed, and cast aside. The life and action of people necessarily change in line with the changes taking place in their world of objects.

THE HUMAN BEING AS AN ACTING ORGANISM

Symbolic interactionism recognizes that human beings must have a makeup that fits the nature of social interaction. The human being is seen not only as an organism that responds to others on the nonsymbolic level but as one that makes indications to others and interprets their indications. He can do this, as Mead has shown so emphatically, only by virtue of possessing a "self." Nothing esoteric is meant by this expression. It means merely that a human being can be an object of his own action. Thus, he can recognize himself, for instance, as being a man, young in age, a student, in debt, trying to become a doctor, coming from an undistinguished family, and so forth. In all such instances he is an object to himself; and he acts toward himself and guides himself in his actions toward others on the basis of the kind of object he is to himself. This notion of oneself as an object fits into the earlier discussion of objects. Like other objects, the self-object emerges from the process of social interaction in which other people are defining a person to himself. Mead has traced the way in which this occurs in his discussion of role taking. He points out that in order to become an object to himself a person has to see himself from the outside. One can do this only by placing himself in the position of others and viewing himself or acting toward himself from that position. The roles the person takes range from that of discrete individuals (the "play stage"), through that of discrete organized groups (the "game stage") to that of the abstract community (the "generalized other"). In taking such roles the person is in a position to address or approach himself—as in the case of a young girl who in "playing mother" talks to herself as her mother would do, or in the case of a young priest who sees himself through the eyes of the priesthood. We form our objects of ourselves through such a process of role taking. It follows that we see ourselves through the way in which others see or define us—or, more precisely, we see ourselves by taking one of the three types of roles of others that have been mentioned. That one forms an object of himself through the ways in which others define one to himself is recognized fairly well in the literature today, so despite the great significance of this point, I shall not comment on it further.

There is an even more important matter that stems from the fact that the human being has a self, namely that this enables him to interact with himself. This interaction is not in the form of interaction between two or more parts of a psychological system, as between needs, or between emotions, or between ideas, or between the id and the ego in the Freudian scheme. Instead, the interaction is social—a form of communication, with the person addressing himself as a person and responding thereto. We can clearly recognize such interaction in ourselves as each of us notes that he is angry with himself, or that he has to spur himself on in his tasks, or that he reminds himself to do this or that, or that he is talking to himself in working out some plan of action. As such instances suggest, self-interaction exists fundamentally as a process of making indications to oneself. This process is in play continuously during one's waking life, as one notes and considers one or another matter, or observes this or that happening. Indeed, for the human being to be conscious or aware of anything is equivalent to his indicating the thing to himself—he is identifying it as a given kind of object and considering its relevance or importance to his line of action. One's waking life consists of a series of such indications that the person is making to himself, indications that he uses to direct his action.

We have, then, a picture of the human being as an organism that interacts with itself through a social process of making indications to itself. This is a radically different view of the human being from that which dominates contemporary social and psychological science. The dominant prevailing view sees the human being as a complex organism whose behavior is a response to factors playing on the organization of the organism. Schools of thought in the social and psychological sciences differ enormously in which of such factors they regard as significant, as is shown in such a diverse array as stimuli, organic drives, need-dispositions, conscious motives, unconscious motives, emotions, attitudes, ideas, cultural prescriptions, norms, values, status demands, social roles, reference-group affiliations, and institutional pressures. Schools of thought differ also in how they view the organization of the human being, whether as a kind of biological organization, a kind of psychological organization, or a kind of imported societal organization incorporated from the social structure of one's group. Nevertheless, these schools of thought are alike in seeing the human being as a responding organism, with its behavior being a product of the factors playing on its organization or an expression of the interplay of parts of its organization. Under this widely shared view the human being is "social" only in the sense either of being a member of social species, or of responding to others (social stimuli), or of having incorporated within it the organization of his group.

The view of the human being held in symbolic interactionism is fundamentally different. The human being is seen as "social" in a much more profound sense—in the sense of an organism that engages in social interaction with itself by making indications to itself and responding to such indications. By virtue of engaging in self-interaction the human being stands in a markedly different relation to his environment than is presupposed by the widespread conventional view described above. Instead of being regarded as merely an organism that responds to the play of factors on or through it, the human being is seen as an organism that has to deal with what it notes. It meets what it so notes by engaging in a process of self-indication in which it makes an object of what it notes, gives it a meaning, and uses the meaning as the basis for directing its action. Its behavior with regard to what it notes is not a response called forth by the presentation of what it notes but instead is an action that arises out of the interpretation made through the process of self-indication. In this sense, the human being who is engaging in self-interaction is not a mere responding organism but an acting organism—an organism that has to mold a line of action on the basis of what it takes into account instead of merely releasing a response to the play of some factor on its organization.

Nature of Human Action

The capacity of the human being to make indications to himself gives a distinctive character to human action. It means that the human individual confronts a world that he must interpret in order to act instead of an environment to which he responds because of his organization. He has to cope with the situations in which he is called on to act, ascertaining the meaning of the actions of others and mapping out his own line of action in the light of such interpretation. He has to construct and guide his action instead of merely releasing it in response to factors playing on him or operating through him. He may do a miserable job in constructing his action, but he has to construct it.

This view of the human being directing his action by making indications to himself stands sharply in contrast to the view of human action that dominates current psychological and social science. This dominant view, as already stated, ascribes human action to an initiating factor or a combination of such factors as motives, attitudes, need-dispositions, unconscious complexes, stimuli configurations, status demands, role requirements, and situational demands. To link the action to one or more of such initiating agents is regarded as fulfilling the scientific task. Yet, such an approach ignores the process of self-interaction through which the individual handles his world and constructs his action. The door is closed to the vital process of interpretation in which the individual notes and assesses what is presented to him and through which he maps out lines of overt behavior prior to their execution.

Fundamentally, action on the part of a human being consists of taking account of various things that he notes and forging a line of conduct on the basis of how he interprets them. The things taken into account cover such matters as his wishes and wants, his objectives, the available means for their achievement, the actions and anticipated actions of others, his image of himself, and the likely result of a given line of action. His conduct is formed and guided through such a process of indication and interpretation. In this process, given lines of action may be started or stopped, they may be abandoned or postponed, they may be confined to mere planning or to an inner life of reverie, or if initiated, they may be transformed. My purpose is not to analyze this process but to call attention to its presence and operation in the formation of human action. We must recognize that the activity of human beings consists of meeting a flow of situations in which they have to act and that their action is built on the basis of what they note, how they assess and interpret what they note, and what kind of projected lines of action they map out. This process is not caught by ascribing action to some kind of factor (for example, motives, need-dispositions, role requirements, social expectations, or social rules) that is thought to initiate the action and propel it to its conclusion; such a factor, or some expression of it, is a matter the human actor takes into account in mapping his line of action. The initiating factor does not embrace or explain how it and other matters are taken into account in the situation that calls for action. One has to get inside of the defining process of the actor in order to understand his action.

This view of human action applies equally well to joint or collective action in which numbers of individuals are implicated. Joint or collective action constitutes the domain of sociological concern, as exemplified in the behavior of groups, institutions, organizations, and social classes. Such instances of societal behavior, whatever they may be, consist of individuals fitting their lines of action to one another. It is both proper and possible to view and study such behavior in its joint or collective character instead of in its individual components. Such joint behavior does not lose its character of being constructed through an interpretative process in meeting the situations in which the collectivity is called on to act. Whether the collectivity be an army engaged in a campaign, a corporation seeking to expand its operations, or a nation trying to correct an unfavorable balance of trade, it needs to construct its action through an interpretation of what is happening in its area of operation. The interpretative process takes place by participants making indications to one another, not merely each to himself. Joint or collective action is an outcome of such a process of interpretative interaction.

Interlinkage of Action

As stated earlier, human group life consists of, and exists in, the fitting of lines of action to one another by the members of the group. Such articulation of lines of action gives rise to and constitutes "joint action"—a societal organization of conduct of different acts by diverse participants. A joint action, while made up of diverse component acts, is different from any one of them and from their mere aggregation. The joint action has a distinctive character in its own right, a character that lies in the articulation or linkage as apart from what may be articulated or linked. Thus, the joint action may be identified as such and may be spoken of and handled without having to break it down into the separate acts that comprise it. This is what we do when we speak of such things as marriage, a trading transaction, war, a parliamentary discussion, or a church service. Similarly, we can speak of the collectivity that engages in joint action without having to identify the individual members of that collectivity, as we do in speaking of a family, a business corporation, a church, a university, or a nation. It is evident that the domain of the social scientist is constituted precisely by the study of joint action and of the collectivities that engage in joint action.

In dealing with collectivities and with joint action, one can easily be trapped in an erroneous position by failing to recognize that the joint action of the collectivity is an interlinkage of the separate acts of the participants. This failure leads one to overlook the fact that a joint action always has to undergo a process of formation; even though it may be a well-established and repetitive form of social action, each instance of it has to be formed anew. Further, this career of formation through which it comes into being necessarily takes place through the dual process of designation and interpretation that was discussed above. The participants still have to guide their respective acts for forming and using meanings.

With these remarks as a background I wish to make three observations on the implications of the interlinkage that constitutes joint action. I wish to consider first those instances of joint action that are repetitive and stable. The preponderant portion of social action in a human society, particularly in a settled society, exists in the form of recurrent patterns of joint action. In most situations in which people act toward one another they have in advance a firm understanding of how to act and of how other people will act. They share common and preestablished meanings of what is expected in the action of the participants, and each participant is able to guide his own behavior accordingly. Instances of repetitive and preestablished forms of joint action are so frequent that it is easy to understand why scholars have viewed them as the essence or natural form of human group life. Such a view is especially apparent in the concepts of "culture" and "social order" that are so dominant in social-science literature. Most sociological schemes rest on the belief that a human society exists in the form of an established order of living, with that order resolvable into adherence to sets of rules, norms, values, and sanctions that specify to people how they are to act in their different situations.

Several comments are in order with regard to this neat scheme. First, it is just not true that the full expanse of life in a human society, in any human society, is but an expression of preestablished forms of joint action. New situations are constantly arising within the scope of group life that are problematic and for which existing rules are inadequate. I have never heard of any society that was free of problems nor any society in which members did not have to engage in discussion to work out ways of action. Such areas of unprescribed conduct are just as indigenous and recurrent in human group life as are those areas covered by preestablished and faithfully followed prescriptions of joint action. Second, we have to recognize that even in the case of preestablished and repetitive joint action each instance of such joint action has to be formed anew. The participants still have to build up their lines of action and fit them to one another through the dual process of designation and interpretation. They do this in the case of repetitive joint action, of course, by using the same recurrent and constant meanings. If we recognize this, we are forced to realize that the play and fate of meanings are what is important, not the joint action in its established form. Repetitive and stable joint action is just as much a result of an interpretative process as is a new form of joint action that is being developed for the first time. This is not an idle or pedantic point; the meanings that underlie established and recurrent joint action are themselves subject to pressure as well as to reinforcement, to incipient dissatisfaction as well as to indifference; they may be challenged as well as affirmed, allowed to slip along without concern as well as subjected to infusions of new vigor. Behind the facade of the objectively perceived joint action the set of meanings that sustains that joint action has a life that the social scientists can ill afford to ignore. A gratuitous acceptance of the concepts of norms, values, social rules, and the like should not blind the social scientist to the fact that any one of them is subtended by a process of social interaction—a process that is necessary not only for their change but equally for their retention in a fixed form. It is the social process in group life that creates and upholds the rules, not the rules that create and uphold group life.

The second observation on the interlinkage that constitutes joint action refers to the extended connection of actions that make up much of human group life. We are familiar with these large, complex networks of action involving an interlinkage and interdependency of diverse actions of diverse people—as in the division of labor extending from the growing of grain by the farmer to an eventual sale of bread in a store, or in the elaborate chain extending from the arrest of a suspect to his eventual release from a penitentiary. These networks with their regularized participation of diverse people by diverse action at diverse points yield a picture of institutions that have been appropriately a major concern of sociologists. They also give substance to the idea that human group life has the character of a system. In seeing such a large complex of diversified activities, all hanging together in a regularized operation, and in seeing the complementary organization of participants in well-knit interdependent relationships, it is easy to understand why so many scholars view such networks or institutions as self-operating entities, following their own dynamics and not requiring that attention be given to the participants within the network. Most of the sociological analysis of institutions and social organization adhere to this view. Such adherence, in my judgment, is a serious mistake. One should recognize what is true, namely, that the diverse array of participants occupying different points in the network engage in their actions at those points on the basis of using given sets of meanings. A network or an institution does not function automatically because of some inner dynamics or system requirements; it functions because people at different points do something, and what they do is a result of how they define the situation in which they are called on to act. A limited appreciation of this point is reflected today in some of the work on decision making, but on the whole, the point is grossly ignored. It is necessary to recognize that the sets of meanings that lead participants to act as they do at their stationed points in the network have their own setting in a localized process of social interaction—and that these meanings are formed, sustained, weakened, strengthened, or transformed, as the case may be, through a socially defining process. Both the functioning and the fate of institutions are set by this process of interpretation as it takes place among the diverse sets of participants.

A third important observation needs to be made, namely, that any instance of joint action, whether newly formed or long established, has necessarily arisen out of a background of previous actions of the participants. A new kind of joint action never comes into existence apart from such a background. The participants involved in the formation of the new joint action always bring to that formation the world of objects, the sets of meanings, and the schemes of interpretation that they already possess. Thus, the new form of joint action always emerges out of and is connected with a context of previous joint action. It cannot be understood apart from that context; one has to bring into one's consideration this linkage with preceding forms of joint action. One is on treacherous and empirically invalid ground if he thinks that any given form of joint action can be sliced off from its historical linkage, as if its makeup and character arose out of the air through spontaneous generation instead of growing out of what went before. One cannot understand the new form without incorporating knowledge of this continuity into one's analysis of the new form. Joint action not only represents a horizontal linkage, so to speak, of the activities of the participants, but also a vertical linkage with previous joint action.

Summary Remarks

The general perspective of symbolic interactionism should be clear from our brief sketch of its root images. This approach sees a human society as people engaged in living. Such living is a process of ongoing activity in which participants are developing lines of action in the multitudinous situations they encounter. They are caught up in a vast process of interaction in which they have to fit their developing actions to one another. This process of interaction consists in making indications to others of what to do and in interpreting the indications made by others. They live in worlds of objects and are guided in their orientation and action by the meaning of these objects. Their objects, including objects of themselves, are formed, sustained, weakened, and transformed in their interaction with one another. This general process should be seen, of course, in the differentiated character which it necessarily has by virtue of the fact that people cluster in different groups, belong to different associations, and occupy different positions. They accordingly approach each other differently, live in different worlds, and guide themselves by different sets of meanings. Nevertheless, whether one is dealing with a family, a boys' gang, an industrial corporation, or a political party, one must see the activities of the collectivity as being formed through a process of designation and interpretation.

SUGGESTED READINGS

1. Blumer, Herbert, "Attitudes and the Social Act," *Social Problems,* Vol. 3, October, 1955.
2. Blumer, Herbert, "Society as Symbolic Interaction," in *Human Behavior and Social Processes,* ed. by Arnold Rose. Boston: Houghton Mifflin, 1962.
3. Blumer, Herbert, "Sociological Implications of the Thought of George Herbert Mead," *American Journal of Sociology,* Vol. 71, March, 1966.
4. Blumer, Herbert, *Symbolic Interactionism: Perspective and Method.* Englewood Cliffs, N.J.: Prentice-Hall, 1969.
5. Bonner, Hubert, *Social Psychology.* New York: American Book, 1953.
6. Cooley, Charles H., *Human Nature and Social Order.* New York: Scribner, 1902.
7. Coutu, Walter, *Emergent Human Behavior: A Symbolic Field Interpretation.* New York: Knopf, 1949.
8. Dewey, John, "Communication, Individual and Society," in *Symbolic Interaction,* ed. by J. G. Manis and B. N. Meltzer. Boston: Allyn and Bacon, 1967.
9. Dewey, John, *Experience and Nature.* New York: Dover, 1958.
10. Dewey, John, *Human Nature and Conduct.* New York: Holt, Rinehart and Winston, 1950.
11. Faris, Robert E. L., *Social Psychology.* New York: Ronald Press, 1952.
12. Farberman, Harvey A., and Gregory Stone, *Social Psychology Through Symbolic Interaction.* Waltham, Mass.: Ginn-Blaisdell, 1970.

418   *Approaches to Human Communication*

13. Gerth, Hans, and C. Wright Mills, *Character and Social Structure*. New York: Harcourt, Brace, 1953.
14. Goffman, Erving, *Behavior in Public Places*. New York: Free Press, 1963.
15. Goffman, Erving, *Encounters*. Indianapolis: Bobbs-Merrill, 1961.
16. Goffman, Erving, *Interaction Ritual*. Garden City, N.Y.: Doubleday, 1967.
17. Goffman, Erving, "The Nature of Deference and Demeanor," *American Anthropologist*, Vol. 58, June, 1956.
18. Goffman, Erving, *The Presentation of Self in Everyday Life*. Garden City, N.Y.: Doubleday, 1959.
19. Goffman, Erving, *Stigma*. Englewood Cliffs, N.J.: Prentice-Hall, 1963.
20. Goffman, Erving, *Strategic Interaction*. Philadelphia: University of Pennsylvania Press, 1969.
21. Homans, George C., "Social Behavior as Exchange," *American Journal of Sociology*, May, 1958.
22. House, Floyd Nelson, *The Development of Sociology*. New York: McGraw-Hill, 1936.
23. Karpf, Fay Berger, *American Social Psychology*. New York: McGraw-Hill, 1932.
24. Krueger, E. T., and Walter C. Reckless, *Social Psychology*. London: Longmans, 1930.
25. Kuhn, Manford H., "Major Trends in Symbolic Interaction in the Past Twenty-Five Years," *The Sociological Quarterly*, Vol. 5, Winter, 1964.
26. Kuhn, Manford H., "The Reference Group Considered," *The Sociological Quarterly*, Vol. 5, Winter, 1964.
27. Lindesmith, Alfred R., and Anselm L. Strauss, eds., *Readings in Social Psychology*. New York: Holt, Rinehart and Winston, 1962.
28. Manis, Jerome G., and Bernard N. Meltzer, *Symbolic Interaction: A Reader in Social Psychology*. Boston: Allyn and Bacon, 1967.
29. Martindale, Don, *The Nature and Types of Sociological Theory*. Boston: Houghton Mifflin, 1960.
30. Mead, George Herbert, *Mind, Self and Society*, ed. by Charles W. Morris. Chicago: University of Chicago Press, 1934.
31. Mead, George Herbert, *The Philosophy of the Act*, ed. by Charles W. Morris. Chicago: University of Chicago Press, 1938.
32. Rose, Arnold M., ed., *Human Behavior and Social Processes*. Boston: Houghton Mifflin, 1962.
33. Secord, Paul F., and Carl W. Backman, *Social Psychology*. New York: McGraw-Hill, 1964.
34. Shibutani, Tamotsu, *Human Behavior and Collective Behavior: Papers in Honor of Herbert Blumer*. Englewood Cliffs, N.J.: Prentice-Hall, 1970.
35. Shibutani, Tamotsu, *Society and Personality: An Interactionist's Approach to Social Psychology*. Englewood Cliffs, N.J.: Prentice-Hall, 1961.
36. Stone, Gregory, "Appearance and Self," *Human Behavior and Social Processes*, ed. by Arnold M. Rose. Boston: Houghton Mifflin, 1962.
37. Stone, Gregory, and Edward Gross, "Embarrassment and the Analysis of Role Requirements," *American Journal of Sociology*, Vol. 70, July, 1964.
38. Strauss, Anselm, and Barney G. Glaser, "Awareness Contexts and Social Interaction," *American Sociological Review*, Vol. 29, October, 1964.
39. Strauss, Anselm, ed., *George Herbert Mead: On Social Psychology*. Chicago: University of Chicago Press, 1964.

40. Stryker, Sheldon, "Symbolic Interaction as an Approach to Family Research," *Marriage and Family Living,* Vol. 21, May, 1959.

41. Turner, Ralph H., "Role-Taking: Process Versus Conformity," in *Human Behavior and Social Process,* ed. by Arnold M. Rose. Boston: Houghton Mifflin, 1962.

42. Turner, Ralph H., "The Self-Conception in Social Interaction," in *The Self in Social Interaction,* ed. by Chard Gordon and K. J. Gergen. New York: Wiley, 1968.

Dr. Daniel E. Costello is Assistant Professor of Communication at the University of Iowa. His research interest focuses upon the relationship between communication theory and human action. He has contributed articles and papers on this subject, including "Communication Patterns in Family Systems" in *The Journal of the Nursing Clinics of North America*. Dr. Costello also edited a volume entitled *Communication: On Being Human*.

23

THERAPEUTIC TRANSACTIONS: AN APPROACH TO HUMAN COMMUNICATION

DANIEL E. COSTELLO

Communication is a universal function of man that is not tied to any particular place, time, or context; and basically communication which produces a therapeutic effect in no way differs from what happens in ordinary exchanges. Therapeutic communication, therefore, is not confined to an appointed hour in the doctor's office. On the contrary, it occurs almost anywhere—on the playfield, in battle, in the ward, at home, or at work. Neither is it bound to the use of certain props such as couch or chair, nor does it run off according to a special formula. Generally therapeutic communication involves more than just the therapist and the patient. A child can be therapeutic for the mother and a boss can be therapeutic for his employee; therapy is done all day long by many people who do not know that they act as therapists, and many people benefit from such experiences without knowing it. Therapeutic communication is not a method invented by physicians to combat illness; it is simply something that occurs spontaneously everywhere in daily life, and the physician is challenged to make these naturally occurring events happen more frequently. (53, p. 30)

T HIS STATEMENT by Jurgen Ruesch represents a challenge; it suggests that our present-day social ills are the responsibility of every one of us. In order to overcome everyday stress, to get along with other people, to adjust to the unalterable and to change the alterable, man must be able to understand and use his ability to participate in communication.

At times, this process of communication is called therapy, at other times education; some call it counseling, others simply friendship. There are people such as ministers, social workers, teachers, counselors, and psychiatrists who have undertaken the challenge to help others improve their ability to function alone, with other persons, and in groups. The difference between therapeutic communication and the kind that is carried on between people under ordinary circumstances is that in therapeutic situations the intention of one or more of the participants is clearly directed at bringing about a change in relationships and manner of communication. In many such situations, the persons in charge of bringing about a change are licensed practitioners, called therapists; the others are called patients. The term *patient,* however, may refer to an individual or to larger systems such as a family, group, or community. In any case, the therapist concerns himself with constructing communication situations for the patient that will bring about more beneficial social relations. For the most part, the procedures used to initiate such changes differ very little from the methods of communication used in daily life.

Matching

Basically, the role of the therapist is to match the individual with the social systems in which he participates. Lennard and Bernstein [38] describe a therapist as a professional who interacts with other persons designated as patients or clients, for the purposes of changing them in some beneficial way. Through a communicational exchange, the person is helped to accept the physical, psychological, and social constraints of his existence; he learns not to deplore what he is or what he has but to make the best of it.

Most therapists are trained physicians, yet beyond this point the similarity between the duties of a therapist and of a doctor of medicine becomes slight. The physician treats illnesses of the body, while the therapist works with illnesses of the mind. For many years the two types of illnesses were thought to be very similar in nature and their differences went unrecognized. As Szasz [63] has argued, many of the analogies made between mental and physical illness are intellectually untenable. Mental stress or illness is affected by one's social environment and often reflects an individual's failure to adapt to or to change that environment. Few physical illnesses, on the other hand, can be directly attributed to such social environments.

The therapist's mode of treatment has little resemblance to that of the physician. In the treatment of patients, the therapist has to rely on his ability to communicate with his patient to determine the nature of the disorder. In a one-to-one situation the therapist questions his patient, listens to him, probes into his patient's feelings and general background, and helps the patient develop some communication behavior that will help him function more effectively. In order for a patient to find a better life, the therapist must be able to construct a communication situation that will allow the patient to develop an understanding of his own problems.

Only through the patient's communication behavior is the therapist able to analyze and diagnose the patient's ills. Unlike the general physician, who deals with a patient's physical symptoms, the therapist must deal with "symbolic" symptoms. In any case, the desired outcome of the treatment is change. The tactic of most therapists is to change the patient's attitudes or behavior, so that the patient can be better able to adjust to society and thereby find a fulfilling and meaningful life.

The Individual and Society

Traditionally, the therapy process is directed toward changing the patient rather than changing his environment. The mere fact that the person selects himself or is selected for treatment places the major impetus for change on him. This mode of treatment usually helps preserve the status quo, since the patient will probably not challenge his environment, but simply become more accepting of it.,

Pinel's creation of the mental-hospital model and Freud's invention of two-person psychotherapy have been the major conceptual frameworks guiding the efforts of therapists. The primary question to which therapists have sought an answer is why some people perceive and react to certain stresses as though they were severe, while others experience them as mild. In the past, therapists seeking this answer focused upon the misery a patient created for himself or his internal system. However, with more and more people seeking out the services of therapists, many therapists are scrapping their individual-defect model and are looking to the patient's environment and his interaction with it for the causes of human suffering.

Thus one of the major conceptual shifts is in considering behavior in terms of how man creates his environment. The point is that the most important environmental stresses are those imposed upon man by other men or by man-created social institutions. Thus the role of the therapist is to help an individual understand the stresses of his environment and, if need be, to find ways of changing not only himself but perhaps also the environment.

In this sense, the therapist faces the question of whether to reinforce the status quo or facilitate change. In part this issue involves the recognition by therapists that their own beliefs about what is good for society affect the nature of the problem which they define for their patient.

Increasingly, therapists are being asked to help change some of society's institutions. One to which a great deal of attention is being given is the family. Therapists now recognize, for example, that members of a family, at times, communicate with each other in a paradoxical manner.[30] They know that a family member, faced with contradictory messages, and in no position to comment or correct, may be under great stress. An example would be a mother who tells her daughter to go out and have a good time (first message), but indicates she doesn't know what she will do if she becomes ill while the daughter is away (second message). This manner of communication over a period of time could lead to difficulties for the daughter and other members of the family. If called upon, the therapist must decide whether to work with the daughter and help her adapt to the family environment or work with the total family and attempt to change the environment. On a slightly different level, the therapist who works in a ghetto must decide whether to help a few individuals adapt to the environment or attempt to alter those social institutions which degrade the environment in which the individuals live.

The major problem may be how man thinks about organizing himself with other men, and how well our institutions serve those needs. The ways individuals communicate with each other within a system determine the nature and amount of stress generated. For example, a husband may openly abuse or reject his wife, or a child may single out one of his parents as a target for harassment. However, an individual may not always know the source of his stress; a wife may reject her husband's physical display of attention while verbalizing how much she loves him.

Some stresses which impact the lives of individuals come about indirectly because we are part of social institutions. An example is the selection of young men for the military. Other stresses stem from our direct communication with family members, friends, or fellow workers. A therapist is interested mainly in the relationship between the individual and his social environment and how this relationship is formed, maintained, and changed in and through communication.

Labeling

When therapists become part of a therapy situation, their own communication behavior becomes crucial to the eventual outcome. The phenomenon of "labeling" is one example. The manner in which a therapist goes about labeling problems is an issue that has been discussed at length by professionals such as Szasz,[61] Leifer,[37] and Menninger.[41] While labeling is necessary for man to make sense out of a diverse and complex world, it is important to realize that man's labels can be functional or dysfunctional, depending upon how they are used.

The therapist's decisions are crucial, since his labeling may have very serious ramifications in regard to man's ability to communicate with others. For instance, when an individual or group is labeled as deviant, the community or society is encouraged to think of them as dangerous or inferior, and therapists point out that the use of restrictive labels such as "deviant," "delinquent," or "sick" inhibits the expression of autonomous behavior on the part of people. Even though labels such as "paranoia," "alcoholism," "schizophrenia," or "psychopathy" do not refer to a precise set of behavior symptoms or treatments, thousands of people each year are being fitted into categories based on the assumption that these labels refer to distinctive and agreed-upon characteristics.

The danger in this assumption manifests itself when individuals or groups, because they are not quite in the mainstream of society, are treated as if they were dangerous or defective. A person's behavior or so-called "symptoms" usually arise from a need to influence what is perceived as a troublesome environment. In this sense, symptoms are usually indirect, "symbolic" attempts to communicate.

In a rapidly changing society the question of what the criteria of normality ought to be and who should determine those criteria seems crucial. At present, mental health professionals are not obliged to reveal their own criteria. Most lay people probably assume that therapists make their judgments based on medical "fact" rather than what they believe to be best for society, but it is important to recognize that a therapist cannot avoid working from his perception of what is best for others. Through the relationship developed between the therapist and patient, the patient cannot avoid being influenced by the values of his therapist. The values a professional brings to bear on his practice have always been a highly controversial issue.[21; 2]

CONTEXTS OF THERAPY

Individual Therapy

As we have already discussed, the major mode of treatment in American therapy is a one-to-one situation. To a certain extent, this form of treatment denies the role of the family and community in producing and perpetuating a person's disturbance. The person may lose any opportunity to interact with his environment in a manner that might produce beneficial change. However, with the advent of the sociotherapist, other types of therapeutic systems have been recognized.

Family Therapy

One of the new modes of therapy developed within the last ten years has been the treatment of families.[44; 28] Family therapy represents the first attempt at a systems-oriented way of treatment. It enables family members to learn how they are presently communicating with one another and how communication can be used in working out their problems. For some families, it is the first time individual family members have attempted to listen to someone within their family without withdrawing or becoming violent.

Usually this type of situation allows the therapist to expose the power alignments within the family. Helping family members to understand the indirect or unintended aspects of their oppressive behavior usually leads the members to communicate more directly with one another. Furthermore, the consequence of the therapy sessions is not likely to be the maintenance of the status quo. For many therapists, this is the first instance in which they have had to play the role of the social reformer or change agent.

When dealing with a social unit rather than an individual, it sometimes becomes very difficult to determine who the patient is. Unlike individual therapy, family therapy gives the members involved the advantage of not being labeled "the patient." It also allows the family members an opportunity to test new ways of communicating with one another in a therapeutic context of relatively low risk.

Group Therapy

Another mode of treatment is that of an individual exploring his problems within an artificial group context. This group context is constructed in order to help individuals learn ways of coping with their emotional problems. Some groups are not intentionally set up for therapeutic purposes, but to provide the group members with training in human relations.[12; 50] Participants in such groups do not define themselves as patients, but as individuals interested in a learning experience which will help them understand their own communication behavior and that of others. The group sessions focus upon interpersonal conflicts and attempt to help each participant examine his position within the group.

There seem to be a number of advantages of the group encounter over individual therapy. First of all, it allows a person to take into account and weigh the reactions of a variety of people to his behavior. Some of the reactions may produce stress within the individual, and the group situation encourages each participant to deal with that openly.

Since in most groups the participants do not know one another, the conflicts that develop will not necessarily be the same type that may develop in a natural setting such as the family. However, these groups can be very useful practice sessions for learning how to deal with the more prolonged, natural conflicts that arise within one's family and community.

A number of therapists have been very critical of the so-called sensitivity-training groups.[36; 60] Most critics emphasize the mishandling of the anxiety that is aroused within group sessions and point out that some members could be left emotionally disturbed by the experience. Others point out that when the participant confronts a power struggle, he may find himself in the position of having to conform to the norms of the group. Without proper guidance, a participant may find that he is unable to deal with his own problems because they are not in line with the direction of the group. Most of the criticism is related to the qualifications of the group leader necessary to provide proper guidance. This matter is still unresolved.

Community Therapy

It wasn't until the early 1960s that some therapists became concerned with the emotional distresses suffered by large groups of people. Some have even called this movement a "psychiatric revolution." [17]

Community therapists could be characterized as concerned with finding solutions to system ills rather than treating the problem as one of individual illness. These therapists are concerned with the broader problems of society, such as crime, alcoholism, the needs of the aged, and care for retarded children. Attempts have been made to improve handling of mental cases in general, to treat as many as possible outside the hospital in the community.

In addition to open-door hospitals and therapeutic communities, lecture and discussion groups have been established for the purpose of informing people about the psychological basis of deviant behavior and the dynamics of interpersonal communication. Aid is being given to entire universities, corporations, and neighborhoods in order to take care of the mental health problems of those who cannot otherwise afford therapy.

Some therapists contend that the community therapist must actively try to create a society which will impose as little oppression as possible on its people. [31] Programs for fostering social change, political involvement, and community planning, as well as efforts aimed toward influencing laws and regulations, are but a few of the directions of this movement. [49; 13]

Of all those involved with therapy, the community therapist probably has the greatest opportunity to directly change oppressive environments. [16] At the same time many community therapists have warned against forgetting the need to maintain some form of social control. [9; 52] Nevertheless, the community therapist is helping to shape the lives of people he has probably never seen. The therapist who advises courts, welfare agencies, or universities on issues such as sex, drug abuse, or delinquency has an indirect but powerful effect on people within the community.

Communication

With the emphasis of therapeutic study changing from an individual-defect model to a system-pathology model, therapists have found the process of communication their major focal point of inquiry. Many now realize that human communication provides the medium through which all social systems perform their functions. No social system can exist without communication among its members.

How communication functions in social systems is the key to man's survival.[65] Yet, even beyond communication in the service of survival and protection, man is characterized by his striving for and dependence upon communication with other men. Communication becomes an end in itself. Most individuals need to communicate with others in order to preserve their own identities. By social recognition and by other's responses, the individual participating in communication gains membership in a class of persons similar to himself, and thus acquires an identity. Goffman [25] suggests that the dehumanization of persons defined as insane proceeds in much the same way. Communication authenticates the identity assumed by an individual and facilitates his orientation vis-à-vis others.

Questions about how individuals are shaped and transformed by their participation in communication systems is the major concern of community therapists. The relationship between social systems and communication behavior becomes increasingly important as one ponders the nature, cause, and cure of so-called deviant behavior. The nature of the solutions arrived at is dependent upon whether pathology is conceived to inhere in an individual or within the systems in which he lives.

The requirements of a society dictate the creation or demise of social systems. Since people group together to cope with problems, their communication relationships represent particular solutions to the problems posed. At times, however, the communication patterns that are formed become dysfunctional either in regard to the accomplishments of the system's goals or to the individual members of the system, or both.

Therapists work with social systems that display communication patterns inimical either to the well-being of the individual or to the full development of the system itself. Some family systems reduce internal conflict by keeping members in a closed family system which remains impervious to external demands. For example, by not requiring a child to adapt his behavior as he gets older, communicational struggles can be avoided within the family system. However, immature individuals may have serious problems in maintaining social and work relationships outside the family.

When something goes wrong in a communication system, it results in a strain on the system which one or more of its members may perceive. For example, if a child adopts a hair or dress style which is unacceptable to the other family members, they may take steps to coax or induce the child to change in keeping with their expectations. However, all persons within a system are important in maintaining that system, so that deficiencies in one may be compensated for by others in order to maintain balance in the system.

A minimum level of communication seems to be needed for a system to accomplish its objectives. Systems may fail either because some members do not increase their contributions when deficits in the system occur or because some members fail to maintain their individual contributions.

Social systems are constantly exposed to inputs from other systems, some of which impose a stress upon the system. In order to deal with external influences, a system must develop mechanisms for adapting to new inputs. For instance, the son who comes home from college may exert stress on the family system due to some of his newly acquired values. The quality of a system might be judged on how well it can adapt through internal communication without becoming disrupted.

Some researchers [1; 70] suggest that, in general, disturbed families are too isolated from the outside world and that their boundaries are inappropriately rigid. In this instance the communication process fails to serve adaptive functions for the family members. At the same time, other researchers [6; 8] suggest that some disturbed families suffer from ill-defined and loose boundaries and that the impact from the outside world has a disorganizing effect upon the communication behaviors of the members within.

Therapists have made major strides in the study of the family, community, and other social institutions. From this perspective, new insights into how people communicate with each other have been constructed. As Birdwhistell has put it:

> An individual does not communicate; he engages in or becomes part of communication. He may move, or make noises . . . but he does not communicate. In a parallel fashion, he may see, he may hear, smell, taste, or feel—but he does not originate communication; he participates in it. Communication as a system, then, is not to be understood on a simple model of action and reaction, however complexly stated. As a system it is to be comprehended on the transactional level. [11, p. 104]

It becomes increasingly clear that only through an understanding of communication will man be able to come to grips with the stresses and frustrations that are inherent in our attempts to organize with one another.

Communication is thought of as a transactive, interrelational concept. The emphasis is not on a single message or an individual, but on the interrelationship of at least two people. This relationship involves the receipt of and response to as well as the emission of messages. Thus, an individual is constantly in the process of interpreting messages that impinge upon him.

The context or system within which people are relating plays a significant role in how the messages will be interpreted. The interpretation of messages in a work situation is different from that within a family, which is, in turn, different from that found in therapy. When we participate in communication, there is never a single message, but a multiplicity of possible interpretations or messages. Verbal messages, facial expressions, bodily gestures, and the context all become part of the analysis of communication, since they are crucial to interpretation and response. This suggests that one never knows what the "real" message is, since the intended message is not the totality of what a person receives.

These conceptions about communication provide a viewpoint on behavior which is quite different from our usual commonsense way of thinking. From this viewpoint, one can assert that all behavior can be interpreted as communication. Watzlawick and Beavin exemplify this point by the following situation:

> If woman A points to woman B's necklace and asks, "Are those real pearls?" the content of her question is a request for information about an object. But at the same time she also gives—indeed, cannot *not* give—her definition of their relationship. How she asks (especially in this case, the tone and stress of voice, facial expression, and context) would indicate comfortable friendliness, competitiveness, formal business relations, etc. B can accept, reject, or redefine but cannot under any circumstances—even by silence—not respond to A's message. A's definition may, for instance, be a catty, condescending one; B, on the other hand, may react to it with defensiveness. It should be noticed that this part of their interaction has nothing to do with the genuineness of pearls at all, but with their respective definitions of the nature of their relationship, although they may continue to talk about pearls. (68, p. 5)

Thus, we see that it is possible for two people to disagree about an issue they are discussing while understanding the nature of their relationship together. Also, two people might agree on an issue, but totally misunderstand their relationship. Or two people may agree or disagree on both levels.

Therapeutic Communication

This perspective introduces a challenging task for those interested in therapeutic communication, namely, to influence communication processes and transactive arrangements in social systems. To develop a strategy for changing institutional structures which will favor the emergence of optimal communicational environments is a task of the highest priority for those concerned with bringing about therapeutic communication and increases in social learning. As Ruesch suggests in the quotation opening this chapter, however, one does not have to be a professional therapist to participate in therapeutic communication.

One of the features of therapeutic communication is that people set aside a period of time for the purpose of communicating about communication in order to become more aware of their own communicative behavior. The presence of several people is the key aspect in this situation, since communication behavior does not develop fully unless at least one other person is willing to be present and participate. Furthermore, there is no one method which produces better communication development than another; the process cannot be reduced to techniques or summed up in a nice, neat formula. Therapeutic communication consists of the utilization of naturally existing conditions and practices. It does, however, involve a heightened sensitivity to oneself and others in a transactional milieu. The skill is to develop an awareness of the appropriate spacing, timing, and selection of one's own messages in reply to the messages of others.

Ruesch states:

> The closer the understanding, acknowledgement, and reply of the therapist match the empirical experience of the patient, the more effective therapy becomes. The working hypothesis is based upon the following observations:
>
> —That understanding is based upon the mutual appreciation of actions and words.
> —That verbal or action signals, if they are to be mutually understood, have to be coded in ways that are intelligible to all.
> —That a reply amplifies, connects, or alters the initial statement of the patient.
> —That such a reply is effective the more it is phrased in the language of the patient. (53, p. 36)

Therapeutic communication thus requires adaptive behavior by the people involved in the situation. Not only do they have to understand the messages of others but they have to construct messages in reply that are comprehensible to others. The desired consequence for each person involved is some degree of self-realization. This requires people to accept differences and to recognize that interpersonal difficulties are settled by means of communication rather than by withdrawal or violence.

The emphasis of therapeutic communication is on the problems of people. We need therefore to develop an understanding of the present and to utilize the past only insofar as it helps a person understand the present. This understanding entails more than a person's asking "Why did I do that?" Far greater importance is placed on asking "What can I do about it?" In searching for explanations of his behavior, a person uses other's reactions to him in order to be able to look at his own behavior. People must come to realize that therapeutic communication can take place under everyday conditions and practices. They must become aware of how communication functions within their family, the groups to which they belong, and the community in which they live.

Future Trends

At the present, most therapists are still concerned with the treatment of individuals rather than with systems of people. There are those who are pioneering in the areas of family, group, and community therapy. These therapists, both as private citizens and as professionals, are trying to change some of our social conditions that produce misery and frustration among groups of people. Environmental oppressions in our ghettoes, prisons, and educational institutions, as well as those based on skin color, sex, age, and harmless social deviation, are some primary targets.

An increasing number of therapists are becoming aware of the inadequacy of an individual-defect model as they search for a way of conceptualizing the problems of society. Important strides have already been made toward the integration of systems theory and communication theory. The recognition that human communication cannot be understood by utilizing a simple cause-and-effect model has opened up new avenues of investigation and inquiry.[15] A redefinition of communication behavior to include more than just verbal utterances has led to questions about "real" messages and man's subjective interpretation of reality. Furthermore, a greater emphasis is being placed on the functions of communication for man in an ever-changing, complex society, with particular regard to the moral and political ramifications of the therapist's role.

With the advancement of communication technology, it is now possible for people to know about numerous happenings all over the world. Television provides local, state, national, and international news for most people within our society. More than ever before, people have an opportunity to observe and detect flaws within the major institutions of society. Issues of political sincerity, objective news reporting, goals of education, and the justification of war are but a few of the standards which people are beginning to question.

How to deal with the interrelatedness of societal issues is probably the most formidable problem man has to face. Planning for the future will require that man deal with the interdependence of the entire social system, rather than treating the issues independently. Many social philosophers and social scientists feel that through the study of the ecology of social communication we can create a more humane and efficient society.[10]

Those who have power to determine the direction of society will have to develop long-range goals that focus on systems of events. The rapid change of technological growth and the complexities involved in man's ability to create social institutions compel man to think more precisely about his own destiny. The need for a vision of what is best for man is the survival issue facing us now. Maybe what Toffler[66] has called "future shock" will be lessened through such an awareness.

Many scholars have recognized this need for long-range planning and have speculated on the goals for the human race.[19; 42; 14] Their general thesis is that man's future will be decided by what man wants to do. For example, our present knowledge about genetic codes may eventually enable us to control man's evolution. With advances in space technology, artificial transplants, and communication technology, we must acknowledge that any direction is possible. What this means is that people who feel that they are responsible for social reform must try to anticipate and direct man's future.

If we agree that the most important stresses in life are those imposed upon man by other men or by man-created social institutions, and that these stresses manifest themselves in and through communication, then what we know about and how we use communication becomes of primary importance. Our participation in communication with our fellowman can lead either to greater stresses in life or to a more useful matching of individual needs and aspirations with those of the social systems man has created to fulfill the needs of a society of men. Each one of us, through communication, has the responsibility to demand the most viable social systems, in which we can grow and develop throughout our lifetime. For these social systems will affect not only us, but those yet to come.

REFERENCES AND SUGGESTED READINGS

1. Ackerman, N., "Preventive Implications of Family Research," in *Prevention of Mental Disorders in Children,* ed. by G. Caplan. New York: Basic Books, 1961.
2. Bandura, A., *Principles of Behavior Modification.* New York: Holt, Rinehart and Winston, 1969.
3. Bateson, Gregory, "Exchange of Information about Patterns of Human Behavior," in *Information Storage and Neural Control,* ed. by William S. Fields and Walter Abbot. Springfield, Ill.: Charles C Thomas, 1963.
4. Bateson, Gregory, Don D. Jackson, Jay Haley, and John Weakland, "Toward a Theory of Schizophrenia," *Behavioral Science,* Vol. 1, 1956.
5. Barker, R., *The Stream of Behavior.* New York: Appleton-Century-Crofts, 1963.
6. Bell, N., "Extended Family Relations of Disturbed and Well Families," *Family Process,* Vol. 1, 1962.
7. Bellack, L., ed., *Handbook of Community Psychiatry and Community Mental Health.* New York: Grune & Stratton, 1964.
8. Bettelheim, B., and E. Sylvester, "Parental Occupations and Children's Symptoms," in *The Family,* ed. by N. Bell and E. Vogel. New York: Free Press, 1960.
9. Brody, E., "Psychiatry and the Social Order," *American Journal of Psychiatry,* Vol. 12, 1965.
10. Buckley, William, *Modern Systems Research for the Behavioral Scientists.* Chicago: Aldine, 1968.

11. Birdwhistell, Ray L., "Contributions of Linguistic-Kinesic Studies to the Understanding of Schizophrenia," in *Schizophrenia: An Integrated Approach,* ed. by Alfred Auerback. New York: Ronald Press, 1959.
12. Burton, A., *Encounter.* San Francisco: Jossey-Bass, 1969.
13. Caplan, G., *Principles of Preventive Psychiatry.* New York: Basic Books, 1964.
14. Chase, S., *The Most Probable World.* New York: Harper & Row, 1968.
15. Costello, Daniel E., "Communication Patterns in Family Systems," *Nursing Clinics of North America,* Vol. 4, 1969.
16. Dumont, Matthew, *The Absurd Healer.* New York: Science House, 1969.
17. Ekman, P., "Body Position, Facial Expression and Verbal Behavior During Interviews," *Journal of Abnormal and Social Psychology,* Vol. 68, March, 1964.
18. Ekman, P., "Nonverbal Behavior in Psychotherapy Research," in *Research on Psychotherapy,* III, ed. by J. Shlien. American Psychological Association, 1967.
19. Feinberg, G., *The Prometheus Project.* Garden City, N.Y.: Doubleday, 1968.
20. Frank H., *Sanity and Survival.* New York: Random House, Vintage Books, 1967.
21. Frank, J., *Persuasion and Healing.* Baltimore: Johns Hopkins Press, 1961.
22. Frank, Lawrence K., "Tactile Communication," in *Exploration and Communication,* ed. by E. Carpenter and M. McLuhan. Boston: Beacon Press, 1960.
23. Freud, Sigmund, *Psychopathology of Everyday Life.* New York: New American Library, 1959.
24. Fuller, Buckminster, *Operating Manual for Spaceship Earth.* Carbondale: Southern Illinois University Press, 1969.
25. Goffman, Erving, *Asylums.* Garden City, N.Y.: Doubleday, 1961.
26. Gray, William, Frederic J. Duhl, and Nicholas D. Rizzo, eds., *General Systems Theory and Psychiatry.* Boston: Little, Brown, 1969.
27. Grier, W., and P. Cobbs, *Black Rage.* New York: Basic Books, 1968.
28. Group for the Advancement of Psychiatry, *Treatment of Families in Conflict.* New York: Science House, 1970.
29. Haley, Jay, "An Interactional Description of Schizophrenia," *Psychiatry,* Vol. 22, 1959, pp. 321–332.
30. Haley, Jay, *Strategies of Psychotherapy.* New York: Grune & Stratton, 1963.
31. Halleck, S. L., "Community Psychiatry: Some Troubling Questions," in *Community Psychiatry,* ed. by L. M. Roberts, S. L. Halleck, and M. B. Loeb. Garden City, N.Y.: Doubleday, Anchor Books, 1969.
32. Laing, R. D., *The Divided Self: A Study of Sanity and Madness.* London: Tavistock Press, 1960.
33. Laing, R. D., *The Politics of Experience.* London: Penguin Books, 1967.
34. Laing, R. D., *The Self and Others.* London: Tavistock Press, 1962.
35. Laing, R. D., H. Phillipson, and A. R. Lee, *Interpersonal Perception.* New York: Springer, 1966.
36. Lakin, M., "Some Ethical Issues in Sensitivity Training," *American Psychologist,* Vol. 24, 1969.
37. Leifer, R., *In the Name of Mental Health.* New York: Science House, 1969.
38. Lennard, Henry L., and Arnold Bernstein, *Patterns in Human Interaction.* San Francisco: Jossey-Bass, 1969.
39. Lidz, T., *The Family and Human Adaptation.* New York: International Universities, 1963.
40. Menninger, Karl, *The Crime of Punishment.* New York: Viking, 1969.

41. Menninger, Karl, *The Vital Balance*. New York: Viking, 1967.
42. Michael, D., *The Unprepared Society*. New York: Basic Books, 1968.
43. Miller, D. R., "The Study of Social Relationships: Situation, Identity and Social Interaction," in *Psychology: A Study of a Science*, Vol. 5, ed. by S. Koch. New York: McGraw-Hill, 1963.
44. Mishler, E. G., and N. E. Waxler, *Interaction in Families*. New York: Wiley, 1968.
45. Nelson, M. C., B. Nelson, M. H. Sherman, and H. S. Strean, *Roles and Paradigms in Psychology*. New York: Grune & Stratton, 1968.
46. Pittenger, R. E., Charles F. Hockett, and J. J. Danehy, *The First Five Minutes*. Ithaca: Paul Martineau Publishers, 1960.
47. Rausch, H., "Interaction Sequences," *Journal of Abnormal and Social Psychology*, Vol. 2, 1965.
48. Redlich, F. C., and D. X. Freedman, *The Theory and Practice of Psychiatry*. New York: Basic Books, 1966.
49. Roberts, L. M., *Introduction to Community Psychiatry*, ed. by L. M. Roberts, S. L. Halleck, and M. B. Loeb. Garden City, N.Y.: Doubleday, Anchor Books, 1969.
50. Rogers, Carl, "The Group Comes of Age," *Psychology Today*, December, 1969.
51. Ruesch, Jurgen, *Disturbed Communication*. New York: Norton, 1957.
52. Ruesch, Jurgen, "Social Psychiatry: An Overview," *Archives of General Psychiatry*, Vol. 12, 1965.
53. Ruesch, Jurgen, *Therapeutic Communication*. New York: Norton, 1961.
54. Ruesch, Jurgen, and G. Bateson, *Communication: The Matrix of Psychiatry*. New York: Norton, 1951.
55. Scheflen, Albert E., "Communication and Regulation in Psychotherapy," *Psychiatry*, Vol. 26, 1963.
56. Scheflen, Albert E., "Natural History Method in Psychotherapy: Communicational Research," in *Methods of Research in Psychotherapy*, ed. by L. A. Gottschalk and A. H. Auerback. New York: Appleton-Century-Crofts, 1966.
57. Scheflen, Albert E., "The Significance of Posture in Communication Systems," *Psychiatry*, Vol. 27, 1964.
58. Scheflen, Albert E., *Stream and Structure of Communicational Behavior, Context Analysis of a Psychotherapy Session*, Behavioral Studies Monograph No. 1, Eastern Pennsylvania Psychiatric Institute, Philadelphia, 1965.
59. Shands, Harley C., "Psychoanalysis and the Twentieth-Century Revolution in Psychiatry," in *Modern Psychoanalysis: New Directions and Perspectives*, ed. by J. Marmor. New York: Basic Books, 1968.
60. Shastrom, E. L., "Group Therapy: Let the Buyer Beware," *Psychology Today*, May, 1969.
61. Szasz, Thomas S., *Law, Liberty and Psychiatry*. New York: Macmillan, 1963.
62. Szasz, Thomas S., *The Manufacture of Madness*. New York: Harper & Row, 1970.
63. Szasz, Thomas S., *The Myth of Mental Illness*. New York: Harper & Row, 1961.
64. Taylor, G. R., *The Biological Time Bomb*. New York: New American Library, Signet Books, 1969.
65. Thayer, Lee, *Communication and Communication Systems*. Homewood, Ill.: Irwin, 1968.
66. Toffler, A., *Future Shock*. New York: Random House, 1970.

67. Watson, J. D., *The Molecular Biology of the Gene.* New York: New American Library, Signet Books, 1969.
68. Watzlawick, Paul, Janet Beavin, and Don D. Jackson, "Some Formal Aspects of Communication," *American Behavioral Scientist,* Vol. 10, 1967.
69. Wertham, F., "Praetorian Psychiatry," *American Journal of Psychotherapy,* Vol. 17, 1963.
70. Wynne, L. *et al.,* "Pseudo-Mutuality in the Family Relations of Schizophrenics," *Psychiatry,* Vol. 21. 1958.

Dr. Hubert Frings is Professor of Zoology at the University of Oklahoma. His research activities have focused on the area of sensory physiology and the behavior of birds and insects. In addition to a variety of book chapters, articles, and papers, Dr. Frings is author of *Animal Communication*.

24

ZOOLOGY: AN APPROACH TO HUMAN COMMUNICATION

HUBERT FRINGS

DEFINITIONS AND PROBLEMS

AN exact definition of animal communication is not possible—indeed, may never be possible.[7; 12, pp. 5–18; 26] It is generally agreed, however, that an operant definition can be formulated. Communication between two animals is said to occur when one animal produces a chemical or physical change in the environment (*signal*) that influences the behavior of another. The study of animal communication has received no generally accepted single name, being engaged in by students in many fields: sensory and nervous physiology, ecology, animal behavior (ethology), and comparative psychology. Sebeok [24; 26] has suggested the term *zoosemiotics* for this field of research, but it is still too early to see whether this will be adopted generally.

While some students of animal behavior would restrict communication to intraspecific relationships only, others would include any case in which the behavior of one animal influences that of another, thus including warning colors, and the like. An interesting case in point is that of echolocation: the ability of some animals—for example, bats and porpoises—to locate unseen objects by reflected pulsed sounds. Some consider this a form of autocommunication; others consider it not communication at all. We shall not discuss echolocation here, not because it is unworthy of discussion or should necessarily be excluded from communication, but for the much more prosaic reason that there are enough other matters to occupy us.

Up to now, studies on animal communication have not in themselves led to generalizations that aid our understanding of human communication. When comparisons between human and animal communication have been made, they have invariably been by someone trying to decide whether animals actually have languages, and the criteria used have been those proposed by students of human language (cf., for instance, Hockett in Ref. 14 and Count in Ref. 26). Studies on animal communication are still generally empirical and have not resulted in many theoretical concepts. As for the question of animal language, one's view of its existence or nonexistence depends entirely upon the criteria he selects as critical, and these vary from worker to worker. Luckily the matter does not concern us practically, and studies proceed fruitfully without a decision.

GENERAL DESCRIPTION OF ANIMAL COMMUNICATION

As with all communication systems, three essential parts are necessary: (1) an individual that produces some chemical or physical change, the *sender,* also called source, addresser, and so forth; (2) a chemical or physical entity produced, the *signal;* and (3) an individual that receives the signal and responds to it, the *receiver,* also called reactor, addressee, and the like. Each of these may be studied scientifically.

Two facets of the sender's activities have received special attention: (1) what might be called the *motivation* of the sender, that is, those internal states and external stimuli that initiate production of signals; and (2) the *mechanisms of signal production* and the effects of environmental factors, such as temperature, upon these. As an example of the first, it is well known that signals involved in communication during reproduction of mammals and birds are generally produced only at times of sexual activity, and are often evoked by such features of the environment as day length, presence of other individuals, and the like. As an example of the second, the best-studied cases are probably production of acoustic signals by various insects. Since insects are poikilothermal, the rate of production of sound by males is directly related to temperature, creating an interesting situation, for the feature of greatest significance in the signals is the emission rate. Thus females, the receivers, must also have behavioral adjustments to correct for this inexactness in the males.

The chemical or physical properties of signals have also been studied, often by chemists and physicists as well as zoologists. Where chemical signals, such as sex odors of insects, may be useful for control of pests, these studies have been especially numerous.[10; 11] Some attention, but much less, has been given to the range of transmission of various signals and the effects of the environment on this.

Two facets of the receiver's activities have been the subject of special study: (1) the nature and functions of *receptor organs* and (2) the induced *behavioral responses.* Much more work is needed on the first, for the limits and properties of receptors are known for only a very few animals, and poorly known for most of these. It is by no means safe to assume, as many have done, that the critical features of a signal reaching an animal are those that impress themselves most upon man. Some insects (e.g., honeybees) receive ultraviolet light, and others (e.g., moths and some grasshoppers) are sensitive to ultrasonic sounds. Furthermore, the responses of receptors of animals other than man are by no means necessarily similar to those of the receptors of man. For example, many insect phonoreceptors act as filtering units, rectifying the fundamental acoustic frequencies, here used as carrier waves, to produce nerve impulses determined only by temporal patterns of the sound pulses. Without precise information on receptive capacities, studies of the receiver's behavior may lead to erroneous conclusions.

No really new experimental techniques have been evolved for these studies.[25] The usual physiological methods are used for studies on mechanisms of production and reception of signals; the usual methods of study in animal behavior are adopted for that aspect. Perhaps the only characteristic feature of many studies on animal communication is the extensive use of constructed or recorded dummies—models of body structure or animal sounds—to stimulate potential or suspected receivers. Even this, however, stems directly from earlier ethological work. Students of animal communication, however, are usually much more interested than ethologists in the exact chemical and physical nature of the signals; therefore, many become involved in chemical and physical analyses. There is no question that all aspects of research in animal communication have been greatly aided by recent developments in microchemical methods, tape recording, and cinematography.

PLACE OF COMMUNICATION IN ANIMAL LIFE

Communication between members of a species, at least for most higher animals, infuses every aspect of existence from birth to death. Most young vertebrates react almost at hatching or birth to food and alarm signals of the parents, and these reactions increase in precision and variety as life progresses. To these are added, in maturity, sexual reactions generally governed by complex communication signals. While most invertebrates do not live in such close social units as do vertebrates, they too usually have signals for reproduction and often for other aspects of life. We may, for convenience, classify communication systems into those involved in nonsexual activities and those involved in sexual activities.

Nonsexual Activities

Species identification is an important aspect of life for most animals. For many (e.g., some fish and birds, social insects, and barnacles), members of the same species form specific *aggregations.* This obviously necessitates recognition of other members of the same species, generally through specific body patterns or sounds which act as aggregational signals. For many others (e.g., some birds, spiders, and marine annelids), individuals of the same species practice *dispersion,* except during reproduction, each with its own *territory.* Since members of other species are usually not excluded from the territory, this too necessitates species recognition. In this case, the signals are mostly chemical or acoustical, the most studied being the territorial songs of birds.

Social facilitation between members of aggregations is common among animals. Warnings of danger, by alarm or distress signals, are found among social insects, fish, birds, and mammals. These are usually acoustical, but may be chemical. Most birds, for instance, have staccato calls that they emit when they sight a cat or other predator, which cause other individuals of the species to flee. In a few cases, a special type of alarm signal occurs, first discovered in grasshoppers and now known for a few birds. In this case, an individual leaving a group utters a special sound if there is no danger, the *departing call,* to which the others respond by remaining. If the departer leaves suddenly, without giving the signal, the others leave also. In highly developed social animals (e.g., honeybees, and many birds and mammals), signals are developed that serve for *guidance* to food or to homes. Among the most studied of these are the guidance signals of honeybees, through which scout bees alert hive-mates to the presence of food at a distance from the hive and communicate to them the distance, nature, and direction.

Sexual Activities

Attraction and *recognition* of a mate are generally the first steps in reproduction. Few species, apparently, depend merely upon chance wandering to bring the sexes together; almost all animals have means whereby at least one sex attracts the other through signals, mostly chemical or acoustical. Birds, grasshoppers, and crickets with songs, and mammals and moths with odors, to mention only a few, combine attraction and species identification in specific signals. Even in protozoans, chemical attraction of mating partners—conjugants—has been found. Slime molds, whose name reflects their questionable position as animals, have chemical signals that bring individuals together for reproduction. In these organisms, individual "animals" are amoebalike forms creeping about on the forest floor. To reproduce, they come together and fuse into a multinucleate mass. One individual releases puffs of a chemical, now known for at least one species to be cyclic adenosine monophosphate, to which others respond by crawling to the "caller" and fusing with it. Amazingly enough, it is not the chemical itself that identifies the species, but the rhythm of puffs. This is actually a more sophisticated use of chemical signals than that of many mammals, which simply give off a continuous scent.

Courtship behavior is, for most higher animals at least, a preliminary to *mating,* and in both activities, communication signals are prominent. Courtship usually serves two purposes—confirmation of species and sexual identification, and arousal of the mating partner. The most elaborate courtship patterns are found among birds, mammals, fish, insects, spiders, and mollusks. Since the partners are usually near each other, almost any type of signal may be used. Thus birds have both visual signals (posture, flashing colors) and sounds (courtship duets). Jumping spiders and crabs have poses or dances by which the male identifies himself to the female and arouses her to mating pitch. Male crickets and grasshoppers, after calling in the female by a so-called ordinary, or calling, song, change to a courtship song when the female is in sight. Male web-spinning spiders of some species pluck the strands of the female's web and thus identify themselves and diminish her normally aggressive reactions, so that mating can take place. Males of one group of flies prepare balloonlike structures to present to the females. Male tree-crickets produce a secretion from a gland on their back on which females feed during mating. Certain land snails shoot pointed projectiles, fancifully called "love-darts," into their partners before mating. Even animals such as oysters and marine worms, that cannot come together for mating, release chemicals into the water that induce others to discharge eggs or sperm for external fertilization.

Parent-young relationships, while not directly sexual, are related to sexual activities and may be considered to be derived from sexual acts. These relationships are also facilitated by communication patterns, at least among higher animals. Many invertebrates, and vertebrates such as amphibians, reptiles, and fish, usually have no contact with their offspring. However, social insects, birds, and mammals have intergenerational contacts, and these are carried out through communication signals.

In honeybees, as long as a queen is present in the hive, the workers— all her sexually incompetent daughters—usually produce no new queen.[3] But if the colony becomes too large or if the queen dies, the workers produce another queen, as if they know that the queen is insufficient or gone. The signal here is a chemical called Queen Substance (now known to be 9-oxodec-trans-2-enoic acid) given by the queen to the workers and passed by them from one to another. When enough of this is present to go around, the workers produce only more workers. When the supply decreases, they produce new queens.

Among birds and mammals, the development periods of offspring are to a great degree regulated by signals from the parents and feedback from the young. Often the reactions of the young are quite different from those of older animals, and adult reactions develop or are learned. The earliest reaction to alarm signals of baby birds and mammals is usually immobility. This changes, as the babies leave the nest or lair, to the adult pattern, usually flight. A young male bird may learn to imitate the song of an adult male, usually his father, generating a local tradition in song pattern.

Communication thus plays an important role in the life of almost every, if not every, animal. Generally, the degree depends upon the development of the sensorimotor capabilities of the animal. Sessile or pelagic beasts, such as sponges and jellyfish, seem to have few methods for communication, while mobile animals with well-developed receptors and nervous systems, such as bees, birds, and mammals, have all of life guided in large measure by communication systems. The exact nature of the systems likewise depends upon potentialities. Thus animals with well-developed eyes tend to have highly evolved visual communication signals, and those with well-developed ears tend to have highly evolved acoustical signals. Since almost all animals are sensitive to chemicals, systems based on these are the most widespread of all. The channels available, therefore, fundamentally determine the nature of the communication systems.

COMMUNICATIVE CHANNELS AND THEIR USES

Tactile

The tactile channel is restricted to animals in contact with one another. Other than that restriction, however, the potential variability of signals is very great, from simple contact to elaborate dances, especially favorable for analog-type codes. Tactile signals are used chiefly in courtship and mating, but a notable exception is the remarkable guidance system of honeybees, involving so-called dances. We may recognize three categories of tactile signals, employing (1) touching, bumping, and so forth, (2) vibration, and (3) so-called dancing.

Touching, bumping, and the like, in some form, are found throughout almost the whole animal kingdom as a part of courtship and mating. Even in man, the language of love is often tactile. Most other mammals likewise rub, stroke, or lick sexual partners. Even porpoises and whales nuzzle their mates. Conversely, ritualized fighting often takes the form of pushing and bumping. Similarly, in birds, mutual preening or solicitation of preening is an important part of courtship rituals. Allowing oneself to be preened or fed signifies suppression of aggression, and thus readiness for mating. It has been suggested that the dull colors and submissive postures of so-called parasitic birds, which lay their eggs in other birds' nests, turn aside the aggression that might otherwise be their lot.

Among insects, many species engage in mutual stroking or titillation before mating. Some male insects, for instance, have special organs associated with their external genital organs that stroke the genitalia of the female in patterned fashion and cause the female organs to admit the male intromittent organ. Ants have an alarm system that is based on rapid and excited running about. Twining of mating pairs, with secretion of mucus envelopes, is usual in many species of leeches and slugs. We have already noted the love-dart of some land snails, seemingly an extreme example of tactile stimulation. From simple touching or stroking to puncturing, the sexual behavior of animals is permeated with tactile signals.

Vibration of a substrate is much less common as a signaling means than touching and bumping. As an example, we may note the warning rattle of frogs. Male frogs call in females by their breeding choruses in ponds and puddles. When the females contact the males, the males mount them. Actually, whenever anything frog-size contacts the male, he mounts it. Sometimes this is another male. In this case, the under frog vibrates his body with a warning rattle, and the upper one releases. Vibrations may be used, as are sounds, for sexual identification and courtship. Thus, in land leeches, a sexually ready animal taps the leaf on which it rests and so attracts another for mating. The most elaborate vibration signals are found in orb-web-spinning spiders. In most of these, the male is much smaller than the female, and the female attacks without hesitation any small creature that vibrates the web. It is necessary, therefore, for the male to identify himself to the female before entering the web. This he does by plucking the strands at the edge of the web in a specific rhythm. If his rhythm is correct and the female is receptive, she remains quiet—usually after a few abortive attacks—and he enters and mates with her.

Dancing is a term used for various patterns of movement and contact found in birds, insects, spiders, and so forth. So-called dances of birds, such as those of gooney birds, usually involve visual and auditory signals, but the partners do nibble each other. In scorpions, there is an elaborate mating dance involving ritualized back-and-forth movements by the partners. These seem basically to give the male a chance to pull the female across a spermatophore, which he has already deposited on the ground, allowing its hook to catch in her genital opening and thus to fertilize her.

By far the best-known and most carefully studied dances of animals are those of honeybees, discovered by von Frisch.[8; 9] These are used by scout bees to convey to their hive-mates information about food sources or suitable places for hive construction. We shall summarize only very, very briefly the impressive body of data that von Frisch and his students have accumulated about these dances.

If a scout bee has found food within about 50 meters of the hive, she performs a round-dance on the comb. In this, the bee runs excitedly to and fro in a circular pattern, bumping into other bees. This movement conveys the information that the food source is close. The degree of persistence and excitement gives information about the quality and quantity of the source, and the odor on the bee's body identifies the flower source. If the food has no odor itself (e.g., if it is an experimental food dish), the bee deposits its own odor on it. Thus informed, other workers can easily find the food by systematic coverage of a relatively small area.

If the food is at a greater distance, the scout performs a waggle-dance. In this, the bee runs for a short distance in a straight line, waggling the abdomen, then in a circle right or left, back to the starting point, after which she repeats the straight run, then around on the other side to start, and so on. The nature of the dance informs the bees that the distance is greater than about 50 meters. The exact distance to the food is indicated by the duration of the waggle run, and possibly by other items which vary simultaneously. The direction to the source is indicated by the direction of the straight run on the comb—directly upward indicating directly toward the sun, directly downward away, and angles between appropriate angles right and left. As before, the vigor and persistence indicate quality and quantity, and odors are used as markers.

This elaborate system is still being subjected to detailed analysis by von Frisch and his students [9; 16] and has been analyzed, in a preliminary fashion, using methods developed for communication systems of man. As the studies proceed, the complexity of this system is being unfolded, and data being obtained on inaccuracies and differences among strains of honeybees may soon lead to a full theoretical analysis. It is, without doubt, one of the most fascinating and highly developed communication systems in the animal kingdom, rivaling in complexity that of primitive peoples.

Visual

To so visually oriented an animal as man, this might seem to be the channel of choice. Actually, for animals in general, it is of restricted use, for the visual apparatus needed to receive coded light messages is found only in cephalopod mollusks, higher arthropods, and vertebrates. Visual signals, unlike tactile, can operate at a distance, but generally not a great distance. They are particularly suited for a digital type of code, unless highly developed eyes are present, and allow considerable variability and control. In short, where the proper receptors are present, visual signals become of great importance for close-range signaling. We may recognize three categories of visual signals, employing: (1) variations in body shape or color, (2) body postures and movements, and (3) production of light (luminescence).

Body shapes and colors of animals are usually so characteristic of species that taxonomists use them routinely for identification. In many species, males and females are differently colored, thus allowing visual discrimination of sex. Where animals have well-developed eyes, these clues to identity and sex form important parts of the social and sexual patterns. Thus, many mammals, most birds, many reptiles and salamanders, and most fish, display characteristic body patterns or colors in some phases of courtship or social relations. An interesting case of use of body-color pattern for sexual communication is found in certain fish that hold the developing eggs in the mouth for incubation. In these, the female takes the eggs into her mouth after she has deposited them outside. While she is picking up the eggs, the male, who has egg-shaped spots on his body near his cloacal opening, displays these near her. As she picks at them, he discharges sperm into her mouth, fertilizing the eggs. It is quite possible that some insects identify mates by body shape or color, but this has been little studied. It is known that certain crabs can identify the general form of the body of mates and react to this. The cuttlefish *Sepia* and some octopods can change color patterns rapidly, and males thus display special patterns to females in courtship.

Postures and movements add further variables to shape and size and, where eyes are well developed, form an important, and so far too little studied, facet of communication. We are most familiar with facial expression in man and other mammals, reflecting aggression or submission. These are matched by aggressive and sexual displays, usually involving intention movements—that is, movements adumbrating the actual activities —such as baring the teeth, displaying claws, or preliminary sexual movements. Alarm may also be communicated by special gaits or movements. Facial expression in birds is, to our eyes, rather limited. However, birds have many other visual signals, such as wing flashing, display of brightly colored tail feathers, and threat postures. In most birds, much of courtship, which can be very elaborate, involves displays of brightly colored areas or adoption of submissive or aggressive postures. In sea gulls, a typical pattern of flight over a source of food signals the presence of this to others. Many reptiles, likewise, use display in their courtship or defense of territory. The displays of male fish, often, as in sticklebacks, induced by the body pattern of the female, involve special postures and displays of bright areas by fin flashing. Male Siamese fighting fish, likewise, spread their brilliantly colored fins at the appearance of another male—a threat gesture—or at the appearance of a female—a courtship gesture.

Among invertebrates, visual displays are found only in those with well-developed eyes—insects, spiders, crabs, and a few mollusks. Male butterflies of some species have on their front wings striking flash patterns. When a male or female of the species appears, the wings are flicked apart, revealing the telltale markings. The wings thus act as semaphores, identifiying species and sex. Male jumping spiders and other hunting spiders with good eyes may use their eyes for signaling by moving a reflecting layer, the tapetum, back and forth, causing the eyes to flash. They also assume special postures and make patterned movements with their legs. In some male wolf spiders, as the front legs are held aloft before the female the internal pressure is increased causing the hairs on the legs to be erected in a brushlike fashion. These movements are usually rhythmic, and so are often called dances. Similarly, males of many species of crabs, such as fiddler crabs, display their large claws, usually by waving them in rhythmic patterns. These movements may be accompanied by sounds, as the appendages are thumped against the ground.

Luminescence requires a highly specialized system for production of cold light. This has been intensively studied by physiologists and biochemists, mostly because of interest in the phenomenon itself, rather than in behavior. Luminescence is rather widespread in animals, but in most cases our knowledge of the communicative significance, if any, is meager. A wide variety of invertebrates luminesce: fireflies and many other insects, a few millipedes, many crustaceans, some mollusks, a number of marine annelids, and many lower forms, such as protozoans, ctenophores, and coelenterates. In most cases, the significance of light production is unknown. There are, of course, a number of theories—mere illumination, warning, sexual signaling, and so on. In fireflies (really beetles, not flies) the males are generally winged, while the females are not. The males flash, as they fly, in rhythms characteristic of each species, and the females answer, often at set intervals of time after the male's flash. Thus, the sexes identify themselves and set up a mutual-attraction system. Luminescence could be involved in communication of other animals, particularly in ocean depths or open terrestrial areas, for signaling at considerable distances. How much this advantage has been exploited, if at all, is for future work to determine.

Chemical

Chemical signals, chiefly odors in terrestrial animals and similar substances in aquatic forms, are characterized by persistence and action at a distance. While many chemicals are quite evanescent, most dissipate slowly and so preclude rapid changes of temporal patterns. They are usually used as markers, rather than off-on signals. These have been given a special name, *pheromones,* by some biologists, chiefly those studying insects.[10; 11] The similarity of this word to the word *hormone* is intentional, supposedly indicating a similarity in mechanism of action. This seems, however, more an analogy than a homology. Chemical signals may not be pure chemical compounds, or they may act only with other signals.

Their supposed targetlike actions are not unique, for other communication signals may bring about the same results. For instance, the effects of chemical signals on development of sexual maturity or activity is emphasized by the originators of the term to justify a hormonelike designation. Yet, in many animals, visual or acoustical contacts, without odors, produce exactly the same effects. While the coining of the name gives a convenient term, and probably has led to some extra research, its use has also suggested a special character for these materials that is unwarranted. If an international single term shorter than *chemical communication signal* is desired, it would seem preferable to base it on a general root, such as *semant* (from the Greek, a signal) to which prefixes, such as chemo-, phono-, and photo-, could be attached. This usage would not suggest a separation of chemical signals from other types of signals which have the same effects, and it would avoid the almost certainly spurious suggestion of homology with hormones that the word *pheromone* suggests. We may recognize two categories of chemical signals, those employing: (1) body odors, and (2) special chemicals produced by glands.

Body odors for identification of species or sex are common among mammals, possibly fish and salamanders, and many invertebrates, particularly insects. In all of these cases, there is no sharp distinction possible between these and specially produced odors, for most body odors are glandularly produced. However, we can distinguish between the constant odor of the body of an animal and special odors produced only occasionally at certain spots on the body. In mammals, use of body odor for identification, particularly of species and in parent-young identification, is general. Ants and bees acquire the odor of the nest or hive, and this serves as a password. An individual without the colony odor is rejected, and one with the odor, even though of a foreign species, is accepted. Barnacles form aggregations consisting of only one species, apparently brought together by chemical signals released from settled individuals. Similar aggregations are formed by other aquatic invertebrates, presumably mediated by chemicals given off by the animals. Wolf spiders, which are wandering species, as the name suggests, have good eyes and their visual courtship we have already mentioned. They are, however, ordinarily as solitary as possible. Males locate females by following the silken draglines that the females lay down as they walk about. The males can, with receptors on their feet, detect the species and sex of the individual that laid down the dragline, even the direction taken, much as a dog can detect recent from older tracks. When the male has found the female by following her dragline and has placed himself in her view, he begins courtship posturing to identify himself to her.

Special chemicals produced by glands in the skin are widespread among animals. Perhaps all animals have them, and where unknown they merely need to be discovered. Among mammals, many have alarm scents or sexual odors produced by special glands, usually near the genital organs, or scents used for marking territories. Sometimes urine is used by mammals, as in dogs, as a territorial marker. Certain salamanders, when sexually ready, give off chemicals into the water that identify them to other members of the species. These animals may use their bodies or tails to stir the water and thus carry the chemical to the other individual. Some fish, when injured, give off a material from the skin, called *Schreckstoff,* a warning and alarming substance. It has been shown that release of this material into the water by marine fish attracts sharks, an interesting example of a little-studied facet of communication: the detection or deception of one species by another through communication signals.

Among invertebrates, chemical signaling systems are common, and are best studied by far among insects.[3; 8; 9; 10; 11; 12; 22] Of particular interest are the materials, usually secreted by females, that attract sexual partners. The high interest here arises from the possibility that these might be used for insect control. These sexual odors are surprisingly effective. Male moths have been attracted from distances up to five miles downwind. One investigator reports that a glass vial which had contained two female *Plodia* (cereal-infesting moths) for only four minutes still excited courtship behavior in males after lying open for two days. Some of these insect sex attractants have been prepared in pure form, and their chemical structure is known. Female silkworm moths give off an attractant (hexadecadiene $(10, 12)$-ol-1) which is still active in inducing male reactions when presented to them on a glass rod dipped in a solution containing 10^{-10} micrograms per milliliter. These facts well illustrate the persistence and carrying power of odors. There are many other examples of chemical use for communication by insects—alarm odors of ants and bees, marking odors of male bumblebees, guidance odors of ants and bees that are used to produce scent trails for cohorts, to mention a few.

Acoustical

As with visual signals, acoustical signals require the presence of rather specialized receptors. They are excellent for distances, easy to control for production of pulses and other time-related patterns, and offering almost infinite variability. Because specialized phonoreceptors are present only in vertebrates and insects, acoustical communication systems are practically limited to these, but in these groups they are second to none in importance. We may recognize three categories of acoustical signals, those employing: (1) incidental sounds, (2) stridulatory or other mechanically produced sounds, and (3) vocal sounds.

Incidental sounds are those that accompany activities other than special sound production. Thus, birds and insects cannot fly without wing sounds, large animals cannot walk without footfalls, fish cannot swim without swishing. In many cases, these sounds are merely incidental, or even accidental, and have no communicatory significance, but in others they are included in signaling systems. Two examples will suffice. In some birds, the whirring noise of the wings, as the animals fly up suddenly, is an alarm signal, causing other birds also to fly away. In mosquitoes, the flight sound of the female attracts males and induces mating. In the latter case, males can be induced to come to a tuning fork emitting a frequency of sound like that of the female's flight. The receptors are bulblike organs at the bases of the antennae, the Johnston's Organs, whose reactive characteristics are quite different from those of human ears. Some attempts by biologists to induce reactions in male mosquitoes have failed because the size relation of the sound projector was inappropriate. A female mosquito is small, and her wings produce sound fields with characteristic intensity patterns and wave forms. The male's receptors enable him to detect these, so the sound projector must approximate them. These facts illustrate the problems one may encounter in making adequate dummies for behavioral tests.

Stridulatory sounds are produced by drawing a toothlike structure over a filelike structure. These are produced by some fish and most grasshoppers and crickets. Other mechanically produced sounds are those made by: drumming in grouse and some grasshoppers; snapping the beak in birds; rattling or tail-swishing in reptiles; vibrating the air bladder in fish; thumping the ground in crabs, insects, and spiders; snapping tymbal-like areas of the body wall in cicadas. Together, stridulation and other mechanical methods of sound production comprise the largest and most varied group of acoustical signal-producing mechanisms in the animal kingdom. We can discuss only a few examples.

Grasshoppers and crickets are famous for their songs. Male short-horned grasshoppers (the familiar common grasshoppers or locusts) rub the hind legs against the wing covers, usually a set of teeth on the legs over a scraping ridge on the wing covers, producing rustling sounds. Male long-horned grasshoppers (often called katydids) and crickets have a file and tooth on the forewings and rub these together, producing generally musical tones, in some cases almost completely ultrasonic. Katydids may have highly specialized areas on the wings near the stridulatory apparatus, creating special acoustical conditions. All of these produce specific, temporally patterned sequences—their songs. The ordinary—or calling—song of the males attracts the females, which are variously tuned to the song (tuned receptors, receptors acting as filters, or specific behavior patterns). However, the males can produce other songs—rival's song if a male appears, mating song during copulation, warning notes, departing song when jumping but not in haste, and so forth. For one species of European grasshopper, 14 songs, separable in sound to man and in behavioral accompaniments, have been cataloged. For about 60 European species over 400 different songs have been found. The vocabulary is fairly large.

There have been many studies on insect sounds. In 1960 [5] we listed about 1,800 papers, and since then at least 800 more have appeared. The sounds of insects afford challenging material for physicists, as well as for students of animal behavior. The temporal coding patterns are various, basically trains of pulses produced by tooth impacts. In general, the receptors are resonant with the major frequencies, where such are present, but the nerve impulses finally produced are synchronous with the pulses. So the parameter most noted by man—frequency—is of little direct informational significance to the insects. Again, use of equipment for recording the projecting sounds—equipment that is almost always designed primarily for human speech and music—may give deceptive results, or none at all. For instance, in a European study, broadcasts of recorded grasshopper sounds through an ordinary loudspeaker were ineffective in inducing responses in females. It was necessary to use a special, corona-type speaker, with no inertia, so that the sounds could be sharply enough pulsed.

One factor of the environment affecting insect songs that has attracted considerable attention is temperature. Since insects have approximately the same temperature as the environment and singing is muscular, the chirp-rate is faster at higher temperatures than at lower. The exact nature of the relationship is still uncertain. This could create a problem for females, for their responses are to the temporal patterns of the songs. Actually their responses also vary with temperature, such that they respond to the rate appropriate for their body temperature. Experimentally, females at, let us say, 15 degrees Centigrade will not respond to the male song at 25 degrees Centigrade. In nature, of course, no such situation ordinarily arises.

Cicadas produce sounds by snapping areas of the body wall in and out, much as one can snap the bottom of a tin can. Each snap produces a pulse of sound. The frequency of snapping ranges from about 100 to 500 times per second, thus fusing the snaps for the human ear. The muscle driving this device is, like the flight muscles of insects, a special type, requiring only occasional neural feed-in to keep going at its own rate, determined by its innate rate and the constraints placed upon it by the tymbal. The muscle snaps the tymbal in, thus releasing tension on the muscle, causing it to relax, after which, as the tymbal snaps out, the muscle is again put under tension and again contracts. Nerve impulses are needed merely to start the train; once going, only occasional impulses keep it going until stopped. It is remarkable what a variety of sound patterns can be produced by so simple a device. Again the males sing, and the females are attracted; and there are other than the calling songs, too, such as protest notes.

These are the best-known insect musicians, but many others produce stridulatory sounds. Many beetles have ridges on the thorax against which they rub the wing covers, producing sounds that seem primarily to repel predators, but they may also be used in mating. Many species of ants and termites produce squeaks by rubbing together specialized areas of the abdomen and thorax. The significance of these sounds is unknown, but they are suspected of being used as alarm calls. Many insects can produce high-pitched buzzing sounds by vibrating the thorax with the wings closed. The best studied of these are the piping sounds of queen honeybees. All bees can produce sounds like these, and recent work makes it seem quite possible that the sounds produced by scout bees during the waggle run are the informational parameter rather than the more easily noted rates of turning. The queen pipes when another queen is present in the colony, or when a new queen is about ready to emerge. This seems to be a challenge to the new queen, and usually the new queen answers and a fight may ensue, or one queen may be driven away with part of the colony. Piping is equivalent to a territorial marker for the queen, therefore. Bees do not have ears and apparently receive the sounds as vibrations through the hive via their excellently developed subgenual organs—strands of tension-sensitive neurons extending across the leg joint and picking up the slightest movement of exoskeleton.

Vocal sounds are those produced, as in man, by passage of air over or through vibrating or resonating structures. Except for one case in insects —a moth that produces sound by driving air over a vibrating membrane near the mouth—voiced sounds are restricted to terrestrial vertebrates. The most studied are those of mammals and birds, and their use in communication in these groups is well known.

The singing of frogs and toads, produced by vibration of bladderlike parts of the mouth cavity, has likewise been noted from antiquity. The male sings, an almost universal situation among animals with acoustical communication systems. The songs are temporally structured, generally quite specific. While it has long been assumed that male choruses of frogs and toads in ponds on spring evenings call in females, it has only been recently that direct proof, through recordings, has been obtained. Besides the calling songs, frogs and toads also have various other notes, including warning and protest notes.

The variety of sounds produced by mammals has been appreciated by man as a "language" since earliest times. With the mobile lips and tongue of most mammals, the wonder is that these systems have not been much more highly developed. Considering the complex systems found in some insects with ridiculously simple sound-producing equipment, the paucity of separable acoustical signals produced by, let us say, dogs or cattle, is noteworthy. Perhaps the strong dependence of mammals upon smell or vision, and the fact that so many species are hunted or hunt, make sounds less valuable, for sounds tend, once released, to carry, and their origin is easily determined. The primates form something of an exception to this, for even in monkeys there is a variety of communicative acoustical signals. And man has taken advantage of the lips and tongue to develop subtle languages.

The songs and calls of birds have likewise attracted attention, even from nonscientists, since earliest times. The variety of sounds and the many patterns of songs of birds almost immediately suggest that they represent a protomusic; much of the earlier writing was in this vein. Actually the songs of male birds are territorial markers and signals to the females. Thus they correspond with the ordinary songs of male crickets and grasshoppers. The song gives notification of territory, identification of species (for the song of each species is usually distinct), identification of sex (for only the males sing), and in breeding season notification of readiness to mate. This is far from being mere music. Bird songs are probably the most studied of all animal sounds, but still much remains to be learned.

Generally the timbre and temporal pattern are the distinctive features of a bird's song. Some birds seem to have the song mostly innate, and even if raised in solitude sing like other males of the species; they do not try to imitate others that they hear. Other birds seemingly inherit only the general vocal structures and the patterns of the song. If raised in isolation, the males sing only a skeleton song. As soon as they can hear other males, they imitate them and ultimately build their own individual patterns as a sort of pastiche. Some, such as mockingbirds, carry this to great lengths, and the so-called talking birds, such as parrots and mynahs, mimic human sounds. In cases where young males learn the distinctive features of their songs from other males, generally their father, the way is open for development of local dialects, and a number of cases of these have been discovered—in meadowlarks, song sparrows, chaffinches, etc.

Far less studied have been the calls, or call notes of birds. These are generally short, often not at all musical in quality to us. Yet they are much more important in the daily lives of birds than are the territorial songs. Too few birds have been studied for generalizations to be very useful. Thorpe [29] lists 17 classes of call notes, based on reactions to these, including alarm, distress, and food-begging. Except for domestic chickens, there has not been any detailed study of acoustical systems in parent-young relations in birds, a most fruitful area, it would seem. Generally, parents and young are quite silent when humans are visible nearby, even, it would seem, when the observers consider themselves to be unobserved. However, if a microphone is concealed near a nest, with wires leading to a distant tape recorder, it quickly reveals to a listener the great variety of sounds of very low intensity that are used by both parents and young in normal activities.

Generally the call notes of birds are specifically distinctive, as are the songs. They are, however, usually shorter and much more simply structured, so that similarities among species are noticeable. Thus, alarm notes tend to be short and staccato, suggesting danger even to human ears. It is, therefore, relatively easy for different species living together to learn to respond to each other's calls; this cross-reactivity has been studied, particularly in crows and gulls. At the same time, calls lend themselves, as do songs, to the development of local dialects. Thus, herring gulls in Holland do not respond to the call notes of the same species recorded in Maine. A detailed, carefully monitored study of the call notes of a single species would probably turn up at least 25 to 50 separable categories, with a tremendous range in variability and intensity. So far no such complete study has been made.

An interesting case of cross-reactivity, bird-mammal, is that of the African honey guides. These small birds feed upon beeswax, but are apparently incapable of withstanding the stings of bees to get it. Instead, when a bird has found a bee colony, it seeks out a mammal, generally a badger-like animal, the ratel, and flies over it emitting a special call which induces the ratel to follow and thus get to the bees. There the ratel tears up the nest, eats the bees and larvae, apparently little affected by the bees, and leaves the wax for the honey guide. This system has been invaded by man too; honey guides often summon human beings the same way for the same purpose. There are many examples also of mammals being alerted by alarm notes of birds, and vice versa.

The development of the tape recorder and modern high-fidelity sound-projecting equipment has made possible scientific studies of bioacoustics that are in their merest infancy. Except for the lower aquatic invertebrates, acoustical communication systems are almost universal in animals, and along with chemical systems are the most important for informational transfer at a distance.

Other Possibilities

The ability of animals to find their way about where man cannot (e.g., bats and owls in the dark), and their aggregation, dispersion, or migration without signals that are obvious to us, have led to postulation of use of channels other than those already discussed. In the case of bats, the discovery of their use of ultrasonic pulses inaudible to man to guide their nocturnal flight made an extrasensory channel unnecessary as an explanation. This type of location of obstacles and prey, using a form of sonar (echolocation), has now been found also in porpoises, sea lions, and oil birds. Some biologists consider it to be a type of autocommunication. It involves no supernormal receptive capacities, except possibly extended frequency ranges for hearing.

Electrical and magnetic fields have been postulated many times as agents in animal behavior, but generally the evidence is negative. Recently, however, it has been shown that fish produce electrical discharges and have receptors for them. These are used as means for detecting objects in the external environment through alterations by the objects of the external fields. And, recently, reactions of various animals to magnetic fields have also been reported. It is difficult to see how an animal could produce magnetic signals, but the possibility is there.

It is rather surprising that there are no reported cases of communication in thermal channels. It must be admitted that thermal changes would seem to have little virtue over other more readily controllable types. Thermal changes are hard to produce (almost impossible in water). They would have very short ranges, and they do not lend themselves to pulsed coding. It is possible that changes in body temperature in mammals during sexual excitement (the common language notes these with the term "in heat") might be involved in courtship and mating, but so far no clear-cut evidence has been presented. Pit vipers have temperature receptors of astonishing sensitivity, capable of detecting differences of as little as 0.1 degree Centigrade between external objects. These are near the mouth and enable them to strike prey accurately. Similarly, mosquitoes respond to the heat given off by their hosts, and moths seem to respond to infrared emanations of food plants. But these cases would not represent communication in the usual sense. However, the generality of temperature sensitivity among animals and the existence of specialized thermoreceptors in many groups suggest that this channel for communication may be exploited too.

As for suggestions that animals communicate by a type of extrasensory perception, little can be said. Since ESP in man is not accepted by many scientists, and its presence in animals would be many times more difficult (if not impossible) to demonstrate, prudence dictates, for animals, the assumption of communication in channels whose presence is known.

Multichannel Communication

Most communication in animals involves more than one channel simultaneously. This is the familiar principle of redundancy, insuring signal transmission. We can mention just a few cases.

In most mammals, courtship is fairly elaborate, involving a number of communication systems. Odors and sometimes accompanying sounds are usual as distance attractants, bringing the sexes together and carrying information about the species, location, and sexual state. When the individuals are near each other, confirmation of identification involves at least specific odors and body forms or color patterns. This is usually facilitated by postures and movements: caressing, licking, or nuzzling and bumping, as well as by special sounds. If the possibility of detection of the "heat" of the female is included, it is obvious that the preparation for mating in this case takes advantage of all channels for communication.

Insect courtship is similar but by no means simpler. Attraction of the sexes usually comes about through chemical or acoustical signals, in the first case with the female usually as sender, in the second the male. Since all insects have body odors, it is quite possible that, even when sounds are produced, odors are important. When the presumptive partners are near each other, courtship may turn to visual signals, to other chemical and acoustical signals, or to a variety of tactile signals. In crickets, for example, males call the females in with a specific song. When the male and female are near each other, the male song changes; identification apparently involves both song and vision. In some singing grasshoppers, the system changes at this point from song to vibration of the plant on which the animals stand. The female tree-cricket approaches the male from behind (in many species of singing insects the pattern of the sound field, produced by erection of the wings or by sound reflectors, guides her), and feeds from a gland on his thorax. While she is thus engaged, the male, aided by tactile exciters, achieves copulation.

Courtship, of course, is not the only complicated signaling system in insects. We need only mention the guidance signals of honeybees, involving, as we have seen, chemical markers (primitive bees,[16] unlike honeybees, use only scent trails to guide their hive-mates), tactile stimuli, and possibly acoustical signals. The operant stimulus pattern transmitted by the dance of the scout through direction on the comb is the pattern of ultraviolet polarized light of the sky. All usual sensory channels are thus involved.

Another example of multiple-channel use is the alarm complex of many birds. Our knowledge of this is really quite fragmentary, but the indications are that every channel, except possibly chemical (and this has been suggested for starlings) is used. The simplest alarm signal is often sudden silent flight from a group. If one bird departs precipitously, the others do too. While this may be mostly visual, often accentuated by flashing of white wing bars or tail feathers, the whirring of the wings in this maneuver is also important. Other visual alarm signals involve a series of body postures communicating varying degrees of alarm. There are almost invariably also alarm notes, emitted generally when a bird, itself safely in a tree or in the air, sees approaching danger. The alarm calls of a species may be various, different for ground predators and for aerial predators. And finally there is often a type of call (the assembly or mobbing call) given when a bird sights a cat, owl, or hawk, which induces others to fly in and mob the predator. And these are not all. In crows and possibly gulls, as in some grasshoppers, there seems to be a call whose absence denotes alarm —the departing call. This is of low intensity, given by an individual that is leaving the flock without alarm. It serves to maintain the status quo, and is therefore hard to test for. If a bird flies away suddenly without giving this call, the others leave too. This is an example of absence of a signal communicating information. In essence, the queen substance of honeybees does the same; its absence signifies absence of the queen. Almost always, however, such signals are part of a complex of overlapping, multichannel communication systems.

EVOLUTIONARY SIGNIFICANCE OF COMMUNICATION

For most biologists, the key to speciation in animal evolution is isola- tion, allowing the development of separate gene pools in isolated popula- tions originally the same species. For instance, two populations of a spe- cies—one on a continent, the other on an island separated so far from the continent that cross-breeding is impossible—gradually accumulate different mutations. Since the conditions of life are also different, variations within the populations have different survival values, and so different genes are favored. Gradually, the gene pools of these two populations diverge, until, at some point, even if individuals from the two populations come together, they are no longer able to produce viable offspring; they are two species.

It is obvious to all biologists that geographic isolation is effective in pro- ducing speciation in this way. But what about other types of isolation? If these are strict enough to absolutely prevent sharing of genes, they should function also. Many students of animal communication believe that differ- ences in identification signals may be sufficient to keep populations of the same species from interbreeding, even though they live at the same place. We might imagine that the first evidence of differences within a once mono- specific population could be what we have called *dialects:* small differ- ences in signals which only some members of the population produce and to which only some react. Gradual intensification of the differences could occur through genetic changes or, in animals such as birds and mammals, through "inheritance" of learned traditions, as in song patterns learned by offspring from parents. Finally, the differences would become great enough that members of the two groups could not "recognize" each other as of the same species. At this point, even if they occupy the same geographic locality, they no longer share genetic material and are essentially isolated. From there the path to separateness of species is the same as in the case of geographic isolation.

Since behavior patterns are generally much more labile than morphological characters, any population of animals has many variants already present. In the case of a signaling system such as that of crickets, for instance, the individual males differ in rate, tonality, number of pulses, and so forth. If one works with a group of grasshoppers or crickets, recording their songs and later playing them over and over for study, he finds that he can identify each by the individuality of its song—slight elisions or extensions, various degrees of time regularity, subtle variation in tonality, and the like. Similarly, females vary in response to different aspects of the song. This could very well mean that the first steps toward speciation are taken when the signals of the sender deviate far enough from the norm that only correspondingly deviant receivers respond, gradually fixing the difference genetically and so creating the situation postulated for behavioral isolation. There is evidence of this now in crickets, frogs, and some birds. This matter is of such importance to zoologists that we can confidently expect much future work on such matters as the nature of signal variations, the inheritance of signal patterns, and the inheritance of and learning of behavioral responses.

PRACTICAL VALUES IN STUDIES OF ANIMAL COMMUNICATION

We might say just a word, finally, on possible practical (that is, anthropocentrically valuable) aspects of these studies.

The first use of communication signals for economic purposes was in pest control. At present, the most extensive use is probably of insect sexual odors (pheromones) to attract pests to their death.[10; 11] Male gypsy moths, for example, are attracted by the scent of females and can be trapped and killed. So far, attempts to use sounds produced by insects—with the possible exception of those produced by mosquitoes—have not been successful.[4; 6]

Since the discovery in 1954 that starlings could be driven from roosts by broadcasting recordings of their distress call, acoustical controls for birds using communication signals have been slowly evolving. At present, starlings, sparrows, crows, gulls, and a few other species of birds are being kept from places where they are not desired by broadcasts of their alarm or distress calls. The development has been somewhat impeded by misunderstanding of the actions of the signals, even by some scientists. It is not enough just to broadcast a call, no matter how effective, to control a pest bird. Similarly, the synthesis of a drug or insecticide, no matter how potent, does not automatically insure disease or pest control. The discovery of acoustical signals that influence bird behavior represents only a beginning. One must know the ecology and behavior, at least, of the pest birds before he can decide upon times and durations of broadcasts, placement of speakers, and other such considerations. Furthermore, the broadcast sounds must be "understandable" to the birds, which means consideration of acoustical and electronic aspects. These are often foreign to biologists. The biological aspects often seem unimportant to acousticians or electronics specialists. So the scene is set for attempts at acoustical control to fail through lack of appreciation of acoustical problems by one group, or of the subtlety of animal social life by the other. At present, in France and Germany, teams of workers are attacking the problems, and effective controls are being developed. In the United States progress has been slow, but there is increasing interest, for usually killing birds, even when they are pests, is considered undesirable, and alternative methods of control are not fully effective.

Studies on animal communication should also increase our knowledge of communication in general and may thus lead to better understanding or an extension of human means of communication. As an example, for the blind we doubly transform the spoken work, first to ordinary writing, then to a derived tactile system. But why? Why not a direct transformation of acoustical to tactile signals, taking full advantage of the special characteristics of the latter?

So far, studies on animal communication have led to few generalizations, and attempts at theoretical analysis have invariably started with ideas derived from studies on man, rather than the other way around. No doubt the diversity of animal communication systems has made it difficult to derive generalizations, and the tendency of zoologists to study only one group of animals has also contributed. As research proceeds, however, generalizations derived from studies on animals themselves and valid for all species should be formulated. A deepened understanding of human communication may be possible. Arguments over whether or not animals have language will then be seen to have no relevance, for the differences and similarities between human and animal communication will be obvious.

REFERENCES AND SUGGESTED READINGS

1. Armstrong, E. A., *A Study of Bird Song*. London: Oxford University Press, 1963.
2. Busnel, R. G., ed., *Acoustic Behavior of Animals*. Amsterdam: Elsevier, 1963.
3. Butler, C. G., *The World of the Honeybee*. London: Collins, 1954.
4. Frings, H., and M. Frings, "Uses of Sounds by Insects," *Annual Review of Entomology*, Vol. 3, 1958.
5. Frings, M., and H. Frings, *Sound Production and Sound Reception by Insects— A Bibliography*. University Park: Pennsylvania State University Press, 1960.
6. Frings, H., and M. Frings, "Pest Control with Sound," Parts I and II, *Sound*, Vols. 1 and 2, 1962–1963.

7. Frings, H., and M. Frings, *Animal Communication.* New York: Blaisdell, 1964.
8. Frisch, Von, K., *Bees—Their Vision, Chemical Senses, and Language.* Ithaca, N.Y.: Cornell University Press, 1950.
9. Frisch, Von, K., *The Dance Language and Orientation of Bees,* trans. by L. Chadwick. Cambridge, Mass.: Harvard University Press, 1967.
10. Jacobson, M., *Insect Sex Attractants.* New York: Wiley-Interscience, 1965.
11. Jacobson, M., "Chemical Insect Attractants and Repellents," *Annual Review of Entomology,* Vol. 11, 1966.
12. Johnston, J. W., Jr., D. G. Moulton, and A. Turk, *Advances in Chemoreception,* Vol. 1, *Communication by Chemical Signals.* New York: Appleton-Century-Crofts, 1970.
13. Kainz, F., *Die "Sprache" der Tiere.* Stuttgart: Ferdin and Enke Verlag, 1961.
14. Klopfer, P. H., *Behavioral Ecology.* Belmont, Calif.: Dickenson, 1970.
15. Lanyon, W. E., and W. M. Tavolga, eds., *Animal Sounds and Communication.* Washington, D.C.: American Institute of Biological Sciences, 1960.
16. Lindauer, M., *Communication Among Social Bees.* Cambridge, Mass.: Harvard University Press, 1961.
17. Marler, P., "Developments in the Study of Animal Communication," in *Darwin's Biological Work: Some Aspects Reconsidered,* ed. by P. R. Bell *et al.,* Cambridge, England: Cambridge University Press, 1959.
18. Marler, P., "The Logical Analysis of Animal Communication," *Journal of Theoretical Biology,* Vol. 1, 1961.
19. Marler, P., and W. J. Hamilton, III, *Mechanisms of Animal Behavior.* New York: Wiley, 1966.
20. Moulton, J. M., "Underwater Sound: Biological Aspects," *Oceanography Marine Biology Annual Review,* Vol. 2, 1964.
21. Reese, E. A., "Ethology and Marine Zoology," *Oceanography Marine Biology Annual Review,* Vol. 2, 1964.
22. Ribbands, C. R., *The Behaviour and Social Life of Honey-bees.* London: Bee Research Association, Ltd., 1953.
23. Roe, A., and G. G. Simpson, eds., *Behavior and Evolution.* New Haven, Conn.: Yale University Press, 1958.
24. Sebeok, T. A., "Animal Communication," *Science,* Vol. 147, 1965.
25. Sebeok, T. A., *Animal Communication: Techniques of Study and Results of Research.* Bloomington: Indiana University Press, 1968.
26. Sebeok, T. A., and A. Ramsay, *Approaches to Animal Communication.* The Hague: Mouton, 1969.
27. Tavolga, W. N., ed., *Marine Bio-acoustics.* New York: Pergamon Press, 1964.
28. Tembrock, G., *Tierstimmen: Eine Einführung in die Bioakustik.* Wittenberg Lutherstadt: A. Ziemsen Verlag, 1959.
29. Thorpe, W. H., *Bird Song.* Cambridge, England: Cambridge University Press, 1961.
30. Thorpe, W. H., and O. L. Zangwill, eds., *Current Problems in Animal Behaviour.* Cambridge, England: Cambridge University Press, 1961.
31. Tinbergen, N., *The Study of Instinct.* Oxford: Clarendon, 1952.
32. Tinbergen, N., *Social Behaviour in Animals, with Special Reference to Vertebrates.* London: Methuen, 1953.

INDEX

459